INTERSECTING INEQUALITIES

Class, Race, Sex, and Sexualities

Edited by

Peter Kivisto
Augustana College

Elizabeth Hartung
California State University—Channel Islands

PEARSON

Prentice
Hall

Upper Saddle River, New Jersey 07458

Library of Congress Cataloging-in-Publication Data

Intersecting inequalities : class, race, sex, and sexualities / [edited by]
Peter Kivisto, Elizabeth Hartung.
   p. cm.
 ISBN 0-13-183958-6
 1. Equality. 2. Social stratification. I. Kivisto, Peter II.
Hartung, Elizabeth.
HM821.I58 2006
305—dc22

2006007233

For Richard Freimuth (1950–1993)

Publisher: Nancy Roberts
Editorial Assistant: Lee Peterson
Full Service Production Liaison: Joanne Hakim
Senior Marketing Manager: Marissa Feliberty
Marketing Assistant: Anthony DeCosta
Manufacturing Buyer: Brian Mackey
Cover Art Director: Jayne Conte
Cover Design: Studio Indigo
Cover Photo: Diego Rivera "The Making of a Fresco Showing the Building of a City" 1931/San Francisco
Art Institute
Manager, Cover Visual Research & Permissions: Karen Sanatar
Full-Service Project Management: Patty Donovan/Pine Tree Composition
Composition: Laserwords Private Limited
Printer/Binder: RR Donnelley & Sons Company

Pearson Education LTD., London
Pearson Education Singapore, Pte. Ltd
Pearson Education, Canada, Ltd
Pearson Education–Japan
Pearson Education Australia PTY, Limited

Pearson Education North Asia Ltd
Pearson Educación de Mexico, S.A. de C.V.
Pearson Education Malaysia, Pte. Ltd
Pearson Education, Upper Saddle River, New Jersey

10 9 8 7 6 5 4 3 2 1
ISBN 0-13-183958-6

Contents

Preface

HOW DO WE MAKE SENSE OF INTERSECTING INEQUALITIES?

This collection of essays and excerpts from classical sociological texts and those that we think are destined to be classics begins with a fundamental question in stratification research: Is inequality inevitable? It certainly seems to be so, both in contemporary American society and globally. Some individuals seem touched by good fortune, while others struggle; some nations suffer drought, monsoons, and famine, while others have such an excess of potential calories that childhood and adult obesity are a growing health threat.

We focus this collection of readings on three, and sometimes four, sets of "intersecting inequalities"—that is, those things that cannot be separated from who we as individuals fundamentally are: our social class, our racial and/or ethnic identity, our sex, and how we define ourselves as sexual beings. In this book, its contributors and editors try to make clear connections between how social class inequalities are sometimes subtly and sometimes dramatically modified by looking at the inequalities of race, sex, and sexual preference. This simultaneously complicates and amplifies what we know about inequality.

Herein lies a paradox: sociology, as Anthony Giddens (1998) once put it, is a "*generalizing* discipline about modernity." That is, sociologists generalize from a subset of experiences to draw larger social patterns about master statuses. At the same time, if we each focus on the intersection of those patterns in our own lives, the extent to which we can generalize shrinks considerably, like the overlapping shaded circles in a Venn diagram. Since the 1980s, many sociologists have written about the importance of understanding connections between race, class, and gender. *Race,* as sociologists use it, really means how physical characteristics like skin color take on social meaning and affect how limited resources (jobs, housing, and education) are likely to be distributed. Complicating matters further is the troublesome fact that for some "racial" groups, patterned social and economic disparities are more apparent and persistent than for others. And for the moment, please notice that we are not defining *ethnicity,* or within national boundary cultural distinctions; recency of arrival to an area, or *immigration* status; or *nationality. Social class* is generally taken to mean social divisions based on the kinds of resources an individual has at his or her disposal and what those resources can buy beyond tangible goods. Finally, *gender* is generally used to mean the social significance of the physical characteristic of sex. *Sex* status, once assumed to be clearly dichotomous (male or female), is no longer so clear cut. That is, a person may be born into a particular sex but feel compelled to become, at least socially, a member of the other (for example, a female man) (Lorber, 1994), or a person may in fact be intersexed, neither clearly male nor female (Fausto-Sterling, 2000).

Thus, quite a lot of potential meaning is packed into the rather facile phrase "race, class, and gender." A focus on race, class, and gender won't lead to greater insights into inequality unless we can truly and carefully examine the interaction effects between them. For example, how is the experience of being an upper-class African American woman different from that of her white counterpart? How does she experience the advantages of her social class, and does her class "trump" the disadvantages of her race and sex? We have much to learn. To that end, we have organized this text by looking first at the idea of inequality and then at various models and measures of social class as a standalone concept. We then turn to class as mediated and modified by race and ethnicity; then by sex (and race and ethnicity), and by sexual preference. Finally, we look at how citizenship affects life chances, broadening our scope to the complicating concept of globalization.

WHY INEQUALITY DISTURBS US

Research about inequality and the rules of resource distribution raises several uncomfortable issues. First, of course, the simple act of studying inequality is an acknowledgment that an unfair distribution of goods—material and nonmaterial—persists in both relatively open and free societies like the United States and elsewhere. Second, to acknowledge inequality means we must carefully define it, and this is not such a straightforward task. As Richard Sennett notes in the first selection of our text, there is a big difference between everyone having enough of something and everyone needing to "feel special" so that our sense of superiority is reinforced. Inequality gives rise to envy, and envy may result in wanting to take away the goods that some have or spoil their pleasure in having them (see Lyman, 1978 on envy). A third issue involves what we plan to do about inequality. Are we are simply content to study the form and substance of inequality? Each sociologist must ask herself if she is a dispassionate, value-free observer or a scholar-activist, or if she can be both. If we are mere observers of inequality, do we contribute to its maintenance? Are economic or racial or sex inequalities topics that we *can* examine dispassionately? The student of sociology is in good company as he struggles with these questions. For more than two hundred years, intellectuals involved in the development of the social sciences have asked whether scholarship should lead the way to social justice and the good society.

A fourth issue is one often raised by students. If we talk about a specific group, say, African Americans, and the issues that group faces, is it racist to point out distinct differences between African Americans and whites, or is it racist to ignore differences? Should the point of stratification research be to diminish all differences between groups both descriptively and in practice? Too often, talking about sets of problems can be seen as endorsing the system that created the problem.

These are all challenging questions, and while we don't plan to resolve them, we will try always to identify our own biases as sociologists and citizens.

SOCIOLOGY BEGINS WITH AN ANALYSIS OF SOCIAL INEQUALITY

What would the good society look like? This question was at the basis of the early "science of society" that would later become sociology. During the Enlightenment, philosophers and scientists challenged traditional authority, particularly in the forms of both the monarchy and the church. Europe experienced a series of political revolutions in the 1700s, culminating most notably in the French Revolution. Indeed, many who fought against the British in the American Revolution earlier in the century, like the threadbare aristocrat and visionary Claude-Henri, Comte de Saint-Simon, would return to France ready to participate in overthrowing a corrupt monarchy. Some of the startling breakthroughs in science and encounters with indigenous peoples in the Americas and elsewhere challenged ideas about the natural order. Charles Darwin's provocative theory of evolution ultimately upended the idea of a "clockwork universe" run by God. New miracles in technology transformed communications and transportation, thereby connecting people previously isolated from one another. Technological change was linked to the Industrial Revolution, which has been rightly viewed as the second-most profound transformation in human history, along with the shift from hunting and gathering to agrarian societies.

This climate of political, economic, technological, and intellectual revolution also spurred new and troubling social problems. What kind of society would be the ultimate goal? Saint-Simon, who spent a year in prison despite giving up his aristocratic title (*Comte,* or Count), was enthusiastic about the gains made in the realm of science and technology, as well as the possibilities brought about by industrialism. He envisioned a good society in which industrial leaders, bankers, scientists, and artists would replace the superstition of the church and the state would provide for all of the needs of the individuals residing within it. After his death, his messianic followers (the Saint-Simonians) attempted to apply his principles in intentional communities based on a secular religion of science. The thinkers that today we would call professional sociologists were to be the priests of the movement. Auguste Comte, who coined the term sociology, extended the ideas of his mentor and rival Saint-Simon and suggested that better living would be possible if only the rules of social life could be ascertained.

Certainly Karl Marx, part of whose *Communist Manifesto* co-authored with Friedrich Engels appears later in this collection, posed a model of a good society based on assumptions of the goodness of human nature (Stevenson and Haberman, 2004). Although Marx was not an "Enlightenment" scholar, his optimism and faith in progress place him firmly in that tradition. In the final stage of his model, working people would build the kind of society in which eventually the state would not be needed. Capitalists, after all, it was argued, need the state to pass laws and to maintain the forces of order (i.e., the police and the military) that will insure that their property is protected. In a socialist alternative to capitalism, each person, perhaps not exactly "equal" in capability, would want to contribute according to "his abilities" and would receive "according to his needs." Marx suggested, then, that after centuries of struggle against domination of one group by another, the liberated poor laborers would be more inclined to share the resources of society—in other words, the proletariat had the potential to be "good" in a way that prior dominating classes were not.

Many of the "positive philosophers" who shaped the discipline of sociology took comfort in the belief that with the end of a paternalist and traditional order based on inheritance and justified by God's divine authority, a new society would emerge moving toward the possibility of perfection. But they didn't agree on the contours of the good society. From Saint-Simon's inner circle of industrial leaders and bankers setting (unselfish) public policy to Marx's cadre of virtuous workers untainted by the temptations of private property to Herbert Spencer's faith that "social selection" would weed out unfit individuals like poor people and dissolute drunkards, sociology has led us to envision both utopias and dystopias.

We're still asking many of the same questions, including what kind of society we would like to shape as well as study. What would the good society look like? What is fair and equitable as we look at struggling peoples and nations? Is inequality inevitable?

REFERENCES

Fausto-Sterling, Anne. (2000). *Sexing the body: gender politics and the construction of sexuality.* New York: Basic Books.

Giddens, Anthony. (1996). *In defense of sociology: essays, interpretations and rejoinders.* Cambridge, UK, and Cambridge, MA: Polity Press.

Lorber, Judith. (1994). *Paradoxes of gender.* New Haven: Yale University Press.

Lyman, Stanford M. (1978). *The seven deadly sins: society and evil.* New York: St. Martin's Press.

Stevenson, Leslie, and David L. Haberman. (2004). *Ten theories of human nature* (4th ed.). New York and Oxford: Oxford University Press.

ACKNOWLEDGMENTS

Elizabeth Hartung would like to thank the students in her Sociology 151 classes at California State University at Fresno over the years for their insights on stratification and social class, and to her new students at Channel Islands. They have all inspired her to do her best and to be a good and honest thinker. She also wants to thank her former colleagues at Fresno State, especially her good friends John Tinker and Manuel Figueroa. And last, but not least, she gives thanks to her husband and partner, Ignacio Mendiguren, who always believes in her.

Peter Kivisto appreciates the advice and support he has received from a number of colleagues and former colleagues, including Jeff Abernathy, Margaret Farrar, John Guidry, Mwenda Ntarangwi, and Bill Swatos. As always, the unconditional love he receives from his family—Susan, Sarah, and Aaron—keeps him going. Once again, his departmental secretary Jean Sottos has gone beyond the call of duty to help out. Finally, he wants to extend a special note of gratitude to Sonia Hanson, his former student assistant and young scholar extraordinaire, whose contribution to this volume has been invaluable.

We would also like to thank the following reviewers: Susan E. Chase, University of Tulsa; Trudie Coker, Florida Atlantic University; Mariella Squire, University of Maine at Fort Kent; and Magaline Harris Taylor, University of Arkansas.

CHAPTER

1

Is Inequality Inevitable?

The question that underlies much of stratification research is whether inequality is, in fact, inevitable. A related question then has to do with how much inequality must we accept in society. In this chapter, we offer several selections that answer the first question distinctly, and almost none of them serve up a simple yes or no. Some of them contain reflections about whether inequality can be desirable. Richard Sennett, in a selection from his book *Respect in a World of Inequality,* provides our lead article. Sennett suggests that one of the things that fuels inequality is a desire to be "special" and "different." In modern society, we are constantly invited to compare ourselves to others, and too often we come up short: not pretty or handsome enough, smart enough, rich enough, tall enough. Comparison invites envy, and envy leads us to a set of moral quandaries as well as makes us absolutely miserable. As noted earlier, in its worst manifestation, it is not enough to want to emulate the admirable characteristics of others. Sometimes we may want to cross the line and take their pleasure away. Sennett invites us to think about inequality differently by asking us to contemplate why we are afraid of ordinariness. Inequality, for him, is something that is part of our humanity because nature distributes attributes unequally. What does it mean that we live in a society that has blurred the distinction between Rousseau's self-*confidence* (*amour de soi*) and self-*love* (*amour-propre*), which requires the admiration of others along with the need to be superior to them?

The two pieces that follow, by Kingsley Davis and Wilbert Moore, and the reply by Melvin Tumin, often appear in texts like this one but perhaps are not always carefully read. In 1945, Davis and Moore proposed "Some Principles of Stratification," namely, that inequality serves a purpose by motivating people into performing needed jobs that might otherwise be hard to fill. Indeed, they make two especially important points: first, that the reward offered for a job is based both on the need for that job in a society *and* the scarcity of people available to do it. In other words, if a job was needed but many people were willing to do it, it would not need to be highly rewarded. The second point is one they make in the second part of their argument, wherein they look at how *what* is valued varies as societies change over time. Take their example of priests and preachers. Many people feel "called" to a religious life of service, but that calling is not something that can be quantified. In fact, it can be faked. Religious leaders are especially important in societies where literacy is limited, and leaders are called

1

upon to interpret the word of God. In most modern societies, priests and preachers are not likely to be highly rewarded as a group because they are not the sole possessors of special knowledge about God. (Weber's *The Protestant Ethic and the Spirit of Capitalism* elucidates this point.) Indeed, many people feel that they have a special relationship with God and don't need an intermediary. Today, say Davis and Moore, we most frequently reward people with technical skills and know-how. As you read Davis and Moore, pay close attention to whether they are saying that inequality is a social good, a social necessity, or both.

Melvin Tumin's response, published several years after the original piece, restates Davis and Moore's argument as he reads it. You may not read the argument in the same way. Tumin is really mounting a critique about the existence (and the immorality) of social stratification as much as he is critiquing Davis and Moore's piece. Along the way he raises intriguing questions about what we value. Certainly he does not feel that stratification is a social "good" but rather is a way to artificially limit competition. Tumin wrote in the early 1950s, and some of his examples may seem strained to contemporary university students. He talks about the prestige of being a student and the sacrifice of parents to put students through school. Bear in mind that in the 1950s, relatively fewer high school graduates entered college and completed a B.A., let alone pursued graduate work, and few undergraduate students were juggling job and family responsibilities.

E. Franklin Frazier's look at "Biracial Organizations" is contained in his book *Race and Culture Contacts in the Modern World,* first published in 1957. Biracial organizations, as he used the term, refer to parallel but manifestly unequal racial systems brought about by racial ideology and prejudice. Frazier wrote at a time when racial segregation was very much alive, both in the United States and elsewhere, and his work foreshadows that of later commentators on *de facto* segregation, such as William Julius Wilson (1980). Frazier's discussion of the contact of indigenous peoples with European economic adventurers takes us through a brief history of the development of racial ideology. As Marx observed, ideology almost always suits the needs of a dominant group, and certainly there were economic reasons for the subjugation of entire peoples on the basis of race. In revisiting Frazier's analysis of parallel communities, however, we have to ask to what extent such divisions continue to mark our own and other societies. Frazier sees a pattern in the global divide between black and white. One pertinent question to be raised in this regard is whether such a pattern persists today in the post–civil rights, post–affirmative action era.

Race and sex inequities, while sharing some features in common, are actually quite different. Moreover, as a generation of feminist scholars has pointed out, by focusing on one to the exclusion of the other, the experiences of women of color are eradicated (Collins, 1990). Both race and sex are experienced by all of us as *identities,* and so also is our sexual preference keenly a part of who we are. But we will experience our race, sex, or sexual preference differently depending on where we fall in the social structures that shape our lives: work, family, school, politics, and so on. Iris Marion Young begins her selection with a simple and true observation: what some call identity politics has much to do with place in the social structure. But how do you get a handle on an institution that is oppressive; or on a job market that systematically excludes members of particular groups? To begin to answer such questions, Young suggests a geometrically complex model, following Peter Blau, Anthony Giddens and others, that is hard to pin down in time and space. That is, one identity/status that you hold will have an impact on another, and another, and so on. One identity/status may lead an individual to make a choice that is rather easier than another; for example, a woman might "choose" a job that will accommodate the child she hasn't had yet. Social structure is like a series of interwoven cords. Taken separately, the cords may flex and give, but woven together they take on a solid form with the strength to contain—and restrict—our freedom. And economic class is at its base determinative of whether we shall work at all, work at something we love, or work because we must.

We conclude this chapter with an excerpt from Charles Tilley's *Durable Inequalities.* Why are some inequalities enduring ones? Tilley states that "categorical inequality" was invented millennia ago, established by the processes of exploitation (with one group benefiting at the expense of another) and by opportunity hoarding. Two additional processes, emulation (or copying relations from one system to another) and adaptation (of one system to another) complete the process.

If inequality is nearly universal, and it takes the multiple and interlocking forms of limiting class resources to particular racial/ethnic groups (not yet delineated) and to a sex class group (women), and adds the dimension of disparagement of sexual minorities (gays, lesbians, transsexual and transgendered individuals), let us continue to look more deeply at various explanations, starting with the origins of class.

REFERENCES

Collins, Patricia Hill. (1990). *Black feminist thought.* New York: Routledge Press.

Wilson, William J. (1980). *The declining significance of race: Blacks and changing American institutions.* Chicago: University of Chicago Press.

pg. 2
interwoven
cords of inequality

The Seductions of Inequality

RICHARD SENNETT

The perverse, seductive power of inequality formed the subject of one of Rousseau's greatest essays, *Discourse on the Origin of Inequality* (as it was finally published in 1755), and the arguments he advances are of such contemporary importance that I want to present them in some detail.

Rousseau's starting point is this: invidious comparison could not hurt if we did not want to be someone different from the person we are. Different not just in material circumstances—a different person. Envy is a way of expressing that desire to become someone else. Modern society invites us to envy; in a world bent on destroying tradition and inherited place, on affirming the possibility of making something of ourselves through our own merits, what keeps us from becoming another person? All we have to do is imitate the sort of person we would like to be.

If we take up this invitation, however, we lose our self-respect. We are not innocent victims; no one is forcing us to be envious.

To explain how people participate in their own loss of self-respect, Rousseau draws a distinction between *amour de soi* and *amour-propre*. The French phrases separate, first of all, the ability to take care of oneself from the capacity to draw attention to oneself. In Rousseau's words:

> Amour propre and amour de soi . . . must not be confused. Amour de soi is a natural sentiment which inclines every

Source: "The Seductions of Inequality from Unequal Talent," from *Respect in a World of Inequality* by Richard Sennett. Copyright © 2003 by Richard Sennett. Used by permission of W. W. Norton & Company, Inc.

> animal to watch over its own preservation. . . . Amour propre is only a relative sentiment, artificial and born in Society, which inclines each individual to have a greater esteem for himself than for anyone else.[1]

So *amour de soi* is not "self-love"; it would better be expressed as "self-confidence," the conviction that we can maintain ourselves in the world. This confidence we acquire through the exercise of those solid craft labors which are our life support. And *amour-propre* is not merely a display of superiority, the demonstration of an inequality. Rousseau's biographer Maurice Cranston pithily defines *amour-propre* as "the desire to be superior to others *and* to be esteemed by them."[2] The second half requires their seduction; Rousseau focuses on their willingness to be seduced.

As *Discourse on the Origin of Inequality* unfolds, Rousseau works out how the self-respect of ordinary people fades through responding to the example set by others:

> He who sings or dances the best, he who is the most handsome, the strongest, and most adroit or the most eloquent becomes the most highly regarded; and this is the first step towards inequality, and at the same time towards vice.[3]

There seems nothing exceptional in this passage until we compare it to Nietzsche's in *Beyond Good and Evil:* "We have to force morals to bow down before hierarchy." Nietzsche's counsel is just to be strong, to take pride in yourself.[4] For Rousseau, the superior is not indifferent to the weak: their envy confirms he has something of value. How can he elicit it?

The superior is like a guard standing at a border crossing, simultaneously beckoning to others while refusing to accept their passports as valid. They insist; he then says, "Let me show you what a valid passport looks like." Now they are hooked: "But my passport looks just like that!" The seduction is about to occur: the guard ruefully demurs, "Well, it looks the same, but I'm not sure." And then is consummated; the immigrant looks at his documents and ruefully reflects, "My passport, although genuine, was not good enough."

I've put crudely the mechanics of invidious comparison which Rousseau descried in the Paris of his time, a city where elderly men dye their hair even though they know other people only notice the fact it is dyed; where solid bourgeois families ruin themselves to provide the carriages, houses, and clothes which, they also know, will yield them at most the ironic smiles of aristocrats willing occasionally to dine with them or condescend to borrow their money. More consequently for Rousseau, the same mechanics will lead the poor to abandon those pursuits which can sustain them—abandon them for chances in the street, for some magical encounter, some elevation of fortune which they keep a secret, knowing that those who know them well and wish them well would be appalled. Envy has the power to suspend one's judgment of reality. As a result, a person's *amour de soi,* be it graceful acceptance of age, station, or confidence in his or her own abilities, founders.

We may think that self-respect is the bedrock of character, but Rousseau did not. Desire for what one lacks seemed to him a much stronger force, and so *amour-propre* will always prevail over *amour de soi.*

The seductions of inequality seemed not only to Rousseau but to many of his contemporaries the dark side of the doctrine of careers open to talent.

In *The Wealth of Nations,* Smith wrote of the "overweening conceit which the greater part of men have of their abilities" and asserted, "The chance of gain is by every man more or less overvalued, and the chance of loss is by most men undervalued."[5] Competitive struggle in the marketplace would expose the cruel illusion of this "overweening conceit." Yet from envy the masses would persist, trying to emulate the risk-taking only the truly wealthy could afford. They would be seduced by possibility even though they had little chance of success.

The market economy also seemed to darken the word "open" in the call to arms "careers open to talent." The talented would form a self-righteous elect, invalidating the passports of the masses, a condition summoned to mind today by the phrase "the liberal elite." This is what worried, early on, the Scottish Enlightenment philosopher Adam Ferguson, who wrote in *An Essay on the History of Civil Society:*

> The separation of the professions, while it seems to promise improvement of skill . . . serves in some measure to break the bonds of society, to substitute mere forms and rules of art in place of ingenuity, and to withdraw individuals from the common scene of occupation on which the sentiments of the heart and the mind are most happily employed.[6]

Rousseau understood the other side of elitism: the fear of being identified with the mass. The superior's *amour-propre* depends on never being taken to be ordinary. While the liberal elite may indeed identify with extremes of poverty or pain, the ordinary person—the "loser," in American slang—arouses anxiety. That anxiety takes on a peculiar twist in the modern emphasis on potential ability; this is an educational and labor regime in which it becomes hard to develop something like *amour de soi,* a realistic assessment and engagement of one's own capacities. So fantasy, of the sort Smith also feared, is unleashed.

Against the seduction of envy, Rousseau argued for the virtue of *amour de soi,* of craft, of the self-respect which consists in doing something well for its own sake. His essay concludes on a note of pessimism, however, just because he feared the dynamics of seduction to be more powerful than those of self-respect.[7] Other people have been taken too seriously, oneself not enough.

These are some of the complications inequality raises in the experience of respect, complications bred particularly by unequal talents. As realistic egalitarians have been the first to admit, nature distributes brains unequally, like beauty or art. The question is what society makes of that fact "Careers open to talent" was a way to honor that inequality; it arose in an era when talent could be framed and defined. Modern concepts of potential ability take away the definition but not the inequality.

Talent itself, whether great or small, has an ambiguous relation to character, character which relates oneself to others. The crafting of self-respect can deny this connection, through inward obsession or object fixation. Displays of mastery can in principle provide a stronger connection, through furnishing models for guidance and imitation. In practice, however, imitation and competition have long been yoked together, the connection becoming an adversarial relation. And again, the display of mastery can trigger a dynamic of seduction in which the weak, when imitating the strong, only ratify inequality through envy.

NOTES

1. Jean-Jacques Rousseau, *Discourse on the Origin of Inequality,* in *The Collected Writings of Rousseau,* ed. Roger D. Masters and Christopher Kelly (Hanover, N.H.: University Press of New England, 1991), 3:91, note 12.

2. Maurice Cranston, *The Noble Savage,* vol.2 of *The Life of Jean-Jacques Rousseau* (Chicago: University of Chicago Press, 1991), p. 304.

3. Jean-Jacques Rousseau, *Discourse on the Origin of Inequality,* ed. Maurice Cranston (New York: Penguin Books, 1984), p. 114.

4. Friedrich Nietzsche, *Beyond Good and Evil,* trans. Walter Kaufmann (New York: Vintage, 1966), #221.

5. Adam Smith, *The Wealth of Nations,* (1776; London: Methuen, 1961), pp. 107, 109.

6. Adam Ferguson, *An Essay on the History of Civil Society* (New York: Cambridge University Press, 1996), p. 364.

7. I am particularly indebted in this reading of Rousseau to Marshall Berman, *The Politics of Authenticity* (New York: Atheneum, 1970).

Some Principals of Stratification

KINGSLEY DAVIS AND WILBERT E. MOORE

In a previous paper some concepts for handling the phenomena of social inequality were presented.[1] In the present paper a further step in stratification theory is undertaken—an attempt to show the relationship between stratification and the rest of the social order.[2] Starting from the proposition that no society is "classless," or unstratified, an effort is made to explain, in functional terms, the universal necessity which calls forth stratification in any social system. Next, an attempt is made to explain the roughly uniform distribution of prestige as between the major types of positions in every society. Since, however, there occur between one society and another great differences in the degree and kind of stratification, some attention is also given to the varieties of social inequality and the variable factors that give rise to them.

Clearly, the present task requires two different lines of analysis—one to understand the universal, the other to understand the variable features of stratification. Naturally each line of inquiry aids the other and is indispensable, and in the treatment that follows the two will be interwoven, although, because of space limitations, the emphasis will be on the universals.

Throughout, it will be necessary to keep in mind one thing—namely, that the discussion relates to the system of positions, not to the individuals occupying those positions. It is one thing to ask why different positions carry different degrees of prestige, and quite another to ask how certain individuals get into those positions. Although, as the argument will try to show, both questions are related, it is essential to keep them separate in our thinking. Most of the literature on stratification has tried to answer the second question (particularly with regard to the ease or difficulty of mobility between strata) without tackling the first. The first question, however, is logically prior and, in the case of any particular individual or group, factually prior.

THE FUNCTIONAL NECESSITY OF STRATIFICATION

Curiously, however, the main functional necessity explaining the universal presence of stratification is precisely the requirement faced by any society of placing and motivating individuals in the social structure. As a functioning mechanism a society must somehow distribute its members in social positions and induce them to perform the duties of these positions. It must thus concern itself with motivation at two different levels: to instill in the proper individuals the desire to fill certain positions, and, once in these positions, the desire to

[1]Kingsley Davis, "A Conceptual Analysis of Stratification," *American Sociological Review.* 7: 309–321, June, 1942.
[2]The writers regret (and beg indulgence) that the present essay, a condensation of a longer study, covers so much in such short space that adequate evidence and qualification cannot be given and that as a result what is actually very tentative is presented in an unfortunately dogmatic manner.

Source: Kingsley Davis and Wilbert E. Moore, "Some Principles of Stratification," *American Sociological Review*, Vol. 10, No. 2, 1944: 242–249.

perform the duties attached to them. Even though the social order may be relatively static in form, there is a continuous process of metabolism as new individuals are born into it, shift with age, and die off. Their absorption into the positional system must somehow be arranged and motivated. This is true whether the system is competitive or non-competitive. A competitive system gives greater importance to the motivation to achieve positions, whereas a non-competitive system gives perhaps greater importance to the motivation to perform the duties of the positions; but in any system both types of motivation are required.

If the duties associated with the various positions were all equally pleasant to the human organism, all equally important to societal survival, and all equally in need of the same ability or talent, it would make no difference who got into which positions, and the problem of social placement would be greatly reduced. But actually it does make a great deal of difference who gets into which positions, not only because some positions are inherently more agreeable than others, but also because some require special talents or training and some are functionally more important than others. Also, it is essential that the duties of the positions be performed with the diligence that their importance requires. Inevitably, then, a society must have, first, some kind of rewards that it can use as inducements, and, second, some way of distributing these rewards differentially according to positions. The rewards and their distribution become a part of the social order, and thus give rise to stratification.

One may ask what kind of rewards a society has at its disposal in distributing its personnel and securing essential services. It has, first of all, the things that contribute to sustenance and comfort. It has, second, the things that contribute to humor and diversion. And it has, finally, the things that contribute to self respect and ego expansion. The last, because of the peculiarly social character of the self, is largely a function of the opinion of others, but it nonetheless ranks in importance with the first two. In any social system all three kinds of rewards must be dispensed differentially according to positions.

In a sense the rewards are "built into" the position. They consist in the "rights" associated with the position, plus what may be called its accompaniments or perquisites. Often the rights, and sometimes the accompaniments, are functionally related to the duties of the position. (Rights as viewed by the incumbent are usually duties as viewed by other members of the community.) However, there may be a host of subsidiary rights and perquisites that are not essential to the function of the position and have only an indirect and symbolic connection with its duties, but which still may be of considerable importance in inducing people to seek the positions and fulfil the essential duties.

If the rights and perquisites of different positions in a society must be unequal, then the society must be stratified, because that is precisely what stratification means. Social inequality is thus an unconsciously evolved device by which societies insure that the most important positions are conscientiously filled by the most qualified persons. Hence every society, no matter how simple or complex, must differentiate persons in terms of both prestige and esteem, and must therefore possess a certain amount of institutionalized inequality.

It does not follow that the amount or type of inequality need be the same in all societies. This is largely a function of factors that will be discussed presently.

THE TWO DETERMINANTS OF POSITIONAL RANK

Granting the general function that inequality subserves, one can specify the two factors that determine the relative rank of different positions. In general those positions convey the best reward, and hence have the highest rank, which (a) have the greatest importance for the society and (b) require the greatest training or talent. The first factor concerns function and is a matter of relative significance; the second concerns means and is a matter of scarcity.

Differential Functional Importance.   Actually a society does not need to reward positions in proportion to their functional importance. It merely needs to give sufficient reward to them to insure that they will be filled competently. In other words, it must see that less essential positions do not compete successfully with more essential ones. If a position is easily filled, it need not be heavily rewarded, even though important. On the other hand, if it is important but hard to fill, the reward must be high enough to get it filled anyway. Functional importance is therefore a necessary but not a sufficient cause of high rank being assigned to a position.[3]

Differential Scarcity of Personnel. Practically all positions, no matter how acquired, require some form of skill or capacity for performance. This is implicit in the very notion of position, which implies that the incumbent must, by virtue of his incumbency, accomplish certain things.

There are, ultimately, only two ways in which a person's qualifications come about: through inherent capacity or through training. Obviously, in concrete activities both are always necessary, but from a practical standpoint the scarcity may lie primarily in one or the other, as well as in both. Some positions require innate talents of such high degree that the persons who fill them are bound to be rare. In many cases, however, talent is fairly abundant in the population but the training process is so long,

costly, and elaborate that relatively few can qualify. Modern medicine, for example, is within the mental capacity of most individuals, but a medical education is so burdensome and expensive that virtually none would undertake it if the position of the M.D. did not carry a reward commensurate with the sacrifice.

If the talents required for a position are abundant and the training easy, the method of acquiring the position may have little to do with its duties. There may be, in fact, a virtually accidental relationship. But if the skills required are scarce by reason of the rarity of talent or the costliness of training, the position, if functionally important, must have an attractive power that will draw the necessary skills in competition with other positions. This means, in effect, that the position must be high in the social scale—must command great prestige, high salary, ample leisure, and the like.

How Variations Are to Be Understood. In so far as there is a difference between one system of stratification and another, it is attributable to whatever factors affect the two determinants of differential reward—namely, functional importance and scarcity of personnel. Positions important in one society may not be important in another, because the conditions faced by the societies, or their degree of internal development, may be different. The same conditions, in turn, may affect the question of scarcity; for in some societies the stage of development, or the external situation, may wholly obviate the necessity of certain kinds of skill or talent. Any particular system of stratification, then, can be understood as a product of the special conditions affecting the two aforementioned grounds of differential reward.

MAJOR SOCIETAL FUNCTIONS AND STRATIFICATION

Religion. The reason why religion is necessary is apparently to be found in the fact that human society achieves its unity primarily through the

---

[3]Unfortunately, functional importance is difficult to establish. To use the position's prestige to establish it, as is often unconsciously done, constitutes circular reasoning from our point of view. There are, however, two independent clues: (a) the degree to which a position is functionally unique, there being no other positions that can perform the same function satisfactorily; (b) the degree to which other positions are dependent on the one in question. Both clues are best exemplified in organized systems of positions built around one major function. Thus, in most complex societies the religious, political, economic, and educational functions are handled by distinct structures not easily interchangeable. In addition, each structure possesses many different positions, some clearly dependent on, if not subordinate to, others. In sum, when an institutional nucleus becomes differentiated around one main function, and at the same time organizes a large portion of the population into its relationships, the *key* positions in it are of the highest functional importance. The absence of such specialization does not prove functional unimportance, for the whole society may be relatively unspecialized; but it is safe to assume that the more important functions receive the first and clearest structural differentiation.

possession by its members of certain ultimate values and ends in common. Although these values and ends are subjective, they influence behavior, and their integration enables the society to operate as a system. Derived neither from inherited nor from external nature, they have evolved as a part of culture by communication and moral pressure. They must, however, appear to the members of the society to have some reality, and it is the role of religious belief and ritual to supply and reinforce this appearance of reality. Through belief and ritual the common ends and values are connected with an imaginary world symbolized by concrete sacred objects, which world in turn is related in a meaningful way to the facts and trials of the individual's life. Through the worship of the sacred objects and the beings they symbolize, and the acceptance of supernatural prescriptions that are at the same time codes of behavior, a powerful control over human conduct is exercised, guiding it along lines sustaining the institutional structure and conforming to the ultimate ends and values.

If this conception of the role of religion is true, one can understand why in every known society the religious activities tend to be under the charge of particular persons, who tend thereby to enjoy greater rewards than the ordinary societal member. Certain of the rewards and special privileges may attach to only the highest religious functionaries, but others usually apply, if such exists, to the entire sacerdotal class.

Moreover, there is a peculiar relation between the duties of the religious official and the special privileges he enjoys. If the supernatural world governs the destinies of men more ultimately than does the real world, its earthly representative, the person through whom one may communicate with the supernatural, must be a powerful individual. He is a keeper of sacred tradition, a skilled performer of the ritual, and an interpreter of lore and myth. He is in such close contact with the gods that he is viewed as possessing some of their characteristics. He is, in short, a bit sacred, and hence free from some of the more vulgar necessities and controls.

It is no accident, therefore, that religious functionaries have been associated with the very highest positions of power, as in theocratic regimes. Indeed, looking at it from this point of view, one may wonder why it is that they do not get *entire* control over their societies. The factors that prevent this are worthy of note.

In the first place, the amount of technical competence necessary for the performance of religious duties is small. Scientific or artistic capacity is not required. Anyone can set himself up as enjoying an intimate relation with deities, and nobody can successfully dispute him. Therefore, the factor of scarcity of personnel does not operate in the technical sense.

One may assert, on the other hand, that religious ritual is often elaborate and religious lore abstruse, and that priestly ministrations require tact, if not intelligence. This is true, but the technical requirements of the profession are for the most part adventitious, not related to the end in the same way that science is related to air travel. The priest can never be free from competition, since the criteria of whether or not one has genuine contact with the supernatural are never strictly clear. It is this competition that debases the priestly position below what might be expected at first glance. That is why priestly prestige is highest in those societies where membership in the profession is rigidly controlled by the priestly guild itself. That is why, in part at least, elaborate devices are utilized to stress the identification of the person with his office—spectacular costume, abnormal conduct, special diet, segregated residence, celibacy, conspicuous leisure, and the like. In fact, the priest is always in danger of becoming somewhat discredited—as happens in a secularized society—because in a world of stubborn fact, ritual and sacred knowledge alone will not grow crops or build houses. Furthermore, unless he is protected by a professional guild, the priest's identification with the supernatural tends to preclude his acquisition of abundant wordly goods.

As between one society and another it seems that the highest general position awarded the priest occurs in the medieval type of social order.

Here there is enough economic production to afford a surplus, which can be used to support a numerous and highly organized priesthood; and yet the populace is unlettered and therefore credulous to a high degree. Perhaps the most extreme example is to be found in the Buddhism of Tibet, but others are encountered in the Catholicism of feudal Europe, the Inca regime of Peru, the Brahminism of India, and the Mayan priesthood of Yucatan. On the other hand, if the society is so crude as to have no surplus and little differentiation, so that every priest must be also a cultivator or hunter, the separation of the priestly status from the others has hardly gone far enough for priestly prestige to mean much. When the priest actually has high prestige under these circumstances, it is because he also performs other important functions (usually political and medical).

In an extremely advanced society built on scientific technology, the priesthood tends to lose status, because sacred tradition and supernaturalism drop into the background. The ultimate values and common ends of the society tend to be expressed in less anthropomorphic ways, by officials who occupy fundamentally political, economic, or educational rather than religious positions. Nevertheless, it is easily possible for intellectuals to exaggerate the degree to which the priesthood in a presumably secular milieu has lost prestige. When the matter is closely examined the urban proletariat, as well as the rural citizenry, proves to be suprisingly god-fearing and priest-ridden. No society has become so completely secularized as to liquidate entirely the belief in transcendental ends and supernatural entities. Even in a secularized society some system must exist for the integration of ultimate values, for their ritualistic expression, and for the emotional adjustments required by disappointment, death, and disaster.

Government.   Like religion, government plays a unique and indispensable part in society. But in contrast to religion, which provides integration in terms of sentiments, beliefs, and rituals, it organizes the society in terms of law and authority.

Furthermore, it orients the society to the actual rather than the unseen world.

The main functions of government are, internally, the ultimate enforcement of norms, the final arbitration of conflicting interests, and the overall planning and direction of society; and externally, the handling of war and diplomacy. To carry out these functions it acts as the agent of the entire people, enjoys a monopoly of force, and controls all individuals within its territory.

Political action, by definition, implies authority. An official can command because he has authority, and the citizen must obey because he is subject to that authority. For this reason stratification is inherent in the nature of political relationships.

So clear is the power embodied in political position that political inequality is sometimes thought to comprise all inequality. But it can be shown that there are other bases of stratification, that the following controls operate in practice to keep political power from becoming complete: (a) The fact that the actual holders of political office, and especially those determining top policy must necessarily be few in number compared to the total population. (b) The fact that the rulers represent the interest of the group rather than of themselves, and are therefore restricted in their behavior by rules and mores designed to enforce this limitation of interest. (c) The fact that the holder of political office has his authority by virtue of his office and nothing else, and therefore any special knowledge, talent, or capacity he may claim is purely incidental, so that he often has to depend upon others for technical assistance.

In view of these limiting factors, it is not strange that the rulers often have less power and prestige than a literal enumeration of their formal rights would lead one to expect.

Wealth, Property, and Labor.   Every position that secures for its incumbent a livelihood is, by definition, economically rewarded. For this reason there is an economic aspect to those positions (e.g. political and religious) the main function of which is not economic. It therefore becomes convenient for the society to use unequal economic returns as a principal means of controlling the entrance of persons into positions and stimulating the performance of their duties. The amount of the economic return therefore becomes one of the main indices of social status.

It should be stressed, however, that a position does not bring power and prestige *because* it draws a high income. Rather, it draws a high income because it is functionally important and the available personnel is for one reason or another scarce. It is therefore superficial and erroneous to regard high income as the cause of a man's power and prestige, just as it is erroneous to think that a man's fever is the cause of his disease.[4]

The economic source of power and prestige is not income primarily, but the ownership of capital goods (including patents, good will, and professional reputation). Such ownership should be distinguished from the possession of consumers' goods, which is an index rather than a cause of social standing. In other words, the ownership of producers' goods is properly speaking, a source of income like other positions, the income itself remaining an index. Even in situations where social values are widely commercialized and earnings are the readiest method of judging social position, income does not confer prestige on a position so much as it induces people to compete for the position. It is true that a man who has a high income as a result of one position may find this money helpful in climbing into another position as well, but this again reflects the effect of his initial, economically advantageous status, which exercises its influence through the medium of money.

In a system of private property in productive enterprise, an income above what an individual spends can give rise to possession of capital wealth.

Presumably such possession is a reward for the proper management of one's finances originally and of the productive enterprise later. But as social differentiation becomes highly advanced and yet the institution of inheritance persists, the phenomenon of pure ownership, and reward for pure ownership, emerges. In such a case it is difficult to prove that the position is functionally important or that the scarcity involved is anything other than extrinsic and accidental. It is for this reason, doubtless, that the institution of private property in productive goods becomes more subject to criticism as social development proceeds toward industrialization. It is only this pure, that is, strictly legal and functionless ownership, however, that is open to attack; for some form of active ownership, whether private or public, is indispensable.

One kind of ownership of production goods consists in rights over the labor of others. The most extremely concentrated and exclusive of such rights are found in slavery, but the essential principle remains in serfdom, peonage, encomienda, and indenture. Naturally this kind of ownership has the greatest significance for stratification, because it necessarily entails an unequal relationship.

But property in capital goods inevitably introduces a compulsive element even into the nominally free contractual relationship. Indeed, in some respects the authority of the contractual employer is greater than that of the feudal landlord, inasmuch as the latter is more limited by traditional reciprocities. Even the classical economics recognized that competitors would fare unequally, but it did not pursue this fact to its necessary conclusion that, however it might be acquired, unequal control of goods and services must give unequal advantage to the parties to a contract.

Technical Knowledge. The function of finding means to single goals, without any concern with the choice between goals, is the exclusively technical sphere. The explanation of why positions requiring great technical skill receive fairly high rewards is easy to see, for it is the simplest case of the rewards being so distributed as to draw talent and motivate training. Why they seldom if ever receive the highest

---

[4]The symbolic rather than intrinsic role of income in social stratification has been succinctly summarized by Talcott Parsons, "An Analytical Approach to the Theory of Social Stratification," *American Journal of Sociology.* 45:841–862, May, 1940.

rewards is also clear: the importance of technical knowledge from a societal point of view is never so great as the integration of goals, which takes place on the religious, political, and economic levels. Since the technological level is concerned solely with means, a purely technical position must ultimately be subordinate to other positions that are religious, political, or economic in character.

Nevertheless, the distinction between expert and layman in any social order is fundamental, and cannot be entirely reduced to other terms. Methods of recruitment, as well as of reward, sometimes lead to the erroneous interpretation that technical positions are economically determined. Actually, however, the acquisition of knowledge and skill cannot be accomplished by purchase, although the opportunity to learn may be. The control of the avenues of training may inhere as a sort of property right in certain families or classes, giving them power and prestige in consequence. Such a situation adds an artificial scarcity to the natural scarcity of skills and talents. On the other hand, it is possible for an opposite situation to arise. The rewards of technical position may be so great that a condition of excess supply is created, leading to at least temporary devaluation of the rewards. Thus "unemployment in the learned professions" may result in a debasement of the prestige of those positions. Such adjustments and readjustments are constantly occurring in changing societies; and it is always well to bear in mind that the efficiency of a stratified structure may be affected by the modes of recruitment for positions. The social order itself, however, sets limits to the inflation or deflation of the prestige of experts: an oversupply tends to debase the rewards and discourage recruitment or produce revolution, whereas an under-supply tends to increase the rewards or weaken the society in competition with other societies.

Particular systems of stratification show a wide range with respect to the exact position of technically competent persons. This range is perhaps most evident in the degree of specialization. Extreme division of labor tends to create many specialists

without high prestige since the training is short and the required native capacity relatively small. On the other hand it also tends to accentuate the high position of the true experts—scientists, engineers, and administrators—by increasing their authority relative to other functionally important positions. But the idea of a technocratic social order or a government or priesthood of engineers or social scientists neglects the limitations of knowledge and skills as a basic for performing social functions. To the extent that the social structure is truly specialized the prestige of the technical person must also be circumscribed.

VARIATION IN STRATIFIED SYSTEMS

The generalized principles of stratification here suggested form a necessary preliminary to a consideration of types of stratified systems, because it is in terms of these principles that the types must be described. This can be seen by trying to delineate types according to certain modes of variation. For instance, some of the most important modes (together with the polar types in terms of them) seem to be as follows:

a. *The Degree of Specialization.* The degree of specialization affects the fineness and multiplicity of the gradations in power and prestige. It also influences the extent to which particular functions may be emphasized in the invidious system, since a given function cannot receive much emphasis in the hierarchy until it has achieved structural separation from the other functions. Finally, the amount of specialization influences the bases of selection. Polar types: *Specialized, Unspecialized.*

b. *The Nature of the Functional Emphasis.* In general when emphasis is put on sacred matters, a rigidity is introduced that tends to limit specialization and hence the development of technology. In addition, a brake is placed on social mobility, and on the development of bureaucracy. When the preoccupation with the sacred is withdrawn, leaving greater scope for purely secular preoccupations, a great development, and rise in status, of economic and technological positions seemingly takes place. Curiously, a concomitant rise in political position is not likely, because it has usually been allied with the religious and stands to gain little by the decline of the latter. It is also possible for a society to emphasize family functions—as in relatively undifferentiated societies where high mortality requires high fertility and kinship forms the main basis of social organization. Main types: *Familistic, Authoritarian (Theocratic* or *sacred,* and *Totalitarian* or *secular), Capitalistic.*

c. *The Magnitude of Invidious Differences.* What may be called the amount of social distance between positions, taking into account the entire scale, is something that should lend itself to quantitative measurement. Considerable differences apparently exist between different societies in this regard, and also between parts of the same society. Polar types: *Equalitarian, Inequalitarian.*

d. *The Degree of Opportunity.* The familiar question of the amount of mobility is different from the question of the comparative equality or inequality of rewards posed above, because the two criteria may vary independently up to a point. For instance, the tremendous divergences in monetary income in the United States are far greater than those found in primitive societies, yet the equality of opportunity to move from one rung to the other in the social scale may also be greater in the United States than in a hereditary tribal kingdom. Polar types: *Mobile* (open), *Immobile* (closed).

e. *The Degree of Stratum Solidarity.* Again, the degree of "class solidarity" (or the presence of specific organizations to promote class interests) may vary to some extent independently of the other criteria, and hence is an important principle in classifying systems of stratification. Polar types: *Class organized, Class unorganized.*

EXTERNAL CONDITIONS

What state any particular system of stratification is in with reference to each of these modes of variation depends on two things: (I) its state with reference to the other ranges of variation, and (2) the conditions outside the system of stratification which nevertheless influence that system. Among the latter are the following:

a. *The Stage of Cultural Development.* As the cultural heritage grows, increased specialization becomes necessary, which in turn contributes to the enhancement of mobility, a decline of stratum solidarity, and a change of functional emphasis.

b. *Situation with Respect to Other Societies.* The presence or absence of open conflict with other societies, of free trade relations or cultural diffusion, all influence the class structure to some extent. A chronic state of warfare tends to place emphasis upon the military functions, especially when the opponents are more or less equal. Free trade, on the other hand, strengthens the hand of the trader at the expense of the warrior and priest. Free movement of ideas generally has an equalitarian effect. Migration and conquest create special circumstances.

c. *Size of the Society.* A small society limits the degree to which functional specialization can go, the degree of segregation of different strata, and the magnitude of inequality.

COMPOSITE TYPES

Much of the literature on stratification has attempted to classify concrete systems into a certain number of types. This task is deceptively simple, however, and should come at the end of an analysis of elements and principles, rather than at the beginning. If the preceding discussion has any validity, it indicates that there are a number of modes of variation between different systems, and that any one system is a composite of the society's status with reference to all these modes of variation. The danger of trying to classify whole societies under such rubrics as *caste, feudal,* or *open class* is that one or two criteria are selected and others ignored, the result being an unsatisfactory solution to the problem posed. The present discussion has been offered as a possible approach to the more systematic classification of composite types.

Some Principals of Stratification:
A Critical Analysis

MELVIN M. TUMIN

The fact of social inequality in human society is marked by its ubiquity and its antiquity. Every known society, past and present, distributes its scarce and demanded goods and services unequally. And there are attached to the positions which command unequal amounts of such goods and services certain highly morally-toned evaluations of their importance for the society.

The ubiquity and the antiquity of such inequality has given rise to the assumption that there must be something both inevitable and positively functional about such social arrangements.

Clearly, the truth or falsity of such an assumption is a strategic question for any general theory of social organization. It is therefore most curious that the basic premises and implications of the assumption have only been most casually explored by American sociologists.

The most systematic treatment is to be found in the well-known article by Kingsley Davis and Wilbert Moore, entitled "Some Principles of Stratification."[1] More than twelve years have passed since its publication, and though it is one of the very few treatments of stratification on a high level of generalization, it is difficult to locate a single systematic analysis of its reasoning. It will be the principal concern of this paper to present the beginnings of such an analysis.

Source: Melvin M. Tumin, "Some Principles of Stratification: A Critical Analysis," *American Sociological Review*, Vol. 18, No. 4, 1953: 387–394.

The central argument advanced by Davis and Moore can be stated in a number of sequential propositions, as follows:

1. Certain positions in any society are functionally more important than others, and require special skills for their performance.
2. Only a limited number of individuals in any society have the talents which can be trained into the skills appropriate to these positions.
3. The conversion of talents into skills involves a training period during which sacrifices of one kind or another are made by those undergoing the training.

---

*The writer has had the benefit of a most helpful criticism of the main portions of this paper by Professor W. J. Goode of Columbia University. In addition, he has had the opportunity to expose this paper to criticism by the Staff Seminar of the Sociology Section at Princeton. In deference to a possible rejoinder by Professors Moore and Davis, the writer has not revised the paper to meet the criticisms which Moore has already offered personally.

[1] *American Sociological Review,* X (April, 1945), pp. 242–249. An earlier article by Kingsley Davis, entitled, "A Conceptual Analysis of Stratification," *American Sociological Review,* VII (June, 1942), pp. 309–321, is devoted primarily to setting forth a vocabulary for stratification analysis. A still earlier article by Talcott Parsons, "An Analytical Approach to the Theory of Social Stratification," *American Journal of Sociology,* XLV (November, 1940), pp. 849–862, approaches the problem in terms of why "differential ranking is considered a really fundamental phenomenon of social systems and what are the respects in which such ranking is important." The principal line of integration asserted by Parsons is with the fact of the normative orientation of any society. Certain crucial lines of connection are left unexplained, however, in this article, and in the Davis and Moore article of 1945 only some of these lines are made explicit.

4. In order to induce the talented persons to undergo these sacrifices and acquire the training, their future positions must carry an inducement value in the form of differential, i.e., privileged and disproportionate access to the scarce and desired rewards which the society has to offer.[2]

5. These scarce and desired goods consist of the rights and perquisites attached to, or built into, the positions, and can be classified into those things which contribute to (a) sustenance and comfort, (b) humor and diversion, (c) self-respect and ego expansion.

6. This differential access to the basic rewards of the society has as a consequence the differentiation of the prestige and esteem which various strata acquire. This may be said, along with the rights and perquisites, to constitute institutionalized social inequality, i.e., stratification.

7. Therefore, social inequality among different strata in the amounts of scarce and desired goods, and the amounts of prestige and esteem which they receive, is both positively functional and inevitable in any society.

Let us take these propositions and examine them *seriatim.*[3]

(1) Certain positions in any society are more functionally important than others and require special skills for their performance.

The key term here is "functionally important." The functionalist theory of social organization is by no means clear and explicit about this term. The minimum common referent is to something known as the "survival value" of a social structure.[4] This

concept immediately involves a number of perplexing questions. Among these are: (a) the issue of minimum vs. maximum survival, and the possible empirical referents which can be given to those terms; (b) whether such a proposition is a useless tautology since any *status quo* at any given moment is nothing more and nothing less than everything present in the *status quo.* In these terms, all acts and structures must be judged positively functional in that they constitute essential portions of the *status quo;* (c) what kind of calculus of functionality exists which will enable us, at this point in our development, to add and subtract long and short range consequences, with their mixed qualities, and arrive at some summative judgment regarding the rating an act or structure should receive on a scale of greater or lesser functionality? At best, we tend to make primarily intuitive judgments. Often enough, these judgments involve the use of value-laden criteria, or, at least, criteria which are chosen in preference to others not for any sociologically systematic reasons but by reason of certain implicit value preferences.

Thus, to judge that the engineers in a factory are functionally more important to the factory than the unskilled workmen involves a notion regarding the dispensability of the unskilled workmen, or their replaceability, relative to that of the engineers. But this is not a process of choice with infinite time dimensions. For at some point along the line one must face the problem of adequate motivation for *all* workers at all levels of skill in the factory. In the long run, *some* labor force of unskilled workmen is as important and as indispensable to the factory as *some* labor force of engineers. Often enough, the labor force situation is such that this fact is brought home sharply to the entrepreneur in the short run rather than in the long run.

Moreover, the judgment as to the relative indispensability and replaceability of a particular segment of skills in the population involves a prior judgment about the bargaining-power of that segment. But this power is itself a culturally shaped *consequence* of the existing system of rating, rather than something inevitable in the nature of social

---

[2]The "scarcity and demand" qualities of goods and services are never explicitly mentioned by Davis and Moore. But it seems to the writer that the argument makes no sense unless the goods and services are so characterized. For if rewards are to function as differential inducements they must not only be differentially distributed but they must be both scarce and demanded as well. Neither the scarcity of an item by itself nor the fact of its being in demand is sufficient to allow it to function as a differential inducement in a system of unequal rewards. Leprosy is scarce and oxygen is highly demanded.
[3]The arguments to be advanced here are condensed versions of a much longer analysis entitled, *An Essay on Social Stratification.* Perforce, all the reasoning necessary to support some of the contentions cannot be offered within the space limits of this article.
[4]Davis and Moore are explicitly aware of the difficulties involved here and suggest two "independent clues" other than survival value. See footnote 3 on p. 244 of their article.

organization. At least the contrary of this has never been demonstrated, but only assumed.

A generalized theory of social stratification must recognize that the prevailing system of inducements and rewards is only one of many variants in the whole range of possible systems of motivation which, at least theoretically, are capable of working in human society. It is quite conceivable, of course, that a system of norms could be institutionalized in which the idea of threatened withdrawal of services, except under the most extreme circumstances, would be considered as absolute moral anathema. In such a case, the whole notion of relative functionality, as advanced by Davis and Moore, would have to be radically revised.

(2) Only a limited number of individuals in any society have the talents which can be trained into the skills appropriate to these positions (i.e., the more functionally important positions).

The truth of this proposition depends at least in part on the truth of proposition 1 above. It is, therefore, subject to all the limitations indicated above. But for the moment, let us assume the validity of the first proposition and concentrate on the question of the rarity of appropriate talent.

If all that is meant is that in every society there is a *range* of talent, and that some members of any society are by nature more talented than others, no sensible contradiction can be offered, but a question must be raised here regarding the amount of sound knowledge present in any society concerning the presence of talent in the population.

For, in every society there is some demonstrable ignorance regarding the amount of talent present in the population. *And the more rigidly stratified a society is, the less chance does that society have of discovering any new facts about the talents of its members.* Smoothly working and stable systems of stratification, wherever found, tend to build-in obstacles to the further exploration of the range of available talent. This is especially true in those societies where the opportunity to discover talent in any one generation varies with the differential resources of the parent generation.

Where, for instance, access to education depends upon the wealth of one's parents, and where wealth is differentially distributed, large segments of the population are likely to be deprived of the chance even to *discover* what are their talents.

Whether or not differential rewards and opportunities are functional in any one generation, it is clear that if those differentials are allowed to be socially inherited by the next generation, then, the stratification system is specifically dysfunctional for the discovery of talents in the next generation. In this fashion, systems of social stratification tend to limit the chances available to maximize the efficiency of discovery, recruitment and training of "functionally important talent."[5]

Additionally, the unequal distribution of rewards in one generation tends to result in the unequal distribution of motivation in the succeeding generation. Since motivation to succeed is clearly an important element in the entire process of education, the unequal distribution of motivation tends to set limits on the possible extensions of the educational system, and hence, upon the efficient recruitment and training of the widest body of skills available in the population.[6]

Lastly, in this context, it may be asserted that there is some noticeable tendency for elites to restrict further access to their privileged positions, once they have sufficient power to enforce such restrictions. This is especially true in a culture where it is possible for an elite to contrive a high demand and a proportionately higher reward for its work by restricting the numbers of the elite available to do the work. The recruitment and training of doctors in modern United States is at least partly a case in point.

---

[5]Davis and Moore state this point briefly on p. 248 but do not elaborate it.

[6]In the United States, for instance, we are only now becoming aware of the amount of productivity we, as a society, lose by allocating inferior opportunities and rewards, and hence, inferior motivation, to our Negro population. The actual amount of loss is difficult to specify precisely. Some rough estimate can be made, however, on the assumption that there is present in the Negro population about the same range of talent that is found in the White population.

Here, then, are three ways, among others which could be cited, in which stratification systems, once operative, tend to reduce the survival value of a society by limiting the search, recruitment and training of functionally important personnel far more sharply than the facts of available talent would appear to justify. It is only when there is genuinely equal access to recruitment and training for all potentially talented persons that differential rewards can conceivably be justified as functional. And stratification systems are apparently *inherently antagonistic* to the development of such full equality of opportunity.

(3) The conversion of talents into skills involves a training period during which sacrifices of one kind or another are made by those undergoing the training.

Davis and Moore introduce here a concept, "sacrifice" which comes closer than any of the rest of their vocabulary of analysis to being a direct reflection of the rationalizations, offered by the more fortunate members of a society, of the rightness of their occupancy of privileged positions. It is the least critically thought-out concept in the repertoire, and can also be shown to be least supported by the actual facts.

In our present society, for example, what are the sacrifices which talented persons undergo in the training period? The possibly serious losses involve the surrender of earning power and the cost of the training. The latter is generally borne by the parents of the talented youth undergoing training, and not by the trainees themselves. But this cost tends to be paid out of income which the parents were able to earn generally by virtue of *their* privileged positions in the hierarchy of stratification. That is to say, the parents' ability to pay for the training of their children is part of the differential *reward* they, the parents, received for their privileged positions in the society. And to charge this sum up against sacrifices made by the youth is falsely to perpetrate a bill or a debt already paid by the society to the parents.

So far as the sacrifice of earning power by the trainees themselves is concerned, the loss may be measured relative to what they might have earned had they gone into the labor market instead of into advanced training for the "important" skills. There are several ways to judge this. One way is to take all the average earnings of age peers who did go into the labor market for a period equal to the average length of the training period. The total income, so calculated, roughly equals an amount which the elite can, on the average, earn back in the first decade of professional work, over and above the earnings of his age peers who are not trained. Ten years is probably the maximum amount needed to equalize the differential.[7] There remains, on the average, twenty years of work during each of which the skilled person then goes on to earn far more than his unskilled age peers. And, what is often forgotten, there is then still another ten or fifteen year period during which the skilled person continues to work and earn when his unskilled age peer is either totally or partially out of the labor market by virtue of the attrition of his strength and capabilities.

One might say that the first ten years of differential pay is perhaps justified, in order to regain for the trained person what he lost during his training period. But it is difficult to imagine what would justify continuing such differential rewards beyond that period.

Another and probably sounder way to measure how much is lost during the training period is to compare the per capita income available to the trainee with the per capita income of the age peer on the untrained labor market during the so-called sacrificial period. If one takes into account the earlier marriage of untrained persons, and the earlier acquisition of family dependents, it is highly dubious that the per capita income of the wage worker is significantly larger than that of the trainee. Even assuming, for the moment, that there is a difference, the amount is by no means sufficient to justify a lifetime of continuing differentials.

---

[7]These are only very rough estimates, of course, and it is certain that there is considerable income variation within the so-called elite group. So that the proposition holds only relatively more or less.

What tends to be completely overlooked, in addition, are the psychic and spiritual rewards which are available to the elite trainees by comparison with their age peers in the labor force. There is, first, the much higher prestige enjoyed by the college student and the professional-school student as compared with persons in shops and offices. There is, second, the extremely highly valued privilege of having greater opportunity for self-development. There is, third, all the psychic gain involved in being allowed to delay the assumption of adult responsibilities such as earning a living and supporting a family. There is, fourth, the access to leisure and freedom of a kind not likely to be experienced by the persons already at work.

If these are never taken into account as rewards of the training period it is not because they are not concretely present, but because the emphasis in American concepts of reward is almost exclusively placed on the material returns of positions. The emphases on enjoyment, entertainment, ego enhancement, prestige and esteem are introduced only when the differentials in these which accrue to the skilled positions need to be justified. If these other rewards were taken into account, it would be much more difficult to demonstrate that the training period, as presently operative, is really sacrificial. Indeed, it might turn out to be the case that even at this point in their careers, the elite trainees were being differentially rewarded relative to their age peers in the labor force.

All of the foregoing concerns the quality of the training period under our present system of motivation and rewards. Whatever may turn out to be the factual case about the present system—and the factual case is moot—the more important theoretical question concerns the assumption that the training period under *any* system must be sacrificial.

There seem to be no good theoretical grounds for insisting on this assumption. For, while under any system certain costs will be involved in training persons for skilled positions, these costs could easily be assumed by the society-at-large. Under these circumstances, there would be no need to compensate anyone in terms of differential rewards once the skilled positions were staffed. In short, there would be no need or justification for stratifying social positions on *these* grounds.

(4) In order to induce the talented persons to undergo these sacrifices and acquire the training, their future positions must carry an inducement value in the form of differential, i.e., privileged and disproportionate access to the scarce and desired rewards which the society has to offer.

Let us assume, for the purposes of the discussion, that the training period is sacrificial and the talent is rare in every conceivable human society. There is still the basic problem as to whether the allocation of differential rewards in scarce and desired goods and services is the only or the most efficient way of recruiting the appropriate talent to these positions.

For there are a number of alternative motivational schemes whose efficiency and adequacy ought at least to be considered in this context. What can be said, for instance, on behalf of the motivation which De Man called "joy in work," Veblen termed "instinct for workmanship" and which we latterly have come to identify as "intrinsic work satisfaction?" Or, to what extent could the motivation of "social duty" be institutionalized in such a fashion that self interest and social interest come closely to coincide? Or, how much prospective confidence can be placed in the possibilities of institutionalizing "social service" as a widespread motivation for seeking one's appropriate position and fulfilling it conscientiously?

Are not these types of motivations, we may ask, likely to prove most appropriate for precisely the "most functionally important positions?" Especially in a mass industrial society, where the vast majority of positions become standardized and routinized, it is the skilled jobs which are likely to retain most of the quality of "intrinsic job satisfaction" and be most readily identifiable as socially serviceable. Is it indeed impossible then to build these motivations into the socialization pattern to which we expose our talented youth?

To deny that such motivations could be institutionalized would be to overclaim our present knowledge. In part, also, such a claim would seem to deprive from an assumption that what has not been institutionalized yet in human affairs is incapable of institutionalization. Admittedly, historical experience affords us evidence we cannot afford to ignore. But such evidence cannot legitimately be used to deny absolutely the possibility of heretofore untried alternatives. Social innovation is as important a feature of human societies as social stability.

On the basis of these observations, it seems that Davis and Moore have stated the case much too strongly when they insist that a "functionally important position" which requires skills that are scarce, "must command great prestige, high salary, ample leisure, and the like," if the appropriate talents are to be attracted to the position. Here, clearly, the authors are postulating the unavoidability of very specific types of rewards and, by implication, denying the possibility of others.

(5) These scarce and desired goods consist of rights and perquisites attached to, or built into, the positions and can be classified into those things which contribute to (a) sustenance and comfort; (b) humor and diversion; (c) self respect and ego expansion.

(6) This differential access to the basic rewards of the society has as a consequence the differentiation of the prestige and esteem which various strata acquire. This may be said, along with the rights and perquisites, to constitute institutionalized social inequality, i.e., stratification.

With the classification of the rewards offered by Davis and Moore there need be little argument. Some question must be raised, however, as to whether any reward system, built into a general stratification system, must allocate equal amounts of all three types of reward in order to function effectively, or whether one type of reward may be emphasized to the virtual neglect of others. This raises the further question regarding which type of emphasis is likely to prove most effective as a differential inducer. Nothing in the known facts about human motivation impels us to favor one

type of reward over the other, or to insist that all three types of reward must be built into the positions in comparable amounts if the position is to have an inducement value.

It is well known, of course, that societies differ considerably in the kinds of rewards they emphasize in their efforts to maintain a reasonable balance between responsibility and reward. There are, for instance, numerous societies in which the conspicuous display of differential economic advantage is considered extremely bad taste. In short, our present knowledge commends to us the possibility of considerable plasticity in the way in which different types of rewards can be structured into a functioning society. This is to say, it cannot yet be demonstrated that it is *unavoidable* that differential prestige and esteem shall accrue to positions which command differential rewards in power and property.

What does seem to be unavoidable is that differential prestige shall be given to those in any society who conform to the normative order as against those who deviate from that order in a way judged immoral and detrimental. On the assumption that the continuity of a society depends on the continuity and stability of its normative order, some such distinction between conformists and deviants seems inescapable.

It also seems to be unavoidable that in any society, no matter how literate its tradition, the older, wiser and more experienced individuals who are charged with the enculturation and socialization of the young must have more power than the young, on the assumption that the task of effective socialization demands such differential power.

But this differentiation in prestige between the conformist and the deviant is by no means the same distinction as that between strata of individuals each of which operates *within* the normative order, and is composed of adults. The *latter* distinction, in the form of differentiated rewards and prestige between social strata is what Davis and Moore, and most sociologists, consider the structure of a stratification system. The *former* distinctions have nothing necessarily to do with the workings of such a system nor with the efficiency of motivation and recruitment of functionally important personnel.

Nor does the differentiation of power between young and old necessarily create differentially valued strata. For no society rates its young as less morally worthy than its older persons, no matter how much differential power the older ones may temporarily enjoy.

(7) Therefore, social inequality among different strata in the amounts of scarce and desired goods, and the amounts of prestige and esteem which they receive, is both positively functional and inevitable in any society.

If the objections which have heretofore been raised are taken as reasonable, then it may be stated that the only items which any society *must* distribute unequally are the power and property necessary for the performance of different tasks. If such differential power and property are viewed by all as commensurate with the differential responsibilities, and if they are culturally defined as *resources* and not as rewards, then, no differentials in prestige and esteem need follow.

Historically, the evidence seems to be that every time power and property are distributed unequally, no matter what the cultural definition, prestige and esteem differentiations have tended to result as well. Historically, however, no systematic effort has ever been made, under propitious circumstances, to develop the tradition that each man is as socially worthy as all other men so long as he performs his appropriate tasks conscientiously. While such a tradition seems utterly utopian, no known facts in psychological or social science have yet demonstrated its impossibility or its dysfunctionality for the continuity of a society. The achievement of a full institutionalization of such a tradition seems far too remote to contemplate. Some successive approximations at such a tradition, however, are not out of the range of prospective social innovation.

What, then, of the "positive functionality" of social stratification? Are there other, negative, functions of institutionalized social inequality which can be identified, if only tentatively? Some such dysfunctions of stratification have already been suggested in the body of this paper. Along with others they may now be stated, in the form of provisional assertions, as follows:

1. Social stratification systems function to limit the possibility of discovery of the full range of talent available in a society. This results from the fact of unequal access to appropriate motivation, channels of recruitment and centers of training.

2. In foreshortening the range of available talent, social stratification systems function to set limits upon the possibility of expanding the productive resources of the society, at least relative to what might be the case under conditions of greater equality of opportunity.

3. Social stratification systems function to provide the elite with the political power necessary to procure acceptance and dominance of an ideology which rationalizes the *status quo*, whatever it may be, as "logical," "natural" and "morally right." In this manner, social stratification systems function as essentially conservative influences in the societies in which they are found.

4. Social stratification systems function to distribute favorable self-images unequally throughout a population. To the extent that such favorable self-images are requisite to the development of the creative potential inherent in men, to that extent stratification systems function to limit the development of this creative potential.

5. To the extent that inequalities in social rewards cannot be made fully acceptable to the less privileged in a society, social stratification systems function to encourage hostility, suspicion and distrust among the various segments of a society and thus to limit the possibilities of extensive social integration.

6. To the extent that the sense of significant membership in a society depends on one's place on the prestige ladder of the society, social stratification systems function to distribute unequally the sense of significant membership in the population.

7. To the extent that loyalty to a society depends on a sense of significant membership in the society, social stratification systems function to distribute loyalty unequally in the population.

8. To the extent that participation and apathy depend upon the sense of significant membership in the society, social stratification systems function to distribute the motivation to participate unequally in a population.

Each of the eight foregoing propositions contains implicit hypotheses regarding the consequences of unequal distribution of rewards in a society in accordance with some notion of the functional importance of various positions. These are empirical hypotheses, subject to test. They are offered here only as exemplary of the kinds of consequences of social stratification which are not often taken into account in dealing with the problem. They should also serve to reinforce the doubt that social inequality is a device which is uniformly functional for the role of guaranteeing that the most important tasks in a society will be performed conscientiously by the most competent persons.

The obviously mixed character of the functions of social inequality should come as no surprise to anyone. If sociology is sophisticated in any sense, it is certainly with regard to its awareness of the mixed nature of any social arrangement, when the observer takes into account long as well as short range consequences and latent as well as manifest dimensions.

SUMMARY

In this paper, an effort has been made to raise questions regarding the inevitability and positive functionality of stratification, or institutionalized social inequality in rewards, allocated in accordance with some notion of the greater and lesser functional importance of various positions. The possible alternative meanings of the concept "functional importance" has been shown to be one difficulty. The question of the scarcity or abundance of available talent has been indicated as a principal source of possible variation. The extent to which the period of training for skilled positions may reasonably be viewed as sacrificial has been called into question. The possibility has been suggested that very different types of motivational schemes might conceivably be made to function. The separability of differentials in power and property considered as resources appropriate to a task from such differentials considered as rewards for the performance of a task has also been suggested. It has also been maintained that differentials in prestige and esteem do not necessarily follow upon differentials in power and property when the latter are considered as appropriate resources rather than rewards. Finally, some negative functions, or dysfunctions, of institutionalized social inequality have been tentatively identified, revealing the mixed character of the outcome of social stratification, and casting doubt on the contention that

> Social inequality is thus an unconsciously evolved device by which societies insure that the most important positions are conscientiously filled by the most qualified persons.[8]

---

[8]Davis and Moore, *op. cit.,* p. 243.

Biracial Organizations

E. FRANKLIN FRAZIER

Unlike caste, the biracial organization of race relations does not imply, at least theoretically, that one race is inferior or subordinate to the other. It is said to be a means of keeping races distinct while at the same time enabling each race to develop completely its potentialities. Since the biracial organization of race relations is based upon certain theories about race as well as certain racial attitudes, this chapter will give attention first to racial ideologies as a basis of social organization. It will consider next the phenomenon of race prejudice or racial attitudes in relation to social organization. In the remaining sections of the chapter an analysis will be made of the various patterns of racial segregation, which is an essential feature of biracial organizations, and of racial segregation in relation to social status.

RACE AS A BASIS OF SOCIAL ORGANIZATION

Racial ideologies developed as a consequence of the contacts of European peoples with the peoples of Africa, America, and Asia. However, at the beginning of these contacts religion rather than race played an important role in defining the relationship of Europeans to non-Europeans. "Natives were outside the pale of humanity, but this was regarded as a consequence of the fact that they were not Christians, not of the fact that they belonged to the darker races."[1] When Europeans began to compete with the Arabs for the trade with Asia, the Christian merchants of Europe were inspired by a religious zeal to drive the infidel from the Indian Ocean and the Pacific Ocean. When slaves were first brought from Africa, the Europeans could justify their aggression by converting the heathen to Christianity. It was said that the zeal of Prince Henry the Navigator for religion:

> led him to rejoice when a company of adventurers brought back cargoes of natives, because of the salvation of those souls that before were lost. He gave away those that fell to his share, for slavery was not in his design, though it was then and for centuries later considered lawful.[2]

But as the trade in black flesh brought wealth to Europe and as the Africans became Christians, the "racial" inferiority of Africans provided new justification of their enslavement. In fact, with the spread of European dominance in America, Asia, and Africa, the alleged superiority of the white race became the main justification of European control over the non-European world.

The European adventurers who engaged in the slave trade and established plantations with colored labor in Africa, America, and Asia were never

---

Source: E. Franklin Frazier, "Biracial Organizations," In *Race and Culture Contacts in the Modern World,* Boston: Beacon Press (1965): 269–287.

[1]Ruth Benedict, *Race: Science and Politics* (New York: The Viking Press, Inc., 1943), p. 168.
[2]Quoted in I. D. MacCrone, *Race Attitudes in South Africa* (London: Andrew Melrose, 1953), p. 7.

influenced by the romantic notion of the "noble savage" which captivated the minds of Europeans who remained at home.[3] They were engaged in a struggle to subjugate colored people in order to make a fortune or, if they could not subjugate them, to exterminate them. Although, as we have seen, the relations of Europeans to natives differed from area to area, nevertheless the spread of European economic and political control was justified on the ground that Europeans were dealing with inferior races. This was amply demonstrated in the case of the African. In the West Indies, in South Africa, and in the southern states, the idea of the racial inferiority of the African developed and became more deeply rooted as the exploitation of African labor and the subordination of the African became tied up with the economic interests of the whites.

However, the development of racial ideologies began with the Aryan myth when European philologists discovered the similarities between the Sanskrit, Greek, Latin, German, English, and Celtic languages.[4] It was, however, Count Gobineau who, in his famous four volume work, *Essai sur l' Inégalité des Races Humaines,* provided the ideological basis of the superiority of the white race, especially the Nordic branch.[5] Since he formulated his theory in the 1850's before the evolutionary hypothesis had been accepted, he assumed that the violence of climatic forms had brought about the differentiation of man into three races during 7,000 years between creation and the birth of Christ. The three races were the Negroid which was animal-like and derived from Africa; the yellow, stubborn and apathetic, which originated in America and spread across Asia to Europe; and the white, endowed with reason and excelling all others in physical beauty, which originated in the Hindu Kush region of Asia. Although Gobineau was not consistent about the characteristics of the Aryan branch of the white race, he claimed that

Aryans were responsible for seven of the ten civilizations that had arisen among mankind. The cult of Gobineau found a warm welcome in Germany.[6] According to Gobineau, though the Germans were being diluted by racial amalgamation, they were the last of the Aryans. A Gobineau Society was founded in Germany which propagated the doctrine of divinely ordained Germanic superiority. The works of scholars and literary men and artists, outstanding among whom was Wagner, supported the new racial patriotism. By the close of the nineteenth century, "the original mysticism of Gobineau had been raised to the exalted level of a holy and increasingly militant faith. In 1899 this was given a powerful expression in the writings of Houston-Stewart Chamberlain, another poet-musician-philosopher."[7]

Gobineau thought that there was some hope for mankind in the fact that Anglo-Saxons dominated Britain and America. However, the myth of Anglo-Saxon superiority was fostered in Britain by philologists, historians, publicists, and poets.[8] The historians were especially influential in disseminating the idea that the achievements of the English people were due to their Anglo-Saxon racial heritage. It was the mission of the Anglo-Saxon race, according to Carlyle, to take over the control of the backward regions of the world. With the election of Disraeli in 1874, the Conservatives preached the doctrine of the racial superiority of the Anglo-Saxons. One Conservative leader declared that the Anglo-Saxons would displace the colored races in the world. The most important literary figure who helped to establish the myth of Anglo-Saxon superiority was Rudyard Kipling, in whose poetry the Anglo-Saxon was exhorted to take up the "white man's burden" and bring the benefits of a higher civilization to the backward colored peoples of the earth. This mission of the Anglo-Saxon became

[3]Benedict, *op. cit.,* p. 167.
[4]See Frank H. Hankins, *The Racial Basis of Civilization* (New York: Alfred A. Knopf, Inc., 1926), Chap. II.
[5]*Ibid.,* Chap. III.
[6]*Ibid.,* Chap. IV.
[7]*Ibid.,* p. 64.
[8]See Louis L. Snyder, *Race: A History of Modern Ethnic Theories* (New York: Longmans, Green and Co., Inc., 1939), pp. 212 ff.

the main justification for imperialism. At the same time, however, Kipling in his famous line contending that East and West would never meet, gave classic expression to the idea of a racial barrier between the white and colored races, destruction of which would lead to the degradation of the white race.

During the nineteenth century, anthropologists were beginning to study in an objective and scientific manner the phenomenon of race.[9] But most people paid little attention to the new science except in so far as it tended to support their interests and their prejudices. They were more impressed by Herbert Spencer's statement of the classical theory of anthropology. In his attempt to apply the evolutionary explanation of the natural world to the social world, he placed the European at the top of the evolutionary scale, the Asians at an intermediate stage, and the Africans at the bottom. The defenders of slavery in the United States eagerly seized upon the myth of Anglo-Saxon superiority as a justification for Negro slavery. After the Civil War the myth was invoked constantly to justify the disfranchisement of Negroes, the system of legal segregation, and a narrow industrial education for Negro children.

These attempts to identify race and culture and to make a particular type of political or social organization the expression of race established the notion that white and colored people could not mingle freely in the same community or be a part of the same social organization. A corollary to this idea of racial determinism was the notion that an innate reaction generally known as race prejudice served to protect the superior white race against mingling freely with the inferior colored races.

In undertaking to answer the question of why race prejudice exists, Miss Benedict was led to conclude that "in order to understand race persecution, we do not need to investigate race; we need to investigate *persecution*."[10] Faris stated the paradox in another way when he wrote that "race prejudice is a phenomenon that is not essentially connected with race."[11] Then he went on to explain the apparent paradox:

> Another way to say the same thing would be to assert that as races are dealt with and as races are disliked, there is little or no connection with the scientific concept of race. Not that this is without justification, for, in this crude world in which we live, it is of importance to determine not what races are, but what men call races when they manifest racial antipathy. And it is an extremely easy task to show in this connection that race prejudice is contingent upon a certain type of group consciousness which may have no defense in a scientific classification, but which does determine in large measure what men live by and what they do when they live.[12]

This statement places in clear focus the fact that the behavior and emotional attitudes which are generally defined as race prejudice are not related to the biological factors that physical anthropologists and geneticists have used as a basis for classifying the races of mankind.[13] Moreover, it reveals in a striking manner how little Vacher de Lapouge, a French pro-Aryan, understood the attitudes and behavior of men in regard to race when he wrote in the 1880's, "I am convinced that in the next century millions will cut each other's throats because of 1 or 2 degrees more or less of cephalic index."[14]

The attempts to explain race prejudice as an instinctive reaction have been abandoned because

---

[9]A controversy, obviously of political origin, split the anthropologists over the question of slavery when James Hunt read a paper on "The Negro's Place in Nature" in 1863. The thesis of the paper was that the Negro became "more humanized when in his natural subordination to the European" and that "European civilization is not suited to the negro's requirements of character." See Alfred C. Haddon, *History of Anthropology* (London: Watts and Co., 1910), p. 66 ff.

[10]Benedict, *op. cit.,* p. 230.
[11]Ellsworth Faris, *The Nature of Human Nature* (New York: McGraw-Hill Book Co., 1937), p. 317.
[12]By permission from *The Nature of Human Nature,* by Ellsworth Faris, p. 317. Copyright, 1937. McGraw-Hill Book Company, Inc.
[13]For an analysis of the present status of anthropological theories concerning races see A. L. Kroeber, *Anthropology* (New York: Harcourt, Brace and Company, 1948), Chaps. IV, V. See also M. F. Ashley Montagu, *Man's Most Dangerous Myth: The Fallacy of Race* (New York: Columbia University Press, 1945).
[14]Quoted in Benedict, *op. cit.,* p. 3.

studies of children have revealed that race prejudice is acquired behavior. However, there is still lack of agreement concerning the nature of race prejudice. According to one widespread theory, race prejudice arises as the result of economic factors or when the exploiting race propagates race prejudice in its own interest.[15] There are psychological theories, according to which race prejudice is a reaction to frustration or some psychic need. There are also theories which emphasize the role of socio-cultural factors in the genesis of prejudice. In fact, in accounting for the existence of race prejudice in any specific situation, it is necessary to study both the economic and socio-cultural factors. On the other hand, the psychological approach to the problem of race prejudice is useful in discovering the differential responses of individuals to the milieu in which race prejudice exists.

Race prejudice is a social attitude with an emotional bias.[16] The object of race prejudice is not necessarily an individual with certain observable characteristics but an individual who is identified as a member of a racial group. It has often been said that race prejudice has resulted from some unpleasant experience with an individual of a different race. But it is more likely that the unpleasant experience has evoked a latent attitude which has been acquired from one's own group. The latent attitude is directed against the "categoric picture" or, as Faris has pointed out, the concept of the individual as a member of a different race.[17] We know that a person who has race prejudice does not perceive any specific individual of a different race but rather sees each one in terms of the categoric picture. Hence all Chinese or Negroes look alike to white people. Since race

prejudice is a social attitude, it comes into existence as the result of the relations which develop between different races. It is propagated through the channels of communication in a society and becomes a part of the social heritage. Race prejudice is generally supported by rationalizations which bear no relation to the real causes of race prejudice. The rationalizations represent an attempt on the part of prejudiced people to make their prejudices appear logical and just. This will become apparent during the course of our discussion of race prejudice in relation to a biracial organization.

MacCrone, who regards racial attitudes as essentially social attitudes, shows how racial prejudices grew out of a conflict situation in South Africa.[18] Out of this conflict have developed the dominance of the white group and the subordination of the Africans. The racial attitudes serve to "protect and preserve" the dominant position of the European with its "attendant social, political and economic privileges against any threat from the members of the dominated races."[19] Therefore, the European is extremely sensitive in regard to any behavior on the part of the non-European which offers a threat to his privileged position. This accounts for the fears and anxieties on the part of the European when he considers the large numbers of Africans by whom he is surrounded. Moreover, it explains the various racial myths, stereotypes and rationalizations, and the whole psychopathology which characterize race and color prejudice.[20]

In the United States the prejudice of whites against Negroes has exhibited very much the same characteristics. In order to understand the manner in which it has developed and spread and been modified in recent years, it is necessary to study it

---

[15]For theories concerning race prejudice see Brewton Berry, *Race Relations* (New York: Houghton Mifflin Co., 1951), pp. 104–16. See also Gordon W. Allport, *The Nature of Prejudice* (Cambridge: Addison-Wesley Publishing Company, Inc., 1954), Chap. 13.

[16]See Louis Wirth, "Race and Public Policy," *Scientific Monthly,* LVIII (1944), p. 303.

[17]Faris, *op. cit.,* p. 324.

[18]I. D. MacCrone, "Race Attitudes: An Analysis and Interpretation," in Ellen Hellmann (ed.), *Handbook on Race Relations in South Africa* (New York: Oxford University Press, Inc., 1949), pp. 675–6.

[19]*Ibid.,* p. 687.

[20]*Ibid.,* p. 120. See also MacCrone, *Race Attitudes in South Africa,* Part III.

in relation to certain economic, social, and political factors in American society. It should be indicated in the beginning that explanations which attribute race prejudice to slavery are completely misleading. In the United States, as in Brazil, slavery provided a modus vivendi for whites and blacks and therefore race prejudice tended to disappear, especially where the plantation acquired the character of a social institution. It was, to be sure, a paternalistic regime, but the Negro was regarded as a person and some degree of human solidarity developed between whites and blacks. The significance of this was pointed out by Thomas when he observed:

> Of the relation of black to white in this country it is perhaps true that the antipathy of the southerner for the negro is rather caste-feeling than race-prejudice, while the feeling of the northerner is race-prejudice proper. In the North, where there has been no contact with the negro and no activity connections, there is no caste-feeling, but there exists a sort of skin-prejudice—a horror of the external aspect of the negro—and many northerners report that they have a feeling against eating from a dish handled by a negro. The association of master and slave in the South was, however, close, even if not intimate, and much of the feeling of physical repulsion for a black skin disappeared.[21]

This observation emphasizes an important fact concerning race prejudice in the South, namely, that it is not based upon physical repulsion. Some of the white people who objected to the mixing of the blood plasma of Negroes and whites during World War II would express their love of Negroes by saying that they had been nurtured by a "black mammy."

After the Civil War and emancipation when conflict developed over the status of the Negro in southern society, race prejudice developed on a wider scale than during slavery. But even then, race prejudice did not become as intense and widespread as it did later during the class struggle between the white landowning and new industrial and commercial classes on one hand, and the landless poor whites on the other. This struggle was resolved by the demagogic leaders of the poor whites who made the Negro the scapegoat. From 1890 to 1915, the Negro became the object of a systematic campaign of defamation in which he was represented as subhuman. During this period there was a marked increase in race prejudice among the masses of white people in the South. They became convinced that the only way that southern society could be saved from the moral and physical contamination of the Negro was by establishing a legalized system of segregation.

PATTERNS OF SEGREGATION

Even in a society like Brazil where there is a minimum of race prejudice and no laws requiring racial segregation, there is some segregation growing out of the Negroes' low economic status and the fact that they have not been drawn completely into the main stream of Brazilian culture. In Bahia, for example:

> The residential pattern suggests a gradually evolving, freely competitive society in which Europeans settled on the ridges, and the Africans and their descendants, as propertyless slaves, as impoverished freemen, were relegated to less desirable territory. Although the Europeans have still today, to a considerable extent, maintained their original advantage, the blacks and darker mixed-bloods have gradually pushed themselves up the slopes from their less favored locations until now they have come, in some cases, to share a portion of the Europeans' favored position.[22]

The cultural segregation of Negroes has resulted partly from the survival of African culture in the *candomblé* which embodies customs and traditions associated with religious sentiments.[23] The members of these cults, which represent to some extent the fusion of Catholicism and African religion, are often members of the Catholic

---

[21]William I. Thomas, "The Psychology of Race-Prejudice," *American Journal of Sociology,* IX, 609–10. Published by the University of Chicago Press, and copyright 1904 by the University of Chicago.

[22]Donald Pierson, *Negroes in Brazil* (Chicago: University of Chicago Press, 1942), pp. 21–2. Copyright 1942 by the University of Chicago.
[23]*Ibid.,* Chap. X.

Church. As the cults disintegrate because of the economic and social changes in Brazil, this last stronghold of racial segregation is breaking down.

On the other hand, in the Union of South Africa, the most extreme form of biracial organization is being undertaken by the Nationalist Party. A form of biracial organization had, of course, existed before the Nationalist Party came to power. From 1920 onward all legislation concerning native Africans was designed to "more clearly define the separate provinces of white and black existence."[24] These laws were designed to place the native outside the political organization of South Africa and to make him subject to discretionary powers on the part of the government. The native chiefs were restored to some of the authority which had been taken from them in the nineteenth century and the once criticized customs, such as the *lobola* or bride price, were restored.[25] Whereas once the Europeans had complained about the menace of tribalism, the tribe was now declared to be the only basis of native existence that would serve as a protection for the whites.

The determination to prevent the native from having the same place in urban life and industry as the European "carried with it the plain implication that the future of the native population was primarily on the land."[26] The rationalization that was used to support this policy was that if the natives were held to the soil and allowed to develop their own institutions, cooperation between whites and blacks would be encouraged and racial tensions would be reduced. According to the report of a competent commission:

> It would be wise to develop the wealth producing capacity of these excellent areas and thus secure a larger amount to go round, rather than to allow a continuance of the present struggle between black and white for a larger share in the wealth being produced from the developed areas. With these areas developed to a reasonably productive level there

should be enough to make possible friendly co-operation between the races.[27]

Then in 1936 the policy of segregation culminated in the passage of the Natives Land and Trust Act and the Representation of Natives Acts. The first of these was supposed to restore to the native the land which had been taken from him in order that he might have an economic basis for his segregated existence. The second act extended the disfranchisement of the natives in the Republics (Transvaal and Orange Free State) to Natal and took away the right of franchise which the African had once enjoyed in the Cape Province. The acts of 1936 were a failure from the standpoint of segregation. In response to the demands of industry, the natives continued to move into urban areas in search of money to pay their taxes as well as an opportunity to lead a fuller life. Moreover, "not even the 15,300,000 acres of 'released' land were enough to permit the development of the native population as a self-sustaining peasantry."[28] The changes which had already transformed the native could not be undone by legislation.

The aim of the apartheid program, which the Nationalist Party is attempting to put into effect, is to bring about complete segregation of the races. The natives would be confined to their reserves and their tribal system would be "revitalized."[29] Only those natives required by industry would be allowed to remain in urban areas while the bulk of cheap native labor would be imported.[30] A system of native councils within the reserves and within urban areas would provide the limit of the political activities of the natives. In addition, this program would stop the duplication of European organizations and institutions among natives, a process similar to what has occurred in the Negro community in the United States.

[24]C. W. DeKiewiet, *A History of South Africa* (New York: Oxford University Press, Inc., 1946), p. 236.
[25]*Ibid.*, p. 237.
[26]*Ibid.*, p. 336.

[27]Quoted in *ibid.*, p. 237. Reprinted by permission of the publisher.
[28]*Ibid.*, p. 243.
[29]Eugene P. Dvorin, *Racial Separation in South Africa* (Chicago: University of Chicago Press, 1952), Chap. IV.
[30]*Ibid.*, Chap. VII.

It is in the United States, especially in the southern states, that a thoroughgoing system of racial segregation has developed, with the result that as far as possible all the forms of organized and institutional life which exist in the white community have been duplicated within the Negro community. A systematic study of the patterns of racial segregation has shown the most conspicuous forms of racial segregation to be:

(1) in residential areas, (2) in educational, recreational, and other public institutions, (3) in quasi-public institutions or privately operated institutions under public control, such as railroads, steamship lines, streetcar and bus systems, and hospitals, (4) in private business establishments, such as hotels and restaurants under customary or legal mandate to prevent racial contact on a level implying social equality or permitting social intimacy, (5) in other private commercial and professional services, such as department stores, undertaking establishments and doctors' offices[31]

The residential segregation of Negroes has resulted from the interplay of economic, social, and political factors. In the North, except during periods when there was a large influx of southern Negroes, economic and social factors rather than race have been chiefly responsible for the residential segregation of Negroes. The location of Negroes in the ecological pattern of northern cities has been due, on the whole, to the same economic and social factors as those which have determined the location of immigrant European groups. Contrary to popular notions, the Negro was not segregated in the older cities of the South. They were brought to these cities by their white owners before the Civil War and it became customary for Negroes and whites to live in the same residential areas. It was in the border cities, where the location of Negroes was determined neither by economic factors nor by historical conditions and custom, that the residential segregation of Negroes became a matter for legislation. It may be said that the problem of residential segregation became an acute racial problem when, during and following World War I,

Negroes began to move into cities in large numbers.[32] When laws providing for the residential segregation of Negroes were declared unconstitutional, whites resorted to covenants or agreements among themselves to achieve the same end. These covenants were in turn declared unenforceable by the courts. This has tended to undermine the residential segregation of Negroes but racial conflicts over housing have not disappeared. These conflicts are often due to political and economic considerations rather than to social factors involving the contacts of Negroes and whites. One of the factors tending to undermine residential segregation is government-supported housing with provisions against racial segregation.

In the other four areas of segregation listed by Johnson, as in the case of housing, the pattern of racial segregation is being broken down. Educational, recreational, and other public institutions in the North and in the border states are gradually removing racial barriers. In the South, where there is still much vocal opposition to breaking down the pattern of segregation, educational institutions in some states are opening their doors to Negroes. Decisions of the Supreme Court have removed one phase after another of the segregation pattern in transportation. While there is no evidence that hotels and restaurants in the South are more inclined than formerly to accept and serve Negro patrons, in the North and to some extent even in border states, on the other hand, racial barriers have been removed in recent years. It is difficult to make generalizations concerning the segregation pattern in private commercial and professional establishments. In the North and in border states the pattern of segregation has generally been broken down in department stores, but in the case of a professional service like undertaking, the pattern of racial segregation holds as well in the North as in the South. One could say almost the same in regard to barbershops although in rare

---

[31]Charles S. Johnson, *Patterns of Negro Segregation* (New York: Harper & Brothers, 1943), p. 7.

[32]For a comprehensive study of the residential segregation of the Negro in the United States see Robert C. Weaver, *The Negro Ghetto* (New York: Harcourt, Brace and Company, 1948).

cases in the North a Negro may be served by some barbers who serve whites.

The most important result of the pattern of segregation has been growth in institutions in the Negro community which duplicate the institutions in the white community.[33] There are Negro churches of the same denominations as the white churches. The Negro church organizations are, with a few exceptions, independent of the white organizations. There are separate mutual aid organizations chiefly among the rural folk, large fraternal organizations, and college Greek-letter fraternities. There are Negro newspapers and magazines, all designed to carry stories of happenings within the Negro community and to give the Negro's outlook and conception of the world at large. There are some Negro schools, especially church schools, which represent the efforts of Negroes; on the whole, however, the segregated private as well as the public schools and colleges represent the control of the white community over the Negro community. Finally, when one considers the futile attempts of Negroes to establish banks and other business enterprises within the Negro community, one realizes the limits of biracialism in an urban industrial community.

RACIAL SEGREGATION AND SOCIAL STATUS

In discussing the change in race relations in the southern states, Park observed that with the development of industrial and professional classes within the Negro group, a biracial organization was coming into existence in which the social distance which separated the races would be preserved but the attitudes would be different in that the races would no longer look up and down; they would look across at each other.[34] Anyone who is acquainted with race relations in the southern states would agree that there is some truth in this observation. As the Negro acquires education and as new industrial and professional classes emerge within the Negro group, the Negro is freed from a certain amount of dependence upon whites, he is able to avoid some of the cruder forms of racial discrimination, and he is not forced to observe to the same extent as formerly the etiquette of race relations.[35] The implications of Park's observation are that there has been a change in the social status of Negroes and that when a biracial organization has completely evolved there would be no suggestion of superiority and inferiority. In fact, these are the assumptions upon which every system of biracial organization, or parallel development as it is sometimes called, is based.

When one studies the actual method of operation of a biracial organization, it is apparent that equality does not and cannot exist between white and colored people. First of all, the biracial organization is imposed by whites. In South Africa, Prime Minister Malan told a delegation of natives in 1948:

> I regard the Bantu not as strangers and not as a menace to the white people, but as our children for whose welfare we are responsible, and as an asset to the country. My Government has no intention of depriving you of your rights or oppressing you. Nothing will be taken from you without giving you something better in its place.
>
> Your reserves will remain intact and when necessary will be enlarged. Your lands will be restored and your young men and women trained to improved methods of cultivation so that your reserves will be capable of supporting a larger population. What you want is a rehabilitation of your own national life, and not competition and intermixture and equality with the white man in his particular part of the country.[36]

In the United States, as in South Africa, it has been the white man who has been responsible for a biracial organization. Moreover, the white man

---

[33]Concerning the origin and growth of the major institutions in the Negro community see E. Franklin Frazier, *The Negro in the United States* (New York: The Macmillan Co., 1949), Chaps. XIV, XV, XVI, XVIII, XIX.

[34]Robert E. Park, *Race and Culture* (Glencoe: The Free Press, 1950), p. 243.

[35]An etiquette which implied his social subordination.

[36]Quoted in Eugene P. Dvorin, *Racial Separation in South Africa* (Chicago: University of Chicago Press, 1952), p. 95. Copyright 1952 by the University of Chicago.

has claimed, as has Malan, to have established a biracial organization in the interest in the Negro. But wherever a biracial organization exists, there are discriminations in favor of the whites.[37] In South Africa, a biracial organization has meant and will mean poor land, poor housing, menial occupations, and low wages for non-Europeans. Likewise, in the United States a biracial organization has meant poor land, inadequate housing, unpaved streets, lack of sanitation, low wages, and unskilled occupations for Negroes. This has been the inevitable consequence of a biracial organization in an urban industrial civilization, which depends upon economic and social mobility for its existence. A biracial organization in such a society can only result in the elimination of competition between white and colored people since it is impossible to divide the economy into two insulated sectors. Moreover, white and colored workers cannot follow the same pursuits without associating in the same unions. White and colored professional men and women cannot confine their practice to one race and fail to associate with whites in the same clinics or hospitals or courts of laws or universities. White and colored businessmen and women must seek customers among both races, and white and colored people must have access to the same stores and other facilities of the community.

There is another aspect of a biracial organization which prevents it from offering any solution of the problem of race relations. Despite the theory that there is no implication of difference in social status in a biracial organization, the colored section of the organization is always stigmatized as unfit or ineligible for normal human association. Any attempts on the part of colored leaders to stimulate race pride can only be a type of compensation for the stigma of race or for implied inferior social status. When whites lend their support to such efforts they are practicing a form of patronizing that only emphasizes the stigma of race. In the United States, after over a half century of the supposed acceptance of the principle of a biracial organization, Negroes are more determined than ever to break down every form of the existing biracial organization. Their acceptance of a biracial system in the past was a form of accommodation to a situation that they could not change, but they were never unconscious of the social implications. Some of the Negro elite may have acquired a vested interest in the biracial organization but they had to deny it in public and assert the belief in a nonsegregated form of race relations.

The social implications of a biracial organization have been realized to some extent by those who formulate the foreign policy of the United States. This has resulted in a change in the official racial policy within the United States in recent years. The most significant expression of the new racial policy was the outlawing of segregation in public education. For it is realized that the most important factor in the relation of the white and colored races all over the world is the deep longing on the part of colored people for "freedom from contempt."[38]

---

[37]Racial discriminations, which grow out of race prejudice, are objective conditions such as laws in regard to employment, intermarriage, and transportation or customary practices based upon racial distinctions.

[38]Hans J. Morgenthau, "United States Policy Towards Africa," in Calvin W. Stillman (ed.), *Africa in the Modern World* (Chicago: University of Chicago Press, 1955), p. 325. Copyright 1955 by the University of Chicago.

Structural Difference and Inequality

IRIS MARION YOUNG

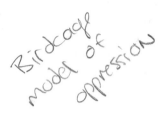

Appeal to a structural level of social life, as distinct from a level of individual experience and action, is common among social critics.[1] Appeal to structure invokes the institutionalized background which conditions much individual action and expression, but over which individuals by themselves have little control. Yet the concept of structure is notoriously difficult to pin down. I will define social structure, and more specifically structural inequality, by rebuilding elements from different accounts.

Marilyn Frye likens oppression to a birdcage. The cage makes the bird entirely unfree to fly. If one studies the causes of this imprisonment by looking at one wire at a time, however, it appears puzzling. How does a wire only a couple of centimetres wide prevent a bird's flight? One wire at a time, we can neither describe nor explain the inhibition of the bird's flight. Only a large number of wires arranged in a specific way and connected to one another to enclose the bird and reinforce one another's rigidity can explain why the bird is unable to fly freely.[2]

At a first level of intuition, this is what I mean by social structures that inhibit the capacities of some people. An account of someone's life circumstances contains many strands of difficulty or difference from others that, taken one by one, can appear to be the result of decision, preferences, or accidents. When considered together, however, and when compared with the life story of others, they reveal a net of restricting and reinforcing relationships. Let me illustrate.

Susan Okin gives an account of women's oppression as grounded in a gender division of labour in the family. She argues that gender roles and expectations structure men's and women's lives in thoroughgoing ways that result in disadvantage and vulnerability for many women and their children. Institutionally, the entire society continues to be organized around the expectation that children and other dependent people ought to be cared for primarily by family members without formal compensation. Good jobs, on the other hand, assume that workers are available at least forty hours per week year round. Women are usually the primary caretakers of children and other dependent persons, due to a combination of factors: their socialization disposes them to choose to do it, and/or their job options pay worse than those available to their male partners, or her male partner's work allows him little time for care work. As a consequence the attachment of many women to the world of employment outside the

Source: Iris Marion Young, "Structural Difference and Inequality," in *Inclusion and Democracy,* Oxford University Press, 2000: 92–99. ISBN: 0-19-829754-8. "By permission of Oxford University Press."

---

[1] See e.g., William Julius Wilson, *When Work Disappears* (New York: Knopf, 1997); see also Jean Hampton, *Political Philosophy* (Boulder, Colo.: Westview Press, 1997), 189–90.
[2] Marilyn Frye, 'Oppression', in *The Politics of Reality* (Trumansburg, NY: Crossing Press, 1983).

home is more episodic, less prestigious, and less well paid than men's. This fact in turn often makes women dependent on male earnings for primary support of themselves and their children. Women's economic dependence gives many men unequal power in the family. If the couple separates, moreover, prior dependence on male earnings coupled with the assumptions of the judicial system makes women and their children vulnerable to poverty. Schools', media, and employers' assumptions all mirror the expectation that domestic work is done primarily by women, which assumptions in turn help reproduce those unequal structures.[3]

This is an account of gender difference as structural difference. The account shows gender difference as structured by a set of relationships and interactions that act together to produce specific possibilities and preclude others, and which operate in a reinforcing circle. One can quarrel with the content or completeness of the account. To it I would add, for example, the structures that organize the social dominance of norms of heterosexual desire, and the consequences of this heterosexual matrix for people of both sexes and multiple desires. The example can show at an intuitive level the meaning of structural social group difference. Social groups defined by race or class are also positioned in structures; shortly I will elaborate these examples. Now I will systematize the notion of structure by building up definitions from several social theorists.

Peter Blau offers the following definition. 'A social structure can be defined as a multidimensional space of differentiated social positions among which a population is distributed. The social associations of people provide both the criterion for distinguishing social positions and the connections among them that make them elements of a single social structure.'[4] Blau exploits the spatial metaphor implied by the concept of structure.

Individual people occupy varying *positions* in the social space, and their positions stand in determinate relation to other positions. The structure consists in the connections among the positions and their relationships, and the way the attributes of positions internally constitute one another through those relationships.

Basic social structures consist in determinate social positions that people occupy which condition their opportunities and life chances. These life chances are constituted by the ways the positions are related to one another to create systematic constraints or opportunities that reinforce one another, like wires in a cage. Structural social groups are constituted through the social organization of labour and production, the organization of desire and sexuality, the institutionalized rules of authority and subordination, and the constitution of prestige. Structural social groups are relationally constituted in the sense that one position in structural relations does not exist apart from a differentiated relation to other positions. Priests, for example, have a particular social function and status in a particular society by virtue of their structured and interdependent relations with others who believe they need specialists in spiritual service and are willing to support that specialization materially. The prestige associated with a caste, to take another example, is bought only through reproduced relations of denigration with lower castes. The castes exist by virtue of their interactive relations with one another, enacted and re-enacted through rituals of deference and superiority enforced through distributions, material dependencies, and threats of force.

More generally, a person's social location in structures differentiated by class, gender, age, ability, race, or caste often implies predictable status in law, educational possibility, occupation, access to resources, political power, and prestige. Not only do each of these factors enable or constrain self-determination and self-development, they also tend to reinforce the others. One reason to call these structural is that they are relatively permanent. Though the specific content and detail of the

---

[3] Susan Okin, *Justice, Gender and the Family* (New York: Basic Books, 1989).

[4] Peter Blau, *Inequality and Heterogeneity* (New York: Free Press, 1977), 4.

positions and relationships are frequently reinterpreted, evolving, and even contested, the basic social locations and their relations to one another tend to be reproduced.

It is certainly misleading, however, to reify the metaphor of structure, that is, to think of social structures as entities independent of social actors, lying passively around them, easing or inhibiting their movement. On the contrary, social structures exist only in the action and interaction of persons; they exist not as states, but as processes. Thus Anthony Giddens defines social structures in terms of 'rules and resources, recursively implicated in the reproduction of social systems'.[5] In the idea of the duality of structure, Giddens theorizes how people act on the basis of their knowledge of pre-existing structures and in so acting reproduce those structures. We do so because we act according to rules and expectations and because our relationally constituted positions make or do not make certain resources available to us.

Economic class is the paradigm of structural relations in this sense. Understood as a form of structural differentiation, class analysis begins with an account of positions in the functioning of systems of ownership, finance, investment, production, and service provision. Even when they have shares of stock or participate in pension funds, those who are not in a position to live independently and control the movement of capital must depend on employment by others in order to gain a livelihood. These positions of capitalist and worker are themselves highly differentiated by income and occupation, but their basic structural relation is an interdependency; most people depend on employment by private enterprises for their livelihoods, and the owners and managers depend on the competence and co-operation of their employees for revenues. Important recent scholarship has argued that a bipolar understanding of economic class in contemporary societies is too simple, and we must also analysis the structural

differences of professional and non-professional employees, as well as self-employed, and those more or less permanently excluded from employment.[6]

People are born into a particular class position, and this accident of birth has enormous consequences for the opportunities and privileges they have for the rest of their lives. Without a doubt, some born to wealth-owner families die paupers, and others born poor die rich. Nevertheless, a massive empirical literature shows that the most consistent predictor of adult income level, educational attainment, occupation, and ownership of assets is the class situation of one's parents. While class position is defined first in terms of relations of production, class privilege also produces and is supported by an array of assets such as residence, social networks, access to high-quality education and cultural supplements, and so on. All of these operate to reinforce the structural differentiations of class.

Defining structures in terms of the rules and resources brought to actions and interactions, however, makes the reproduction of structures sound too much like the product of individual and intentional action. The concept of social structure must also include conditions under which actors act, which are often a *collective* outcome of action impressed onto the physical environment. Jean-Paul Sartre calls this aspect of social structural the *practico-inert*.[7] Most of the conditions under which people act are socio-historical: they are the products of previous actions, usually products of many co-ordinated and uncoordinated but mutually influenced actions over them. Those collective actions have produced determinate effects on the physical and cultural environment which condition future action in specific ways. As I understand the term, social structures include this practico-inert physical organization of buildings,

---

[5]Anthony Giddens, *The Constitution of Society* (Berkeley: University of California Press, 1984).

[6]For a clear and thorough account of class in a contemporary Marxist mode, see Eric Olin Wright, *Class Counts* (Cambridge: Cambridge University Press, 1997).

[7]Jean-Paul Sartre, *Critique of Dialectical Reason, trans.* Alan Sheridan-Smith (London: New Left Books, 1976), bk. 1, ch. 3.

but also modes of transport and communication, trees, rivers, and rocks, and their relation to human action.

Processes that produce and reproduce residential racial segregation illustrate how structural relations become inscribed in the physicality of the environment, often without anyone intending this outcome, thereby conditioning future action and interaction. A plurality of expectations and actions and their effects operate to limit the options of many inner-city dwellers in the United States. Racially discriminatory behaviour and policies limit the housing options of people of colour, confining many of them to neighbourhoods from which many of those whites who are able to leave do. Property-owners fail to keep up their buildings, and new investment is hard to attract because the value of property appears to decline. Because of more concentrated poverty and lay-off policies that disadvantage Blacks or Latinos, the effects of an economic downturn in minority neighbourhoods are often felt more severely, and more businesses fail or leave. Politicians often are more responsive to the neighbourhoods where more affluent and white people live; thus schools, fire protection, policing, snow removal, garbage pick-up, are poor in the ghetto neighbourhoods. The spatial concentration of poorly maintained buildings and infrastructure that results reinforces the isolation and disadvantage of those there because people are reluctant to invest in them. Economic restructuring independent of these racialized processes contributes to the closing of major employers near the segregated neighbourhoods and the opening of employers in faraway suburbs. As a result of the confluence of all these actions and processes, many Black and Latino children are poorly educated, live around a higher concentration of demoralized people in dilapidated and dangerous circumstances, and have few prospects for employment.[8]

Reference to the physical aspects of social structures helps to lead us to a final aspect of the concept. The actions and interactions which take place among persons differently situated in social structures using rules and resources do not only take place on the basis of past actions whose collective effects mark the physical conditions of action. They also often have future effects beyond the immediate purposes and intentions of the actors. Structured social action and interaction often have collective results that no one intends, and which may even be counter to the best intentions of the actors.[9] Even though no one intends them, they become given circumstances that help structure future actions. Presumably no one intends the vulnerability of many children to poverty that Okin argues the normal gender division of labour produces.

In summary, a structural social group is a collection of persons who are similarly positioned in interactive and institutional relations that condition their opportunities and life prospects. This conditioning occurs because of the way that actions and interactions conditioning that position in one situation reinforce the rules and resources available for other actions and interactions involving people in the structural positions. The unintended consequences of the confluence of many actions often produce and reinforce such opportunities and constraints, and these often make their mark on the physical conditions of future actions, as well as on the habits and expectations of actors. This mutually reinforcing process means that the positional relations and the way they condition individual lives are difficult to change.

Structural groups sometimes build on or overlap with cultural groups, as in most structures of racialized differentiation or ethnic based privilege. Thus cultural groups and structural groups cannot be considered mutually exclusive or opposing concepts. Later I will elaborate on the interaction of cultural groups with structures, in the context

---

[8]See Douglas Massey and Nancy Denton, *American Apartheid* (Cambridge, Mass.: Harvard University Press, 1993).

[9]Sartre calls such effects counter-finalities; see *Critique of Dialectical Reason,* 277–92.

of evaluating what should and should not be called identity politics. Not all ethnic or cultural group difference, however, generates structural group difference. Some structural difference, moreover, is built not on differences of cultural practice and perception, but instead on bodily differences like sex or physical ability. Some structures position bodies with particular attributes in relations that have consequences for how people are treated, the assumptions made about them, and their opportunities to realize their plans. In so far as it makes sense to say that people with disabilities are a social group, for example, despite their vast bodily differences, this is in virtue of social structures that normalize certain functions in the tools, built environment, and expectations of many people.[10]

People differently positioned in social structures have differing experiences and understandings of social relationships and the operations of the society because of their structural situation. Often such differences derive from the structural inequalities that privilege some people in certain respects and relatively disadvantage others. Structural *inequality* consists in the relative constraints some people encounter in their freedom and material well-being as the cumulative effect of the possibilities of their social positions, as compared with others who in their social positions have more options or easier access to benefits. These constraints or possibilities by no means determine outcomes for individuals in their ability to enact their plans or gain access to benefits. Some of those in more constrained situations are particularly lucky or unusually hardworking and clever, while some of those with an open road have bad luck or squander their opportunities by being lazy or stupid. Those who successfully overcome obstacles, however, cannot be judged as equal to those who have faced fewer structural obstacles, even if at a given time they have roughly equivalent incomes, authority, or prestige.

---

[10]Anita Silvers develops a thorough and persuasive account of why issues of justice regarding people with disabilities should focus on the relation of bodies to physical and social environments, rather than on the needs and capacities of individuals called disabled. See Silvers, 'Formal Justice', in Anita Silvers, David Wasserman, and Mary B. Mahowald (eds.), *Disability, Difference, Discrimination: Perspectives on Justice in Bioethics and Public Policy* (Lanham, MD: Rowman & Littlefield, 1998).

Of Essences and Bonds

CHARLES TILLY

Humans invented categorical inequality millennia ago and have applied it to a wide range of social situations. People establish systems of categorical inequality, however inadvertently, chiefly by means of these two causal mechanisms:

- *Exploitation,* which operates when powerful, connected people command resources from which they draw significantly increased returns by coordinating the effort of outsiders whom they exclude from the full value added by that effort.
- *Opportunity hoarding,* which operates when members of a categorically bounded network acquire access to a resource that is valuable, renewable, subject to monopoly, supportive of network activities, and enhanced by the network's modus operandi.

The two mechanisms obviously parallel each other, but people who lack great power can pursue the second if encouraged, tolerated, or ignored by the powerful. Often the two parties gain complementary, if unequal, benefits from jointly excluding others.

Two further mechanisms cement such arrangements in place: *emulation,* the copying of established organizational models and/or the transplanting of existing social relations from one setting to another; and *adaptation,* the elaboration of daily routines such as mutual aid, political influence, courtship, and information gathering on the

Source: Charles Tilly, "Of Essences and Bonds," in *Durable Inequality,* Berkeley, University of California Press, Copyright © 1998: 10–15. Used with permission of University of California Press.

basis of categorically unequal structures. Exploitation and opportunity hoarding favor the installation of categorical inequality, while emulation and adaptation generalize its influence.

A certain kind of inequality therefore becomes prevalent over a large population in two complementary ways. Either the categorical pair in question—male/female, legitimate/illegitimate, black/white, citizen/noncitizen, and so on—operates in organizations that control major resources affecting welfare, and its effects spread from there; or the categorical pair repeats in a great many similar organizations, regardless of their power.

In the first case, organizations that produce work and wield coercive power—corporations and states, plantations and mercenary forces, textile mills and drug rings, depending on the context—take pride of place because they ordinarily control the largest concentrations of deployable resources within large populations. In some settings of ideological hegemony, religious organizations and their own categorical distinctions can also have similar effects on inequality around them.

In the second case, households, kin groups, and local communities hold crucial positions for two reasons: within a given population, they form and change according to similar principles, and they strongly influence biological and social reproduction. Gender and age distinctions, for example, do not ordinarily separate lineages from one another, but the repetition of these distinctions in many lineages lends them influence throughout the population. The basic mechanisms that generate inequality operate in a similar fashion over a wide variety of organizational settings as well as over a great range of unequal outcomes: income, wealth, power, deference, fame, privilege, and more.

People who create or sustain categorical inequality by means of the four basic mechanisms rarely set out to manufacture inequality as such. Instead they solve other organizational problems by establishing categorically unequal access to valued outcomes. More than anything else, they seek to secure rewards from sequestered resources. Both exploitation and opportunity hoarding provide a means of doing so. But, once undertaken, exploitation and opportunity hoarding pose their own organizational problems: how to maintain distinctions between insiders and outsiders; how to ensure solidarity, loyalty, control, and succession; how to monopolize knowledge that favors profitable use of sequestered resources. The installation of explicitly categorical boundaries helps to solve such organizational problems, especially if the boundaries in question incorporate forms of inequality that are already well established in the surrounding world. Emulation and adaptation lock such distinctions into place, making them habitual and sometimes even essential to exploiters and exploited alike.

To be sure, widely applicable categories accumulate their own histories and relations to other social structures: male/female distinctions have acquired enormous, slow-moving cultural carapaces yet reappear within almost all social structures of any scale, whereas in the United States the distinction Hispanic/white remains a disputed, politically driven division of uncertain cultural content. Such categorical pairs therefore operate with characteristic differences when imported into new settings. The distinction citizen/foreigner, for instance, does a variety of organizational work— separating temporary from long-term employees, differentiating access to public benefits, managing rights to intervene in political processes, and so on—but everywhere and always its existence and effectiveness depend on the present capacity of a relatively centralized government. The power of a differentiator based on membership or nonmembership in a political party (notable cases being communist parties in state socialist regimes) similarly depends on the existence of a hegemonic party exercising extensive state power and controlling a wide variety of valued resources.

Divisions based on preference for sexual partners—gay, lesbian, straight, and so on—depend far less on governmental structure. As compared to those who differentiate based on citizenship or party membership, those who install sexual preference as a local basis of inequality have less access to governmental backing as well as a lower likelihood of governmental intervention. Sexual preference distinctions, however, do import extensive mythologies, practices, relations, and understandings that significantly affect how the distinctions work within a new setting.

Categorical inequality, in short, has some very general properties. But one of those properties, paradoxically, is to vary in practical operation with the historically accumulated understandings, practices, and social relations already attached to a given set of distinctions.

Consider some quick examples. Josef Stalin knits together an effective political machine by recruiting ethnically identified regional leaders, training them in Moscow, making them regional party bosses, and giving their ethnic identifications priority within semiautonomous political jurisdictions. When the Soviet center later relaxes its grip, political entrepreneurs within regions mobilize followings around those ethnic identities, others mobilize against them, and ostensibly age-old ethnic conflicts flame into civil war.

Again, the founder of a small manufacturing firm, following models already established in the trade, divides the firm's work into clusters of jobs viewed as distinct in character and qualifications and then recruits workers for those jobs within well-marked categories. As turnover occurs and the firm expands, established workers pass word of available jobs among friends and relatives, collaborating with and supporting them once they join the work force. Those new workers therefore prove more reliable and effective than others hired off the street, and all concerned come to associate job with category, so much so that owner and workers come to believe in the superior fitness of that category's members for the particular line of work.

Another case in point. Householders in an urban neighborhood build up a precarious system of trust on the basis of common backgrounds and shared relations to third parties, live with persons and property at risk to that system of trust, and then react violently when newcomers whom they cannot easily integrate into the same networks threaten to occupy part of the territory. In the process, members of the two groups elaborate compelling stories about each other's perfidy and utter incompatibility.

Members of an immigrant stream, finally, peddle craft goods from their home region on big-city streets, and some of them set up businesses as suppliers, manufacturers, or retail merchants. New immigrants find work in the expanding trade, and not only an immigrant niche but an ethnically specific international connection provides exclusive opportunities for the next generation. In all these cases, organizational improvisations lead to durable categorical inequality. In all these cases, but with variable weight, exploitation and opportunity hoarding favor the installation of categorical inequality, while emulation and adaptation generalize its influence.

When it comes to the determinants of durable inequality, are these special cases or the general rule? There are sound reasons for thinking that categorical inequality in general results from varying intersections of exploitation, opportunity hoarding, emulation, and adaptation. Some might argue further that much of the inequality that seems to result from individual or group differences in ability actually stems from the same causes:

- Authoritatively organized categorical differences in current performance (e.g., categorically differentiated cooperation or sabotage by fellow workers, subordinates, and supervisors)
- Authoritatively organized categorical differences in *rewards* for performance (e.g., systematically lower pay for blacks than for whites doing similar work)
- Authoritatively organized differences in the acquisition of *capacities* for performance (e.g., categorically segregated and unequal schools)

It can be argued that the social mechanisms which generate inequality with respect to a wide range of advantages—wealth, income, esteem, protection, power, and more—are similar. Although historical accumulations of institutions, social relations, and shared understandings produce differences in the day-to-day operation of various sorts of categories (gender, race, citizenship, and so on) as well as differences in various sorts of outcomes (e.g., landed wealth versus cash income), ultimately interactions of exploitation, opportunity hoarding, emulation, and adaptation explain them all.

Nutrition turns out to provide a useful general model for categorical inequality, since in most settings feeding differs with categorical membership, and since in many cases the cumulative effects of feeding elsewhere help to explain categorical differences in performance in the current case. In direct parallel, the information and social ties that individuals and groups can currently acquire differ categorically, but previous categorical experience also strongly affects the information and social ties these individuals and groups already have at their disposal, not to mention the means they have of acquiring new information and social ties. Unequal treatment of females and males in a wide range of social lives creates female/male differences in the qualifications and social ties prospective workers bring to workplaces; those differences interact with (and generally reinforce) gender distinctions built into the allocation and supervision of work.

Again, categorically differentiated family experience strongly affects children's school performance and teachers' evaluations of that performance, which in turn channel children into categorically differentiated, career-shaping educational streams (Hout and Dohan 1996; Taubman 1991). To the extent that teachers, employers, public officials, and other authorities differentiate their responses to performances categorically, they contribute to durable, authoritatively organized categorical differences. More generally, apparent third parties to the inequality in question—state officials, legislatures, owners of firms, and other powerholders—significantly influence the operation of categorical inequality and sometimes take the initiative in creating it. Authorities do, in fact, frequently solve their own organizational problems—how to sort students, whom to hire, what rights to honor—in categorical ways.

Feelings of identity, on one side, and intergroup hostility, on the other, may well accompany, promote, or result from the use of categorical differences to solve organizational problems. But the relative prevalence of such attitudes plays a secondary part in inequality's extent and form. Mistaken beliefs reinforce exploitation, opportunity hoarding, emulation, and adaptation but exercise little independent influence on their initiation—or so I will argue. It follows that the reduction or intensification of racist, sexist, or xenophobic attitudes will have relatively little impact on durable inequality, whereas the introduction of certain new organizational forms—for example, installing different categories or changing the

relation between categories and rewards—will have great impact.

If so, the identification of such organizational forms becomes a significant challenge for social scientists. It also follows that similar organizational problems generate parallel solutions in very different settings, in articulation with very different sets of categories. Thus matches of positions with categories, and the justifications for such matches, vary much more than recurrent structural arrangements—for example, when similar clusters of jobs acquire contrasting racial, ethnic, or gender identifications in different labor markets. Causal mechanisms resemble each other greatly, while outcomes differ dramatically, thus inviting very different rationalizations or condemnations after the fact. Social scientists dealing with such durable forms of inequality must hack through dense ideological overgrowth to reach structural roots.

REFERENCES

Hout, Michael and Daniel P. Dohan. 1996. "Two Paths to Educational Opportunity in the 'Age of Extremes.'" *Demography* 33:421-425.

Taubman, Paul S. 1991. "Discrimination within the Family: The Treatment of Daughters and Sons." In *Essays on the Economics of Discrimination,* Emily P. Hoffman (ed.) Kalamazoo, MI: W.E. Upjohn Institute for Employment Research.

CHAPTER

2

Class

Social class is often framed in two ways in sociology: either as a *relationship* to capital, as Karl Marx and Friedrich Engels saw it, or as a *category* based on measurable items like income and education. Class is assumed to be meaningful in determining not only people's quality of life (Weber's life chances) but the kinds of decisions we make politically, as consumers, and so on. Our selections on defining social class begin with sociology's classical era of the late nineteenth and early twentieth centuries and include some of our finest thinkers.

Although it may seem that class analysis begins with Marx and Engels, it didn't. Europeans of Marx and Engels's generation were very well aware of the existence of social class and the privileges of birth. It is fair to say, however, that the earliest class analyst claimed by sociology is Marx. The selection we include from the *Communist Manifesto* is an early statement of what would become Marxist class theory written by a very young Marx and Engels. The tone is youthful: angry, stirring, direct, and passionate. Marx and Engels identify the two main divisions resulting from industrial capitalism: a *bourgeoisie,* or capitalist class, and a *proletariat,* or laboring class. They provide an overview of the historic role of the bourgeoisie as it emerged from feudalism. There is also a summary of the dialectic of change, which they depict in terms of the conflict between opposing class interests that move history forward. Marx and Engels write in the language of adept propagandists in this selection. There's something of the street preacher in the cadence of the section that begins, "The bourgeoisie, historically, has played a most revolutionary part [in social transformation]." Try reading this selection out loud. One has a clear sense that Marx and Engels are not altogether contemptuous of some of the changes that the bourgeoisie brought about in its earliest moment.

Max Weber's classic essay, "Class, Status, Party," is also included here as an important foundation in understanding how sociologists see class. Weber would have been influenced by Marx, and although he wasn't fully in agreement with him on the nature of social change, he makes the same distinction as Marx and Engels in conceptualizing social class: the great divide is between those who are owners (of business, of land) and those who are not. This selection introduces Weber's well-known idea of life chances, that social classes determine the quality of life that we are able to purchase. Weber introduces the idea of status and status honor separate from social class, or market standing. Status, says Weber, may not be directly connected to the market principle; that is, it may not be directly tied to social class standing. Several times in this selection, Weber alludes to Marx, sometimes directly ("a talented author") and sometimes more subtly. You may want to consider, however, whether Weber is really so far removed in his analysis from Marx and Engels (see Collins, 1994).

A very different approach to looking at class comes from Thorstein Veblen's 1899 text, *A Theory of the Leisure Class*. In the chapter we selected, on pecuniary emulation, Veblen looks at how consumption became, to paraphrase Marx, a thing-in-itself. Veblen's jaundiced view of humanity, and especially of the upper and upper-middle classes, gives a different perspective still on social class as measured by the ability and desire to conspicuously consume both goods and time, something Weber's Puritans would have found morally repugnant. His idea that the more we (any of us) consume, the more we want to consume, and the less we enjoy it, is not only remarkably contemporary but suggests that, rich or poor, we are never fully satisfied with what we have. Consider how Veblen might have responded to Marx's revolutionary proletariat!

Erik Olin Wright is a current Marxist theorist who has spent his career reconfiguring Marx's ideas about class to better explain contemporary capitalist economies. In the reading included here, Wright elaborates and contrasts what he sees as the differences between Weberian and Marxist models of class and describes the uses of class analysis in sociology. This selection also provides some important clarification about how to distinguish among historical Marxism, political Marxism, and Marxist theories of class.

Moving from the classical period and responses to it, we include excerpts from a midcentury text in stratification, *The American Occupational Structure* (1967), by Peter Blau and Otis Dudley Duncan with Andrea Tyree. Blau and Duncan's work continues our understanding about social class by focusing on the categorical difference between occupations and professions. Recall the earlier analysis by Davis and Moore and their allegation that "all jobs are not created equal because some are more vital than others". Leaving functional imperatives of jobs aside, Blau and Duncan look at occupations as an important component of class standing and of social mobility across generations. The American Dream of nineteenth-century immigrants, still powerful in the middle years of the twentieth century, was a strong belief in perpetual upward mobility. If you didn't do particularly well, at least you could be reasonably assured that your children would do better than you did. Blau and Duncan, through their examination of the American occupational structure, set out to measure the truth about American social mobility and some factors that could reasonably explain it, at least in comparing the cross-generational mobility of fathers and sons.

Having examined theories about social class, this section changes tone with a set of selections about specific social classes written by sociologists working today. Robert Perrucci and Earl Wysong, in their book *The New Class Society: Goodbye American Dream?* (2003), pose a "double diamond" model of social class based on the kind of capital individuals can access. They conclude that a new kind of privileged class dominates consumption capital, investment capital, skill capital, and social capital. Their effort takes into account one of the areas hardest to pin down in stratification analysis: wealth, or resources not directly associated with earned income. The documentation for their model is provided in an excerpt from Lisa Keister's book *Wealth in America* (2000) in which Keister examines wealth distribution in the United States over time. Like Perrucci and Wysong's data, Keister's data suggests a striking division between the top 20 percent and the rest of the population in the distribution of wealth. There is a clear and present divide, then, between the richest Americans and others. These authors argue that the divide is more palpable now than in previous decades.

The increasing separation between the extremely wealthy and other groups leads us to examine the "fragile middle class," to borrow from the title of Teresa Sullivan, Elizabeth Warren, and Jay Lawrence

Westbrook's book (2000). We've also included a chapter from Alan Wolfe's (1998) intriguing effort to measure the middle class in his project on middle-class morality. Wolfe asks how the vast middle really feels about key moral issues. Is the middle class deeply divided in "culture wars" that pit conservative against liberal? The middle class, a recent historical development, is also the most insecure of classes. Sullivan, Warren, and Westbrook document one of the reasons for this: all middle-class individuals depend on a steady paycheck and on the extension of credit to maintain middle-class status. To a large extent, then middle-class lives are built on a house of credit cards and second mortgages. Sullivan, Warren, and Westbrook look at the multiple causes for the upsurge in bankruptcy proceedings and analyze the meaning of bankruptcy itself as the ultimate free-market solution to excessive debt accumulation.

Veblen insinuates, and Sullivan, Warren, and Westbrook document, that consumption takes on a meaning beyond the item purchased. A home, specifically home "ownership," represents the achievement of stable adulthood and is the ticket to enter the middle class. On a very different level, a dress from last season but still in fashion, purchased well below the going retail rate, is the end result of a kind of moral quest by the suburban shopper. The history of that dress, and the resurgence of appalling conditions in the garment industry, is detailed in Edna Bonacich and Richard Appelbaum's "The Return of the Sweatshop." Poorly paid, unskilled, often immigrant laborers represent another important social class segment, the working poor, of which we will say more later in the text. We end this section on class with a commentary by Harvard sociologist Barbara Reskin, "The Proximate Causes of Employment Discrimination." Reskin here makes the point that sociology's effort to explain and understand inequality is our most important contribution to public policy. Reskin's research has focused on understanding, specifically, labor market mechanisms that contribute to inequality. Here she pushes beyond the conflict model of dominant privilege and subordinate capitulation to examine some of the social psychological reasons that may better explain the enduring nature of discrimination.

Bourgeois and Proletarians[1]

KARL MARX AND FRIEDRICH ENGELS

The history of all hitherto existing society[2] is the history of class struggles.

Freeman and slave, patrician and plebeian, lord and serf, guild-master[3] and journeyman, in a word, oppressor and oppressed, stood in constant opposition to one another, carried on an uninterrupted, now hidden, now open fight, a fight that each time ended, either in a revolutionary re-constitution of society at large, or in the common ruin of the contending classes.

In the earlier epochs of history, we find almost everywhere a complicated arrangement of society into various orders, a manifold gradation of social rank. In ancient Rome we have patricians, knights, plebeians, slaves; in the Middle Ages, feudal lords, vassals, guild-masters, journeymen, apprentices, serfs; in almost all of these classes, again, subordinate gradations.

The modern bourgeois society that has sprouted from the ruins of feudal society has not done away with class antagonisms. It has but established new classes, new conditions of oppression, new forms of struggle in place of the old ones.

Our epoch, the epoch of the bourgeoisie, possesses, however, this distinctive feature: it has simplified the class antagonisms: Society as a whole is more and more splitting up into two great hostile camps, into two great classes directly facing each other: Bourgeoisie and Proletariat.

From the serfs of the Middle Ages sprang the chartered burghers of the earliest towns. From these burgesses the first elements of the bourgeoisie were developed.

The discovery of America, the rounding of the Cape, opened up fresh ground for the rising bourgeoisie. The East-Indian and Chinese markets, the colonisation of America, trade with the colonies, the increase in the means of exchange and in commodities generally, gave to commerce, to navigation, to

---

[1]By bourgeoisie is meant the class of modern Capitalists, owners of the means of social production and employers of wage-labour. By proletariat, the class of modern wage-labourers who, having no means of production of their own, are reduced to selling their labour-power in order to live. [*Engels, English edition of 1888*]

[2]That is, all *written* history. In 1847, the pre-history of society, the social organisation existing previous to recorded history, was all but unknown. Since then, Haxthausen discovered common ownership of land in Russia, Maurer proved it to be the social foundation from which all Teutonic races started in history, and by and by village communities were found to be, or to have been the primitive form of society everywhere from India to Ireland. The inner organisation of this primitive Communistic society was laid bare, in its typical form, by Morgan's crowning discovery of the true nature of the *gens* and its relation to the *tribe*. With the dissolution of these primaeval communities society begins to be differentiated into separate and finally antagonistic classes. I have attempted to retrace this process of dissolution in: "Der Ursprung der Familie, des Privateigenthums und des Staats" [*The Origin of the Family, Private Property and the State*], 2nd edition, Stuttgart 1886. [*Engels, English edition of 1888*]

[3]Guild-master, that is, a full member of a guild, a master within, not a head of a guild. [*Engels, English edition of 1888*]

---

industry, an impulse never before known, and thereby, to the revolutionary element in the tottering feudal society, a rapid development.

The feudal system of industry, under which industrial production was monopolised by closed guilds, now no longer sufficed for the growing wants of the new markets. The manufacturing system took its place. The guild-masters were pushed on one side by the manufacturing middle class; division of labour between the different corporate guilds vanished in the face of division of labour in each single workshop.

Meantime the markets kept ever growing, the demand ever rising. Even manufacture no longer sufficed. Thereupon, steam and machinery revolutionised industrial production. The place of manufacture was taken by the giant, Modern Industry, the place of the industrial middle class, by industrial millionaires, the leaders of whole industrial armies, the modern bourgeois.

Modern industry has established the world-market, for which the discovery of America paved the way. This market has given an immense development to commerce, to navigation, to communication by land. This development has, in its turn, reacted on the extension of industry; and in proportion as industry, commerce, navigation, railways extended, in the same proportion the bourgeoisie developed, increased its capital, and pushed into the background every class handed down from the Middle Ages.

We see, therefore, how the modern bourgeoisie is itself the product of a long course of development, of a series of revolutions in the modes of production and of exchange.

Each step in the development of the bourgeoisie was accompanied by a corresponding political advance of that class. An oppressed class under the sway of the feudal nobility, an armed and self-governing association in the medieval commune;[4]

here independent urban republic (as in Italy and Germany), there taxable "third estate" of the monarchy (as in France), afterwards, in the period of manufacture proper, serving either the semi-feudal or the absolute monarchy as a counterpoise against the nobility, and, in fact, corner-stone of the great monarchies in general, the bourgeoisie has at last, since the establishment of Modern Industry and of the world-market, conquered for itself, in the modern representative State, exclusive political sway. The executive of the modern State is but a committee for managing the common affairs of the whole bourgeoisie.

The bourgeoisie, historically, has played a most revolutionary part.

The bourgeoisie, wherever it has got the upper hand, has put an end to all feudal, patriarchal, idyllic relations. It has pitilessly torn asunder the motley feudal ties that bound man to his "natural superiors," and has left remaining no other nexus between man and man than naked self-interest, than callous "cash payment." It has drowned the most heavenly ecstasies of religious fervour, of chivalrous enthusiasm, of philistine sentimentalism, in the icy water of egotistical calculation. It has resolved personal worth into exchange value, and in place of the numberless indefeasible chartered freedoms, has set up that single, unconscionable freedom—Free Trade. In one word, for exploitation, veiled by religious and political illusions, it has substituted naked, shameless, direct, brutal exploitation.

The bourgeoisie has stripped of its halo every occupation hitherto honoured and looked up to with reverent awe. It has converted the physician, the lawyer, the priest, the poet, the man of science, into its paid wage-labourers.

The bourgeoisie has torn away from the family its sentimental veil, and has reduced the family relation to a mere money relation.

---

[4]"Commune" was the name taken, in France, by the nascent towns even before they had conquered from their feudal lords and masters local self-government and political rights as the "Third Estate." Generally speaking, for the economical development of the bourgeoisie, England is here taken as the typical country; for

its political development, France. [*Engels, English edition of 1888*]

This was the name given their urban communities by the townsmen of Italy and France, after they had purchased or wrested their initial rights of self-government from their feudal lords. [*Engels, German edition of 1890*]

The bourgeoisie has disclosed how it came to pass that the brutal display of vigour in the Middle Ages, which Reactionists so much admire, found its fitting complement in the most slothful indolence. It has been the first to show what man's activity can bring about. It has accomplished wonders far surpassing Egyptian pyramids, Roman aqueducts, and Gothic cathedrals; it has conducted expeditions that put in the shade all former Exoduses of nations and crusades.

The bourgeoisie cannot exist without constantly revolutionising the instruments of production, and thereby the relations of production, and with them the whole relations of society. Conservation of the old modes of production in unaltered form, was, on the contrary, the first condition of existence for all earlier industrial classes. Constant revolutionising of production, uninterrupted disturbance of all social conditions, everlasting uncertainty and agitation distinguish the bourgeois epoch from all earlier ones. All fixed, fast-frozen relations, with their train of ancient and venerable prejudices and opinions, are swept away, all new-formed ones become antiquated before they can ossify. All that is solid melts into air, all that is holy is profaned, and man is at last compelled to face with sober senses, his real conditions of life, and his relations with his kind.

The need of a constantly expanding market for its products chases the bourgeoisie over the whole surface of the globe. It must nestle everywhere, settle everywhere, establish connexions everywhere.

The bourgeoisie has through its exploitation of the world-market given a cosmopolitan character to production and consumption in every country. To the great chagrin of Reactionists, it has drawn from under the feet of industry the national ground on which it stood. All old-established national industries have been destroyed or are daily being destroyed. They are dislodged by new industries, whose introduction becomes a life and death question for all civilised nations, by industries that no longer work up indigenous raw material, but raw material drawn from the remotest zones; industries whose products are consumed, not only at home, but in every quarter of the globe. In place of the old wants, satisfied by the productions of the country, we find new wants, requiring for their satisfaction the products of distant lands and climes. In place of the old local and national seclusion and self-sufficiency, we have intercourse in every direction, universal inter-dependence of nations. And as in material, so also in intellectual production. The intellectual creations of individual nations become common property. National one-sidedness and narrow-mindedness become more and more impossible, and from the numerous national and local literatures, there arises a world literature.

The bourgeoisie, by the rapid improvement of all instruments of production, by the immensely facilitated means of communication, draws all, even the most barbarian, nations into civilisation. The cheap prices of its commodities are the heavy artillery with which it batters down all Chinese walls, with which it forces the barbarians' intensely obstinate hatred of foreigners to capitulate. It compels all nations, on pain of extinction, to adopt the bourgeois mode of production; it compels them to introduce what it calls civilisation into their midst, *i.e.,* to become bourgeois themselves. In one word, it creates a world after its own image.

The bourgeoisie has subjected the country to the rule of the towns. It has created enormous cities, has greatly increased the urban population as compared with the rural, and has thus rescued a considerable part of the population from the idiocy of rural life. Just as it has made the country dependent on the towns, so it has made barbarian and semi-barbarian countries dependent on the civilised ones, nations and peasants on nations of bourgeois, the East on the West.

The bourgeoisie keeps more and more doing away with the scattered state of the population, of the means of production, and of property. It has agglomerated population, centralised means of production, and has concentrated property in a few hands. The necessary consequence of this was political centralisation. Independent, or but loosely connected provinces, with separate interests, laws, governments and systems of taxation, became lumped together into one nation, with one government, one code of laws, one national class-interest, one frontier and one customs-tariff.

The bourgeoisie, during its rule of scarce one hundred years, has created more massive and more colossal productive forces than have all preceding generations together. Subjection of Nature's forces to man, machinery, application of chemistry to industry and agriculture, steam-navigation, railways, electric telegraphs, clearing of whole continents for cultivation, canalisation of rivers, whole populations conjured out of the ground—what earlier century had even a presentiment that such productive forces slumbered in the lap of social labour?

We see then: the means of production and of exchange, on whose foundation the bourgeoisie built itself up, were generated in feudal society. At a certain stage in the development of these means of production and of exchange, the conditions under which feudal society produced and exchanged, the feudal organisation of agriculture and manufacturing industry, in one word, the feudal relations of property became no longer compatible with the already developed productive forces; they became so many fetters. They had to be burst asunder; they were burst asunder.

Into their place stepped free competition, accompanied by a social and political constitution adapted to it, and by the economical and political sway of the bourgeois class.

A similar movement is going on before our own eyes. Modern bourgeois society with its relations of production, of exchange and of property, a society that has conjured up such gigantic means of production and of exchange, is like the sorcerer, who is no longer able to control the powers of the nether world whom he has called up by his spells. For many a decade past the history of industry and commerce is but the history of the revolt of modern productive forces against modern conditions of production, against the property relations that are the conditions for the existence of the bourgeoisie and of its rule. It is enough to mention the commercial crises that by their periodical return put on its trial, each time more threateningly, the existence of the entire bourgeois society. In these crises a great part not only of the existing products, but also of the previously created productive forces, are periodically destroyed. In these crises there breaks out an epidemic that, in all earlier epochs, would have seemed an absurdity—the epidemic of over-production. Society suddenly finds itself put back into a state of momentary barbarism; it appears as if a famine, a universal war of devastation had cut off the supply of every means of subsistence; industry and commerce seem to be destroyed; and why? Because there is too much civilisation, too much means of subsistence, too much industry, too much commerce. The productive forces at the disposal of society no longer tend to further the development of the conditions of bourgeois property; on the contrary, they have become too powerful for these conditions, by which they are fettered, and so soon as they overcome these fetters, they bring disorder into the whole of bourgeois society, endanger the existence of bourgeois property. The conditions of bourgeois society are too narrow to comprise the wealth created by them. And how does the bourgeoisie get over these crises? On the one hand by enforced destruction of a mass of productive forces; on the other, by the conquest of new markets, and by the more thorough exploitation of the old ones. That is to say, by paving the way for more extensive and more destructive crises, and by diminishing the means whereby crises are prevented.

The weapons with which the bourgeoisie felled feudalism to the ground are now turned against the bourgeoisie itself.

But not only has the bourgeoisie forged the weapons that bring death to itself; it has also called into existence the men who are to wield those weapons—the modern working class—the proletarians.

In proportion as the bourgeoisie, *i.e.,* capital, is developed, in the same proportion is the proletariat, the modern working class, developed—a class of labourers, who live only so long as they find work, and who find work only so long as their labour increases capital. These labourers, who must sell themselves piece-meal, are a commodity, like every other article of commerce, and are consequently exposed to all the vicissitudes of competition, to all the fluctuations of the market.

Owing to the extensive use of machinery and to division of labour, the work of the proletarians has lost all individual character, and consequently, all charm for the workman. He becomes an appendage of the machine, and it is only the most simple, most monotonous, and most easily acquired knack, that is required of him. Hence, the cost of production of a workman is restricted, almost entirely, to the means of subsistence that he requires for his maintenance, and for the propagation of his race. But the price of a commodity, and therefore also of labour,[5] is equal to its cost of production. In proportion, therefore, as the repulsiveness of the work increases, the wage decreases. Nay more, in proportion as the use of machinery and division of labour increases, in the same proportion the burden of toil also increases, whether by prolongation of the working hours, by increase of the work exacted in a given time or by increased speed of the machinery, etc.

Modern industry has converted the little work-shop of the patriarchal master into the great factory of the industrial capitalist. Masses of labourers, crowded into the factory, are organised like sol-diers. As privates of the industrial army they are placed under the command of a perfect hierarchy of officers and sergeants. Not only are they slaves of the bourgeois class, and of the bourgeois State; they are daily and hourly enslaved by the machine, by the over-looker, and, above all, by the individual bourgeois manufacturer himself. The more openly this despotism proclaims gain to be its end and aim, the more petty, the more hateful and the more embittering it is.

The less the skill and exertion of strength implied in manual labour, in other words, the more modern industry becomes developed, the more is the labour of men superseded by that of women. Differences of age and sex have no longer any dis-tinctive social validity for the working class. All are instruments of labour, more or less expensive to use, according to their age and sex.

No sooner is the exploitation of the labourer by the manufacturer, so far, at an end, that he receives his wages in cash, than he is set upon by the other portions of the bourgeoisie, the landlord, the shop-keeper, the pawnbroker, etc.

The lower strata of the middle class—the small tradespeople, shopkeepers, and retired tradesmen generally, the handicraftsmen and peasants—all these sink gradually into the proletariat, partly because their diminutive capital does not suffice for the scale on which Modern Industry is carried on, and is swamped in the competition with the large capitalists, partly because their specialised skill is rendered worthless by new methods of production. Thus the proletariat is recruited from all classes of the population.

The proletariat goes through various stages of development. With its birth begins its struggle with the bourgeoisie. At first the contest is carried on by individual labourers, then by the workpeople of a factory, then by the operatives of one trade, in one locality, against the individual bourgeois who directly exploits them. They direct their attacks not against the bourgeois conditions of production, but against the instruments of production themselves; they destroy imported wares that compete with their labour, they smash to pieces machinery, they set factories ablaze, they seek to restore by force the vanished status of the workman of the Middle Ages.

At this stage the labourers still form an incoher-ent mass scattered over the whole country, and bro-ken up by their mutual competition. If anywhere they unite to form more compact bodies, this is not yet the consequence of their own active union, but of the union of the bourgeoisie, which class, in order to attain its own political ends, is compelled to set the whole proletariat in motion, and is more-over yet, for a time, able to do so. At this stage, therefore, the proletarians do not fight their ene-mies, but the enemies of their enemies, the rem-nants of absolute monarchy, the landowners, the non-industrial bourgeois, the petty bourgeoisie. Thus the whole historical movement is concentrated

---

[5] Subsequently Marx pointed out that the worker sells not his labour but his labour power.

in the hands of the bourgeoisie; every victory so obtained is a victory for the bourgeoisie.

But with the development of industry the proletariat not only increases in number; it becomes concentrated in greater masses, its strength grows, and it feels that strength more. The various interests and conditions of life within the ranks of the proletariat are more and more equalised, in proportion as machinery obliterates all distinctions of labour, and nearly everywhere reduces wages to the same low level. The growing competition among the bourgeois, and the resulting commercial crises, make the wages of the workers ever more fluctuating. The unceasing improvement of machinery, ever more rapidly developing, makes their livelihood more and more precarious; the collisions between individual workmen and individual bourgeois take more and more the character of collisions between two classes. Thereupon the workers begin to form combinations (Trades Unions) against the bourgeois; they club together in order to keep up the rate of wages; they found permanent associations in order to make provision beforehand for these occasional revolts. Here and there the contest breaks out into riots.

Now and then the workers are victorious, but only for a time. The real fruit of their battles lies, not in the immediate result, but in the ever-expanding union of the workers. This union is helped on by the improved means of communication that are created by modern industry and that place the workers of different localities in contact with one another. It was just this contact that was needed to centralise the numerous local struggles, all of the same character, into one national struggle between classes. But every class struggle is a political struggle. And that union, to attain which the burghers of the Middle Ages, with their miserable highways, required centuries, the modern proletarians, thanks to railways, achieve in a few years.

This organisation of the proletarians into a class, and consequently into a political party, is continually being upset again by the competition between the workers themselves. But it ever rises up again, stronger, firmer, mightier. It compels legislative recognition of particular interests of the workers, by taking advantage of the divisions among the bourgeoisie itself. Thus the ten-hours' bill in England was carried.

Altogether collisions between the classes of the old society further, in many ways, the course of development of the proletariat. The bourgeoisie finds itself involved in a constant battle. At first with the aristocracy; later on, with those portions of the bourgeoisie itself, whose interests have become antagonistic to the progress of industry; at all times, with the bourgeoisie of foreign countries. In all these battles it sees itself compelled to appeal to the proletariat, to ask for its help, and thus, to drag it into the political arena. The bourgeoisie itself, therefore, supplies the proletariat with its own elements of political and general education, in other words, it furnishes the proletariat with weapons for fighting the bourgeoisie.

Further, as we have already seen, entire sections of the ruling classes are, by the advance of industry, precipitated into the proletariat, or are at least threatened in their conditions of existence. These also supply the proletariat with fresh elements of enlightenment and progress.

Finally, in times when the class struggle nears the decisive hour, the process of dissolution going on within the ruling class, in fact within the whole range of society, assumes such a violent, glaring character, that a small section of the ruling class cuts itself adrift, and joins the revolutionary class, the class that holds the future in its hands. Just as, therefore, at an earlier period, a section of the nobility went over to the bourgeoisie, so now a portion of the bourgeoisie goes over to the proletariat, and in particular, a portion of the bourgeois ideologists, who have raised themselves to the level of comprehending theoretically the historical movement as a whole.

Of all the classes that stand face to face with the bourgeoisie today, the proletariat alone is a really revolutionary class. The other classes decay and finally disappear in the face of Modern Industry; the proletariat is its special and essential product.

The lower middle class, the small manufacturer, the shopkeeper, the artisan, the peasant, all these fight against the bourgeoisie, to save from extinction their existence as fractions of the middle class. They are therefore not revolutionary, but conservative. Nay more, they are reactionary, for they try to roll back the wheel of history. If by chance they are revolutionary, they are so only in view of their impending transfer into the proletariat, they thus defend not their present, but their future interests, they desert their own standpoint to place themselves at that of the proletariat.

The "dangerous class," the social scum, that passively rotting mass thrown off by the lowest layers of old society, may, here and there, be swept into the movement by a proletarian revolution; its conditions of life, however, prepare it far more for the part of a bribed tool of reactionary intrigue.

In the conditions of the proletariat, those of old society at large are already virtually swamped. The proletarian is without property; his relation to his wife and children has no longer anything in common with the bourgeois family-relations; modern industrial labour, modern subjection to capital, the same in England as in France, in America as in Germany, has stripped him of every trace of national character. Law, morality, religion, are to him so many bourgeois prejudices, behind which lurk in ambush just as many bourgeois interests.

All the preceding classes that got the upper hand, sought to fortify their already acquired status by subjecting society at large to their conditions of appropriation. The proletarians cannot become masters of the productive forces of society, except by abolishing their own previous mode of appropriation, and thereby also every other previous mode of appropriation. They have nothing of their own to secure and to fortify; their mission is to destroy all previous securities for, and insurances of, individual property.

All previous historical movements were movements of minorities, or in the interests of minorities. The proletarian movement is the self-conscious, independent movement of the immense majority, in the interests of the immense majority. The proletariat, the lowest stratum of our present society, cannot stir, cannot raise itself up, without the whole superincumbent strata of official society being sprung into the air.

Though not in substance, yet in form, the struggle of the proletariat with the bourgeoisie is at first a national struggle. The proletariat of each country must, of course, first of all settle matters with its own bourgeoisie.

In depicting the most general phases of the development of the proletariat, we traced the more or less veiled civil war, raging within existing society, up to the point where that war breaks out into open revolution, and where the violent overthrow of the bourgeoisie lays the foundation for the sway of the proletariat.

Hitherto, every form of society has been based, as we have already seen, on the antagonism of oppressing and oppressed classes. But in order to oppress a class, certain conditions must be assured to it under which it can, at least, continue its slavish existence. The serf, in the period of serfdom, raised himself to membership in the commune, just as the petty bourgeois, under the yoke of feudal absolutism, managed to develop into a bourgeois. The modern labourer, on the contrary, instead of rising with the progress of industry, sinks deeper and deeper below the conditions of existence of his own class. He becomes a pauper, and pauperism develops more rapidly than population and wealth. And here it becomes evident, that the bourgeoisie is unfit any longer to be the ruling class in society, and to impose its conditions of existence upon society as an over-riding law. It is unfit to rule because it is incompetent to assure an existence to its slave within his slavery, because it cannot help letting him sink into such a state, that it has to feed him, instead of being fed by him. Society can no longer live under this bourgeoisie, in other words, its existence is no longer compatible with society.

The essential condition for the existence, and for the sway of the bourgeois class, is the formation and augmentation of capital; the condition for capital is wage-labour. Wage-labour rests exclusively on competition between the labourers. The advance of industry, whose involuntary promoter is the bourgeoisie, replaces the isolation of the labourers, due to competition, by their revolutionary combination, due to association. The development of Modern Industry, therefore, cuts from under its feet the very foundation on which the bourgeoisie produces and appropriates products. What the bourgeoisie, therefore, produces, above all, is its own grave-diggers. Its fall and the victory of the proletariat are equally inevitable.

Class, Status, Party

MAX WEBER

1: ECONOMICALLY DETERMINED POWER AND THE SOCIAL ORDER

Law exists when there is a probability that an order will be upheld by a specific staff of men who will use physical or psychical compulsion with the intention of obtaining conformity with the order, or of inflicting sanctions for infringement of it.* The structure of every legal order directly influences the distribution of power, economic or otherwise, within its respective community. This is true of all legal orders and not only that of the state. In general, we understand by 'power' the chance of a man or of a number of men to realize their own will in a communal action even against the resistance of others who are participating in the action.

'Economically conditioned' power is not, of course, identical with 'power' as such. On the contrary, the emergence of economic power may be the consequence of power existing on other grounds. Man does not strive for power only in order to enrich himself economically. Power, including economic power, may be valued 'for its own sake.' Very frequently the striving for power is also conditioned by the social 'honor' it entails. Not all power, however, entails social honor: The typical American Boss, as well as the typical big speculator, deliberately relinquishes social honor. Quite generally, 'mere economic' power, and especially 'naked' money power, is by no means a recognized basis of social honor. Nor is power the only basis of social honor. Indeed, social honor, or prestige, may even be the basis of political or economic power, and very frequently has been. Power, as well as honor, may be guaranteed by the legal order, but, at least normally, it is not their primary source. The legal order is rather an additional factor that enhances the chance to hold power or honor; but it cannot always secure them.

The way in which social honor is distributed in a community between typical groups participating in this distribution we may call the 'social order.' The social order and the economic order are, of course, similarly related to the 'legal order.' However, the social and the economic order are not identical. The economic order is for us merely the way in which economic goods and services are distributed and used. The social order is of course conditioned by the economic order to a high degree, and in its turn reacts upon it.

Now: 'classes,' 'status groups,' and 'parties' are phenomena of the distribution of power within a community.

Source: "Class, Status, Party pp. 180–195", *From Max Weber: Essays in Sociology* by Max Weber, edited by H. H. Gerth & C. Wright Mills, translated by H. H. Gerth & C. Wright Mills, copyright 1946, 1958, 1973 by H. H. Gerth and C. Wright Mills. Used by permission of Oxford University Press, Inc.

Wirtschaft und Gesellschaft, part III, chap. 4, pp. 631–40. The first sentence in paragraph one and the several definitions in this chapter which are in brackets do not appear in the original text. They have been taken from other contexts of *Wirtschaft und Gesellschaft.*

2: DETERMINATION OF CLASS-SITUATION BY MARKET-SITUATION

In our terminology, 'classes' are not communities; they merely represent possible, and frequent, bases for communal action. We may speak of a 'class' when (1) a number of people have in common a specific causal component of their life chances, in so far as (2) this component is represented exclusively by economic interests in the possession of goods and opportunities for income, and (3) is represented under the conditions of the commodity or labor markets. [These points refer to 'class situation,' which we may express more briefly as the typical chance for a supply of goods, external living conditions, and personal life experiences, in so far as this chance is determined by the amount and kind of power, or lack of such, to dispose of goods or skills for the sake of income in a given economic order. The term 'class' refers to any group of people that is found in the same class situation.]

It is the most elemental economic fact that the way in which the disposition over material property is distributed among a plurality of people, meeting competitively in the market for the purpose of exchange, in itself creates specific life chances. According to the law of marginal utility this mode of distribution excludes the non-owners from competing for highly valued goods; it favors the owners and, in fact, gives to them a monopoly to acquire such goods. Other things being equal, this mode of distribution monopolizes the opportunities for profitable deals for all those who, provided with goods, do not necessarily have to exchange them. It increases, at least generally, their power in price wars with those who, being propertyless, have nothing to offer but their services in native form or goods in a form constituted through their own labor, and who above all are compelled to get rid of these products in order barely to subsist. This mode of distribution gives to the propertied a monopoly on the possibility of transferring property from the sphere of use as a 'fortune,' to the sphere of 'capital goods'; that is, it gives them the entrepreneurial function and all chances to share directly or indirectly in returns on capital. All this holds true within the area in which pure market conditions prevail. 'Property' and 'lack of property' are, therefore, the basic categories of all class situations. It does not matter whether these two categories become effective in price wars or in competitive struggles.

Within these categories, however, class situations are further differentiated: on the one hand, according to the kind of property that is usable for returns; and, on the other hand, according to the kind of services that can be offered in the market. Ownership of domestic buildings; productive establishments; warehouses; stores; agriculturally usable land, large and small holdings—quantitative differences with possibly qualitative consequences—; ownership of mines; cattle; men (slaves); disposition over mobile instruments of production, or capital goods of all sorts, especially money or objects that can be exchanged for money easily and at any time; disposition over products of one's own labor or of others' labor differing according to their various distances from consumability; disposition over transferable monopolies of any kind—all these distinctions differentiate the class situations of the propertied just as does the 'meaning' which they can and do give to the utilization of property, especially to property which has money equivalence. Accordingly, the propertied, for instance, may belong to the class of rentiers or to the class of entrepreneurs.

Those who have no property but who offer services are differentiated just as much according to their kinds of services as according to the way in which they make use of these services, in a continuous or discontinuous relation to a recipient. But always this is the generic connotation of the concept of class: that the kind of chance in the *market* is the decisive moment which presents a common condition for the individual's fate. 'Class situation' is, in this sense, ultimately 'market situation.' The effect of naked possession *per se,* which among cattle breeders gives the non-owning slave or serf into the power of the cattle owner, is only a fore-runner of real 'class' formation. However, in the cattle loan and in the naked severity of the law of debts in such communities, for the first time mere 'possession' as such emerges as decisive for the fate of the individual. This is very much in contrast to the agricultural communities based on labor. The creditor-debtor relation becomes the basis of 'class situations' only in those cities where a 'credit market,' however primitive, with rates of interest increasing according to the extent of dearth and a factual monopolization of credits, is developed by a plutocracy. Therewith 'class struggles' begin.

Those men whose fate is not determined by the chance of using goods or services for themselves on the market, e.g. slaves, are not, however, a 'class' in the technical sense of the term. They are, rather, a 'status group.'

3: COMMUNAL ACTION FLOWING FROM CLASS INTEREST

According to our terminology, the factor that creates 'class' is unambiguously economic interest, and indeed, only those interests involved in the existence of the 'market.' Nevertheless, the concept of 'class-interest' is an ambiguous one: even as an empirical concept it is ambiguous as soon as one understands by it something other than the factual direction of interests following with a certain probability from the class situation for a certain 'average' of those people subjected to the class situation. The class situation and other circumstances remaining the same, the direction in which the individual worker, for instance, is likely to pursue his interests may vary widely, according to whether he is constitutionally qualified for the task at hand to a high, to an average, or to a low degree. In the same way, the direction of interests may vary according to whether or not a *communal* action of a larger or smaller portion of those commonly affected by the 'class situation,' or even an association among them, e.g. a 'trade union,' has grown out of the class situation from which the individual may or may not expect promising results. [Communal action refers to that action which is oriented to the feeling of the actors that they belong together. Societal action, on the other hand, is oriented to a rationally motivated adjustment of interests.] The rise of societal or even of communal action from a common class situation is by no means a universal phenomenon.

The class situation may be restricted in its effects to the generation of essentially *similar* reactions, that is to say, within our terminology, of 'mass actions.' However, it may not have even this result. Furthermore, often merely an amorphous communal action emerges. For example, the 'murmuring' of the workers known in ancient oriental ethics: the moral disapproval of the work-master's conduct, which in its practical significance was probably equivalent to an increasingly typical phenomenon of precisely the latest industrial development, namely, the 'slow down' (the deliberate limiting of work effort) of laborers by virtue of tacit agreement. The degree in which 'communal action' and possibly 'societal action,' emerges from the 'mass actions' of the members of a class is linked to general cultural conditions, especially to those of an intellectual sort. It is also linked to the extent of the contrasts that have already evolved, and is especially linked to the *transparency* of the connections between the causes and the consequences of the 'class situation.' For however different life chances may be, this fact in itself, according to all experience, by no means gives birth to 'class action' (communal action by the members of a class). The fact of being conditioned and the results of the class situation must be distinctly recognizable. For only then the contrast of life chances can be felt not as an absolutely given fact to be accepted, but as a resultant from either (1) the given distribution of property, or (2) the structure of the concrete economic order. It is only then that people may react against the class structure not only through acts of an intermittent and irrational protest, but in the form of rational association. There have been 'class situations' of the first category (1), of a specifically naked and transparent sort, in the urban centers of Antiquity and during the Middle Ages; especially then, when great fortunes were accumulated by factually monopolized trading in industrial products of these localities or in foodstuffs. Furthermore, under certain circumstances, in the rural economy of the most diverse periods, when agriculture was increasingly exploited in a profit-making manner. The most important historical example of the second category (2) is the class situation of the modern 'proletariat.'

4: TYPES OF 'CLASS STRUGGLE'

Thus every class may be the carrier of any one of the possibly innumerable forms of 'class action,' but this is not necessarily so. In any case, a class does not in itself constitute a community. To treat 'class' conceptually as having the same value as 'community' leads to distortion. That men in the same class situation regularly react in mass actions to such tangible situations as economic ones in the direction of those interests that are most adequate to their average number is an important and after all simple fact for the understanding of historical events. Above all, this fact must not lead to that kind of pseudo-scientific operation with the concepts of 'class' and 'class interests' so frequently found these days, and which has found its most classic expression in the statement of a talented author, that the individual may be in error concerning his interests but that the 'class' is 'infallible' about its interests. Yet, if classes as such are not communities, nevertheless class situations emerge only on the basis of communalization. The communal action that brings forth class situations, however, is not basically action between members of the identical class; it is an action between members of different classes. Communal actions that directly determine the class situation of the worker and the entrepreneur are: the labor market, the commodities market, and the capitalistic enterprise. But, in its turn, the existence of a capitalistic enterprise presupposes that a very specific communal action exists and that it is specifically structured to protect the possession of goods *per se,* and especially the power of individuals to dispose, in principle freely, over the means of production. The existence of a capitalistic enterprise is preconditioned by a specific kind of 'legal order.' Each kind of class situation, and above all when it rests upon the power of property *per se,* will become

most clearly efficacious when all other determinants of reciprocal relations are, as far as possible, eliminated in their significance. It is in this way that the utilization of the power of property in the market obtains its most sovereign importance.

Now 'status groups' hinder the strict carrying through of the sheer market principle. In the present context they are of interest to us only from this one point of view. Before we briefly consider them, note that not much of a general nature can be said about the more specific kinds of antagonism between 'classes' (in our meaning of the term). The great shift, which has been going on continuously in the past, and up to our times, may be summarized, although at the cost of some precision: the struggle in which class situations are effective has progressively shifted from consumption credit toward, first, competitive struggles in the commodity market and, then, toward price wars on the labor market. The 'class struggles' of antiquity—to the extent that they were genuine class struggles and not struggles between status groups—were initially carried on by indebted peasants, and perhaps also by artisans threatened by debt bondage and struggling against urban creditors. For debt bondage is the normal result of the differentiation of wealth in commercial cities, especially in seaport cities. A similar situation has existed among cattle breeders. Debt relationships as such produced class action up to the time of Cataline. Along with this, and with an increase in provision of grain for the city by transporting it from the outside, the struggle over the means of sustenance emerged. It centered in the first place around the provision of bread and the determination of the price of bread. It lasted throughout antiquity and the entire Middle Ages. The propertyless as such flocked together against those who actually and supposedly were interested in the dearth of bread. This fight spread until it involved all those commodities essential to the way of life and to handicraft production. There were only incipient discussions of wage disputes in antiquity and in the Middle Ages. But they have been slowly increasing up into modern times. In the earlier periods they were completely secondary to slave rebellions as well as to fights in the commodity market.

The propertyless of antiquity and of the Middle Ages protested against monopolies, pre-emption, forestalling, and the withholding of goods from the market in order to raise prices. Today the central issue is the determination of the price of labor.

This transition is represented by the fight for access to the market and for the determination of the price of products. Such fights went on between merchants and workers in the putting-out system of domestic handicraft during the transition to modern times. Since it is quite a general phenomenon we must mention here that the class antagonisms that are conditioned through the market situation are usually most bitter between those who actually and directly participate as opponents in price wars. It is not the rentier, the share-holder, and the banker who suffer the ill will of the worker, but almost exclusively the manufacturer and the business executives who are the direct opponents of workers in price wars. This is so in spite of the fact that it is precisely the cash boxes of the rentier, the share-holder, and the banker into which the more or less 'unearned' gains flow, rather than into the pockets of the manufacturers or of the business executives. This simple state of affairs has very frequently been decisive for the role the class situation has played in the formation of political parties. For example, it has made possible the varieties of patriarchal socialism and the frequent attempts—formerly, at least—of threatened status groups to form alliances with the proletariat against the 'bourgeoisie.'

5: STATUS HONOR

In contrast to classes, *status groups* are normally communities. They are, however, often of an amorphous kind. In contrast to the purely economically determined 'class situation' we wish to designate as 'status situation' every typical component of the life fate of men that is determined by a specific, positive or negative, social estimation of *honor*. This honor may be connected with any quality shared by a plurality, and, of course,

it can be knit to a class situation: class distinctions are linked in the most varied ways with status distinctions. Property as such is not always recognized as a status qualification, but in the long run it is, and with extraordinary regularity. In the subsistence economy of the organized neighborhood, very often the richest man is simply the chieftain. However, this often means only an honorific preference. For example, in the so-called pure modern 'democracy,' that is, one devoid of any expressly ordered status privileges for individuals, it may be that only the families coming under approximately the same tax class dance with one another. This example is reported of certain smaller Swiss cities. But status honor need not necessarily be linked with a 'class situation.' On the contrary, it normally stands in sharp opposition to the pretensions of sheer property.

Both propertied and propertyless people can belong to the same status group, and frequently they do with very tangible consequences. This 'equality' of social esteem may, however, in the long run become quite precarious. The 'equality' of status among the American 'gentlemen,' for instance, is expressed by the fact that outside the subordination determined by the different functions of 'business,' it would be considered strictly repugnant—wherever the old tradition still prevails—if even the richest 'chief,' while playing billiards or cards in his club in the evening, would not treat his 'clerk' as in every sense fully his equal in birthright. It would be repugnant if the American 'chief' would bestow upon his 'clerk' the condescending 'benevolence' marking a distinction of 'position,' which the German chief can never dissever from his attitude. This is one of the most important reasons why in America the German 'clubby-ness' has never been able to attain the attraction that the American clubs have.

6: GUARANTEES OF STATUS STRATIFICATION

In content, status honor is normally expressed by the fact that above all else a specific *style of life* can be expected from all those who wish to belong to the circle. Linked with this expectation are restrictions on 'social' intercourse (that is, intercourse which is not subservient to economic or any other of business's 'functional' purposes). These restrictions may confine normal marriages to within the status circle and may lead to complete endogamous closure. As soon as there is not a mere individual and socially irrelevant imitation of another style of life, but an agreed-upon communal action of this closing character, the 'status' development is under way.

In its characteristic form, stratification by 'status groups' on the basis of conventional styles of life evolves at the present time in the United States out of the traditional democracy. For example, only the resident of a certain street ('the street') is considered as belonging to 'society,' is qualified for social intercourse, and is visited and invited. Above all, this differentiation evolves in such a way as to make for strict submission to the fashion that is dominant at a given time in society. This submission to fashion also exists among men in America to a degree unknown in Germany. Such submission is considered to be an indication of the fact that a given man *pretends* to qualify as a gentleman. This submission decides, at least *prima facie,* that he will be treated as such. And this recognition becomes just as important for his employment chances in 'swank' establishments, and above all, for social intercourse and marriage with 'esteemed' families, as the qualification for dueling among Germans in the Kaiser's day. As for the rest: certain families resident for a long time, and, of course, correspondingly wealthy, e.g. 'F. F. V., i.e. First Families of Virginia,' or the actual or alleged descendants of the 'Indian Princess' Pocahontas, of the Pilgrim fathers, or of the Knickerbockers, the members of almost inaccessible sects and all sorts of circles setting themselves apart by means of any other characteristics and badges . . . all these elements usurp 'status' honor. The development of status is essentially a question of stratification resting upon usurpation. Such usurpation is the normal origin of almost all status honor. But the road from this purely conventional situation to legal privilege, positive or negative, is easily traveled as soon as a certain stratification of the social order has in fact been 'lived in' and has achieved stability by virtue of a stable distribution of economic power.

7: 'ETHNIC' SEGREGATION AND 'CASTE'

Where the consequences have been realized to their full extent, the status group evolves into a closed 'caste.' Status distinctions are then guaranteed not merely by conventions and laws, but also by *rituals.* This occurs in such a way that every physical contact with a member of any caste that is considered to be 'lower' by the members of a 'higher' caste is considered as making for a ritualistic impurity and to be a stigma which must be expiated by a religious act. Individual castes develop quite distinct cults and gods.

In general, however, the status structure reaches such extreme consequences only where there are underlying differences which are held to be 'ethnic.' The 'caste' is, indeed, the normal form in which ethnic communities usually live side by side in a 'societalized' manner. These ethnic communities believe in blood relationship and exclude exogamous marriage and social intercourse. Such a caste situation is part of the phenomenon of 'pariah' peoples and is found all over the world. These people form communities, acquire specific occupational traditions of handicrafts or of other arts, and cultivate a belief in their ethnic community. They live in a 'diaspora' strictly segregated from all personal intercourse, except that of an unavoidable sort, and their situation is legally precarious. Yet, by virtue of their economic indispensability, they are tolerated, indeed, frequently privileged, and they live in interspersed political communities. The Jews are the most impressive historical example.

A 'status' segregation grown into a 'caste' differs in its structure from a mere 'ethnic' segregation: the caste structure transforms the horizontal and unconnected coexistences of ethnically segregated groups into a vertical social system of super- and subordination. Correctly formulated: a comprehensive societalization integrates the ethnically divided communities into specific political and communal action. In their consequences they differ precisely in this way: ethnic coexistences condition a mutual repulsion and disdain but allow each ethnic community to consider its own honor as the highest one; the caste structure brings about a social subordination and an acknowledgment of 'more honor' in favor of the privileged caste and status groups. This is due to the fact that in the caste structure ethnic distinctions as such have become 'functional' distinctions within the political societalization (warriors, priests, artisans that are politically important for war and for building, and so on). But even pariah people who are most despised are usually apt to continue cultivating in some manner that which is equally peculiar to ethnic and to status communities: the belief in their own specific 'honor.' This is the case with the Jews.

Only with the negatively privileged status groups does the 'sense of dignity' take a specific deviation. A sense of dignity is the precipitation in individuals of social honor and of conventional demands which a positively privileged status group raises for the deportment of its members. The sense of dignity that characterizes positively privileged status groups is naturally related to their 'being' which does not transcend itself, that is, it is to their 'beauty and excellence' ($\chi\alpha\lambda o-\chi\dot{\alpha}\gamma\alpha\vartheta\iota\alpha$). Their kingdom is 'of this world.' They live for the present and by exploiting their great past. The sense of dignity of the negatively privileged strata naturally refers to a future lying beyond the present, whether it is of this life or of another. In other words, it must be nurtured by the belief in a providential 'mission' and by a belief in a specific honor before God. The 'chosen people's' dignity is nurtured by a belief either that in the beyond 'the last will be the first,' or that in this life a Messiah will appear to bring forth into the light of the world which has cast them out the hidden honor of the pariah people. This simple state of affairs, and not the 'resentment' which is so strongly emphasized in Nietzsche's much admired construction in the *Genealogy of Morals,* is the source of the religiosity cultivated by pariah status groups. In passing, we may note that resentment may be accurately applied only to a limited extent; for one of Nietzsche's main examples, Buddhism, it is not at all applicable.

Incidentally, the development of status groups from ethnic segregations is by no means the normal phenomenon. On the contrary, since objective 'racial differences' are by no means basic to every subjective sentiment of an ethnic community, the ultimately racial foundation of status structure is rightly and absolutely a question of the concrete individual case. Very frequently a status group is instrumental in the production of a thoroughbred anthropological type. Certainly a status group is to a high degree effective in producing extreme types, for they select personally qualified individuals (e.g. the Knighthood selects those who are fit for warfare, physically and psychically). But selection is far from being the only, or the predominant, way in which status groups are formed: Political membership or class situation has at all times been at least as frequently decisive. And today the class situation is by far the predominant factor, for of course the possibility of a style of life expected for members of a status group is usually conditioned economically.

8: STATUS PRIVILEGES

For all practical purposes, stratification by status goes hand in hand with a monopolization of ideal and material goods or opportunities, in a manner we have come to know as typical. Besides the specific status honor, which always rests upon distance and exclusiveness, we find all sorts of material monopolies. Such honorific preferences may consist of the privilege of wearing special costumes, of eating special dishes taboo to others, of carrying arms—which is most obvious in its consequences—the right to pursue certain non-professional dilettante artistic practices, e.g. to play certain musical instruments. Of course, material monopolies provide the most effective motives for the exclusiveness of a status group; although, in themselves, they are rarely sufficient, almost always they come into play to some extent. Within a status circle there is the question of intermarriage: the interest of the families in the monopolization of potential bridegrooms is at least of equal importance and is parallel to the interest in the monopolization of daughters. The daughters of the circle must be provided for. With an increased inclosure of the status group, the conventional preferential opportunities for special employment grow into a legal monopoly of special offices for the members. Certain goods become objects for monopolization by status groups. In the typical fashion these include 'entailed estates' and frequently also the possessions of serfs or bondsmen and, finally, special trades. This monopolization occurs positively when the status group is exclusively entitled to own and to manage them; and negatively when, in order to maintain its specific way of life, the status group must *not* own and manage them.

The decisive role of a 'style of life' in status 'honor' means that status groups are the specific bearers of all 'conventions.' In whatever way it may be manifest, all 'stylization' of life either originates in status groups or is at least conserved by them. Even if the principles of status conventions differ greatly, they reveal certain typical traits, especially among those strata which are most privileged. Quite generally, among privileged status groups there is a status disqualification that operates against the performance of common physical labor. This disqualification is now 'setting in' in America against the old tradition of esteem for labor. Very frequently every rational economic pursuit, and especially 'entrepreneurial activity,' is looked upon as a disqualification of status. Artistic and literary activity is also considered as degrading work as soon as it is exploited for income, or at least when it is connected with hard physical exertion. An example is the sculptor working like a mason in his dusty smock as over against the painter in his salon-like 'studio' and those forms of musical practice that are acceptable to the status group.

9: ECONOMIC CONDITIONS AND EFFECTS OF STATUS STRATIFICATION

The frequent disqualification of the gainfully employed as such is a direct result of the principle of status stratification peculiar to the social order, and of course, of this principle's opposition to a distribution of power which is regulated exclusively through the market. These two factors operate along with various individual ones, which will be touched upon below.

We have seen above that the market and its processes 'knows no personal distinctions': 'functional' interests dominate it. It knows nothing of 'honor.' The status order means precisely the reverse, viz.: stratification in terms of 'honor' and of styles of life peculiar to status groups as such. If mere economic acquisition and naked economic power still bearing the stigma of its extra-status origin could bestow upon anyone who has won it the same honor as those who are interested in status by virtue of style of life claim for themselves, the status order would be threatened at its very root. This is the more so as, given equality of status honor, property *per se* represents an addition even if it is not overtly acknowledged to be such. Yet if such economic acquisition and power gave the agent any honor at all, his wealth would result in his attaining more honor than those who successfully claim honor by virtue of style of life. Therefore all groups having interests in the status order react with special sharpness precisely against the pretensions of purely economic acquisition. In most cases they react the more vigorously the more they feel themselves threatened. Calderon's respectful treatment of the peasant, for instance, as opposed to Shakespeare's simultaneous and ostensible disdain of the *canaille* illustrates the different way in which a firmly structured status order reacts as compared with a status order that has become economically precarious. This is an example of a state of affairs that recurs everywhere. Precisely because of the rigorous reactions against the claims of property *per se,* the 'parvenu' is never accepted, personally and without reservation, by the privileged status groups, no matter how completely his style of life has been adjusted to theirs. They will only accept his descendants who have been educated in the conventions of their status group and who have never besmirched its honor by their own economic labor.

As to the general *effect* of the status order, only one consequence can be stated, but it is a very important one: the hindrance of the free development of the market occurs first for those goods which status groups directly withheld from free exchange by monopolization. This monopolization may be effected either legally or conventionally. For example, in many Hellenic cities during the epoch of status groups, and also originally in Rome, the inherited estate (as is shown by the old formula for indiction against spendthrifts) was monopolized just as were the estates of knights, peasants, priests, and especially the clientele of the craft and merchant guilds. The market is restricted, and the power of naked property *per se,* which gives its stamp to 'class formation,' is pushed into the background. The results of this process can be most varied. Of course, they do not necessarily weaken the contrasts in the economic situation. Frequently they strengthen these contrasts, and in any case, where stratification by status permeates a community as strongly as was the case in all political communities of antiquity and of the Middle Ages, one can never speak of a genuinely free market competition as we understand it today. There are wider effects than this direct exclusion of special goods from the market. From the contrariety between the status order and the purely economic order mentioned above, it follows that in most instances the notion of honor peculiar to status absolutely abhors that which is essential to the market: higgling. Honor abhors higgling among peers and occasionally it taboos higgling for the members of a status group in general. Therefore, everywhere some status groups, and usually the most influential, consider almost any kind of overt participation in economic acquisition as absolutely stigmatizing.

With some over-simplification, one might thus say that 'classes' are stratified according to their relations to the production and acquisition of goods; whereas 'status groups' are stratified according to the principles of their *consumption* of goods as represented by special 'styles of life.'

An 'occupational group' is also a status group. For normally, it successfully claims social honor only by virtue of the special style of life which may be determined by it. The differences between classes and status groups frequently overlap. It is precisely those status communities most strictly segregated in terms of honor (viz. the Indian castes) who today show, although within very rigid limits, a relatively high degree of indifference to pecuniary income. However, the Brahmins seek such income in many different ways.

As to the general economic conditions making for the predominance of stratification by 'status,' only very little can be said. When the bases of the acquisition and distribution of goods are relatively stable, stratification by status is favored. Every technological repercussion and economic transformation threatens stratification by status and pushes the class situation into the foreground. Epochs and countries in which the naked class situation is of predominant significance are regularly the periods of technical and economic transformations. And every slowing down of the shifting of economic stratifications leads, in due course, to the growth of status structures and makes for a resuscitation of the important role of social honor.

10: PARTIES

Whereas the genuine place of 'classes' is within the economic order, the place of 'status groups' is within the social order, that is, within the sphere of the distribution of 'honor.' From within these spheres, classes and status groups influence one another and they influence the legal order and are in turn influenced by it. But 'parties' live in a house of 'power.'

Their action is oriented toward the acquisition of social 'power,' that is to say, toward influencing a communal action no matter what its content may be. In principle, parties may exist in a social 'club' as well as in a 'state.' As over against the actions of classes and status groups, for which this is not necessarily the case, the communal actions of 'parties' always mean a societalization. For party actions are always directed toward a goal which is striven for in planned manner. This goal may be a 'cause' (the party may aim at realizing a program for ideal or material purposes), or the goal may be 'personal' (sinecures, power, and from these, honor for the leader and the followers of the party). Usually the party action aims at all these simultaneously. Parties are, therefore, only possible within communities that are societalized, that is, which have some rational order and a staff of persons available who are ready to enforce it. For parties aim precisely at influencing this staff, and if possible, to recruit it from party followers.

In any individual case, parties may represent interests determined through 'class situation' or 'status situation,' and they may recruit their following respectively from one or the other. But they need be neither purely 'class' nor purely 'status' parties. In most cases they are partly class parties and partly status parties, but sometimes they are neither. They may represent ephemeral or enduring structures. Their means of attaining power may be quite varied, ranging from naked violence of any sort to canvassing for votes with coarse or subtle means: money, social influence, the force of speech, suggestion, clumsy hoax, and so on to the rougher or more artful tactics of obstruction in parliamentary bodies.

The sociological structure of parties differs in a basic way according to the kind of communal action which they struggle to influence. Parties also differ according to whether or not the community is stratified by status or by classes. Above all else, they vary according to the structure of domination within the community. For their leaders normally deal with the conquest of a community. They are, in the general concept which is maintained here, not only products of specially modern forms of domination. We shall also designate as parties the ancient and medieval 'parties,' despite the fact that their structure differs basically from the structure of modern parties. By virtue of these structural differences of domination it is impossible to say anything about the structure of parties without discussing the structural forms of social domination *per se.* Parties, which are always structures struggling for domination, are very frequently organized in a very strict 'authoritarian' fashion. . .

Concerning 'classes,' 'status groups,' and 'parties,' it must be said in general that they necessarily presuppose a comprehensive societalization, and especially a political framework of communal action, within which they operate. This does not mean that parties would be confined by the frontiers of any individual political community. On the contrary, at all times it has been the order of the day that the societalization (even when it aims at the use of military force in common) reaches beyond the frontiers of politics. This has been the case in the solidarity of interests among the Oligarchs and among the democrats in Hellas, among the Guelfs and among Ghibellines in the Middle Ages, and within the Calvinist party during the period of religious struggles. It has been the case up to the solidarity of the landlords (international congress of agrarian landlords), and has continued among princes (holy alliance, Karlsbad decrees), socialist workers, conservatives (the longing of Prussian conservatives for Russian intervention in 1850). But their aim is not necessarily the establishment of new international political, i.e. *territorial,* dominion. In the main they aim to influence the existing dominion.*

---

*The posthumously published text breaks off here. We omit an incomplete sketch of types of 'warrior estates.'

Pecuniary Emulation

THORSTEIN VEBLEN

In the sequence of cultural evolution the emergence of a leisure class coincides with the beginning of ownership. This is necessarily the case, for these two institutions result from the same set of economic forces. In the inchoate phase of their development they are but different aspects of the same general facts of social structure.

It is as elements of social structure—conventional facts—that leisure and ownership are matters of interest for the purpose in hand. An habitual neglect of work does not constitute a leisure class; neither does the mechanical fact of use and consumption constitute ownership. The present inquiry, therefore, is not concerned with the beginning of indolence, nor with the beginning of the appropriation of useful articles to individual consumption. The point in question is the origin and nature of a conventional leisure class on the one hand and the beginnings of individual ownership as a conventional right or equitable claim on the other hand.

The early differentiation out of which the distinction between a leisure and a working class arises is a division maintained between men's and women's work in the lower stages of barbarism. Likewise the earliest form of ownership is an ownership of the women by the able-bodied men of the community. The facts may be expressed in more general terms, and truer to the import of the barbarian theory of life, by saying that it is an ownership of the woman by the man.

There was undoubtedly some appropriation of useful articles before the custom of appropriating women arose. The usages of existing archaic communities in which there is no ownership of women is warrant for such a view. In all communities the members, both male and female, habitually appropriate to their individual use a variety of useful things; but these useful things are not thought of as owned by the person who appropriates and consumes them. The habitual appropriation and consumption of certain slight personal effects goes on without raising the question of ownership; that is to say, the question of a conventional, equitable claim to extraneous things.

The ownership of women begins in the lower barbarian stages of culture, apparently with the seizure of female captives. The original reason for the seizure and appropriation of women seems to have been their usefulness as trophies. The practice of seizing women from the enemy as trophies, gave rise to a form of ownership-marriage, resulting in a household with a male head. This was followed by an extension of slavery to other captives and inferiors, besides women, and by an extension of ownership-marriage to other women than those seized from the enemy. The outcome of emulation under the circumstances of a predatory life, therefore, has been on the one hand a form of marriage resting on coercion, and on the other hand the custom of ownership. The two institutions are not distinguishable in the initial phase of their development; both arise from the desire of the successful men to put their prowess in evidence by exhibiting

Source: From *The Theory of the Leisure Class* by Thorstein Veblen (Amherst, NY: Prometheus Books). Published 1998.

some durable result of their exploits. Both also minister to that propensity for mastery which pervades all predatory communities. From the ownership of women the concept of ownership extends itself to include the products of their industry, and so there arises the ownership of things as well as of persons.

In this way a consistent system of property in goods is gradually installed. And although in the latest stages of the development, the serviceability of goods for consumption has come to be the most obtrusive element of their value, still, wealth has by no means yet lost its utility as a honorific evidence of the owner's prepotence.

Wherever the institution of private property is found, even in a slightly developed form, the economic process bears the character of a struggle between men for the possession of goods. It has been customary in economic theory, and especially among those economists who adhere with least faltering to the body of modernised classical doctrines, to construe this struggle for wealth as being substantially a struggle for subsistence. Such is, no doubt, its character in large part during the earlier and less efficient phases of industry. Such is also its character in all cases where the "niggardliness of nature" is so strict as to afford but a scanty livelihood to the community in return for strenuous and unremitting application to the business of getting the means of subsistence. But in all progressing communities an advance is presently made beyond this early stage of technological development. Industrial efficiency is presently carried to such a pitch as to afford something appreciably more than a bare livelihood to those engaged in the industrial process. It has not been unusual for economic theory to speak of the further struggle for wealth on this new industrial basis as a competition for an increase of the comforts of life,—primarily for an increase of the physical comforts which the consumption of goods affords.

The end of acquisition and accumulation is conventionally held to be the consumption of the goods accumulated—whether it is consumption directly by the owner of the goods or by the household attached to him and for this purpose identified with him in theory. This is at least felt to be the economically legitimate end of acquisition, which alone it is incumbent on the theory to take account of. Such consumption may of course be conceived to serve the consumer's physical wants—his physical comfort—or his so-called higher wants—spiritual, æsthetic, intellectual, or what not; the latter class of wants being served indirectly by an expenditure of goods, after the fashion familiar to all economic readers.

But it is only when taken in a sense far removed from its naïve meaning that consumption of goods can be said to afford the incentive from which accumulation invariably proceeds. The motive that lies at the root of ownership is emulation; and the same motive of emulation continues active in the further development of the institution to which it has given rise and in the development of all those features of the social structure which this institution of ownership touches. The possession of wealth confers honour; it is an invidious distinction. Nothing equally cogent can be said for the consumption of goods, nor for any other conceivable incentive to acquisition, and especially not for any incentive to the accumulation of wealth.

It is of course not to be overlooked that in a community where nearly all goods are private property the necessity of earning a livelihood is a powerful and ever-present incentive for the poorer members of the community. The need of subsistence and of an increase of physical comfort may for a time be the dominant motive of acquisition for those classes who are habitually employed at manual labour, whose subsistence is on a precarious footing, who possess little and ordinarily accumulate little; but it will appear in the course of the discussion that even in the case of these impecunious classes the predominance of the motive of physical want is not so decided as has sometimes been assumed. On the other hand, so far as regards those members and classes of the community who are chiefly concerned in the accumulation of wealth, the incentive of subsistence or of physical comfort never plays a considerable part. Ownership began and grew into a human institution on grounds unrelated to the subsistence minimum. The dominant incentive was from the outset the invidious distinction attaching to wealth, and, save temporarily and by exception, no other motive has usurped the primacy at any later stage of the development.

Property set out with being booty held as trophies of the successful raid. So long as the group had departed but little from the primitive communal organisation, and so long as it still stood in close contact with other hostile groups, the utility of things or persons owned lay chiefly in an invidious comparison between their possessor and the enemy from whom they were taken. The habit of distinguishing between the interests of the individual and those of the group to which he belongs is apparently a later growth. Invidious comparison between the possessor of the honorific booty and his less successful neighbours within the group was no doubt present early as an element of the utility of the things possessed, though this was not at the outset the chief element of their value. The man's prowess was still primarily the group's prowess, and the possessor of the booty felt himself to be primarily the keeper of the honour of his group. This appreciation of exploit from the communal point of view is met with also at later stages of social growth, especially as regards the laurels of war.

But so soon as the custom of individual ownership begins to gain consistency, the point of view taken in making the invidious comparison on which private property rests will begin to change. Indeed, the one change is but the reflex of the other. The initial phase of ownership, the phase of acquisition by naïve seizure and conversion, begins to pass into the subsequent stage of an incipient organisation of industry on the basis of private property (in slaves); the horde develops into a more or less self-sufficing industrial community; possessions then come to be valued not so much as evidence of successful foray, but rather as evidence of the prepotence of the possessor of these goods over other individuals within the community. The

invidious comparison now becomes primarily a comparison of the owner with the other members of the group. Property is still of the nature of trophy, but, with the cultural advance, it becomes more and more a trophy of successes scored in the game of ownership carried on between the members of the group under the quasipeaceable methods of nomadic life.

Gradually, as industrial activity further displaces predatory activity in the community's everyday life and in men's habits of thought, accumulated property more and more replaces trophies of predatory exploit as the conventional exponent of prepotence and success. With the growth of settled industry, therefore, the possession of wealth gains in relative importance and effectiveness as a customary basis of repute and esteem. Not that esteem ceases to be awarded on the basis of other, more direct evidence of prowess; not that successful predatory aggression or warlike exploit ceases to call out the approval and admiration of the crowd, or to stir the envy of the less successful competitors; but the opportunities for gaining distinction by means of this direct manifestation of superior force grow less available both in scope and frequency. At the same time opportunities for industrial aggression, and for the accumulation of property by the quasi-peaceable methods of nomadic industry, increase in scope and availability. And it is even more to the point that property now becomes the most easily recognised evidence of a reputable degree of success as distinguished from heroic or signal achievement. It therefore becomes the conventional basis of esteem. Its possession in some amount becomes necessary in order to any reputable standing in the community. It becomes indispensable to accumulate, to acquire property, in order to retain one's good name. When accumulated goods have in this way once become the accepted badge of efficiency, the possession of wealth presently assumes the character of an independent and definitive basis of esteem. The possession of goods, whether acquired aggressively by one's own exertion or passively by transmission through inheritance from others, becomes a conventional basis of reputability. The possession of wealth, which was at the outset valued simply as an evidence of efficiency, becomes, in popular apprehension, itself a meritorious act. Wealth is now itself intrinsically honourable and confers honour on its possessor. By a further refinement, wealth acquired passively by transmission from ancestors or other antecedents presently becomes even more honorific than wealth acquired by the possessor's own effort; but this distinction belongs at a later stage in the evolution of the pecuniary culture and will be spoken of in its place.

Prowess and exploit may still remain the basis of award of the highest popular esteem, although the possession of wealth has become the basis of commonplace reputability and of a blameless social standing. The predatory instinct and the consequent approbation of predatory efficiency are deeply ingrained in the habits of thought of those peoples who have passed under the discipline of a protracted predatory culture. According to popular award, the highest honours within human reach may, even yet, be those gained by an unfolding of extraordinary predatory efficiency in war, or by a quasi-predatory efficiency in statecraft; but for the purposes of a commonplace decent standing in the community these means of repute have been replaced by the acquisition and accumulation of goods. In order to stand well in the eyes of the community, it is necessary to come up to a certain, somewhat indefinite, conventional standard of wealth; just as in the earlier predatory stage it is necessary for the barbarian man to come up to the tribe's standard of physical endurance, cunning, and skill at arms. A certain standard of wealth in the one case, and of prowess in the other, is a necessary condition of reputability, and anything in excess of this normal amount is meritorious.

Those members of the community who fall short of this, somewhat indefinite, normal degree of prowess or of property suffer in the esteem of their fellow-men; and consequently they suffer also in their own esteem, since the usual basis of self-respect is the respect accorded by one's neighbours. Only individuals with an aberrant temperament can in the long run retain their self-esteem in the face of the disesteem of their fellows. Apparent exceptions to the rule are met with, especially among people with strong religious convictions. But these apparent exceptions are scarcely real exceptions, since such persons commonly fall back on the putative approbation of some supernatural witness of their deeds.

So soon as the possession of property becomes the basis of popular esteem, therefore, it becomes also a requisite to that complacency which we call self-respect. In any community where goods are held in severalty it is necessary, in order to his own peace of mind, that an individual should possess as large a portion of goods as others with whom he is accustomed to class himself; and it is extremely gratifying to possess something more than others. But as fast as a person makes new acquisitions, and becomes accustomed to the resulting new standard of wealth, the new standard forthwith ceases to afford appreciably greater satisfaction than the earlier standard did. The tendency in any case is constantly to make the present pecuniary standard the point of departure for a fresh increase of wealth; and this in turn gives rise to a new standard of sufficiency and a new pecuniary classification of one's self as compared with one's neighbours. So far as concerns the present question, the end sought by accumulation is to rank high in comparison with the rest of the community in point of pecuniary strength. So long as the comparison is distinctly unfavourable to himself, the normal, average individual will live in chronic dissatisfaction with his present lot; and when he has reached what may be called the normal pecuniary standard of the community, or of his class in the community, this chronic dissatisfaction will give place to a restless straining to place a wider and ever-widening pecuniary interval between himself and this average standard. The invidious comparison can never become so favourable to the individual making it that he would not gladly rate himself still higher relatively to his competitors in the struggle for pecuniary reputability.

In the nature of the case, the desire for wealth can scarcely be satiated in any individual instance, and evidently a satiation of the average or general desire for wealth is out of the question. However widely, or equally, or "fairly," it may be distributed, no general increase of the community's wealth can make any approach to satiating this need, the ground of which is the desire of every one to excel every one else in the accumulation of goods. If, as is sometimes assumed, the incentive to accumulation were the want of subsistence or of physical comfort, then the aggregate economic wants of a community might conceivably be satisfied at some point in the advance of industrial efficiency; but since the struggle is substantially a race for reputability on the basis of an invidious comparison, no approach to a definitive attainment is possible.

What has just been said must not be taken to mean that there are no other incentives to acquisition and accumulation than this desire to excel in pecuniary standing and so gain the esteem and envy of one's fellow-men. The desire for added comfort and security from want is present as a motive at every stage of the process of accumulation in a modern industrial community; although the standard of sufficiency in these respects is in turn greatly affected by the habit of pecuniary emulation. To a great extent this emulation shapes the methods and selects the objects of expenditure for personal comfort and decent livelihood.

Besides this, the power conferred by wealth also affords a motive to accumulation. That propensity for purposeful activity and that repugnance to all futility of effort which belong to man by virtue of his character as an agent do not desert him when he emerges from the naïve communal culture where the dominant note of life is the unanalysed and undifferentiated solidarity of the individual with the group with which his life is bound up. When he enters upon the predatory stage, where self-seeking in the narrower sense becomes the dominant note, this propensity goes with him still, as the pervasive trait that shapes his scheme of life. The propensity for achievement and the repugnance to futility remain the underlying economic motive. The propensity changes only in the form of its expression and in the proximate objects to which it directs the man's activity. Under the régime of individual ownership the most available means of visibly achieving a purpose is that afforded by the acquisition and accumulation of goods; and as the self-regarding antithesis between man and man reaches fuller consciousness, the propensity for achievement—the instinct of workmanship—tends more and more to shape itself into a straining to excel others in pecuniary achievement. Relative success, tested by an invidious pecuniary comparison with other men, becomes the conventional end of action. The currently accepted legitimate end of effort becomes the achievement of a favourable comparison with other men; and therefore the repugnance to futility to a good extent coalesces with the incentive of emulation. It acts to accentuate the struggle for pecuniary reputability by visiting with a sharper disapproval all shortcoming and all evidence of shortcoming in point of pecuniary success. Purposeful effort comes to mean, primarily, effort directed to or resulting in a more creditable showing of accumulated wealth. Among the motives which lead men to accumulate wealth, the primacy, both in scope and intensity, therefore, continues to belong to this motive of pecuniary emulation.

In making use of the term "invidious," it may perhaps be unnecessary to remark, there is no intention to extol or depreciate, or to commend or deplore any of the phenomena which the word is used to characterise. The term is used in a technical sense as describing a comparison of persons with a view to rating and grading them in respect of relative worth or value—in an æsthetic or moral sense—and so awarding and defining the relative degrees of complacency with which they may legitimately be contemplated by themselves and by others. An invidious comparison is a process of valuation of persons in respect of worth.

Foundations of Class Analysis:
A Marxist Perspective

ERIK OLIN WRIGHT

If "class" is the answer, what is the question? The word "class" is deployed in a wide range of explanatory contexts in sociology, and, depending on that explanatory context, different concepts of class may be needed. Three broad kinds of questions are particularly common for which the word "class" figures centrally in the answer. First, the word "class" sometimes figures in the answers to questions such as "How do people locate themselves within a social structure of inequality?" Class is one of the possible answers to the question. In this case, the concept would be defined something like "a social category sharing a common set of subjectively salient attributes within a system of stratification." Second, class is offered as part of the answer to the question "What explains inequalities in economically defined standards of living?" Here, typically, the concept of class would not be defined by subjectively salient attributes of a social location but rather by the relationship of people to income-generating resources or assets of various sorts. Third, class plays a central role in answering the question "What sorts of struggles have the potential to transform capitalist economic oppressions in an emancipatory direction?" This is the distinctively Marxist question. Marxists may share with Weberians the second question concerning the

explanation of economic inequalities, and, as we will see, the Marxist concept of class shares much with the Weberian concept in terms of its role in explaining such inequality. Marxists may also use the concept of class in the account of people's subjective understandings of their location in systems of stratification, as in the first question. However, it is the third question that imparts to the Marxist concept of class a distinctive explanatory and normative agenda. It suggests a concept of class that is not simply defined in terms of relations to economic resources but that elaborates these relations in terms of mechanisms of economic oppression. The problem of specifying the theoretical foundations of the concept of class, therefore, crucially depends on what explanatory work the concept is called on to do.

In these terms, the concept of class has greater explanatory ambitions within the Marxist tradition than in any other tradition of social theory, and this, in turn, places greater burdens on its theoretical foundations. In its most ambitious form, classical historical materialism argued that class—or very closely linked concepts such as "mode of production" or "the economic base"—constituted the primary explanation of the epochal trajectory of social change as well as social conflicts located within concrete time and place, and of the macrolevel institutional form of the state along with the microlevel subjective beliefs of individuals. Expressions such as "class struggle is the motor of history" and "the executive of the modern state is but a committee of the bourgeoisie" captured this ambitious claim of explanatory primacy for the concept of class.

Most Marxist scholars today have pulled back significantly from the grandiose explanatory claims of historical materialism (if not necessarily from its explanatory aspirations). Few today defend stark versions of "class primacy." Nevertheless, it remains the case that class retains a distinctive centrality within the Marxist tradition and is called on to do much more arduous explanatory work than in other theoretical traditions. Indeed, a good argument can be made that this, along with a specific orientation to radically egalitarian normative principles, is a large part of what defines the remaining distinctiveness and vitality of the Marxist tradition as a body of thought, particularly within sociology. It is for this reason that I have argued that "Marxism as class analysis" defines the core agenda of Marxist sociology (see Wright, Levine, and Sober, 1992: chap. 8).

The task of this [essay] is to lay out the central analytical foundations of the concept of class in a way that is broadly consistent with the Marxist tradition. This is a tricky business, for within Marxism there is no consensus on any of the core concepts of class analysis. What defines the tradition is more a loose commitment to the importance of class analysis for understanding the conditions for challenging capitalist oppressions and the language within which debates are waged—what Alvin Gouldner (1970) aptly called a "speech community"—than a precise set of definitions and propositions. Any claims about the analytical foundations of Marxist class analysis that I make, therefore, will reflect my specific stance within that tradition rather than an authoritative account of "Marxism" in general or of the work of Karl Marx in particular.

I proceed in the following manner. First, I lay out a series of conceptual elements that underlie the kind of Marxist class analysis that I have pursued. Many of these elements apply, perhaps with some rhetorical modification, to Weberian-inspired class analysis as well as Marxist, although as a package they reflect the background assumptions characteristic of the Marxist agenda. Some of the points I make here may be quite obvious, but nevertheless I think it is useful to lay these out step by step. Second, I specify what I feel is the core common explanatory claim of class analysis in both the Marxist and the Weberian tradition. Third, I identify what I believe to be the distinctive hallmark of the Marxist concept, which differentiates from its Weberian cousins and anchors the broader theoretical claims and agenda of Marxist class analysis. This involves, above all, elaborating the specific causal mechanisms through which Marxists claim that class relations generate social effects. Finally, I briefly lay out what I see as the advantages of the Marxian-inspired form of class analysis.

CONCEPTUAL ELEMENTS

Five conceptual elements need to be clarified in order to give specificity to the Marxist approach to class analysis: (1) the concept of social relations of production, (2) the idea of class as a specific form of such relations, (3) the problem of the forms of variation of class relations, (4) the meaning of a "location" within class relations, and (5) the distinction between micro and macro levels of class analysis.

Relations of Production

Any system of production requires the deployment of a range of assets or resources or factors of production: tools, machines, land, raw materials, labor power, skills, information, and so forth. This deployment can be described in technical terms as a production function—so many inputs of different kinds are combined in a specific process to produce an output of a specific kind. The deployment can also be described in social relational terms: The individual actors that participate in production have different kinds of rights and powers over the use of the inputs and over the results of their use. Rights and powers over resources, of course, are attributes of social relations, not descriptions of the relationship of people to things as such: To have rights and powers with respect to land defines one's social relationship to other people with respect to the use of the land and the appropriation of the fruits of using the land productively. The sum total of these rights and powers constitutes the "social relations of production."

Class Relations as a Form of Relations of Production

When the rights and powers of people over productive resources are unequally distributed—when some people have greater rights/powers with respect to specific kinds of productive resources than do others—these relations can be described as class relations. The classic contrast in capitalist societies is between owners of means of production and owners of labor power since "owning" is a description of rights and powers with respect to a resource deployed in production.

Let us be quite precise here: The rights and powers in question are not defined with respect to the ownership or control of things in general but only of resources or assets insofar as they are deployed in production. A capitalist is not someone who owns machines but someone who owns machines, deploys those machines in a production process, hires owners of labor power to use them, and appropriates the profits from the use of those machines. A collector of machines is not, by virtue of owning those machines, a capitalist. To count as a class relation, it is therefore not sufficient that there be unequal rights and powers over the sheer physical use of a resource. There must also be unequal rights and powers over the appropriation of the results of that use. In general, this implies appropriating income generated by the deployment of the resource in question.

Variations in Class Relations

Different kinds of class relations are defined by the kinds of rights and powers that are embodied in the relations of production. For example, in some systems of production, people are allowed to own the labor power of other people. When the rights accompanying such ownership are absolute, the class relation is called "slavery." When the rights and powers over labor power are jointly owned by the laborer and someone else, the class relation is called "feudalism." In capitalist societies, in contrast, such absolute or shared ownership of other people is prohibited.

Because of the specific role that class analysis played in historical materialism, Marxists have traditionally limited the range of variation of types of class relations to a very few abstract forms, slavery, feudalism, and capitalism being the main types. Once the restrictions of historical materialism are relaxed, the basic concept of class relations allows for a much richer array of variations. The rights and powers that constitute "ownership" can be decomposed, with different rights and powers going to different actors. Just as feudalism is characterized by a decomposition of rights and powers over labor power—some belonging to feudal lords, others to serfs—so too can there be a decomposition of the rights and powers over means of production. Government restrictions on workplace practices, union representation on boards of directors, codetermination schemes, employee stock options, delegations of power to managerial hierarchies, and so on all constitute various ways in which the property rights and powers embodied in the idea of "owning the means of production" are decomposed and redistributed. Such redistribution of rights and powers constitutes a form of variation in class relations. To be sure, such systems of redistributed rights and powers are complex and move class relations away from the simple, abstract form of perfectly polarized relations. One of the objectives of class analysis is to understand the consequences of these forms of variation of class relations. Such complexity, however, is still complexity in the form of class relations, not some other sort of social relation, since the social relations still govern the unequal rights and powers of people over economically relevant assets.

The sum total of the class relations in a given unit of analysis can be called the "class structure" of that unit of analysis. One can thus speak of the class structure of a firm, of a city, of a country, and perhaps of the world. A class structure generally does not consist of a single type of class relation. Typically, a variety of forms of class relations are combined in various ways, further adding to the complexity of class structures.

Class Locations within Class Relations

"Class locations" can be understood as the social positions occupied by individuals—and, in some contexts, families—within class relations. Again, these class locations need not be polarized—locations in which there is an absolute disjuncture between the rights and powers of the different locations within relations. A characteristic feature of many class structures is the existence of what I have termed "contradictory locations within class relations." The claim of a class analysis of such social locations is that the specific pattern of rights and powers over productive resources that are combined in a given location defines a set of real and significant causal processes. Contradictory locations are like a chemical compound in which its properties can best be explained by uncovering the specific way in which different elements—different rights and powers with respect to the various assets used in production—are combined rather than treating such locations as unitary, one-dimensional categories.

Micro- and Macro-Class Analysis

The micro level of class analysis attempts to understand the ways in which class impacts on individuals. At its core is the analysis of the effects of class locations on various aspects of individual lives. Analyses of labor market strategies of unskilled workers or political contributions of corporate executives would be examples of micro-level class analysis as long as the rights and powers of these actors over economic resources figured in the analysis. The macro level of analysis centers on the effects of class structures on the unit of analysis in

which they are defined. The analysis of how the international mobility of capital constrains the policy options of states, for example, constitutes a macro-level investigation of the effects of a particular kind of class structure on states.

THE EXPLANATORY CLAIMS: THE FUNDAMENTAL METATHESIS OF CLASS ANALYSIS

The fundamental metathesis of class analysis is that class, understood in the way described here, has systematic and significant consequences for both the lives of individuals and the dynamics of institutions. One might say "class counts" as a slogan. At the micro level, whether one sells one's labor power on a labor market, whether one has the power to tell other people what to do in the labor process, whether one owns large amounts of capital, whether one possesses a legally certified valuable credential, and so on have real consequences in the lives of people. At the macro level, it is consequential for the functioning of a variety of institutions whether the rights over the allocation and use of means of production are highly concentrated in the hands of a few people, whether certain of these rights have been appropriated by public authority or remain privately controlled, whether there are significant barriers to the acquisition of different kinds of assets by people who lack them, and so on. To say that class counts, then, is to claim that the distribution of rights and powers over the basic productive resources of the society have significant, systematic consequences.

What, then, are the specific mechanisms through which these effects are generated? By virtue of what are class relations, as defined here, explanatory? At the most general and abstract level, the causal processes embedded in class relations help explain two kinds of proximate effects: what people get and what they have to do to get what they get. The first of these concerns, above all, the distribution of income. The class analysis claim is, therefore, that the rights and powers that people have over productive assets constitute a systematic and significant determinant of their standards of living: What you have determines what you get. The second of these causal processes concerns, above all, the distribution of economic activities. Again, the class analysis thesis is that the rights and powers over productive assets constitute a systematic and significant determinant of the strategies and practices in which people engage to acquire their income: whether they have to pound the pavement looking for a job, whether they make decisions about the allocation of investments around the world, whether they have to worry about making payments on bank loans to keep a farm afloat, and so on. What you have determines what you have to do to get what you get. Other kinds of consequences that are linked to class—voting patterns, attitudes, friendship formation, health, and so on—are second-order effects of these two primary processes.

These are not trivial claims. It could be the case, for example, that the distribution of the rights and powers of individuals over productive resources has relatively little to do with their income or economic activities. Suppose that the welfare state provided a universal basic income to everyone sufficient to sustain a decent standard of living. In such a society, what people get would be significantly, although not entirely, decoupled from what they own. Similarly, if the world became like a continual lottery in which there was virtually no stability either within or across generations to the distribution of assets, then, even if it were still the case that relations to such assets statically mattered for income, it might make sense to say that class did not matter very much. Or, suppose that the central determinant of what you had to do to get what you get was race or sex or religion and that ownership of economically relevant assets was of marginal significance in explaining anyone's economic activities or conditions. Again, in such a society, class might not be very explanatory (unless, of course, the main way in which gender or race affects these outcomes was by allocating people to class positions on the basis of their race and gender). The sheer fact of inequalities of income or of domination and subordination within work is not proof that class counts; what has to be shown is that the rights and powers of people over productive assets have a systematic bearing on these phenomena.

MARXIST CLASS ANALYSIS

As formulated above, there is nothing uniquely Marxist about the explanatory claims of class analysis. "What people get" and "what people have to do to get what they get" sounds very much like "life chances." Weberian class analysts would say very much the same thing. It is for this reason that there is a close affinity between Marxist and Weberian concepts of class (although less affinity in the broader theoretical frameworks within which these concepts figure or in the explanatory reach class is thought to have).

What makes class analysis distinctively Marxist is the account of specific mechanisms that are seen as generating these two kinds of consequences. Here the pivotal concepts are exploitation and domination. These are the conceptual elements that anchor the Marxist concept of class in the distinctive Marxist question of class analysis.

Exploitation is a complex and challenging concept. It is meant to designate a particular form of interdependence of the material interests of people, namely, a situation that satisfies three criteria:

1. *The inverse interdependent welfare principle:* The material welfare of exploiters causally depends on the material deprivations of the exploited.
2. *The exclusion principle:* This inverse interdependence of welfares of exploiters and exploited depends on the exclusion of the exploited from access to certain productive resources.
3. *The appropriation principle:* Exclusion generates material advantage to exploiters because it enables them to appropriate the labor effort of the exploited.

Exploitation is thus a diagnosis of the process through which the inequalities in incomes are generated by inequalities in rights and powers over productive resources: The inequalities occur, at least in part, through the ways in which exploiters, by virtue of their exclusionary rights and powers over resources, are able to appropriate surplus generated by the effort of the exploited. If the first two of these principles are present, but not the third, economic oppression may exist, but not exploitation. The crucial difference is that in nonexploitative economic oppression, the privileged social category does not itself need the excluded category. While their welfare does depend on the exclusion, there is no ongoing interdependence of their activities. In the case of exploitation, the exploiters actively need the exploited: Exploiters depend on the effort of the exploited for their own welfare.

This deep interdependence makes exploitation a particularly explosive form of social relation for two reasons. First, exploitation constitutes a social relation that simultaneously pits the interests of one group against another and that requires their ongoing interactions. Second, it confers on the disadvantaged group a real form of power with which to challenge the interests of exploiters. This is an important point. Exploitation depends on the appropriation of labor effort. Because human beings are conscious agents, not robots, they always retain significant levels of real control over their expenditure of effort. The extraction of effort within exploitative relations is thus always to a greater or lesser extent problematic and precarious, requiring active institutional devices for its reproduction. Such devices can become quite costly to exploiters in the form of the costs of supervision, surveillance, sanctions, and so on. The ability to impose such costs constitutes a form of power among the exploited.

Domination is a simpler idea. It identifies one dimension of the interdependence of the activities within production itself rather than simply the interdependence of material interests generated by those activities. Here the issue is that, by virtue of the relations into which people enter as a result of their rights and powers that they have over productive resources, some people are in a position to control the activities of others—to direct them, to boss them, to monitor their activities, to hire and fire them, or to advance or deny them credit. The Marxist class analysis thesis, therefore, is not simply

that "what you have determines what you have to do to get what you get" but, rather, "what you have determines the extent to which you are dominated or dominating when you do what you have to do to get what you get."

In Weberian class analysis, just as much as in Marxist class analysis, the rights and powers that individuals have over productive assets define the material basis of class relations. However, for Weberian-inspired class analysis, these rights and powers are consequential primarily because of the ways they shape life chances, most notably life chances within market exchanges, rather than the ways they structure patterns of exploitation and domination. Control over resources affects bargaining capacity within processes of exchange, and this in turn affects the results of such exchanges, especially income. Exploitation and domination are not centerpieces of this argument.

This suggests the contrast between Marxist and Weberian frameworks of class analysis illustrated in Figure 1. Both Marxist and Weberian class analysis differ sharply from simple gradational accounts of class in which class is itself directly identified within inequalities in income since both begin with the problem of the social relations that determine the access of people to economic resources. In a sense, therefore, Marxist and Weberian definitions of class in capitalist society share the same definitional criteria. Where they differ is in the theoretical elaboration and specification of the implications of this common set of criteria: The Marxist model sees two causal paths being systematically generated by these relations—one operating through market exchanges and the other through the process of production itself—whereas the Weberian model traces only one causal path; and the Marxist model elaborates the mechanisms of these causal paths in terms of exploitation and domination as well as bargaining capacity within exchange, whereas the Weberian model deals only with the last of these. In a sense, then, the Weberian strategy of class analysis is contained within the Marxist model.

Of course, any Weberian can include an analysis of class-based domination and exploitation within

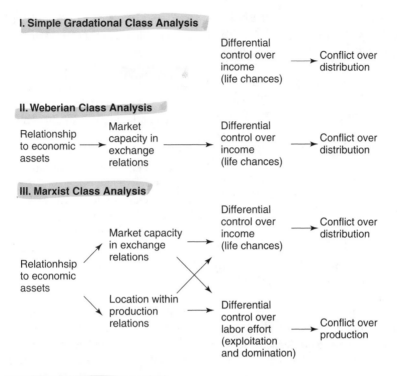

FIGURE 1   Three Models of Class Analysis.

any specific sociological inquiry. One of the charms of the Weberian analytical framework is that it is entirely permissive about the inclusion of additional causal processes. Such an inclusion, however, represents the importation of Marxist themes into the Weberian model; the model itself does not imply any particular importance to these issues. Frank Parkin (1979:25) once made a well-known quip in a book about class theory: "Inside every neo-Marxist is a Weberian struggling to get out." The argument presented here suggests a complementary proposition: "Inside every leftist neo-Weberian is a Marxist struggling to stay hidden."

THE PAYOFF: WHAT ARE THE ADVANTAGES OF THE MARXIST STRATEGY OF CLASS ANALYSIS?

Elaborating the concept of class in terms of exploitation and domination clearly facilitates its analytical relevance to the agenda embedded in the distinctive Marxist question: "What sorts of struggles have the potential to challenge and transform capitalist economic oppressions in an emancipatory direction?" Class struggles have this potential because of the way class relations shape the interests and capacities of actors with respect to those oppressions. Saying this, of course, does not define the conclusion of the Marxist agenda but only its starting point. It does not prejudge the problem of what social conditions enable or impede such struggles or determine their effectiveness, of how class struggles are linked to other kinds of social conflicts, whether class compromises are possible within such struggles, or even of the historically possible extent to which capitalist economic oppressions can be eliminated. I am claiming, however, that the answer to these questions is facilitated when class is understood in terms of exploitation and domination.

However, what if one is not particularly interested in the foundational Marxist question? What if one believes that emancipatory transformations of capitalism, however morally attractive, are utopian fantasies? Or, even more critically, what if one believes that capitalism is not especially oppressive? If one rejects the relevance of the Marxist question, does this necessarily imply a complete rejection of the Marxist conceptualization of class as well? I think not. There are a number of reasons that elaborating the concept of class in terms of exploitation and domination has theoretical payoffs beyond the specific normative agenda of Marxist class analysis itself:

1. *Linking exchange and production.* The Marxist logic of class analysis affirms the intimate link between the way in which social relations are organized within exchange and within production. This is a substantive, not a definitional, point: The social relations that organize the rights and powers of individuals with respect to productive resources systematically shape their location both within exchange relations and within the process of production itself. This does not mean, of course, that there is no independent variation of exchange and production, but it does imply that this variation is structured by class relations.

2. *Conflict.* One of the standard claims about Marxist class analysis is that it foregrounds conflict within class relations. Indeed, a conventional way of describing Marxism in sociological textbooks is to see it as a variety of "conflict theory." This characterization, however, is not quite precise enough, for conflict is certainly a prominent feature of Weberian views of class as well. The distinctive feature of the Marxist account of class relations in these terms is not simply that it gives prominence to class conflict but that it understands conflict as generated by inherent properties of those relations rather than simply contingent factors. Exploitation defines a structure of interdependent interests in which advancing the interests of exploiters depends on their capacity to impose deprivations on the exploited. This is a stronger antagonism of interests than simple competition,

and it underwrites a strong prediction within Marxist class analysis that class systems will be conflict ridden.

3. *Power.* At the very core of the Marxist construction of class analysis is the claim not simply that class relations generate deeply antagonistic interests but that they also give people in subordinate class locations forms of power with which to struggle for their interests. As already noted, since exploitation rests on the extraction of labor effort and since people always retain some measure of control over their own effort, they always confront their exploiters with capacities to resist exploitation. This is a crucial form of power reflected in the complex counterstrategies that exploiting classes are forced to adopt through the elaboration of instruments of supervision, surveillance, monitoring, and sanctioning. It is only by virtue of this inherent capacity for resistance—a form of social power rooted in the interdependencies of exploitation—that exploiting capacities are forced to devote some of their resources to ensure their ability to appropriate labor effort.

4. *Coercion and consent.* Marxist class analysis contains the rudiments of what might be termed an endogenous theory of the formation of consent. The argument is basically this: The extraction of labor effort in systems of exploitation is costly for exploiting classes because of the inherent capacity of people to resist their own exploitation. Purely coercively backed systems of exploitation will often tend to be suboptimal since under many conditions it is too easy for workers to withhold diligent performance of labor effort. Exploiting classes will therefore have a tendency to seek ways of reducing those costs. One of the ways of reducing the overhead costs of extracting labor effort is to do things that elicit the active consent of the exploited. These range from the development of internal labor markets that strengthen the identification and loyalty of workers to the firms in which they work to the support for ideological positions that proclaim the practical and moral desirability of capitalist institutions. Such consent-producing practices, however, also have costs attached to them, and thus systems of exploitation can be seen as always involving trade-offs between coercion and consent as mechanisms for extracting labor effort.

This argument points to a crucial difference between systems of non-exploitative oppression and exploitative class relations. In nonexploitative oppression, there is no dependency of the oppressing group on the extraction of labor effort of the oppressed and thus much less need to elicit their active consent. Purely repressive reactions to resistance—including genocidal repression—are therefore feasible. This is embodied in the abhorrent nineteenth-century American folk expression that "the only good Indian is a dead Indian," an expression that reflects the fact that Native Americans were generally not exploited, although they were certainly oppressed. The comparable, if less catchy, expression for workers would be that "the only good worker is an obedient worker"; it would make no sense to say that "the only good worker is a dead worker." This contrast points to the ways in which an exploitation-centered class analysis suggests an endogenous understanding of the construction of consent.

5. *Historical/comparative analysis.* As originally conceived, Marxist class analysis was an integral part of a sweeping theory of the epochal structure and historical trajectory of social change. However, even if one rejects historical materialism, the Marxist exploitation-centered strategy of class analysis still provides a rich menu of concepts for historical and comparative analysis. Different kinds of class relations are defined by the specific mechanisms through which exploitation is accomplished,

and these differences in turn imply different problems faced by exploiting classes for the reproduction of their class advantage and different opportunities for exploited classes to resist. Variations in these mechanisms and in the specific ways in which they are combined in concrete societies provide an analytically powerful road map for comparative research.

These are all reasons why a concept of class rooted in the linkage between social relations of production on the one hand and exploitation and domination on the other should be of sociological interest. Still, the most fundamental payoff of these conceptual foundations is the way in which it infuses class analysis with moral critique. The characterization of the mechanisms underlying class relations in terms of exploitation and domination focuses attention on the moral implications of class analysis. Exploitation and domination identify ways in which these relations are oppressive and create harms, not simply inequalities. Class analysis can thus function as part not simply of a scientific theory of interests and conflicts but also of an emancipatory theory of alternatives and social justice. Even if socialism is off the historical agenda, the idea of countering the exploitative logic of capitalism is not.

REFERENCES

Frank Parkin, *Marxism and Class Theory: A Bourgeois Critique.* New York: Columbia University Press, 1979.

Gouldner, Alvin. 1970. *The Coming Crisis of Western Sociology.* New York: Avon Books.

Wright, Erik Olin, Andrew Levine and Elliot Sober. 1992. *Re-Constructing Marxism: Essays on Explanation and the Theory of History.* London: Verso.

Occupational Structure and Social Mobility

PETER M. BLAU AND OTIS DUDLEY DUNCAN WITH ANDREA TYREE

To say that the sons of the elite are superior in ability to the entire group of sons of other strata does not imply that they are superior to those sons of other strata who succeed in moving up into the elite. The population of nonelite sons constitutes a large pool of human resources that is sifted in the process of selection entailed in upward mobility, which makes it likely that the ones who do achieve elite status are more outstanding than the initially superior but unselected elite sons, just as the more selected large-family college graduates are more successful in pursuing higher degrees than the initially advantaged small-family college graduates. Moreover Sorokin himself notes that "a greater versatility and plasticity of human behavior is a natural result of social mobility,"[1] and he points out that this encourages intellectual endeavors and creativity. These qualities would give the upwardly mobile a further advantage over those who have inherited elite status. Given the existing family structure it is hardly conceivable that men in the elite would not attempt to assure that their sons remain in this top stratum, and their resources and power often enable them to do so. Differential fertility makes it possible, without any change in the institution of the family, for the elite to be invigorated by fresh blood and for sons from lower strata

to have opportunities to move into the elite. Unless we assume that the non-elite sons with the highest potential are inferior to the elite sons with the lowest qualifications, the process of selection inherent in upward mobility can be expected to have the result that the most successful men from lower strata bring not only new perspectives but also superior qualifications to the elite.

OCCUPATIONAL STRUCTURE AND HISTORICAL TRENDS

The movements of individuals from various origins to different occupational destinations, conditioned by the factors that influence chances of achievement, find expression in the occupational structure of the society. The occupational structure can be studied in its own right, and so can its development over time. Any structure consists of relations among parts, and two crucial questions are how the parts are distinguished and what the criterion for defining relation is. In our analysis of the occupational structure the parts are the ten major occupational groups or, more usually, a subdivision of them into 17 occupational strata, and the criterion of relation is the flow of manpower from occupational origins to occupational destinations.

As a starting point let us distinguish the 10 major occupational groups on the basis of their growth

[1]Pitirim A. Sorokin, *Social Mobility,* New York: Harper, 1927, pp. 509–515.

or decline since the beginning of this century and the patterns of mobility associated with this change in size. It should be noted that the aggregate trend in an occupation, which is most strongly influenced by differences between successive age cohorts, cannot be inferred from the patterns of intergenerational mobility, because the generation of fathers does not represent a distinctive age cohort but overlaps many (and similar considerations apply to first jobs with respect to intragenerational mobility). The expansion of an occupation may be associated with the intergenerational inflow of men into it, the intragenerational inflow of men into it, or both, and the contraction of an occupation may be associated with the intergenerational outflow of men from it, the intragenerational outflow of men from it, or both. This schema yields six types of occupational groups.

The first type is an occupation that has expanded in the last half-century as increasing numbers of sons have moved into it, despite the fact that intragenerational mobility exhibits a net outflow, that is, in the course of their lifetime careers more men moved out of than into this occupation. The prototype of such an occupation expanded by intergenerational inflow notwithstanding intragenerational outflow is clerical work, and two other cases are salesmen and operatives. The second kind is an occupation that has increased in size because disproportionate numbers of men from other pursuits moved into it in the course of their careers, although the number of sons starting this career line falls short of the number of fathers who pursued it. Many of the occupations in the three groups that manifest this type—managers, proprietors, and officials (combined into one group), craftsmen, and service workers—require some resources, experience, or apprenticeship. Third, one occupational group has grown rapidly as the result of both intergenerational and intragenerational mobility into it, namely, professional, technical, and kindred workers. Fourth, farming is an occupation that has declined since decreasing numbers of sons choose it as their career, despite the fact that there is a net inflow of men who had started to

work elsewhere—typically in farm labor—into it. The fifth type is an occupation that has declined as disproportionate numbers who started to work in it later left for other careers, although the number of men starting to work in this occupation exceeds the number of fathers in it. Labor and farm labor represent this type. A final possibility is an occupation whose decline is produced by both intergenerational and intragenerational outflow, but there is no empirical case representing this type. In sum only the two farm occupations and nonfarm labor have decreased in size during this century, whereas the seven other major groups have expanded by various processes and in varying degree.

Turning now to the patterns of mobility themselves, and using 17 occupational strata for this purpose, two basic features can be observed in every matrix, whether intergenerational or intragenerational mobility is considered, and whatever the specific measure employed. There is much upward mobility in the United States, but most of it involves relatively short social distances. Men are much more likely to experience upward than downward mobility, inasmuch as the rapidly expanding salaried professions with low fertility and the contracting farm occupations with high fertility create a vacuum in the form of occupational demand near the top and a pressure of manpower supply at the bottom that have repercussions throughout the occupational structure. An important reason why the growth of high-status professions and the decline of low-status farming have repercussions for the mobility of intermediate strata is that very few men originating in a bottom stratum themselves move all the way to the top, because most upward mobility involves short social distances of two or three steps in the hierarchy.

The socioeconomic rank of occupations, indicated by the education they require and the income they yield, influences mobility among them profoundly, as the preponderance of short-distance movements shows. The similarity between any pair of occupational origins in respect to their destinations, and between any pair of occupational destinations in respect to their origins, can be used as a measure of social distance that is entirely independent of the rank order based on education and income. The major underlying dimension of social distance defined by this similarity measure is the socioeconomic status of occupations, which confirms the assumption that socioeconomic differences are an important determinant of the patterns of mobility among occupations. A second dimension, which is only evident in the similarities of social origins with respect to destination, may refer to whether work is governed by universalistic principles or particularistic skills. Such differences in the organization of work seem to influence the orientation toward occupational life fathers transmit to their sons and hence the career lines sons are likely to follow.

Two class boundaries are manifest in the intergenerational as well as the intragenerational mobility matrix, which divide white-collar from blue-collar and blue-collar from farm occupations. These boundaries restrict downward mobility between virtually any two categories below the level expected on the assumption of independence, although they permit upward mobility in excess of this level. Occupations just below a class boundary, such as skilled crafts, have unexpectedly low recruitment from higher strata, because occupations just above a boundary, such as retail sales, provide opportunities for the unsuccessful from higher strata who are anxious to avoid losing white-collar respectability to find relatively unskilled jobs at low pay within the higher social class. The class boundaries also find expression in excessive social distances between occupations on either side, as shown by the dissimilarity measure discussed above. If the boundaries between the three major social classes restrict occupational mobility, we would also expect them to restrict various forms of social intercourse. As far as intermarriage is concerned, we have data to test this inference.

There is some homogamy by social origins, and it does reflect the class boundaries, as hypothesized. The prediction is that intermarriage exceeds expectations (on the assumption of independence)

if the occupations of husband's and wife's father are in the same broad occupational class (white-collar, blue-collar, or farm) but falls short of expectations if the occupations of the two fathers are in different classes. The data essentially confirm this prediction, the major exceptions being that children of craftsmen and of service workers marry children of some of the white-collar strata more frequently than expected. Assortative mating with respect to the education of the spouses themselves, however, is much more pronounced than assortative mating by their occupational origins. These findings suggest that similarities in education and other personal characteristics directly influence marriage, and that origin homogamy is an indirect product of these influences. Although origin homogamy is only reduced and does not entirely disappear when educational homogamy is controlled, this result is not incompatible with the conclusion that similarities in the spouses themselves, which may be related to their social background, are what directly affects selective mating. Because education and other personal characteristics are influenced by social origins, however, mate selection on the basis of these characteristics simultaneously assures some origin homogamy, and parents take this into account when they live in the right neighborhoods and send their children to proper schools in terms of their style of life.

The flow of manpower is not evenly distributed among occupations. Some occupational groups may be considered to be distributive of manpower, inasmuch as they recruit much manpower from different origins and supply disproportionate numbers of sons to different occupational destinations. Other occupations are relatively self-contained, and neither recruit nor supply very much manpower. The occupations located just above one of the two class boundaries—the lowest white-collar and the lowest blue-collar groups—have high rates of both inflow, especially from lower strata, and outflow, especially to higher strata, thus serving as channels for upward mobility. The three self-employed occupational groups—free professionals, proprietors, and farmers—are the most self-contained, implying that proprietorship discourages the inflow of men into as well as their outflow from an occupation. Since self-employment restricts mobility, its decline over time may well have contributed to the high rates of mobility today.

To study the degree of dispersion in the flow of manpower, two different measures were developed. The second was initially intended simply as a refined substitute for the first, but analysis revealed that the two refer to distinct aspects of dispersion that have different properties. The admittedly crude measure is indicative of the width of the recruitment base or of the supply section of an occupation, from how many different origins it recruits more than its share of men or to how many different destinations it supplies disproportionate numbers of men. The refined measure, on the other hand, signifies whether the men recruited into an occupation from the outside or supplied by it to different ones are concentrated in a few other occupations or randomly distributed over all of them.

The width of the recruitment base of an occupation is inversely related to the width of its supply sector in the intergenerational flow of men. Occupational groups that attract more than their proportionate share of men from many different origins send more than their proportionate share to only a few different destinations. This finding has been interpreted with the aid of another, namely, that recruitment from a wide base is directly related to the growth an occupational group has experienced in recent decades. For an occupation to expand in response to an increased demand for its services it must recruit more men than it has in the past. The assumption is that a growing demand can broaden recruitment and effect expansion only by raising income or improving other employment conditions. This increment in rewards does not, of course, obliterate the basic differences in rewards between occupations associated with variations in skill requirements and status. But the heightened incentives presumably attract some men from various backgrounds who otherwise would have gone into different career lines, enabling the occupation to recruit more than its share of manpower from many other origins. The superior economic conditions

that outsiders find attractive undoubtedly are also attractive to the occupational group's own sons and, therefore, discourage some of these sons who would otherwise have moved into a variety of other occupations from doing so. This interpretation, though it cannot be tested with our data, would explain the negative correlation between an occupation's recruitment base and its supply sector.

There is a positive correlation between the dispersion in recruitment and the dispersion in supply—that is, between the degree to which the origins of the men recruited into an occupation are dispersed rather than concentrated and the degree to which the destinations of the men supplied by it to others are dispersed rather than concentrated. Moreover intragenerational movements reveal the same direct association between dispersion in inflow and in outflow as intergenerational movements. All these manifestations of the degree of dispersion in the flow of manpower have similar nonmonotonic relations to the status rank order of occupations. The higher blue-collar strata, which constitute the intermediate ranks in the hierarchy, exhibit most dispersion of movement of all kinds. The white-collar strata nearer the top as well as the lower blue-collar and farm strata nearer the bottom have less dispersed patterns of occupational mobility, whatever aspect of mobility is considered. These differences reflect in part the prevalence of short-distance mobility, which restricts the range of likely origins or destinations for those occupational groups located near the top or near the bottom of the hierarchy. The higher degree of dispersion in the social mobility of the intermediate blue-collar workers, however, is also a sign of the poorer chances of upward mobility of these strata.

An important issue is whether the working class has poorer chances of upward mobility than the middle class. It is not easy to answer such a question, as indicated earlier, because even standardized measures of mobility are not free from the pervasive influence of ceiling effects, which makes any direct comparison of the mobility of occupations differently ranked of dubious value.

An indirect approach makes it possible, however, to give at least a partial answer to this question. The problem must be reformulated first. Taking advantage of the fact that we have information on father's, first, and 1962 occupation, we ask how men who *enter* careers on different levels compare with respect to the net *inter*generational mobility they experience from father's occupation to their own in 1962. Abstracting from the many compensating moves in opposite direction, the index of net mobility shows how the 1962 occupational distribution of the members of a group entering careers on a certain level differs from the occupational distribution of their fathers. Although information on the direction of mobility is not included in the index, inferences about it can be derived from the analysis.

The reformulated question is whether men who start their careers in manual work are less likely than others to achieve an occupational status that differs from that of their fathers. The answer the data give to this question is yes. Men who start their careers on high white-collar levels as well as those starting to work on farms experience more net mobility from social origins to 1962 occupational destinations than do men entering the labor force as blue-collar workers. The source of the high rates of net mobility of the white-collar and the farm strata is not the same, however, Men who start their working lives in higher white-collar jobs have already experienced much mobility from their social origins, most of which must have been upward mobility, given the elevated destinations. Men who first work on farms have as yet experienced little mobility but experience much subsequently in their careers, most of which also must be upward mobility, given the low positions of the origins. Men who begin their working lives in the working class, by contrast, seem to have a less fortunate fate and end up in occupational positions that differ little from those of their fathers.

Shifting attention to an examination of historical trends, the conservative conclusion is that we find no indication of increasing rigidity in the American occupational structure. Three methods have been used to estimate recent trends in mobility. First, the OCG data were compared with those from national surveys conducted 5, 10, and 15 years earlier, after making needed adjustments in one of these sets of data, though we do not claim that this fully removes the hazards of comparing surveys carried out by different investigators using different procedures. The findings reveal a small increase in occupational mobility, primarily owing to higher rates of upward mobility. Second, to make indirect inferences from the OCG data, supplemented by other sources, the transition matrix for each younger cohort was applied to the origin distribution of the cohort 10 years older, and the destination distribution so derived was compared with that observed. The results suggest that upward mobility has somewhat increased. Third, the correlations between the status of father's occupation and of first job were computed for four age cohorts, 25 to 34, 35 to 44, 45 to 54, and 55 to 64. These data show that the influence of social origins on career beginnings has not changed at all in the last 40 years. None of these comparisons reveals any decrease in social mobility, and two of them imply that there may have been a slight increase in it.

A few other trends deserve brief mention. There is some indication, though the evidence is by no means conclusive, that the influence of educational attainments on occupational achievements has increased in recent decades. Migration apparently has become more pervasive and more selective of men with high potential for success than was the case in the past, making occupational chances less dependent on the accident of a man's birth place. These trends signify an extension of universalistic principles in contemporary occupational life—as does another phenomenon.

Discrimination against Negroes seems to have subsided somewhat, enabling them to begin to narrow the gap between themselves and whites, though only on lower levels of attainment and not on higher ones. The OCG data indicate that the differences between Negroes and whites in average education and in first jobs have decreased, particularly in the North. But resort to census data on education for more refined analysis discloses a different picture. To be sure the gap between the two groups in the proportion who completed eight years of schooling has narrowed since the early part of this century, in both the North and the South. However the differences between Negroes and whites in the likelihood of graduating from high school and in the likelihood of graduating from college have widened, in the North as well as in the South, and so has the difference in income. It would be misleading to interpret these findings as the result of an intensification of discrimination, for which there is no evidence. Yet even if Negroes were not at all discriminated against today, and this surely is still far from the true state of affairs, they would not thereby be enabled to overcome the consequences of centuries of slavery and subjugation and in one big leap jump to the level of the whites. Equitable treatment in terms of universalistic standards is not sufficient for a seriously underprivileged and deprived group to catch up with the rest or, for that matter, to keep abreast of their progress. It requires a helping hand.

CAUSES OF SOCIAL MOBILITY IN CONTEMPORARY SOCIETY

"The land where the streets are paved with gold"— that is how Europeans traditionally have thought of America, meaning the United States. The allegory had some basis in fact. The expanding continent with its open frontier combined with the impact of the industrial revolution, which could be fully exploited in the absence of an aristocracy with a feudal heritage, to create unheard-of opportunities for economic advancement. After the closing of the frontier itself vast open spaces and a rapidly expanding industrial economy absorbed still larger numbers of immigrants and continued to supply much opportunity for social mobility.

The high rates of upward mobility in the United States have been attributed to these and other special historical circumstances, for example by Sibley: "Technological progress, immigration, and differential fertility contributed to a great excess of upward over downward circulation in American Society."[2] The substitution of manual work by machines resulting from technological developments greatly reduced the need for men to perform physical labor and made it possible for a larger proportion of the labor force to be engaged in white-collar work, thus fostering upward mobility. As millions of disadvantaged immigrants moved in disproportionate numbers into the lower ranks of the occupational hierarchy, they freed many sons of men in these lower strata to move up to higher occupational levels. The relatively low birth rates of the white-collar class, finally, opened up additional opportunities for upward mobility.

Two of these three historical conditions that gave a strong impetus to upward mobility in this country, however, no longer exist to the extent that they did in the early part of this century. The once huge stream of immigrants to the United States has declined to a mere rivulet. Differential fertility also has become less pronounced, as we have seen, with the birth rates of the higher white-collar strata now exceeding those of the lower ones. Although technological progress has continued, its further development has not always served to replace more men by machines but often to simplify tasks for the sake of efficiency, thereby lowering rather than raising the skill level of the labor force, as exemplified by assembly-line production, which substitutes semi-skilled operatives for skilled craftsmen. In brief upward mobility no longer benefits from large numbers of immigrants to this country; there is less class differential in fertility to promote it; and the influence of technological advances on it has become equivocal.

The rates of upward mobility in the United States today are still high, however, notwithstanding the changes in the historical circumstances that have been held responsible for the high mobility rates in the past. To be sure we have no way of knowing whether the opportunities for upward mobility in the last century were not much superior

---

[2]Elbridge Sibley, "Some Demographic Clues to Stratification," *American Sociological Review,* 7(1942), p. 322.

to those now, although the data do show that the chances of upward mobility have by no means declined in recent years. Be that as it may, the special historical conditions in the nineteenth century that ceased to exist early in the twentieth cannot explain the high rates of social mobility observable in the middle of the twentieth century. The interpretation to be advanced is that basic structural features of contemporary industrial society are the source of its high rates of occupational mobility, and that the three historical causes of mobility discussed were merely special cases of these generic structural causes, though these special historical conditions may have produced particularly high chances of mobility in nineteenth-century America.

Superior opportunities for occupational achievements attract migrants from other places in which conditions are not so favorable. The poorer environment in which the migrants were raised makes their qualifications inferior to those of the natives, enabling the natives to move to higher positions as the newcomers fill lower ones in the hierarchy. Whereas immigrants from Europe, who used to play this role, have ceased to arrive in large numbers in American metropolitan centers, in-migrants from rural areas have taken their place. Although chances are that the stream of migrants from farms to urban centers will dwindle in the future as the farm population becomes an increasingly smaller proportion of the total population, this would not alter the general principle, only its specific manifestation. Occupational opportunities will unquestionably continue to vary substantially in different places, and they will continue to change as new industries develop in some urban centers and technological advances make the industrial activities in another obsolete. These variations give men incentives to migrate from areas with lesser to areas with better opportunities, and the flow of migrants from disadvantaged environments acts as a catalyst for occupational mobility.

The class differential in fertility has been delining, and prospets are that it will decline further. Thus the inverse relationship between education and birth rate is less pronounced for younger women than for older ones, and it is less pronounced for those who do not have a farm background than for those who do, from which we can infer that this inverse association will further diminish as decreasing proportions of the population have a farm background. Nevertheless there is reason to believe, on theoretical grounds, that some differential fertility is an ingrained characteristic of industrialized and urbanized society and will persist. We have speculated above that an important determinant of lower differential fertility as well as lower fertility rates is the calculating orientation toward human relations typical of *Gesellschafts* structures. Whereas *Gemeinschaft* implies that men derive their major gratification from the intimate social bonds in which their whole existence is rooted, *Gesellschaft* involves a predominant orientation toward achievement and success without which men cannot find satisfaction. The ceaseless and unsatiable striving for success that sometimes results has often been satirized in modern fiction. These extremes only highlight the supreme value achievement assumes generally. Not everybody can be equally successful in the competitive struggle for superior status, however, regardless of the affluence of a society and the equality of opportunity in it.

Men who attain positions of superior prestige and power in the occupational hierarchy receive supportive and gratifying social acknowledgment of their prowess, but those who fail to attain superior status must find other sources of social support and gratification. The very importance of success makes failure to achieve it a threatening experience against which men seek to defend themselves lest it debilitate them, often by denying institutional values. Unsuccessful men may reject the political values of their society and organize an opposition against its government. Alternatively they may reject the prevailing *Gesellschafts* orientation and seek satisfaction and support from their families. Having many children not only expresses the rejection of a calculating approach in the most intimate sexual relation but also supplies a man with a group whose ascribed status as children requires them to submit to his authority. Whereas successful achievers have their status as adult men supported by their superior occupational roles and authority, the unsuccessful find a substitute in the authority they exercise in their role as fathers over a number of children. The significance parental authority has for lower strata is manifest in the tendency of these strata to treat their children in more authoritarian fashion than do higher strata, as students of child rearing have found.[3] If these speculations have any validity, it follows that differential achievement in societies strongly oriented toward achievement will continue to be mirrored in differential fertility.[4]

Technological advances have sometimes led to serious economic depressions, which worsened chances of upward mobility and seriously disrupted careers in general, and they have sometimes effected routinization of formerly skilled tasks, which can only have an adverse effect on mobility. In the long run, however, technological progress has undoubtedly improved chances of upward mobility and will do so in the future. Technical improvements in production and farming have made possible the tremendous expansion of the labor force in tertiary industries—those other than agriculture or manufacturing—and, particularly, in professional and semiprofessional services since the turn of the century. For example, the number of professional, technical, and kindred workers was less than one-tenth the number working on farms in 1900; today the first group outnumbers the second nearly two to one. This great expansion of the occupational group at the top of the hierarchy,[5] in combination with the simultaneous contraction of the bottom strata, has been a major generator of upward mobility. The elimination

of routine jobs by automation, though it may well immediately set back the careers of some men, should ultimately open up additional avenues of upward mobility. The general principle is that as long as some jobs are more routine and less rewarding than others—and the time is hardly foreseeable when this will not be the case—incentives exist to apply scientific and engineering talents to the task of developing mechanical procedures for doing them or finding some other substitute for human labor. The recurrent elimination of the least-skilled occupations is a continual source of upward mobility in advanced industrial societies.

The basic assumption underlying these conjectures is that a fundamental trend toward expanding universalism characterizes industrial society. Objective criteria of evaluation that are universally accepted increasingly pervade all spheres of life and displace particularistic standards of diverse ingroups, intuitive judgments, and humanistic values not susceptible to empirical verification.[6] The growing emphasis on rationality and efficiency inherent in this spread of universalism finds expression in rapid technological progress and increasing division of labor and differentiation generally, as standards of efficiency are applied to the performance of tasks and the allocation of manpower for them.[7] The strong interdependence among men and groups engendered by the extensive division of labor becomes the source of their organic solidarity, to use Durkheim's term, inasmuch as social differentiation weakens the particularistic ingroup values that unite men in common bonds of mechanical solidarity.[8] The attenuation of particularistic ties of ingroup

---

[3]See, for example, Robert R. Sears, Eleanor E. Maccoby and Harry Levin, *Patterns of Child Rearing,* Evanston: Row, Peterson, 1957, pp. 426–447.

[4]We had expected, in accordance with these notions, that downward mobility raises fertility, but the data disconfirm this prediction, which weakens the interpretation suggested.

[5]When the professional group is divided into the self-employed and the salaried, the latter are seen to account for the great expansion of this occupational group, whereas self-employed professionals have expanded very little.

[6]The last point is particularly stressed in Pitirim A. Sorokin, *Social and Cultural Dynamics,* 4 volumes, New York: American Book, 1937–41, *passim.*

[7]Talcott Parsons' theory of social change, modifying Weber's principle of progressive rationalization, focuses on progressive differentiation; *The Social System,* Glencoe: Free Press, 1951, pp. 480–535. For the concepts of universalism and particularism, see *ibid.,* pp. 58–67, 101–112.

[8]Emile Durkheim, *On the Division of Labor in Society,* New York: Macmillan, 1933.

solidarity, in turn, frees men to apply universalistic considerations of efficiency and achievement to ever-widening areas of their lives.

Heightened universalism has profound implications for the stratification system. The achieved status of a man, what he has accomplished in terms of some objective criteria, becomes more important than his ascribed status, who he is in the sense of what family he comes from. This does not mean that family background no longer influences careers. What it does imply is that superior status cannot any more be directly inherited but must be legitimated by actual achievements that are socially acknowledged. Education assumes increasing significance for social status in general and for the transmission of social standing from fathers to sons in particular. Superior family origins increase a son's chances of attaining superior occupational status in the United States in large part because they help him to obtain a better education, whereas in less industrialized societies the influence of family origin on status does not seem to be primarily mediated by education.[9] Universalism also discourages discrimination against ethnic minorities, though it does not furnish incentives for giving them the assistance they may need to overcome the handicaps produced by long periods of deprivation and suppression. At the same time, universalism fosters a concern with materialistic values at the expense of spiritual ones; an interest in achievement and efficiency rather than religious devotion, philosophical contemplation, or artistic creation; a preoccupation with the outward signs of success and little patience for probing the deeper meanings of life. The crass materialism and invidious striving for status in today's world that have often been deplored are an integral part of the universalistic system that has also helped produce many things we cherish,

including technological progress, a high standard of living, and greater equality of opportunity.

The three structural causes of upward mobility in industrialized society discussed above have their roots in the predominance of universalism. A pervasive concern with efficiency is an essential incentive for devoting much energy to accelerating technological progress, and such progress helps raise standards of living and promote upward mobility from obsolete lower occupational positions to expanding higher ones. The weakening of particularistic ties to kin and neighbor that would keep a man in the community where he was raised encourages migration to places with better opportunities for achievement, and this migration stimulates occupational mobility. The counterforces set in motion by the dominant significance of occupational achievement among those who cannot achieve superior status in their careers may constrain them to have larger families from whom they can obtain, in their role as fathers, the status support and gratification denied them in their occupational roles. The resulting differential fertility gives another impetus to upward mobility. According to these speculations—and this is all they are, of course—the structural conditions in our industrialized society governed by universalistic principles, and not merely the special historical circumstances in which they find expression at one time or another, are the causes of its high rate of occupational mobility.

The great potential of society's human resources can be more fully exploited in a fluid class structure with a high degree of mobility than in a rigid social system. Class lines that restrict mobility and prevent men born into the lower strata from even discovering what their capacities might be constitute a far more serious waste of human talent than the often deplored lower birth rates of the higher strata. In previous periods the knowledge and skills society was able to utilize were severely limited, which made this waste of talent regrettable from the standpoint of individuals but unavoidable from the perspective of the social order. Indeed Simmel has suggested that the major reason for the inevitable discrepancy between

---

[9]Even in Sweden, where the levels of industrialization and education are high but not so high as in the United States, "differential access to educational facilities as such does not go very far in explaining . . . the correlation between parental and filial status." Gösta Carlsson, *Social Mobility and Class Structure,* Lund: Gleerup, 1958, p. 135.

personal qualifications and social positions "is that there are always more people qualified for superordinate positions than there are such positions."[10] This is much less true in today's highly industrialized society than it was in earlier times, for technological progress has created a need for advanced knowledge and skills on the part of a large proportion of the labor force, not merely a small professional elite. Under these conditions society cannot any longer afford the waste of human resources a rigid class structure entails. Universalistic principles have penetrated deep into the fabric of modern society and given rise to high rates of occupational mobility in response to this need. The improvements in opportunities for social mobility resulting from the wider application of universalistic standards permit greater utilization of society's human potential, and they have important implications for the stability of democracy.

---

[10]Georg Simmel, *The Sociology of Georg Simmel,* Glencoe: Free Press, 1950, p. 300.

The Contemporary American Class Structure

ROBERT PERRUCCI AND EARL WYSONG

GENERATIVE CAPITAL AND CLASS STRUCTURE

Our image of a double-diamond class structure is based on the way that vital life-sustaining resources are distributed and the availability of these resources over time. In some societies the most important resource is land, because it allows one to grow food to eat and to exchange the surplus food for housing, health care, and seeds to grow more food. Peasant farmers in Central America are permanently impoverished because most land is held in large estates. These estates produce coffee or cotton for export; that is, they produce for foreign exchange or money. Peasants, without land, face the choice of starvation, working for the owner of a large landholding, or moving to the city in search of work.

In American society today, capital is the main resource used in exchange for what we need and want, and it is found in four forms: consumption capital, investment capital, skill capital, and social capital. We call these resources *generative capital* because they can produce more of the same resource when invested, or they can contribute to the production of another resource (e.g., social capital can produce investment capital).

Source: Robert Perrucci and Earl Wysong. *The New Class Society: Goodbye American Dream?* 2nd ed, Rowman and Littlefield Publishers, Inc. 2003; 10–30. Used with permission of Rowman and Littlefield Publishers, Inc.

Consumption Capital

Consumption capital is usually thought of as income—what we get in our wages and salary, unemployment check, social security, or welfare check. The lucky people have enough of it to buy food and clothing, pay the rent or mortgage, and make payments on the furniture or car. The really lucky people have a little money left over. But for most people, there is plenty of month left over when the money runs out.

When thinking about how much consumption capital families have and how they spend it, we immediately recognize that food can mean lobster or macaroni and cheese; clothing can mean second-hand from the thrift shop or name brands and fashionable labels. People vary in their weekly or monthly consumption capital, and two families with the same monthly income may choose to spend it in very different ways.

Consumption capital is closely linked to position in the system of production, or occupation. Some jobs pay a lot more than others, but there is also large variation in the incomes of people with the same occupation. Salaries of lawyers, professors, or engineers may vary from upper six figures at the high end to incomes barely above the national average for wage and salaried workers (e.g., $31,000 in 1998). Thus, position in the system of production is important, but it does not tell us the full story when considering the question of income. Attempts to map the class structure by using only occupational categories or occupational prestige rankings will invariably combine persons who are getting vastly different returns on their educational assets. The salaries of lawyers, professors, or engineers will be due partly to their occupation and partly to the particular organizations in which they do their work (in addition to other resources discussed later).

Investment Capital

Investment capital is what people use to create more capital. If you have a surplus of consumption capital (the money left over when the month runs out), you can save it and earn interest each month. You can buy a house, or you can invest in stocks or bonds and earn dividends and capital gains. You can buy an old house, a "fixer-upper," renovate it, divide it into apartments, and collect rent. If your annual rent receipts exceed the combined cost of mortgage payments, property taxes, insurance, and maintenance costs, you will earn a profit.

If you have a great deal of investment capital, you can live off returns on investments in stocks or investments in a business. If you own a business, it probably means that you will employ others and will have to decide how much to pay workers and whether or not to provide them with health insurance or retirement plans. The less you need to pay them, the more you will have for yourself.

The varied ways in which investment capital is used produce wealth, which provides power and independence and is a major source of well-being for families. Wealth is determined by the total current value of financial assets (bank accounts, stocks, bonds, life insurance, pensions) plus durable assets such as houses or cars, minus all liabilities such as mortgages and consumer debt. Thus, we can describe a family's wealth in terms of *total net worth* (financial assets, plus durable assets, minus liabilities) or *total financial wealth* (only financial assets). The distinction is important, because financial assets can generate income (interest, dividends) but durable assets like homes or cars are "lived in" or for "driving around."

The level of wealth inequality in the United States is much greater than the level of income inequality. Much less is known about wealth than about income distribution in the United States, but wealth is probably a more significant indicator of inequality because of its role in transmitting privilege across generations. Wealth provides security, well-being, independence, and power to a privileged minority in American society, who can use that wealth to advance their privileged-class interests. The members of this privileged class have accumulated wealth while in positions that are at the intersection of an occupation and an organizational position. Consider the case of a new Ph.D. in business from the University of Chicago who received a starting salary of at least $100,000 at Columbia University, while another Ph.D. recipient from an obscure business school may receive $50,000 for a starting salary at a less prestigious university. This same new Ph.D. from the University of Chicago received comparable offers from Harvard, Duke, and the University of North Carolina. This is clearly a case of elite universities preparing their graduates for positions in elite universities, and paying salaries that serve to enhance the salaries of everyone else at those elite universities.

Those with significant wealth are likely to be the corporate elite, top managers, doctors and corporate lawyers, members of Congress, White House staff, cabinet officials, professors at elite universities, media elite, "talking heads" on television, and assorted cultural elites. They are Democrats and Republicans, conservatives and liberals, Christians and Jews, pro-choice and antiabortion, radical feminists and Promise Keepers. They have a common commitment to keeping 80 percent of the population "bamboozled" while pretending to represent their interests. They have a common bond, which is high income, job security, and wealth, and they will rig the rules of the game in order to preserve and extend their privilege.

Skill Capital

Skill capital is the specialized knowledge that people accumulate through their work experience, training, or education. Skilled plumbers learn their craft through apprenticeship programs and years of on-the-job experience. Skilled doctors learn their craft primarily in medical schools, but their skills are developed further through work experience.

Skill capital is exchanged in a labor market, just as investment capital is used in connection with a financial market. Both plumbers and doctors try to get the highest return for their skill in the form of wages or fees, and they do this through collective associations like labor unions (United Auto Workers) or medical societies (American Medical Association). When skill capital is organized in the form of collective associations, there is greater likelihood of job security or high wages. Workers with unorganized skills (i.e., nonunion) or with low levels of skill are more vulnerable when dealing with employers or clients.

The most important source of skill capital in today's society is located in the elite universities that provide the credentials for the privileged class. For example, the path into corporate law with six-figure salaries and million-dollar partnerships is provided by about two dozen elite law schools where the children of the privileged class enroll. Similar patterns exist for medical school graduates, research scientists, and those holding professional degrees in management and business. After the credentialed skill is provided by elite universities, the market value of that skill (and its income- and wealth-producing capability) is protected by powerful corporations and professional associations. People in high income- and wealth-producing professions will seek to protect their market value not only for themselves but also for their children who will enter similar fields.

Social Capital

Social capital is the network of social ties that people have to family, friends, and acquaintances. These ties can provide emotional support, financial assistance, and information about jobs. Social capital is used by immigrants in deciding which communities they will settle in when they come to the United States. These same immigrants use social capital to get settled and to find jobs. Social ties are also used by doctors, lawyers, and other professionals to facilitate their affiliations with more or less prestigious organizations where they will begin to "practice" their work.

The basis of social ties can be found in school ties and in kinship, religious, and political affiliations. For example, graduates of elite universities often become the new recruits at national law firms, major corporations, foundations, and government agencies. A study by the Office of Management and Budget reports that 40 percent of foreign service professionals in the State Department come from eight Ivy League colleges. Another example is found in a story in the *New York Times* (November 10, 1995) about some of the appointments made of new lawyers to join the staff of New York State's new attorney general. One new employee is the daughter of the best friend of the state's U.S. senator; she is paid $75,000 a year. Another employee just admitted to the bar is the daughter of another lawyer who served on the attorney general's election committee; she is paid $60,000 a year.

But social capital is used for more than just getting high-paid secure jobs. It is also used to solidify class interests by making sure that people marry within their corporate or professional class. For example, consider the type of "personal ad" that appears in many upscale magazines for the young urban professional:

> Join the Ivy League of Dating. Graduates and faculty of the Ivies, Seven Sisters, Johns Hopkins, M.I.T., Stanford, U. of Chicago, CAL Tech, Duke, U.C. Berkeley, Northwestern, meet alumni and academics. The Right Stuff! Call XXX–XXX–XXXX.

One has to wonder what the "right stuff" is. These ads may appeal to people who are simply trying to meet someone on their intellectual level; but they could instead join MENSA, an association of people with high IQ. More likely it is an effort to match same-class individuals with credentialed skills. This is the way to get dual-earner-household doctors, attorneys, and corporate elites or the "mixed marriages" of doctors and fashion designers or artists who become the "darlings" of *People* magazine fare.

Although everyone has at least a minimal level of social capital, it should be clear that access to different forms of social capital (like consumption, investment, and skill capital) is distributed very unequally. Having a family member able to loan you $100 or a friend who works in a retail store and can tell you about a job opening is not the same as being a member of a fraternity or sorority at an elite university. Social capital refers to current memberships people hold in social networks that are linked to varying levels of organizational power, prestige, and opportunities. Individuals can be connected by strong ties (e.g., family members) or weak ties (e.g., acquaintances) to formal and informal social networks that are associated with varying levels of organizational resources and power. A person's position in these social networks provides access to information and opportunities that can be converted into important financial and social benefits. For example, the extent of investment capital owned or controlled can be the result of holding high positions in large organizations; paid and unpaid leadership positions in economic, political, or cultural organizations can be used to advance personal careers or provide opportunities for relatives and friends. Thus, social capital must be viewed as a class-linked resource that both protects and advances privilege and provides a barrier for those "upstarts" seeking to expand their generative capital.

GENERATIVE CAPITAL AND POWER

The residents of one zip code—10021—on New York City's Upper West Side contributed more money to Congress during the 1994 elections than did all the residents of 24 states.

—Ellen Miller and Randy Kehler,
Dollars and Sense, July–August 1996

The distribution of these scarce and valued resources—consumption capital, investment capital, skill capital, and social capital—is the basis for class inequality among individuals and families in America. This inequality is revealed when resources are converted into economic power, political power, and social power. Economic power is based on the resource of money (consumption capital and investment capital), and it usually is used to provide food, shelter, and clothing. People who have more economic power can buy more things and better things and thereby make their lives more comfortable and enjoyable. Money can be converted into other valued things like health care, which enables those with more money to live longer and healthier lives. Money can protect people when unfortunate or unforeseen events occur, like an earthquake, tornado, or flood. Recovering from these natural disasters and from human disasters like unemployment or illness is possible when you have economic power. Money also has the special quality of being transferable to others and can also be used to transmit advantage.

Consumption capital can be used to procure social capital. For example, families with money can use it to help secure the futures of their children by purchasing special experiences through travel, tennis lessons, scuba diving, dance, and creative arts in the hope that such experiences will foster or strengthen social relationships with others having similar experiences. It is also done by buying entry into prestigious educational institutions that provide their students with lifelong advantages. Families who buy elite educational degrees for their children are using their consumption capital to develop both social capital and skill capital. Graduates of elite universities have a special advantage in converting their credentialed skill capital into better jobs. They establish the social contacts that can be used later in life to solidify or enhance their social position. Many families, recognizing the payoff that comes with a degree from an elite college, prepare their children with SAT prep courses in the eighth grade and private school education. In 2000–01, Harvard University received 19,009 applications for 1,650 places in the entering class. Those lucky enough to be selected can expect annual costs of $35,400 per year for tuition, fees, room and board, and personal expenses. Clearly, these families are using their consumption capital to invest in the education of their children.

Three out of four families in the United States have very little economic power. Even so-called middle-class families on the "brink of comfort" times described; see *New York Times* story by Charisse Jones, February 18, 1995) find themselves in a constant struggle to make ends meet. There are thousands of anecdotal stories about how people struggle to meet family expenses, but the most systematic evidence is provided by the U.S. Department of Labor in its preparation of a consumption budget for an average married couple with two children.

Monthly Budget for Family of Four (1998 dollars)

Housing	$793	27.3%
Utilities	247	8.5
Furnishings	109	3.7
House operations	73	2.5
Food	555	19.1
Auto	558	19.2
Clothing	137	4.7
Health care	165	5.6
Entertainment	207	7.1
Other	64	2.2

This monthly budget totals $2,908, or $34,896 annually. In order to have this much money to spend each month, the household's gross annual income (before taxes) would have to be about $40,000. Moreover, this budget assumes one wage earner, because a number of monthly expenditures would increase with two wage earners. Less than one-half of American families earn enough money to live by the U.S. Department of Labor budget, and when they do, they are often two-earner families. Two people working full-time, each earning about $10 per hour, will have a combined annual gross income of about $41,000. If two people with children are working to make this income, then you will have to add childcare to the consumption budget, which can be from $100 to $300 a week. This middle-class budget for a family on the "brink of comfort" will produce nothing for savings, and

little for retirement beyond social security taxes. If one or both of the wage earners in this family should experience unemployment for a month or longer, the family would be in serious difficulty.

If the hypothetical family just described is on the brink of comfort, what must things be like in a female-headed household with one or two children where the mother brings home about $1,000 a month from a $7.00-an-hour job as a retail clerk? This family is sitting on the official poverty line, or maybe one paycheck above or below it. Clearly, a household budget for three or four persons of $1,000 a month generates no economic power.

The problem facing three of every four families in the United States is not simply that they are just making ends meet—whether on $30,000 a year or $12,000 a year—but that their consumption capital is limited, unstable, and unpredictable. They cannot count on these resources over time in any predictable way, and if they should experience any period of joblessness they will face a serious crisis. Possession of stable and secure resources over time is the key to economic power. The predictability of resources allows people to plan and save in order to provide for the future. They can think about buying a home, sending a child to college, saving for retirement, or starting a business. Most American workers have very unstable incomes, even if they are sometimes earning what seems like a "high" salary. For example, take the case of the United Auto Worker employed in a General Motors assembly plant. During periods of peak production and heavy overtime, a worker might earn $5,000 per month. This is a $60,000-a-year job, assuming that the monthly salary continues all year. But that's the rub. When overtime disappears and production schedules are cut back because of overproduction, that $60,000 may be quickly cut to $40,000; or layoffs might reduce that income even more; at worst, the plant may be shut down and production moved to a lower-wage area in the United States or some other country—which is exactly what happened to hundreds of thousands of high-wage blue-collar workers in the 1970s, 1980s, and 1990s.

Political power is the result of collective actions to shape or determine decisions that limit or enhance peoples' opportunities. The tenants of a housing project can combine their time to collect signatures on a petition calling on the housing director to provide better services. Corporations in a particular sector of the economy can combine their money (economic power) to hire lobbyists who will seek to influence members of Congress to support or oppose legislation that will affect those corporations. Individuals and organizations with more economic power have a different set of opportunities for exercising political power than groups without economic power.

The clearest examples of how collective economic power can be converted into political power are in the area of corporate welfare—the practice of congressional action that provides billions of dollars in federal loans and subsidies to specific industries. More than $100 million a year goes to corporations like McDonald's, Pillsbury, and Sunkist to help them advertise their products in foreign countries. The Pentagon provides another $100 million a year to a group of semiconductor firms to help them compete internationally. This money goes not to small, struggling firms but to giants like Intel and National Semiconductor Corporation. The total annual corporate welfare bill just from business tax preferences from the federal government was estimated at $195 billion in fiscal 2000.

Groups with little economic power usually try to exercise political power through mass mobilization of persons with grievances. Bringing together hundreds or thousands of persons for a march on city hall conveys a visible sense of a perceived problem and an implied threat of disruption. The capacity to disrupt may be the only organized weapon available to those without economic resources. Such actions usually get the attention of political leaders, although it does not always produce the results desired by aggrieved groups.

Social power involves access to public services and the interpersonal networks that can be used to solve many of the day-to-day problems that confront most families. Public services like police, fire protection, and public transportation can provide people with the security to use public space for living, leisure, and getting to and from work, stores, and day-care facilities. Interpersonal networks consist of the informal groups and formal associations that are available in a community for persons with certain interests and concerns. The availability of community groups concerned about the presence of toxic waste dumps, the spread of crime, and the quality of the schools in their community provides opportunities for people to learn about many things in addition to toxic waste, police protection, and education. Such groups often provide links to information about jobs, or how to approach a local banker for a loan, or how to obtain information about financial aid for college students.

Opportunities to develop social power vary widely across groups. People who have jobs that provide little flexibility in their work schedules or are physically demanding may have little time or inclination for participating in community groups at the end of a hard day. Similarly, some jobs offer more opportunities than others to develop the interpersonal networks that can be drawn upon to help a family member find a job or to help in finding good and affordable legal assistance.

There is considerable evidence from social research that Americans with greater economic resources, and those holding upper managerial positions in organizations, are more likely to actively participate in a variety of community affairs. These active participants accumulate information about community affairs and social contacts that can be used to advance or solidify the interests of one's social group. Some of the key players in this process of accumulating social power have been identified as women from professional families who are out of the labor force and have the discretionary time for civic affairs.

An interesting example of how social power operates among the privileged classes is provided by the case of the Morrison Knudsen Corporation. It happened that the chairman's spouse started a private charity organization to provide young women with alternatives to abortion. The spouse served as unpaid executive director of the charity and was apparently successful in obtaining donors to support its activities. The success of the charity could perhaps be traced to the fact that five of the charity's directors are the spouses of directors of Morrison Knudsen, and three of the directors of the charity are senior executives of the corporation. Thus, the spouse of the board chairman of Morrison Knudsen was able to use her social power to put together a charity organization capable of drawing upon the political and economic power of directors from the privileged elite. Such opportunities would certainly not be available to a community organization trying to oppose the location of toxic waste sites in their area or one trying to get the local police to be more responsive to the concerns of local citizens.

CLASS STRUCTURE AND CLASS SEGMENTS

The combination of capital and power can be used to describe the class structure of American society. One popular way of describing the class structure of a society is with a physical or geometric shape or image. The shape or image conveys the relative proportions of people in a society who have some valued thing, like money or education. The pyramid (Figure 1), for example, illustrates a class structure in which a small percentage of a society (10 percent) has a great deal of the commodity, another 30 percent has a little less, and the majority (60 percent) has the least amount of the valued commodity.

Another frequently used image is the diamond (Figure 2), which provides a different picture of the way valued things are distributed. The diamond image says that a small percentage (10 percent) of a society has a lot of something, another small percentage (10 percent) has very little of something, and most of the people (80 percent) are in the middle, with moderate amounts of the valued commodity.

In each of these class structures, the class positions of people can be simply designated as upper class, middle class, or lower class. Thus, the pyramid image represents a society in which most persons are lower class, and the diamond image represents a middle-class society. If asked to choose between the two societies depicted here, most people would probably choose the society represented by the diamond image, because most of the people are in the middle class. If you chose to live in the pyramid society, you would have a 60 percent chance of being in the lower class.

However, before choosing one of these societies in which to live, you might want a little more information. You might want to know about the particular attribute or characteristic that puts people in each class. Is it something they are born with, like skin color or physical size, or is it some characteristic they learn or acquire, like being a good hunter or a skilled craft worker? You might also want to

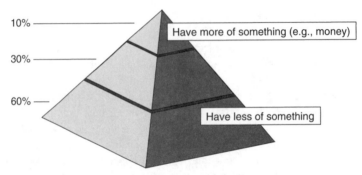

FIGURE 1   Pyramid Diagram of Class Structure and Class Segments.

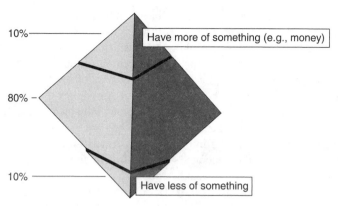

FIGURE 2   Diamond Diagram of Class Structure and Class Segments.

know something about how people in each class live, in terms of basic necessities, material comforts, physical security, and freedom. Finally, it might be important to know if it is possible for people to change their class position within a lifetime or across generations, or if there are opportunities for their children to rise above the class into which they were born.

Thus, the image of a society as pyramidal or diamond-shaped provides an overall view of how people in that society are distributed on some valued characteristic or attribute. But it does not tell about the society's "rules" for determining or changing their class position.

Let us try to make all this a little more concrete by examining American society. Most efforts to portray the American class structure have focused on occupations as the main determinant of the class structure and of people's positions in that structure. Occupations have been classified according to the public's opinion of the social standing or prestige associated with being a public school teacher, or a dentist, or a mechanic, or a machine operator. When large numbers of Americans are asked to rate occupations on a scale ranging from "excellent" to "poor" in social standing, they consistently place U.S. Supreme Court Justice, physician, and corporate manager at the top of the list; at the bottom are garbage collector, filling station attendant, and janitor. The prestige hierarchy of

occupations has remained pretty stable in studies done over several decades and in different countries. This has led some analysts to see occupational prestige as the basis of class structure in American society. They also assert that the term *class* is not meaningful because prestige is determined according to a continuous system of rankings of occupations, without any sharp boundaries or divisions between occupations.

However, if you look behind these prestige rankings to ask what it is that people are actually ranking, you will find that what is being evaluated is not simply the prestige of an occupation but also its income and power. In our society, the occupational structure as embedded in organizations is the key to understanding the class structure, and a person's occupation is one aspect of class position. But how do the hundreds of different occupations combine to create a structure of distinct classes with different amounts of economic, political, and social power? What aspects of occupations determine their position in the class structure?

People often speak of their occupation or their job as what they do for a living. An occupation or job describes how a person is related to the economy in a society or what one does in the process of the production of goods and services. An occupation or job provides people with the means to sustain life ("to make a living"); and the sum total of the work done by people in their occupations or jobs is the wealth generated by the economic system. In one sense there is a parallel or symmetric relation between the availability of jobs and the amount of wealth that is generated. The more people in a society are working at making a living, the better the economic health of the total society. But there is also a sense in which there is an asymmetric relationship between the well-being of working people ("how much of a living they make") and the total wealth that is generated. Some people contribute more to the total wealth than they receive for their work, as in the case of some workers whose wages are a fraction of the value of their products when they are sold. And some people may receive ten or twenty times more in income for their work than that received by others. So although there may be 130 million Americans involved in occupations and jobs for which they are compensated, their amount of compensation varies widely according to how they are related to the production process. There are a variety of ways in which people are related to the production process in today's economy.

The Privileged Class

The activity of some people in the system of production is focused on their role as owners of investment capital. Such a person may be referred to colloquially as the "boss" or, in more respectful circles, as a "captain of industry," an "entrepreneur," or a "creator of wealth," but in the language of class analysis they are all owner-employers. The owner may actually be the sole proprietor of the XYZ Corporation and be involved in the day-to-day decisions of running that corporation. But ownership may also consist in the possession of a large number of shares of stock in one or several corporations in which many other persons may also own stock. However, the ownership of stock is socially and economically meaningful only when (1) the value of shares owned is sufficient to constitute "making a living," or (2) the percentage of shares of stock owned relative to all shares is large enough to permit the owner of said shares to

have some say in how the company is run. Members of this group (along with the managers and professionals) control most of the wealth in America. The point of this discussion is to distinguish owners of investment capital from the millions of Americans who own shares of stock in companies, who own mutual funds, or whose pension funds are invested in the stock market. The typical American stock owner does not make a living from that ownership and has nothing to say about the activities of the companies they "own."

On the lower rungs of the owner-employer group are the proprietors of small but growing high-tech firms that bring together venture capital and specialized knowledge in areas involving biomedical products or services and computer software forms. These are "small" businesses only in Department of Commerce classifications (less than $500,000 in sales), for they bear no resemblance to the Korean grocer, the Mexican restaurant owner, or the African American hair salon found in many American cities. They are more typically spin-off firms created by technical specialists who have accumulated some capital from years of employment in an industrial lab or a university and have obtained other investment capital from friends, family, or private investors.

A second activity in the system of production is that of manager, the person who makes the day-to-day decisions involved in running a corporation, a firm, a division of a corporation, or a section within a company. Increasingly, managers have educational credentials and degrees in business, management, economics, or finance. Managers make decisions about how to use the millions of dollars of investment capital made available to them by the owners of investment capital.

The upper levels of the managerial group include the top management of the largest manufacturing, financial, and commercial firms in the United States. These managers receive substantial salaries and bonuses, along with additional opportunities to accumulate wealth. Table 1 presents a typical pattern of "modest" compensation for the officers of a large firm in 2000. We refer

TABLE 1 Compensation for Corporate Executives (2000)

Position	Annual Compensation	Bonus	Stock Awards
President and CEO	$745,385	$450,000	$2,028,125
Executive vice pres.	299,897	119,000	745,000
Executive vice pres.	273,846	120,000	558,750
Senior vice pres. and General Counsel	242,885	34,000	447,000
Senior vice pres. and CFO	275,192	128,000	558,750
Vice president	342,029	174,760	—
Executive vice pres.	322,400	5,000	—

Source: Based on data from the Annual Report and Proxy Statements, Great Lakes Chemical Corporation, 2001, Indianapolis, Ind.

to this compensation as "modest" because it is far below the multimillion-dollar packages of compensation for CEOs at IBM, AT&T, Disney or Coca-Cola (which range from $20 million to $50 million). But such distinctions are probably pointless, because we are describing executives whose wealth is enormous in comparison with others not in their class. For example, the top CEO in the group just listed also owns 100,000 shares of stock and has options for another 100,000 shares in the corporation he heads. The value of these shares fluctuates with the market value of the stock, which in the summer of 2001 was $31 a share, or about $3 million for the 100,000 shares.

The lower levels of the managerial group carry out the important function of supervising the work done by millions of workers who produce goods and services in the economy. The success of this group, and their level of rewards, is determined by their ability to get workers to be more productive, which means to produce more at a lower cost.

Professionals carry out a third activity in the economic system. This group's power is based on the possession of credentialed knowledge or skill, such as an engineering degree, a teaching degree, or a degree in public relations. Some may work as "independent professionals," providing service for a fee, such as declining numbers of doctors, dentists, and lawyers. But most professionals work for corporations, providing their specialized knowledge to enhance the profit-making potential of their firm or of firms that buy their services. The professional group is made up of university graduates with degrees in the professional schools of

medicine, law, business, and engineering and in a variety of newly emerging fields (e.g., computer sciences) that serve the corporate sector. The possession of credentialed knowledge unifies an otherwise diverse group, which includes doctors who may earn $500,000 a year and computer specialists who earn $60,000 a year.

The potential to accumulate wealth is very great among certain segments of professionals. The mean net salary in 2001 for all physicians surveyed in one report was $196,000. There were great differences between the incomes of family practice physicians, who averaged $145,496 in 2001, and specialty physicians such as radiologists and oncologists, who averaged $255,223. Unfortunately, these averages hide the salaries of graduates from elite medical schools and those affiliated with the most prestigious hospitals. Also absent is information about doctor's entrepreneurial activities such as ownership of nursing homes or pharmaceutical firms.

Similar opportunities for high income exist among lawyers, where partners at the nation's elite law firms average $335,000 and associates average $80,000 (1998). Even law professors at prestigious law schools have a chance to amass a small fortune while teaching and practicing law or consulting. A recent *New York Times* story reported that a professor at Harvard Law School gave the school a bequest of $5 million. The *Times* reported that the professor is "not one of the school's prominent moonlighters" and is "unlike Prof. Alan M. Dershowitz, the courtroom deity who has defended Leona Helmsley and Mike Tyson and is on the

O. J. Simpson defense team." So how did the professor do it? By "writing and consulting."

Professors at elite universities who are in selected fields like law, medicine, business, biomedical engineering, or electrical engineering have opportunities to start high-tech firms and to consult for industry in ways that can significantly enhance income. Even "modest" activities, like becoming an outside director for a bank or industrial firm, can be very rewarding. A colleague in a business school at a Big Ten university who is a professor of management has been on the board of directors of a chemical corporation for twenty years. His annual retainer is $26,000. He gets an additional $1,000 a day for attending meetings of the board or committee meetings and $500 a day for participating in telephone conference meetings (the board meets six times a year, and committees convene from one to six times a year). Each nonemployee director gets a $50,000 term life insurance policy and a $200,000 accidental death and dismemberment insurance policy. After serving on the board for a minimum of five years, directors are eligible for retirement benefits equal to the amount of the annual retainer at the time of retirement. Retirement benefits begin at the time of the director's retirement from the board and continue for life.

Why does the president of this university, or its board of trustees, allow a professor to engage in such lucrative "outside activities"? Maybe it's because the president, whose annual salary is $200,000, holds four director positions that give him more than $100,000 a year in additional income.

Professionals in elite settings not only make six-figure salaries, but they have enough "discretionary time" to pursue a second line of activity that may double or triple their basic salaries. Not a bad deal for the professional class.

Not everyone with a credentialed skill is in the privileged professional class. We exclude from this group workers like teachers, social workers, and nurses, who despite their professional training and dedication fail to get the material rewards accorded to other professionals. Moreover, they are usually labeled as "semiprofessions," implying that they somehow fall short of the full professionals. This may be due to the fact that most of these "semiprofessionals" are women, and that their services do not provide direct benefits to the privileged class. They deal with people in nonproductive roles as students, patients, or human service clients, and they deal mostly with people without much in the way of consumption or investment capital. We also exclude university professors at nonelite schools. They are excluded because of the large number of faculty at hundreds of nonelite colleges and universities who make modest salaries; and many of them are not even employed in tenure track positions. We also exclude the thousands of attorneys working for legal services agencies, franchise law firms, and in public defender positions. Professionals in these positions are excluded because of limited job security, modest levels of income, and little investment capital. Thus, we distinguish between elite and marginalized professional groups, with only the former being in the privileged class.

The New Working Class

Finally, there is the large majority of Americans—employees who sell their capacity to work to an employer in return for wages. This group typically carries out their daily work activities under the supervision of the managerial group. They have limited skills and limited job security. Such workers can see their jobs terminated with virtually no notice. The exception to this rule is the approximately 14 percent of workers who are unionized; but even union members are vulnerable to having their jobs eliminated by new technology, restructuring and downsizing, or the movement of production to overseas firms.

This working group also consists of the many thousands of very small businesses that include self-employed persons, and family stores based on little more than "sweat equity." Many of these people have been "driven" to try self-employment as a protection against limited opportunities in the general labor market. But many are attracted to the idea of owning their own business, an idea that has a special place in the American value system: It means freedom from the insecurity and subservience of being an employee. For the wage worker, the opportunities for starting a business are severely limited by the absence of capital. Aspirations may be directed at a family business in a neighborhood where one has lived, such as a dry-cleaning store, a beauty shop, a gas station, or a convenience store. Prospects for such businesses may depend upon an ethnic "niche" where the service, the customer, and the entrepreneur are tied together in a common cultural system relating to food or some personal service. The failure rate of these small businesses is very high, making self-employment a vulnerable, high-risk activity.

Another sizable segment of wage earners, perhaps 10–15 percent, has very weak links to the labor market. For these workers, working for wages takes place between long stretches of unemployment, when there may be shifts to welfare benefits or unemployment compensation. This latter group typically falls well below official poverty levels and should not be considered as part of the "working poor." The working poor consists of persons who are working full time at low wages, with earnings of about $12,000 a year—what you get for working full time at $6.00 an hour.

Table 2 summarizes these major segments of Americans with different standing in the current economy. The groups are distinguished as (1) those who own capital and businesses; (2) those who control corporations and the workers in those corporations; (3) those who possess credentialed knowledge that provides a protected place in the labor market; (4) the self-employed, small business-owners who operate as solo entrepreneurs with limited capital; and (5) those with varying skills who have little to offer in the labor market but their capacity to work.

These segments of the class structure are defined by their access to essential life-sustaining resources and the stability of those resources over time. As discussed earlier, these resources include consumption capital, investment capital, skill capital, and social capital. The class segments differ in their access to stable resources over time, and they represent what

TABLE 2   Class Structure in America

Class Position	Class Characteristics	Percentage of Population
Privileged Class Superclass	Owners and employers. Make a living from investments or business ownership; incomes at six- to seven-figure level, yielding sizable consumption and investment capital.	1–2%
Credentialed Class Managers	Mid- and upper-level managers and CEOs of corporations and public organizations. Incomes for upper-level CEOs in seven-figure range, others six figures.	13–15%
Professionals	Possess credentialed skill in form of college and professional degrees. Use of social capital and organizational ties to advance interests. Incomes from 100K to upper-six figures.	4–5%
New Working Class Comfort class	Nurses, teachers, civil servants, very-small- business owners, and skilled and union carpenters, machinists, or electricians. Incomes in the $35–50K range but little investment capital.	10%
Contingent Class Wage earners	Work for wages in clerical and sales jobs, personal services, and transportation and as skilled craft workers, machine operators, and assemblers. Members of this group are often college graduates. Incomes at $30K and lower.	50%
Self-employed	Usually self-employed with no employees, or family workers. Very modest incomes, with high potential for failure.	3–4%
Excluded class	In and out of the labor force in a variety of unskilled, temporary jobs.	10–15%

is, for all practical purposes, a two-class structure, represented by a double-diamond (see Figure 3). The top diamond represents the privileged class, composed of those who have stable and secure resources that they can expect will be available to them over time. This privileged class can be subdivided into the superclass of owners, employers, and CEOs, who directly or indirectly control enormous economic resources, and the credentialed class of managers and professionals with the knowledge and expertise that is essential to major industrial, financial, commercial, and media corporations and key agencies of government. The bottom diamond is the new working class, composed of those who have unstable and insecure resources over time. One segment of this class has a level of consumption capital

that provides income sufficient for home ownership and for consumption patterns that suggest they are "comfortable." Thus, we label this segment the comfort class, represented by school teachers, civil servants, social workers, nurses, some small-business owners, and skilled unionized carpenters, machinists or electricians. Despite their relatively "high" incomes ($35,000–60,000), the comfort class is vulnerable to major economic downturns or unforeseen crises (e.g., health problems) and has limited investment capital to buffer such crises.

The largest segment of the new working class is composed of the wage earners with modest skills and unpredictable job security. This group includes, for example, machine operators in manufacturing plants, bank clerks, and the supervisors who could

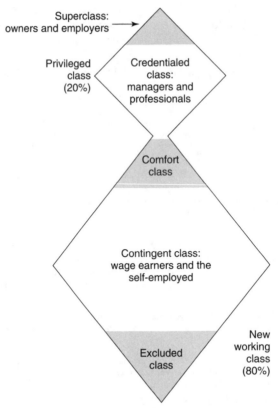

FIGURE 3   Double-Diamond Diagram of Class Structure and Class Segments.

be displaced by new production technology, computerized information systems, or other "smart" machines. Their job insecurity is similar to that of the growing segment of temporary and part-time workers, thereby making them the contingent class.

At the bottom of the new working class are those without marketable skills who move in and out of the labor force in temporary jobs or in seasonal employment. They are the excluded class, who either are treated as "waste," because they are no longer needed as either cheap labor or as consumers, or fill the most undesirable jobs in restaurant kitchens or as nighttime cleaners of downtown buildings. It is important to keep in mind that a person's location in the double-diamond class structure is related to his or her occupation but not determined by that occupation (as is the case in the production and functionalist models of class, discussed earlier in this chapter). Some lawyers are in the top diamond, and some in the bottom. Some engineers, scientists, and professors are in the privileged class, and some in the new working class. It is not occupation that determines class position but access to generative capital—stable, secure resources over time.

Who Owns What? The Changing Distribution of Wealth

LISA A. KEISTER

Men (in the United States) are nearer equality in wealth and mental endowments, or, in other words, more nearly equally powerful, than in any other country of the world or in any other age in recorded history.

(de Tocqueville, 1841)

Who owns what? How is the ownership of wealth distributed among families? Both basic research and practical concerns demand information about how many families are among the top wealth holders, how many families are truly asset-poor, and how many fall somewhere in the middle. Understanding wealth inequality also demands that we know how much these families own and how both levels of ownership and the extent of inequality have changed over time. What did the distribution of wealth look like in past decades, and what does it look like now? Few would expect wealth to be distributed evenly. Life-cycle patterns, baby booms, and other demographic trends affect the number of people earning income and accumulating assets at any time. Individual preferences for owning certain types of assets and debts vary over time as well as across generations at single points in time. Structural constraints limit the ability of entire groups of people to do the things necessary to accumulate assets and may even make them more likely to own debt. The availability of financial instruments varies over time, and laws regarding saving, investment, and related taxes affect the propensity of households to save. Of course, luck also plays an important role in distributing wealth unevenly. There is, of course, luck involved in even the most strategic stock investment decisions that can project some into the ranks of the top wealth holders and send others down to the bottom of the distribution.

Even if we accept some level of inequality as inevitable, it is disturbing to find either very extreme levels of inequality or sharp rises in inequality in a short period of time. Clearly the first step in understanding how and why wealth inequality exists is to get a sense of how much inequality there is. Only once we understand the basic trends in the distribution of wealth can we begin to understand the economic and social processes that have accounted for these trends. In this [work], I examine how wealth was distributed in the United States between 1962 and 1995. I identify the percentage of families that were among the richest wealth owners, how many had little or no wealth, and how many families were left somewhere in the middle. I use both survey data and the simulation model to explore the distribution of household wealth over these three decades. In the first section, I examine the mean and median household net worth. In the next sections, I use both survey data and simulated data to investigate the percentage of wealth held by households in various sections of the wealth distribution, and I examine changes in the composition of the typical family's net worth portfolio. I briefly discuss trends in wealth mobility, that is, trends in movement of families from one segment of the distribution to another over time. . . .

In addition to exploring trends in the distribution of wealth . . . , I also compare estimates of basic patterns from the survey data to those produced by the simulation model. The comparisons

Source: Lisa A. Keister, "Who Owns What? The Changing Distribution of Wealth," in *Wealth in America: Trends in Wealth Inequality,* Cambridge University Press, 2000. 55–66. Reprinted with the permission of Cambridge University Press.

demonstrate that the simulation model is highly consistent with indicators of wealth ownership and accumulation that we obtain from standard data sources prior to any manipulations of the model. My intention is to demonstrate the model's abilities to re-create historical estimates while lending credibility to its postmanipulation estimates. In the final section . . . I introduce the results of such a simulation experiment. Specifically the experiment simulates the distributional impact of a historic increase in middle-class stock ownership and finds some indication of a resulting increase in inequality.[1]

NET WORTH AND FINANCIAL WEALTH

While levels of wealth ownership vary from year to year, long-term trends in mean and median holdings of net worth and financial assets are good indicators of the general level of household well-being. Looking at trends over long periods of time highlights the influence of short-term fluctuations in inflation, rates of return, levels of employment, and other economic indicators. Likewise, a long-term view accents the influence of demographic trends that affect the proportion of families that are in various stages of the life cycle. For example, we would expect levels of wealth ownership to vary as baby boomers move through the life cycle. Looking at both levels of net worth and financial wealth provides a more complete picture of well-being than either indicator alone. Net worth, total assets less total debts, is a good summary indicator of household finances; while financial wealth, total financial assets, indicates the savings that are immediately available to the household.

Historical data on aggregate household wealth and net worth suggest that aggregate levels of

household wealth holdings have grown consistently since the early 1920s. Despite the methodological challenges that arise in collecting, synthesizing, and interpreting any data, particularly wealth data, over such long periods, Wolff and Marley (1989) were able to amass estimates of wealth ownership spanning the 1922–1983 period. Relying on both survey data and government estimates of aggregate wealth, they found that total household wealth per capita and net worth both grew dramatically in real terms over that period. Wolff and Marley used four separate definitions of wealth to investigate trends in wealth ownership. Because their concern was largely methodological, the use of separate definitions was sensible. In discussing their results, I refer to their first, basic definition of wealth, or total assets. There is little substantive difference in the trends that Wolff and Marley find across their different definitions. Ruggles and Ruggles (1982) used a similar methodology to estimate long-term historical trends in wealth ownership. While there are important differences in the findings of the two studies, the general trend in wealth ownership is the same in both. Wolff and Marley (1989:773) discussed the differences between the two studies in greater detail.

Between 1922 and 1983, real household per capita wealth and household net worth each increased more than three times (Wolff and Marley (1989). In the early 1920s, total household assets, or real wealth, was approximately $309 billion (in 1967 dollars).[2] By 1983, that number had increased to over $11 trillion. Similarly, total household net worth increased from $292 billion to nearly $9.4 trillion. Remarkably, while there are certainly downturns in this trend during difficult economic times, even during the worst times, only slight decreases are evident. During the 1930s, for example, both total wealth and net worth declined slightly, but the downturn appears as a minor jump in an otherwise steadily increasing trend. Wolff and Marley also used scattered survey

---

[1] I chose this experiment among many that I might have presented because portfolio behavior is relatively easily altered with policy changes and because middle-class stock ownership appears to have affected wealth distribution in the final years covered by this book. I might have presented the results of various other experiments, but I chose this because it is more practical (i.e., less abstract) than others.

---

[2] This is the sum of all assets owned by all families.

and census data to estimate that these trends were evident across the components of total wealth as well. Their estimates of the value of owner-occupied housing from census data demonstrated that the value of the primary residence increased remarkably over the 1922–1983 period, with the greatest increases in the later years.

At the household level, there have also been dramatic increases in net worth and financial wealth historically. Between 1962 and 1995, the period for which survey data is available, mean and median household wealth increased markedly. Table 1 compares mean and median household net worth and financial wealth for 1962, 1983, 1989, 1992, and 1995. The survey estimates for 1962 are from the Survey of the Financial Characteristics of Consumers for 1962 (Wolff 1992). For the other years, the survey estimates are from the Surveys of Consumer Finances (Avery, Elliehausen, Canner, and Gustafson 1986; Kennickell and Shack-Marquez 1992; Kennickell and Starr-McCluer 1994; Wolff 1994, 1998). In these estimates, net worth refers to wealth that is marketable. That is, the current market value of all fungible assets less the current value of all debts. Assets include the value of the principle residence, other real estate, stocks and mutual funds, all bonds, cash accounts such as checking and savings accounts, certificates of deposit and money market accounts, Individual Retirement Accounts and Keogh accounts, other pension plans, the cash surrender value of whole life insurance, and trust accounts. Debts include all mortgage and non-mortgage liabilities held by the household. Financial wealth is defined as net worth less equity in owner-occupied housing. Financial wealth is a measure of a household's liquid assets and indicates resources available for immediate use. I use both measures for two reasons. First, while net worth is the standard measure of wealth, the financial wealth measure is a better indicator of available resources. Second, both are somewhat standard in the literature, allowing for relatively easy comparisons of my estimates with other published estimates. The numbers in Table 1 are my own estimates, but they are consistent with other published estimates from these data sources (Wolff 1992, 1995, 1998).

Mean net worth increased by more than 50 percent between 1962 and 1995, and while the general trend was a steady increase in mean net worth, the 1990s saw a downturn in this measure of wealth. In 1962, mean net worth was just under $116,000 (in 1990 dollars). By 1983 it had increased to more than $170,000, and the mean was nearly $200,000 by the end of the 1980s. In the early 1990s, however, mean net worth began to decline. By 1992, the mean was just under $190,000, and it fell to about

TABLE 1   Household Net Worth and Financial Wealth, 1962–1995

	1962		1983		1989		1992		1995	
	Survey	*Simulated*	*Survey*	*Simulated*	*Survey*	*Simulated*	*Survey*	*Simulated*	*Survey*	*Simulated*
Net worth										
Mean	115,995	117,000	170,550	173,200	195,382	195,379	189,948	190,700	175,485	176,385
Median	30,996	35,218	43,801	48,700	46,881	47,181	39,995	40,721	39,146	41,000
Percent with zero or negative	11	12	16	17	18	19	18	19	19	19
Financial wealth										
Mean	92,243	93,181	123,762	124,501	145,839	146,750	144,804	146,175	134,650	135,050
Median	8,358	8,200	9,459	9,580	11,166	11,212	9,366	9,418	8,537	8,613
Percent with zero or negative	21	22	26	27	27	27	28	29	29	29

Note: Survey estimates are author's calculations from the Survey of the Financial Characteristics of Consumers for 1962 and the Surveys of Consumer Finances for other years. Simulated results are from the simulation model. All values are adjusted to 1990 dollars, based on a standard CPI-U.

widening wealth gap!

$175,000 by 1995. Median net worth, of course, is much lower, one-quarter to one-fifth as large as mean net worth. However, the 1962–1995 trend in median values was similar to that of mean values. Median net worth increased from 1962 to 1983 and again from 1983 through 1989. But in the 1990s, median net worth also began to decline, although the decline was less than the decline in mean net worth in both absolute and relative terms. One reason for the decline in net worth during the 1990s is apparent from the table. That is, the percentage of households with zero or negative net worth rose steadily from 1962 through 1995, including during the 1990s.

Financial wealth also increased steadily between 1962 and 1989 and then started to decline. Mean financial wealth is, again, much greater than median financial wealth; in fact, it is 13 to 17 times greater. However, both mean and median financial wealth followed the same basic pattern that was evident in net worth values. Again, one of the reasons for this trend in wealth ownership was the increase in the number of families that had zero or negative financial wealth during the early 1990s. Between 1989 and 1995, the percentage of families with no financial wealth rose from 27 to 29 percent. What is perhaps most astonishing about the estimates included in this table is the magnitude of financial wealth that families owned during this period. That is, the median family had, at most, $11,000 of financial wealth at their disposal. In the worst years, the median was much less than this, as low as $8,300.

While the estimates from the Surveys of Consumer Finances (SCF) reported in this table suggest that most families had very little wealth, other sources of wealth data paint an even bleaker picture. For example, the Survey of Income and Program Participation (SIPP) estimates that household net worth for 1984 and 1988 was far less than estimates derived from the SCF (Wolff 1993). Moreover, according to the SIPP, mean household net worth grew much slower during the 1980s than SCF estimates indicate. The reason for the differences in these estimates likely originates with

sampling methods. The SIPP is collected by the Bureau of the Census and is designed to gather information on income and household participation in government programs. The SIPP produces lower estimates of wealth ownership because it is based on a representative sample of the population, while the SCF oversamples high-income earners. Because this oversampled group contains many top wealth holders, the SCF sample includes more of the households that own the bulk of the country's wealth. The estimates I report in Table 1 are weighted by the Federal Reserve Board's weight that controls for the oversampling (Kennickell and Woodburn 1992).

One large gap in the information presented in Table 1 is the years between 1962 and 1983. I do not include estimates of net worth and financial wealth for those years because the Federal Reserve Board had essentially suspended the Survey of Consumer Finances during that period. There were other surveys of wealth information, but it is difficult to reconcile them with the SCF information. One method of estimating wealth during this gap is to use the estate tax data that I discussed in the previous chapter in my explanation of the simulation model. Smith (1987) used estate tax data and the estate multiplier method to estimate trends in wealth ownership between 1958 and 1976. His estimates indicate that total wealth ownership increased rather steadily during that period, consistent with the Wolff and Marley estimates discussed above. My own estimates of trends in net worth from the 1970 and 1977 Surveys of Consumer Finances (surveys that were scaled back from the primary years I discuss in this book and that are viewed as generally less reliable) indicate that mean and median net worth and financial wealth did, indeed, continue to increase during the 1962–1983 gap. However, the recessionary years of the 1970s slowed the growth of wealth considerably. Again, this trend can only be regarded as a preliminary finding as the data may be unreliable. At the same time, the estimates suggest that there was a rather interesting relation between aggregate growth and wealth during the 1970s.

Estimates of mean and median net worth and financial wealth from the simulation model that are also depicted in Table 1 are highly consistent with the survey estimates included in that table. The comparability of the survey and simulated estimates speaks to the ability of the model to produce historically consistent estimates of household wealth. Because the simulation model synthesizes survey data, estate tax data, and aggregate national balance sheets data, the model estimates are also consistent with historical estimates from each of these sources. The model estimates depict the same general trend in mean and median net worth over the 1962–1995 period. Both mean and median net worth increased from 1962 through 1989 and then began to decline. The difference between mean and median net worth is also substantial in the model estimates, and this difference is consistent in magnitude with the difference in the survey data. Likewise, the simulated estimates of trends in financial wealth and the percentage of households with zero or negative net worth and financial assets are also consistent with the survey estimates. One way in which the simulated estimates consistently diverge from the survey estimates is in magnitude. The simulation model consistently estimates moderately higher mean and median net worth and financial wealth than the survey. The differences are slight and not consistently statistically significant, but they are apparent. The slightly higher estimates are likely the result of alignment with the estate tax data, which tends to estimate higher wealth holdings for top wealth holders who are often not accurately represented in standard surveys. Interestingly, those who file estate taxes likely underreport their wealth even in their estate tax returns, so the true value of wealth holdings and the actual degree of wealth inequality may be greater than even the bleakest surveys indicate.

WEALTH DISTRIBUTION

Historical evidence indicates that while the levels of inequality in the distribution of household wealth varied dramatically during the first part of the twentieth century, inequality in wealth ownership was consistently severe. Lampman (1962) was one of the first researchers to point to inequalities in wealth distribution as a source of social problems. Using estate tax data and the estate multiplier method, Lampman investigated trends in wealth ownership and inequality in the decades between 1920 and 1960. His findings indicated that between 1922 and 1953, the top 1 percent of wealth holders owned an average of 30 percent of total household sector wealth. While inequalities varied with macroeconomic trends during the decades Lampman studied, he provided convincing evidence that inequality was consistently extreme throughout that period.

Other historical estimates have produced similar evidence of inequality during the early twentieth century, even in the absence of systematic survey data. Wolff and Marley (1989) used various data sources, including Lampman's 1962 data and data compiled by Smith (1984, 1987), to study wealth inequality over the entire 1920–1990 period. For the early part of the century, their results are consistent with Lampman's findings. They demonstrate that the top 1 percent of wealth owners owned an average of 30 percent of total net worth between 1922 and the early 1950s. Between 1922 and the 1929 stock market crash, the share of wealth owned by the top 1 percent increased from about 29 percent to about 32 percent. During the 1930s and 1940s, the concentration of wealth declined, so that the top 1 percent owned less than 30 percent by the late 1940s. During the 1950s, economic prosperity brought with it increased wealth inequality, and by the late 1950s, estimates suggest that the top 1 percent of households owned nearly 35 percent of total wealth.

In 1962, the Survey of the Financial Characteristics of Consumers (SFCC) supplied a uniquely comprehensive look into the wealth holdings of Americans and contributed unequivocal evidence that wealth inequality was quite severe. The estimates in Table 2 demonstrate just how unequal the distribution of wealth was between 1962 and 1995. The table includes estimates of the percentage of

TABLE 2   Distribution of Net Worth and Financial Wealth, 1962–1995: Survey Estimates

	Gini Coefficient	Top 1%	Next 4%	Next 5%	Next 10%	Top 20%	2nd 20%	3rd 20%	Bottom 40%
Net Worth									
1962	0.80	33.5	21.2	12.5	14.0	81.2	13.5	5.0	0.3
1983	0.80	33.8	22.3	12.1	13.1	81.3	12.6	5.2	0.9
1989	0.85	37.4	21.6	11.6	13.0	83.6	12.3	4.8	−0.7
1992	0.85	37.2	22.9	11.8	12.0	83.9	11.4	4.5	0.2
1995	0.87	38.5	21.8	11.5	12.1	83.9	11.4	4.5	0.2
Financial Wealth									
1962	0.88	40.3	23.8	12.8	12.7	89.6	9.6	2.1	−1.4
1983	0.90	42.9	25.1	12.3	11.0	91.3	7.9	1.7	−0.9
1989	0.93	46.9	23.9	11.6	10.9	93.4	7.4	1.7	−2.4
1992	0.92	45.6	25.0	11.5	10.2	92.3	7.3	1.5	−1.1
1995	0.94	47.2	24.6	11.2	10.1	93.0	6.9	1.4	−1.3

Note: Author's estimates from Survey of the Characteristics of Consumers for 1962 and the Survey of Consumer Finances for other years. Cells indicate the percentage of net worth or financial wealth held by households in each segment of the distribution.

total net worth and total financial wealth owned by households in various segments of the wealth distribution. The 1962 estimates in this table are from the SFCC and, again, the estimates for other years are from the Surveys of Consumer Finances (SCF). Net worth and financial wealth are defined as they were in Table 1. This table also includes estimates of the wealth Gini coefficient, derived from the same survey data. The Gini coefficient is an indicator of the degree of inequality. It ranges from 0 to 1, with 0 indicating perfect equality and 1 indicating perfect inequality. Conceptually, if a single household were to own all wealth, the Gini coefficient would equal unity (Weicher 1995, 1997). The Gini coefficient is a convenient, single indicator of inequality that reflects changes in inequality in any segment of the distribution. As Weicher points out, however, the Gini's primary drawback is that it does not have an intuitive interpretation. For instance, a Gini of 0.5 does not mean that the distribution is halfway between equal and unequal, even if such a statement made any sense. Yet the coefficient has become widely used, as it is in the measurement of income inequality, as a single measure of the degree of inequality in the distribution of wealth. Thus I include estimates of it in the table.

From the estimates presented in Table 2, it is apparent that a very small portion of households

has consistently owned the vast majority of household wealth. In 1962, the top 1 percent of wealth owners owned 33.5 percent of total net worth. The next 4 percent owned an additional 21.2 percent, with the top quintile accounting for more than 80 percent of net worth holdings. The second quintile owned the next 13.5 percent, and the remaining 60 percent of the population shared only 5 percent of total net worth. The Gini coefficient for net worth in 1962 was 0.80, reflecting the story of extreme inequality that the distributional numbers in Table 2 tell. The distribution of financial wealth was even more unequal in 1962. The Gini coefficient was 0.88, and the top 1 percent of financial wealth holders owned more than 40 percent of total financial wealth. In 1962, the top quintile owned nearly 90 percent of total financial wealth, and the other 80 percent of the population shared the remaining 10 percent. The bottom 40 percent of the population actually owned negative financial wealth.

Wealth inequality remained unequally distributed but relatively constant between 1962 and the mid-1970s due to an extended stock market slump and the growth of welfare programs such as AFDC and Social Security (Smith 1987). Using estate tax data, Smith found evidence that after 1973 wealth inequality began to drop once again.

Other researchers, using similar methodologies, have found that between 1972 and 1976, the share of total wealth owned by the top 1 percent of wealth owners declined from approximately 29 to about 19 percent of total wealth (Smith 1987; Wolff 1992). As with the estimates in Table 1, I do not include estimates of wealth distribution in Table 2 because there are not consistent sources of survey data from which to derive the estimates. . . .

Wealth inequality began to rise considerably after 1979, a trend that continued throughout the 1980s. By 1983, wealth inequality had returned to and, indeed, surpassed, 1962 levels on some measures. By 1983, the Gini coefficient for net worth had returned to 0.80, and it was 0.90 for financial wealth. The share of wealth owned by the top 1 percent of wealth holders was 33.8 percent in 1983 and 37.4 percent by 1989. Real mean wealth grew at 3.4 percent annually during this six-year period, a rate that was nearly double the rate of wealth growth between 1962 and 1983. Others have found similar trends. Wolff (1993) found that mean family wealth increased 23 percent in real terms, but that median wealth grew by only 8 percent over that period. His research also suggested that the share of the top one-half of 1 percent of wealth owners rose 5 percent during this period, from 26.2 percent of total household sector wealth in 1983 to 31.4 percent in 1989. The wealth of the next half percent remained relatively constant at about 7.5 percent of total household wealth, but the share of the next 9 percent decreased from 34.4 percent in 1983 to 33.4 percent in 1989. Thus, the rich became richer and the poor became poorer.

Most striking is evidence of the decline in the wealth of the poorest 80 percent of households. The wealth of this group decreased by almost 3 percent, from 18.7 percent of total wealth in 1983 to 16.4 percent in 1989. Moreover, nearly all growth in real wealth between 1983 and 1989 was accumulated by the top 20 percent of wealth holders who gained 3.3 percent in their total wealth holdings. The second 20 percent lost 0.9 percent, the middle 20 percent lost 0.6 percent, the next 20 percent lost 0.4 percent, and the bottom group

lost 0.9 percent. Wolff (1995) found similar results in his examination of trends in wealth inequality. Existing research also indicates that in the 1980s, wealth inequality in the United States became severe relative to that found in European nations. Studies of wealth in the 1920s suggested that wealth was much more equally distributed in the United State than in Western European nations. By the late 1980s, however, research suggests that household sector wealth in the United States was considerably more concentrated than in Western Europe (Wolff 1995).

While mean and median household net worth and financial wealth declined during the 1990s (Table 1), the distribution of wealth continued to worsen. By 1995, the Gini coefficient for net worth had increased to 0.87, an increase of 7 percent since 1962 and 2 percent since the late 1980s. Likewise, the Gini coefficient for financial wealth reached 0.94 by 1995, a steady increase from 0.88 in 1962. As a Gini coefficient of 1.0 would indicate perfect inequality, wealth ownership in the United States at that point was not far from being perfectly unequally distributed. The Gini coefficient accurately reflected trends in the distribution: As the estimates in Table 2 indicate, wealth ownership was highly concentrated by the mid-1990s. The top 1 percent of wealth owners owned 38.5 percent of net worth and 47.2 (nearly half!) of financial wealth. The next 4 percent owned 21.8 percent of net worth and nearly 25 percent of financial wealth. The extreme inequality that these numbers reflect is most evident in the proportion of total wealth owned by the top quintile: The top 20 percent of households owned nearly 84 percent of net worth and 93 percent of financial wealth in 1995. Of course, the most striking message these estimates convey is that the remaining 80 percent of households owned only 16 percent of net worth and only 7 percent of financial wealth. . . .

REFERENCES

Avery, Robert B., Gregory E. Elliehausen, Glenn B. Canner, and Thomas A Gostafson. 1986. "Survey of Consumer Finances, 1983." *Federal Reserve Bulletin* March: 163–177.

Kennickell, Arthur B., Martha Starr-McCluer. 1997. "Household Saving and Portfolio Change: Evidence from the 1983–89 SCF Panel." *Review of Income and Wealth* December: 381–399.

Kennickell, Arthur B., and R. Louise Woodburn. 1992. "Estimation of Household Net Worth Using Model-Based and Design-Based Weights: Evidence from the 1989 Survey of Consumer Finances." Unpublished Federal Reserve Board Manuscript.

Lampman, Robert J. 1962. *The Share of Top Wealth-Holders in national Wealth, 1922–56.* Princeton, NJ: Princeton University Press.

Ruggles, Richard, and Nancy Ruggles. 1982. "Integrated Economic Accounts for the United States, 1947–1980." *Survey of Current Business* 62:1–53.

Smith, James D. 1984. "Trends in the Concentration of Wealth in the United States, 1958–1976." *Review of Income and Wealth* December: 419–428.

Smith, James D. 1987. "Recent Trends in the Distribution of Wealth in the United States: Data, Research Problems, and Prosepcts." Pp. 72–90 in *International Comparisons of the Distribution of Household Wealth,* edited by E. N. Wolff. New York: Oxford University Press.

Weicher, John C. 1997. "Wealth and Its Distribution: 1983–1992: Secular Growth, Cyclical Stability." *Federal Reserve Bank of St. Louis Review* 79: 3–23.

Wolff, Edward N. 1992. "Changing Inequality of Wealth." *American Economic Review* 82:552–558.

Wolff, Edward N. 1993. "Trends in Household Wealth in the United States During the 1980s." Unpublished manuscript. New York: New York University.

Wolff, Edward N. 1994. "Trends in Household Wealth in the United States 1962–1983 and 1983–1994." C.V. Starr Center for Applied Economics, New York University, #94–03.

Wolff, Edward N. 1995. *Top Heavy: A Study of the Increasing Inequality of Wealth in America.* New York: Twentieth Century Fund.

Wolff, Edward N. 1998. "Recent Trends in the Size Distribution of Household Wealth." *Journal of Economic Perspectives* 12:131–150.

Wolff, Edward N., and Maria Marley. 1989. "Long Term Trends in U.S. Wealth Inequality: Methodological Issues and Results." Pp. 765–839 in *The Measurement of Saving, Investment, and Wealth,* edited by R. Lipsey and H. S. Tice. Chicago: University of Chicago Press.

The Middle Class and Its Discontents

ALAN WOLFE

THE MIDDLE CLASS AND ITS DISCONTENTS

The adage that America is a middle-class nation, long taken for granted in self-perception, came about as close to reality as it ever would in the years after World War II. No doubt far too many Americans during those years faced poverty and indefensible racial and gender discrimination, but it is also true that unprecedented economic growth, an expansion of home ownership, inflation-proof contracts between companies and their workers, the democratization of higher education, successful Keynesian stabilization policies, social and geographic mobility, and impressive technological accomplishments allowed an astonishing number of Americans to make plausible claims for middle-class status. A level of physical and psychological security unimaginable to all but the very few a hundred years ago seemed within the grasp of the overwhelming many. Under those conditions, the promise of middle-class life—independence from the whims, blessings, and ill designs of others—seemed a reality.

How distant those years after World War II seem from the American mood in the last decade of the twentieth century! Now, according to a large number of critics, journalists, and social scientists, the middle class acts as if it has reached middle age. Those who take the pulse of the American middle class these days find the patient on the one hand lethargic, sunk into civic apathy and private withdrawal, and on the other hand hyperactive, loudly protesting its condition in support for populistic anger and collective revenge. Emerging from all corners of the political spectrum comes a rather depressing story about recent middle-class experience. The story runs roughly as follows.

First and foremost, we are told, the middle class is getting smaller. Writing during the 1980s, economists Bennett Harrison and Barry Bluestone noted with alarm that the "deindustrialization of America" was bound to depress wages, shrink managerial positions, and eventually result in a pattern of income distribution tilted toward the extremes rather than the middle. Given the importance of the charge, others challenged the data, pointing to the emergence of new jobs, as well as the ability of two-income families to make up for any losses experienced by once highly paid male workers, which in turn prompted a criticism of the critics' data and interpretations. Debates of this kind are rarely ever resolved, including this one. Nonetheless, sorting carefully through the passions involved, Frank Levy and Richard Murnane, economists at MIT and Harvard, concluded that a "hollowing out" of middle-class jobs produced "larger percentages of workers at the top and bottom of the distribution and a smaller percentage in the middle. At least for men, it is now clear that there were fewer middle-class jobs in the mid-1980s than a decade earlier." A more recent study, focusing on the distribution of overall wealth rather than income, demonstrated a pattern in which the extremes of rich and poor have grown in America at the expense of the middle. That conclusion has also been challenged by conservatives. They point out that the years in which the distribution of wealth allegedly became more polarized were also years in which significant amounts of new wealth were created.

However the statistics are interpreted, the story of middle-class shrinkage received a major boost when it was picked up by a conservative Republican, Patrick Buchanan, who made it the theme of his unsuccessful effort to win the Republican nomination for president in 1996. At a time when politicians of both parties were searching in vain for ways to strike a responsive chord in the electorate, Buchanan single-handedly launched a national discussion of whether American corporations, to meet global challenges, should be allowed to "downsize," no matter what the effects of such efforts on American jobs and communities. Devoting an unusually large number of pages to the subject, the *New York Times* published a series of stories that, in personalizing the experience of middle-class Americans suddenly finding themselves with neither income nor moorings, left the clear impression that the dream of middle-class security was fading fast in the United States.

Even those lucky enough to protect their middle-class lifestyles in the 1990s, analyses of this sort continue, found the meaning of their accomplishment ambiguous at best. The seemingly endless economic growth of the 1960s and early 1970s had led a generation of Americans to believe that middle-class status was like academic tenure: once you got it, no one could ever take it away. But in the 1990s that picture changed dramatically and those who remained in the middle class found that the price for their success was a speeding up and intensification of just about everything. Both spouses now worked to keep up, as did some of the children. Long commuting hours became routine, child care emotionally complicated and an additional source of time pressure, and public schools no longer the bargain they once were.

Under these more competitive conditions, critics argued that changes in the moral and political outlook of the middle class were inevitable. Whereas middle-class Americans were once characterized as forward-looking, optimistic, even (according to the social critics of the 1950s) too comfortable and complacent, now they were increasingly pictured as self-interested to the point of selfishness. Americans in general, and middle-class Americans in particular, had entered what *Newsweek* writer Robert Samuelson called "the age of entitlement," relying on expanded governmental programs to subsidize their housing and transportation, for example, while protesting the taxes involved in paying for them. No longer living within their means as a nation—Samuelson called this tendency of government to overpromise things "suicidal"—they also were financing their personal lifestyles, not through their earnings, but by using expanded forms of credit and speculative investment. Their lives, the critics charged, were premised on illusions; as the realities of economic downturns and the limits to government subsidies hit them, their response would be one of anger and frustration.

There are polling data available to support the proposition that Americans are indeed angry, especially about their public life. Indicative is a 1995 poll that asked whether "the American dream of equal opportunity, personal freedom, and social mobility has become easier or harder to achieve in the past 10 years"; 67 percent responded that it had become harder, while 31 percent said easier. Surveys from a wide variety of sources revealed a sense of deep hostility to American political institutions. For example, 66 percent of the American people told a 1995 Gallup poll that they were dissatisfied "with the way things are going in the United States at this time," compared with 30 percent in 1986, while a *U.S. News & World Report* survey of 1994 indicated that 75 percent of Americans believed that "middle-class families can't make ends meet."

Interpreting the mood of the middle class means finding a plausible story to explain its discontents. One such story dominates the discussion taking place among social and political theorists. The key characters in this story are large-scale social and political forces that sociologists call tradition and modernity. In a world characterized by tradition, people believed in God and considered God's commands as binding standards for right and wrong, not only for themselves, but also for others. The family was viewed as sacrosanct: divorce was highly unusual and children were expected to be grateful for the sacrifices that parents, who postponed their own gratifications in forming a family, made on their behalf. Patriotism was a strongly inscribed value in a more traditional society; people not only served in the armed forces when called, but were expected to support their country without reservation, for America, one of the world's truly successful democracies, was worthy of such support. Hard work and upward striving, virtues often identified with the Protestant ethic, were considered important in a traditionalist world. So was active civic involvement, taking pride in the voluntary ties one formed with neighbors and friends. The moral rules of a traditional world, according to its defenders, were clear, unchanging, and accepted by most people as fair.

Around the turn of the twentieth century, although the exact date cannot be specified, as this story continues, something called modernity entered, and ultimately threatened to destroy, the world of tradition. When sociologists use the term, "modernity" is often a slippery concept, sometimes referring to the ways people think, sometimes to the ways they act, and sometimes to anything that takes place at the present time. Still, the term is an important one, because something did happen to upset the world of traditional middle-class morality. We are best off thinking of that something as a very powerful idea, so powerful that it was capable of changing the way people act. Modernity means freedom, but not in the narrow sense of voting for candidates of one's own choice. The freedom associated with modernity is the freedom to construct one's own life as one best sees fit. Concretely, that means not accepting God's commands regarding right and wrong, but developing one's own personal ethical standards. It means thinking of marriage as a union of consenting equals to be dissolved when it oppresses one or both of the parties involved. A modern person loves his or her country but reserves the right to criticize it. In the modern world, we recognize the importance of working hard but also understand that work may not be available to all, requiring government involvement to insure that the gap between the rich and poor never becomes too great. Finally, modern people are mobile people, no longer sufficiently tied to their neighborhoods that they become "joiners," always ready to lend a hand building the neighbor's barn. The moral rules of modernity cannot provide the security of fixed standards, but, as those who justify them understand them, they recognize that people in the modern world are determined to choose what's best for them.

If this story of how modernity is replacing tradition is generally accepted by sociologists to be true, its implications are subject to heated debate. Around the story have developed two accounts, one that prefers traditional society and views modernity as suspect and one, not surprisingly, that reverses the evaluation. For lack of better terms, the first account can be called conservative, the second liberal.

The middle class, in contemporary conservative theory, is the moral class. As conservatives see it, middle-class Americans are ordinary people trying to live by traditional rules of working hard, saving for the future, and being loyal to family and country. As early as 1972, the neoconservative social theorist Irving Kristol wrote that "it is only the common people who remain loyal to the bourgeois ethos." Not that Kristol was completely enamored of that ethos; its lack of appreciation for the spiritual and heroic virtues rendered it inappropriate for answering deep questions about man's role in the universe. Still, the commonsense values of the working and lower-middle class had "an intimate and enduring relation to mundane realities that was relatively immune to speculative enthusiasm," he wrote. The middle-class ideal of the common good, "consisting mainly of personal security under the law, personal liberty under the law, and a steadily increasing material prosperity for those who apply themselves to that end," is not all that bad, Kristol concluded, especially when compared with the pretensions of intellectuals.

Kristol's formulation of the issue was enormously important for contemporary American politics. So long as conservatism is understood as the defense of the rich, it will always be a minority taste in middle-class America. By arguing that conservatives needed to respect the power of middle-class ideas among lower-middle-class—and even working-class—Americans, Kristol was outlining a path toward majority status for the conservative view of the world. Contemporary American conversatism can literally be defined as the defense of middle-class morality, an effort to protect the traditional neighborhoods, family ideals, religious beliefs, work ethic, schools, love of country, and security concerns of the lower-middle class, no matter how impolitically expressed, from the welfare state on the one hand and the liberal defense of modernity on the other. From such a perspective, middle-class morality is good; the only thing that is bad is its continual decline.

For liberals, by contrast, a world without fixed moral guidelines is one that offers individuals greater choice. True of everyone, liberals believe, such expanded choices are especially true of those whose needs were ignored by traditionalists. As conservatives rallied to a defense of the middle-class morality they associated with hardworking sobriety, liberals responded by finding traditional neighborhoods hostile to excluded racial minorities, traditional religiosity intolerant of nonbelievers, and traditional families first oppressive to women and later to homosexuals. Because they identify so strongly with those who were outsiders in the world of tradition, American intellectuals and activists on the left have never had much sympathy for the middle-class morality praised by the right. The left tends to believe that middle-class morality is bad, and the only good thing is that it might become obsolete. Yet, since so many Americans view themselves as middle class, by dismissing middle-class morality so blithely, the left moved rapidly toward dismissing itself as a majority force in American life.

After the Reagan administration came to power, however, liberals found a way to shift the discussion from morality to declining incomes and a lack of middle-class jobs. Economic polarization suggested that the middle class was splitting into two wings. One, the liberal theory held, was composed of comfortable financial analysts, real estate brokers, and Yuppies driving expensive cars and purchasing summer houses, while the other contained economically insecure midlevel employees and well-paid, if anything but rich, union members. If true, this split in the middle class offered liberals, like conservatives, a plausible way to talk about why middle-class Americans, including those in the lower ranks, were fed up: the left could prevent the right from monopolizing the loyalties of the lower-middle class, not by praising its moral outlook on the world, but instead by criticizing the way the upper-middle class led its life.

"The nervous, uphill financial climb of the professional middle class accelerates the downward spiral of the society as a whole: toward cruelly widening inequalities, toward heightened estrangement along lines of class and race, and toward the moral anesthesia that estrangement requires," wrote social critic Barbara Ehrenreich in this vein. Left to its own devices, critics from the left concluded, well-off Americans separate themselves physically, emotionally, and politically from the less fortunate. Using one of the most emotionally laden terms in American history, Robert Reich, before he became secretary of labor in the Clinton administration, wrote that in the new world economy that came into being in the 1980s, upper-middle-class people "are quietly *seceding* from the large and diverse publics of America into homogeneous enclaves, within

cultural war

which their earnings need not be redistributed to people less fortunate than themselves." Let's call this phenomenon the "middle-class withdrawal symptom." From a liberal perspective, no cultural change in America was more important than this effort by those with means to detach themselves from their obligations to those without them. Since liberals believe so strongly in a society in which everyone should have an equal capacity to determine how best to lead their lives, the conservative insistence that middle-class morality needs respect is seen by liberals as an effort to detract attention from what liberals believe to be the *real* problems facing America: economic polarization and the increasing conservatism of upper-middle-class selfishness.

Conservatives and liberals, then, disagree about the causes of middle-class anger, but in their description of the empirical reality of that anger, all agree that the middle class is in a severe state of discontent, either because it has lost jobs and income (liberals), religious belief, moral bearings, and physical safety (conservatives), or both (populists). It is what one is angry about, and not whether one is angry, that seems to define positions on America's political spectrum. Rather than picturing the middle class as unified in its disdain for the way both the poor and the rich led their lives, which is historically how the middle class understood itself, critics from both ends of the political spectrum focused instead on what seemed to be a radical split within the middle class, each identifying in some way with one side or the other. The name that came to be given to this split was the "culture war."

It has by now become something close to an accepted fact, due in no small part to the foresight of conservative writers such as Irving Kristol, that a wide gap exists in the United States between people who retain strong religious beliefs, adhere to the traditional family, possess unquestioned loyalty to their country, dislike immigration, denounce pornography, and are suspicious of cultural relativism and those—often called a new class or a cultural elite—who have accepted the

basic axioms of feminism, support principles of multiculturalism, express cosmopolitan values, and place a high priority on civil liberties. At one level, such a culture war represents nothing new: the Scopes trial, battles over immigration, and McCarthyism were earlier encounters in what has been a very long conflict. But such earlier encounters took place between classes: those on the conservative, and eventually the losing, side in those battles represented forces—fundamentalist faithful, displaced farmers, segregationists— seemingly on their way to economic and cultural obsolescence.

Now the cultural conflict alleged to be spreading through America is understood to be taking place within just one class: those in the middle. Upper-middle-class people who have prospered in the speculative 1980s and 1990s appear to be disproportionately represented on the liberal side, and those lower-middle-class Americans who still believe in savings accounts and family-oriented neighborhoods find themselves on the traditional side. Or so, at least, argues Christopher Lasch. The culture war, in his view, represents an alliance between the inner city and the outer city against those caught in between: hard-pressed Americans earning enough to move to the outskirts, but not so much that they can escape the costs of liberal experiments in social justice. In a similar way, Michael Lind views the culture war as an alliance between the overclass and the underclass, both of whom support multiculturalism, against the forgotten Americans in the middle. Scholars have been writing about the "radical center" of American politics for some time, and what they generally have found is that such middle Americans lean toward cautious support of the welfare state on the one hand and toward equally cautious cultural conservatism on the other, a sociological insight put to great use by politicians such as Richard Nixon in his appeals to the "forgotten" American. This time, what seems to be at stake in debates over the radical middle is the very future of middle-class morality: will middle-class Americans such as Judy Vogel shift toward that part of their worldview that emphasizes dismay at the character of people on welfare or toward that side that emphasizes a generous conception of membership in a larger social world? Divided between the abstractions of its upper end and the nitty-gritty realities of its lower, the middle class faces its most serious rupture of all: disappearance as a cohesive set of values in the face of simultaneous pulls and pushes from all directions.

If even part of this story about middle-class decline and fracturing is true, the implications could not be greater. The issue is simple to state: an angry, inward-looking, and hopelessly divided middle class is not a middle class at all—not in the way Americans have traditionally understood their aspirations. To be middle class in this country is to believe in the future; asked whether a person who works hard has a chance to become rich, Americans respond very positively, while Britons respond very negatively. Strip away the vibrancy, the sense of expectancy, the open-ended character of middle-class life, and America becomes more like Europe—even at a time when Europe becomes more like America. Other countries in the world, it is generally believed, experience castelike immobility, bitterly contested ideological politics, class envy and resentment, and support for parties of nostalgia—not the United States. If middle-class America is as morally divided as so many accounts from all across the political spectrum would have it, we all lose. For then, our future as a nation will be marked by incessant conflicts between irreconcilable worldviews, raising the prospect that the democratic stability that has kept the country together since the Civil War will no longer be attainable.

BUT IS IT TRUE?

The trouble is that we do not know for sure whether any of these accounts of middle-class discontent are true. Even the seemingly obvious idea that middle-class Americans are angry and frustrated as they watch their economic prospects shrink, and are shrinking their sense of generosity

and obligation along with it, suffers from a number of problems. Although Patrick Buchanan made downsizing the theme of his 1996 campaign for the Republican nomination, the question disappeared from the general election; if anything, President Clinton's reelection was due to the fact that so many Americans believed the economy was moving along fine and did not need the stimulus offered by the Republican challenger. Furthermore, the 1996 presidential campaign was not marked by cultural and moral conflict over such issues as abortion and affirmative action, in large part because Americans made it clear that they do not like extremism and polarization in their politics. And Ross Perot's third-party efforts to capitalize on populist frustrations made little splash in 1996 compared with his showing four years earlier. Whatever may have motivated voters in 1996, anger was conspicuously missing.

Nor is it true, as the left perversely tends to insist, that the right has won the battle for the mind of the middle class. Americans did not became more conservative during the 1970s and 1980s; on questions of race and the acceptance of feminist goals, they moved to the left, just as on crime or immigration they moved to the right. It is also incorrect to say that, in their newfound conservatism, Americans turned against government and liberal social programs such as welfare; instead, what their mood registered, in political scientist William Mayer's words, "was simply a few modest adjustments within the present system: a little less domestic spending (or perhaps a slower rate of growth), a slight relaxation of environmental regulations in order to produce more energy, a little more reliance on individual initiative in dealing with the problems of poverty." As Mayer's sophisticated reading of three decades of polling data suggests, Americans may not be withdrawing from a sense of obligation so much as they are trying to find more effective ways to express it.

Less angry than they are often taken to be, Americans may also not be quite as engaged in a culture war as intellectuals claim. A number of books by distinguished sociologists have appeared, demonstrating, with the use of polling and other kinds of data, that there is a culture war taking place in the United States. But, then again, other studies have appeared, based on equally (if not more) impressive evidence suggesting that, with the possible exception of abortion, no such culture war exists in America. To be sure, a society divided by race and gender, dealing with such issues as immigration and welfare, and undergoing a revision of its constitutional principles on church and state, is experiencing some kind of cultural conflict. But how much conflict is simply part of the basic disagreement essential to a democracy and how much represents a country literally at war? No one has yet provided a satisfactory answer to that question. . . .

The Middle Class in Debt

TERESA A. SULLIVAN, ELIZABETH WARREN, AND JAY LAWRENCE WESTBROOK

Stability is the essence of the middle class. It is the source of disdain for the bourgeoisie as well as its goal and glory. But the economic dynamics of recent decades have placed important portions of the middle class at risk. Bankruptcy is a middle-class phenomenon, and the dramatic increases in bankruptcy filings must be understood to reveal a middle-class pathology. Something is amiss, at least financially, at the heart of American society. Although many middle-class people are prosperous in the midst of one of the longest economic booms in United States history, the middle class is not so secure as it once seemed.

More than one million bankruptcy filings a year means that more than a million American households are directly affected by bankruptcy annually. With about one hundred million households in the United States, in the space of a decade, even allowing for some overlap, that rate would imply that about 10 percent of the country would have lived through a personal bankruptcy. Of course, that is the rate in a boom time. The rate may change if bad times return, as they always have in the past.

One explanation offered for the sharp increase in bankruptcies is that the bankruptcy law is "too easy." People are filing for bankruptcy frivolously, when they really could pay their debts if they

would just buckle down and take some responsibility. The difficulty with this argument is that it flies in the face of known facts. If people nowadays are filing bankruptcy more from convenience than from desperation, two things must be true: many bankrupts must have relatively payable debts, and there must be a growing number of such "can pay" bankrupts. In fact, the figures from our study, and the others we report in this book, show that the great majority of debtors in bankruptcy are overwhelmed by debt they could not possibly pay. These data also show that their incomes are lower and they are just as deeply indebted as were their predecessors in our 1981 study. If the explanation based on easy laws and strategic behavior by debtors is not sufficient, what is the answer?

Studies of bankruptcy filings in the 1990s have begun to explore the leading causes of the financial collapse of middle-class households. The most important, beyond doubt, are the loss of income and long-term reduction in income that result from job loss and job changes. The central economic problem for ordinary, middle-class salaried workers is the risk of job loss. For the middle-aged middle class, job loss may be tantamount to forced retirement. The resulting trauma may be the most plausible explanation for the stability of wage rates (and the consequent lack of inflation) at a time of record-low unemployment: people are afraid to demand higher wages and slow to move to new opportunities at a time of increasing volatility in the employment market. The danger in this rapidly shifting economy is not

Source: Teresa A. Sullivan, Elizabeth Warren, 9/27 Jay Lawrence Westbrook, "The Middle Class in Debt." In *The Fragile Middle Class: Americans in Debt*, New Haven: Yale University Press, 2000: 238-261.

only unemployment but changing employment and landing on a lower rung on the economic ladder.

Americans seem to react with profound ambivalence to the increasing volatility of employment. Our mixed emotions are nicely captured in the *New Yorker* cartoon in which Hermes and two other gods are talking. Hermes says, "It's called monotheism, but it looks like downsizing to me." We pat ourselves on the back for downsizing our way back to competitiveness and pity the Europeans for their staggering unemployment rates. At the same time, we shake our heads over the stories of fifty-year-old former factory foremen and bank managers tending airport kiosks and delivering pizza. Consistent with our history, Americans have opted for overall economic success at the price of severe economic inequality and serious economic hardship for some. In the past we have exchanged economic security for political and social mobility and economic opportunity. In the 1990s and into the new millennium, we have done it again. One consequence may be a loss of middle-class stability.

The point highlighted by our findings in the bankruptcy courts is the role of the *rate* of change. Only in the 1970s did the financial world finally discover that the rate of change in investment value—the beta—is a key aspect of financial analysis. Our findings may contribute to an appreciation that the same thing is true with respect to the central investment in the lives of most middle-class people: their jobs. It is the volatility of the job market; not necessarily the end result, that is an essential factor in explaining the bankruptcies of the 1990s. Debts may have seemed reasonable (even if at the high end of reasonable) when acquired, but they may have suddenly become crushing when the future held lesser prospects. Even if a laid-off employee lands an equivalent salary in a new job, the interval between jobs, with high interest rates running, may dig a debt hole that is too deep to escape.

To these difficulties we must often add the inevitable lag in adjustment to disaster. Human beings seem to require some period in which to accept the consequences of calamity, so that

debts may actually increase (especially on credit cards thrust through the mailbox daily) while the head of a household reluctantly begins to absorb the fact that things are not going to get better soon.

Closely related to job loss as a cause of bankruptcy are medical problems. Our debtors report that the most serious consequence of illness or injury is loss of income, whether temporarily during recovery or rehabilitation or permanently following disability. In significant part, this result follows from the very structure of America's safety nets for the ill or injured. Worker's compensation and public and private disability plans are deliberately designed to provide a fraction of the employee's previous salary. Such support may provide enough to live on, but it leaves little margin for repaying debts, especially if the debts were stretching the available resources back at the previous income level. Even if recovery or rehabilitation makes the loss of income temporary, the accumulation of consumer interest during that period will make the debts very hard to repay.

Although loss of income was the most important consequence of medical problems, our debtors say that unpayable medical debts were also a major factor. The striking increase in medical costs over the past two decades has been well documented and much discussed. Despite the prevalence of third-party payers in the form of employer-provided benefits, many middle-class Americans are still paying a lot of their own medical bills. That number grows every time people are laid off from long-term jobs with benefits and reemployed as temporary or contract workers without benefits. Although many doctors and hospitals perform a substantial amount of charity work, there are still many people burdened with large medical debts.

Just as bankruptcy is our primary indicator of financial crisis in middle America, so the divorce rate signals its social turmoil. The family is the center of middle-class life, but nowadays many families break up and re-form, increasing social volatility in tandem with increased economic volatility. A standard of living established by two living together—and most often contributing two salaries—must decline when the two separate. The change in circumstances is even greater when children are involved. The most profound human emotions and the most serious disruption of personal context are inextricably linked with great financial pressure.

The financial results are all too often measured in bankruptcy. The financial burden falls more heavily on women, who are typically the custodial parents for the children of the marriage and who usually have lower earnings than their ex-husbands. Although there is some dispute about the size of the divorce penalty, most researchers agree that divorce has serious adverse financial consequences for men and women and that the consequences for women are much more serious than they are for men. There is also agreement that the key to financial recovery from divorce is remarriage, especially for women. Thus it is not surprising that we find a far higher percentage of unmarried people in our bankruptcy sample than among Americans generally.

The basic reason that we frequently find the shards of a broken marriage in the bankruptcy courts is familiar: the debts incurred at one level of net disposable income are too great to be satisfied by a lower income. In this context, the calculation may also change because even if the income(s) remain the same, the expenses of living apart are greater. The net result is identical. The husband heavily burdened with alimony and support payments, whether made willingly or under threat of jail, may find that bankruptcy, by eliminating his other debts, provides the only way to focus enough of his earnings on those divorce obligations he cannot escape. The wife left with rusty job skills, children to raise, and unstable support payments may find herself in bankruptcy as well, using the filing to erase old debts if her family is to free up enough income to put a roof over their heads, groceries on the table, and otherwise survive financially. There are no doubt many others who manage to stay out of the bankruptcy courts who are severely burdened in much the

same ways, but the financial pressures on families in the aftermath of divorce are unmistakable.

It seems strange to think of homeownership as part of the litany of middle-class woe, but our research indicates that it holds an important place in financial distress. Homes join credit card debt as one of the voluntary sources of money troubles. No one wants to be laid off or to become sick or injured, and the mix of fault that leads to each divorce is unique to every marriage. But homes are bought and credit charges are run up voluntarily, even eagerly. Like credit card debt, home mortgages are the subject of a constant hard sell, but homeownership is different in its respectability. Friends are unlikely to send congratulations for maxing out a Visa card, but they will buy a drink to celebrate qualifying for a mortgage on the soon-to-be-purchased dream house. Even in the frenzy of modern credit use, there is a widespread feeling that credit cards are dangerous and that their overuse signals irresponsibility. Buying a home, by contrast, is rarely condemned and often applauded.

Yet homeownership gets people into financial trouble in similar ways: they buy more than they can truly afford and they have too little margin left when disaster strikes. The initial difference is the social cachet; the long-term difference is the personal and social attachment to the home. When trouble strikes homeowners, some will file for bankruptcy because their mortgage obligations have become unmanageable. As with support obligations, by eliminating all other debt they can focus their incomes on making the mortgage payments and saving their homes. For many, the desperation to keep a home extends beyond their attachment to the kitchen wallpaper and the barbecue in the backyard. If they are unable to pay other debts, their neighbors and friends may never know, but leaving a home for an apartment is hard to explain away. The move is a public announcement of downward mobility.

It must be significant that second-mortgage lending has increased so dramatically in the past decade or so, a development related to the fact that the amount of mortgage debt has climbed much faster than the value of the homes securing that debt. In 1998 Texas became the last state to abolish most of its stringent limitations on second mortgages. In the ensuing months, the state has seen an explosion of advertising urging Texans to create second mortgages as a source of credit. Because Texas is the second-most populous state, a further, rapid rise in second mortgages nationally seems very likely. Debtors are using their homes to secure loans for home improvements, college tuition, and taking care of elderly parents, but they are also putting their homes at risk for what has long been considered ordinary consumer debt—credit cards and other lines of credit to be drawn on one charge at a time. In spite of their potentially revolutionary impact, the implications of second mortgages—and third and fourth mortgages in many cases—are largely unexplored. For whatever reasons, with about half the debtors in bankruptcy identified as homeowners, it is clear that the American dream of homestead security is in serious jeopardy. More homeowners are struggling harder than ever to hang on to their chief symbol of participation in the middle class, and the bankruptcy courts are often their last stop to try to stabilize economically before they face foreclosure.

We have identified five factors contributing to consumer bankruptcy: job and income loss, sickness and injury, divorce, homeownership, and too much credit. When we look at the data we have gathered on these bankrupt debtors and put it in the context of larger economic trends, we conclude that the first four of these are the necessary preconditions to increasing financial failure, and frequently the triggering causes, but they are not sufficient in themselves to explain a 400 percent increase in bankruptcy filings since 1985. Increasing job volatility and the rising cost of medical debts have undoubtedly contributed, not just to the failure, but to the increasing rate of failure, of middle-class families. They are important, but are probably not enough by themselves to explain the rapid rise in financial failure. Historically high divorce rates have also contributed, but they have

remained relatively stable for nearly twenty years. Mortgage rates have fallen steadily since the sky-high rates of the early 1980s, giving homeowners the opportunity to reduce somewhat the financial risks associated with homeownership. Concluding that these factors, important as they are, do not seem sufficient to explain the increase in financial failure, we look to two additional factors: the real-location of national wealth away from the middle of the middle class and the dramatic rise in consumer credit, especially credit cards.

The central paradox we address is the rise in middle-class financial failure in the midst of prosperity. The paradox is to some extent only apparent, because much of the middle class is not enjoying most of that prosperity. It is a cliche, but also a truth, that the top and the bottom of the income scale have done much better in the past twenty years than the middle class. To a large extent, the income side of debt-income ratios has remained almost stagnant for most middle-class people.

Our data fit together with a number of other sources to suggest strongly that greatly increased consumer debt is the crucial additional explanation for the great increase in economic distress leading to bankruptcy. Every financial problem confronting every family is made worse by an overlay of consumer debt. During the past decades, with a sharp rise since the mid-1980s, American families, collectively and individually, have increased their debt burdens, making themselves vulnerable to every other problem that may come their way. Any job loss can be devastating, but a working family can withstand a short time without a paycheck coming in or can adjust to a smaller check—if there is some flexibility in the weekly budget. But for every week of income that is committed to pay off last month's fast-food purchases and last year's nursery furniture, a family's chance of withstanding an economic collapse goes down. A divorce that divided $40,000 of income to support two households was painful, but much more manageable, in 1973 when the family owed about $250 in credit card debt. By 1998, when a similar family might owe about $11,500 in such debt, a trip to the divorce court would be much more likely to be accompanied by a second trip to the bankruptcy court. Medical debts of $10,000 can stagger any family, but when they are piled on top of $20,000 of credit card debt, the house of cards collapses. The same pattern is true for every problem, from the most catastrophic to the mildest. As more families carry more debt, the number of Americans ripe for financial implosion grows exponentially.

Our data show that the amount of unsecured debt that carries into bankruptcy as a proportion of peoples' income has stayed about the same. At the same time, that same ratio—unsecured, mostly installment debt as a percentage of income—has risen greatly in the general population. Thus it is reasonable to conclude that more people are reaching the "tip point" of debt-income ratios that leads many of them to file for bankruptcy. Why is this debt rising?

The most persuasive explanation, from our data and other sources, is the dramatic rise of the credit card. In the studies we report, the proportion of ordinary consumer debt incurred on credit cards carried into bankruptcy rose substantially from 1981 through 1991 to 1997. Although the ratio of total unsecured debt to incomes remained steady for the debtors in bankruptcy, the fraction of debt that was devoted to credit cards climbed sharply. From six weeks' worth of income in 1981 to six months' worth of income in 1991 to nine months' worth of income in 1997, the debtors in bankruptcy demonstrate that they follow the growing national trend to charge more and more of their expenses on credit cards.

In a world in which credit cards are rapidly taking over much of the world of unsecured credit (now used to pay department stores, drug stores, doctors, lawyers, and even the Internal Revenue Service), they stand surrogate for almost the whole universe of everyday consumer credit. Although big-ticket items, such as automobiles, are often financed by specialist companies and a fair number of loans, especially "consolidation" loans, are made by finance companies in the traditional way, there is

a strong push toward a day when all or most non-mortgage credit will revolve around credit cards and their issuers. Both in bankruptcy and out of bankruptcy, the credit card category is swallowing the entire consumer credit industry, so that speaking of "credit cards" comes closer to describing all consumer credit.

Technically, credit card debt is merely one category of consumer debt, along with the personal loans from finance companies and banks and the installment sales of cars, furniture, and appliances. But three characteristics of credit card debt make such debt very different from other consumer debt. First, the credit decision is different. Unlike traditional loans, credit card debt continues to be extended long after the initial application, at a time when the lender knows little about the borrower's current finances. Second, the borrowing decision is different. The debt itself is incurred a little bit at a time, so that even large amounts of debt do not involve a single, sober decision to take on $25,000 or even $2,500 of debt. And third, the payment schedules are different. The user may become ever more indebted while paying the minimum required every month exactly on time. Together the three characteristics suggest that credit card debt endangers the financial health of the middle class.

There has been much complaint about the fact that card issuers obtain relatively little information about consumers before issuing lines of credit of thousands of dollars. About half of all new solicitations are preapproved, indicating that the decision to extend credit has been made with no information other than a zip code or ordering preferences from certain mail order catalogues. Often creditors rely on "credit scores" obtained from credit agencies whose information is incomplete, dated, and often inaccurate. If the issuers do ask debtors for information, it is often no more than to name the current employer and state annual income, so they frequently have little idea of the consumer's existing obligations to other creditors. To a large extent, all they know is that the debtor has had an income of a certain amount and a payment record identified by a credit agency as good, fair, or poor.

Although lack of preissuance investigation is a serious problem, this complaint overlooks the more profound difference between traditional loans and credit card credit. Traditional loans are discrete, but a credit card invites a continuous flow of borrowing. The credit card issuer is like the lender in making some judgment at the start of the relationship but is very unlike the lender in that the bulk of the credit is actually extended at a later time—often years later. Most issuers, it appears, make little or no attempt to review the borrower's financial status after the initial issuance of the card except to raise the limit. The result is an absence of the credit judgment we have traditionally associated with lending, an almost complete disconnection between the circumstances of the borrower and the granting of the credit at the time it is granted. Modern credit has become like life insurance: after the initial exam, you keep the benefit as long as you pay the premium. For credit cards the premium is the minimum payment. The credit line is extended on an actuarial basis, like insurance. The issuer is lending to a category of people, most of whom will pay. Any individual borrower is a statistical black marble or a red one, suggests that asking how to fix the fragile state of the American middle class is to ask the wrong question. There is no fix. There is only a question about how a government should deal with the risks facing its citizens. For those who believe that the risk itself should be borne collectively rather than individually, the obvious answer is to increase the strength of the social safety net and restrict consumer lending. Bankruptcy laws can be rather modest, reserved only for the most extraordinary cases. For those who believe that the risk should be borne individually, however, consumer bankruptcy provides critical relief that heads off social unrest and keeps the maximum number of players in the economic game.

Bankruptcy is the ultimate free-market solution to bad debt. It forces individual creditors who made voluntary lending decisions to bear the costs of their bad credit decisions out of the profits from their good loans. So far, that part of the equation has worked extraordinarily well, with consumer lenders enjoying more than a decade of the lending industry's highest profits, despite writing off more bad loans than ever. Bankruptcy is the market-driven choice to deal with privatized, rather than socialized, risk. For the family facing financial collapse, however, a trip to the bankruptcy court may be considerably less attractive than standing in line at an unemployment office or using an identification card to obtain free medical care. Bankruptcy may be ameliorative, but it is not pleasant. The sting of losing is still sharply felt by those who must publicly declare that they are "bankrupt." Not all ways to deal with risk are equally attractive to the losers.

One of the redeeming paradoxes of this country is that a people so individualistic and so competitive nonetheless overwhelmingly identify themselves as members of a single class, the middle class. Some see it as glorious and some as boring, but it is within the perceived reach of nearly all citizens. A clerk and a secretary sharing a one-room apartment in Newark will give the same response to a question about class identification on a survey questionnaire as a hard-charging executive and a management consultant spouse in a fourteen-room manse in Grosse Pointe. The social reality may be considerably more complex, but the perception has a profound importance of its own.

One consequence of the Great Depression was a federal commitment to protect and extend this great, amorphous middle class. Literally hundreds of government programs, from housing subsidies and tax breaks to small business loans, were designed to further that end. Indeed, one way to describe the New Deal as a reaction to the Great Depression is that the federal government became committed to maintaining middle-class stability in the face of economic change and to expanding the ranks of the middle class to include as many Americans as possible. One way to describe the political direction of the country since the Reagan Revolution is the dismantling of that government structure in favor of one with more flexibility, more inequality, more opportunity, and more risk. On that basis, one inevitable cost can be seen to be the increased vulnerability of the American middle class to financial catastrophe.

There is no easy fix for the fragile middle class. As we opt for deregulation and higher profits, we also opt for higher rates of personal failure. The tradeoff is thrilling for some and offensive to others. At this juncture, we can do little more than understand that in every choice to deal with risk, a game that produces winners also produces losers, and that for every policy to encourage winning, there must be some thought about mechanisms to deal with losing. . . .

Bankruptcy is not merely the passive lens through which we might see the failure. It appropriately belongs near the center of the economic policy stage, offering itself as the treatment for those injured in a competitive, high-risk game. Correctly calibrating the kind and amount of bankruptcy treatment is central to the long-term survival of the always interesting, often dangerous American Experiment.

The Return of the Sweatshop

EDNA BONACICH AND RICHARD P. APPELBAUM

The apparel industry is probably the hardest industry the United States Department of Labor has ever faced.

Gerald M. Hall
District Director
U.S. Department of Labor

Where does the money from the sale of a $100 dress actually go? The wholesale cost of a $100 dress made in the United States is about $50; half of the $100 sales price goes to the retailer. Of the $50 wholesale cost, 45 percent, or $22.50, is spent by the manufacturer on the fabric. Twenty-five percent, or $12.50, is profit and overhead for the manufacturer. The remaining 30 percent, or $15, goes to the contractor, and covers both the cost of direct labor and the contractor's other expenses, and profit. Only 6 percent, $6, goes to the person who actually sewed the garment. Furthermore, this individual was more than likely to have been paid by the number of sewing operations performed than by the hour and to have received no benefits of any kind.

Sweatshops have indeed returned to the United States. A phenomenon of the apparel industry considered long past is back, not as a minor aberration, but as a prominent way of doing business. Every once in a while, an especially dramatic story hits the news: an Orange County family is found sewing in their home, where a seven-year-old child works next to his mother. Thai workers in El Monte are found in an apartment complex, held against their will under conditions of semi-enslavement while earning subminimum wages.

Source: Edna Bonacich and Richard P. Appelbaum. "The Return of the Sweatshop," in *Behind the Label: Inequality in the Los Angeles Apparel Industry,* Berkeley: University of California Press, 2000: 1–8. Used with permission of University of California Press.

Kathie Lee Gifford, celebrity endorser of a Wal-Mart label, discovers that her line is being produced in sweatshops both offshore and in the United States and cries in shame on national television. The United States Department of Labor develops a program to make apparel manufacturers take responsibility for sweatshop violations. The President of the United States establishes the Apparel Industry Partnership to see if a solution can be found to the growth of sweatshops here and abroad. The nation is becoming aware that the scourge of sweatshops has returned.

Sweatshops first emerged in the United States apparel industry in the last decades of the nineteenth century with the development of the mass production of garments in New York City. Immigrant workers, mainly young women, slaved for long hours over their sewing machines in cramped and unsanitary factories, for very low wages. Workers eventually rebelled. In 1909 a major strike by shirtwaist factory workers, sometimes called the uprising of the 20,000, was the first mass strike by women workers in the United States. (Shirtwaists, a style of women's blouse, were the first mass-produced fashion items.) It was followed by strikes in other sectors of the industry. In 1911 the infamous Triangle Shirtwaist factory fire in New York resulted in the deaths of 146 young garment workers, and provoked public outrage. Organized, militant, and supported by an aroused public, the workers founded the garment unions and demanded contracts that would protect them against sweatshop production. New Deal legislation reinforced basic standards of labor for workers and protected their right to join or form independent unions. A combination of government protection and strong apparel unions helped to relegate garment sweatshops to the margins of the industry until the 1970s, when they began to reappear.

What exactly is a "sweatshop"? A sweatshop is usually defined as a factory or a homework operation that engages in multiple violations of the law, typically the non-payment of minimum or overtime wages and various violations of health and safety regulations. According to this definition, many of the garment factories in Los Angeles are sweatshops. In a sample survey conducted by the United States Department of Labor in January 1998, 61 percent of the garment firms in Los Angeles were found to be violating wage and hour regulations. Workers were underpaid by an estimated $73 million dollars per year. Health and safety violations were not examined in that study, but in a survey completed in 1997, 96 percent of the firms were found to be in violation, 54 percent with deficiencies that could lead to serious injuries or death.

An emphasis merely on violations of the law fails to capture the full extent of what has been happening. In recent years the garment industry has been moving its production offshore to countries where workers earn much lower wages than are paid in the United States. In offshore production, some manufacturers may follow local laws, but the legal standard is so low that the workers, often including young teenagers, live in poverty, although they are working full time. The same problem arises in the United States. Even if a factory follows the letter of the law in every detail, workers may suffer abuse, job insecurity, and poverty. In 1990, according to the United States census, the average garment worker in Los Angeles made only $7,200, less than three-quarters of the poverty-level income for a family of three in that year. Thus we wish to broaden the definition of sweatshops to include factories that fail to pay a "living wage," meaning a wage that enables a family to support itself at a socially defined, decent standard of living. We include in the concept of a living wage the idea that people should be able to afford decent housing, given the local housing market, and that a family should be covered by health insurance. If wages fail to cover these minima, and if families with working members still fall below the official poverty line, they are, we claim, working in sweatshops.

Why are sweatshops returning to the apparel industry a number of decades after they had more or less disappeared? Why have their numbers grown so rapidly, especially in the last two decades of the twentieth century? And why has Los Angeles, in particular, become a center of garment sweatshops?

GLOBAL, FLEXIBLE CAPITALISM

The reemergence of apparel industry sweatshops is part of a much broader phenomenon, namely, the restructuring of global capitalism—a phenomenon we refer to as the new global capitalism. Starting in the 1970s, and accelerating rapidly especially in the 1980s and 1990s, the restructuring included a series of complex changes: a decline in the welfare state in most of the developed industrial countries; a growth in multinational corporations and an increase in global production; entry into manufacturing for export by many countries, among them some of the poorest in the world; a rise in world trade and intensification of competition; deindustrialization in the developed countries; a decrease in job security and an increase in part-time work; a rise in immigration from poorer countries to the richer ones; and renewed pressure on what remains of the welfare state.

These changes are all interconnected, and it is difficult to establish a first cause. Combined, they are associated with an effort by capitalists, supported by national governments, to increase profits and push back the effects of egalitarian movements that emerged in the 1960s and 1970s and that achieved some redistributive policies. The new global capitalism is characterized by an effort to let the free market operate with a minimum of government interference. At the same time, nations are themselves promoting the hegemony of the free market and imposing it as a standard for the entire world.

Among policies that foster the free market are the elimination of trade barriers and the encouragement of international free trade, as exemplified by the North American Free Trade Agreement (NAFTA) and the World Trade Organization (WTO); the insistence by strong states on the rights of their corporations to invest abroad with a minimum of local regulation; and pressure by state-backed, world financial institutions on developing countries that they restructure their political economies so as to foster free markets. Internal policies associated with the disestablishment of the welfare state have included deregulation, the privatization of state functions, and the minimization of state interference in business practices. In the United States, for example, affirmative action, welfare, and other efforts to increase equality through state intervention have come under attack.

The new global capitalism is often touted for its so-called flexibility. The decades of the 1980s and 1990s have been described as post-Fordist; i.e., we have moved beyond huge, mass-production plants making standardized products on the assembly line to a system in which smaller batches of specialized goods are made for an increasingly diverse consumer market. New systems of production, including contracting out the manufacture of specialized goods and services, and the ability to source goods and services wherever they can most efficiently be provided, enhance this flexibility. It is sometimes argued that the new, flexible production allows for more participation by the workers, by enabling them to develop several skills and encouraging them to use their initiative. Instead of repeating the same boring task, as did the workers on the Fordist assembly line, workers in the new factories may engage in more interesting, well-rounded activities. Critics have pointed out that,

while some workers may benefit from the new, flexible production arrangements, others face increased job insecurity, more part-time and temporary work, a greater likelihood of working for subcontractors, and less opportunity for unionization. Flexibility for the employer may lead to the expansion of the contingent labor force, which must shift around to find short-term jobs as they arise.

One of the starkest areas of social change in the post–welfare state period has been the attack on organized labor. In the United States, for example, during the postwar period of the late 1940s and continuing until the 1960s, an accommodation was reached between industries and trade unions, whereby both sides accepted that the unions would help to eliminate industrial warfare under a "social contract." The tacit agreement was simple: In exchange for union-demanded wages and benefits, workers would cede control over industrial production to management. The cost of this arrangement would be paid for in the marketplace, through higher prices for goods, rather than in narrower profit margins. This arrangement particularly benefited workers in large, oligopolistic industries, where unions were strong and profits were substantial. The entire economy was seen to benefit from this arrangement because the workers would have enough expendable income to buy the products, thereby stimulating production, creating more jobs, and generating a spiraling prosperity. Even though unions were never popular with business, the major industries, including the apparel industry, came to accept them and accept the fact that they made an important contribution to the well-being of the economy at large.

This view of organized labor has collapsed. Business leaders in the United States now see unions as having pushed the price of American labor too high, thereby limiting the competitiveness of firms that maintain a workforce in this country. Firms in certain industries have increasingly moved offshore to seek out low-wage labor in less developed countries. Business owners and managers also see unions as irrelevant to the new flexible systems of production. Unions grew strong in response to the Fordist production regimes, but with more decentralized systems of production, they are viewed as rigid and impractical. Besides, argue the owners and managers, more engaged and multiskilled workers no longer need union protection, as they share in a commitment to the firm's goals. Unions interfere with a company's flexibility and therefore hurt everyone, including the firm's employees.

Organized labor has been weakened by various federal policies, among them, President Ronald Reagan's dismissal of the air traffic controllers, the appointment of antiunion members to the National Labor Relations Board, the acceptance of the right of firms to hire permanent replacements for strikers, the passage of NAFTA without adequate protections for workers in any of the three countries involved, and the encouragement of offshore contracting by special tariff provisions. The development of flexible production, with its contracting out and dispersion of production around the globe, has also served to undermine unions because it is much more difficult to organize workers in a decentralized system. As a result, the proportion of the workforce that is unionized has dropped, not only in the United States, but also in other industrial countries: in the United States from a high of 37 percent in 1946 to less than 15 percent of the total workforce in 1995, and only 11 percent of the private sector workforce. These figures are much lower than for the rest of the industrial world.

Another significant aspect of the new global economy has been the rise of immigration from the less developed to the industrialized countries. Local economies have been disrupted by the arrival of multinational corporations, and many people see no alternative but to seek a means of survival elsewhere. The involvement of the more developed countries in the economies and governments of the Third World is not a new phenomenon, and it has long been associated with emigration. The countervailing movements of capital and labor in opposite directions have often been noted.

What is new about the recent phase of global capitalism is the accelerated proletarianization of much of the world's remaining peasantry. Young women, in particular, have been drawn into the labor force to become the main workers in plants that engage in manufacturing for export. In many ways they are the ideal workforce, as they frequently lack the experience and alternatives that would enable them to demand higher wages and better treatment. The poor working conditions are exacerbated by political regimes, often supported by the United States, that have restricted the workers' ability to organize and demand change.

The increased exploitation of workers in the Third World has a mirror image in the movement of immigrant workers to the more developed countries. Immigrants come not only because of economic dislocations that arise, in part, from the presence of foreign capital in their homelands, but also because of political struggles that have ensued in connection with the Cold War and its aftermath. A paradox of the new global capitalism is that, although the right of capital to move freely is touted by the supporters of the free market, no such right is afforded labor. Immigration is restricted by state policies. One consequence has been the creation of so-called illegal workers, who are stripped of many basic legal rights. Immigrant workers, especially the undocumented, are more easily exploited than are native workers.

In sum, there has been a shift in the balance of power between capital and labor. Although the working class, including women and people of color, made important gains during the three postwar decades (from the late 1940s through the early 1970s), a backlash began developing in the 1970s and achieved full momentum by the 1980s. This backlash corresponds closely to the "great U-turn" in the United States and other capitalist economies, as a broadly shared postwar rise in living standards came to a halt. Conservative governments in the United States and Europe have implemented policies that favor capital and the free market over labor and other disadvantaged groups. Even political parties that have traditionally supported the working class, such as the Democrats in the United States and the Labour Party in Britain, have shifted to the right.

The reappearance of sweatshops is a feature of the new global, flexible capitalism. The original sweatshops disappeared with the growth of unions and the development of the welfare state. Today, with both of those institutions weakened, markets have been able to drive down wages and reduce working conditions to substandard levels in many labor-intensive industries, such as electronics, toys, shoes, and sports equipment. Indeed, almost every manufacturing industry and some services are pressed to reduce labor costs by minimizing job stability, by contracting out, by using more contingent (part-time and temporary) workers, by reducing benefits, and by attacking unions. But the apparel industry is leading the way.

The Proximate Causes
of Employment Discrimination*

BARBARA F. RESKIN

High on the agenda of sociology is to understand the origins and consequences of inequality. This understanding is potentially one of our important contributions to public policy. Examples of such sociological research topics include access to quality education, welfare "reform" and poverty, and the amount of job competition between immigrants and native-born low-wage workers. In this essay, which focuses on gender and race/ethnic discrimination in the workplace, I argue that the standard sociological approaches to explaining workplace discrimination have not been very fruitful in producing knowledge that can be used to eradicate job discrimination. If sociological research is to contribute to the battle against injustice, we need to direct more attention to how inequality is produced. In the following pages, I suggest that research findings from our sister discipline, social psychology, can help us understand both the original and the proximate causes of employment discrimination. This (sometimes interdisciplinary) approach that distinguishes original and proximate causes may be useful and even necessary in other specialty areas where sociologists seek to create a more just society.

In the twentieth century, most sociologists concerned with reducing employment discrimination assumed that once we demonstrated that discrimination persisted, our evidence would find its way to policymakers who would eradicate this discrimination. Thus, sociologists and other social scientists developed a variety of innovative techniques to assess the extent of employment discrimination. Researchers conducted sophisticated analyses establishing race and gender disparities in various employment outcomes, net of qualifications; confirmed through surveys employers' aversion to hiring people of color (Kirschenman and Neckerman 1991; Bobo, Oliver, Valenzuela, and Johnson 2000); and designed ingenious ways to estimate the prevalence of discriminatory treatment (Fix and Struyk 1993; Blumrosen, Bendick, Miller, and Blumrosen 1998). In terms of our policy impact, however, we might have spent our time better in counseling labor market entrants or working as human resource specialists. If we want to use sociology to reduce discrimination in the twenty-first century, we need to move beyond demonstrating that employment discrimination exists, and investigate why it persists in work organizations. To do this, we need to expand our conceptualization of discrimination to recognize that it occurs as a result of nonconscious cognitive processes, as well as from the deliberate negative treatment of people of color and white women.

The prominent sociological explanations for discrimination at the beginning of the new century are grounded in conflict theory (e.g., Blumer 1958;

*These ideas benefited from the comments of Lowell Hargens and William Bielby and of the *Contemporary Sociology* editors and editorial board members. I was also helped by talking with Marilynn Brewer. Any logical or factual errors are entirely my responsibility.

Source: Barbara Reskin, "The Proximate Causes of Employment Discrimination," *Contemporary Sociology*. Vol. 29, No. 2, March, 2000 319–328.

Blalock 1967, 1982; Reskin 1988; Martin 1992; Jackman 1994; Tomaskovic-Devey 1993; Tilly 1998). According to a conflict-theory perspective, the beneficiaries of systems of inequality protect their privileges by using the resources they control to exclude members of subordinate groups. Thus, these theories explain discrimination in terms of the strategic, self-interested actions by members of privileged groups who intentionally exclude and exploit subordinate-group members to protect or advance their own interests. However, conflict-theoretic approaches to discrimination are deficient in important respects. Most important, they do not identify the specific processes through which group motives give rise to outcomes that preserve group interests, and they cannot explain the variation in employment discrimination across contemporary workplaces.[1] As a result, they have not proven fruitful in identifying remedying mechanisms.

I should note that most of my past research assumes that intergroup competition prompts dominant groups to discriminate against members of subordinate groups. I remain convinced that this theoretical perspective accurately characterizes the behavior of some people. But intergroup conflict is not the only source of discrimination, or even the most important one. By conceptualizing discrimination as the result of conflict-based behavior, we cannot identify the proximate causes of discrimination that results from other processes. In sum, I argue that the theoretical approach that many sociologists embrace intellectually has not generated explanatory models of the causes of employment discrimination. If our goal in studying discrimination is to discover how to reduce it, conflict theories are not particularly fruitful in helping us to understand *why* discrimination occurs regularly in tens of thousands of work organizations.

In this essay, I argue that we should turn our attention to *how* as well as *why* discrimination occurs, and I propose that social cognition theory can answer both these questions. I make two

claims. First, although some employment discrimination results from people pursuing their group-based interests or prejudices, much discrimination stems from normal cognitive processes (the subject of social cognition theory) that occur regardless of individuals' motives.[2] Second, the *proximate cause* of most discrimination is whether and how personnel practices in work organizations constrain the biasing effects of these automatic cognitive processes.

In brief, social cognition theory holds that people automatically categorize others into ingroups and outgroups. The visibility and cultural importance of sex and race and their role as core bases of stratification make them almost automatic bases of categorization.[3] Having categorized others, people tend to automatically "feel, think, and behave toward [particular members of the category] the same way they . . . feel, think, and behave toward members of that social category more generally" (Fiske, Lin, and Neuberg 1999). Importantly, categorization is accompanied by stereotyping, attribution bias, and evaluation bias. These, in turn, introduce sex, race, and ethnic biases into our perceptions, interpretations, recollections, and evaluations of others. These biases are cognitive rather than motivational; in other words, they occur independently of decision makers' group interests or their conscious desire to favor or harm others (Krieger 1995: 1188).

The expected outcomes of these habitual cognitive processes are race and sex discrimination. But discrimination is not inevitable. Organizational arrangements can activate or suppress social psychological and cognitive processes (Baron and Pfeffer 1994: 191). We cannot rid work organizations of discrimination until we recognize both that much employment discrimination originates in automatic cognitive processes, and that it occurs because of work organizations' personnel practices.

---

[1] In addition, they do not generate research hypotheses that are falsifiable.

[2] In describing these processes as "normal," I mean only that normal mental functioning requires cognitive simplification.
[3] In this essay I use the term *race* as shorthand for race, color, ethnicity, and national origin.

Sociologists' knowledge of social and organizational behavior qualifies us for this task. After summarizing the cognitive processes that produce employment discrimination, I propose that sociology in the twenty-first century should examine how employment practices mediate whether these processes give rise to discriminatory outcomes.

SOCIAL COGNITION PROCESSES AS THE EXOGENOUS CAUSES OF DISCRIMINATION

A large body of research in cognitive psychology suggests that to cope in a complex and demanding environment, people are "cognitive misers" who economize by through categorization, ingroup preference, stereotyping, and attribution bias (Fiske 1998: 362). These processes, sometimes characterized as cognitive "short-cuts," occur regardless of people's feelings toward other groups or their desires to protect or improve their own status (Fiske 1998: 364).[4] If unchecked, they can produce outcomes that "perpetrators" neither intend nor recognize.

SOCIAL CATEGORIZATION

The categorization of people into ingroups and outgroups is a rapid, automatic, nonconscious process. By conserving cognitive resources, automatic categorization helps people manage an enormous volume of incoming stimuli (Fiske 1998: 364, 375). In keeping with cognitive impulses toward efficiency, categorization into in- and outgroups often is based on sex and race because of their widespread availability as "master statuses" that have long been the bases for differential treatment (Hughes 1945).[5] However, I propose that it is primarily through categorization and its concomitants that sex and race are bases for unequal treatment.

Inherent in the categorization of people into in- and outgroups is the tendency to exaggerate between-group differences, while minimizing within-group differences, especially among members of the outgroup. (An example of this is the phenomenon: "I know an X [outgroup category] said it, but I can't remember which X" [Fiske 1998: 372]). Conceptually, social categorization resembles the sociological concept of differentiation, but each plays a different role in theoretical accounts of discrimination. While a social psychological perspective sees categorization as automatic and not necessarily group-serving, sociologists view differentiation as a fundamental mechanism of stratification through which dominant groups preserve their privileged position (e.g., to divide and conquer [Edwards 1988]).

INGROUP PREFERENCE

Categorization is more than a data-reduction device that our brains use to deal with the barrage of stimuli to which they are exposed. Classifying people into ingroups and outgroups leads more or less automatically to distorted perceptions and biased evaluation of ingroup and outgroup members, and hence to discrimination (Brewer and Brown 1998). In- versus outgroup membership defines the pool of others to whom people are attracted, with whom they seek equal treatment, and who serve as their reference group (Baron and Pfeffer 1994). In general, people are more comfortable with, have more trust in, hold more positive views of, and feel more obligated to members of their own group (Perdue, Dovidio, Gurtman, and Tyler 1990). As a result, people try to avoid outgroup members, and they favor ingroup members in evaluations and rewards (Brewer and Brown 1998: 567; Fiske 1998: 361). Thus, at least in the lab, the unequal treatment

---

[4]For a demonstration, take the Implicit Association Tests for racism, sexism, and ageism at www.yale.edu//implicit// (Greenwald and Banaji 1999).

[5]Ridgeway (1997) offers a related analysis. While she concurs with the psychologists whose work I cite on the importance of categorization, she construes categorization as an emergent property of interaction. Although she does not address the effect of sex categorization except through interactional processes, her conclusions on the consequences of categorization resemble some of those reviewed here. She also provides a useful account of the effect of gender categorization on gender status beliefs.

associated with group membership results more often from ingroup preference than outgroup antipathy.

Given white men's predominance in many workplaces, minorities' and white women's status as outgroup members probably contributes to the devaluation of jobs that are predominantly female and predominantly minority. This account of devaluation suggests that we should observe the overvaluation of men's and whites' activities in settings in which men and whites are the ingroup as a job-level phenomenon.

STEREOTYPING

Stereotypes are unconscious habits of thought that link personal attributes to group membership. Stereotyping is an inevitable concomitant of categorization: As soon as an observer notices that a "target" belongs to a stereotyped group (especially an outgroup), characteristics that are stereotypically linked to the group are activated in the observer's mind, *even among people who consciously reject the stereotypes* (Bodenhausen, Macrae, and Garst 1998). To appreciate the importance of stereotyping for discriminatory outcomes, it is helpful to distinguish descriptive and prescriptive stereotypes.

Descriptive stereotypes, which characterize how group members *are,* influence how we perceive others and interpret their behavior. Descriptive stereotyping can precipitate discrimination because it predisposes observers toward interpretations that conform to stereotypes and blinds them to disconfirming possibilities (Fiske 1998: 367), especially when the behavior that observers must make sense of is subject to multiple interpretations (e.g., she worked late because women are helpful, rather than she worked late because she wants a promotion). Thus, descriptive stereotypes distort observers' impressions of the behavior of members of stereotyped groups.

Prescriptive stereotypes are generalizations about how members of a group *are supposed to be,* based usually on descriptive stereotypes of how they are. These normative stereotypes serve as standards against which observers evaluate others'

behavior. Both descriptive and prescriptive stereotypes influence what we remember about others and the inferences we draw about their behavior (Heilman 1995: 6). Thus, stereotypes serve as "implicit theories, biasing in predictable ways the perception, interpretation, encoding, retention, and recall of information about other people" (Krieger 1995: 1188).

The cognitive processes involved in stereotyping make stereotypes tenacious. People unconsciously pursue, prefer, and remember "information" that supports their stereotypes (including remembering events that did not occur), and ignore, discount, and forget information that challenges them (Fiske 1998). From the standpoint of social cognition theory, stereotypes are adaptive: People process information that conforms to their stereotypes more quickly than inconsistent information, and they are more likely to stereotype when they are under time pressure, partly because stereotyping conserves mental resources (Fiske 1998: 366; Fiske et al. 1999: 244). Research on people's efforts to suppress stereotypes is relevant.[6] In one study, subjects instructed to avoid sexist statements in a sentence-completion task could comply when they had enough time, but when they had to act quickly the statements they constructed were more sexist than those of subjects who had not been told to avoid making sexist statements. And according to a comparison of subjects who were and were not instructed to suppress stereotypes, the former could refrain from expressing stereotypes, but in a "rebound effect," they expressed stronger stereotypes in subsequent judgments than did subjects who had not tried to suppress their stereotypes in the first place (Bodenhausen et al. 1998: 326).

EVALUATION BIAS
AND ATTRIBUTION BIAS

Stereotype-based expectations and ingroup favoritism act as distorting lenses through which

---

[6]When "attentional resources" are limited, stereotyping increases (Fiske et al. 1999: 237).

observers assess others' performance and account for their successes and failures (Crocker, Major, and Steele 1998: 539). Descriptive stereotypes affect observers' expectations and hence the explanations they construct. When the actions of others conform to our expectations, we tend to attribute their behavior to *stable, internal* propensities (e.g., ability), while we attribute actions that are inconsistent with our stereotype-based expectations to *situational* (i.e., external) or *transient* factors (e.g., task difficulty, luck, or effort). In this way, stereotype-based expectations give rise to biased attributions. For example, given the stereotype that men are good at customarily male tasks, competent performance by men doesn't require an explanation; men's failures do, however, and observers tend to attribute these unexpected outcomes to situational factors such as bad luck or lack of effort, none of which predict future failure. In contrast, women are stereotypically not expected to do well at customarily male endeavors, so explaining their failure is easy: They lack the requisite ability (an internal trait) and hence are likely to fail in the future. In contrast, their successes are unexpected, so they must have resulted from situational factors that do not predict future success (Swim and Sanna 1996; Brewer and Brown 1998: 560).

Ingroup preference and outgroup derogation lead to similar attribution processes. Because observers expect ingroup members to succeed and outgroup members to fail, they attribute ingroup success and outgroup failure to internal factors, and ingroup failure and outgroup success to situational factors. Observers also tend to characterize behavior that is consistent with their expectations in abstract terms and unexpected behavior in concrete terms. For example, given the same act—arriving late for a meeting—an observer would recall that an ingroup member was delayed, but that an outgroup member is a tardy person. Once a behavior has been interpreted and encoded into memory, it is the interpretation, not the initial behavior, to which people have ready access (Krieger 1995: 1203).

Thus, observers would predict that the outgroup member, but not the ingroup member, would be tardy in the future.

POWER AND COGNITIVE BIASES

Up to this point, I have treated discrimination motivated by status politics or antipathy and discrimination that results automatically from unconscious cognitive processes as if they were mutually exclusive. Although cognition researchers have given relatively little attention to their relationship, a handful of experimental studies indicate that power differentials condition these cognitive processes. These studies have shown that although the propensity to categorize is universal, occupying a position of power may prompt people to invest extra effort into categorizing others (Goodwin, Operario, and Fiske 1998). In addition, power affects the degree to which people act on the propensity to stereotype. People can't afford to stereotype others on whom they depend because they need to assess them accurately, but they can afford to stereotype subordinate groups and are more likely do so than subordinate group members are to stereotype members of dominant groups (Fiske et al. 1999: 241). In addition, under conditions of perceived threat, the more stake observers have in the status quo, and hence the more to lose, the more likely they are to stereotype outgroups (Operario, Goodwin, and Fiske 1998: 168). The sense of entitlement that accompanies dominant-group status is likely to give dominant group members particular confidence in their stereotypes. This propensity is reinforced by the fact that powerful observers actively seek information that confirms their stereotypes and disregard disconfirming information. However, priming the powerful with egalitarian values leads them to pay closer attention to information that contradicts outgroup stereotypes (Operario et al. 1998: 172–73). Finally, members of high-status ingroups show more bias in favor of ingroup members than do members of low-status ingroups (Brewer and Brown 1998: 570).

THE PROXIMATE CAUSES
OF DISCRIMINATION

According to social cognition theory, bias and discrimination result from the individual-level cognitive processes summarized above. Cognitive psychologists agree, however, that these biases can be controlled (Fiske 1998: 375). Thus, the proximate causes of discrimination are the contextual factors that permit or counter the effects of these habits of the brain. The course I urge for sociology in the twenty-first century is to investigate how organizational practices can check these factors. Experimental research on contextual factors that appear to minimize the likelihood of stereotyping and its biasing effects provides a starting point for this enterprise. These factors include constructing heterogeneous groups, creating interdependence among ingroup and outgroup members, minimizing the salience of ascribed status dimensions in personnel decisions, replacing subjective data with objective data, and making decision makers accountable for their decisions.

Of course, organizations' ability to apply the findings from experimental research to the exogenous causes of discrimination depends on the external validity of the experimental results described above. Work organizations are vastly more complex than laboratory experiments. In particular, work organizations are hothouses that nurture power and status differences. Thus, the first task for sociologists—perhaps in collaboration with social psychologists—is to determine whether the cognitive processes that I have reviewed operate the same way in work organizations as they do in the lab.[7] If they do, the next step is to investigate the proximate causes of employment discrimination: the social, contextual, and organizational mechanisms that suppress or exacerbate these exogenous causes. Below I summarize the experimental research. I hope readers view this summary as a set of propositions that specify how organizations can prevent

nonconscious cognitive processes from culminating in employment discrimination.

HETEROGENEITY OF WORK GROUPS

Categorization is too fundamental to cognitive processing to be prevented, and ingroup favoritism is remarkably hard to eradicate, even for people with a material stake in ending it (Brewer and Brown 1998: 566). But organizations can discourage the categorization of people based on their sex, race, and ethnicity, and thus reduce sex and race discrimination. Creating work groups and decision-making groups that are heterogeneous with respect to these ascriptive characteristics should suppress ingroup preference and outgroup derogation, stereotyping, and concomitant bias personnel decisions. (In addition, if neither ingroup nor outgroup members numerically dominate decision-making groups, personnel outcomes are less likely to be linked to group membership.)

Of course, organizations whose work groups are well integrated by sex and race are not the ones in which discrimination is a serious problem. Organizations in which work groups are segregated may be able to create superordinate identities (i.e., more inclusive ingroups) that are independent of sex and race (Brewer and Brown 1998: 583). In laboratory experiments, researchers can artificially create categories to which subjects become attached, even on the most trivial basis, so workers should be receptive to recategorization based on characteristics that are contextually salient (Fiske 1998: 361). Organizations may be able to create such categories by using existing functional categories that are relevant and hence cognitively available to workers, or they may be able to create new categories that supplant ascriptively defined categories as the basis for the cognitive processes discussed here. Among possible bases of categorization are teams, divisions or branches, job groups, and the organization itself.[8]

---

[7]Bielby (2000) believes they should be even stronger in work organizations than in laboratory experiments.

[8]Of course, for these categories to supplant sex- and race-based categorization, category membership cannot be associated with sex or race.

With respect to the last of these, the more organizations emphasize organizational culture, the easier it should be to expand the ingroup to encompass all employees. Organizations can maximize the impact of heterogeneous groupings by reinforcing ingroup identification through task interdependence, job rotation, and other collective activities. Sociology should place high on its agenda for the twenty-first century a study of organizations' ability to minimize ascriptively based categorization by emphasizing other categories and the impact of such re-engineered groups on stereotypes and attribution bias.

INTERDEPENDENCE

Intergroup contact that exposes people to individuating information about outgroup members challenges outgroup stereotypes, and hence should reduce bias. But for intergroup contact to change ingroup members' perceptions, the latter must attend to information about outgroup members (Goodwin et al. 1998: 681). The conditions that should foster such attention are enumerated in the contact hypothesis. This hypothesis argues that intergroup contact alters ingroup members' attitudes only if the groups come together with a common goal, have institutional support for their joint enterprise, and have close and sustained contact in equal-status positions (Brewer and Brown 1998: 576–78).

The logic of the contact hypothesis assumes that ingroup members' interdependence with outgroup members encourages the former to notice counter-stereotypic information about the latter and thus to form more individuated and accurate impressions.[9] By the same logic, ingroup members' dependence on outgroup members should motivate the former to seek accurate information about the latter. Based on this expected association, Goodwin and his colleagues (1998: 694) contended that supervisors who know that their salaries depend on their subordinates' productivity or evaluations will judge their subordinates more accurately.

Intergroup competition based on status characteristics is counterproductive because it encourages each group to stereotype the other. Fiske and her colleagues (1999: 241–42) speculated that this happens because group members devote most of their available cognitive resources to obtaining accurate information about their teammates, rather than about their opponents.[10] Thus, cooperative interdependence can reduce stereotyping, while competitive interdependence increases it.

SALIENCE

Anything that focuses observers' attention on a stereotyped category "primes" stereotyping, and it does so without the observer's awareness (Heilman 1995; Fiske 1998: 366). For example, men who were primed with stereotypic statements about women were more likely to ask a female job applicant "sexist" questions and exhibit sexualized behavior (and it took them longer than non-primed men to recognize nonsexist words; Fiske et al. 1999). Thus, a comment about pregnancy, a sex discrimination lawsuit, or diversity immediately before a committee evaluates a female job candidate is likely to exacerbate sex stereotyping in the evaluation (Heilman 1995). The process of priming may mean that injunctions to a search committee to look closely at female or minority candidates can backfire, tainting the evaluations of women and minorities. Similarly, when women and men are interacting and gender is relevant to purpose of the interaction, cultural gender stereotypes become "effectively salient" (Ridgeway

---

[9]Workers may initially resist these collective arrangements, however. In addition, when the context changes, the former groupings are likely to re-emerge (Brewer and Brown 1998: 582–83). In other words, intergroup contact is not a quick fix; it makes a difference only when it occurs through a permanent transformation of the workplace.

[10]Interpersonal (i.e., one-on-one) competition reduces stereotyping, because competitors' success depends on having accurate information about their opponent.

[11]As Ridgeway (1997: 221) observed, the diffuse nature of sex stereotypes makes them relevant in many situations.

1997: 221).[11] Organizational contexts can also make category membership salient. A highly skewed sex or race composition in a work group is likely to activate stereotypes (Bodenhausen et al. 1998: 317).

FORMALIZED EVALUATION SYSTEMS

Stereotyping and its concomitants distort how we interpret the behavior of outgroups, and the vaguer the information to which we are responding, the more subject it is to misinterpretation. In work settings, this means that recollections and evaluations that are based on unstructured observations are particularly vulnerable to race or sex bias (Fiske, Bersoff, Borgida, Deaux, and Heilman 1991). Organizations should be able to minimize race and sex bias in personnel decisions by using objective, reliable, and timely information that is directly relevant to job performance (Heilman 1995). For objective measures to minimize intergroup bias, organizations must provide a detailed specification of all performance criteria along with precise information for each candidate for each criterion (Krieger 1995: 1246). Employers should further reduce attribution errors by routinely collecting concrete performance data and implementing evaluation procedures in which evaluators rely exclusively on these data *without attributions* explaining them.

ACCOUNTABILITY

The biasing effects of stereotypes and other cognitive distortions on evaluative judgments are reduced when decision makers know that they will be held accountable for the criteria they use to make decisions and for the accuracy of the information upon which they base their decisions (Salancik and Pfeffer 1978; Tetlock 1992; Tetlock and Lerner 1999).[12] If evaluators know that they will be held accountable for their judgments before

being exposed to the information on which they will base their judgment, accountability not only reduces the expression of biases, it also reduces bias in nonconscious cognitive processes, such as the encoding of information (Tetlock 1992). The benefits of accountability vanish under time pressure, however (Tetlock and Lerner 1999). Indeed, time pressure, mental "busyness," and information overload—all common in contemporary work organizations—exacerbate the effects of stereotypes on judgment and memory (Bodenhausen et al. 1998: 319).

The processes underlying the importance of accountability no doubt help explain how antidiscrimination and affirmative action laws and regulations increase job access for people of color and white women. Goals, timetables, and monitoring—all effective affirmative action mechanisms—hold organizations responsible for sex- and race-balanced hiring and the sex and race composition of their job assignments (Reskin 1998). Hypothetically, organizations can achieve similar results through programs that make decision makers at all levels responsible for ensuring that their decisions are not tainted by ingroup preference and for the outcomes of those decisions.

CONCLUSIONS

All common social scientific theories of discrimination, as well as the dominant legal approach to discrimination (Krieger 1995, 1998), locate its source in intrapsychic processes such as prejudice, ignorance, the sense of threat, and the desire to maintain or improve one's position. They differ, however, in whether they view the consequences of intrapsychic processes as motivated or automatic. Theories that assume that discrimination is motivated by antipathy toward or fear of another group view discrimination as an aberration within a generally fair reward system (Black 1989). According to social cognition theory, in contrast, the basic cognitive processes through which everyone's brain sorts through data distort all our perceptions, bias all our attributions, and induce all of us to favor

---

[12]See DiTomaso (1993) for a description of Xerox's successful use of accountability.

ingroup members. *Laissez-faire* decision making in work organizations—and other domains, including schools, voluntary organizations, and the family—transforms these biases into discrimination against outgroup members. If the cognitive processes that lead to discrimination are universal, as experimental evidence suggests, then they cause a huge amount of employment discrimination that is neither intended nor motivated by conscious negative feelings toward outgroups. And the organizational practices that determine how the input of individuals contribute to personnel decisions, and hence precipitate, permit, or prevent the activation of cognitive biases, are the proximate causes of most employment discrimination.

Although I and others suspect that most employment discrimination originates in the cognitive processes I have summarized, we should not lose sight of the fact that discrimination also results from conscious actions that are motivated by ignorance, prejudice, or the deliberate efforts by dominant group members to preserve their privileged status. Twentieth-century sociology has focused on these conscious processes of exploitation and exclusion, as well as on structures that preserve a discriminatory status quo.[13] This approach assumes that dominant group members intentionally create work structures and organizational arrangements whose purpose is to preserve or enhance their position. Among many examples I could offer is the widespread and deliberate exclusion of minorities and women from police and fire departments (Chetkovich 1997; also see Reskin 2000). When people's group position motivates them to discriminate, exclusionary organizational practices are *superficial* causes of discrimination, and they require different interventions.[14] Organizations, I have argued, can reduce discrimination issuing from nonconscious cognitive processes. Remedying discrimination that results from dominant group members' deliberate construction of exclusionary personnel practices will require race- and gender-conscious interventions, including formal charges of sex-/race-based discrimination, collective action organized on the basis of status groups,[15] or intervention by regulatory agencies, including sex- and race-conscious remedial affirmative action.

The same characteristics—sex, race, ethnicity—are the primary bases of both automatic cognitive categorization and social stratification; indeed, their centrality in each process reinforces them in the other process. Moreover, automatic cognitive categorization and race- or sex-based social stratification have the same result: privileging ingroup members who are usually white males of European ancestry. Moreover, both cognitive-based and conflict-group-based processes comprise "countless small acts by a changing cast of characters, . . . that incrementally and consistently limit the employment prospects of one group of workers compared with those of another" (Nelson and Bridges 1999: 243). Individually, either process leads to the accumulation of advantages and disadvantages. Sometimes both cognitive biases and prejudice- or conflict-based discrimination are at work, with reinforcing effects. Ridgeway's (1997: 227) analysis illustrates this with respect to gender: "Only occasionally will gender be so salient in the situation that men will act self-consciously as men to preserve their interests[, but] the repeated background activation of gender status over many workplace interactions, biasing behavior in subtle or more substantial degrees, produces the effect of men acting in their gender interest, even when many men feel no special loyalty to their sex."

---

[13]At least one social psychological theory, "realistic group conflict" theory, attributes discrimination to group conflict (Brewer and Brown 1998: 565).

[14]For discussion of superficial causes, see Lieberson (1985) or Reskin (1988).

[15]For example, in challenging intentional, bias-based racial discrimination by Shoney's Restaurants, the NAACP Legal Defense Fund publicized an 800 number for complaints against Shoney's, generating both the basis for a class action lawsuit and supporting evidence from white supervisory employees who supported the lawsuit (Watkins 1993).

As I said above, some members of the dominant group actively discriminate against people based on their race, sex, national origin, as well as other characteristics such as age, sexual orientation, weight, and religion. Here I have questioned the assumption that I and many other sociologists brought to the study of workplace inequality in the twentieth century: that most discrimination results from the purposive actions by dominant group members who seek to preserve and expand their privileges. While dominant group members benefit from such discrimination, the salience of race and sex in contemporary society and in cognitive processes such as categorization and stereotyping allows most dominant group members to benefit without their having to take any action. By assuming that discrimination is largely the result of purposive action, we are on the wrong track for reducing discrimination. Plaintiffs routinely lose discrimination lawsuits because they cannot prove that their employer intended to discriminate against them (for examples, see Krieger 1995; Reskin 2000).[16] And employers, who share our view that discrimination involves deliberate attempts to harm people because of their status, find discrimination charges implausible and reject them out of hand. The recognition that discrimination often stems from universal cognitive processes may make organizations less resistant to charges of discrimination and more receptive to modifying their employment practices to remove the effect of cognitive biases against people of color and white women.

Sociology's history of trying to expose, understand, and reduce discrimination is to our discipline's credit. Most of our progress in the last several decades of the twentieth century has been in documenting discrimination's extent and persistence. We have made less headway in understanding its persistence and very little in figuring out how to reduce it because we have not correctly theorized

how or why discrimination occurs. I have argued that much of it results from nonconscious cognitive processes. If I'm right, then its proximate cause is the organizational practices that permit or prevent it. Exactly how and when organizations contain the effects of cognitive biases should be high on the discipline's agenda for the twenty-first century.

REFERENCES

Baron, James N. and Jeffrey Pfeffer. 1994. "The Social Psychology of Organizations and Inequality." *Social Psychology Quarterly 57:* 190–209.

Bielby, William T. 2000. "How to Minimize Workplace Gender and Racial Bias." *Contemporary Sociology* 29: 120–29.

Black, Donald. 1989. *Sociological Justice.* New York: Oxford University Press.

Blalock, Hubert M. 1967. *Toward a Theory of Minority-Group Relations.* New York: Wiley.

———. 1982. *Race and Ethnic Relations.* Englewood Cliffs, NJ: Prentice Hall.

Blumer, Herbert. 1958. "Race Prejudice as a Sense of Group Position." *Pacific Sociological Review* 1: 3–7.

Blumrosen, Alfred W., Marc Bendick, John J. Miller, and Ruth Blumrosen. 1998. "Employment Discrimination against Women in Washington State, 1997." Employment Discrimination Project Report Number 3. Newark, NJ: Rutgers University School of Law.

Bobo, Larry D., Melvin L. Oliver, A. Valenzuela, and J. H. Johnson. 2000. *Prismatic Metropolis: Race, Segregation and Inequality in Los Angeles.* New York: Russell Sage Foundation.

Bodenhausen, Galen V., C. Neil Macrae, and Jennifer Garst. 1998. "Stereotypes in Thought and Deed: Social-Cognitive Origins of Intergroup Discrimination." Pp. 311–35 in *Intergroup Cognition and Intergroup Behavior,* edited by Constantine Sedikides, John Schopler, and Chester A. Insko. Mahwah, NJ: Lawrence Erlbaum Associates.

Brewer, Marilyn B. and Rupert J. Brown. 1998. "Intergroup Relations." Pp. 554–94 in *Handbook of Social Psychology,* edited by D. T. Gilbert, S. T. Fiske, and G. Lindzey. New York: McGraw-Hill.

Chetkovich, C. 1997. *Real Heat: Gender and Race in the Urban Fire Service.* New Brunswick, NJ: Rutgers University Press.

Crocker, Jennifer, Brenda Major, and Claude Steele. 1998. "Social Stigma." Pp. 504–53 in *Handbook of Social Psychology,* edited by D. T. Gilbert, S. T. Fiske, and G. Lindzey. New York: McGraw-Hill.

DiTomaso, Nancy. 1993. Notes on Xerox Case: Balanced Work Force at Xerox. Unpublished.

Edwards, Richard. 1979. *Contested Terrain.* New York: Basic Books.

---

[16]For a discussion of the legal limitations associated with the standard conception of discrimination as actions intended to harm people based on their sex, race, or color, see Krieger (1995).

Fiske, Susan T. 1998. "Stereotyping, Prejudice and Discrimination." Pp. 357–411 in *Handbook of Social Psychology,* edited by D. T. Gilbert, S. T. Fiske, and G. Lindzey. New York: McGraw-Hill.

Fiske, Susan T., Donald N. Bersoff, Eugene Borgida, Kay Deaux, and Madeline E. Heilman. 1991. "Social Science Research on Trial. Use of Sex Stereotyping Research in Price Waterhouse v. Hopkins." *American Psychologist* 46: 1049–60.

Fiske, Susan T., Monica Lin, and Steven L. Neuberg. 1999. "The Continuum Model: Ten Years Later." Pp. 231–54 in *Dual Process Theories in Social Psychology,* edited by Shelly Chaiken and Yaacov Trope. New York: Guilford Press.

Fix, Michael and Raymond J. Struyk, eds. 1993. *Clear and Convincing Evidence. Measurement of Discrimination in America.* Washington, DC: Urban Institute.

Goodwin, Stephanie A., Don Operario, and Susan T. Fiske. 1998. "Situational Power and Interpersonal Dominance Facilitate Bias and Inequality." *Journal of Social Issues* 54: 677–98.

Greenwald, Anthony and Mahzarin Banaji. 1999. "Implicit Association Test." *www.yale.edu/implicit/*.

Heilman, M. E. 1995. "Sex Stereotypes and Their Effects in the Workplace: What We Know and What We Don't Know." *Journal of Social Issues* 10: 3–26.

Hughes, Everett C. 1945. "Dilemmas and Contradictions of Status." *American Journal of Sociology* 50: 353–59.

Jackman, Mary R. 1994. *The Velvet Glove.* Berkeley: University of California Press.

Kirschenman, Joleen and Kathryn M. Neckerman. 1991. "'We'd Love to Hire Them but . . .': The Meaning of Race for Employers." Pp. 203–34 in *The Urban Underclass,* edited by Christopher Jencks and Paul Peterson. Washington, DC: Brookings Institution.

Krieger, Linda Hamilton. 1995. "The Contents of Our Categories: A Cognitive Bias Approach to Discrimination and Equal Employment Opportunity." *Stanford Law Review* 47: 1161–248.

——. 1998. "Civil Rights Perestroika: Intergroup Relations after Affirmative Action." *California Law Review* 86: 1253–1333.

Lieberson, Stanley. 1985. *Making It Count.* Berkeley: University of California Press.

Martin, Patricia Yancey. 1992. "Gender Interaction and Inequality in Organizations." Pp. 208–31 in *Gender Interaction and Inequality,* edited by Cecilia Ridgeway. New York: Springer-Verlag.

Nelson, Robert L. and William P. Bridges. 1999. *Legalizing Gender Inequality: Courts, Markets, and Unequal Pay for Women in America.* Cambridge: Cambridge University Press.

Operario, Don, Stephanie A. Goodwin, and Susan T. Fiske. 1998. "Power Is Everywhere: Social Control and Personal Control Both Operate at Stereotype Activation, Interpretation, and Inhibition." Pp. 163–75 in *Stereotype Activation and Inhibition,* edited by Robert S. Wyer. Mahway, NJ: Lawrence Erlbaum Associates.

Perdue, C. W., J. F. Dovidio, M. B. Gurtman, and R. B. Tyler. 1990. "'Us' and 'Them': Social Categorization and the Process of Intergroup Bias." *Journal of Personality and Social Psychology* 59: 475–86.

Reskin, Barbara F. 1988. "Bringing the Men Back In: Sex Differentiation and the Devaluation of Women's Work." *Gender & Society* 2: 58–81.

——. 1998. *The Realities of Affirmative Action.* Washington, DC: American Sociological Association.

——. 2000. "Employment Discrimination and Its Remedies." Forthcoming in *Handbook on Labor Market Research,* edited by Ivar Berg and Arne Kalleberg. New York: Plenum.

Ridgeway, Cecilia. 1997. "Interaction and the Conservation of Gender Inequality." *American Sociological Review* 62: 218–35.

Salancik, Gerald R. and Jeffrey Pfeffer. 1978. "Uncertainty, Secrecy, and the Choice of Similar Others." *Social Psychology* 41: 246–55.

Swim, Janet K. and Lawrence J. Sanna. 1996. "He's Skilled, She's Lucky: A Meta-Analysis of Observers' Attributions for Women's and Men's Successes and Failures." *Personality and Social Psychology Bulletin* 22: 507–19.

Tetlock, Phillip E. 1992. "The Impact of Accountability on Judgment and Choice: Toward a Social Contingency Model." *Advances in Experimental Social Psychology* 25: 331–76.

Tetlock, Phillip E. and Jennifer S. Lerner. 1999. "The Social Contingency Model: Identifying Empirical and Normative Boundary Conditions on the Error-and-Bias Portrait of Human Nature." Pp. 571–85 in *Dual Process Theories in Social Psychology,* edited by Shelly Chaiken and Yaacov Trope. New York: Guilford Press.

Tilly, Charles. 1998. *Durable Inequality.* Berkeley: University of California Press.

Tomaskovic-Devey, Donald. 1993. *Gender and Racial Inequality at Work: The Sources and Consequences of Job Segregation.* Ithaca, NY: ILR Press.

Watkins, Steve. 1993. "Racism *du jour* at Shoney's." *The Nation,* October 18.

CHAPTER

3

Race, Ethnicity, and Class

Does our understanding of social class focus more sharply or blur when we look at it in tandem with a focus on race, ethnicity, and nationality? The readings in Chapter 2 make it fairly clear that when we talk about social class and social class membership, we are also talking about all aspects of people's lives. And people have a racial designation, an ethnic identification, a sex, a sexual preference, an age—in other words, a complete set of identifying master statuses. This section extends the preceding analysis by including readings that look explicitly at how race, ethnicity, nationality, and immigration status shape the experience of social class. The defining characteristics for understanding how race and ethnicity intersect with class appear to be where people can afford to live, the kinds of jobs they are likely to find in their neighborhood or nearby, and whether or not they are welcomed into mainstream societal institutions.

Often, newly arrived immigrants are housed in the urban ghettos or the "bad" parts of town where they can *afford* to live. Thus, native-born racial minorities and newcomers come into contact and into competition with each other for the scarce resources available. Some who live in the burned-over neighborhoods of inner cities have lived there for generations; others will be able to use a poor neighborhood as a staging area and get out as soon as their fortunes improve. The native-born group to whom we refer are mostly African Americans who, on virtually every gauge of stratification, continue to suffer greater deprivations than other minority groups. Why? This is a perplexing question and has raised various responses over the years, ranging from motivational factors, to human capital differences in quality and amount of education, social capital differences, to a variety of differential structural features. The authors in this section offer three related answers for the increasing isolation of a poor group of inner city blacks, all hinging on the real estate broker's homily of "location, location, location."

Melvin Oliver and Thomas Shapiro's work taps a dimension of social class that is particularly challenging to document. Wealth (or capital), as seen in Chapter 2, can produce greater wealth. In other words, disparities in wealth distribution tend to be readily perpetuated over time. Income is what we earn. While there are great disparities in income distribution among races, differences in wealth distribution are even more pronounced. Oliver and Shapiro look at the cumulative impact of the differences in wealth across various racial-ethnic groups, building on their original analysis in *Black Wealth/White*

Wealth (1995). In their view, the most important distinction between wealth and income is that wealth can be passed down across generations. An asset like a home becomes important not only to the family who lives there right now but to a subsequent generation who may profit from the sale of the family home and who will pass on the profits to their children, and so on. Obviously, where you live determines property value, and residential segregation has a tremendous and depressing impact on what homes will be worth in areas dominated by African American residents. This is one of the real and tangible costs of racism. Oliver and Shapiro show that the economic effects of racism are both historically rooted and continue to have a profound impact on the fortunes of minority groups.

The theme of residential segregation and its impact on all aspects of our lives is explicitly addressed by Massey and Denton in their book *American Apartheid* (1993). Wherever you live, you know which parts of town are extremely desirable and which are not. In fact, if you've grown up in your town, you could probably map neighborhoods by social class and the race of residents. The characteristics of undesirable neighborhoods are easy enough to supply: dangerous, dirty, ugly, with little to no green space, limited businesses and shopping to meet residents' food and clothing needs, but scores of liquor stores and pawn shops and storefront government agencies. These are the parts of town cut in two by freeway developments, or the parts left behind as commercial and residential developers build away from what used to be a city's center. These are the areas where majestic Victorian homes, now abandoned, are silent witnesses to the movement of the better-off to other parts of town or to the suburbs. The human consequences of these changes are documented in this chapter. Simply put, those without social mobility are left behind. Indeed, as Massey and Denton show, in the city of Philadelphia in the 1980s, even relatively affluent blacks were "mired" in neighborhoods that didn't provide good public education or maintain housing value. Both Oliver and Shapiro, and Massey and Denton make a good argument for the structural underpinnings of racism, especially as it pertains to African Americans.

William Julius Wilson's most recent original book, *When Work Disappears* (1996), looks at what happens to neighborhoods when employers leave. Relying on extensive interviews with inner-city residents *and* their potential employers, the excerpt we include looks at the meaning of one's home address for employment opportunities and the impact of prevailing and damning stereotypes for black men. The inner city is, again, the place where poor African Americans and newly arrived immigrants meet. The immigrants, initially at least, are willing to work for poor wages, although interestingly, African Americans actually have lower "reservation" wages—that is, the lowest wage a worker is willing to accept—than do immigrants. Much of the problem, as Wilson has documented in his other works, *The Declining Significance of Race* (1980) and *The Truly Disadvantaged* (1987), revolves around the loss of blue-collar manufacturing jobs and a shift to low-paying service work, the loss of vibrant social institutions in the inner city, and the loss of a black professional class as the civil rights movement enabled them to exit into more attractive, integrated neighborhoods.

Those low-paid service workers provide the focus of the following three selections. Waldinger and Lichter's interviews with managers offer a fascinating look at the folk wisdom regarding native-born American workers ("spoiled") versus immigrant labor ("hard-working"). Their patronizing compliments about immigrant labor have an underbelly of condemnation (why would someone stay in a "dead-end" job for years on end?). Clearly, in these interviews, "they"—be they Mexican, Thai, or Lao—are desirable workers because they have no choice but to accept the less-than-ideal conditions of the job. African American workers who might be competing for low-skill work are not desired nor are they expected to want to fill these routine jobs. Katherine Newman, an anthropologist who specializes in stratification, looks at fast-food workers in the inner city in her book *No Shame in My Game* (2003). On the one hand, service work is despised as low status; indeed, "flipping burgers" has become parlance for having failed in the job market. On the other hand, any job is preferable to none in the harsh moral metric of American values. And in the inner city, the only jobs available to the young and middle-aged may be in fast-food places.

Jill Quadagno's commentary on the state of the welfare state takes issues of race, ethnicity, nationality, and immigration up a level to the policy arena. Across the European Union and within North America, immigrants who differ from the dominant population linguistically, religiously, and ethnically challenge established patterns regarding the delivery of and entitlement to state aid. Quadagno broadens the dimensions of inequality to include crossnational analyses of material conditions (wealth, income, poverty), inequality in agency (or political representation), and inequality in policy institutions. For centuries, communities and nations have divided poor populations into the "deserving" and "nondeserving" poor; increasingly, this debate involves broad shifts in global movement—such as Turkish immigrants residing in Germany, Algerians in France, Indians (Asians) in Great Britain, and so forth.

We conclude this chapter on the intersecting inequalities of race, ethnicity, nationality, and class with a selection that touches on the philosophical ideal of *meritocracy.* The idea of meritocracy, like functionalism, assumes that each individual can be fairly and solely judged on the basis of merit (talents, ability, education, and the like). As attacks on affirmative action as a race-based preferential treatment system, or non-meritocratic system, mounted in state legislatures and elsewhere in the late 1990s, William Bowen and Derek Bok undertook an ambitious survey of former students at prestigious institutions. Bowen is former president of Princeton University, and Bok is former president of Harvard. In their book, *The Shape of the River* (1998), the "river" refers to the flow of students into higher education and from there into the job market. The authors mount a defense of race-based policy. In the chapter we include here, Bowen and Bok address several questions raised by opponents of affirmative action. Such questions include the matter of harm: that is, does affirmative action demoralize those it is intended to help, thereby doing more harm than good?

REFERENCES

Wilson, William Julius. 1987. *The Truly Disadvantaged: The Inner City, the Underclass, and Public Policy.* Chicago: University of Chicago Press.

Wilson, William Julius. 1980. *The Declining Significance of Race: Blacks and Changing American Institutions.* Chicago: University of Chicago Press.

Wealth and Racial Stratification

MELVIN L. OLIVER AND THOMAS M. SHAPIRO

Income is what the average American family uses to reproduce daily existence in the form of shelter, food, clothing, and other necessities. In contrast, *wealth* is a storehouse of resources, it's what families own and use to produce income. Wealth signifies a control of financial resources that, when combined with income, provides the means and the opportunity to secure the "good life" in whatever form is needed—education, business, training, justice, health, material comfort, and so on. In this sense, wealth is a special form of money not usually used to purchase milk and shoes or other life necessities; rather it is used to create opportunities, secure a desired stature and standard of living, and pass class status along to one's children.

Wealth has been a neglected dimension of social science's concern with the economic and social status of Americans in general and racial minorities in particular. Social scientists have been much more comfortable describing and analyzing occupational, educational, and income distributions than examining the economic bedrock of a capitalist society—"private property." During the past decade, sociologists and economists have begun to pay more attention to the issue of wealth. The growing concentration of wealth at the top, and the growing racial wealth gap, have become important public-policy issues that undergird many

Source: Reprinted with permission from *America Becoming: Racial Trends and Their Consequences, Volume II* © (2001) by the National Academy of Sciences, courtesy of the National Academics Press, Washington, D.C.

political debates but, unfortunately, not many policy discussions. Our work takes up this challenge. This paper begins with a summary of the social science findings on race and wealth. The data are strongest regarding Black–White differences, but reference is made to findings and data that refer to Hispanics, Asians, and American Indians as well.

This paper focuses on three key contributions. First, an indispensable contribution to the current understanding of racial stratification is an examination of wealth, distinct from labor-market indicators, which this paper offers. Second, the paper makes an evidentiary contribution to the theory that current racial trends in inequality result, to a significant extent, from past racial policies and practices; and that the racial inequality of today, if left unattended, will contribute to continued racial stratification for the next generation. Third, by looking at new evidence concerning wealth and racial stratification, this paper contributes an impetus to push forward the research and policy agenda concerned with America's racial wealth gap. Thus, a wealth perspective provides a fresh way to examine the "playing field." Consequently, a standard part of the American credo—that similar accomplishments result in roughly equal rewards—may need reexamination.

RACIAL STRATIFICATION AND THE ASSET PERSPECTIVE

Understanding racial inequality, with respect to the distribution of power, economic resources, and life chances, is a prime concern of the social sciences. Most empirical research on racial inequality has focused on the economic dimension, which is not surprising considering the centrality of this component for life chances and well-being in an industrial society. The concerted emphasis of this economic component has been labor-market processes and their outcomes, especially earnings, occupational prestige, and social mobility. Until recently, the social sciences and the policy arena neglected wealth, intergenerational transfers, and policy processes that result in differential life chances based on racial criteria. Our ongoing work attempts to redress this severe imbalance.

The data and the social science understanding are strongest for income inequality in relation to race. For most, income is a quintessential labor-market outcome indicator. It refers to a flow of resources over time, representing the value of labor in the contemporary labor market and the value of social assistance and pensions. As such, income is a tidy and valuable gauge of the state of present economic inequality. Indeed, a strong case can be made that reducing racial discrimination in the labor market has resulted in increasing the income of racial minorities and, thus, narrowing the hourly wage gap between minorities and Whites. The command of resources that wealth entails, however, is more encompassing than income or education, and closer in meaning and theoretical significance to the traditional connotation of economic well-being and access to life chances as depicted in the classic conceptualizations of Marx, Weber, Simmel, and Tawney.[1]

As important is the fact that wealth taps not only contemporary resources, but also material assets that have historic origins and future implications. Private wealth thus captures inequality that is the product of the past, often passed down from generation to generation. Conceptualizing racial inequality through wealth revolutionizes the concept of the nature and magnitude of inequality, and of whether it is decreasing or increasing. Although most recent analyses have concluded that contemporary class-based factors are most important in understanding the sources of continuing racial inequality, a focus on wealth sheds light on both the historical and the contemporary impacts not only of class but also of race. Income is an important indicator of racial inequality; wealth allows an examination of racial stratification.

A wealth perspective contends that continued neglect of wealth as a dimension of racial stratification will result in a seriously underestimated racial inequality. Tragically, policies based solely on narrow differences in labor-market factors will fail to close that breach. Taken together, however, asset-building and labor-market approaches open new windows of opportunity.

HISTORICAL TRENDS AND CONTEXT OF WEALTH DISTRIBUTION IN THE UNITED STATES

Wealth inequality is today, and always has been, more extreme than income inequality. Wealth inequality is more lopsided in the United States than in Europe. Recent trends in asset ownership do not alleviate inequality concerns or issues. In general, inequality in asset ownership in the United States between the bottom and top of the distribution domain has been growing. Wealth inequality was at a 60-year high in 1989, with the top 1 percent of U.S. citizens controlling 39 percent of total U.S. household wealth. The richest 1 percent owned 48 percent of the total. These themes have been amply described in the work of Wolff (1994, 1996a, 1996b). Household wealth inequality increased sharply between 1983 and 1989. There was a modest attenuation in 1992, but the level of wealth concentration was still greater in 1992 than in 1983.

Until recently, few analyses looked at racial differences in wealth holding. Recent work, however,

---

[1]See Marx, K., and F. Engels, 1947, *The German Ideology,* New York: International Publishers; Weber, M., 1958, *The Protestant Ethic and the Spirit of Capitalism,* New York: Scribner's; Simmel, G., 1990, *The Philosophy of Money,* London: Routledge; Tawny, R.H., 1952, *Equality,* London: Allen and Unwin.

suggests that inequality is as pronounced—or more pronounced—between racial and ethnic groups in the dimension of wealth than income. The case of Blacks is paradigmatic of this inequality. Eller and Fraser (1995) report that Blacks had only 9.7 percent of the median net worth (all assets minus liabilities) of Whites in 1993 ($4,418 compared to $45,740); in contrast, their comparable figure for median family income was 62 percent of White income. Using 1988 data from the same source, Oliver and Shapiro (1995a) established that these differences are not the result of social-class factors. Even among the Black middle class, levels of net worth and net financial assets (all assets minus liabilities excluding home and vehicle equity) are drastically lower than for Whites. The comparable ratio of net worth for college-educated Blacks is only 0.24; even for two-income Black couples, the ratio is just 0.37. Clearly there are factors other than what we understand as "class" that led to these low levels of asset accumulation.

Black Wealth/White Wealth (Oliver and Shapiro, 1995a) decomposed the results of a regression analysis to give Blacks and Whites the same level of income, human capital, demographic, family, and other characteristics. The rationale for this was to examine the extent to which the huge racial wealth gap was a product of other differences between Whites and Blacks. Given the skewness of the wealth distribution, researchers agree that median figures best represent a typical American family; however, it should be noted, that regressions conventionally use means. A potent $43,143 difference in mean net worth remains, with 71 percent of the difference left unexplained. Only about 25 percent of the difference in net financial assets is explained. Taking the average Black household and endowing it with the same income, age, occupational, educational, and other attributes as the average White household still leaves a $25,794 racial gap in mean net financial assets. These residual gaps should not be cast wholly to racial dynamics; nonetheless, the regression analyses offer a powerful argument to directly link race in the American experience to the wealth-creation process.

As important is the finding that more than two-thirds of Blacks have no net financial assets, compared to less than one-third of Whites. This near absence of assets has extreme consequences for the economic and social well-being of the Black community, and of the ability of families to plan for future social mobility. If the average Black household were to lose an income stream, the family would not be able to support itself without access to public support. At their current levels of net financial assets, nearly 80 percent of Black families would not be able to survive at poverty-level consumption for three months. Comparable figures for Whites—although large in their own right—are one-half that of Blacks. Thinking about the social welfare of children, these figures take on more urgency. Nine out of ten Black children live in households that have less than three months of poverty-level net financial assets; nearly two-thirds live in households with zero or negative net financial assets (Oliver and Shapiro, 1989, 1990, 1995a, 1995b).

Because home ownership plays such a large role in the wealth portfolios of American families, it is a prime source of the differences between Black and White net worth. Home ownership rates for Blacks are 20 percent lower than rates for Whites; hence, Blacks possess less of this important source of equity. Discrimination in the process of securing home ownership plays a significant role in how assets are generated and accumulated. The reality of residential segregation also plays an important role in the way home ownership figures in the wealth portfolio of Blacks. Because Blacks live, for the most part, in segregated areas, the value of their homes is less, demand for them is less, and thus their equity is less (Oliver and Shapiro, 1995b; Massey and Denton, 1994). (Because the area of home ownership is so central to the wealth accumulation process, the most current data will be analyzed in a later section of this paper.)

Similar findings on gross differences between Hispanics and Whites also have been uncovered (Eller and Fraser, 1995; Flippen and Tienda, 1997; O'Toole, 1998; Grant, 2000). Hispanics have slightly higher, but not statistically different, net worth figures than Blacks, based on the 1993 Survey of Income and Program Participation (SIPP); however, these findings are not sufficiently nuanced to capture the diversity of the Hispanic population. Data from the Los Angeles Survey of Urban Inequality show substantial differences in assets and net financial assets between recent immigrants who are primarily from Mexico and Central America and U.S.-born Hispanics (Grant, 2000).

Likewise, place of birth and regional differences among Hispanic groups also complicate a straightforward interpretation of this national-level finding. For example, Cuban Americans, we would hypothesize, have net worth figures comparable to Whites because of their dominance in an ethnic economy in which they own small and medium-sized businesses (Portes and Rumbaut, 1990). They have a far different set of economic life chances than Blacks and other recent Hispanic immigrants by way of their more significant wealth accumulation. For recent Hispanic immigrants, these figures suggest real vulnerability for the economic security of their households and children.

Finally, it is important to point out findings by Flippen and Tienda (1997) that attempt to explain the Black-White and Hispanic-White gap in wealth. Substituting White means for all the variables in a complex Tobit model, Flippen and Tienda found that the model "reduces asset inequality more for Hispanics than for Blacks." This is particularly the case for housing equity; for Hispanics, mean substitution reduced the gap by 80 percent, compared to only 62 percent for Blacks. As Flippen and Tienda note, "This suggests the importance of residential segregation and discrimination in the housing and lending market in hindering the accumulation of housing assets for Black households" (1997:18). Although their findings for Hispanics may be true for "White Hispanics," they may not apply to Black Puerto Ricans, who share social space with non-Hispanic Blacks and, therefore, may also be targeted for institutionalized racism in housing markets and financial

institutions. Preliminary data from the Greater Boston Social Survey suggest that Hispanics in that region, the majority of whom are Puerto Rican, have even lower levels of net worth and financial assets than Blacks (O'Toole, 1998).

The case of Asians is quite similar to that for Hispanics, in that it is necessary to be mindful of their diversity, in terms of both national origin and immigrant status. Changes in immigration rules have favored those who bring assets into the country over those without assets; as a consequence, recent immigrants, from Korea, for example, are primarily individuals and families with assets, and once they arrive, they convert these assets into other asset-producing activities—e.g., small businesses. Bates' (1998) analysis of SIPP points out that Koreans who started businesses had significant assets and were able to use those assets to secure loans for business startups. Data from Los Angeles again underscore the importance of immigrant status and place of birth. U.S.-born Asians have both net worth and net financial assets approaching those of White Los Angelenos; foreign-born Asians, however, report lower wealth than U.S.-born Asians but higher wealth than all other ethnic and racial groups (Grant, 2000).

American Indians form a unique case when it comes to assets. They are asset rich but control little of these assets. Most Indian assets are held in tribal or individual Indian trust (Office of Trust Responsibilities, 1995). Thus, any accounting of the assets of individual Indian households is nearly impossible to calculate, given their small population and these "hidden" assets.

The dearth of studies of wealth in the United States has hampered efforts to develop both wealth theory and information. For more than 100 years, the prime sources concerning wealth status came from estate tax records, biographies of the super rich, various listings of the wealthiest, and like sources. In other words, something was known about those who possessed abundant amounts of wealth, but virtually nothing was known about the wealth status of average American families. During the 1980s, several data sources were developed based on field surveys of the American population. Most notable are SIPP, the Panel Study of Income Dynamics (PSID), the Federal Reserve Board's Survey of Consumer Finances (SCF), and the Health and Retirement Study (HRS). Thus, it is only relatively recently that any data at all were available to characterize the asset well-being of American families.

RACE, INCOME, AND WEALTH

The empirical presentation begins with a fundamental examination of the most current income and wealth data for Whites, Blacks, Hispanics, and Asians. The data displayed in Table 1 are taken from the 1993 SIPP, Wave 7. Drawing attention first to income comparisons, the household income ratio of Blacks, compared to Whites, is 0.61:1, and the Hispanic ratio, 0.67:1. Asians fare considerably better in this comparison, earning close to 125 percent of White income. (It is important, here, to mind the caution from the literature review: the Hispanic and Asian data are aggregated, subsuming important dimensions of country of origin and immigrant status.) These income comparisons closely match other national data and provide an effective indicator of current racial and ethnic material inequality. Changing the lens of analysis to wealth dramatically shifts the perspective. Black families possess only 14 cents for every dollar of wealth (median net worth) held by White families. The issue is no

longer how to think about closing the gap from 0.61 but how to think about going from 14 cents on the dollar to something approaching parity. Nearly half of all Black families do not possess any net financial assets, compared to $7,400 for the average White family. These figures represent some asset accumulation for both Whites and Blacks between 1988 and 1994; nonetheless, the wealth perspective reveals an economic fragility for the entire American population, as it demonstrates the continuing racial wealth gap.

The data for Hispanics resemble the Black–White comparisons in one important respect and diverge in another. The median figures for both net worth and net financial assets reveal similar gaps in comparison with Whites, but the mean figures for net worth and net financial assets bump Hispanics "ahead" of Blacks. This apparent peculiarity most likely illustrates differences in experiences, country of origin, and immigrant status referred to earlier.

Mindful that the Asian data also are grouped, the figures for Asian wealth show an even more exaggerated pattern. The median-wealth figures indicate that Asians possess about three-quarters of the net worth and two-thirds of the net financial assets that Whites own. Commentators could seize on this piece of the story, noting that Asian family income is greater than Whites', and wonder why the wealth gap exists. An examination of mean wealth figures proves this exercise unnecessary— indeed, the data indicate parity in wealth between

TABLE 1 Income, Wealth, Race, and Ethnicity: 1994

	Median Income	*Median NW*[a]	*Mean NW*	*Median NFA*[b]	*Mean NFA*
White	$33,600	$52,944	$109,511	$7,400	$56,199
Black	$20,508	$6,127	$28,643	$100	$7,611
Ratio to White	0.61	0.12	0.26	0.01	0.14
Hispanic	$22,644	$6,723	$40,033	$300	$15,709
Ratio to White	0.67	0.13	0.37	0.03	0.27
Asian	$40,998	$39,846	$117,916	$4,898	$57,782
Ratio to White	1.22	0.67	1.02	0.51	0.98

[a]Net worth.
[b]Net financial assets.

Source: 1993 SIPP, Wave 7.

White and Asian families. Like the Hispanic data, but to an even greater extent, the Asian aggregate data mask different historical immigrant experiences, country of origin, and immigration status. The divergence between median and mean figures also most likely indicates that a sizable portion of the Asian community is relatively well off alongside a sizable portion of the community whose asset resources are far less than the average White family's. In other words, in parts of the Asian community, the wealth resources more closely resemble Black and Hispanic wealth profiles, while some segments of the Asian community virtually mirror the White profile.

These data provide a baseline of information regarding racial and ethnic differences in income and wealth resources. Not only do they update previous analyses in a simple way, they also bolster the previous findings. More important, the wealth data consistently indicate a far greater chasm in and pattern of racial and ethnic inequality than when income alone is examined.

INCOME AND WEALTH

A starting point for building on the basic analysis is a further examination of the connection between income and wealth. One leading economic perspective contends that the racial wealth gap predominantly results from income inequality. Do differences in income explain nearly all the racial differences in wealth? If so, then policies need to continue a primarily labor-market orientation that further narrows income inequality. If not, however, then social policy must address dynamics outside the labor market as well as income-generating, labor-market dynamics. Thus, it is critically important to address whether the wealth of Blacks is similar to Whites with similar incomes.

The strong income-wealth relationship is recognized in previous analysis of the 1984 SIPP data. *Black Wealth/White Wealth* (Oliver and Shapiro, 1995a) identified income as a significant variable determining wealth accumulation,

next only to age in the wealth regressions. Looking at wealth by income ranges, however, showed that a powerful racial wealth gap remained. A regression analysis similarly indicated a highly significant differential wealth return to Whites and Blacks from income. The idea that wealth is quite similar when controlling for income, nonetheless, still holds some currency; so a direct empirical examination that uses the most recently available data should provide some evidence of, and resolution of, this issue. An empirical examination can be done in two ways.

The first way to address this issue can be demonstrated by using the data in Table 2, which show median measured net worth and net financial assets by income quintile, race, and Hispanic origin. White households in every income quintile had significantly higher levels of median wealth than Black and Hispanic households in the same income quintiles. In the lowest quintile, the median net worth for White households was $17,066, while that of Black and Hispanic households was $2,500 and $1,298, respectively. For the highest quintile households, median net worth for White households was $133,607; significantly lower was the median for Black households, $43,806. The median net financial assets data are just as revealing. At the middle quintile, for example, the median net financial assets for White households were $6,800, which was markedly higher than for Black ($800) and Hispanic ($1,000) households.

It is important to observe that controlling for income in this manner does, indeed, significantly lessen the Black-White/Hispanic-White wealth ratios. The overall median Black-White net worth ratio was 0.14:1, but this narrows when comparing White and Black households in similar income quintiles. The gap, as expressed in ratios, stays about the same for the two lowest income quintiles but narrows to 0.3:1, 0.45:1, and 0.33:1 for the next three income quintiles. In brief, as shown by this comparative procedure, controlling for income narrows the gap; but a significantly large gap persists, even when incomes are roughly equal. This evidence does not support the proposition that

TABLE 2 Wealth by Race and Hispanic Origin and Income Quintiles: 1994

	Total		White		Black		Hispanic	
	NW^a	NFA^b	NW	NFA	NW	NFA	NW	NFA
All households								
Median	$40,172		$52,944	$7,400	$7,400	$100	$ 6,723	$ 300
Ratio to white:					0.14		0.13	
Lowest income quintile								
Median	8,032	185	17,066	551	2,500		1,298	0
Ratio to white:					0.15		0.08	
Second income quintile								
Median	27,638	1,848	39,908	3,599	6,879	249	5,250	250
Ratio to white:					0.17	0.07	0.13	0.07
Third income quintile								
Median	40,665	4,599	50,350	6,800	14,902	800	12,555	1,000
Ratio to white:					0.30	0.12	0.25	0.15
Fourth income quintile								
Median	59,599	10,339	65,998	13,362	29,851	2,699	26,328	2,125
Ratio to white:					0.45	0.20	0.4	0.16
Highest income quintile								
Median	126,923	36,851	133,607	40,465	43,806	7,448	91,102	11,485
Ratio to white:					0.33	0.18	0.68	0.28

[a]Net worth.

[b]Net financial assets.

Source: 1993 SIPP, Wave 7.

Whites and Blacks at similar income levels possess similar wealth.

Another way to address the income and wealth connection is to examine wealth at precisely similar income points for Whites and Blacks. New worth for Whites and Blacks is examined first at distribution percentiles—i.e., leaving income uncontrolled. Figures 1 and 2, drawn from 1994 SIPP data, show that median White wealth totaled $7,671 and Black wealth totaled $0 at the 25th percentile of each distribution. At the 50th percentile, White net worth was $52,944, compared with $6,126 for Blacks. At the 75th percentile, White net worth was $141,491 versus $40,315 for Blacks. How much of this gap is closed by controlling for income? Will Black–White wealth become actually quite similar, or will substantial, dramatic racial wealth inequality persist? At stake here is a

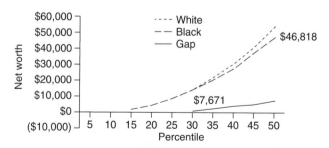

FIGURE 1   Wealth Gap in 1994 with No Control of Income: $0–$60,000.

Source: 1993 SIPP, Wave 7.

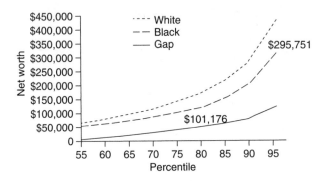

FIGURE 2   Wealth Gap in 1994 with No Control of Income: $0–$450,000.
Source: 1993 SIPP, Wave 7.

test of two contending claims—(1) wealth inequality fundamentally derives from income inequality versus (2) wealth inequality derives from accumulations within historically and racially structured contexts. The claim is that Black wealth would be near parity with Whites' if incomes were equal; therefore, the logic is to compare net worth while controlling for income. Calibrating the White-to-Black income distributions means, for example, comparing the 25th percentile of the White wealth data to the 45th percentile of the Black distribution, the 50th White to the 70th Black, and the 75th White to the 88th Black.

Figure 3 graph this income-wealth relationship. A summary that captures some major data points should guide any interpretation. At the 25th percentile for Whites, median net worth is $7,671; controlling for income, the Black net worth adjusts

upward to $3,548. At the 50th percentile for Whites, net worth is $52,944, compared to $30,000 for Blacks earning equivalent incomes. At the 75th percentile for Whites, wealth stands at $141,491 versus $72,761 for Blacks.

At the 50th percentile, then, the original uncontrolled gap weighs in at $46,817 with a ratio of 0.12:1. Controlling for income reduces this gap to $22,944. The Black/White wealth ratio closes as well to 0.57. Let us be clear: controlling for income significantly reduces the wealth gap; at the same time, however, even if incomes are equal, a consequential racial wealth gap remains. Indeed, after controlling for income, it is prudent to note that the remaining wealth gap is about as large as the racial income inequality gap. So if this exercise is correct, something akin to the original racial income gap remains unexplained after equalizing incomes.

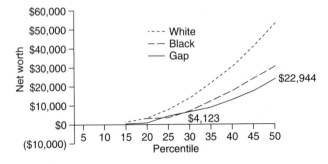

FIGURE 3   Wealth Gap in 1994 Controlled for Income: $0–$60,000.
Source: 1993 SIPP, Wave 7.

REFERENCES

Avery, R., and M. Rendell. 1993. Estimating the size and distribution of the baby boomers' prospective inheritances. Pp. 11–19 in *American Statistical Association: 1993 Proceedings of the Social Science Section*. Alexandria, Va.: American Statistical Association.

Bates, T. 1998. *Race, Self-Employment, and Upward Mobility: An Illusive American Dream*. Baltimore: Johns Hopkins University Press.

Butler, J. 1991. *Entrepreneurship and Self-Help Among Black Americans: A Reconsideration of Race and Economics*. Albany, N.Y.: State University of New York Press.

Corporation for Enterprise Development 1996. *Universal Savings Accounts—USAs: A Route to National Economic Growth and Family Economic Security*. Washington, D.C.: Corporation for Enterprise Development.

Darity, W., Jr., and P. Mason. 1998. Evidence on discrimination in employment: Codes of color, codes of gender. *Journal of Economic Perspectives* 12(2): 63–90.

Eller, T., and W. Fraser. 1995. Asset Ownership of Households: 1993. *U.S. Bureau of the Census. Current Population Reports, P70–47*. Washington, D.C.: U.S. Government Printing Office.

Flippen, C., and M. Tienda. 1997. Racial and Ethnic Differences in Wealth Among the Elderly. Paper presented at the 1997 Annual Meeting of the Population Association of America, Washington, D.C.

Gale, W., and J. Scholz. 1994. Intergenerational transfers and the accumulation of wealth. *Journal of Economic Perspectives* 8(4): 145–160.

Grant, D. 2000. A demographic portrait of Los Angeles, 1970–1990. In *Prismatic Metropolis: Analyzing Inequality in Los Angeles*, L. Bobo, M. Oliver, J. Johnson Jr., and A. Valenzuela, eds. New York: Russell Sage Foundation.

Howard, C. 1997. *The Hidden Welfare State: Tax Expenditures and Social Policy in the United States*. Princeton: Princeton University Press.

Jackman, M., and R. Jackman. 1980. Racial inequalities in home ownership. *Social Forces* 58: 1221–1233.

Jackson, K. 1985. *Crabgrass Frontier: The Suburbanization of the United States*. New York: Oxford University Press.

Koltikoff, L., and L. Sommers. 1981. The role of intergenerational transfers in aggregate capital accumulation. *Journal of Political Economy* 89:706–732.

Ladd, H. 1998. Evidence on discrimination in mortgage lending. *Journal of Economic Perspectives* 12(2):41–62.

Leiberson, S. 1980. *A Piece of the Pie*. Berkeley: University of California Press.

Massey, D., and N. Denton. 1994. *American Apartheid: Segregation and the Making of the Underclass*. Cambridge: Harvard University Press.

McNamee, S., and R. Miller, Jr. 1998. Inheritance and stratification. In *Inheritance and Wealth in America*, R. Miller, Jr., and S. McNamee, eds. New York: Plenum Press.

Mink, G. 1990. The lady and the tramp: Gender, race, and the origins of the American welfare state. Pp. 92–122 in *Women, the State, and Welfare*, L. Gordon, ed. Madison: University of Wisconsin Press.

Modigliana, F., and R. Brumberg. 1954. Utility analysis and the consumption function: An interpretation of cross-section data. In *Post-Keynesian Economics*, K. Kurihara, ed. New Brunswick: Rutgers University Press.

National Research Council 1989. *A Common Destiny: Blacks and American Society*, G. Jaynes and R. Williams, eds. Washington, D.C.: National Academy Press.

O'Toole, B. 1998. Family net asset levels in the greater Boston region. Paper presented at the Greater Boston Social Survey Community Conference, John F. Kennedy Library, Boston, Mass., November.

Office of Trust Responsibilities 1995. *Annual Report of Indian Lands*. Washington, D.C.: U.S. Department of the Interior.

Oliver, M., and T. Shapiro. 1989. Race and wealth. *Review of Black Political Economy* 17: 5–25.

———. 1990. Wealth of a nation: At least one-third of households are asset poor. *American Journal of Economics and Sociology* 49: 129–151.

———. 1995a. *Black Wealth/White Wealth: A New Perspective on Racial Inequality*. New York: Routledge.

———. 1995b. Them that's got shall get. In *Research in Politics and Society*, M. Oliver, R. Ratcliff, and T. Shapiro, eds. Greenwich, Conn.: JAI Press Vol. 5.

Ong, P. and E. Grigsby. 1988. Race and life cycle effects on home ownership in Los Angeles, 1970 to 1980. *Urban Affairs Quarterly* 23: 601–615.

Oubre, C. 1978. *Forty Acres and a Mule: The Freedman's Bureau and Black Land Ownership*. Baton Rouge: Louisiana State University Press.

Portes, A., and Rumbaut, R. 1990. *Immigrant America*. Berkeley: University of California Press.

Quadagno, J. 1994. *The Color of Welfare*. New York: Oxford University Press.

Sherraden, M. 1991. *Assets and the Poor: A New American Welfare Policy*. New York: Sharpe.

Wilhelm, M. 1998. The role of intergenerational transfers in spreading asset ownership. Prepared for *Ford Foundation Conference on The Benefits and Mechanisms for Spreading Assets*, New York, December 10–12.

Wolff, E. 1994. Trends in household wealth in the United States, 1962–1983 and 1983–1989. *Review of Income and Wealth* 40: 143–174.

———. 1996a. *Top Heavy: A Study of Increasing Inequality of Wealth in America*. Updated and expanded edition. New York: Free Press.

———. 1996b. International comparisons of wealth inequality. *Review of Income and Wealth* 42: 433–451.

Yinger, J.1995. *Closed Doors, Opportunities Lost: The Continuing Costs of Housing Discrimination*. New York: Russell Sage Foundation.

———. 1998. Evidence on discrimination in consumer markets. *Journal of Economic Perspectives* 12(2): 23–40.

The Perpetuation of the Underclass

DOUGLAS S. MASSEY AND NANCY A. DENTON

One notable difference appears between the immigrant and Negro populations. In the case of the former, there is the possibility of escape, with improvement in economic status in the second generation.

1931 report to President Herbert Hoover
by the Committee on Negro Housing

If the black ghetto was deliberately constructed by whites through a series of private decisions and institutional practices, if racial discrimination persists at remarkably high levels in U.S. housing markets, if intensive residential segregation continues to be imposed on blacks by virtue of their skin color, and if segregation concentrates poverty to build a self-perpetuating spiral of decay into black neighborhoods, then a variety of deleterious consequences automatically follow for individual African Americans. A racially segregated society cannot be a race-blind society, as long as U.S. cities remain segregated—indeed, hypersegregated—the United States cannot claim to have equalized opportunities for blacks and whites. In a segregated world, the deck is stacked against black socioeconomic progress, political empowerment, and full participation in the mainstream of American life.

In considering how individuals fare in the world, social scientists make a fundamental distinction between individual, family, and structural characteristics. To a great extent, of course, a person's success depends on individual traits such as motivation, intelligence, and especially, education. Other things equal, those who are more highly motivated, smarter, and better educated will be rewarded more highly in the labor market and will achieve greater socioeconomic success.

Other things generally are not equal, however, because individual traits such as motivation and education are strongly affected by family background. Parents who are themselves educated, motivated, and economically successful tend to pass these traits on to their children. Children who enter the middle and upper classes through the accident of birth are more likely than other, equally intelligent children from other classes to acquire the schooling, motivation, and cultural knowledge required for socioeconomic success in contemporary society. Other aspects of family background, moreover, such as wealth and social connections, open the doors of opportunity irrespective of education or motivation.

Yet even when one adjusts for family background, other things are still not equal, because the structural organization of society also plays a profound role in shaping the life chances of individuals. Structural variables are elements of social and economic organization that lie beyond individual control, that are built into the way society is organized. Structural characteristics affect the fate of large numbers of people and families who share common locations in the social order.

Among the most important structural variables are those that are geographically defined. Where one lives—especially, where one grows up—exerts a profound effect on one's life chances. Identical individuals with similar family backgrounds and personal characteristics will lead very different

Source: "The Perpetuation of the Underclass" reprinted by permission of the publisher from *American Apartheid: Segregation and the Making of the Underclass* by Douglas S. Massey and Nancy A. Denton, pp. 148–160, Cambridge, Mass.: Harvard University Press, Copyright © 1993 by the President and Fellows of Harvard College.

lives and achieve different rates of socioeconomic success depending on where they reside. Because racial segregation confines blacks to a circumscribed and disadvantaged niche in the urban spatial order, it has profound consequences for individual and family well-being.

SOCIAL AND SPATIAL MOBILITY

In a market society such as the United States, opportunities, resources, and benefits are not distributed evenly across the urban landscape. Rather, certain residential areas have more prestige, greater affluence, higher home values, better services, and safer streets than others. Marketing consultants have grown rich by taking advantage of this "clustering of America" to target specific groups of consumers for wealthy corporate clients. The geographic differentiation of American cities by socioeconomic status does more than conveniently rank neighborhoods for the benefit of demographers, however; it also creates a crucial connection between social and spatial mobility.

As people get ahead, they not only move up the economic ladder, they move up the residential ladder as well. As early as the 1920s, sociologists at the University of Chicago noted this close connection between social and spatial mobility, a link that has been verified many times since. As socioeconomic status improves, families relocate to take advantage of opportunities and resources that are available in greater abundance elsewhere. By drawing on benefits acquired through residential mobility, aspiring parents not only consolidate their own class position but enhance their and their children's prospects for additional social mobility.

In a very real way, therefore, barriers to spatial mobility are barriers to social mobility, and where one lives determines a variety of salient factors that affect individual well-being: the quality of schooling, the value of housing, exposure to crime, the quality of public services, and the character of children's peers. As a result, residential integration has been a crucial component in the broader process of socioeconomic advancement among immigrants

and their children. By moving to successively better neighborhoods, other racial and ethnic groups have gradually become integrated into American society. Although rates of spatial assimilation have varied, levels of segregation have fallen for each immigrant group as socioeconomic status and generations in the United States have increased.

The residential integration of most ethnic groups has been achieved as a by-product of broader processes of socioeconomic attainment, not because group members sought to live among native whites per se. The desire for integration is only one of a larger set of motivations, and not necessarily the most important. Some minorities may even be antagonistic to the idea of integration, but for spatial assimilation to occur, they need only be willing to put up with integration in order to gain access to socioeconomic resources that are more abundant in areas in which white families predominate.

To the extent that white prejudice and discrimination restrict the residential mobility of blacks and confine them to areas with poor schools, low home values, inferior services, high crime, and low educational aspirations, segregation undermines their social and economic well-being. The persistence of racial segregation makes it difficult for aspiring black families to escape the concentrated poverty of the ghetto and puts them at a distinct disadvantage in the larger competition for education, jobs, wealth, and power. The central issue is not whether African Americans "prefer" to live near white people or whether integration is a desirable social goal, but how the restrictions on individual liberty implied by severe segregation undermine the social and economic well-being of individuals.

Extensive research demonstrates that blacks face strong barriers to spatial assimilation within American society. Compared with other minority groups, they are markedly less able to convert their socioeconomic attainments into residential contact with whites, and because of this fact they are unable to gain access to crucial resources and benefits that are distributed through housing markets. Dollar for dollar, blacks are able to buy fewer neighborhood amenities with their income than other groups.

Among all groups in the United States, only Puerto Ricans share blacks' relative inability to assimilate spatially; but this disadvantage stems from the fact that many are of African origin. Although white Puerto Ricans achieve rates of spatial assimilation that are comparable with those found among other ethnic groups, those of African or racially mixed origins experience markedly lower abilities to convert socioeconomic attainments into contact with whites. Once race is controlled, the "paradox of Puerto Rican segregation" disappears.

Given the close connection between social and spatial mobility, the persistence of racial barriers implies the systematic exclusion of blacks from benefits and resources that are distributed through housing markets. We illustrate the severity of this black disadvantage with data specially compiled for the city of Philadelphia in 1980 (see Table 1). The data allow us to consider the socioeconomic character of neighborhoods that poor, middle-income, and affluent blacks and whites can be expected to inhabit, holding education and occupational status constant.

In Philadelphia, poor blacks and poor whites both experience very bleak neighborhood environments; both groups live in areas where about 40% of the births are to unwed mothers, where median home values are under $30,000, and where nearly 40% of high school students score under the 15th percentile on a standardized achievement test. Families in such an environment would be unlikely to build wealth through home equity, and children growing up in such an environment would be exposed to a peer environment where unwed parenthood was common and where educational performance and aspirations were low.

As income rises, however, whites are able to escape this disadvantaged setting by relocating to a more advantaged setting. With a middle-class income ($20,000 1979 dollars), whites no longer reside in a neighborhood where unwed parenthood predominates (only 10% of births are to single mothers) and housing values are well above $30,000. At the same time, school performance is markedly better: only 17% of students in the local high school score below the 15th percentile.

Once whites achieve affluence, moreover, negative residential conditions are left far behind.

TABLE 1   Characteristics of Neighborhoods Inhabited by Blacks and Whites at Different Income Levels in Philadelphia, 1980

	Level of Household Income					
	Poor ($8,000)		*Middle ($20,000)*		*Affluent ($32,000)*	
	Whites	**Blacks**	**Whites**	**Blacks**	**Whites**	**Blacks**
Percentage of births to unwed mothers	40.7	37.6	10.3	25.8	1.9	16.7
Median value of homes (in thousands of 1980 dollars)	$19.4	$27.1	$38.0	$29.5	$56.6	$31.9
Percentage of students scoring below 15th percentile on CAT in local high school	39.3	35.5	16.5	26.6	5.7	19.2

Note: Household income is in 1979 dollars.

Source: Douglas S. Massey, Gretchen A. Condran, and Nancy A. Denton, "The Effect of Residential Segregation on Black Social and Economic Well-Being," *Social Forces* 66 (1987): 46–47, 50.

Affluent whites in Philadelphia (those with a 1979 income of $32,000) live in neighborhoods where only 2% of the births are to unwed mothers, where the median home value is $57,000, and where a mere 6% of high school students score below the 15th percentile on achievement tests. Upwardly mobile whites, in essence, capitalize on their higher incomes to buy their way into improved residential circumstances.

Blacks, in contrast, remain mired in disadvantage no matter what income they achieve. Middle-income blacks live in an area where more than a quarter of the births are to unwed mothers, where housing values languish below $30,000, and where 27% of all students in the local high school score below the 15th percentile. Even with affluence, blacks achieve neighborhood environments that compare unfavorably with those attained by whites. With an income of $32,000, a black family can expect to live in a neighborhood where 17% of all births are to unwed mothers, home values are barely over $30,000, and where a fifth of high school students score below the 15th percentile.

For blacks, in other words, high incomes do not buy entrée to residential circumstances that can serve as springboards for future socioeconomic mobility; in particular, blacks are unable to achieve a school environment conducive to later academic success. In Philadelphia, children from an affluent black family are likely to attend a public school where the percentage of low-achieving students is three times greater than the percentage in schools attended by affluent white children. Small wonder, then, that controlling for income in no way erases the large racial gap in SAT scores. Because of segregation, the same income buys black and white families educational environments that are of vastly different quality.

Given these limitations on the ability of black families to gain access to neighborhood resources, it is hardly surprising that government surveys reveal blacks to be less satisfied with their residential circumstances than socioeconomically equivalent whites. This negative evaluation reflects an accurate appraisal of their circumstances rather than different values or ideals on the part of blacks. Both races want the same things in homes and neighborhoods; blacks are just less able to achieve them. Compared with whites, blacks are less likely to be homeowners, and the homes they do own are of poorer quality, in poorer neighborhoods, and of lower value. Moreover, given the close connection between home equity and family wealth, the net worth of blacks is a small fraction of that of whites, even though their incomes have converged over the years. Finally, blacks tend to occupy older, more crowded dwellings that are structurally inadequate compared to those inhabited by whites; and because these racial differentials stem from segregation rather income, adjusting for socioeconomic status does not erase them.

THE POLITICS OF SEGREGATION

Socioeconomic achievement is not only a matter of individual aspirations and effort, however; it is also a matter of collective action in the political arena. Generations of immigrants have entered American cities and struggled to acquire political power as a means to enhance individual mobility. Ultimately most were incorporated into the pluralist political structure of American cities. In return for support at the polls, ethnic groups were awarded a share of public services, city contracts, and municipal jobs in rough proportion to their share of the electorate. The receipt of these public resources, in turn, helped groups consolidate their class position and gave their members a secure economic base from which to advance further.

The process of political incorporation that followed each immigrant wave grew out of shared political interests that were, to a large extent, geographically determined. Although neighborhoods may have been labeled "Polish," "Italian," or "Jewish," neighborhoods in which one ethnic group constituted a majority were rare, and most immigrants of European origin never lived in them. As a result, levels of ethnic segregation never reached the heights typical of black-white segregation today.

This geographic diversification of ethnicity created a situation in which ethnic groups necessarily shared common political interests. In distributing public works, municipal services, and patronage jobs to ethnic groups in return for their political support, resources were also allocated to specific neighborhoods, which typically contained a diverse array of ethnicities. Given the degree of ethnic mixing within neighborhoods, political patronage provided to one group yielded substantial benefits for others as well. Building a new subway stop in an "Italian" neighborhood, for example, also provided benefits to Jews, Poles, and Lithuanians who shared the area; and allocating municipal jobs to Poles not only benefited merchants in "Polish" communities but generated extra business for nearby shopkeepers who were Hungarian, Italian, or Czech.

At the same time, threats to curtail municipal services encouraged the formation of broad, interethnic coalitions built around common neighborhood interests. A plan to close a firehouse in a "Jewish" neighborhood, for example, brought protests not only from Jews but from Scandinavians, Italians, and Slovaks who shared the neighborhood and relied on its facilities. These other ethnics, moreover, were invariably connected to friends and relatives in other neighborhoods or to co-ethnic politicians from other districts who could assist them in applying political pressure to forestall the closure. In this way, residential integration structurally supported the formation of interethnic coalitions, providing a firm base for the emergence of pluralist political machines.

Residential integration also made it possible for ethnic groups to compete for political leadership throughout the city, no matter what their size. Because no single group dominated numerically in most neighborhoods, politicians from a variety of backgrounds found the door open to make a bid for elective office. Moreover, representatives elected from ethnically diverse neighborhoods had to pay attention to all voters irrespective of ethnic affiliation. The geographic distribution of political power across ethnically heterogeneous districts spread political influence widely among groups and ensured that all were given a political voice.

The residential segregation of blacks, in contrast, provided no basis for pluralist politics because it precluded the emergence of common neighborhood interests; the geographic isolation of blacks instead forced nearly all issues to cleave along racial lines. When a library, firehouse, police station, or school was built in a black neighborhood, other ethnic groups derived few, if any, benefits; and when important services were threatened with reduction or removal, blacks could find few coalition partners with whom to protest the cuts. Since no one except blacks lived in the ghetto, no other ethnic group had a self-interest in seeing them provided with public services or political patronage.

On the contrary, resources allocated to black neighborhoods detracted from the benefits going to white ethnic groups; and because patronage was the glue that held white political coalitions together, resources allocated to the ghetto automatically undermined the stability of the pluralist machine. As long as whites controlled city politics, their political interests lay in providing as few resources as possible to African Americans and as many as possible to white ethnic groups. Although blacks occasionally formed alliances with white reformers, the latter acted more from moral conviction than from self-interest. Because altruism is notoriously unreliable as a basis for political cooperation, interracial coalitions were unstable and of limited effectiveness in representing black interests.

The historical confinement of blacks to the ghetto thus meant that blacks shared few political interests with whites. As a result, their incorporation into local political structures differed fundamentally from the pluralist model followed by other groups. The geographic and political isolation of blacks meant that they had virtually no power when their numbers were small; only when their numbers increased enough to dominate one or more wards did they acquire any influence at all. But rather than entering the pluralist coalition as an equal partner, the black community was incorporated in a very different way: as a machine within a machine.

The existence of solid black electoral districts, while undermining interracial coalition-building, did create the potential for bloc voting along racial lines. In a close citywide election, the delivery of a large number of black votes could be extremely useful to white politicians, and inevitably black political bosses arose to control and deliver this vote in return for political favors. Unlike whites, who exercised power through politicians of diverse ethnicities, blacks were typically represented by one boss, always black, who developed a symbiotic and dependent relationship with the larger white power structure.

In return for black political support, white politicians granted black bosses such as Oscar DePriest or William Dawson of Chicago and Charles Anderson of Harlem a share of jobs and patronage that they could, in turn, distribute within the ghetto. Although these bosses wielded considerable power and status within the black community, they occupied a very tenuous position in the larger white polity. On issues that threatened the white machine or its constituents, the black bosses could easily be outvoted. Thus patronage, services, and jobs were allocated to the ghetto only as long as black bosses controlled racial agitation and didn't threaten the color line, and the resources they received typically compared unfavorably to those provided to white politicians and their neighborhoods.

As with black business owners and professionals, the pragmatic adaptation of black politicians to the realities of segregation gave them a vested interest in the ghetto and its perpetuation. During the 1950s, for example, William Dawson joined with white ethnic politicians to oppose the construction of public housing projects in white neighborhoods, not because of an ideological objection to public housing per se, but because integration would antagonize his white political sponsors and take voters outside of wards that he controlled.

The status quo of a powerful white machine and a separate but dependent black machine was built on shifting sand, however. It remained viable only as long as cities dominated state politics, patronage was plentiful, and blacks comprised a minority of the population. During the 1950s and 1960s, white suburbanization and black in-migration systematically undermined these foundations, and white machine politicians became progressively less able to accommodate black demands while simultaneously maintaining the color line. Given the declining political clout of cities, the erosion of their tax base, and the rising proportion of blacks in cities, municipal politics became a racially charged zero-sum game that pitted politically disenfranchised blacks against a faltering coalition of ethnic whites.

In cities where blacks came to achieve an absolute majority—such as Baltimore, Newark, Gary, Detroit, Cleveland, and Washington, D.C.—the white political machine was destroyed as blacks assumed power and ended white patronage. In cities where the share of blacks peaked at around 40%—as in Chicago and Philadelphia—blacks were able to acquire power only by pulling liberal whites and disaffected Hispanics into a tenuous coalition, but given prevailing patterns of segregation these alliances were not politically stable. Chicago, for example, quickly reverted to white control in a way that succinctly illustrates the vulnerability of black politicians under conditions of racial segregation.

By the beginning of the 1980s, black in-migration to Chicago had stopped, white out-migration had leveled off, and the movement of Hispanics into the city was accelerating. As the share of blacks stalled at just above 40%, it became clear that they would not soon, if ever, comprise a majority of the Chicago's population. Latinos had become the swing voters and whoever pulled them into a coalition would rule the city. Mexican Americans and Puerto Ricans, however, had traditionally been ignored by the city's white machine politicians, and in frustration they joined with blacks in 1983 to elect the city's first black mayor, Harold Washington.

But under black leadership the fruits of political power did not come fast enough to satisfy rising

Latino expectations. Given the high degree of residential segregation between blacks and Hispanics, resources provided to black constituents had few spillover benefits for Mexican Americans or Puerto Ricans, and when Mayor Washington died early in his second term, they bolted from the black politicians to form a new coalition with the chastened and now politically receptive ethnic whites. Together Latinos and European whites constituted a working majority of voters who elected a new white mayor, Richard M. Daley, son of the city's last white political boss. Given their relative integration, moreover, white Europeans and Latinos found a stable basis for coalition politics based on geographically structured self-interest.

Chicago's Latinos now appear to be following the pluralist political model of earlier European immigrant groups; and because they are the only major group in the city whose numbers are growing, their political power and influence can only be expected to increase. As long as the working coalition between Latinos and European whites holds, blacks will be unable to win citywide power. The political isolation of blacks continues because of the structural limitations imposed on them by racial segregation, which guarantees that they have few interests in common with other groups.

Even in cities where blacks have assumed political leadership by virtue of becoming a majority, the structural constraints of segregation still remain decisive. Indeed, the political isolation experienced by blacks in places such as Newark and Detroit is probably more severe than that experienced earlier in the century, when ghetto votes were at least useful to white politicians in citywide elections. Once blacks gained control of the central city and whites completed their withdrawal to the surrounding suburbs, virtually all structural supports for interracial cooperation ended.

In the suburbs surrounding places such as Newark and Detroit, white politicians are administratively and politically insulated from black voters in central cities, and they have no direct political interest in their welfare. Indeed, money that flows into black central cities generally means increased taxes and lower net incomes for suburban whites. Because suburbanites now form a majority of most state populations—and a majority of the national electorate—the "chocolate city–vanilla suburb" pattern of contemporary racial segregation gives white politicians a strong interest in limiting the flow of public resources to black-controlled cities.

In an era of fiscal austerity and declining urban resources, therefore, the political isolation of blacks makes them extremely vulnerable to cutbacks in governmental services and public investments. If cuts must be made to balance strained city budgets, it makes political sense for white politicians to concentrate the cuts in black neighborhoods, where the political damage will be minimal; and if state budgets must be trimmed, it is in white legislators' interests to cut subventions to black-controlled central cities, which now represent a minority of most states' voters. The spatial and political isolation of blacks interacts with declining public resources to create a powerful dynamic for disinvestment in the black community.

The destructiveness of this dynamic has been forcefully illustrated by Rodrick and Deborah Wallace, who trace the direct and indirect results of a political decision in New York City to reduce the number of fire companies in black and Puerto Rican neighborhoods during the early 1970s.[1] Faced with a shortage of funds during the city's financial crisis, the Fire Department eliminated thirty-five fire companies between 1969 and 1976, twenty-seven of which were in poor minority areas located in the Bronx, Manhattan, and

---

[1] Deborah Wallace, "Roots of Increased Health Care Inequality in New York," *Social Science and Medicine* 31 (1990):1219–27; Rodrick Wallace, "Urban Desertification, Public Health and Public Order: 'Planned Shrinkage,' Violent Death, Substance Abuse, and AIDS in the Bronx," *Social Science and Medicine* 32 (1991):801–813; Rodrick Wallace, " 'Planned Shrinkage,' Contagious Urban Decay, and Violent Death in the Bronx: The Implications of Synergism," Epidemiology of Mental Disorders Research Department, New York State Psychiatric Institute, 1990.

Brooklyn, areas where the risk of fire was, in fact, quite high. Confronted with the unpleasant task of cutting services, white politicians confined the reductions to segregated ghetto and barrio wards where the political damage could be contained. The geographic and political isolation of blacks and Puerto Ricans meant that their representatives were unable to prevent the cuts.

As soon as the closings were implemented, the number of residential fires increased dramatically. An epidemic of building fires occurred within black and Puerto Rican neighborhoods. As housing was systematically destroyed, social networks were fractured and institutions collapsed; churches, block associations, youth programs, and political clubs vanished. The destruction of housing, networks, and social institutions, in turn, caused a massive flight of destitute families out of core minority areas. Some affected areas lost 80% of their residents between 1970 and 1980, putting a severe strain on housing in adjacent neighborhoods, which had been stable until then. As families doubled up in response to the influx of fire refugees, overcrowding increased, which led to additional fires and the diffusion of the chaos into adjacent areas. Black ghettos and Puerto Rican barrios were hollowed out from their cores.

The overcrowded housing, collapsed institutions, and ruptured support networks overwhelmed municipal disease prevention efforts and swamped medical care facilities. Within affected neighborhoods, infant mortality rates rose, as did the incidence of cirrhosis, gonorrhea, tuberculosis, and drug use. The destruction of the social fabric of black and Puerto Rican neighborhoods led to an increase in the number of unsupervised young males, which contributed to a sharp increase in crime, followed by an increase in the rate of violent deaths among young men. By 1990, this chain reaction of social and economic collapse had turned vast areas of the Bronx, Harlem, and Brooklyn into "urban deserts" bereft of normal community life.

Despite the havoc that followed in the wake of New York's fire service reductions, the cuts were never rescinded. The only people affected were minority members who were politically marginalized by segregation and thereby prevented, structurally, from finding allies to oppose the service reductions. Although residential segregation paradoxically made it easier for blacks and Puerto Ricans to elect city councillors by creating homogeneous districts, it left those that were elected relatively weak, dependent, and unable to protect the interests of their constituents.

As a result of their residential segregation and resultant political isolation, therefore, black politicians in New York and elsewhere have been forced into a strategy of angrily demanding that whites give them more public resources. Given their geographic isolation, however, these appeals cannot be made on the basis of whites' self-interest, but must rely on appeals to altruism, guilt, or fear. Because altruism, guilt, and fear do not provide a good foundation for concerted political action, the downward spiral of black neighborhoods continues and black hostility and bitterness grow while white fears are progressively reinforced. Segregation creates a political impasse that deepens the chasm of race in American society.

Under the best of circumstances, segregation undermines the ability of blacks to advance their interests because it provides ethnic whites with no immediate self-interest in their welfare. The circumstances of U.S. race relations, however, can hardly be described as "best," for not only do whites have little self-interest in promoting black welfare, but a significant share must be assumed to be racially prejudiced and supportive of policies injurious to blacks. To the extent that racism exists, of course, the geographic and political isolation of the ghetto makes it easier for racists to act on their prejudices. In a segregated society, blacks become easy targets for racist actions and policies.

The Meaning and Significance of Race

WILLIAM JULIUS WILSON

Many inner-city residents have a strong sense of the negative attitudes which employers tend to have toward them. A 33-year-old employed janitor from a poor South Side neighborhood had this observation: "I went to a coupla jobs where a couple of the receptionists told me in confidence: 'You know what they do with these applications from blacks as soon as the day is over?' Say 'we rip them and throw 'em in the garbage.'" In addition to concerns about being rejected because of race, the fears that some inner-city residents have of being denied employment simply because of their inner-city address or neighborhood are not unfounded. A welfare mother who lives in a large public housing project put it this way:

> Honestly, I believe they look at the address and the—your attitudes, your address, your surround—you know, your environment has a lot to do with your employment status. The people with the best addresses have the best chances, I feel so, I feel so.

Another welfare mother of two children from a South Side neighborhood expressed a similar view:

> I think that a lot of peoples don't get jobs over here because they lives—they live in the projects. They think that just 'cause people living in the projects they no good. Yes, yes. I think so! I think so! I think a lot of people might judge a person because you out—because they got a project address. You know, when you put it on an application, they might not even hire you because you live over here.

A 34-year-old single and unemployed black man put it this way: "If you're from a nice neighborhood I believe it's easier for you to get a job and stuff. I have been on jobs and such and gotten looks from folks and such, 'I wonder if he is the type who do those things that happen in that neighborhood.'"

Although the employers' perceptions of inner-city workers make it difficult for low-income blacks to find or retain employment, it is interesting to note that there is one area where the views of employers and those of many inner-city residents converge—namely, in their attitudes toward inner-city black males. Inner-city residents are aware of the problems of male joblessness in their neighborhoods. For example, more than half the black UPFLS survey respondents from neighborhoods with poverty rates of at least 40 percent felt that very few or none of the men in their neighborhood were working steadily. More than one-third of the respondents from neighborhoods with poverty rates of at least 30 percent expressed that view as well. Forty percent of the black respondents in all neighborhoods in the UPFLS felt that the number of men with jobs has steadily decreased over the past ten years. However, responses to the open-ended questions in our Social Opportunity Survey and data from our ethnographic field interviews reveal a consistent pattern of negative views among the respondents concerning inner-city black males, especially young black males.

Some provided explanations in which they acknowledged the constraints that black men face.

An employed 25-year-old unmarried father of one child from North Lawndale stated:

> I know a lot of guys that's my age, that don't work and I know some that works temporary, but wanna work, they just can't get the jobs. You know, they got a high school diploma and that . . . but the thing is, these jobs always say: Not enough experience. How can you get some experience if you never had a chance to get any experience?

Others, however, expressed views that echoed those of the employers. For example, a 30-year-old married father of three children who lives in North Lawndale and works the night shift in a factory stated:

> I say about 65 percent—of black males, I say, don't wanna work, and when I say don't wanna work I say don't wanna work hard—they want a real easy job, making big bucks—see? And, and when you start talking about hard labor and earning your money with sweat or just once in a while you gotta put out a little bit—you know, that extra effort, I don't, I don't think the guys really wanna do that. And sometimes it comes from, really, not having a, a steady job or, really, not being out in the work field and just been sittin' back, being comfortable all the time and hanging out.

A 35-year-old welfare mother of eight children from the Englewood neighborhood on the South Side agreed:

> Well, I mean see you got all these dudes around here, they don't even work, they don't even try, they don't wanna work. You know what I mean, I wanna work, but I can't work. Then you got people here that, in this neighborhood, can get up and do somethin', they just don't wanna do nothin'—they really don't.

The deterioration of the socioeconomic status of black men may have led to the negative perceptions of both the employers and the inner-city residents. Are these perceptions merely stereotypical or do they have any basis in fact? Data from the UPFLS survey show that variables measuring differences in social context (neighborhoods, social networks, and households) accounted for substantially more of the gap in the employment rates of black and Mexican men than did variables measuring individual attitudes. Also, data from the survey reveal that jobless black men have a lower

"reservation wage" than the jobless men in the other ethnic groups. They were willing to work for less than $6.00 per hour, whereas Mexican and Puerto Rican jobless men expected $6.20 and $7.20, respectively, as a condition for working; white men, on the other hand, expected over $9.00 per hour. This would appear to cast some doubt on the characterization of black inner-city men as wanting "something for nothing," of holding out for high pay.

But surveys are not the best way to get at underlying attitudes and values. Accordingly, to gain a better grasp of the cultural issues, I examined the UPFLS ethnographic research that involved establishing long-term contacts and conducting interviews with residents from several neighborhoods. Richard Taub points out:

> Anybody who studies subgroups within the American population knows that there are cultural patterns which are distinctive to the subgroups and which have consequences for social outcomes. The challenge for those concerned about poverty and cultural variation is to link cultural arrangements to larger structural realities and to understand the interaction between the consequences of one's structural position on the one hand and pattern group behavior on the other. It is important to understand that the process works both ways. Cultures are forged in part on the basis of adaptation to both structural and material environments.

Analysis of the ethnographic data reveals identifiable and consistent patterns of attitudes and beliefs among inner-city ethnic groups. The data, systematically analyzed by Taub, reveal that the black men are more hostile than the Mexican men with respect to the low-paying jobs they hold, less willing to be flexible in taking assignments or tasks not considered part of their job, and less willing to work as hard for the same low wages. These contrasts in the behavior of the two groups of men are sharp because many of the Mexicans interviewed were recent immigrants.

"Immigrants, particularly Third World immigrants," will often "tolerate harsher conditions, lower pay, fewer upward trajectories, and other job related characteristics that deter native workers, and thereby exhibit a better 'work ethic' than others." The ethnographic data from the UPFLS suggest that the Mexican immigrants are harder workers because they "come from areas of intense poverty and that even boring, hard, dead-end jobs look, by contrast, good to them." They also fear being deported if they fail to find employment.

Once again, it should be emphasized that the contrasts between blacks and Mexicans in our ethnographic sample are sharp because most of the latter in our sample were recent immigrants. Our ethnographic research was conducted mainly in black and Latino inner-city neighborhoods, and the ethnographic data that were sufficient to draw systematic comparisons concerning work attitudes were those based on intensive field interviews with Mexican men and African-American men. However, as indicated earlier, the large UPFLS survey revealed that white men in the inner city have a much higher reservation wage than either African-American or Latino inner-city men. Accordingly, there is no reason to assume that their attitude toward dead-end menial jobs is any less negative than that of black men.

Since our sample was largely drawn from poverty areas, it includes a disproportionate number of immigrants, who tend to settle initially in poverty areas. As previous research has consistently shown, migrants who leave a poorer economy for a more developed economy in the hope of improving their standard of living tend to accept, willingly, the kinds of employment that the indigenous workers detest or have come to reject. It is reasonable to hypothesize that the more "Americanized" they become, the less inclined they will be to accept menial low-wage and hazardous jobs.

In contrast to the Mexican men, the inner-city black men complained that they get assigned the heaviest or dirtiest work on the job, are overworked, and are paid less than nonblacks. They strongly feel that they are victims of discrimination. "The Mexican-American men also report that they feel exploited," states Taub, "but somehow that comes with the territory." Taub argues that the inner-city black men have a greater sense of "honor" and often see the work, pay, and treatment from bosses as insulting and degrading.

Accordingly, a heightened sensitivity to exploitation fuels their anger and gives rise to a tendency to "just walk off the job."

One has to look at the growing exclusion of black men from higher-paying blue-collar jobs in manufacturing and other industries and their increasing confinement to low-paying service laboring jobs to understand these attitudes and how they developed. Many low-paying jobs have predictably low retention rates. For example, one of the respondents in the UPFLS employer survey reported turnover rates at his firm that exceeded 50 percent. When asked if he had considered doing anything about this problem, the employer acknowledged that the company had made a rational decision to tolerate a high turnover rather than increasing the starting salary and improving working conditions to attract higher-caliber workers: "Our practice has been that we'll keep hiring and, hopefully, one or two of them are going to wind up being good."

As Kathryn Neckerman points out, "This employer, and others like him, can afford such high turnover because the work is simple and can be taught in a couple of days. On average, jobs paying under $5.00 or $6.00 an hour were characterized by high quit rates. In higher-paying jobs, by contrast, the proportion of employees resigning fell to less than 20 percent per year." Yet UPFLS data show that the proportion of inner-city black males in the higher-paying blue-collar positions has declined far more sharply than that of Latinos and whites. Increasingly displaced from manufacturing industries, inner-city black males are more confined to low-paying service work. Annual turnover rates of 50 to 100 percent are common in low-skill service jobs in Chicago, regardless of the race or ethnicity of the employees.

Thus, the attitudes that many inner-city black males express about their jobs and job prospects reflect their plummeting position in a changing labor market. The more they complain and manifest their dissatisfaction, the less desirable they seem to employers. They therefore experience greater rejection when they seek employment and clash more often with supervisors when they secure employment.

Residence in highly concentrated poverty neighborhoods aggravates the weak labor-force attachment of black males. The absence of effective informal job networks and the frequency of many illegal activities increases nonmainstream behavior such as hustling. As Sharon Hicks-Bartlett, another member of the UPFLS research team, points out, "Hustling is making money by doing whatever is necessary to survive or simply make ends meet. It can be legal or extra-legal work and may transpire in the formal or informal economy. While both men and women hustle, men are more conspicuous in the illegal arena of hustling."

In a review of the research literature on the experiences of black men in the labor market, Philip Moss and Christopher Tilly point out that criminal activity in urban areas has become more attractive because of the disappearance of legitimate jobs. They refer to a recent study in Boston that showed that while "black youth in Boston were evenly split on whether they could make more money in a straight job or on the street, by 1989 a three-to-one majority of young black people expressed the opinion that they could make more on the street."

The restructuring of the economy will continue to compound the negative effects of the prevailing perceptions of inner-city black males. Because of the increasing shift away from manufacturing and toward service industries, employers have a greater need for workers who can effectively serve and relate to the consumer. Inner-city black men are not perceived as having these qualities.

The restructuring of the urban economy could also have long-term consequences for inner-city black women. Neckerman argues that a change in work cultures accompanied the transformation of the economy, resulting in a mismatch between the old and new ways of succeeding in the labor market. In other words, there is a growing difference between the practices of blue-collar and service employers and the practices of white-collar employers. This mismatch is important in assessing the labor-market success of inner-city workers.

Low-skilled individuals from the inner city tend to be the children of blue-collar workers or service workers, and their work experience is thus largely confined to blue-collar or service jobs. What happens "when employees socialized to approach jobs and careers in ways that make sense in a blue-collar or service context enter the white-collar world?" The employer interviews suggest that workers from blue-collar or service settings seek positions that carry high entry-level salaries that provide all the necessary training on the job and that grant privileges and promotion in accordance with both seniority and performance. But in a white-collar setting, inner-city workers face entry-level positions that require more and continuous training and employers who are looking for people who are energetic, intelligent, and possess good language skills. Promotions in this environment seldom depend on seniority. Accordingly, "their advancement may depend on fairly subtle standards of evaluation, and on behavior that is irrelevant or even negatively sanctioned in the blue-collar and service settings." Interviews with inner-city workers revealed that most recognize the changing nature of the labor market and that a greater premium is placed on education and training for success, but many "did indeed espouse blue-collar ways of getting ahead."

In summary, the issue of race in the labor market cannot simply be reduced to the presence of discrimination. Although our data suggest that inner-city blacks, especially African-American males, are experiencing increasing problems in the labor market, the reasons for those problems are seen in a complex web of interrelated factors, including those that are race-neutral.

The loss of traditional manufacturing and other blue-collar jobs in Chicago resulted in increased joblessness among inner-city black males and a concentration in low-wage, high-turnover laborer and service-sector jobs. Embedded in ghetto neighborhoods, social networks, and households that are not conducive to employment, inner-city black males fall further behind their white and Hispanic counterparts, especially when the labor market is slack. Hispanics "continue to funnel into manufacturing because employers prefer Hispanics over blacks and they like to hire by referrals from current employees, which Hispanics can readily furnish, being already embedded in migration networks." Inner-city black men grow bitter and resentful in the face of their employment prospects and often manifest or express these feelings in their harsh, often dehumanizing, low-wage work settings.

Their attitudes and actions, combined with erratic work histories in high-turnover jobs, create the widely shared perception that they are undesirable workers. The perception in turn becomes the basis for employers' negative hiring decisions, which sharply increase when the economy is weak. The rejection of inner-city black male workers gradually grows over the long term not only because employers are turning more to the expanding immigrant and female labor force, but also because the number of jobs that require contact with the public continues to climb.

The position of inner-city black women in the labor market is also problematic. Their high degree of social isolation in impoverished neighborhoods reduces their employment prospects. Although Chicago employers consider them more acceptable as workers than the inner-city black men, their social isolation is likely to strengthen involvement in a work culture that has few supports allowing a move into white-collar employment. Also, impoverished neighborhoods, weak networks, and weak household supports decrease their ability to develop language and other job-related skills necessary in an economy that increasingly rewards employees who can work and communicate effectively with the public.

Despite the attitudes of employers, joblessness in inner-city ghetto neighborhoods would decline if the U.S. economy could sustain high levels of employment over a long period of time. In a slack labor market—a labor market with high unemployment—employers are—and indeed, can afford to be—more selective in recruiting and in granting promotions. They overemphasize job prerequisites and exaggerate the value of experience. In such an economic climate, disadvantaged minorities suffer disproportionately and the level of employer discrimination rises. In a tight labor market, job vacancies are numerous, unemployment is of short duration, and wages are higher. Moreover, in a tight labor market the labor force expands because increased job opportunities not only reduce unemployment but also draw into the labor force those workers who, in periods when the labor market is slack, respond to fading job prospects by dropping out of the labor force altogether. Conversely, in a tight labor market the status of all workers—including disadvantaged minorities—improves because of lower unemployment, higher wages, and better jobs.

The economic recovery during the first half of the 1990s lowered the unemployment rates among blacks in general. For the first time in more than two decades, the unemployment rate for African-Americans dipped below 10 percent in December 1994. Indeed, "the unemployment rate for black adults dropped faster in 1994 than it did for white adults." This was in part due to a brief expansion of manufacturing jobs. By contrast, the economy saw a slight decrease in manufacturing jobs during the economic recovery period in the late 1980s and more than 1.5 million positions were eliminated from January 1989 to September 1993. However, 301,000 manufacturing jobs were created during the next sixteen months, significantly benefiting black workers who are heavily concentrated in manufacturing.

Nonetheless, the unemployment rate represents only the percentage of workers in the labor force—that is, those who are actively looking for work. A more significant measure is the employment-to-population ratio, which corresponds to the percentage of adult workers 16 and older who are working. For example, whereas the unemployment rate for black youths 16 years old and older was 34.6 percent in December of 1994, compared with a white youth unemployment rate of 14.7 percent, only 23.9 percent of all black youths were actually working, compared with 48.5 percent of white youths. In previous years, labor-market demand stimulated by fiscal or monetary policy not only absorbed the technically unemployed (that is, those jobless workers who are in the official labor force) but also enlarged the employment ranks by drawing back workers who were not in or had dropped out of the labor force. Today, it appears that inner-city residents who are not in the labor force tend to be beyond the reach of monetary or fiscal policy. The problem is that in recent years tight labor markets have been of relatively short duration, frequently followed by a recession which either wiped out previous gains for many workers or did not allow others to fully recover from a previous period of economic stagnation. It would take sustained tight labor markets over many years to draw back those discouraged inner-city workers who have dropped out of the labor market altogether, some for very long periods of time. The disappearance of work in the inner-city ghetto presents a serious challenge to society. The consequences of such joblessness are not restricted to the inner-city ghettos, they affect the quality of life and race relations in the larger city as well.

'Us' and 'Them': Employer Preferences in Hiring

ROGER WALDINGER AND MICHAEL I. LICHTER

A NEW ETHNIC ORDER?

Latino Immigrants: "They Like to Work"

One might imagine, especially in the immigrant-dense regions of Southern California, South Florida, or New York, that apprehension over the political and demographic consequences of immigration might lead Euro-Americans to revise their long-held racial antipathy for blacks. Yet Euro-American employers still prove reluctant to hire African Americans, even if the alternative involves recruiting Mexicans or Central Americans, toward whom the same Euro-American bosses often evince considerable aversion.

The distinction . . . between attitudes and preferences does much to illuminate the characteristics of the emergent ethnic hierarchy, as well as the factors influencing employers' selection and ranking criteria. In Los Angeles' multi-ethnic labor market, nativity serves as a crucial marker, although only one of several, distinguishing "us" from "them." . . . [I]ndividualistic understandings of the issue link discrimination to an aversion to others not like oneself: "we" do not hire "them," because "they" are different, hence to be kept at a distance from "us." But, from the employers'

perspective, "we" lack those characteristics that make for a good—that is, hardworking and uncomplaining—low-level worker. Although the employers seemed unlikely to think of themselves as "un-American," they often viewed "American" as shorthand for those qualities to avoid in a worker. "The American people, *we've* been spoiled." Part of the problem was a general disinclination for hard, menial labor: "The American workforce does not want to do physical labor." But the problem lay deeper: "Americans are too damned spoiled and lazy to work. Fifteen, twenty years ago, I wouldn't have said this. Their outlook has changed completely."

"Spoiled" American workers held to the belief that "it's a birthright to have good jobs and good pay. Why on earth would an American clean a hotel for five-fifty an hour? But immigrants see them as good jobs. There's a willingness to take jobs that Americans see as demeaning." Managers were enchanted neither with the American approach to work at the bottom—"It's 3:30, I've done my job. It's 'me, me, me.' "—nor with the prevailing work ethos. "When you say to an American person, 'Do you want to work at McDonald's?' they'll say, 'No way. I don't want to flip burgers,' due to the general laziness of American culture." Worse still was the fact that, as Americans, the native-born workforce was likely to talk back: "And American workers are more concerned with their rights, as opposed to immigrants who just want a job and will settle for minimal pay without a fuss. [Without immigrants] we'd have

Source: Roger Waldinger and Michael I. Lichter, "A New Ethnic Order," in *How the Other Half Works: Immigration and the Social Organization of Labor,* University of California Press, Copyright © 2003; 160–170. Used with permission of University of California Press.

more problems managing workers that would be more difficult and more demanding."

Lack of the experiences, and therefore, expectations, shared by natives made the foreign-born workers different. But this was not such a bad thing, since "having gone without meals gives you motivation," as a fast-fooder explained: "These people have a drive. From where these people are coming from, they are not given the opportunities that they are granted here, so the workers are very motivated to work, and work hard. Even though they are earning low wages."

Rephrased in the language of our respondents, the disparities between *here* and *there* made all the difference: "Where *they* come from, five dollars an hour, at home, is a lot of money to them, where five dollars *here* is nothing"; "From where *they* are coming, working for these wages—*they* think it's great"; "For *them,* the basics is a lot; for people raised *here,* it is not worth it." Or, as clarified by one of our more sophisticated furniture industry respondents, "If *I* consider that relative deprivation,"—the "that" consisting of unskilled work at "six-to-seven-dollar rates"—"*they* consider this a very good opportunity."

Thus, immigrants *were* different from "us," but their differences served as a *positive* signal for selection; the immigrants' "otherness" was associated with a set of behavioral characteristics that employers generally liked. "The 'amigo'," a fast-food manager said bluntly, "comes to work." Noted others:

Yes, the immigrants just want to work, work long hours, just want to do anything. They spend a lot of money coming up from Mexico. They want as many hours as possible. If I called them in for four hours to clean latrines, they'd do it. *They like to work.* They have large families, a big work ethic, and small salaries. The whites have more, so they're willing to work fewer hours. Vacation time is important to them. They get a play and want to get two months off. They want me to rearrange a schedule at a moment's notice. These guys in the back would never dream of that. They would like to go back to Mexico every four years for a month which I [let them] do. The back-of-the-house workers take vacation pay and then work through their vacations. I try to get them to take off a week once a year. But most of them plead poverty. The kids in the front of

the house are still being taken care of by their parents. I'm not trying to disparage them, but *they're spoiled.* (Manager in a French bistro)

Immigrants are here to work, and they're not afraid of hard work. There are a lot of young Americans who don't want to work. If they want work at the minimum wage, they go elsewhere. Immigrants will work for minimum wage and *won't complain, even if you keep them there forever.* They're used to this kind of job. (Coffee shop manager)

They're real good workers and they work lots of overtime. I mean they work and work and work. . . . Maybe some of your natives would say, "Wait a minute, I've already worked, you know, eighty hours this week. I'm kind of tired." Well then, you know, your Asian will go, "Oh yeah, you need me to work? No problem." So I think that the work ethic, you talk about work ethic, is there for them. Because, I mean, compared to what they came from this is paradise. (Public hospital human resources manager)

They're willing to work for a dollar. They don't have an attitude of "you owe me a job." They'll give eight hours work for eight hours of pay, *and they're happy doing it,* especially Hispanics. (Print shop manager)

As indicated by the comments above, employers' assessments were most likely to be couched in contextual terms, praising the immigrants for traits especially valuable in the function that the newcomers filled. As a furniture manufacturer put it, "I think that immigrants as a whole are generally suited for the type of work that we do"—hard, menial, poorly remunerated, and not likely to be seen as suitable by many other, native-born groups. Indeed, the employers tended to describe group characteristics in terms of jobs held, as did the furniture manufacturer who told us that "the Hispanic will work on a repetitive basis," the printer who observed that "Latinos seem to be good with their hands," or the manufacturer who told us that "Hispanics are good in this type of industry." Not only were immigrants considered well-matched for the tasks involved, they also were seen as possessing understandings of the reward/effort relationship that an employer would be especially likely to appreciate. "They are willing to come and do whatever job you tell them without question." Unlike the natives, the immigrants were fully cognizant of the importance of a job, and therefore less likely to quit in search of better prospects. "We have very little turnover in positions that I would think people would not want to stay in for a long period of time, like the Environmental Services Tech position [janitor]," said the HR manager of a large HMO. "The [immigrants] . . . are content to have, to continue working in those positions. So, often we have people who've been here for twenty years."

Even better, the newcomers were unlikely to scoff at the employer's coin: "I think immigrants are very hardworking, they are responsible, and most importantly are willing to receive meager salaries for the work they put in." Finally, they knew their place in the social hierarchy of the workplace, proving more accepting of subordination than were natives, as suggested by the white personnel director of an Asian fast-food chain: "The Latinos in our locations, most are recent arrivals. Most are tenuously here, and here on fragile documents. I see them as very subservient. I see the Asian restaurant managers call them the 'amigos.' That's their name for them. The Asian kitchen people are very hierarchical. There's a place for everyone and it's clear where their place is."

"I Don't Know How They Do It"

As argued above, the managers were quite capable of preferring immigrants to fill the low-level jobs that few others found attractive without actually *liking* the immigrants, or (as we note below) favoring immigration, or holding the immigrants' ethnic groups in high esteem. To some extent, the stigma associated with the job spilled over to the group, with suitability for undesirable work signaling incompatibility with higher functions. Thus, the appreciation involved in a typical comment— "Lots of Spanish people, if they're working for you and feel that they have a fair shake, they stay forever"—had its nastier accompaniment, in the form of respondents' "amazement" over workers who persisted in dead-end jobs for years. "I see a lot of complacency," noted a respondent, referring to "people contented in housekeeping or entry-level jobs and remain in them. I don't know how they do it." Likewise, managers glad to find somebody to

fill their entry-level jobs nonetheless looked down on those persons, whom they saw as "not all that interested in responsibility and advancement." One hotel manager nicely expressed the Janus-faced nature of the evaluations involved in the preference for immigrant labor: "The dishwashers don't have to speak English. They're not driven, not motivated. They don't want to better their life. They're happy, doing a good job, a whole group of non-promotables."

Thus, contrary to what follows from more individualistic perspectives, a preference for immigrant labor could go hand-in-hand with an aversion to immigrants or their communities. "There are so many of them," said a department store personnel manager, who happened to be a native-born woman of Mexican descent. She referred to the immigrants in terms that echoed the protests of many other Californians: "There are also a lot from Mexico that come up to get social services. They're exploiting California's welfare system. They come here and think we should support them. They get Social Security. Especially from Asia. They come in with an immigrant status and they get more money than Americans on Social Security."

A printer who saw no alternatives to hiring immigrants, since "I can't seem to hire whites right now," still thought that immigrants "should be kept out, enough are here already." A furniture manufacturer with a heavily foreign-born workforce conceded that immigration "creates the quality of my life," but also told us that "on a personal level where we live, a lot of us see the quality of life deteriorating and a lot of us feel it is because of immigration." A manager in a printing plant could laud the newcomers as *workers,* but go on to describe the immigrants as *people* in quite unflattering terms:

Field notes: The respondent first tells me, "A lot of people come to me from working in the fields." She goes on to say that they've picked vegetables, milked cows, done whatever they could do to help their family, and are used to hard work. "There's very few lazy immigrant workers." But she then notes that Thais are industrious, more eager to assimilate into American culture than are Hispanics. "Here, everything is set up for Hispanics. They don't have to utter a word in English and can get along fine. Thais want to learn English." She tells me that she lives near a Tianguis supermarket [a subdivision of a major supermarket chain, designed to serve the Hispanic market] and has to make a two-city drive to get to a market where people speak English and she can recognize the food.

Similarly, a contextually related preference might not exclude a negative stereotype or an implied, more abstract, aversion: "[The immigrants are] all pretty much hard workers but relatively lazy when it comes to the language." In general, resentment of the symbolic and cultural changes associated with immigration—as well as of the prominence of Spanish and other "foreign" languages in the workplace and public space—were frequently echoed by managers who had nothing but praise for the immigrants' work ethic.

The Hierarchy of the Bottom

By the same token, as immigrants' "otherness" progressively disappeared—a process quaintly described by the social sciences as "assimilation"—employers came to feel differently about the newcomers, without, however, any gain in affection. Hardly multiculturalists, the managers were ambivalent about Americanization. "[T]he more Americanized the [immigrants] become, they start getting a little bit lazier, once they start to learn the system," said a furniture manufacturer. A hotelier had a similar complaint, praising the "new immigrants, [who] tend to be the most aggressive and hardest workers," but chastising "the more American ones, [who] tend to be less productive." A printer thought that "immigrants come here trying to survive," but that "those who've been here a while see that there are ways to get by." Asked about the second generation, managers were even less enthusiastic: the children of the immigrants were "too damned Americanized"—that is to say, too much like "us." One remarked: "If the sons are raised in the old way of raising children, they are just like their parents. But if they are Americanized, a *pocho,* the majority of them turn out to have an American work ethic."

Managers looked askance at assimilation—"Americanized Mexicans . . . that's the problem"—because the process changed the bench-marks by which immigrant children evaluated both jobs and the terms of compensation. The second generation was seen as not so willing to cooperate with authority: "We tell them that we need you to sweep outside," said a printer; "They say 'that's not what I was hired for.' " Nor were they willing to work as hard, having other options. "The children of immigrants are more cocky. This is probably as a result of the American system. They have an attitude, they are also more familiar with their environment. Confidence is more apparent in the children of immigrants. They are also more inclined to leave the job and not work for a considerable time," said one white furniture manufacturing manager. "Many of the Mexican Americans acquire an education and they don't want to work in these types of jobs. Also the Mexican American is bilingual, so he has other opportunities to work in other settings earning better salaries," said another HR manager, a Latino, also in furniture manufacturing.

Of course, the same characteristics could fit managers' needs in other ways, as noted by a manufacturer who told us that "they are not as hard-working as their parents, although they speak both languages, which is an asset." Consequently, depending on the dimension and its relevance to the tasks at hand, the fading of otherness could make immigrants' children preferable as workers because they had become "like us," just as it could make them unwanted for the same reason.

Since the preference for immigrants was so often contextual, it did not necessarily generalize beyond the workplace or even the specific set of jobs for which particular immigrant groups were thought suited. Whereas employers associated foreign birth with an "otherness" conducive to desired work habits, many were also aware of other distinctions among the immigrant population, providing the basis for a more elaborate ranking. In the words of one furniture manufacturer:

In Southern California, if I had to rank workforces, and give you four racial areas of Caucasian, Asian, blacks, and Hispanics—I would say if I had to rank them I would probably rate the Caucasian with the Asian equal, but for different reasons. The Caucasians because of the communications skills, the flexibility skills, and the comfortness that we would have culturally. The Asians would be here on the basis of hard working, long hours, the ability to do detailed work. The Hispanic would come underneath them, on the basis of their ability to do tedious work over a long period of time, and reasonably good quality, but lacking in flexibility, communication skills, education, and drive. This leaves us with blacks at the bottom, who have no flexibility, no drive, massive personal problems, and no feeling that they want to contribute to the well-being of the company.

Most managers thought that "immigrants are hardworking people, anywhere they come from." Still, their discourse about race and ethnicity at the workplace pointed to a distinct and often quite elaborate hierarchy. Asians vied with whites as the most preferred group; Latinos, taking into account distinctions based on generational status and national origins, were arrayed towards, but not at, the bottom; and blacks were generally the least liked *and* least preferred group. Said one manager, after a long pause: "Based on my observations, I could generalize by saying that Asians are very well-organized and regimented. They are quality workers. They don't distract easily from their work. Hispanics, on the other hand, are more casual, have less intensity. You also have to be motivating the Hispanic group so they will arrive on time. Tardiness is a big problem. Blacks, on the other hand, are even less productive. This is from the very limited experience that I have with this group [blacks]."

As suggested by these remarks, rankings often involved the invocation of prejudices having little if any relationship to the work context, informed only by broader social stereotypes. Employers' praise of Asians took the familiar form of the superego stereotype. They heaped encomiums on Asians' hard-work ethic, desire to get ahead, drive, goal orientation, and so on, only to arrive at the inevitable comparison: "They're able to trade dollars with the best Jewish salesman you ever saw." As displayed also in the quotes above, stereotypes of Hispanics revealed ambivalence with a more negative twist. Wanting a compliant workforce, some employers

discovered that there was such a thing as workers who were *too* subservient. As one department store manager said, "[T]he Hispanic people don't seem to really want to improve themselves as much as some of the other groups do." Of course, stereotypes invoking the image of the dumb and unambitious but eager-to-please worker seemed to entail considerable projection; it was far easier to blame underlings for their lack of skills than oneself or the "bigger bosses" for the pinched purse and unpleasant conditions that deterred more-qualified workers and allowed no outlet for the ambitious.

On the other hand, differences in education and skill between most Asians and Hispanics meant that employers' preferences regarding the two groups were unlikely to enter into hiring decisions for entry-level jobs. Employers were indeed likely to prefer hiring Asians over Hispanics when given the choice, but this opportunity only rarely presented itself. Skill differences ensured that workers of Asian and Hispanic background were typically assigned to different jobs. Asians were found in the office, not in the shop; employed as supervisors, not line workers; involved "in sales and work with computers, while Hispanics are in the pressroom"; "stealing the jobs at the technical level," according to a hospital manager, but never applying for housekeeping positions. Even if many respondents agreed with the printer who contended that "Asians are more productive," this assessment was normally irrelevant to entry-level hiring decisions. As the African-American owner of a small print shop told us, the ethnicity of the worker "depends on the job function. In the United States, you wouldn't find an Asian running a press."

Although employers were also aware of national origin differences among Latino workers, no comparably clear set of feelings or judgments had crystallized around these characteristics. Some respondents did seem to entertain a ranking system, but there was little intensity or much consistency in their comparisons. For the most part, social distance complicated the job of making the fundamental perceptual distinctions needed for such discriminations. "They are all Hispanic to me. I can't distinguish between nationalities." Occasionally, the employers noted a behavioral difference related to some disparity in the immigrant settlement experience, as pointed out by a manufacturer who told us that, "[w]here we see the difference, the Mexicans, during Christmas, tend to want to go home, because it's closer." Such niceties apart, the traits that might distinguish Latino immigrants from one another were not seen as so impressive as those that made these immigrants different from the native-born. As a department store manager tersely responded, "[They are] all hard workers to me."

AFRICAN AMERICANS: DISLIKED AND NOT PREFERRED

If employers prefer immigrants without necessarily liking them, what considerations influence their views of blacks, and with what effects? Dislike for African Americans does a reasonable job of explaining white avoidance of blacks as neighbors, but it obviously cannot explain why some people who will not tolerate a black neighbor will happily employ a black servant. Economic theories of prejudice provide plausible accounts of how white owners can get away with paying lower wages to black than to white workers, but these accounts are of limited help here. . . . [S]tandard economic theory casts owners as motivated by the desire for profit maximization. Instead, however, the economic theory of discrimination contends that they may be driven by a "taste for discrimination," a modification introduced ad hoc and without justification. At its best, the economic theory of discrimination illuminates the trade-off between the psychic benefits of discrimination and the monetary rewards of hiring without prejudice. However, this trade-off only applies to capitalists, not to their agents—that is, managers—who may well put their comfort ahead of any profits foregone as a result of discrimination. In any event, the economic framework is largely irrelevant to the issue at hand, which is not wage inequality *within* any given occupation, but occupational segregation. We want to know why employers

have generally been willing to hire blacks as janitors and hotel maids, but far more resistant to engaging them as bank tellers or sales-persons— not to speak of higher-level, more prestigious positions in the professions or management.

Where Do African Americans Now Fit?

An alternative to the economists' view might be that employers hire under the influence of stereotyped notions of the jobs for which blacks are most fit. But any such hypothesis suffers from circularity, since the fit between traditional stereotype and historical position has been too tight to determine which came first. In the past, long-held stereotypes proved no obstacle when other considerations became important; the historical record shows that employers who previously excluded blacks could quickly turn accepting, particularly when blacks could be deployed as replacements for union-prone and strike-happy whites.

In any case, it is not clear how traditional stereotypes of African Americans would influence decisions in today's labor market. On the one hand, we are asking about factors that affect entry into jobs that have generally been considered right for persons considered inferior, so it is unlikely that views of African-American inferiority would render them ineligible for jobs denoting inferiority (such as janitorial or other unskilled jobs). On the other hand, we are also interested in explaining the declining African-American presence in positions or industries (e.g., hotels and hospitals) where they were previously overrepresented. Since a constant cannot explain a change, one cannot invoke traditional stereotypes as an explanation of why employers of low-skilled help suddenly developed an aversion to black labor. And as these stereotypes served to explain why blacks were confined to the low-skilled sector in the first place, we are locked in circularity.

It may be that employers are impelled by a new set of stereotypes. As Lawrence Bobo, among others, has argued, there is a new form of Euro-American prejudice in play, in which "laissez-faire racism" has replaced the "Jim Crow racism" of old.[1] For Bobo, laissez-faire racism functions as a stratification ideology, explaining black/white inequality in terms of deficiencies of individual blacks, as opposed to the persistent effect of racialized social structures; laissez-faire racism includes *symbolic racism,* a view that "blacks violate such traditional American values as individualism and self-reliance, the work ethic, obedience, and discipline."[2] *Laissez-faire* racism also draws from contemporary conceptions of African Americans bound up with media-popularized notions of the "underclass"—which, to the extent they attempt to explain persistent black poverty, have increased the salience of stereotypic views of blacks as unwilling to work. As opposed to older stereotypes of inherent inferiority, the "underclass" label ascribes the problems of poor African Americans to misguided government attempts to do good, the suburbanization of the well-behaved middle and working classes, and the birth of a "culture of poverty" among those remaining in the urban ghetto. Lingering images from the Black Power movement of the 1960s, videos from the "gangsta rap" movement of the 1990s, and age-old fears of "black thugs and rapists" have combined, within the "underclass" rubric, to identify opposition to authority as the principal expression of black identity. Whereas traditional stereotypes of blacks impeded movement into higher-level positions, while supporting continued black employment in menial jobs, underclass stereotypes may have the opposite effect. Equipped with the new stereotypes, employers filling professional positions may consider well-educated middle-class African Americans, but those seeking deferential less-educated workers are cued to scratch African Americans off the list.

This argument brings us . . . to the Blumerian concept of race as a sense of group position. . . . Traditional stereotypes of African Americans told employers where black workers belonged, producing a contextual preference for persons otherwise disliked. The new stereotypes, by contrast, signal that this earlier fit no longer holds. Black workers should not be assigned to bottom-level tasks, because their sense of group position no longer supports the subordination that such low-level roles require. The new stereotypes associated with low-level labor groups typically combine negative traits (too stupid/too smart, not sufficiently ambitious/too competitive) with some positive evaluation (hardworking). Thus past and present diverge. Employers in the low-skilled sector previously held *negative* attitudes toward blacks as *people* but *positive* preferences for blacks as *workers* for the least desirable jobs. Today, however, both attitudes *and* preferences are negative. Moreover, the weight of the antiblack animus reduces the likelihood that employers' experiences with blacks will be sufficiently common or powerful to undermine the new stereotypes' baneful influence.

[1]Lawrence Bobo, James R. Kluegel, and Ryan A. Smith, "Laissez-faire racism: the crystallization of a 'kinder, gentler' ideology," in *Racial attitudes in the 1990s: continuity and change,* ed. S.A. Tuch and J.K. Martin (Westport, Conn.: Praeger, 1997).
[2]Donald R. Kinder and David O. Sears, "Prejudice and politics: symbolic racism versus racial threats to the good life," *Journal of Personality and Social Psychology* 40 (1981): 416.

No Shame in (This) Game

KATHERINE S. NEWMAN

In the early 1990s, the McDonald's Corporation launched a television ad campaign featuring a young black man named Calvin, who was portrayed sitting atop a Brooklyn stoop in his Golden Arches uniform while his friends down on the sidewalk passed by, giving him a hard time about holding down a "McJob." After brushing off their teasing with good humor, Calvin is approached furtively by one young black man who asks, *sotto voce,* whether Calvin might help him get a job too. He allows that he could use some earnings and that despite the ragging he has just given Calvin, he thinks the uniform is really pretty cool—or at least that having a job is pretty cool.

Every fast food worker we interviewed for this book knew the Calvin series by heart: Calvin on the job, Calvin in the streets, Calvin helping an elderly woman cross the street on his way to work, Calvin getting promoted to management. And they knew what McDonald's was trying to communicate to young people by producing the series in the first place: that the stigma clings to fast food jobs, that it can be overcome, and that even your best friends will come to admire you if you stick with it—after they've finished dissing you in public.

Americans have always been committed to the moral maxim that work defines the person. We carry around in our heads a rough tally that tells us what kinds of jobs are worthy of respect and what kinds are to be disdained, a pyramid organized by the income a job carries, the sort of credentials it takes to secure a particular position, the qualities of an occupation's incumbents—and we use this system of stratification (ruthlessly at times) to boost the status of some and humiliate others. This penchant for ranking by occupation is more pervasive in the United States than in other societies, where there are different ways of evaluating the personal worth of individuals. In these societies, coming from a "good family" counts heavily in the calculus of social standing. Here in America, there is no other metric that matters as much as the kind of job you hold.

Given our tradition of equating moral value with employment, it stands to reason that the most profound dividing line in our culture is that separating the working person from the unemployed. Only after this canyon has been crossed do we begin to make the finer gradations that distinguish white-collar worker from blue-collar worker, CEO from secretary. We attribute a whole host of moral virtues—self-discipline, personal responsibility, maturity—to those who have found and kept a job, almost any job, and dismiss those who haven't as slothful or irresponsible.

We inhabit an unforgiving culture that is blind to the many reasons why some people cross that employment barrier and others are left behind. While we may remember, for a time, that unemployment rates are high, or that particular industries have downsized millions of workers right out of a job, or that racial barriers or negative attitudes

Source: From *No Shame in My Game* by Katherine S. Newman, copyright © 1999 by Russell Sage Foundation. Used by permission of Alfred A. Knopf, a division of Random House, Inc.

toward teenagers make it harder to get a job at some times and for some people, in the end American culture wipes these background truths out in favor of a simpler dichotomy: the worthy and the unworthy, the working stiff and the lazy sloth.

These days, our puritanical attitudes owe some of their force to the resentment the employed bear toward the taxes they must pay to support those who cannot earn on their own. But it has deeper cultural dimensions. From the earliest beginnings of the nation, work has been the *sine qua non* of membership in this society. Adults who work are full-fledged citizens in the truest sense of the term—complete participants in the social world that is most highly valued. No other dimension of life—community, family, religion, voluntary organizations—qualifies Americans for this designation of citizen in the same way.

We express this view in a variety of ways in our social policies. Virtually all our benefits (especially health care but including unemployment insurance, life insurance, child care tax credits, etc.) are provided through the employment system. In Western Europe this is often not the case: health care is provided directly through the tax system and benefits come to people who are political "citizens" whether they work or not. In the United States, however, those outside the employment system are categorized as unworthy and made to feel it by excluding them from these systems of support. To varying degrees, we "take care" of the socially excluded by creating stigmatized categories for their benefits—welfare and Medicaid being prime examples. Yet we never confuse the approved, acceptable Americans with the undeserving, and we underscore the difference by separating them into different bureaucratic worlds.

For those on the positive side of the divide, those who work for a living, the rewards are far greater than a paycheck. The employed enter a social world in which their identities as mainstream Americans are shaped, structured, and reinforced. The workplace is the main institutional setting in which individuals become part of the collective American enterprise that lies at the heart of our

culture: the market. We are so divided in other domains—race, geography, family organization, gender roles, and the like—that common ground along almost any other lines is difficult to achieve. Indeed, only in wartime do Americans tend to cleave to their national origins as a major feature of their self-concept. The French, by contrast, are French whether they work or not. But for our more diverse and divided society, participation in the world of work is the most powerful source of social integration.

It is in the workplace that we are most likely to mix with those who come from different backgrounds, are under the greatest pressure to subordinate individual idiosyncrasy to the requirements of an organization, and are called upon to contribute to goals that eclipse the personal. All workers have these experiences in common; even as segregation constrains the real mix of workers, conformity is expected to a greater degree for people who work in some kinds of jobs than in others, and the organizational goals to which they must subscribe are often elusive, unreachable, or at odds with personal desire.

The creation of an identity as a worker is never achieved by individuals moving along some preordained path. It is a transformation worked by organizations, firms, supervisors, fellow workers, and the whole long search that leads from the desire to find a job to the end point of landing one. This is a particularly dramatic transformation for ghetto youth and adults, for they face a difficult job market, high hurdles in convincing employers to take a chance on them, and relatively poor rewards—from a financial point of view—for their successes. But the crafting of an identity is an important developmental process for them, just as it is for their more privileged counterparts.

Powerful forces work to exclude minorities from full participation in American society. From a school system that provides a substandard education for millions of inner city kids, to an employment system rife with discrimination, to a housing market that segregates minority families, there is almost no truth to the notion that we all begin from the same starting line. Precisely because this is the case, blasting one's way through the job barrier and starting down that road of acquiring a common identity as a mainstream worker is of the greatest importance for the young. It may be one of the few available pipelines into the core of American society, and the one with the greatest payoff, symbolic and material.

THE SOCIAL COSTS OF ACCEPTING LOW-WAGE WORK

Even though we honor the gainfully employed over the unemployed, all jobs are not created equal. Fast food jobs, in particular, are notoriously stigmatized and denigrated. "McJob" has become a common epithet for work without much redeeming value. The reasons for this are worth studying, for the minority workers who figure in this book have a mountain of stigma to overcome if they are to maintain their self-respect. Indeed, the organizational culture they join when they finally land a job at Burger Barn is instrumental in generating conditions and experiences that challenge a worker's self-esteem.

As Robin Leidner has argued,[1] fast food jobs epitomize the assembly-line structure of de-skilled service positions: they are highly routinized and appear to the casual observer to be entirely lacking in discretion—almost military in their scripted nature. The symbolic capital of these assembly-line jobs can be measured in negative numbers. They represent the opposite of the autonomous entrepreneur who is lionized in the popular culture, from *Business Week* to hip-hop.

Burger Barn workers are told that they must, at whatever cost to their own dignity, defer to the public. Customers can be unreasonably demanding, rude, even insulting, and workers must count backwards from a hundred in an effort to stifle their outrage. Servicing the customer with a smile pleases

management because making money depends on keeping the clientele happy, but it can be an exercise in humiliation for teenagers. It is hard for them to refrain from reading this public nastiness as another instance of society's low estimation of their worth. But they soon realize that if they want to hold on to their minimum-wage jobs, they have to tolerate comments that would almost certainly provoke a fistfight outside the workplace.

It is well known among ghetto customers that crew members have to put up with whatever verbal abuse comes across the counter. That knowledge occasionally prompts nasty exchanges designed explicitly to anger the worker, to push him or her to retaliate verbally. Testing those limits is a favorite pastime of teenage customers in particular, for this may be the one opportunity they have to put a peer on the defensive in a public setting, knowing that there is little the victim can do in return.

It is bad enough to be on the receiving end of this kind of abuse from adults, especially white adults, for that has its own significance along race lines. It is even worse to have to accept it from minority peers, for there is much more personal honor at stake, more pride to be lost, and an audience whose opinion matters more. This, no doubt, is why harassment is a continual problem for fast food workers in Harlem. It burns. Their agemates, with plenty of anger bottled up for all kinds of reasons extraneous to the restaurant experience, find counterparts working the cash register convenient targets for venting.

Roberta is a five-year veteran of Burger Barn who has worked her way up to management. A formidable African-American woman, Roberta has always prided herself on her ability to make it on her own. Most of her customers have been perfectly pleasant; many have been longtime repeat visitors to her restaurant. But Roberta has also encountered many who radiate disrespect.

Could you describe some of the people who came into the store during your shift?
The customers? Well, I had alcoholics, derelicts. People that are aggravated with life. I've had people that don't even have jobs curse me out. I've dealt with all kinds.

---

[1] Robin Liedner, *Fast Food, Fast Talk: Service Work and the Routinization of Everyday Life.* Berkeley: University of California Press, 1993.

Sometimes it would get to me. If a person yelled out [in front of] a lobby full of people . . . "Bitch, that's why you work at [Burger Barn]," I would say [to myself], "I'm probably making more than you and your mother." It hurts when people don't even know what you're making and they say those things. Especially in Harlem, they do that to you. They call you all types of names and everything.

Natasha is younger than Roberta and less practiced at these confrontations. But she has had to contend with them nevertheless, especially from customers her age who at least claim to be higher up the status hierarchy. Though she tries, Natasha can't always control her temper and respond the way the firm wants her to.

It's hard dealing with the public. There are good things, like old people. They sweet. But the younger people around my age are always snotty. Think they better than you because they not working at [Burger Barn]. They probably work at something better than you.

How do you deal with rude or unfriendly customers?
They told us that we just suppose to walk to the back and ignore it, but when they in your face like that, you get so upset that you have to say something. . . . I got threatened with a gun one time. 'Cause this customer had threw a piece of straw paper in the back and told me to pick it up like I'm a dog. I said, "No." And he cursed at me. I cursed at him back, and he was like, "Yeah, next time you won't have nothing to say when I come back with my gun and shoot your ass." Oh, excuse me.

Ianna, who had just turned sixteen the summer she found her first job at Burger Barn, has had many of the same kinds of problems Natasha complains of. The customers who are rude to her are just looking for a place to vent their anger about things that have nothing to do with buying lunch. Ianna recognizes that this kind of thing could happen in any restaurant, but believes it is a special problem in Harlem, for ghetto residents have more to be angry about and fewer accessible targets. So cashiers in fast food shops become prime victims.

What I hate about [Burger Barn] is the customers, well, some of them that I can't stand. . . . I don't want to stereotype Harlem . . . but since I only worked in Harlem that's all I can speak for. Some people have a chip on their shoulders. . . . Most of the people that come into the

restaurant are black. Most of them have a lot of kids. It's in the ghetto. Maybe, you know, they are depressed about their lifestyles or whatever else that is going on in their lives and they just . . . I don't know. They just are like, urff! And no matter what you do you cannot please them. I'm not supposed to say anything to the customer, but that's not like me. I have a mouth and I don't take no short from nobody. I don't care who it is, don't take anybody's crap.

Despite this bravado, Ianna knows well that to use her mouth is to risk her job. She has had to work hard to find ways to cope with this frustration that don't get her in trouble with management.

I don't say stuff to people most of the time. Mostly I just look at them like they stupid. Because my mother always told me that as long as you don't say nothin' to nobody, you can't never get in trouble. If you look at them stupid, what are they going to do? If you roll your eyes at somebody like that, I mean, that's really nothing [compared to] . . . cursing at them. Most of the time I try to walk away.

As Ianna observes, there is enough free-floating fury in Harlem to keep a steady supply of customer antagonism coming the way of service employees every day of their work lives. The problem is constant enough to warrant official company policies on how crew members should respond to insults, on what managers should do to help, on the evasive tactics that will work best to quell an ugly situation without losing the business. Management tries to minimize the likelihood of incidents by placing girls on the registers rather than boys, in the apparent belief that young women attract less abuse and find it easier to quash their anger than young men.

Burger Barn does what it can to contend with these problems in the workplace. But the neighborhood is beyond their reach, and there, too, fast food workers are often met with ridicule from the people they grew up with. They have to learn to defend themselves against criticism that they have lowered themselves by taking these jobs, criticism from people they have known all their lives. As Stephanie explains, here too she leans on the divide between the worker and the do-nothing:

People I hang out with, they know me since I was little. We all grew up together. When they see me comin', they laugh and say, "Here come Calvin, here come Calvin sister." I just laugh and keep on going. I say, "You're crazy. But that's okay 'cause I got a job and you all standing out here on the corner." Or I say, "This is my job, it's legal." Something like that. That Calvin commercial show you that even though his friends tease him he just brushed them off, then he got a higher position. Then you see how they change toward him.

Tiffany, also a teen worker in a central Harlem Burger Barn, thinks she knows why kids in her community who don't work give her such a hard time. They don't want her to succeed because if no one is "making it," then no one needs to feel bad about failing. But if someone claws her way up and it looks as if she has a chance to escape the syndrome of failure, it implies that everyone could, in theory, do so as well. The teasing, a thinly veiled attempt to enforce conformity, is designed to drag would-be success stories back into the fold.

> What you will find in any situation, more so in the black community, is that if you are in the community and you try to excel, you will get ridicule from your own peers. It's like the "crab down" syndrome. . . . If you put a bunch of crabs in a big bucket and one crab tries to get out, what do you think the other crabs would do now? According to my thinking, they should pull 'em up or push 'em or help 'em get out. But the crabs pull him back in the barrel. That's just an analogy for what happens in the community a lot.

Keeping everyone down protects against that creeping sense of despair which comes from believing things could be otherwise for oneself.

Swallowing ridicule would be a hardship for almost anyone in this culture, but it is particularly hard on minority youth in the inner city. They have already logged four or five years' worth of interracial and cross-class friction by the time they get behind a Burger Barn cash register. More likely than not, they have also learned from peers that self-respecting people don't allow themselves to be "dissed" without striking back. Yet this is precisely what they must do if they are going to survive in the workplace.

This is one of the main reasons why these jobs carry such a powerful stigma in American popular culture: they fly in the face of a national attraction to autonomy, independence, and the individual's "right" to respond in kind when dignity is threatened. In ghetto communities, this stigma is even more powerful because—ironically—it is in these enclaves that this mainstream value of independence is most vigorously elaborated and embellished. Film characters, rap stars, and local idols base their claim to notoriety on standing above the crowd, going their own way, being free of the ties that bind ordinary mortals. There are white parallels, to be sure, but this is a powerful genre of icons in the black community, not because it is a disconnected subculture but because it is an intensified version of a perfectly recognizable American middle-class and working-class fixation.

It is therefore noteworthy that thousands upon thousands of minority teens, young adults, and even middle-aged adults line up for jobs that will subject them, at least potentially, to a kind of character assassination. They do so not because they start the job-seeking process with a different set of values, one that can withstand society's contempt for fast food workers. They take these jobs because in so many inner-city communities, there is nothing better in the offing. In general, they have already tried to get better jobs and have failed, landing at the door of Burger Barn as a last resort.

Social stigma has other sources besides the constraints of enforced deference. Money and mobility matter as well. Fast food jobs are invariably minimum-wage positions. Salaries rise very little over time, even for first-line management. In ghetto areas, where jobs are scarce and the supply of would-be workers chasing them is relatively large, downward pressure on wages keeps these jobs right down at the bottom of the wage scale.

The public perception (fueled by knowledge of wage conditions) is that there is very little potential for improvement in status or responsibility either. Even though there are Horatio Algers in this industry, there are no myths to prop up a more glorified image. As a result, the epithet "McJob" develops out of the perception that fast food workers are not likely to end up in a prestigious job as a general manager or restaurant owner; they are going to spend their whole lives flipping burgers.

As it happens, this is only half true. The fast food industry is actually very good about internal promotion. Workplace management is nearly always recruited from the ranks of entry-level workers. Carefully planned training programs make it possible for employees to move up, to acquire transferable skills, and to at least take a shot at entrepreneurial ownership. McDonald's, for example, is proud of the fact that half of its board of directors started out as crew members. One couldn't say as much for the rest of the nation's Fortune 500 firms.

However, the vast majority never even get close to management. The typical entry-level worker passes through his or her job in short order, with an industry-average job tenure of less than six months. Since this is an average, it suggests that a large number of employees are there and gone in a matter of weeks. It is this pattern, a planned operation built around low skills and high turnover, that has given fast food jobs such a bad name. In order for the industry to keep functioning with such an unstable labor force, the jobs themselves must be broken down so that each step can be learned, at least at a rudimentary level, in a very short time. A vicious circle develops in which low wages are attached to low skills, encouraging high departure rates. Hence, although it is quite possible to rise above the fray and make a very respectable living as a general manager overseeing a restaurant, most crew members remain at the entry level and leave too soon to see much upward movement. Observing this pattern on such a large scale—in practically every town and city in the country—Americans naturally conclude that one can't get anywhere in a job like this, that there is no real future in it, and that anyone with more "on the ball" wouldn't be caught dead working behind the counter. Mobility isn't necessarily that limited, but since that is not widely known, the negative impression sticks.

The stigma also stems from the low social status of the people who hold these jobs: minorities, teenagers, immigrants who often speak halting English, those with little education, and (increasingly in affluent communities afflicted with labor shortages) the elderly. To the extent that the prestige of a job refracts the social characteristics of its average incumbents, fast food jobs are hobbled by the perception that people with better choices would never purposely opt for a "McJob." Succeeding chapters will show that entry-level jobs of this kind are undeserving of this scorn: more skill, discretion, and responsibility are locked up in a fast food job than is apparent to the public. But this truth hardly matters where public perception is concerned. There is no quicker way to indicate that a person is barely deserving of notice than to point out he or she holds a "chump change" job at Kentucky Fried Chicken or Burger King. We "know" this is the case just by looking at the age, skin color, or educational credentials of the people already on the job: the tautology has a staying power that even the smartest public relations campaign cannot shake.

Ghetto youth are particularly sensitive to the status degradation entailed in stigmatized employment. As Elijah Anderson (in *Streetwise,* University of Chicago Press, 1990) and others have pointed out, a high premium is placed on independence, autonomy, and respect among minority youth in inner-city communities—particularly by young men. No small amount of mayhem is committed every year in the name of injured pride. Hence jobs that routinely demand displays of deference force those who hold them to violate "macho" behavior codes that are central to the definition of teen culture. There are, therefore, considerable social risks involved in seeking a fast food job in the first place, one that the employees and job-seekers are keenly aware of from the very beginning of their search for employment.

It is hard to know the extent to which this stigma discourages young people in places like central Harlem from knocking on the door of a fast food restaurant. It is clear that the other choices aren't much better and that necessity drives thousands, if not millions, of teens and older job-seekers to ignore the stigma or learn to live with it. But no one enters the central Harlem job market without having to face this gauntlet.

Another Face of Inequality: Racial and Ethnic Exclusion in the Welfare State

JILL QUADAGNO

Although there are several studies that document the racial biases in the American welfare state, these issues have received less attention in comparative social policy research (Lieberman 1998; Quadagno 1994; 2000). To some extent this is an artifact of history, since European welfare states developed prior to the postwar flows of racially and ethnically diverse immigrant groups whose presence has created social tensions. Before the war, most migrants were from neighboring countries. Those who settled permanently into the host nations experienced thorough assimilation. Postwar immigrant streams, by contrast, consisted of former colonials and large numbers of manual workers from Third World nations (Ireland 1995). Specific immigrant groups were concentrated in different countries: Algerians in France, Turks in Germany, and West Indians and South Asians in Britain (Gordon 1995). When economic conditions deteriorated after 1974, many "guest" workers stayed, creating resident ethnic communities. Those who originated in nations belonging to the European Community gained political and social rights; the others were excluded as host nations concentrated on maintaining their own welfare states for their own nationals (Garth 1986).

The attention on ethnoracial immigrant groups should not obscure the fact that there are also

indigenous groups who, in many nations, were denied the rights of citizenship, including the right to vote and the right to own property. Among them are African Americans and Native Americans in the United States, the Maori in New Zealand, the Inuit in Canada and Denmark, the Aborigines in Australia, and the Flemish and Walloons in Belgium.

For the most part the incomplete incorporation of racial and ethnic minorities into the polity has been ignored by welfare state theorists. Although many acknowledge that race or ethnicity are dimensions of the stratification process, they rarely develop this insight theoretically. For example, Esping-Anderson's (1999, 42) concept of "intergenerational risk transmission" explicitly recognizes that the life chances of some racial groups are restricted and that these disadvantages are transmitted across generations. Inherited disadvantages produce inequality in social capital. The minimalist solution is to expand the opportunity to obtain human capital through education. A more comprehensive approach is to enact policies that provide "any resource which can be considered vital for life chances . . . the entire complex of social resources necessary to function optimally" (Esping-Anderson 1999, 43). Yet Esping-Anderson never explains what form these policies should take or how social resources can compensate those who have been relegated to an inferior position because of their race. Feminist theorists sometimes mention race in their discussions of inequality, but they fail to specify how the processes that create racial or ethnic inequality might differ from those

Source: Jill Quadagno, "Another Face of Inequality: Racial and Ethnic Exclusion in the Welfare State," *Social Politics,* Vol. 7, No. 2, Summer, 2000: 229-237. Used with permission of Jill Quadagno.

that create gender inequality (O'Connor, Orloff, and Shaver 1999; Orloff 1993).

In his paper in this volume, Korpi (see pp. 127–191) also alludes to race briefly, but always subsumes it into class. Yet the theoretical principles that Korpi derives from gender and class models do provide a useful framework for evaluating ways to understand patterned forms of racial and ethnic inequality across nations. In particular, Korpi identifies three interrelated dimensions of inequality that can be applied in theorizing racial/ethnic inequality. These dimensions include inequality in material conditions of living, inequality in agency, and inequality in policy institutions. Acker's (see pp. 192–214) analysis of workplace organizations provides the basis for explaining how ethnoracial inequality differs from class and gender inequality. In Acker's view, although "class, gender and race are complexly related aspects of the same ongoing practical activities," each has a different basis. Class inequality emerges from the wage relation, gender inequality stems primarily from the segregation of women into certain lower positions in the workplace, but racial inequality results from exclusion.

In the next section I attempt to describe the forms racial/ethnic inequality take in different nations and in different historical contexts. I also explore the ways in which the welfare state intervenes in patterns of distributive processes organized around race or ethnicity. I base my discussion on Korpi's dimensions of inequality, but add to this Acker's concept of exclusion as the mechanism that maintains racial/ethnic inequality.

DIMENSIONS OF INEQUALITY

Inequality in Material Conditions

Korpi defines inequality in *material standards of living* in terms of such direct measures as income, wealth, and poverty, as well as by more indirect indicators including health, escapable morbidity, and premature mortality. The issue, then, is whether racial and ethnic minorities fare more poorly in these indicators than the majority group within a given country.

Since race consciousness is embedded in data gathering procedures in the United States, data on race and ethnic origin are readily available for many of these indicators. Poverty rates in the United States are higher among African Americans and Hispanics than they are for whites. African Americans also have poorer health than whites, particularly among the middle aged and old. Black men and women in their fifties are significantly more likely than whites of the same age to report being in "fair" or "poor" health (Bound, Schoenbaum, and Waidmann 1996). Blacks also experience higher morbidity and mortality than whites (Shea, Miles, and Hayward 1996).

As a general rule, European immigrants have higher rates of poverty than the majority group (Gordon 1995). This is also the case in Canada where poverty rates among immigrants from Latin America and West Asia stand at 41% and 39.4% among immigrants of Arab origin. Among Canadian Aboriginals, too, the poverty rate is 39.4% (Kazemipur and Halli 1997). The causes of higher poverty rates among immigrants are complex. Immigrants may face exclusion and marginalization in the host nation because of racial/ethnic hostility. A Eurobarometer opinion survey conducted in 1989 asked if people believed there were "too many residents of another race" in their country. Thirty-seven percent of Germans, 44% of British, and 43% of French said "yes" (Gordon 1995, 535). Immigrants also often face language barriers, have incompatible educational credentials and nontransferable job skills, and lack job hunting networks (Halli and Kazemipur 1999). Finally, immigrants may bring their poverty with them from their country of origin. Thus it is difficult to determine in a systematic way if a "racialization" of poverty is occurring through processes of exclusion or if these groups will experience social mobility and thorough assimilation by the second or third generation (Halli and Kazemipur 1999).

Inequality in Agency

The second component of inequality in Korpi's model is *agency inequality.* It includes three components: political representation, access to tertiary education, and labor force participation. Agency inequality in political representation may occur at several levels. At the most basic level is the denial of citizenship to members of a racial/ethnic group. This represents the purest form of Acker's concept of exclusion. It is important to recognize that controlling membership in the polity has always been a way of protecting national identity. Determining who has legitimate claims to membership is not derived from "static ethnodemographic" categories but from a dynamic political process. This process can become a mechanism of racial exclusion if host nations establish categories of "privileged" foreigners (Brubaker 1996, 60). In some cases immigrants from ex-colonial territories have been granted citizenship privileges, guaranteeing them rights of residency, political participation, and social benefits (Ireland 1995). By contrast, groups that were admitted on limited work permits often have had none of these rights (Gordon 1995). In Germany, Austria, and Switzerland, for example, guest workers initially had no citizenship rights, although some of these restrictions were loosened in the 1980s. Racial minorities who are natives seem even more likely than immigrants to be victims of exclusionary practices. In the United States, African Americans in the South were denied the right to vote until passage of the Voting Rights Act of 1965. In Denmark, Inuits lacked voting rights until 1950. The Maori could not vote in New Zealand until 1962 (Janowski 1998).

In class-based theories of the welfare state, democratization proceeds in stages, as workers struggle to gain first civil, then political, and finally social rights. The pursuit of rights flows from the power invested in workers as a *numerical majority* (Esping-Anderson 1990; Hicks 1999; Myles 1988). Racial or ethnic minorities, by definition, can never muster a political majority. Rather their votes can only be used at the margins of politics, to swing an election outcome (Quadagno 2000). Although it is possible for racial/ethnic minorities

to win representation, they are frequently underrepresented in political institutions. The lack of political representation is another form of agency inequality measured by numbers of elected officials and level of participation in governing bodies.

Agency inequality may also occur through the systematic denial of equal educational opportunities to racial minorities. In this case, institution-specific forms of exclusion may be operating. In the United States, racial segregation in education was legal until 1954, when the Supreme Court ruled that "separate but equal" was unconstitutional (Schuman, Steeh, Bobo, and Krysan 1997). Inequality in education may be a secondary consequence of housing segregation if minorities are concentrated in school districts where the quality of schooling is inferior to that of the majority group. In the United States, public education is funded primarily through local property taxes. The separation of metropolitan areas by income has created stark inequalities. In Texas, for example, the wealthier school districts spend three times more than the poorest (Weir 1995). Neighborhoods characterized by dense racial segregation are also those with inferior schools (Massey and Denton 1993).

Agency inequality is also produced by unequal access to employment. Acker's paper is organized around the consequences of exclusion from job opportunities. There is considerable evidence that racial/ethnic minorities experience job discrimination in many countries. In The Netherlands, Turks and Moroccans are excluded from high wage jobs because many receive only a primary education (Veenman 1995). In the United States, employers refuse to hire inner city blacks because they hold negative biases against them (Wilson 1996). In Great Britain, young blacks and Asians who are currently entering the labor market are better prepared to compete than their parents' generation. Yet their returns to education are lower than they are for whites because "job opportunities for blacks and Asians have been limited by entrenched inequality and by racial discrimination" (Brown 1995, 590). One study found that one-third of private employers discriminated against Asian and Afro-Caribbean job applicants (Brown 1995).

The consequences of job discrimination may be compounded by residential segregation. In France, Algerian immigrants are housed in "reservation areas" and "dump estates" where maintenance is minimal (Body-Gendrot 1995). In other European countries, "many inner city communities and outer-city public housing estates have been cut off from the mainstream labor market institutions and informal job networks, creating the vicious cycle of weak labor force attachment, growing social exclusion and rising tensions" (Lawson and Wilson 1995, 695). Overall, immigrant unemployment rates are double those of natives for all these reasons.

Inequality in Policy Institutions

The third form of inequality in Korpi's model is inequality in *policy institutions.* Social programs vary in form and in the rules that govern access to benefits. Benefits may be provided on the basis of need via a means test or benefits may be earned. Benefits may also be universal, with eligibility resting on citizenship or long-term residency (Esping-Anderson 1990).

There are many forms of racial/ethnic exclusion from the welfare state. Racial or ethnic disparities in benefits may be merely a by-product of labor market experience or human capital variables. If this is the case, then racial/ethnic minorities may be disproportionately represented in the means-tested programs because of their high rates of poverty. Racial/ethnic minorities may also have lower earnings-related benefits, again reflecting their differential experiences in the labor market. If minorities systematically have lower earnings, fewer years of earnings, or higher rates of disability, then they will receive lower benefits than the majority group.

On the other hand, discriminatory features may be built into the eligibility criteria for benefits. Means-tested benefits empower local relief authorities to determine who receives benefits and how much beneficiaries receive. This discretionary power allows the principle of exclusion to

operate. In the old age assistance program in the United States, for example, African Americans received lower benefits than whites because they were presumed to have a lower standard of living; many poor blacks were deemed ineligible for any benefits (Quadagno 1988).

Racial/ethnic disparities in social insurance benefits may also occur if the eligibility criteria exclude some occupations. For example, the Social Security Act of 1935 excluded agricultural workers and domestic servants. That meant that three-fifths of all black workers in the United States at that time were ineligible for benefits (Quadagno 1988). Also, the spouse benefit in the U.S. Social Security system is biased against black women because they are less likely than white women to be married to high earner males and more likely to be divorced or separated (Harrington Meyer 1996).

Finally, minorities may be excluded entirely from social insurance programs based on their citizenship status. Germany has signed bilateral agreements that allow eastern European companies to operate with their own workers. Although these contract laborers reside in Germany, they remain under their home country's social security system (Ireland 1995).

On a cultural level, social welfare programs have the capacity to unify or divide. If the majority group perceives minorities as consuming a disproportionate share of earned benefits, racial/ethnic resentment may be activated. Hostility to foreigners in some European countries stems from the belief that they are burdening the unemployment system (Gordon 1995). In Germany, the large population of foreigners has become increasingly ghettoized and dependent on means-tested benefits. Whereas only 5% of the native German population used public assistance during 1991, 15% of foreigners did so (Lawson and Wilson 1995). Germans have come to view immigrants as the cause of housing shortages and labor market difficulties, leading to racially motivated attacks and the politicization of anti-immigrant sentiment. As Veenman explains about Dutch social policy:

Feelings of solidarity are stronger when the assisted group is very similar to the population that is taxed for transfer programs. Consequently, in recent years there has been an attempt to emphasize general policies that affect the entire citizenry and a perceptible reluctance to establish new policies aimed only at ethnic minorities. (1995, 626)

CONCLUSION

Just as African Americans have been subject to processes of exclusion in the United States, so the European experience demonstrates that new immigrants can be assigned to economically marginal roles and incomplete citizenship if they are perceived as outsiders and inferior. The postwar flow of ethnically diverse immigrants has challenged traditional concepts of citizenship and social solidarity that have been grounded in similar identity-shaping experiences and social homogeneity (Ireland 1995). The question that remains to be answered is whether racial/ethnic cleavages are hardening. If so, this suggests that ascribed characteristics may be increasingly important in resource allocation.

The economic crises of the past decades have made the task of reducing ethnic/racial inequality more difficult, and indeed economic prosperity may be a precondition for solidarity, social integration, and universality. Declining economic growth means less economic surplus to be distributed, lower levels of well-being, and increased risk that families at the lower end of the income distribution will fall into poverty. If countries are to prevent the emergence of a racialized underclass, they must expand their definition of social citizenship to incorporate minority groups.

Expanding the three dimensions delineated by Korpi captures the parameters of racial/ethnic inequality. These include the following: the extent to which racial/ethnic groups are equal to the majority group in the material conditions of life; the extent to which racial/ethnic minorities have equality of agency in political institutions, in educational opportunity, and in the labor market; and the extent to which racial/ethnic minorities have equal access to policy institutions. In each case Acker's concept

of exclusion helps to explain how minorities are relegated to inferior positions. The task now is to elaborate the social, economic, and political processes of exclusion within specific countries and identify commonalities across nations.

NOTE

I thank John Myles for his helpful comments on a previous draft of the paper.

REFERENCES

Body-Gendrot, Sophie. 1995. "Immigration, Marginality, and French Social Policy." Pp. 571–84 in *Poverty, Inequality and the Future of Social Policy,* eds. Katherine McFate, Roger Lawson, and William Julius Wilson. New York: Russell Sage.

Bound, John, Michael Schoenbaum, and Timothy Waidmann. 1996. "Race Differences in Labor Force Attachment and Disability Status." *The Gerontologist* 36:311–21.

Brown, Colin. 1995. "Poverty, Immigration and Minority Groups: Policies Toward Minorities in Great Britain." Pp. 585–606 in *Poverty, Inequality and the Future of Social Policy,* eds. Katherine McFate, Roger Lawson, and William Julius Wilson. New York: Russell Sage.

Brubaker, Rogers. 1996. *Nationalism Reframed.* Cambridge: Cambridge University Press.

Esping-Andersen, Gosta. 1990. *The Three Worlds of Welfare Capitalism.* Princeton, N.J.: Princeton University Press.

———. 1999. *Social Foundation of Postindustrial Economies.* New York: Oxford University Press.

Garth, Bryant G. 1986. "Migrant Workers and the Rights of Mobility in the European Community and the United States." Pp. 141–46 in *Integration through Law,* eds. Mauro Cappelletti, Monica Secombe, and Joseph Weiler. New York: Walter deGruyter.

Gordon, Ian. 1995. "The Impact of Economic Change on Minorities and Migrants in Western Europe." Pp. 489–520 in *Poverty, Inequality and the Future of Social Policy,* eds. Katherine McFate, Roger Lawson, and William Julius Wilson. New York: Russell Sage.

Halli, S., and A. Kazemipur. 1999. "A Study of Poverty of Immigrants in Canada." Paper presented at the Metropolis Conference, Vancouver, Canada, 15 January 1999.

Harrington Meyer, Madonna. 1996. "Making Claims as Workers or Wives: The Distribution of Social Security Benefits." *American Sociological Review* 61:449–65.

Hicks, Alexander. 1999. *Social Democracy and Welfare Capitalism.* Ithaca, N.Y.: Cornell University Press.

Ireland, Patrick R. 1995. "Migration, Free Movement and Immigrant Integration in the EU: A Bifurcated Policy Response." Pp. 231–66 in *European Social Policy,* eds. Stephan Liebfried and Paul Pierson. Washington, D.C.: Brookings Institution.

Janowski, Thomas. 1998. *Citizenship and Civil Society.* Cambridge: Cambridge University Press.

Kazemipur, A., and S. S. Halli. 1997. "Plight of Immigrants: The Spatial Concentration of Poverty." *Canadian Journal of Regional Science* XX: 11–28.

Lawson, Roger, and William J. Wilson. 1995. "Poverty. Social Rights and the Quality of Citizenship." Pp. 693–713 in *Poverty, Inequality and the Future of Social Policy,* eds. Katherine McFate, Roger Lawson, and William Julius Wilson. New York: Russell Sage.

Lieberman, Robert C. 1998. *Shifting the Color Line: Race and the American Welfare State.* Cambridge, Mass: Harvard University Press.

Massey, Doug, and Nancy Denton. 1993. *American Apartheid.* Cambridge, Mass.: Harvard University Press.

Myles, John. 1988. *Old Age in the Welfare State.* Lawrence: University Press of Kansas.

O'Connor, Julia S., Ann Shola Orloff, and Sheila Shaver. 1999. *States, Labor Markets and Families.* Cambridge: Cambridge University Press.

Orloff, Ann. 1993. "Gender and the Social Rights of Citizenship: The Comparative Analysis of State Policies and Gender Relations." *American Sociological Review* 58:303–28.

Quadagno, Jill. 1988. *The Transformation of Old Age Security.* Chicago: University of Chicago Press.

———. 1994. *The Color of Welfare.* New York: Oxford University Press.

———. 2000. "Promoting Civil Rights through the Welfare State: How Medicare Integrated Southern Hospitals." *Social Problems* 47:68–89.

Schuman, Howard, Charlotte Steeh, Lawrence Bobo, and Maria Krysan. 1997. *Racial Attitudes in America.* Cambridge, Mass.: Harvard University Press.

Shea, Dennis, Toni Miles, and Mark Hayward. 1996. "The Health/Wealth Connection: Racial Differences." *The Gerontologist* 36:342–49.

Veenman, Justus. 1995. "Ethnic Minorities in the Netherlands." Pp. 607–29 in *Poverty, Inequality and the Future of Social Policy,* eds. Katherine McFate, Roger Lawson, and William Julius Wilson. New York: Russell Sage.

Weir, Margaret. 1995. "Poverty, Social Rights and the Politics of Place in the United States." Pp. 329–53 in *European Social Policy,* eds. Stephan Liebfried and Paul Pierson. Washington, D.C.: Brookings Institution.

Wilson, William J. 1996. *When Work Disappears.* Chicago: University of Chicago Press.

Informing the Debate

DEREK BOK AND CHARLES BOWEN

The purpose of [*The Shape of the River*] has been to build a firmer foundation of fact on which to conduct the on-going debate about the race-sensitive admissions policies employed by almost all selective colleges and professional schools in the United States. . . . [O]ur aim [is] to convey a more accurate picture of the long and complicated process—more akin to movement along a river than to a smooth passage through a pipeline—by which young people are educated, and then pursue careers and assume responsibilities in their communities. . . . [W]e now point out how our findings bear upon the arguments commonly made on both sides of the controversy. Of course, information alone cannot resolve all of the issues, since many of them involve differences of values or legal interpretation. Nevertheless, facts often help to confirm some arguments and undermine others. In what ways, then, can the results of this study clarify and advance a debate that has become so heated, so predictable, and yet so inconclusive?

ASSESSING THE PERFORMANCE OF MINORITY STUDENTS

The data assembled in this [study] should dispel any impression that the abilities and performance of the minority students admitted to selective colleges and universities have been disappointing.

On the contrary, our findings contain abundant evidence that these minority students had strong academic credentials when they entered college, that they graduated in large numbers, and that they have done very well after leaving college.

In our intensive study of applications to five selective colleges, more than 75 percent of the black applicants had higher math SAT scores than the national average for white test-takers, and 73 percent had higher verbal SAT scores. Qualifications of black matriculants have improved dramatically: at the SEL-1 colleges and universities, the percentage with combined SAT scores over 1100 rose from 50 percent for the '76 entering cohort to 73 percent for the '89 cohort. Minority students enter selective colleges with test scores and high school grades substantially below those of most of their classmates. Nevertheless, this gap does not prove that they are deficient by any national standard; rather, it reflects the extraordinary quality of the white and Asian applicants who have been attracted to leading institutions in ever greater numbers.

Of the black students who matriculated in 1989 at the twenty-eight selective colleges in the College and Beyond (C&B) database, 75 percent graduated from the college they first entered within six years, and another 4 percent transferred and graduated from some other college within this same period. These figures are far above the averages for all NCAA Division I schools, not only for blacks (of whom only 40 percent graduated from their first school) but also for whites (of

Source: Bowen, William G. and Derek Curtis Bok, *The Shape of the River,* © 1998 Princeton University Press. Reprinted by permission of Princeton University Press.

whom 59 percent graduated). Graduation rates for black students from professional schools are even more impressive. At leading schools of law, business, and medicine, approximately 90 percent of black students complete their studies successfully.

Our research also documents the success of black College and Beyond graduates after they finished college. They were more than five times as likely as all black college graduates nationwide to earn professional degrees or PhDs. Moreover, they were as likely as their white classmates to receive degrees in law, business, or medicine.[1] The attainment of graduate and professional degrees has led large numbers of black graduates into highly productive careers.

Twenty years after entering college, black men who graduated from these selective colleges earned an average of $82,000—*twice* the average earnings of all black men with BAs nationwide; black women graduates of C&B schools earned an average of $58,500—80 percent more than the average earnings of all black women with BAs (. . . these estimates of average annual earnings are for all graduates, not just full-time workers). Earnings for black 1976 matriculants at C&B schools were higher than the average earnings of the "A" students of all races (the top 11 percent of all students in our national control group) who entered colleges nationwide in the same year.

In addition to their economic success, C&B black matriculants have been extensively involved in a wide range of civic and community activities. According to our survey, 1976 black matriculants at selective colleges, especially men, subsequently participated at a higher rate than their white classmates in community and civic undertakings. Black men in this sample are also much more likely than whites to hold leadership positions in civic and community organizations, especially those involving social service, youth, and school-related activities. These findings appear to bear out the assumption of selective institutions that minority students have unusual opportunities to make valuable contributions to their communities and the society. Even more encouraging is the evident willingness of these matriculants to accept such responsibilities.

By any standard, then, the achievements of the black matriculants have been impressive. Even so, critics continue to challenge the central premises of race-sensitive admissions. Some question whether admitting minority applicants to selective colleges actually benefits these students either in college or in later life. Some dispute the claims of educators that diversity on campus increases racial understanding. Still others argue that any admissions policy that attaches special weight to the race of an applicant aggravates tensions in the larger society.

DO RACE-SENSITIVE ADMISSIONS POLICIES HARM THE INTENDED BENEFICIARIES?

Several opponents of race-sensitive admissions claim that such policies harm the minority students they purport to help. This broad line of argument needs to be examined along a number of dimensions, ranging from the academic performance and graduation rates of black matriculants to their record in obtaining advanced degrees and their subsequent careers.

Graduation Rates

Stephan and Abigail Thernstrom assert correctly that "the college dropout rate for black students is at least 50 percent higher than it is for whites."[2] They then add that "misguided affirmative action policies may have done a lot to create the problem. . . . The point is simple. When students are given a

---

[1] We also found that impressionistic reports about black students failing to fulfill their educational aspirations were both partially accurate (because the black C&B population entered college with much higher degree attainment goals than those of their white classmates) and misleading (because, in the end, equal percentages of black and white students were attaining advanced degrees, including the most sought after graduate and professional degrees).

[2] Thernstrom and Thernstrom 1997, pp. 405–6.

preference in admission because of their race or some other extraneous characteristic, it means that they are jumping into a competition for which their academic achievements do not qualify them and many find it hard to keep up."[3]

In fact, the data show that "the point" is anything but "simple." If race-sensitive admissions in selective colleges lead to more dropouts, it is more than a little puzzling that in our sample of twenty-eight selective schools, none had a dropout rate for minority students anywhere near as high as the average attrition of 60 percent for black students at all NCAA Division I colleges, many of which are not selective. Black dropout rates are low at all of the C&B schools (averaging just over 25 percent); moreover, *the more selective the college attended, the lower the black dropout rate.*

Since the C&B schools differ among themselves in their degree of selectivity, as measured by the average SAT score of their students, we were able to perform a much more conclusive test of the claim that black students will do better at schools with average SAT scores more nearly like their own (sometimes called the "fit" hypothesis). We compared how black students *with equivalent test scores* performed at colleges where the average score for all students was much higher than their own scores and at colleges where their scores were more like the average score for the entire school (where the "fit" between the black student and the school was presumably better). The results are completely contrary to the claims made by the critics. The higher the average SAT score of the college in question, the *higher* the graduation rate of black students *within each SAT interval* (including the intervals for students with only very modest SAT scores). More generally, when we predicted graduation rates for black students within the C&B universe on an "other things equal" basis (holding constant socioeconomic status, high school grades and test scores), we found that

graduation rates were highest for those who attended the most selective schools.[4] We also found that black students who did drop out were not embittered or demoralized, as some critics of race-sensitive admissions have alleged. On the contrary, of the relatively small number of black students who dropped out of the most selective schools, a surprisingly large percentage were "very satisfied" with their college experience—indeed, black dropouts from these schools were more likely than white dropouts to be "very satisfied."

A broader test of the effect of race-sensitive admissions on graduation rates was carried out by Thomas Kane. His results confirm our findings. When Kane compared the graduation rates of black students who attended a much wider range of schools, including some that were not selective at all, he found that blacks admitted to selective schools graduated at significantly *higher* rates than blacks with equivalent test scores, high school grades, and family backgrounds who attended non-selective schools.[5]

Incentive Effects

Another complaint sometimes made against race-sensitive admissions practices is that they weaken the incentives for minority students to work hard at their studies because they know that they can gain admission to selective colleges and professional schools with lower grades than those of their white classmates. As Jay B. Howd has put it: "At the college and university level, minorities

---

[3]Ibid., p. 406.

[4]Some critics claim that graduation rates for minorities are overstated because they are more likely than other students to choose allegedly "soft" majors such as Afro-American studies. One of these critics, Lino Graglia, suggests that: "When the specially admitted students discover . . . that they cannot compete with their classmates, no matter how hard they try, . . . they will insist . . . that the game be changed. Thus are born demands for black studies and multiculturalism" (1993, p. 135). Our data indicate that, in general, minority students chose the same array of traditional majors as non-minority students. This tendency seems to have become even more pronounced in recent years.
[5]Kane (1998).

cannot be expected to focus on maximizing their own efforts when rewarded for factors independent of those efforts."[6]

We know of no way to measure directly the effect that race-sensitive admissions policies have on the motivation of minority students. Nevertheless, various findings in our study cast doubt on claims such as Howd's. Even under race-sensitive admissions programs, black applicants have little reason to be complacent about their chances of entering a selective institution. Our analysis of admissions patterns in five selective colleges reveals that less than half of the black applicants were admitted. Approximately 25 percent of blacks with SAT scores between 1350 and 1500 were rejected, although such scores put these students in the top 2 percent of all black test-takers in the nation. In the face of such facts, no sensible black applicant could afford to relax and assume that entry to a selective college would come easily.

Much the same is true of the incentives facing students during their college and professional school years. Most minority students enter selective colleges aspiring to earn a graduate degree, often in law, business or medicine, but competition for admission to such programs is very keen for all applicants. Using national data, Linda Wightman has found that more than half of all black applicants fail to gain acceptance to any law school.[7] The pattern is the same for black applicants to medical school.[8] Once admitted to a professional school, minority students presumably know that the leading law firms and corporations do not seriously consider employing students below the top half, or top third, or even top tenth of the class. It is at least as hard for blacks and Hispanics to achieve these levels of academic achievement as it is for their white classmates, and they presumably focus their efforts accordingly.

The general tenor of these conclusions is supported by other findings. Our results show that black students in the top third of the class are more likely to earn an advanced degree than students in the middle third of their class, while the latter are much more likely than students in the bottom third to obtain such degrees. Moreover, college grades are clearly and positively correlated with subsequent earnings for blacks and whites alike. In fact, blacks appear to pay an even greater financial penalty than whites for receiving low grades in college. For these reasons, there would seem to be ample incentives for blacks and other members of minority groups to do as well as they can academically, both during their undergraduate years and in the course of their graduate and professional studies.

Demoralization and Its Possible Effect on Grades

According to some opponents of race-sensitive admissions, there is yet another way in which such policies harm the very students they purport to help. Knowing that they have been admitted to selective institutions with lower grade averages and test scores than their white classmates, minority students may become demoralized. According to Shelby Steele, "The effect of preferential treatment—the lowering of normal standards to increase black representation—puts blacks at war with an expanding realm of debilitating doubt, so that the doubt itself becomes an unrecognized preoccupation that undermines their ability to perform, especially in integrated situations."[9]

Yet if minority students were truly demoralized, one would expect that they would be less likely than whites to succeed in graduate and professional schools, less likely to appreciate their college experience, and less inclined to report that they benefited intellectually by having attended a selective school. None of these results appears in our data. Blacks are just as likely as whites to attend the most demanding, competitive professional schools. They are as likely as their white

---

[6]Howd 1992, p. 451.
[7]Wightman 1997, p. 16.
[8]Association of American Medical Colleges 1996, p. 69.

[9]Steele 1994, p. 42.

classmates to become doctors, lawyers, and business executives. They are just as appreciative of their college experience, and they tend to believe that they gained more from their undergraduate experience than do their white classmates. Also, contrary to what critics who support the "fit" hypothesis would predict, we found that the more selective the college attended, the *more* satisfied black matriculants were with their college experience—a pattern that holds even for those students with relatively low test scores. . . . If black students admitted to the most academically demanding schools suffered as a result, they certainly don't seem to know it.

There is one kind of evidence, however, that can be read to support claims of demoralization or diminished motivation. A number of studies (including our own) have found that minority students, especially blacks, perform at significantly lower levels academically than their test scores would predict.[10] Indeed, our data show that underperformance plays a slightly greater role than test scores in explaining why the average rank in class for black students is lower than that of whites. Why does this underperformance occur? Could it reflect some form of demoralization resulting from a realization on the part of minority students that they are less qualified academically than their white classmates?

Some experimental evidence does suggest that vulnerability to racial stereotypes helps to explain underperformance by minority students.[11] If this is

so, however, it seems likely that such stereotypes are less a product of race-sensitive admissions policies than of deep-seated prejudices that long antedate these policies and still exist in our society. Another piece of evidence from our study casts further doubt on the hypothesis that *admissions policies* account for underperformance. At least at the SEL-1 schools, underperformance appears to increase as the test scores of black students rise. In other words, it is the *most* academically talented black students (who could be admitted even under a race-blind policy, and who have the *least* reason to feel outmatched intellectually) who perform the furthest below their potential.

Perhaps the fairest conclusion to draw is that no one has yet shown definitively why minority students tend to underperform, although various plausible theories have been advanced to account for this phenomenon. . . . Whatever the explanation, several schools appear to have succeeded in creating programs that have substantially eliminated the problem, even in such academically demanding fields as science and engineering. The success of these programs suggests that the existence of academic underperformance does not justify doing away with race-sensitive admissions. Rather, this evidence illustrates what is possible when schools institute programs designed explicitly to bring the academic achievements of minority students fully in line with their academic potential.

Do Race-Sensitive Admissions Policies Harm Minority Graduates in Their Careers?

Another argument against race-sensitive admissions challenges the claim that colleges and universities can help build stronger leadership for the professions and for society by educating more minority students. According to some critics, race-sensitive policies actually hamper the progress of minorities later in life by inducing them to attend schools for which they were not really qualified and perpetuating the stigma that they are not really as able as whites. In Charles Murray's words, "That is the evil of preferential treatment. It perpetuates

---

[10]For an early statement of this proposition, see Klitgaard (1985, pp. 116–31). More recent evidence is cited in Chapter 3 of this study. These findings have an important bearing on the argument made by some proponents of race-sensitive admissions that differences in test scores should be disregarded because standardized tests, such as the SAT, are culturally biased against members of minority groups. To buttress this claim, opponents of these tests often call attention to particular questions that seem to call for familiarity with words or phrases that have little or no currency in poor urban neighborhoods or minority communities. We have no desire to enter the dense thickets of controversy surrounding the use of standardized tests. What is clear is that the evidence cited here shows that, far from being biased *against* minority students, standardized admissions tests consistently predict higher levels of academic performance than most blacks actually achieve.

[11]See, e.g., Steele and Aronson (1998).

the impression of inferiority."[12] By this reasoning, minority graduates would have achieved more in the long run had they attended colleges with students of comparable ability, where they could have performed better academically and avoided any impression that their academic credentials were inferior to those of whites.

Looking at patterns of graduate study provides an initial test of this argument. Our study of the interrelationships among SAT scores, college grades, and attainment of advanced degrees . . . shows that black matriculants at the most selective schools, including those with modest SAT scores and only average grades in college, were highly successful in earning advanced degrees, far more successful than black men and women in the sample of those who graduated from all four-year institutions. Judged by this criterion, black students who attended the most academically competitive schools do not appear to have been penalized.

Detailed examination of job histories and a considerable amount of earnings data leads to the same conclusion. We find that black graduates of the most selective colleges have done very well indeed in the marketplace. Among black women and black men with modest SAT scores, those who enrolled at the most selective C&B schools had appreciably higher average earnings than those who attended less selective C&B schools; other things being equal, black matriculants appear to have been well advised to attend the most selective school that would admit them. Moreover, black C&B graduates as a group earned far more than other black college graduates. Similarly, Thomas Kane, using national data, has shown that black students who graduate from selective colleges and universities earn more than blacks with similar grades, test scores, and family backgrounds who attended non-selective institutions.[13]

At the same time, black men earn less than white men who graduate from the same selective institutions (a pattern that does not exist for women). In fact, black men earn less than their white classmates even when they have the same grades, college majors, and socioeconomic backgrounds. This persistent earnings gap is troubling,[14] but we have no reason to believe that it has been exacerbated by race-sensitive admissions. On the contrary, the evidence summarized above shows that black matriculants do better in their careers, both absolutely and relative to whites, the more competitive the academic environment. This finding holds within the C&B universe of schools, even after controlling for other variables, and it also holds when we compare C&B graduates as a group with all black graduates nationwide.[15]

One can readily explain why blacks have benefited from attending academically selective colleges and universities. Apart from the quality of education they provide, selective institutions give employers, graduate schools, and others a better-known, more credible basis for judging the capacities of their students. A law school admissions office, a corporate recruiter, or a hospital seeking residents will all give greater weight to transcripts from a selective institution because they are likely to have a clearer sense of what such records mean.

---

[12]Murray 1994, p. 207.
[13]Kane (1998).

[14]It is beyond the scope of this study to analyze the underlying causes of this pattern. There is little doubt that racial discrimination still exists to some degree in the United States and that blacks and Hispanics often suffer the burdens of prejudice and stereotyping on the part of some people with whom they have contact in their working lives. However, Glenn Loury has argued that "imperfect information may be a more pervasive and intractable cause of racial discrimination today than is behavior based on agents' purported distaste for associating with blacks" (1998, p. 1).
[15]These consistent findings rebut assertions that "racial preferences in college admissions systematically mismatch talent and opportunity. . . . Many beneficiaries of preferences have no hope of excelling against their supposed peers, struggle hard merely to keep up, get discouraged, perform poorly by their own standards, and even drop out of school altogether. The modestly successful middle class career they would have enjoyed if they had attended a first-rate second-class school is lost to them, perhaps forever" (O'Sullivan 1998, p. 41).

The more selective the institution, the more reliance employers tend to place on its records of performance ("grade inflation" notwithstanding).

At the same time, race-sensitive admissions policies result in costs as well as benefits for at least some of the intended beneficiaries. The very existence of a process that gives explicit consideration to race can raise questions about the true abilities of even the most talented minority students ("stigmatize" them, some would say). The possibility of such costs is one reason why selective institutions have been reluctant to talk about the degree of preference given black students. Such reticence may be due in part to the desire to avoid criticism and controversy, but some of these institutions may also be concerned that the standing of black students in the eyes of white classmates would be lowered if differences in test scores and high school grades were publicized. More than a few black students unquestionably suffer some degree of discomfort from being beneficiaries of the admissions process (as do some athletes and legacies, even though they are generally less "visible"). It is for this reason that many high-achieving black graduates continue to seek reassurance that they have "made it on their own" and why they complain when job interviewers presume that even the most outstanding black student may well have been helped in this way.

The judgment that has to be made is whether, at the end of the day, it is worth accepting these costs, which are all too real, in exchange for the benefits received. The black matriculants themselves—who are, after all, the ones most affected by any stigmatizing effects—are presumably in the best position to weigh the pros and cons. The C&B survey data are unequivocal. Black students do not seem to *think* they have been harmed as a result of attending selective colleges with race-sensitive policies. Were it otherwise, one would suppose that the ablest black students would be resentful of these policies and the colleges that adopted them. Yet our results show that 75 percent of 1989 black matriculants who scored over 1300 on their SATs believe that

their college should place "a great deal" of emphasis on racial diversity. Similarly, 77 percent of black graduates who ranked in the top third of their class were "*very* satisfied" with their undergraduate educational experience; only 1 percent were dissatisfied.

The charge that race-sensitive admissions stigmatize blacks, and therefore hurt them rather than help them, is an argument that critics frequently make against affirmative action programs of all kinds. If it were true, those who suffered from the stigma would presumably be the ones most likely to feel its effects. Yet Jennifer Hochschild reports that successful blacks do not feel that they have suffered: "Overall, 55 percent of well-off blacks think affirmative action programs help recipients, and only 4 percent think such programs hurt recipients."[16] In the eyes of those best positioned to know, any putative costs of race-based policies have been overwhelmed by the benefits gained through enhanced access to excellent educational opportunities.

DOES DIVERSITY INCREASE RACIAL UNDERSTANDING?

Still another group of arguments holds that racial diversity, when it is deliberately achieved through an institution's admissions policies, does not necessarily enhance the value of education or contribute to the tolerance and understanding of students. Indeed, some critics suggest that such policies help to poison race relations within the larger society.

Effects of Diversity on Campus Life

In their most modest form, these arguments merely note that little or no persuasive evidence exists to show that a racially diverse student body has positive effects on the education of students. We would agree that such evidence has heretofore been limited; this deficiency was an important reason for conducting this study. Most critics of

---

[16]Hochschild 1995, p. 101.

race-sensitive admissions, however, go further, suggesting that the diversity produced by race-sensitive admissions policies tends to aggravate racial tensions and to result in a segregation of blacks and whites that increases hostility and misunderstanding among students.

Stephan and Abigail Thernstrom have made this argument most forcefully. Pointing to racial problems at Stanford University, they observed: "[Stanford] not only instituted an aggressive affirmative action admissions policy; it trained students in racial sensitivity, created dorms with an ethnic 'theme,' and drastically altered the curriculum to meet minority demands. The result was more minorities on campus; a curriculum that included courses on such subjects as black hair; frustrated, bewildered white students; and blacks who felt more alienated, more culturally black, and perhaps more hostile to whites than when they arrived."[17] From this account of a particular period of racial tension on a single campus, the authors proceed to draw much more sweeping conclusions: "The result is precisely that resegregation of campus life so clearly and appallingly on display at Stanford—but certainly not confined to that school. Without an admissions system involving racial preferences, the picture would be quite different."[18]

What light does our study throw on arguments of this kind? Clearly, racial incidents occur periodically on many campuses; feelings occasionally run high, and administrators can make unwise decisions.[19] Such episodes are unfortunate. But they tend to be uncommon, and when they do occur, they sometimes serve as a catalyst to provoke greater thought and understanding among students about problems of race.[20] Rather than focus exclusively on such incidents in isolation, it is more helpful to ask what the entire undergraduate experience of diversity has contributed to those who have lived it. To this end, our surveys record what diversity in its totality has meant to some thirty thousand former students reflecting on their experience at a wide range of selective colleges during two separate periods in the past twenty-five years. These opinions sum up the entire four years of college, and hence presumably include times of racial harmony as well as episodes of tension and misunderstanding.

The results of these surveys speak very clearly and strongly to the value of racial diversity in college. A large number of both white and black respondents felt that their undergraduate experience made a significant contribution to their ability to work with and get along well with members of other races (a 4 or a 5 on a five-point scale where 5 equals "a great deal"). Moreover, in contradiction to claims that racial diversity leads to a rigid self-segregation, 56 percent of white '89 matriculants reported that at college they "knew well" at least two blacks, and 26 percent said they "knew well" at least two Hispanics, even though each of these minority groups made up less than 10 percent of the total undergraduate student body. Blacks were even more likely to know students of other races; 88 percent knew well two or more of their white classmates, and 54 percent reported being similarly well acquainted with two or more Hispanic students.

Other investigators using different methods likewise report that diversity has a number of positive effects for students. The most comprehensive of these investigations surveyed more than twenty-seven thousand students attending a wide range of colleges and tested the effects of 192 separate variables in the campus environment.[21] Of all the items examined, the extent of racial diversity and racial interaction among students turned out to be among the three most influential

---

[17]Thernstrom and Thernstrom 1997, p. 386.

[18]Ibid., p. 388.

[19]The media sometimes give a misleading impression of the prevalence of such incidents. For a critique of the evidence underlying inflated claims of racial tension on campus, see Bernstein (1994, pp. 203–10).

[20]Forty to fifty years ago, when the '51 C&B cohort was enrolled, these campuses were free from racial friction, for the simple reason that there were too few black students on campus to allow for much conflict.

[21]Sax and Astin 1997. (See our discussion in [*The Shape of the River*], Chapter 8, of the limitations of all studies of this kind.)

factors associated with increased student acceptance of other cultures, participation in community service programs, and growth in other aspects of civic responsibility. The weight of the evidence, therefore, points clearly in one direction. As educators have long surmised, racial diversity does appear to bring about positive results in increasing the mutual understanding of whites and minority students, enhancing their ability to live and work together successfully.

Effects on Racial Tensions in the Society

A somewhat similar argument against utilizing race in the admissions process maintains that efforts of any kind that treat people differently because of their race only tend to increase racial animosities in the larger society. Claims of this kind are largely conjectural, since there is no way of knowing what the effect might be on racial tensions in the United States if colleges and universities did *not* practice race-sensitive admissions. Current admissions policies unquestionably create resentment in some families. But it seems at least as plausible to suppose that racial tensions will increase even more if the vast majority of top jobs in government, business, and the professions continue to be held by whites, while one-third of the population is composed of blacks and Hispanics who are largely relegated to less remunerative, less influential positions.

Paul Sniderman and Edward Carmines have reported some experimental evidence to the effect that affirmative action does produce negative reactions among whites that carry over to affect attitudes toward blacks generally.[22] This phenomenon was neither proved nor disproved by our study, since we were not directly concerned with the society as a whole but only with the effects of race-sensitive admissions policies on students at selective institutions. What we did do, however, was to test whether students turned down by their first-choice selective college were more opposed to racial diversity than their classmates, on the assumption that individuals rejected by the college they most wanted to attend would be especially likely to believe that racial diversity should be emphasized less. Our results indicated no tendency of this sort whatsoever.

It is also worth noting that racial attitudes in the society as a whole have continued to improve during the twenty-five to thirty years in which race-sensitive admissions have been widely practiced.[23] Whites may oppose certain policies to deal with racial problems, such as school busing, minority set-asides, or even race-sensitive admissions policies. On questions of racial discrimination, living in integrated neighborhoods, interracial dating, and intermarriage, however, whites have become more tolerant, not less so, since 1970. One can always argue that progress would have been even faster had colleges not made special efforts to diversify their student bodies. Such claims cannot easily be proved or disproved. But if race-sensitive admissions were truly poisoning race relations, one might expect to see some evidence of growing disaffection among the white alumni/ae who were most exposed to these policies and most likely to have experienced them when they applied to graduate school. In fact, the very opposite is true. Support for an institutional emphasis on enrolling a diverse student body is high among both black and white alumni/ae of selective colleges and appears to have grown steadily, not diminished, from the class beginning college in 1951 to the class that enrolled in 1976 and, finally, to the class that entered thirteen years later.

IS THERE A BETTER WAY?

The final cluster of arguments—apart from those involving issues of "fairness" and "merit" . . . comes from representatives on both sides of the affirmative action debate who claim that there are ways of admitting students to achieve a racially

---

[22]Sniderman and Carmines 1997, ch. 2.

[23]Schuman et al. 1997.

diverse student body that do not accord different treatment to members of different races in the admissions process.

More Vigorous Recruitment

An early argument along these lines was expressed in 1972 by Thomas Sowell of the Hoover Institute, who declared that selective institutions were simply not trying hard enough to find qualified minority applicants. In his words, "The belief that there is no substantial pool of capable black students might be understandable if the various colleges, foundations and special programs were seeking the academically ablest black students they could possibly find and were failing to turn up what they were looking for. In fact, however, their recruiting efforts are seldom directed toward ferreting out the most academically accomplished black students and many are explicitly *not* looking for any such thing."[24]

Whether or not this statement was accurate when made, it is almost certainly no longer valid. Professional school and college admissions offices can and regularly do obtain reports of every student in the country who meets whatever academic profile the admissions officers select. Thus a law school can write to the Law School Admissions Council and obtain the names of every black student in the United States with a college grade point average over 3.25 and an admissions test score above 130. A college can obtain from the Educational Testing Service a similar printout containing the names of all minority students with, say, SAT scores above 1100 and high school grade point averages over 3.0. Admissions officers regularly use these lists to contact promising minority students by mail or by phone and to schedule recruiting visits to high schools and colleges where such candidates are regularly found. Because of such lists, together with the extensive efforts made by most selective institutions to recruit minority candidates, it is highly doubtful that any significant

number of black and Hispanic students who are qualified by conventional criteria are overlooked by selective colleges and universities.

Considering Class Rather Than Race

Another argument frequently advanced by participants in the debate over race-sensitive admissions is that universities could attract a suitably diverse class without taking account of race if they simply gave preference to applicants from economically disadvantaged families regardless of race. Such a policy would be based on the generally accepted notion that young people from economically deprived backgrounds have greater obstacles to overcome than do students who grow up in more comfortable circumstances. Because blacks and Hispanics are much more heavily represented among the poor than they are in the population as a whole, proponents argue that a policy based on economic class will automatically result in a significant number of minority students. In the words of Richard Kahlenberg, "Class-based affirmative action is a remedy to the moral and political thicket of affirmative action, a way of meeting the goals racial preferences seek to achieve while avoiding the problems racial preferences create."[25]

Almost every selective institution is committed to the principle that talented students from all income groups should be able to attend regardless of ability to pay the tuition. Indeed, colleges and professional schools make great efforts to act on this principle by raising as much money as they can for scholarships and other forms of financial aid. But it is most unlikely that shifting from race-sensitive to class-based admissions would allow institutions to admit student bodies nearly as racially diverse as they are today. Admitting genuinely poor students is very costly, since such students have few if any resources of their own. As a practical matter, therefore, most selective institutions could not find enough additional financial

---

[24]Sowell 1972, pp. 133–34.

[25]Kahlenberg 1996, p. xii.

aid to increase the number of poor students by more than a limited amount. But even if such an approach could be paid for, it would add little to minority student enrollments, because children from poor black and Hispanic families make up less than half of all poor children and are much less likely than poor whites to excel in school. . . . Kane found that among all students from families with incomes under $20,000 *who also finished in the top tenth of their high school class,* only one in six is black or Hispanic.

Shifting from race-sensitive admissions to class-based admissions, therefore, would substantially reduce the minority enrollments at selective institutions while changing dramatically their overall student profiles. Our data show that students with low socioeconomic backgrounds are less likely than students of equivalent ability from high socioeconomic backgrounds to complete their studies, attain professional or doctoral degrees, and earn high incomes. As a result, although a class-based system might reward applicants handicapped by poor schools, troubled neighborhoods, and similar burdens, it would surely hinder selective institutions in attempting to prepare the most talented minority students for eventual positions of leadership in government, business, and the professions.

Emphasizing Grades, Not Test Scores

The last suggestion for avoiding an explicitly race-sensitive admissions policy has been advanced by proponents of affirmative action. Such advocates argue that selective institutions should abandon the use of standardized tests and admit all students on the basis of their high school class rank or (in the case of graduate schools) their college class rank.[26] The Texas legislature, in the wake of the *Hopwood* decision, has adopted a variant of this approach. Under legislation passed in 1997, the state's premier public universities are required to admit the top 10 percent of seniors from every public high school in Texas; the remaining offers of admission will be based, as they have been in the past, "on applicants' grades, test scores, essays, and other academic and personal factors."[27]

It is too soon to be able to estimate the effects of this policy on the number of minority students who will attend the most selective universities in Texas and even harder to gauge the potential effects of such a policy in other locales. Nationally, we know that blacks are only half as likely as whites to finish in the top 10 percent of the high school class and less than 40 percent as likely to earn an A average.[28] However, as the article in the *Chronicle* cited earlier indicates, such a policy could give many minority students who attend high schools that are *de facto* segregated a much *better* chance of gaining admission to a premier public university than they had before.

One example given is W. H. Adamson High School in Dallas, where 86 percent of the students are Hispanic. In such situations, the actual effects of the "10 percent plan" will depend on the advice given by guidance counselors, one of whom is said to have told her seniors in the top 10 percent: "You can get into the University of Texas at Austin, but do you really want to go there? Do you feel prepared and confident enough to compete?" Another guidance counselor is quoted as warning her students to focus on "where they can graduate, not

---

[26]For a detailed discussion of law school admissions and the weaknesses of traditional indicia, especially the Law School Admissions Test (LSAT), see Sturm and Guinier 1996.

[27]Healy 1998, p. A29. University officials are cited as expecting members of the 10-percent-cohort to receive about 43 percent of offers to freshmen. They also recognize (in personal correspondence) that it remains to be seen how many slots will actually be filled by those receiving acceptances based on class rank; since there are no limits to the number of places allotted by this policy, it is possible that over time, as the policy becomes more widely known within the state, a very large percentage of the class could be filled by this method.

[28]Thernstrom and Thernstrom 1997, p. 402. Presumably, selective colleges could further increase the percentage of minority students in a way that did not rely overtly on race by giving extra points to students with high GPAs from disadvantaged high schools (i.e., schools with average parental incomes below a certain level). But such strategies only underscore the inequalities *in fact* of utilizing policies of this kind.

where they can attend and then feel discouraged and drop out." Also, how many minority students end up enrolling at a school like the University of Texas at Austin will depend on money, since many minority students, in particular, who rank in the top 10 percent of their class cannot afford to attend college in Austin without a state scholarship program that is either race-based itself or sufficiently generous to benefit all those from lower income families who are admitted to the leading universities. As a guidance counselor asked: "Where's the money? Many of our top kids aren't going to go someplace where they don't get a scholarship."[29]

In effect, much of the responsibility for deciding which students are capable of handling the academic work at a university such as the University of Texas at Austin has now passed from the admissions officers at the university to the guidance counselors at high schools and the prospective students themselves. The likelihood of mistakes being made, simply through lack of knowledge, lack of experience in making such determinations, and the absence of comparative data, would seem to be all too real. At the same time, other students, including minority students, who attended highly competitive high schools but did not finish in the top 10 percent of their class, may now be turned down even though they would have been admitted under the previous policy. Having failed to make the 10 percent cutoff, these students will have to compete "at large" for far fewer places even though they possess greater academic ability than many of those who were automatically admitted by virtue of their rank in class. So long as high schools differ so substantially in the academic abilities of their students and the level of difficulty of their courses, treating all applicants alike if they finished above a given high school class rank provides a spurious form of equality that is likely to damage the academic profile of the overall class of students admitted to selective institutions far more than would anything accomplished through race-sensitive admissions policies.

Incentive effects also need to be considered in thinking about the long-term consequences for teaching and learning at all levels. If so much depends on being in the top 10 percent of one's class, many high school students are likely to shy away from tough courses and concentrate even more than they do now simply on "getting good grades." There is also an incentive for parents to find some way to enroll their children in less demanding schools, where they will have a better chance of being in the top 10 percent.

Is a policy of this kind, whatever its shortcomings turn out to be, likely to end controversy over race-sensitive admissions? Some obviously hope so. As the *Chronicle* article noted: "The Texas policy's popularity among both liberal and conservative politicians—who are usually divided over affirmative action—is one of its intriguing qualities." But the article goes on to observe: "The reality, of course, is that new admissions policies create new sets of winners and losers." Already, some applicants from the most competitive high schools are saying that the policy is unfair because it doesn't take account of differences between high schools and is just "another form of affirmative action."[30] As the effects of the new procedure become clear, the debate over appearances versus realities—and over the unintended consequences of the policy—may become even more heated.

We conclude that basing admissions to academically selective institutions on any simple criterion such as being in the top 10 percent of one's high school class (or the top 3 or 4 percent, which would be the required cut-off in situations in which the competition for admission is even more intense than it is in Texas) is unlikely to be an effective substitute for racesensitive admissions policies. On the contrary, this approach could well have the effect of lowering minority graduation rates from college and diminishing the pool of students who can compete effectively for positions of leadership in business, government, and the professions.

---

[29]Healy 1998, p. A29.

[30]Ibid.

The evidence summarized in this [writing] calls into question many of the arguments most frequently made in the debate over race-sensitive admissions. Refuting such arguments, however, does not necessarily resolve the ultimate question of whether or not these admissions policies are desirable. Efforts to answer this question need to take account of the kinds of facts produced by this study. But facts alone are not sufficient for the task. Wise policy decisions require a larger view of the present and future needs of the society, the values that deserve greatest emphasis, the varied missions of leading educational institutions, and an appreciation of where responsibility for educational policy-making should reside. . . .

REFERENCES

Association of American Medical Colleges. 1996. *Minority Students in Medical Education: Facts and Figures X.* Washington, DC: Association of American Medical Colleges.

Bernstein, Richard. 1994. *The Dictatorship of Virtue: Multiculturalism and the Battle for America's Future.* New York: Knopf.

Graglia, Lino A. 1993. "Racial Preferences in Admission to Institutions of Higher Education." In *The Imperiled Academy,* edited by Howard Dickman. New Brunswick, NJ: Transaction Publishers.

Healy, Patrick. 1998. "Admissions Law Changes the Equations for Students and Colleges in Texas." *Chronicle of Higher Education,* April 3, pp. A29–A31.

Hochschild, Jennifer. 1995. *Facing Up to the American Dream: Race, Class, and the Soul of the Nation.* Princeton, NJ: Princeton University Press.

Howd, Jay B. 1992. "Race-Exclusive Scholarships in Federally-Assisted Colleges and Universities—Will They Survive?" *Southern Illinois Law Journal,* 16:451.

Kahlenberg, Richard D. 1996. *The Remedy: Class, Race, and Affirmative Action.* New York: Basic Books.

Kane, Thomas J. 1998. "Racial and Ethnic Preferences in College Admission." In *The Black-White Test Score Gap,* edited by Christopher Jencks and Meredith Phillips. Washington, DC: Brookings Institution.

Klitgaard, Robert. 1985. *Choosing Elites.* New York: Basic Books.

Loury, Glenn C. 1998. "Discrimination in the Post-Civil Rights Era: Beyond Market Interactions." Paper presented at a meeting of the Russell Sage Foundation.

Murray, Charles. 1994. "Affirmative Racism." In *Debating Affirmative Action: Race, Gender, Ethnicity, and the Politics of Inclusion,* edited by Nicholas Mills. New York: Delta.

O'Sullivan, John. 1998. In "Is Affirmative Action on the Way Out? Should It Be? A Symposium." *Commentary,* 105(3): 40–42.

Sax, Linda J. and Alexander W. Astin. 1997. "The Development of 'Civic Virtue' among College Students." In *The Senior Year Experience,* edited by John Gardner and Gretchen Van der Veer. San Francisco: Jossey-Bass.

Schuman, Howard, et al. 1997. *Racial Attitudes in America: Trends and Interpretations.* Cambridge: Harvard University Press.

Sniderman, Paul M. and Edward G. Carmines. 1997. *Reaching Beyond Race.* Cambridge: Harvard University Press.

Sowell, Thomas. 1972. *Black Education: Myths and Tragedies.* New York: McKay.

Steele, Claude and Joshua Aronson. 1998. "Stereotype Threat and the Test Performance of Academically Successful African-Americans." In *The Black-White Test Score Gap,* edited by Christopher Jencks. Washington, DC: Brookings Institution.

Steele, Shelby. 1994. "A Negative Vote on Affirmative Action." In *Debating Affirmative Action: Race, Gender, Ethnicity, and the Politics of Inclusion,* edited by Nicholas Mills. New York: Delta.

Sturm, Susan and Lani Guinier. 1996. "The Future of Affirmative Action: Reclaiming the Innovative Ideal." *California Law Review,* 84: 953.

Thernstrom, Stephan and Abigail Thernstrom. 1997. *America in Black and White: One Nation Indivisible.* New York: Simon & Schuster.

Wightman, Linda F. 1997. "The Threat to Diversity in Legal Education: An Empirical Analysis of the Consequences of Abandoning Race as a Factor in Law School Admissions Decisions." *New York University Law Review,* 72(1): 1–53.

CHAPTER 4

Sex, Sexual Identity, and Class

In Chapter 3, various scholars make a clear point that race and ethnicity influence both an individual's experience of class and the class in which he or she is likely to be located. What happens when we add sex, gender, and sexual identity to the increasingly complex mix of factors contributing to inequality? Looking at the sex, gender, and sexual preference of raced individuals forces a new kind of question not yet raised explicitly: What is or should be our unit of analysis when looking at social class? Do we focus on an individual having a class, as is often the case when looking at men regardless of their race, ethnicity, or immigration status; or do we focus on households and the combined earnings of all parties? Because of the historical reality that many households were organized around a primary wage earner until fairly late in the game and that the ideal through mid-twentieth century was the family wage model, for many sociologists for many years, the class of the family unit was seen to reflect the standing of all members in it.

As Szonja Sylezni (2001) points out, stratification theorists are still struggling with the "woman problem," which has resulted in theories that ignored women altogether, either benignly (focusing on the emotional role of the wife and mother) or with hostility (seeing women as a reserve army of labor who threaten male wages). Some have tried to factor in women's contribution to family class standing as a fraction of what men's higher earnings provided; others have looked at women as men had been looked at: as independent actors with a class location. While there is not yet a satisfactory resolution to the question of whether the family or the individual should be the most basic and appropriate unit of analysis in stratification research, there has been in recent decades an explosion of work on women as economic actors. Most of this scholarship focuses on differences between how women and men earn a living, persistent differences between them in pay and promotional opportunities, and why we continue to see such differences despite legislative changes and shifts in societal attitudes about gender equity. At the margins are questions about how sexuality, specifically homosexuality and especially lesbianism, might impact assumptions about work and family life. The selections we provide in Chapter 4 grapple with this issue (women's classed status), with the persistence of gender hierarchies, with how sex and race influence class location and job opportunities, and finally, with how sexual preference can influence family and job choices.

Cecilia Ridgeway applies an interactionist framework in her analysis of a structural problem: the persistence of gender inequality in labor markets. She notes that while labor markets are structures that generate gender queues (that is, potential workers being ranked by gender and by race/ethnicity), the process that begins the labeling of workers and jobs that in turn result in wage inequality is one based on interaction. Ridgeway walks us through several of these processes to try to explain why the gender of an employee remains so salient. Paula England, a sociologist known for her challenges to neoclassical economic theories, provides an overview of class by households containing women. Through the 1980s, as divorce laws became more liberal, sociologists documented the "feminization of poverty" (see Weitzman, 1985). Women without male incomes, and with the responsibility of rearing children, were more likely to be poor because of lower earning capabilities. In this selection, "Gender and Access to Money," England re-examines the likelihood of female poverty in an era of greater similarity between men's and women's earnings, occupations, and patterns of employment. On an individual level, things are looking up for some women; on a household level, more women and their children remain poor.

The next selections use ethnographic research to explore a range of women's work experiences. These selections are not meant to be comprehensive but illustrate again the rich interplay between immigration status, ethnicity, class, and gender. Pierrette Hondagneu-Sotelo's book *Doméstica* describes the unseen world of live-in domestic labor done by immigrant workers. As Hondagneu-Sotelo acknowledges, housekeeper/nanny work is entry level because it is not desirable work. Historically in the United States, Irish immigrants and African Americans entered home service, but left as soon as other opportunities became available (see Kessler-Harris, 1982). Domestic labor is an extension of the work most women provide in their own families; and like family labor, it is poorly paid and never ending. One of the greatest ironies of living in a home not one's own, as this excerpt reveals, is being hungry in the face of upper middle-class affluence. Behind the exquisite kitchen cabinetry there may be no food. Poorly paid workers buy their own groceries, which their wealthy employers may eat!

Another side of service work is minimum wage labor. Journalist Barbara Ehrenreich's *Nickel and Dimed* (2000) was based on a premise proposed by her editor: to live for several months undercover as a minimum wage worker. The book that resulted is a touching tribute to the working poor, mainly women, among whom Ehrenreich worked for four months. Ehrenreich worked as a maid at a "professional contracting" company, waited tables, cleaned motel rooms, and in the chapter included here, entered the world of retail. At fifty-something, Ehrenreich finds both the physical and the fiscal demands of the jobs daunting. Many of her coworkers don't make enough to pay their rent or eat despite working a forty-hour week or more. Hunger, again, is a constant theme. Safe and affordable housing and transportation are out of reach for the women whose lives Ehrenreich describes; one of her Wal-Mart coworkers lives in her car. Sadly evident, too, is the contempt of generally young male managers hired to enforce arbitrary employment rules who don't really see working women of a certain age as people. Wal-Mart, the retail giant and employer *du jour* of this chapter, has responded to recent bad press with full-page print and television ads describing the opportunities it contends it offers its "associates" and their communities, opting for a public relations campaign in lieu of genuine reform.

While the majority of women today work for pay, volunteer work is still largely a female preserve. Diana Kendall's ethnographic look at privileged women is an interesting peek into a world that isn't open to everyone: the world of philanthropic and other nonprofit organizations that, in Kendall's words, do "good deeds." At the other end of the spectrum of social class, then, are the women from a variety of racial and ethnic backgrounds who, born or married into privilege, seek to give back in some way. How does *noblesse oblige* really work? Kendall offers a glimpse into the organizational structure of groups such as the Junior League (mostly but not exclusively Christian and white) and the Links (African American) and who is likely to be invited to join. Women's service organizations are undergoing tremendous change but offer a parallel formal structure echoed in men's clubs devoted to political power brokerage.

We end this section with a look at how sexuality affects stratification with two theoretical pieces looking explicitly at lesbian and gay identities. Certainly, as Julie Matthaei points out in her historical overview, one can never separate sexuality from sex—that is, lesbians face a different set of economic issues *because they are women* than do gay men. Badgett and King examine how sexual orientation might influence choice of occupation; their sample, drawn from the General Social Survey, is too small to be representative but large enough to point the way to future directions for research. Badgett and King hypothesize that gay men and lesbian women will enter different kinds of jobs based on expectations about discrimination (some jobs will be more hostile to homosexual workers) and about family life (ability to support a family will be particularly important for lesbians). They argue that sexual preference is analogous to facing discrimination about religion or national origin—in some cases, it isn't clear that an employee has the stigmatized characteristic. Under some circumstances, then, an individual may "pass" as heterosexual, but at a price. Likewise, if the worker is forthcoming about her sexuality, she may also pay a high price both socially and financially. The other variable, family life, will effect men and women differently. Lesbians like all women are more likely to earn less than men; the economic affects for family life are obvious.

Matthei provides a closing history for this chapter on how sexuality has been construed historically and socially. Certainly our understanding of sexuality is a work in progress. In the social sciences, sexuality as a building block of stratification has been largely ignored. Matthei builds an argument linking sexuality to capitalism, consumerism, and secularization. Women's fate has been disentangled economically from men's in the United States with mixed results, as we have seen; heterosexuality, however, need not be the automatic default position from an economic standpoint. The final two pieces in this chapter demonstrate that we have far to go in understanding the origins and nature of sexuality (a fascinating topic outside of the purview of this text) and their implications for understanding inequality.

REFERENCES

Kessler-Harris, Alice. (1982). *Out to work: A history of wage-earning women in the United States.* Oxford and New York: Oxford University Press.

Szelenyi, Szonja. (2001). "The 'woman problem' in stratification theory and research." In David B. Grusky, *Social stratification* (2nd ed.). Boulder, CO: Westview Press, pp. 681–688.

Weitzman, Lenore J. (1985). *The divorce revolution: The unexpected social and economic consequences for women and children in America.* New York and London: Free Press.

Interaction and the Conservation of Gender Inequality: Considering Employment

CECILIA RIDGEWAY

How can we explain the persistence of gender hierarchy in our society over major historical transformations in its socio-economic base? A system that advantages men over women in material resources, power, status, and authority (i.e., gender hierarchy) has continued in one form or another despite profound structural changes such as industrialization and the movement of production out of the household, women's accelerated movement into the labor force after World War II, and, most recently, women's entry into male-dominated occupations (Hartmann 1976; Reskin and Roos 1990). What accounts for the chameleon-like ability of gender hierarchy to reassert itself in new forms when its old structural forms erode?

Although there is no single answer, part of the solution may lie in the way gender stratification is mediated by interactional processes that are largely taken for granted. In this paper I argue that interactional gender mechanisms can operate as an "invisible hand" that rewrites gender inequality into new socioeconomic arrangements as they replace the prior socioeconomic bases for gender hierarchy.

I focus on interactional mechanisms that mediate gender inequality in paid employment. Employment is one of two interdependent structural foundations on which our present system of gender hierarchy appears to rest; the other is the

Source: Cecilia Ridgeway, "Interaction and the Conservation of Gender Inequality: Considering Employment," in *American Sociological Review,* 1997, Vol,. 62 April: 216–235. Used with permission from the American Sociological Association.

household division of labor. Some efforts have been made to understand the interactional mediation of the latter (Berk 1985; Risman 1987), but few for the former.

A substantial research industry has sought to explain the persistence of wage inequality and sex segregated jobs. Key processes identified include statistical discrimination, internal labor markets, and the rendering of labor queues into gender queues, but explanations remain incomplete (England 1992; Reskin and Roos 1990). An analysis of mediating interactional mechanisms may improve our answers to several stubborn questions including the reasons for unrelenting gender-labeling of jobs despite occupational change, how employers' apparent preferences for male workers persist even under competitive market pressures, why women's work is devalued, whether and how people act in their gender interests in employment matters, and why women workers accept lower wages than equivalent men.

Like race or class, gender is a multilevel system of differences and disadvantages that includes socioeconomic arrangements and widely held cultural beliefs at the macro level, ways of behaving in relation to others at the interactional level, and acquired traits and identities at the individual level. Interactional processes contribute to all forms of inequality, but there are several reasons for suspecting that they are especially important in gender inequality. First, our system of sex categorization divides the population into two groups of roughly equal size, creating the maximum structural likelihood of a high rate of interaction between men and women (Blau and Schwarz 1984). Sex categorization crosscuts almost all other divisions in the population, including kin and households, and forces regular cross-sex interaction on virtually everyone. In addition, there is growing evidence that our cultural system of gender difference relies heavily on interaction. What Deaux and Kite (1987) call the "now you see them, now you don't" nature of sex differences in behavior suggests that they are situationally and thus interactionally based, as many gender theorists now argue (Deaux and Major 1987; Eagly 1987; West and Zimmerman 1987).

I argue that gender becomes an important component of interactional processes because the problems of organizing interaction evoke cultural schemas that reinforce continual sex categorization. Sex categorization is the process by which actors classify one another as male or female, supposedly on the basis of physical sex criteria, but more commonly on the basis of personal presentation (e.g., clothing, hairstyles) that the audience presumes stands for these sex criteria (West and Zimmerman 1987). As ethnomethodologists have demonstrated, this process is almost entirely socially constructed despite its apparent "naturalness" (Goffman 1977; Kessler and McKenna 1978). Sex categorization in interaction, in turn, can activate a number of gender processes that may recreate gender hierarchy in the organizational and resource-distributing processes that the interaction mediates. I focus on two of these processes—status processes and biased referential processes—that are especially relevant for employment inequality. After describing the interactional gender mechanisms, I discuss the role they play in mediating the persistence of gender inequality in employment.

INTERACTION, GENDER, AND INEQUALITY

Interaction and Sex Categorization

It is striking that people are nearly incapable of interacting with one another when they cannot guess the other's sex. The television program *Saturday Night Live* evoked this situation in its comedy sequence about "Pat," an androgynous person who wreaked interactional havoc even in the most mundane encounters because others couldn't place her/him as a woman or man. Although people usually can interact with others whom they can't place on other major dimensions of inequality, such as class or race, they seem to have difficulty completing even trivial, routine exchanges with someone they can't classify by sex. This suggests that sex categorization is deeply rooted in the cultural rules that organize interaction (West and Zimmerman 1987).

Interaction requires coordinating your behavior with that of another. To act yourself, you need some way of making sense of and anticipating the other's behavior. As symbolic interactionists have long noted, this requires that you develop at least a minimal definition, some initial beginning of "who" you and the other are in this situation (Alexander and Wiley 1981; Stryker 1980). Something can be "seen" only in explicit or implicit contrast to something else; therefore defining self and other requires one to find dimensions by which to categorize the other as similar to or different from self in various ways, as social identity research has demonstrated (Turner 1987).

The process of situating self and other through categorization is a nested process that must begin so that interaction can start but it continues throughout the interaction episode, as documented in recent models of person perception (Brewer 1988; Fiske and Neuberg 1990). Over time, more and more crosscutting classifications are introduced, yielding increasingly complex and nuanced situated identities for self and other. The relevance to action of any given classification waxes and wanes with events, but at least one initial categorization of self and other as similar or different on some dimension is necessary if any interaction is to take place.

This argument implies that sets of interacting individuals are likely to actively construct shared cultural schemas for readily categorizing self and other. Some of these schemas must be so simplified and so apparently obvious that they provide an easy means of initially situating self and almost any other so that interaction may begin at all. Such prior categorization systems in effect are cultural "superschemas" defining a few fundamental categories that can be applied to make sense of any person. They need not be relevant to the specific focus of interaction. They merely render actors sufficiently meaningful to one another to be able to address each other in relation to the focal goals and, by doing so, to introduce more relevant categorizations. Yet, by providing a cognitive starting point from which the rest proceeds, these superschemas can subtly influence the course of interaction even when they are irrelevant to its focus.

Supporting this analysis, research in cognition demonstrates that person perception is hierarchical: It begins with an initial, automatic classification according to a very small number of primary social categories and moves on to more detailed typing depending on the circumstances (Brewer 1988; Fiske and Neuberg 1990). Empirical evidence demonstrates that sex functions as one of these primary categorization systems in Western society (Fiske 1992). Studies show that we automatically and unconsciously sex-categorize any specific other to whom we must relate (Brewer and Lui 1989; Stangor et al. 1992).

As a dimension of variation among individuals, sex may be especially susceptible to social construction as one of a culture's primary systems of self-other categorization. Brewer and Lui (1989) argue that although cultures vary in the specific dimensions of human variation that serve as their few primary person categories, sex is always among them. Once sex is constructed as a simple, roughly dichotomous distinction, its constant use in interaction keeps it always accessible in people's minds (Bargh 1989) and discourages its differentiation into more than two sexes, which would reduce its usefulness as a quick, prior way of classifying self and other.

The social problems of organizing interaction over a wide range of actors and circumstances may facilitate the cultural construction of sex as a simple,

prior categorization system. Once this occurs, however, sex categorization becomes a habitual, automatic part of person perception. In institutional settings, including workplaces, clear social scripts may define self and other (e.g., supervisor and worker). Yet sex categorization continues because the actual process of *enacting* an institutional script with a *concrete* other evokes habitual person perception, and with it, the culture's superschemas that define the basic attributes necessary to make sense of any person. Cognition research shows that when institutional identities and occupational roles are activated in the process of perceiving a specific person, they become nested within the prior, automatic categorization of that person as male or female and take on slightly different meanings as a result (Brewer 1988; Brewer and Lui 1989). Thus, although we may be able to imagine an ungendered institutional script whereby "the student talks to the teacher," we cannot interact with any actual student except as a male or female student. The sex categorization of self and others, even in institutionally scripted settings, is a fundamental process that injects a variety of gender effects into the activities and institutional contexts that people enact.

Gender Stereotypes, Salience, and Behavior

If the cultural construction of sex as a simplified, prior categorization system is related to its uses in interaction, then the cultural development of *gender stereotypes* is likely; these describe what behaviors can be expected from a person of a given category. Given the basis of automatic sex categorization in interactional contrasts, it is likely that whatever specific content is attached to a sex category, it will be organized around polarized traits that differentiate men from women (Deaux and Kite 1987).[1]

---

[1]While sex category remains dichotomous, gender stereotypes are more complex, containing multiple subtypes such as professional woman or traditional woman.

Actors' gender stereotypes are cued by sex categorization, which makes them implicitly accessible (Fiske and Neuberg 1990). But the extent to which these stereotypes shape actors' behaviors in the setting (e.g., their performance scripted roles) depends on the salience of gender in the situation compared with other identities on which they have also categorized self and others (Berger et al. 1977; Deaux and Major 1987; Eagly 1987; Fiske and Taylor 1991). Although sex categorization provides an all-purpose way to begin, its very generality as a social category usually necessitates subsequent, more specific categorizations (Brewer 1991; Turner 1987). As multiple categorizations occur, the cognitive implications of each, weighted by its relevance to the situation and its utility for making sense of the other, are combined by actors into an ongoing impression (Fiske and Neuberg 1990). Therefore stereotypes cued by sex categorization can vary from vague cognitive backgrounds, whose implications for behavior are virtually overcome by more immediate identities in the situation, to powerful determinants of actors' expectations and behavior.

In work settings institutional identities are likely to reside in the foreground for actors. Evidence indicates, however, that even when other identities are the most powerful determinants of behavior in a situation, cultural gender stereotypes become *effectively salient* (i.e., sufficiently salient to measurably modify actors' expectations and behavior) under at least two conditions: when the interactants differ in sex category, and when gender is relevant to the purposes or the social context of the interaction (Berger et al. 1977; Cota and Dion 1986; Deaux and Major 1987). Indeed, gender may shape behavior most commonly as an effectively salient background identity that acts in combination with more situationally salient foreground identities and modifies their performance.

Even when initially they are not effectively salient, gender stereotypes are primed by actors' sex categorization of one another so that they are easily triggered, or made salient, by events in interaction (Bargh 1989; Deaux and Major 1987). This is especially likely because of the diffuse nature of gender stereotypes, which allows them to be construed as relevant to many situations. For these reasons and because of the high rate of mixed-sex interaction, the conditions in which gender stereotypes become salient enough to perceptively modify behavior and judgments are a large subset of all situations.

Gender Status and Behavior

By continually reinforcing sex/gender as a system of presumed difference, interaction creates a salient distinction that can easily become a basis for inequality. Gender *status beliefs* are one form of inequality: These are widely held cultural beliefs that evaluate one sex as generally superior and diffusely more competent than the other. When status beliefs form, they become an important component of gender stereotypes that is also effectively salient (affecting expectations and behavior) in mixed-sex and gender-relevant situations (Carli 1991; Ridgeway 1993). It is well documented that currently accepted gender stereotypes incorporate assumptions of men's greater status value; that is, men's traits are generally viewed as more valuable than women's, and men are diffusely judged as more competent (Broverman et al. 1972; Deaux and Kite 1987; Eagly 1987).

Although other elements of gender stereotypes probably are also important, I focus here on status beliefs because they are directly relevant to inequality. Gender status beliefs have three types of effects on goal-oriented interaction that affect employment inequality. First, when effectively salient, they cause both men and women to implicitly expect (or expect that others will expect) greater competence from men than from women, all other things being equal. These expectations tend to become self-fulfilling, shaping men's and women's assertiveness and confidence, their judgments of each other's competence, their actual performance, and their influence in the situation (Carli 1991; Miller and Turnbull 1986; Pugh and Wahrman 1983; Ridgeway 1993).

Second, activated gender status beliefs create expectations for rewards that reflect an actor's relative status and expected performance and thus favor men over equivalent women (Berger, Fisek, Norman, and Wagner 1985). These reward expectations often acquire the normative, moral quality of a "right" to rewards corresponding to one's status relative to others who are different in status-relevant ways (Berger et al. 1985; Cook 1975). When gender status is effectively salient, men may react negatively if they are placed on the same reward level as a similar woman and may experience this situation as an implicit status threat.

Third, because gender status beliefs advantage men over women who are otherwise their equals, men, on average, have less interest in attending to information that undermines expectations based on gender status. Cognition research suggests that people are "good enough" perceivers; the extent to which they move beyond initial categorizations, incorporate inconsistent information, and develop complex, individuated impressions of the other is mediated by their motives in the situation (Fiske 1992; Fiske and Neuberg 1990). In interaction, men are less likely to notice, and more likely to discount if they do notice, information about self or other that might diminish or eliminate the effects of gender status beliefs on expectations for competence and reward.[2] As a result, women may find it difficult to alter the lower expectations held for them.

Interaction and Gender Status Beliefs

Continual sex categorization in interaction has an especially potent consequence: Under conditions of distributional inequality between the sexes in some valued asset or resource (e.g., access to material resources or coercive power), it drives the social construction of gender status beliefs (Ridgeway

1991). Most important, it does so in a manner that helps maintain these beliefs in spite of changes in the structural conditions that support them.

When people who differ in resources engage in goal-oriented interaction, they usually develop hierarchies of influence and respect in the situation that correspond to their resource differences (Harrod 1980; Stewart and Moore 1992). Experimental evidence shows that when this happens, and when the actors also differ on a distinguishing personal attribute, they form the belief that people in the resource- and influence-advantaged category of the attribute are more highly respected, more competent, and more powerful in most people's eyes than are individuals in the disadvantaged category (Ridgeway et al. 1995). In other words, they form status beliefs about the distinguishing attribute.

This point suggests that because interactional categorization makes sex a salient distinction in mixed-sex encounters, goal-oriented encounters between men and women who differ in resources should foster gender status beliefs. With a gender inequality in the distribution of resources there will be more of these mixed-sex encounters in which the man is resource-advantaged; thus the encounters will produce a predominance of status beliefs favoring men, which diffuse widely (Ridgeway and Balkwell 1997).

If interactional processes, when they occur, are *sufficient* (if not necessary) to create gender status beliefs in the context of gender inequalities in the distribution of a valued resource, then interaction will ensure the continuance of such beliefs as long as some such distributional inequalities exist. Interaction is also likely to conserve gender status beliefs over changes in the original distributional inequalities that supported them. Because status beliefs create expectations that have self-fulfilling effects, they resist change and cannot be eroded except by repeated disconfirming experiences (Harris and Rosenthal 1985; Miller and Turnbull 1986; Rothbart and John 1985). Multiple experiences are required, especially for people who benefit from gender status beliefs because their self

---

[2]Some women also may have an interest in maintaining traditional gender stereotypes, which makes them similarly resistant to disconfirming information.

interest makes them more cognitively resistant to disconfirming information. When structural changes (e.g., economic, technological, or widespread social organizational changes) cause a decline in the original distributional inequalities, people will have more frequent disconfirming interactional experiences—for example, interactions in which a woman has resource advantages large enough to override gender status so that she becomes men's actual superior in situational power and prestige (Pugh and Wahrman 1983). Yet, unless structural change produces a rapid outright reversal in the inequalities (i.e., from favoring most men to favoring most women), the rate at which change produces such reversal interactions may not provide enough people with enough disconfirmations to permanently erode their status beliefs except over a long period. As a result, change in the evaluative content and consensuality of gender status beliefs across the population will be slow and will lag substantially behind the changes in the distributional inequalities that support them.

The lagged effect of gender status beliefs creates a "window" of time during which, even as societal changes mitigate the former distributional inequality, the continued operation of gender status in interaction biases the interactionally mediated allocation of other resources, opportunities, or positions of power. As a result, men will retain their advantage in power and resources within newly emerging organizational forms, although their degree of advantage may change.

Sex Categorization, Interaction, and Comparison Others

Interactionally driven sex categorization activates a second process that also is important for gender inequality in many situations, but particularly in employment. The categorization of self and other establishes a *referential set* of those who are similar to oneself and are therefore appropriate comparison others for evaluating one's rewards or other outcomes in a situation (Suls and Wills 1991).

As Major (1989) observes, when valued rewards are distributed unequally among men and women in a population, the biased selection of comparison others can result in sex differences in the levels of rewards that people feel they are entitled to receive in a given situation.

Research shows that people define the level of rewards they are entitled to receive in a work situation (e.g., pay, promotions, working conditions) in comparison with others who are similar to them in attributes relevant to the situation (Major 1989; Major and Forcey 1985). Information on others' outcomes is acquired primarily by searches (Major 1989). Searches involve talking to others—to coworkers, friends, family, and associates—asking around and evaluating written or observed evidence of others' outcomes. Basically they are interactive, involving a definition of self in relation to a concrete other, and thus searches evoke sex categorization. In turn, however, sex categorization during searches creates a dimension of implicit similarity that biases the search toward same-sex others. Because of the often unconscious bias introduced by sex categorization, people seek out more same-sex than other-sex comparison others and weigh more heavily the evidence of same-sex others with similar job qualifications in establishing the standard of rewards to which they feel entitled in a given situation (Crosby 1982; Major 1989; Moore 1991).

Sex-biased searches for comparison others both encourage and are facilitated by people's tendency to form sex-homophilous social networks (McPherson and Smith-Lovin 1987). They are also encouraged by sex segregation in employment and other social contexts. The strength of the bias in a given actor's search will depend on the availability of proximate same-sex others and on the assumed relevance, to the searcher, of sex category for reward outcomes. Even small biases can result in systematic differences in the comparative reward information acquired by men and by women if rewards are distributed differentially by sex in the population. Evidence in fact shows that women have lower pay expectations than similarly qualified men and that a major determinant of the discrepancy is the difference between the sexes' estimates of what others earn (Major and Konar 1984; Major and Testa 1989).

Information from comparison others is useful in defining two types of referential standards for reward outcomes in a job. First, what is the going rate for "people like me" with the same training, skills, and experience? Second, what range of outcomes do people in jobs like this one receive? Each question implies a search of slightly different others, but both searches are likely to show bias toward same-sex others, particularly the "people like me" search, which selects on attributes of the individual.

Referential standards for both "people like me" and "people in jobs like this" are beliefs about what is typical. From these beliefs people form expectations about the rewards to which they are entitled; these expectations in turn affect their willingness to settle for a given reward in a job or to press for more (see Major, Vanderslice, and McFarlin 1984). Thus expectations for rewards, like performance expectations, tend to become self-fulfilling.

In sum, interaction makes gender a stubbornly available, if often implicit, distinction in the workplace and elsewhere by pushing actors to continually sex-categorize one another. Continual sex categorization, in turn, encourages the formation and use of gender status beliefs, and biases the choice of comparison others toward the same sex. The task now is to consider how these processes help sustain gender inequality in employment.

GENDER AND OCCUPATIONAL INEQUALITY

In the 1950s and 1960s, gender inequality in the United States seemed to rest heavily on two aspects of women's relationship to paid employment: their lower rate of participation in the labor force and the concentration of employed women in a few low-paying, female-labeled jobs (Oppenheimer 1970). Since that time, the first has changed profoundly as

women have flooded into the labor force, and the second has changed considerably as they have moved into several formerly "male" occupations (Reskin and Hartmann 1986:4; Reskin and Roos 1990: 17–18). Yet a significant degree of wage inequality and sex segregation in occupations and jobs has persisted in the face of these profound changes; this reality suggests that other processes are slowing their impact and conserving gender inequality.

A major research industry has attempted to explain continuing wage inequality and job segregation. Differences in male and female workers' work experience (i.e., human capital differences) explain only one-quarter to one-half of the sex gap in pay and account for little of the job segregation (England 1984, 1992; Kilbourne et al. 1994). If the problem is a "taste" for discrimination on the part of employers, competitive market conditions should wipe these out, as economists observe (Becker 1957). England (1992) argues that employment inequality persists despite the flattening effects of the market because it is continually being created anew, even if it is worn down slightly over time.

What mechanisms continually recreate gender inequality in paid employment? England (1992; England and Browne 1992) points to the household division of labor and socialized internal constraints, as well as to employers' prejudice, which devalues women and the activities associated with them. Reskin and Roos (1990) argue that labor queues become gender queues because employers rank males as more valuable workers than females. Strober (1984; Strober and Arnold 1987) points to a cultural system of patriarchy in which employers give men the first pick of the best jobs. Jacobs (1989) shows that socialized tracking affects the sex typing of initial jobs but that there are surprising rates of subsequent mobility; this suggests a "revolving door" process by which occupations remain predominantly the territory of one sex despite a great deal of individual movement. Jacobs argues that the culprit is a diffuse system of gender social control

involving socialization and employment practices in the workplace (Jacobs 1989; Jacobs and
Steinberg 1995).

Thus, researchers maintain that gender arrangements in employment result from structural and
economic factors (e.g., the supply of certain types
of workers, the growth or decline of certain occupations), on the one hand, and some type of gender
status effect, on the other. Two sorts of institutional
processes are important in this regard. First, organizational structures, such as job ladders and internal labor markets, and institutionalized practices,
such as job evaluation systems, incorporate
assumptions about gender status at their inception
and then persist through bureaucratic inertia
(Baron, Jennings, and Dobbin 1988; Kim 1989;
Reskin and Roos 1990; Steinberg 1995). Second,
bureaucratic politics within employing organizations help to maintain inequality because actors in
advantaged positions, often men, represent their
own interests in salary-setting and job-evaluation
processes more strongly than the interests of those
in disadvantaged positions (Bridges and Nelson
1989). As Stone (1995) comments, however, current theories and research "explain how gender
works rather than why gender is such a major force
in the organization of work" (p. 415).

A systematic incorporation of interactionally
driven sex categorization, status, and referential
reward processes can begin to explain why the work
process is so relentlessly gendered and why this
gendering persists in spite of ongoing economic
and organizational change. Perhaps this perspective's most distinctive contribution is its ability to
answer the "why" question—although it can further
specify answers to the "how" questions as well.

Most work-related interaction takes place in
organizational contexts with established job structures and institutionalized practices that heavily
constrain what occurs. Under business-as-usual
conditions, interactional gender status and referential processes are part of the means by which existing gender-biased job structures and practices are
enacted, reinforced, and maintained. Interactional
gender processes, however, become important in

themselves, rather than merely agents of higher-
level structures and rules, at the interstices of organizational structures and under conditions that force
change on organizational structures and practices.
In these transition zones where organizational structures are less clearly defined, sex-categorization,
status, and referential processes play a part in shaping the interactions through which actors create
new organizational rules and structural forms, and
map gender hierarchy into them as they do so.
These transition zones are precisely where bureaucratic politics also have great effect (Bridges and
Nelson 1989); but interactional gender processes
can help explain how and why bureaucratic politics
become gender politics.

INTERACTIONAL MECHANISMS AND OCCUPATIONAL GENDER INEQUALITY

It is useful, first, to recognize the extent to which
occupational arrangements and wage outcomes
are interactionally mediated. Workers gain information about jobs and evaluate them through contact with others. Employers hire workers through
direct interaction (e.g., interviews) or indirect
interaction (e.g., reviewing resumes, records, references). On the job, as Kanter (1977) pointed
out, performance, evaluations, task assignments,
and promotions are mediated in complex ways by
interaction. All of these mediating interactions are
potential sites where interactional mechanisms
may help map gender hierarchy into the occupational patterns that result.[3]

The Sex Labeling of Workers and Jobs

Reskin and Roos (1990) argue that gender
inequality in employment is maintained through the

---

[3]Studies show that actors also sex-categorize others in computer-
mediated interaction (Nass and Steuer 1993; Quist and Wisely
1991). In electronic communication, gender stereotypes affect
actors' judgments of others, but because the sense of audience is
diminished, they constrain actors' own behavior less strongly
than in face-to-face contexts (Sproull and Kiesler 1991).

transformation of labor queues into gender queues. The necessary first step in this transformation is the sex labeling of workers. This point seems so obvious and so natural that we generally do not bother to explain it. But why should sex be such a primary and salient descriptor of workers? The answer lies in the way interaction evokes primary person perception, infusing sex categorization into the hiring process as it mediates employers' recruitment and placement of workers. Because interaction evokes sex categorization, employers can never interview or read the resume of a sex-neutral worker. Similarly, workers cannot interact with a sex-unclassified coworker, boss, or subordinate; thus they create the conditions for writing gender inequality into workplace relations.

This situation begins a process that also leads to the sex labeling of jobs. The difficulty of interacting with workers without categorizing them by sex primes workers and employers alike to infuse gender into the institutional scripts by which the job is enacted, comprehended, and represented to others, effectively constructing it as a "man's" or a "woman's" job. Employers often begin the process by implicitly or explicitly seeking workers of a given sex on the basis of assumptions about labor costs, which themselves are suffused with gender status effects (Milkman 1987; Strober 1984). As the hirees interact with each other, bosses, clients, or customers, automatic sex categorization of self and others causes the employees' enactment of work activities to be perceived as implicitly nested within their prior identities as men or as women and tinge those activities with gender. When hiring creates a predominance of one sex in the job, the gendered connotation of individual job enactments spreads to the shared institutional scripts that represent the job and its activities to actors and others. Because interactional sex categorization primes gender stereotypes to become effectively salient on the job, even in sex-segregated contexts, workers and employers may come to justify in gender stereotypic terms those sex-segregated job activities that originally seemed gender irrelevant (e.g., electronic assembly or selling

securities). This reaction further consolidates the sex labeling of the job in the eyes of its participants and of those who deal with them, and in representations in the media.

As the scripts that represent the job come to be labeled male or female, in either a given organizational culture or a wider culture, the differential status value attached to the sexes and their stereotypic traits spreads to the job as well. Continually reinforced by sex categorization in workplace interaction, the spread of status value affects the performance and reward expectations associated with the job. Experiments show that a job or task, when labeled feminine, is viewed by both job evaluators and job incumbents as requiring less ability and effort and as worth less compensation than the identical job or task when labeled masculine (Major and Forcey 1985; McArthur and Obrant 1986). Other evidence shows that the gender composition of a job alone has a significant impact on wages (Baron and Newman 1990; England 1992), as does the association of the job with stereotypically female tasks such as nurturance (Kilbourne et al. 1994).

Although this labeling process involves shared cultural constructions of a job, it is governed primarily by the situational constructions of workplace interaction; thus it reacts to changes in the context of interaction (e.g., the sex of workers, managers, or trainees). Over time or between organizations, a given activity or job can be relabeled very flexibly from one sex to the other. What does not change, however, is the tendency to apply sex labels; interaction injects sex categorization into the work process and brings in status evaluations as well.

Men and Women as Interested Actors

Employment inequality is also preserved, some observers have concluded, by men acting to maintain their advantages over women (Acker 1989; Bridges and Nelson 1989; Reskin 1988; Stone 1995). How does this actually play out? Part of the answer is structural: The interests of those in more powerful positions in employment organizations are represented more forcefully than the interests of the less powerful, who are more likely to be women (Bridges and Nelson 1989). But writers suggest that more is involved.

Because sex is such an all-encompassing category and crosscuts other differences, it has always been difficult to explain how or in what sense either men or women act in the interests of their gender. This question may be clarified by understanding how sex categorization in interaction tinges work identities with gender stereotypes in various degrees, thus evoking status interests and biasing perceptions.

When gender status is effectively salient in workplace interactions, because of the sex-typed or mixed-sex context, it creates a number of apparently gender-interested behaviors on the part of men, whether as employers, workers, or customers. People (including male actors themselves) will tend to judge male actors as more competent and more worthy of reward than equivalent women, to miss or discount information in the situation that undermines gender stereotypes, and to perceive an implicit status threat in the equal rewarding of equivalent men and women.

All of these effects, however, usually occur as a modification, a biasing, of behavior and judgments during the enactment of a more situationally salient occupational and institutional identity. Thus a man acting in his role as an electrical engineer or a union representative may slightly bias his treatment of other men and of women, usually in an implicit way that he himself does not recognize. Only occasionally will gender be so salient in the situation that men will act self-consciously as men to preserve their interest. Yet, the repeated background activation of gender status over many workplace interactions, biasing behavior in subtle or more substantial degrees, produces the effect of men acting in their gender interest, even when many men feel no special loyalty to their sex. This behavior-biasing process weighs the encounters through which bureaucratic politics are enacted;

it brings an implicit gender dimension to the outcomes in addition to that produced by the differential power of male and female actors.

What about women as interested actors? As indicated by the entrance of women into male occupations and management positions, women pursue their interests in employment settings despite barriers (Jacobs 1992; Reskin and Roos 1990). Even so, they are handicapped by the lower power attached to their positions and by interactional gender mechanisms.

Where gender status is effectively salient, it is in women's interest to introduce added job-relevant information that undermines its effects on perceptions of the competence and reward-worthiness of self and others in the situation. Doing so is difficult, however, precisely because gender usually operates as a background identity in workplace interactions; the participants do not define it explicitly as part of "what is going on here." Its implicitness complicates the task of recognizing its effects and introducing countervailing information in the real time of interaction. The process is difficult as well because men's own status interests tend to make them more cognitively resistant to countervailing information.

As a result, women periodically may sense that something prejudicial is happening to them, but they may be frustrated in their efforts to act effectively against it. They will be vulnerable to "role encapsulation," whereby others define them in their work identities in implicitly gendered terms that limit their effectiveness as actors in their own interests (Kanter 1977). In their analysis of the Washington State pay system, for instance, Bridges and Nelson (1989:645) found that women employees were disadvantaged not only because they had fewer representatives in pay-setting processes, but also because the actors and groups that traditionally represented women (e.g., the Nurses Association) were viewed as "passive and ineffective" on pay issues. Interactional gender mechanisms contribute to the situational construction of women in the workplace as stereotypically more "passive and ineffective" than many men in pursuing their interests.

Preferences for Male Workers

Labor queues become gender queues not simply through the sex labeling of workers but also through employer preferences that rank male workers higher in the queue (Reskin and Roos 1990). The persistence of such preferences is problematic, because many women's wage rates are lower than men's, even when their qualifications are similar. Again, part of the explanation may lie in the interactional mediation of workplace relations and the opportunity this mediation provides for the operation of gender status beliefs.[4] At least four types of sex discrimination have been suggested to account for employers' preferences: tastes, error, statistical discrimination, and group collusion (England 1992:54–68). The first three can be understood as straightforward results of gender status processes. Such processes also create the conditions for collusion.

When an applicant pool contains at least some members of both sexes or when the job has been sex-labeled (as in most hiring situations), sex categorization of applicants activates status beliefs as employers assess applications, interview candidates, and talk to others in the hiring process. If the employer holds these activated gender status beliefs explicitly as a matter of ideology, or believes them to be so held by other workers or customers, status beliefs can function as "tastes" (outright preferences for not hiring a given group) in the hiring process.

For the large majority of jobs, especially "good" jobs involving either stereotypically male or gender-neutral tasks, gender status beliefs create a preference for male workers. At the same time, they create only a weak taste for female workers for jobs defined as involving stereotypically female tasks, such as nursery school teacher. Gender status beliefs contain both general assumptions that men are more competent than women and specific assumptions that men are superior at stereotypically male tasks, while women are better at stereotypically female tasks. For the "female" tasks, however, people appear to combine the general assumptions of male superiority with specific assumptions of female superiority to form expectations that women will be somewhat, but not greatly, better than men at female tasks (Ridgeway 1993).

Probably more common than explicit tastes are the discriminatory effects exerted by activated gender status beliefs through their impact on employers' judgments of workers' potential productivity. Performance expectations based on gender status cause a male worker to appear "better" than an equally qualified woman (see Lott 1985). Furthermore, an equally competent performance by the two appears more indicative of skill and ability in the man than in the woman (Deaux and Emswiller 1974; Foschi, Lai, and Siegerson 1994). On the surface, then, not gender but merit is involved, but worker's sex is connected with merit by the interactional mediation of employers' evaluations of workers, and by the way this mediation injects gender status into the process. In this way interactionally activated status processes create error discrimination, whereby two workers who would perform equally are judged to be different and are paid accordingly.

The operation of gender status beliefs in the workplace can also create the basis for a type of statistical discrimination. Performance expectations created by employers' status beliefs tend to become self-fulfilling, and this tendency often produces employer experiences with male and female workers that confirm such judgments. A competent performance by a female worker appears less competent than by a male worker. Also, and more insidious, the pressure of low expectations actually can interfere with some women workers' performance. Similarly, high expectations of others can improve the performances of some men workers (Harris and Rosenthal 1985). Thus the effect of status-based expectations on some men and some women can create "real" differences in the average performance

---

[4]The agents of employers' preferences are not always the persons authorizing a hire but lower-level functionaries who actually construct ads, screen applicants, recommend placements, and evaluate performances. These individuals engage in more direct and indirect interaction with prospective and actual employees.

and productivity for groups of similar male and female workers. When interactional sex categorization makes gender salient in the hiring process, the employer's experience of these average differences also becomes salient. The employer may react by preferring male workers across the board, thus creating statistical discrimination. Statistical discrimination is especially important for gender inequality because it resists the flattening effects of market forces more strongly than do other types of discrimination (England 1992:61–8).

Gender status processes in interaction also consolidate the conditions for interest-based collusion, a fourth type of discrimination suggested by several writers (Hartmann 1976; Reskin 1988; Strober 1984). Both workers and employers have a wide variety of crosscutting interests. But few are enacted and reinforced in interaction so repeatedly (albeit implicitly) as are gender status interests; therefore these interests are especially fertile ground for explicit collusion. To occur, collusion may need to be triggered by contingent events that threaten gender hierarchy in a work setting, such as organizational or technological change.

As studies of organizational practices show (Steinberg 1995), interaction is not the only source of discriminatory processes or their persistence. But the knowledge that interactional processes are *sufficient* to create most of the observed forms of discrimination clarifies an important (if subtle and even insidious) means by which discrimination is continually recreated in the face of leveling market forces. Especially important here is the capacity of gender status beliefs to lag behind changes in the distributional inequalities that support them; they give interaction a chameleon-like ability to reestablish discrimination in new forms in the face of market forces and structural changes in the work process.

Why Do Women Workers Accept Lower Wages?

Employers' ability to attract and retain women workers for lower wages is also critical for maintaining occupational gender inequality. Why do women settle for less than similarly qualified men? Although some argue that women place less value on money, women step forward when good-paying jobs open up for them, even if these have been labeled men's jobs (Jacobs 1989; Reskin and Roos 1990).

At this juncture, too, interaction plays a role by shaping different senses of entitlement on the part of similarly qualified male and female workers. Although many women work in sex-segregated jobs, their performance is often evaluated through direct or indirect interaction with male supervisors, clients, or customers. Also, their work may be typed as a women's job. In any of these situations, interactionally determined sex categorization will activate status beliefs, affecting women workers' own performance and reward expectations as well as their employers' and fellow workers' expectations for them. Evidence suggests that women underestimate the quality of their performances in comparison with men, and thus are susceptible to arguments that they deserve less pay (Deaux and Kite 1987; Lenny 1977).

Status beliefs create expectations for the relative rewards that male and female workers deserve. Referential standards for rewards, established (like evaluation) through interaction, anchor those relative expectations around a specific reward level. If sex-biased searches of comparison others cause women to estimate the going rate at lower levels than do similar men for given work by people with given qualifications, this effect is a second reason why women judge the compensation they deserve as less than men do. Sex-biased referential standards reduce women's reward expectations even in work situations where status beliefs are not effectively salient. They also reduce the estimates of deserved rewards among women who try to resist the pressures of status expectations by developing very high skill levels about which they can be confident (Major 1989).

If women workers inadvertently underestimate the rewards to which they are entitled, employers can more easily force them to settle for lower wages (Major et al. 1984). If corresponding status- and sex-biased referential processes cause male workers to overestimate what they deserve, employers find it harder to force lower wages on them. This unequal and self-fulfilling entitlement process, which operates within a work organization, is bolstered further by workers' comparisons of their rewards with those in other employment settings (Reskin and Roos 1990). Searches among comparison others in different firms and different jobs are also biased by the interactional sex categorization and sex labeling of jobs. Thus, here, too, women generally will compare themselves to lower paid others than will men.

As a result of these entitlement and comparison processes, which are activated by interactional sex categorization, women settle for lesser rewards than do similar men. Although most women find it unfair that men have higher wages, they are no more likely than men to be dissatisfied with their own rewards and job (Crobsy 1982). This inadvertent acceptance of lower compensation helps sustain the system of gender hierarchy in pay over time by moderating women's resistance (Major 1989). By this analysis, it is a product of interactional gender mechanisms.

Women's Entrance into Male Occupations

Interactional mediation can also help explain why the movement of women into male occupations sometimes results in feminization of the occupation or resegregation by specialty, which reduces the wage benefits to women and moderates the impact on wage inequality (Reskin and Roos 1990). Given employers' general preferences for male workers, it is usually a structural change that opens male occupations to women workers. When the demand for employees in a given occupation outstrips the pool of qualified and interested male workers at the acceptable price, women begin to be hired (Reskin and Roos 1990; Strober and Arnold 1987). Yet aspects of this structural change are also mediated interactionally, just as employers' preferences are, with significant gendering effects that maintain inequality.

Male workers' preferences are a major determinant of the available pool of male workers for a job. These are formed through the same sex-biased referential processes that shape women workers' sense of entitlement. With some exceptions (Wright and Jacobs 1994), case studies suggest that male occupations commonly are opened to women when their pay and working conditions start to deteriorate, often because of technological or organizational change (Reskin and Roos 1990). I suggest that when men in these jobs experience a decline in their work outcomes, this decline triggers a search of comparison others through whom they evaluate their situation. Male workers will start to leave if the search, which is biased by interactional sex categorization, yields a standard for what is available to "people (men) like me" that is higher than the declining outcomes currently available in the job. If the search does not yield such a standard, they will stay with the job and may resist efforts to bring in lower-paid female workers.

As the shortage of male workers brings women into the job, gender-based status interests become increasingly salient in the workplace; sometimes they create tensions that appear greatest at the balance point in the gender mix (Wharton and Baron 1987). Activated gender status beliefs cause women's presence to subtly devalue the status and reward-worthiness of the job in the eyes of both workers and employers. Male workers may react to the perceived threat to status and rewards by hostility toward women in the job. Tensions from male coworkers increase the costs of the job for women, but for many women, given their sex-biased referential standards, the job still will be relatively attractive in both status and pay. Men's sex-biased referential standards, on the other hand, suggest that the job is increasingly less attractive than alternatives. The men's flight from the job will accelerate, and even fewer males will apply for the openings.

As women become more numerous in the job, supervisors' gender status beliefs and women workers' lower sense of entitlement exert self-fulfilling effects on women's reward outcomes, and these effects increasingly spread to the job itself. This situation facilitates employers' introduction of more organizational and technological changes that reduce the status and reward outcomes of the job. Although this scenario is not inevitable, the likely result when it occurs is feminization of the job or resegregation by specialty, with the female jobs and specialties declining in rewards and status (Reskin and Roos 1990).

The point here is that this transition, which maintains gender hierarchy over a change in the structural organization of jobs, is mediated by interactional processes. The combination of interactionally activated status processes and biased referential standards, also a product of interaction, creates a complex mix of discrimination, status-based interest competition, differences in entitlement, and differential perceptions of alternatives. The result is a system of interdependent effects that are everywhere and yet nowhere because they develop through multiple workplace interactions, often in taken-for-granted ways. Their aggregate result is structural: the preservation of wage inequality and the sex segregation of jobs.

An Empirical Prediction

If the interactional perspective presented here is to be more than illustrative, it should provide testable empirical predictions. I have argued that under business-as-usual conditions interactional gender mechanisms are part of the process by which gender-biased organizational structures and institutional practices are implemented. But under more organizationally chaotic conditions, such as those at organizational interstices or those produced by economic change, interactional mechanisms are sufficient in themselves to create gender inequality in pay and power among the participants and to generate sex-typing of work; as a result, any new organizational structures or practices that emerge from actions under these conditions will themselves embody gender hierarchy. Thus a general prediction is: *Wage inequality and sex labeling of work will be present even in employment settings where the usual organizational structures and practices that produce them are relatively absent, such as internal labor markets and biased job evaluation systems.*

Evidence exists to support this prediction. Television writers are employed on short-term contracts through an organizationally unstructured, interpersonally mediated process whereby a few successful writer-producers serve as "brokers" (Bielby and Bielby 1995). Gendering structures such as internal labor markets and job systems are lacking; in addition, human capital effects are blunted because competence is difficult to judge from the products themselves. Yet despite the absence of these usual sources of wage inequality, Bielby and Bielby (1995:224) found that between 1982 and 1990 women television writers had a net earnings disadvantage of 22 to 25 percent less pay than men of similar age, experience, and work histories. Male writers were better known and were perceived as better risks than equally successful female writers (a classic status effect) and women writers tended to be typecast in gender-stereotypical ways as situation comedy writers rather than action writers.

The degree of gender inequality in an organizationally unstructured occupation such as television writing is as large as in bureaucratically organized work. Yet there are differences in the primary mechanisms sustaining the inequality (interpersonal processes or organizational structures) (Bielby and Bielby 1995).[5] This point underscores the multilevel nature of the processes by which gender hierarchy is enacted. As these data show, the power of interactional gender processes is that they are sufficient to maintain gender hierarchy in employment in the absence of the usual gendered organizational structures.

---

[5]The increasing rationalization and explicitness of procedures that attend bureaucratic organization may make the implicit gender inequality of interpersonally organized work difficult to sustain without justification, and thus may encourage the differentiation of job titles by gender (Baron and Pfeffer 1994).

The organizational circumstances of television writers are atypical, but other situations where interactional gender processes should have testable effects are not. These include start-up companies and newly forming professions (e.g., personal financial planners) that draw people from diverse occupational backgrounds. Within organizations, they include interdepartmental and interagency teams charged with change or innovation. In each of these organizationally less highly structured settings, interactional gender mechanisms can be predicted to measurably shape the interpersonal and power politics from which new organizational structures and practices emerge.

CONCLUSION

Adding an interactional account to labor market and organizational accounts of employment inequality helps explain why gender is such a major force in the labor process. Hiring, job searches, placement, performance evaluation, task assignment, promotion, and dealing with customers, clients, bosses, coworkers, and subordinates all involve direct or indirect (e.g., the evaluation of resumes) interaction. Interacting with a concrete other evokes primary cultural rules for making sense of self and of other, pushing actors to sex categorize one another in each of these situations. Sex categorization pumps gender into the interactionally mediated work process by cueing gender stereotypes, including status beliefs, and by biasing the choice of comparison others. The process is insidious because gender is usually an implicit, background identity whose effective salience varies situationally, acting in combination with more salient work identities and modifying their performance. In bureaucratically well-ordered work contexts, interactional gender mechanisms become part of the process for enacting more formal structures that embody gender bias, such as job ladders and evaluation systems. Interactional processes contribute to the sex labeling of jobs, to the devaluation of women's jobs, to forms of sex discrimination, to the construction of men as effectively gender-interested actors, to the control of

women's interests, to differences between men's and women's reward expectations, and to the processes by which women's entrance into male occupations sometimes leads to feminization or resegregation by specialty. In less bureaucratically ordered settings, such as those at organizational interstices, in start-up companies, in newly forming professions, or in some types of work, interpersonal processes come to the fore and are sufficient in themselves to create gender inequality in wages and sex typing of work. As they do so, interactional processes conserve gender inequality over significant changes in the organization of work, writing it into new work structures and practices as they develop.

If this inequality is to be reduced, it is vital to understand the multilevel nature of gender processes and the role of interactional processes in maintaining gender inequality. Structural changes such as the implementation of comparable worth policies, for instance, would change men's and women's referential reward expectations. Yet, changes in gender status beliefs lag behind changes in the distributional inequalities that support them; thus the degree of equality achieved is likely to be substantially undermined by interactional processes mediating the decision making through which comparable worth policies would be adopted and implemented. Concerted intervention is required at both the structural level (e.g., comparable worth) and the interactional level, through policies such as affirmative action that change the interpersonal configuration of actors, and create more stereotype-disconfirming experiences for all. Insofar as commitment to affirmative action creates greater accountability among workplace decision makers, social cognition research suggests that it also will reduce the impact of stereotypes, like gender, on their judgments and evaluations (Fiske and Neuberg 1990).

Gender inequality in employment is maintained not only by the work processes discussed here but by its interdependence with the household division of labor. One of the promises of an interactional approach is that it may clarify how this interdependence works. Accomplishing this goal will necessitate the incorporation of additional gender mechanisms that affect interaction in enduring, intimate relations. It is a promising project for the future.

REFERENCES

Acker, Joan. 1989. *Doing Comparable Worth: Gender, Class, and Pay Equity.* Philadelphia, PA: Temple University Press.

Alexander, C. Norman and Mary Glenn Wiley. 1981. "Situated Activity and Identity Formation." Pp. 269–89 in *Social Psychology: Sociological Perspectives,* edited by M. Rosenberg and R. Turner. New York: Basic Books.

Bargh, John. 1989. "Conditional Automaticity: Varieties of Automatic Influence in Social Perception and Cognition." Pp. 3–51 in *Unintended Thought,* edited by J. Uleman and J. Bargh. New York: Guilford.

Baron, James and Andrew Newman. 1990. "For What It's Worth: Organizations, Occupations, and the Value of Work." *American Sociological Review* 55:155–75.

Baron, James and Jeffrey Pfeffer. 1994. "The Social Psychology of Organizations and Inequality." *Social Psychology Quarterly* 57:190–209.

Baron, James, P. Devereaux Jennings, and Frank Dobbin. 1988. "Mission Control? The Development of Personnel Systems in U.S. Industry." *American Sociological Review* 53:497–514.

Becker, Gary. 1957. *The Economics of Discrimination.* Chicago, IL: University of Chicago.

Berger, Joseph, M. Hamit Fisek, Robert Norman, and David Wagner. 1985. "The Formation of Reward Expectations in Status Situations." Pp. 215–61 in *Status, Rewards, and Influence,* edited by J. Berger and M. Zelditch. San Francisco, CA: Jossey-Bass.

Berger, Joseph, Hamit Fisek, Robert Norman, and Morris Zelditch. 1977. *Status Characteristics and Social Interaction.* New York: Elsevier.

Berk, Sarah Fenstermaker. 1985. *The Gender Factory: The Apportionment of Work in American Households.* New York: Plenum.

Bielby, William and Denise Bielby. 1995. "Cumulative versus Continuous Disadvantage in an Unstructured Labor Market: Gender Differences in the Careers of Television Writers." Pp. 209–30 in *Gender Inequality at Work,* edited by J. Jacobs. Thousand Oaks, CA: Sage.

Blau, Peter and Joseph Schwartz. 1984. *Crosscutting Social Circles: Testing a Macrostructural Theory of Intergroup Relations.* New York: Academic.

Brewer, Marilynn. 1988. "A Dual Process Model of Impression Formation." Pp. 1–36 in *Advances in Social Cognition,* vol. 1, edited by T. Srull and R. Wyer. Hillsdale, NJ: Earlbaum.

———. 1991. "The Social Self: On Being the Same and Different at the Same Time." *Personality and Social Psychology Bulletin* 17:475–82.

Brewer, Marilynn and Layton Lui. 1989. "The Primacy of Age and Sex in the Structure of Person Categories." *Social Cognition* 7:262–74.

Bridges, William and Robert Nelson. 1989. "Markets in Hierarchies: Organizational and Market Influences on Gender Inequality in a State Pay System." *American Journal of Sociology* 95:616–58.

Broverman, Inge, Susan Vogel, Donald Broverman, Frank Clarkson, and Paul Rosenkrantz. 1972. "Sex-Role Stereotypes: A Reappraisal." *Journal of Social Issues* 28:59–78.

Carli, Linda. 1991. "Gender, Status, and Influence." Pp. 89–113 in *Advances in Group Processes,* vol. 8, edited by E. Lawler, B. Markovsky, C. Ridgeway, and H. Walker. Greenwich, CT: JAI.

Cook, Karen. 1975. "Expectations, Evaluations, and Equity." *American Sociological Review* 40:372–88.

Cota, Albert and Kenneth Dion. 1986. "Salience of Gender and Sex Composition of Ad Hoc Groups: An Experimental Test of Distinctiveness Theory." *Journal of Personality and Social Psychology* 50:770–76.

Crosby, Faye. 1982. *Relative Deprivation and Working Women.* New York: Oxford University Press.

Deaux, Kay and Tim Emswiller. 1974. "Explanation of Successful Performance on Sex-Linked Tasks: What Is Skill for the Male Is Luck for the Female." *Journal of Personality and Social Psychology* 29:80–85.

Deaux, Kay and Mary Kite. 1987. "Thinking about Gender." Pp. 92–117 in *Analyzing Gender: A Handbook of Social Science Research,* edited by B. Hess and M. Ferree. Newbury Park, CA: Sage.

Deaux, Kay and Brenda Major. 1987. "Putting Gender into Context: An Interactive Model of Gender-Related Behavior," *Psychological Review* 94:369–89.

Eagly, Alice, 1987. *Sex Differences in Social Behavior: A Social-Role Interpretation.* Hillsdale, NJ: Erlbaum.

England, Paula. 1984. "Wage Appreciation and Depreciation: A Test of Neoclassical Economic Explanations of Occupational Sex Segregation." *Social Forces* 62:726–49.

———. 1992. *Comparable Worth: Theories and Evidence.* New York: Aldine.

England, Paula and Irene Browne. 1992. "Internalization and Constraint in Women's Subordination." *Current Perspectives in Social Theory* 12:97–123.

Fiske, Susan. 1992. "Thinking Is for Doing." *Journal of Personality and Social Psychology* 63:877–89.

Fiske, Susan and Steven Neuberg. 1990. "A Continuum of Impression Formation, from Category-Based to Individuating Processes: Influences of Information and Motivation on Attention and Interpretation." Pp. 1–73 in *Advances in Experimental Social Psychology,* edited by M. Zanna. New York: Academic.

Fiske, Susan and Shelley Taylor. 1991. *Social Cognition.* New York: McGraw-Hill.

Foschi, Martha, Larissa Lai, and Kirsten Sigerson. 1994. "Gender and Double Standards in the Assessment of Job Applicants." *Social Psychology Quarterly* 57:326–39.

Goffman, Erving. 1977. "The Arrangement between the Sexes." *Theory and Society* 4:301–31.

Harris, Monica and Robert Rosenthal. 1985. "Mediation of Interpersonal Expectancy Effects: 31 Meta-Analyses." *Psychological Bulletin* 97:363–86.

Harrod, Wendy. 1980. "Expectations from Unequal Rewards." *Social Psychology Quarterly* 43:126–30.

Hartmann, Heidi. 1976. "Capitalism, Patriarchy, and Job Segregation by Sex." Pp. 137–70 in *Women and the Workplace,* edited by M. Blaxall and B. Reagan. Chicago, IL: University of Chicago.

Jacobs, Jerry. 1989. *Revolving Doors: Sex Segregation and Women's Careers.* Stanford, CA: Stanford University Press.

———. 1992. "Women's Entry into Management: Trends in Earnings, Authority, and Values among Salaried Managers." *Administrative Science Quarterly* 372:282–301.

Jacobs, Jerry and Ronnie Steinberg. 1995. "Further Evidence on Compensating Differentials and the Gender Gap in Wages." Pp. 93–124 in *Gender Inequality at Work,* edited by J. Jacobs. Thousand Oaks, CA: Sage.

Kanter, Rosabeth. 1977. *Men and Women of the Corporation.* New York: Basic Books.

Kessler, Suzanne and Wendy McKenna. 1978. *Gender: An Ethnomethodological Approach.* New York: Wiley.

Kilbourne, Barbara, Paula England, George Farkas, Kurt Beron, and Dorothea Weir. 1994. "Returns to Skill, Compensating Differentials, and Gender Bias: Effects of Occupational Characteristics on the Wages of White Women and Men." *American Journal of Sociology* 100:689–719.

Kim, Marlene. 1989. "Gender Bias in Compensation Structures: A Case Study of Its Historical Basis and Persistence." *Social Issues* 45:39–50.

Lenny, Ellen. 1977. "Women's Self-Confidence in Achievement Settings." *Psychological Bulletin* 84:1–13.

Lott, Bernice. 1985. "The Devaluation of Women's Competence." *Journal of Social Issues* 41:43–60.

Major, Brenda. 1989. "Gender Differences in Comparisons and Entitlement: Implication for Comparable Worth." *Journal of Social Issues* 45:99–115.

Major, Brenda and Blythe Forcey. 1985. "Social Comparisons and Pay Evaluations: Preferences for Same-Sex and Same-Job Wage Comparisons." *Journal of Experimental Social Psychology* 21:393–405.

Major, Brenda and Ellen Konar. 1984. "An Investigation of Sex Differences in Pay Expectations and Their Possible Causes." *Academy of Management Journal* 27:777–92.

Major, Brenda and Maria Testa. 1989. "Social Comparison Processes and Judgments of Entitlement and Satisfaction." *Journal of Experimental Social Psychology* 25:101–20.

Major, Brenda, Virginia Vanderslice, and Dean McFarlin. 1984. "Effects of Pay Expected on Pay Received: The Confirmatory Nature of Initial Expectations." *Journal of Applied Social Psychology* 14:399–412.

McArthur, Leslie and Sarah Obrant. 1986. "Sex Biases in Comparable Worth Analyses." *Journal of Applied Social Psychology* 16:757–70.

McPherson, Miller and Lynn Smith-Lovin. 1987. "Homophily in Voluntary Organizations: Status Distance and the Consequences of Face-to-Face Groups." *American Sociological Review* 52:370–79.

Milkman, Ruth. 1987. *Gender at Work.* Urbana, IL: University of Illinois Press.

Miller, Dale and W. Turnbull. 1986. Expectancies and Interpersonal Processes. *Annual Review of Psychology* 37:233–56.

Moore, Dahlia. 1991. "Entitlement and Justice Evaluation: Who Should Get More and Why?" *Social Psychology Quarterly* 54:208–23.

Nass, Clifford and Jonathan Steuer. 1993. "Voices, Boxes, and Sources of Messages: Computers and Social Actors." *Human Communication Research* 19:504–27.

Oppenheimer, Valerie. 1970. *The Female Labor Force in the United States: Demographic and Economic Factors Governing Its Growth and Changing Composition.* Westport, CT: Greenwood.

Pugh, Meredith and Ralph Wahrman. 1983. "Neutralizing Sexism in Mixed-Sex Groups: Do Women Have to Be Better than Men?" *American Journal of Sociology* 88:746–62.

Quist, Theron and Phillip Wisely. 1991. "Gender Attribution: Structural and Behavioral Power in an Experimental Setting." Paper presented at the annual meeting of the American Sociological Association, August 27, Cincinnati, OH.

Reskin, Barbara. 1988. "Bringing the Men Back in: Sex Differentiation and the Devaluation of Women's Work." *Gender and Society* 2:58–81.

Reskin, Barbara and Heidi Hartmann. 1986. *Women's Work, Men's Work: Sex Segregation on the Job.* Washington, DC: National Academy Press.

Reskin, Barbara and Patricia Roos. 1990. *Job Queues, Gender Queues: Explaining Women's Inroads into Male Occupations.* Philadelphia, PA: Temple University Press.

Ridgeway, Cecilia L. 1991. "The Social Construction of Status Value: Gender and Other Nominal Characteristics." *Social Forces* 70:367–86.

———. 1993. "Gender, Status, and the Social Psychology of Expectations." Pp. 175–98 in *Theory on Gender/Feminism on Theory,* edited by P. England. New York: Aldine.

Ridgeway, Cecilia L. and James Balkwell. 1997. "Groups and the Diffusion of Status Value Beliefs." *Social Psychology Quarterly* 60:14–31.

Ridgeway, Cecilia, Elizabeth H. Boyle, Kathy Kuipers, and Dawn Robinson. 1995. "Interaction and the Construction of Status Value Beliefs." Paper presented at the annual meeting of the American Sociological Association, August 23, Washington, DC.

Risman, Barbara. 1987. "Intimate Relationships from a Microstructural Perspective: Men Who Mother." *Gender and Society* 1:6–32.

Rothbart, Myron and Oliver John. 1985. "Social Categorization and Behavioral Episodes: A Cognitive Analysis of the Effects of Intergroup Contact." *Journal of Social Issues* 41:81–104.

Sproull, Lee and Sara Kiesler. 1991. *Connections: New Ways of Working in the Networked Organization.* Cambridge, MA: MIT Press.

Stangor, Charles, Laure Lynch, Changming Duan, and Beth Glass. 1992. "Categorization of Individuals on the Basis of Multiple Social Features." *Journal of Personality and Social Psychology* 62:207–18.

Steinberg, Ronnie. 1995. "Gendered Instructions: Cultural Lag and Gender Bias in the Hay System of Job Evaluation." Pp. 57–92 in *Gender Inequality at Work,* edited by J. Jacobs. Thousand Oaks, CA: Sage.

Stewart, Penni and James Moore. 1992. "Wage Disparities and Performance Expectations." *Social Psychology Quarterly* 55:78–85.

Stone, Pamela. 1995. "Assessing Gender at Work: Evidence and Issues." Pp. 408–23 in *Gender Inequality at Work,* edited by J. Jacobs. Thousand Oaks, CA: Sage.

Strober, Myra. 1984. "Toward a General Theory of Occupation Sex Segregation: The Case of Public School Teaching." Pp. 144–56 in *Sex Segregation in the Workplace,* edited by B. Reskin. Washington, DC: National Academy Press.

Strober, Myra and Carolyn Arnold. 1987. "The Dynamics of Occupational Segregation among Bank Tellers." Pp. 107–48 in *Gender in the Workplace,* edited by C. Brown and J. Pechman. Washington, DC: Brookings Institution.

Stryker, Sheldon. 1980. *Symbolic Interactionism.* Menlo Park, CA: Benjamin/Cummings.

Suls, Jerry and Thomas Wills. 1991. *Social Comparison: Contemporary Theory and Research.* Hillsdale, NJ: Erlbaum.

Turner, John. 1987. *Rediscovering the Social Group: A Self-Categorization Theory.* Oxford, England: Blackwell.

West, Candace and Don Zimmerman. 1987. "Doing Gender." *Gender and Society* 1:125–51.

Wharton, Amy and James Baron. 1987. "So Happy Together? The Impact of Gender Segregation on Men at Work." *American Sociological Review* 52:574–87.

Wright, Rosemary and Jerry Jacobs. 1994. "Male Flight from Computer Work: A New Look at Occupational Resegregation and Ghettoization." *American Sociological Review* 59:511–36.

Gender and Access to Money
What Do Trends in Earnings and Household Poverty Tell Us?

PAULA ENGLAND

INTRODUCTION

What is the relationship between gender and class? Has this changed in recent decades? Our answer to this depends in good part on what we mean by class and whether we think of individuals or households as having a class location. . . . I examine the extent to which a person's sex, through various gendered processes, affects personal earnings and affects whether the individual lives in a household that is in poverty. Either of these speaks to the relationship between gender and class to the extent that we think that access to money and its fruits is part of what we mean by "class" or results from class position. The first indicator, individual earnings, is relevant if we think that class should be measured at the individual level. The second indicator, poverty, is a household income measure (one that is also dichotomous and size adjusted). It can be argued to be the best measure available to tap an individual's access to a certain minimum level of goods and services. For each of these indicators of class (or results of class position), this [essay] will examine whether class is gendered and whether the "gendering of class" has increased or decreased over time. If the two indicators do not trend in the same direction, what does this mean? My argument

will not be that one indicator is the "true" indicator while the other is inferior but rather that they tell us different things about the outcomes of the overall systems of production (including reproduction) and distribution. For those who prefer not to think of either personal earnings or household poverty as having anything to do with "class," my project . . . is better described as examining trends in whether personal earnings and household poverty show gender inequality and discussing what this means about women's relative access to those things in life that one can buy with money. My observations were formulated largely from study of the United States; however, I also include some comparative discussion of patterns in other affluent nations.

If access to money is our focus, what is the argument for using an individual versus a household measure? The argument for using a household measure is that households (at least families) generally pool and share income, so that an individual's access to the goods and services money can buy on the market is better indexed at the household level. This view is supported, for example, by the observation that the wives of rich men seem to consume a lot even if they do not hold a job. The formal assumption is that all members of a household share the same standard of living. To assume this may be too extreme. Perhaps there is sharing but not perfect sharing. In particular, what if who brings the money into a household affects the relative power of the spouses, including but not limited to power in decisions regarding what to spend money on? If this is true, household income is a misleading indicator that understates male advantage. In data on poor nations, there is evidence that relative earnings affect the amount of food and medical care girls and women get relative to boys and men and how much of family income is devoted to children (more of both when women's relative share is higher). Thus, for these nations, access to even the most necessary goods and services is affected by power within the family and by the fact that all members of a household do not have a common standard of living. I am not aware of evidence for industrialized nations showing effects of relative earnings on access to basic material necessities. However, there is evidence of effects of relative earnings on decision-making power on a number of issues, including how money and time are spent (including who does how much household work and who has more leisure). Such issues presumably affect individuals' utilities and thus are relevant to "standard of living" in a broad sense. This argues for the relevance of women's earnings relative to men's as an indicator of access to those utilities that flow from money.

The discussion I will pursue fits into two of the five categories suggested by Erik Wright . . . as fruitful modes of conceptualizing relations between gender and class. One of his categories is examining gender as a sorting mechanism into class locations. If we consider groups of jobs to be class locations, then the discussion of the sex segregation of jobs and its role in the sex gap in pay is an instance of this category. Here we are interested in sex discrimination in access to jobs or to the qualifications that lead to them, socialization that affects job aspirations, or aspects of household division of labor by sex that affect women's ability to hold certain jobs. To the extent that pay is itself seen as an indicator of "class," the discussion of sex differences in pay that are not generated by segregation of men and women into different jobs but by pay differences within or between jobs that are linked to credentials, productivity, or direct pay discrimination, is also an instance of this category. However, a difference between Wright's perspective and mine

is in what dimensions of job positions are seen as relevant. Wright sees class as positional, and, while his conceptualization of class has changed over the years, in one way or another it is generally linked to the extent to which positions involve ownership of property, authority, autonomy, or expertise. While authority is a very gendered dimension of jobs (with many more men than women in jobs with authority over others), the most important dimensions of gender segregation do not relate to property, autonomy, or amount of expertise. A critical gendered dimension involves whether jobs involve performing a face-to-face service (with women heavily represented in such jobs) or clerical work. Thus, one needs to broaden Wright's conceptualization of the dimensions of jobs relevant to class or see amount earned itself as a dimension of class in order to see much of this analysis as speaking to class. Some readers may prefer a tighter concept of class, together with recognizing that many of the relevant gendered dimensions of inequality are not captured by class.

The second of Wright's categories exemplified [here] is what he calls "gender as mediated linkage to class location." Women are linked to the occupation and earnings-based class locations of their husbands to the extent that status and earnings are shared by all family members. Men's consumption is also affected by the class location, broadly defined, of their wives, insofar as class affects earnings. I will emphasize that women's poverty is affected not only by their own earnings but also by whether they have access to a share of men's earnings through marriage or cohabitation. Here again, however, to see this discussion as relevant to class, one needs a broader (looser) conception of class than characterizes Wright's work.

I begin by reviewing trends in the sex gap in personal (not household) earnings and some of the things that underlie it. The direction of change is toward a convergence between men's and women's employment, occupations, and earnings. We would expect this equalizing trend to disproportionately increase the income of households containing women and thus, if there were no countervailing trends, to decrease the sex gap in poverty rates. I then examine whether women are more likely than men to live in households in poverty in the post–World War II period in the United States. The answer is clearly yes. However, the trend in the ratio of women's to men's poverty rates is nonmonotonic. Poverty was feminizing between 1950 and 1980, a trend captured in the phrase "the feminization of poverty." However, the feminization of poverty has ceased and even reversed in some groups since 1980, particularly nonelderly whites, although women are still more likely to be in poverty than men. How is it possible for women to have lost ground to men in freedom from (household) poverty during some of the time that their personal earnings relative to men's were going up? It is possible because of trends in household structure that led fewer women to live in households with men and thus that led fewer women (and children) to have a secure claim on a share of men's earnings. These trends include later marriage, increased nonmarital childbearing, and increased divorce. It is an empirical question whether the gain in women's own earnings or the loss in access to a share of men's earnings will have a larger effect on women's poverty rates relative to men's; apparently, the latter loss dominated in the first part of the postwar period, whereas the gain from women's increasing relative earnings has dominated more recently.

[Later in this essay] I consider a macro-level model of the causal linkages between some of the variables related to women's relative statuses. I argue that women's increased employment and earnings should raise women's power within marriages, making marriage more satisfactory for women. However, employment and their own earnings also make it more feasible for women to leave unhappy marriages or avoid getting married. While women's roles have changed dramatically, there is much more resistance to changing men's roles in the family to include more traditionally female responsibilities of child care, household work, and emotional work. . . . It is this asymmetry of gender role change that makes

women living apart from men—rather than enduring in egalitarian marriages—the predominant response to women's increased earning power relative to men.

THE ENDURING BUT DECLINING SEX GAP IN PERSONAL EARNINGS

If we measure income at an individual rather than a household level and look only at earned income, women's progress relative to men is unmistakable. Personal earnings are obtained through employment. Thus, trends in employment are relevant to women's access to earnings. In the United States, the proportion of women over 16 years of age in the labor force has increased steadily in the postwar period, increasing from 33 percent in 1950 to 59 percent in 1995 (Blau, Ferber, and Winkler 1998: 80). If we look only at women 15 to 64 in age, half were in the labor force in 1972, up to 69 percent by 1992 (Blau et al. 1998: 336). Thus, more women than ever before have their own earnings, so fewer are entirely reliant on men or the state, the other two major options, for money. If we look at women's trends relative to those of men's, our sense of a declining gender gap is increased because men's labor force participation has decreased: Between 1960 and 1990, the proportion of women who were not employed even for one week in the previous year dropped from 57 to 38 percent, but the corresponding figures for men increased—from 14 to 21 percent (Spain and Bianchi 1996: 84).

Most affluent nations have seen large increases in women's employment in the last few decades and have higher female employment rates than poorer southern nations, although they have seen increases as well (Blau et al. 1998; Clement 2001). The nations with the highest rates of female employment are the Nordic countries (Sweden, Norway, and Denmark). The United States is below most of the Nordic nations but substantially above Austria, Germany, France, Italy, Ireland, Switzerland, and the Netherlands in its female employment rates (Blau et al. 1998).

One might wonder whether figures showing average hours worked per year would show a different story—if, as more women become employed, there would be a higher proportion of those employed working part time. If this were true, simple increases in the percentage of women employed would give an exaggerated impression of the increase in women's involvement in employment. In the United States, this is not true; the proportion of employed women who work part time has been relatively stable since 1970, at between 20 and 25 percent (Kalleberg 1995). Of all women with any employment experience, the proportion of those aged 25 to 54 who were employed both full time and all year increased from 46 percent in 1968 to 57 percent in 1986 (Taeuber 1991: table B1-22). Indeed, the United States is exceptional in how few employed women work part time; most of the nations that have higher female employment rates than the United States also have a higher proportion of employed women working part time (Gornick 1999: fig. 1; Rosenfeld and Birkelund 1995).

One major factor affecting women's earnings relative to men's is less continuous experience (England 1992: 28–35; Wellington 1994). Men and women are converging in experience levels in the United States (England 1992: chap. 1; Wellington 1993). Since most affluent nations have had rising female employment rates, we would expect this to be leading to more continuous experience in successive cohorts.

Another important factor in the sex gap in pay is segregation of jobs by sex (England 1992; Petersen and Morgan 1995). Segregation has been declining in the United States. Studies exploring this generally use the index of dissimilarity, which, roughly speaking, tells us what percentage of men or women would have to change occupations to achieve integration, defined as a state where the percentage female (male) in each occupation is the same as the percentage women (men) constitute of all workers. Segregation changed little between 1950 and 1970 but has declined substantially since. The index declined from 68 to 53 between 1970 and 1990 (Gross 1986: table 2; Spain

and Bianchi 1996: 94). These figures are computed on detailed census categories that divide occupations into several hundred categories. A problem in comparing nations in their segregation is that to find comparable occupational categories, they have to be very broad, which masks segregation (e.g., combining doctors, nurses, pilots, and accountants in "professional"). Studies using very broad categories have found the United States to be lower than many nations in degree of segregation. Indeed, Sweden, which has one of the lowest sex gaps in pay, has relatively high segregation that has not been declining (Blau et al. 1998: 34–35).

Trends in the United States in the sex gap in annual earnings for full-time year-round workers are shown in table 1. Here white women made little progress relative to white men between 1955 and 1980, but since 1980 the women's median as a percentage of men's went from 59 to 71 percent. Black women have made more continuous progress relative to black men, from 55 percent of black men's median in 1955 to 85 percent in 1995.

However, it is important to note that women's relative progress in average earnings has been as much because of declines in men's real earnings than because of increases in their own. Between

TABLE 1   Women's Median Annual Earnings as a Percentage of Men's by Race, 1955–1995

Year	White Women/White Men	Black Women/Black Men
1955	65.3	55.1
1960	60.6	62.2
1965	57.9	62.5
1970	58.6	70.3
1975	58.5	74.8
1980	59.3	78.7
1985	64.1	81.2
1990	69.4	85.4
1995	71.0	85.0

Sources: Figart et al. (1989: 25–33); U.S. Bureau of the Census (1990a); unpublished tabulations from the March 1996 Current Population Survey.

Note: Data are for full-time, year-round workers.
Data for 1955 through 1970 are for all nonwhites; data for blacks are unavailable for these years.

1979 and 1995, if we pool racial groups together, the median annual earnings of men employed full time year-round fell in real terms, from $30,629 to $27,011 in constant 1990 dollars. The comparable figures for women are from $18,274 to $19,294 (although their highest point was $19,972 in 1992). Thus, if we take this entire period from 1979 to 1995, 72 percent of the increase in the ratio of women's to men's median earnings came from declines in men's pay rather than increases in women's. If men's wages had stayed at their 1979 real level but women's had moved as they did, the ratio of women's to men's median would have moved from about 60 to 63 percent rather than from 60 to 71 percent (Institute for Women's Policy Research 1997).

Overall, the convergence in men and women's earnings is explained by declines in men's average earnings caused by restructuring of the economy that has brought men's wages down more than women's, women's increasingly continuous employment experience (Wellington 1993), and the desegregation of occupations, the latter probably encouraged both by declining hiring discrimination and by changes in women's occupational aspirations.

How does the United States compare to other nations in the sex gap in pay? In the 1990s, it was similar to West Germany, in the middle of the pack of affluent nations, with Sweden, Australia, Norway, Finland, Denmark, and France having higher ratios of women's to men's earnings and the United Kingdom, Canada, and Switzerland having slightly lower ratios, while Japan had a much lower ratio (Waldfogel 1998: 140). A look at trends in the sex gap in pay shows no uniformity in what decades had most convergence across affluent nations, although most have seen some convergence since the late 1960s (Waldfogel 1998: 139). While cross-national differences in continuity of experience and segregation probably affect differences in the pay gap, research has not clearly established this. However, one factor that has been shown to affect the sex gap in pay is the overall level of pay inequality in the labor market; other things being equal, this increases the sex gap in pay (Blau and Kahn 1996, 1997). This factor makes the convergence in men and women's pay in the 1980s in the United States all the more surprising since the United States has more overall inequality in its wage structures than most industrial nations, and its inequality grew more rapidly than other nations' since 1980 (Blau and Kahn 1997).

To note the decrease in the sex gap in pay in the United States is not to say that gender has disappeared as a factor influencing an individual's work experiences or earnings. Women are still more likely to spend time out of the labor force for child rearing than men, occupations are still quite segregated, and women still earn less than men. The point is that all these inequalities have decreased. Other aspects of gender inequality in paid work may not have decreased—for example, the sort of discrimination at issue in "comparable worth" in which the sex composition of jobs affects the pay offered, the extent to which nurturant work pays less than other work requiring no more training, or the extent to which organizational rules invented with male workers in mind have an adverse impact on women (Acker 1990; England 1992). Nonetheless, on the "bottom line" indicator of earnings, women's progress relative to men is unmistakable. More women have earnings than previously, and, among men and women who have earnings, women's relative earnings have increased.

Thus, if we were to use individual earnings as an index of class, we would conclude that class is becoming degendered. Both purchasing power between households of single individuals and power differentials between spouses are affected by personal earnings. This is an argument for using individual earnings. On the other hand, to the extent that people who live together generally share income, especially when they are part of the same family, household income, adjusted for household size, is a more appropriate indicator of access to goods and services. Because of this, I turn to a comparison of the overall incomes of the households in which women and men live.

THE SEX GAP IN HOUSEHOLD POVERTY

How is an individual's sex related to household income? To examine this, let us use a measure of household income that is dichotomized at the official U.S. government's "poverty line." The poverty line was originally devised by estimating what a minimally adequate food budget would cost, adjusting this by family size and multiplying by 3 (since data for the 1950s showed poor families spending about a third of their income on food). The poverty lines (for families of various sizes) are adjusted each year by the consumer price index. Thus, it is an absolute, not a relative, measure of poverty. "Poverty," thus measured, applies to households consisting of either families (defined as people related by blood, marriage, or adoption who share a household) or unrelated individuals living alone. It tells us whether the income of the household, before taxes, from all sources (earnings of any household member from employment or self-employment and nonearned income, such as dividends, government transfer payments, or alimony or child support payments) was above or below the poverty line for that year.

Table 2 draws on recent work on the United States by Sara McLanahan and her colleagues (McLanahan and Kelly 1999; McLanahan, Sorensen, and Watson 1989). It shows that a higher percentage of U.S. women than men lived in households in poverty in every year shown from 1950 to 1996. This is true for both blacks and whites and in every age-group, with the exception of whites between the ages of 18 and 24 in 1950 and 1960. Thus, household poverty is gendered.

What drives the higher poverty rate of women than men? To understand this, it is important to remember that this table takes individuals as the units of analysis and reports on the percentages of individual women and men in poverty in various years, but the assessment of whether the individual is in poverty is based not on the individual's income alone but on whether the total income of the person's household puts it in poverty. In husband–wife families (whether or not they include children), either both the husband and the wife are in poverty or both are not. This means that if all adults were married, there could not be any sex gap in poverty, given how the term is defined in U.S. government statistics. The other major types of households are those containing a man living alone or with children and those containing a woman living alone or with children. Let us refer to these three types of households as couple, male headed, and female headed, respectively. Given that there is no sex gap in poverty by definition within couple households, the sex gap in poverty arises from female-headed households being poorer than

TABLE 2   Ratio of Female to Male Poverty Rates for U.S. Whites and Blacks by Age, 1950–1996

	1950 Census	1960 Census	1970 Census	1970 CPS	1980 CPS	1996 CPS
Whites						
Total	1.10	1.23	1.46	1.53	1.56	1.52
Young	0.83	0.99	1.00	1.33	1.48	1.47
Middle aged	1.16	1.24	1.51	1.50	4.43	1.33
Elderly	1.13	1.24	1.45	1.49	1.64	2.33
Blacks						
Total	1.17	1.19	1.37	1.47	1.69	1.71
Young	1.05	1.11	1.11	1.49	1.78	1.65
Middle aged	1.15	1.25	1.56	1.59	1.72	1.68
Elderly	1.05	1.05	1.14	1.16	1.44	2.09

Sources: Census figures from McLanahan, Sorensen, and Watson (1989); CPS figures from McLanahan and Kelly (1999).

Note: The age classifications differ by source. The census figures use 18–24 for young, 25–64 for middle aged, and 65 + for elderly. The Current Population Survey (CPS) figures use 18–30 for young, 31–64 for middle aged, and 65 + for elderly. The only notable effect is the difference for the young age-groups, where the ratio of women's to men's poverty is lower if only 18–24-year-olds are included.

male-headed households, and any given disparity between the poverty rates of these two groups of noncouple households will affect the overall sex gap in poverty more the higher the proportion of all adults that live in non-couple households.

Why are female-headed households more impoverished than male-headed households? This is true for two main reasons. First, women earn less than men, so the earnings of those heading female-headed households are generally less than the earnings of the men heading male-headed households. Thus, since, except for the elderly, earnings are the major source of income for most households, the sex gap in pay contributes to the sex gap in poverty.

A second factor contributing to the sex gap in poverty is sex differences in who lives with children. Since poverty lines are adjusted for household size, the presence of children in a household raises the income necessary for the household to escape poverty, and thus, other things being equal, adults who live with children are more likely to be poor. Single women are much more likely to live with children than single men since women usually have custody of the children in cases of divorce or nonmarital births. Unless this tendency of a higher proportion of adult women than men to live with children is entirely offset by transfers of income from either the nonresident fathers, the government, or someone else, it will increase women's poverty relative to men's. Clearly, such transfers do not fully offset women's responsibility for children. In 1991 in the United States, only 57 percent of divorced mothers received any child support from the children's fathers, and among those receiving support, the average amount received during the year was only $3,623. Separated and never-married mothers were even less likely to receive child support (34 and 20 percent, respectively) and, among those receiving support, received even less per year ($2,735 and $1,534, respectively; figures are from Scoon-Rogers and Lester 1995, as cited in Spain and Bianchi 1996).

Is the gender gap in household poverty unique to the United States? A recent analysis for eight industrialized nations in the 1980s shows that all nations but Sweden have higher poverty among women than men, but the United States has the largest sex gap in poverty (Casper, McLanahan, and Garfinkel 1994). In descending order of the size of their ratio of women's to men's poverty, the United States, Australia, West Germany, Canada, and the United Kingdom all had a sizable gender gap. In Italy and the Netherlands, women's poverty rate was 1.02 times men's, virtually equal. Sweden is the only nation in which a lower proportion of women than men were in poverty; the women's poverty rate was 90 percent of men's. Casper et al. (1994) attribute the low sex gap in poverty in Italy to high marriage and low divorce rates, the low sex gap in the Netherlands to a relatively generous state-provided safety net that brings most single mothers' households above poverty, and women's favorable poverty position in Sweden to high female employment, a relatively small sex gap in pay, and a sturdy safety net. It is also interesting to note that, in general, nations with higher poverty rates have a higher gender disparity in poverty. The United States has both a high poverty rate and the largest gender disparity. The high disparity by gender in the United States results in part from its less generous social welfare programs and a higher ratio of mothers living apart from men (England et al. 1998).

THE FEMINIZATION OF POVERTY: THE MODERN PARADOX

We have seen that women have higher poverty rates than men in the United States and a number of other nations, but what is the trend in the gender gap in poverty in the United States? Has there been a feminization of poverty, as claimed by Diana Pearce (1978), who coined the phrase? If what we mean by the "feminization of poverty" is a "relative feminization"—that is, the extent to which women's poverty rates as a ratio of men's have gone up—table 2 (drawing from McLanahan et al. 1989 and McLanahan and Kelly 1999) answers the question. Focusing on the row pertaining to all ages (18 and over) combined, we can see that for whites the ratio of women's to men's poverty rate went up markedly—over 30 percentage points—between 1950 and 1970 but went up only a few points from 1970 to 1980 and declined about the same few points between 1980 and 1996. Thus, it has been fairly constant since 1970. However, if we break things out by age, we see that the dramatic increase in women's rates relative to men's has continued among the elderly, but the ratio of women's to men's poverty was stable among young adults after 1980 and has declined among those aged 30 to 64 since 1970.

Blacks in the United States showed a continued and dramatic increase in women's poverty rates relative to men's among the elderly. The younger age-groups showed increases in women's relative poverty until 1980, but poverty has "defeminized" a bit since then. When we look at all ages combined, there is a dramatic increase in the ratio of women's to men's poverty rates until 1980 but little increase in the ratio after 1980 (two points). More of the increase in the feminization of poverty for blacks occurred between 1970 and 1980, whereas for whites the increase was almost over by 1970.

This trend in relative poverty gives a very different picture of women's progress relative to men than the figures on women's employment and earnings discussed previously. One might have thought that the great increase in women's employment and earnings would have reduced women's poverty relative to men's among the nonelderly during the whole period. (We would not expect this among the elderly because employment is not the major source of earnings for either men or women in this group.) Had there been no countervailing force, this would have been true. What is the countervailing force that increased women's poverty relative to men's from 1950 to 1980?

The countervailing factor is the increase in the proportion of women living independently from men and the increasing portion of these who have children. As discussed previously, given the low rates and levels of child support payment and levels of government cash subsidy to welfare recipients that seldom bring them above the poverty line, female-headed households containing children are very vulnerable to poverty. Several forces had led to an increased proportion of all women living in such households, and this has detached an increasing proportion of women and children from men's earnings.

Americans have been marrying at later ages since 1960. After a slight decrease in age at marriage during the 1950s, average age at first marriage has increased steadily (Spain and Bianchi 1996: 27). This may not reduce the proportion who never marry. However, it means that women are spending more years of their life living independently of men. This trend is especially pronounced for African Americans (Raley 1996).

The proportion of women living without men in their households is also affected by the divorce rate. In the United States, divorce increased fairly continuously from 1860 to 1940, spiked dramatically during World War II, then came down to its prewar level and was fairly stable during the 1950s. It increased dramatically during the 1960s and 1970s and has declined slightly since 1980 (Cherlin 1996: 353). Even if further increases do not occur (and this is debatable), it has leveled off at a very high level that implies that half or more of all new marriages will end in divorce (Martin and Bumpass 1989). In addition, since the 1970s, divorced women have waited longer to remarry, which also contributes to a higher proportion of women living independently of men (Spain and Bianchi 1996: 34–35).

Another trend affecting women's relative poverty is nonmarital child-bearing. While overall fertility has fallen dramatically since the peak of the baby boom in 1956 (though it rose slightly since 1980) (England and Farkas 1986: 13; Spain and Bianchi 1996), the proportion of births that are to unmarried women has increased continuously since the 1950s. It was under 5 percent in 1950 and is over 30 percent today (Moore 1995).

Both divorce and nonmarital births increase the proportion of single women who are supporting children, and this will, other things being equal, increase women's poverty rates relative to men's since the poverty line is adjusted for household size.

All these trends—later marriage, increased divorce, and an increasing percentage of births to unmarried women—mean that more women, and especially more women with children, are living independently of men. The small amounts that such households get in state transfer payments and in transfers from men outside the household means that many of them are surviving largely on women's earnings. While women's employment and earnings have grown, apparently before 1980 this increase was not great enough to offset the increasing detachment of women (and children) from men's earnings. This is why women's poverty rates increased relative to men's. However, in the United States since 1980, although poverty has gone up for men and women, women's continued gains in employment and earnings and/or men's losses (either being an improvement for women relative to men) have apparently been large enough to offset the continuing increases in the proportion of women living independently of men, and it is these gains that have brought the ratio of women's poverty to men's downward again among the nonelderly over 30. This explanation is consistent with the finding in table 2 that the ratio of women's to men's poverty decreased since 1980 among those aged 30 to 64. We would not expect women's recent gains in employment and earnings, which were concentrated among younger cohorts of women, to affect the poverty of women relative to men among the elderly for many more decades since most of the elderly are not employed and live on Social Security and pensions, the amounts of which were determined by employment records stretching back many decades.

Thus, to summarize the trends for the United States, poverty feminized from 1950 to 1980, but this trend was over among the nonelderly by 1980. Women's poverty as a ratio of men's went up between 1950 and 1980 despite women's increased employment. This is because more women were living in households without men and thus losing access to a share of men's earnings. Since 1980,

among those in the 30-to-64 age-group, trends toward women living independently from men without access to their earnings have continued. But increases in women's earnings and decreases in men's earnings apparently were at least offsetting among blacks and substantially more than offsetting among whites.

A few caveats to the discussion are needed. Table 2 shows sex ratios of poverty rates, not the underlying rates themselves. However, if those are examined, we see that the feminization of poverty does not necessarily mean that women's absolute poverty is increasing (McLanahan et al. 1989; McLanahan and Kelly 1999). Indeed, the basic pattern is that poverty came down for most all groups between 1950 and 1980, but because it came down faster for men than women, women's poverty relative to men's increased. Since 1980, poverty has gone up for all groups, but because it has gone up faster for men than women except among the elderly, women's relative poverty has decreased in nonelderly age-groups. However, we should remember that in virtually every race/age/year combination, women have higher poverty than men. Overall, in 1996, white women had poverty rates 52 percent higher than white men's, and black women had rates 71 percent higher than black men's (table 2).

To return to the terminology of gender and class with which I began, if our interest is on freedom from the deprivation of poverty and we can think of household poverty as one crude measure of class, then class is gendered and became increasingly so from 1950 to 1980 but decreasingly so since 1980. Most of the increase in the "gendering of class," the "feminization of poverty" that occurred through 1980 was, at least in a proximate sense, because of changes in whether men and women live together and pool income.

A MACRO-LEVEL MODEL AND INTERPRETATION

Let us step back from the details discussed so far to consider what theoretical assertions we might make about the causal relationship between the major factors considered. Figure 1 presents my view of the causal linkages. In principle, it is a model that could explain variation over time within a society or variation between societies (or smaller units).

The model starts with women's relative earnings. I am thinking here of a concept that would best be measured as annual earnings of the individual, where those who are not employed have earnings of zero. Thus, the issue is not just relative wage rates but how much the individual earns, letting that amount be impacted by employment versus nonemployment, hours per week and weeks per year of employment, and the wage rate. Earnings would then be aggregated in some measure of central tendency, and a ratio or difference between women's and men's would be computed. As discussed previously, such a measure would show increases for

women's relative earnings in the United States fairly continuously since at least 1950 even though wage rates have converged only since 1980. The model asserts that women's relative earnings affect women's power relative to men in their marriages. . . . I think most of the available evidence suggests this, although further research is clearly needed. (For conceptual discussions of effects of spouses' relative resources, including earnings, on material or other manifestations of marital power, see Behrman 1992; Blumberg 1991; Bourguignon and Chiappori 1992; Browning et al. 1994; England and Kilbourne 1990; Hobcraft 1997; Thomas 1990).

Why would we think that who earns more of the family income would affect power within the family? One relevant set of ideas comes from what sociologists call exchange theory and what economists call a "bargaining" perspective, which is in turn essentially a version of game theory. The

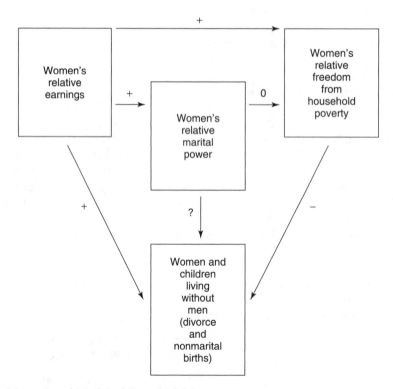

FIGURE 1   Macro-Level Model of Causal Linkages.

basic idea is that what one can successfully bargain for with a spouse is increased the more one's alternatives outside this relationship increase relative to the gains from staying in the relationship and the less one's partner's alternatives outside this relationship increase relative to the partner's gains from the relationship. Thus, contrary to how exchange theory is sometimes portrayed, the notion is not simply that bargaining power is proportional to contributions. If that were true, the conclusion that men have more power by virtue of bringing in money would by no means follow, despite the fact that it is often portrayed as being self-evident. If the issue is relative contributions, who is to say that men are contributing more to the family by bringing in earnings than a woman who is a homemaker is contributing by providing care for children and other household work? From the vantage point of this perspective, the salient way in which earnings differ from homemaking is that earning power is portable if one leaves the marriage. Thus, if there is a divorce, a wife loses access to a husband's earnings and a husband to the wife's earnings (except to whatever extent alimony or child support is enforced); thus, earnings give either spouse power vis-à-vis the other. This suggests that men's higher earnings have been a source of greater marital power. The provision of child rearing is not analogous since women generally continue to take care of the children in the case of divorce. Thus, to the extent that women's contributions to the marriage are to provide things that they would not take away from their husbands in the case of a divorce (child-rearing services) whereas men's role is to provide things that they will largely withdraw if the marriage ends (earnings), women have less power than men. Thus, women's lesser employment and earnings relative to their husbands in marriage give women less credible "external threat points" than men, in the language of game theory, but they have more favorable threat points the higher their own earnings are. At the abstract level, the idea is that the more one could threaten to withdraw from the partner if one left a relationship and the worse

their options outside the relationship, the more one can exercise power within a relationship (for a more extended theoretical discussion, see England and Kilbourne 1990).

This approach differs from Gary Becker's (1991) approach to the family, which assumes a single family utility function and altruism of the family head (for critiques of Becker, see England and Budig 1998; England and Farkas 1986: chaps. 3, 4; Folbre 1994). However, one need not assume complete selfishness of marital partners to think that the bargaining approach has some merit. I believe that there is a mix of altruism and selfishness in most all social relations. To the extent that some degree of selfishness vis-à-vis spouses is present, the bargaining perspective should have some explanatory power.

The bargaining perspective has some empirical support in findings suggesting that employment and/or women's earnings relative to their husbands' affect who gets their way when there is conflict on various issues (Bahr 1974; Blumstein and Schwartz 1983; Duncan and Duncan 1978: 205; McDonald 1980). If we assume that most people would prefer to have more leisure and do less housework, then findings on the division of housework in the United States also provide indirect support for the bargaining model: A spouse having higher earnings is predictive of doing less housework (Brines 1994; Presser 1994).

If relative earnings affect marital power, this may affect how satisfying marriages are to the partners on a large number of dimensions that partners implicitly or explicitly negotiate, things as diverse as how money is to be spent, who will do what household chores, the couple's sex life, when and if they will have children, how children are reared, the timing of children, where the family will live, and so on. If this is true and if an individual's relative power affects how much they can negotiate for what they want within the marriage, we would expect marriages to be more satisfying to women when their earnings are higher.

Marital power should not have any effects on household poverty, so figure 1 shows a 0 on the arrow from marital power to freedom from household level poverty. Figure 1 also shows a positive, direct effect from women's relative earnings to their relative freedom from household poverty. As discussed previously, if household structure is held constant, this is almost definitional. It will be true as long as any increases in women's relative earnings apply to those who head households and thus bring female-headed households out of poverty at higher rates than other households. However, as discussed previously, during the period between 1950 and 1980, when women's employment and earnings were increasing, women's relative freedom from poverty was not always improving. This is because the effect of women's relative earnings on their poverty, operating indirectly through effects on the proportion of women living apart from men, works in opposition to the direct effect, as shown in figure 1.

The lower section of figure 1 says that women's earnings relative to men's lead to more women and children living in households without men, and this decreases women's relative freedom from (household) poverty. Let us examine the first path in the link. Why would women's increased earnings increase women's tendency to live independently of men? One way is through increasing divorce.

Is there evidence that the increase in women's employment and earnings has increased divorce? There is no question about the fact that women's increased employment and increasing divorce have moved upward together over the last century (Greenstein 1990: 659). What is more difficult to assess is whether the increased employment and earnings of women have had a causal effect on divorce through making it possible for women to live independently of men. Many commentators argue for a causal relationship (Cherlin 1981; England and Farkas 1986: chaps. 1, 3) and some time-series (Michael 1988; Ruggles 1997a, 1997b) micro-level analyses (Greenstein 1995; South and Spitze 1986) find effects of either women's employment or earnings on divorce, although the evidence is mixed (Greenstein 1990; Hoffman and Duncan 1995; Tzeng and Mare 1995).

However, divorce is not the only force increasing the number of female-headed households. The movement to a later age at marriage (and some possibly not marrying at all) combined with an increase in the proportion of births that are out of marriage are also important. We might expect that women's increased employment and earnings would also make it more possible for women to choose to forgo marriage, even if they want children. (The evidence, however, on this is weak since there is some evidence that employment encourages rather than discourages first marriage for women [reviewed in Oppenheimer 1997: 471].)

There are at least two theoretical perspectives that can generate a prediction that women's employment increases divorce. From the point of view of the neoclassical "new home economics," Becker (1991) sees increasing divorce to be explained by declining gains from marriage because there is less specialization by sex when both women and men are employed. Specialization, in his view, makes families more efficient in their combined efforts to procure income from the market and to engage in household production (his term for household work and child rearing).

There is another way to look at the same empirical relationships that I find more compelling because it pays more attention to the patriarchal nature of marriage. In any feminist account and in the game theory–informed view mentioned previously, men have had disproportionate power in marriages because of their earning power. This has led many aspects of the relationships to be unsatisfying to women. In this view, what has held marriages together, in part, is women's dependence on men for money. When women's earnings lessen this dependence, women are more free to leave bad marriages or to forgo marriage in the first place. Notice that, on this view, marriages are not made less happy by women's employment (at least not for women). Indeed, employment should increase their satisfactoriness to women. Rather, what changes is whether women can leave unhappy marriage partners without experiencing the worst levels of destitution for themselves and their children.

Of course, if women are freer to divorce, they are also freer to delay or avoid marriage and to have children outside marriage.

It would be consistent with the way I am telling the story to find that it is women's decisions prompting a majority of divorces rather than an increase in men deserting women. Of course, sometimes it is not clear that it was one person who wanted the breakup while another wanted the union preserved; and we definitely cannot rely on data indicating who filed for the divorce since that may not correspond with who really initiated the decision. However, surveys in the United States that have asked people whether one party wanted the divorce find that a majority are prompted by women (Kelly 1986: 309; Kitson 1992; Spanier and Thompson 1984; Wallerstein and Kelly 1980). This is true for England as well (Hobcraft 1997). Swedish data show the same (Svedin 1994). I thus suspect that this may be true in all affluent, industrial nations.

This is not to say that women's employment is the only factor affecting the century-long increase in divorce. Increased emphasis on individualism in the culture may also be a factor (Cherlin 1981, 1996; England and Farkas 1986), perhaps prompted in part by advertising and consumerism; and, of course, any trend tends eventually to become self-reinforcing by producing values consistent with it. If enough people divorce or have nonmarital births, it becomes less stigmatized, and this may prompt further increases.

When more women and children live independently of men, especially in a context of low earnings for women, low state enforcement of child support, a below-poverty state-supported cash payment system for lone mothers, and a lack of universally provided health and child care services by the state, this increases women's poverty relative to men's. In figure 1, the negative effect of women living apart from men on women's relative freedom from poverty, net of women's earnings, results from more single women than men living with children (recall that the poverty threshold is adjusted for household size). Consistent with this,

changes in family structure were behind the increases in the ratio of women's to men's poverty in the United States between 1950 and 1980, and national differences in family structure explain the relative ratio of women's to men's poverty across nations (England et al. 1998).

There is, to be sure, something a bit paradoxical about arguing that women's earnings lead to divorce because it allows more women to leave men without destitution and then to further say that one result of this is women's increased poverty relative to men's. Yet I think that this is what has occurred. While female-headed families with children have always fared badly, more women can support families, and more adequately than previously, even if some fall below the poverty line, at least for a period.

One interesting way to think about the effect of women's relative earnings on both marital power and living independently of men is to use the terms coined by Albert Hirschman (1970). In a classic formulation, he argued that people in a situation that they do not like have three possible responses: exit, voice, or loyalty. According to the model here, women's increased power through increased earnings can be used as "voice" to bargain to make marriages better but can also be used to "exit" unhappy marriages. Presumably, women's increased employment has had both effects, although we do not have trend data on marital power. In earlier decades, women's economic dependence and resulting limited marital power meant that even those deeply dissatisfied with their marriages generally chose "loyalty" (staying married) because their only option was destitution. Men's greater power allowed them to respond to dissatisfaction through either exit or a bargaining "voice" in which their greater power usually brought them concessions. The low divorce rate of the earlier period suggests that men generally chose "voice." If women's power has increased because of their increased employment and earnings, they can choose either to leave unsatisfactory marriages (exit) or to utilize their new power by bargaining harder for what they want in marriage. That the two options of voice and exit go hand and hand is implied by the view that resources one would withdraw from a partner if one decided to end the relationship also lead to power within it.

While we lack trend data on marital power, are there some more indirect indicators that would suggest whether women are successfully bargaining for more satisfactory marriages? One thing that might make us doubt the increase in women's successful utilization of their new power is the fact that as women have increased their employment dramatically, men have increased the time they spend in domestic work much less, and, as a result, women, especially employed mothers, generally enjoy less leisure than men (see literature reviewed in England and Kilbourne 1990). One presumes that employed women would like to use their bargaining power to bring about a more equal sharing of domestic work. There is also evidence that women would like to change the degree to which men provide emotional empathy. Both of these things would require a significant change in men's roles. However, there is much greater resistance, psychologically, culturally, and structurally, to changing men's roles than to changing women's roles. Men grow up and live in a culture that denigrates "feminine" males more than "masculine" females. In addition, employers are more willing to incorporate female workers into male jobs than to redefine "male" jobs that were constructed assuming that men did no domestic work and had wives to do it for them. Thus, women may use exit because of the resistance they encounter when they try to use voice in ways that significantly require changes in men's roles. One result of women using exit rather than voice is to protect men's roles from having to change. As a result, there is a profound asymmetry in gender role change. This is particularly true since women continue to do all the child-rearing work in divorced households and households with nonmarital births. Women have taken on traditionally male responsibilities much more than men have taken on traditionally female responsibilities. Thus, the question of why exit is used more often than effective voice may reduce to the

question of why men's roles are so much harder to change than women's. It may be the resistance that women find to changing men's roles to include more traditionally female activities that leads them to often opt for exit over voice. This is consistent with the evidence that it is disproportionately women who initiate marital breakups. However, the result of the "exit" (or "never enter") decisions, in the aggregate, is to increase women's relative exposure to household poverty, and, given low child support enforcement, this increasingly disconnects children from men's incomes as well.

Thus, a modern paradox is this: Women have gained access to money through increased employment, which improves their marital power, but their ability to use this power to get men to share in traditionally female responsibilities is limited. Thus, many instead use their economic independence to form separate households, often with children. In doing so, they continue to take responsibility for child rearing, but they lose a realistic claim to a share of men's earnings for themselves and their children. Whether, in net, what has been lost or what has been gained is greater is difficult to answer. I suspect, however, that if male resistance to taking on more traditionally female responsibilities were to lessen, the empowerment provided by women's employment and earnings would be more likely to translate into an increased voice within marriages than currently and less likely to lead to divorce and the retreat from marriage.

REFERENCES

Acker, Joan. 1973. "Women and Stratification: A Case of Intellectual Sexism." In J. Huber, ed., *Changing Women in a Changing Society,* pp. 174–183. Chicago: University of Chicago Press.

Acker, Joan. 1990. "Hierarchies, Jobs, Bodies: A Theory of Gendered Organizations." *Gender and Society* 4: 139–158.

Bahr, Stephen J. 1974. "Effects of Power and Division of Labor in the Family." In L. W. Hoffman and F. E. Nye, eds., *Working Mothers,* pp. 167–185. San Francisco: Jossey-Bass.

Becker, Gary S. 1991. *A Treatise on the Family.* Cambridge, Mass.: Harvard University Press.

Behrman, J. R. 1992. "Intra-Household Allocation of Nutrients and Gender Effects: A Survey of Structural and Reduced-Form Estimates." In S. R. Osmani, ed., *Nutrition and Poverty,* pp. 287–320. Oxford: Clarendon Press.

Blau, Francine D., Marianne A. Ferber, and Anne E. Winkler. 1998. *The Economics of Women, Men, and Work.* 3rd ed. Upper Saddle River, N.J.: Prentice Hall.

Blau, Francine D., and Lawrence Kahn. 1996. "Wage Structure and Gender Earnings Differentials: An International Comparison." *Economica* 63 (Supplement): S29–S62.

———. 1997. "Swimming Upstream: Trends in the Gender Wage Differential in the 1980s." *Journal of Economic Literature* 15: 1–42.

Blumberg, Rae Lesser, ed. 1991. *Gender, Family, and Economy: The Triple Overlap.* Newbury Park, Calif.: Sage Publications.

Blumstein P., and P. Schwartz. 1983. *American Couples.* New York: William Morrow.

Bourguigrion, Francois, and Pierre-Andre Chiappori. 1992. "Collective Models of Household Behavior." *European Economic Review* 36: 355–364.

Brines, Julie. 1994. "Economic Dependency, Gender, and the Division of Labor at Home." *American Journal of Sociology* 100: 652–688.

Browning, Martin, Francois Bourguignon, Pierre-Andre Chiappori, and Valerie Lechene. 1994. "Income and Outcomes: A Structural Model of Intrahousehold Allocation." *Journal of Political Economy* 102, no. 6: 1067–1096.

Casper, Lynne M., Sara S. McLanahan, and Irwin Garfinkel. 1994. "The Gender-Poverty Gap: What We Can Learn from Other Countries." *American Sociological Review* 59: 594–605.

Cherlin, Andrew J. 1981. *Marriage, Divorce, Remarriage.* Cambridge, Mass.: Harvard University Press.

———. 1996. *Public and Private Families.* New York: McGraw-Hill.

Clement, Wallace. 2001. "Who Works? Comparing Labor Market Practices." In *Reconfigurations of Class and Gender,* Janeen Baxter and Mark Western (eds.) Stanford, CA: Stanford University Press. Pp. 55–80.

Duncan, Beverly, and Otis Dudley Duncan. 1978. *Sex Typing and Social Roles: A Research Report.* New York: Academic Press.

England, Paula. 1992. *Comparable Worth: Theories and Evidence.* Hawthorne, N.Y.: Aldine de Gruyter.

England, Paula, and Michelle J. Budig. 1998. "Gary Becker on the Family: His Genius, Impact, and Blind Spots." In Dan Clawson, ed., *Required Reading: Sociology's Most Influential Books,* pp. 95–112. Amherst, Mass.: University of Massachusetts Press.

England, Paula, Karen Christopher, Tim Smeeding, Katherine Ross, and Sara McLanahan. 1998. "The Role of State, Family, and Market in the Gender Gap in Poverty in Modern Nations: Findings from the Luxembourg Income Study." Paper presented at the annual meetings of the American Sociological Association, San Francisco, August.

England, Paula, and George Farkas. 1986. *Households, Employment, and Gender: A Social, Economic and Demographic View.* New York: Aldine de Gruyter.

England, Paula, and Barbara Stanek Kilbourne. 1990. "Markets, Marriages, and Other Mates: The Problem of Power." In Roger Friedland and A. F. Robertson, eds., *Beyond the Marketplace: Rethinking Economy and Society,* pp. 163–188. New York: Aldine de Gruyter.

Folbre, Nancy. 1994. *Who Pays for the Kids?* New York: Routledge.

Gornick, Janet C. 1999. "Gender Equality in the Labor Market: Women's Employment and Earnings." In Diane Sainsbury, ed., *Gender Policy Regimes and Welfare States,* pp. 210–242. Oxford: Oxford University Press.

Greenstein, Theodore N. 1990. "Marital Disruption and the Employment of Married Women." *Journal of Marriage and the Family* 52: 657–676.

———. 1995. "Gender Ideology, Marital Disruption, and the Employment of Married Women." *Journal of Marriage and the Family* 57: 31–42.

Gross, E. 1986. "Plus Ca Change. . .? The Sexual Structure of Occupations over Time." *Social Problems* 16: 249–264.

Hirschman, Albert O. 1970. *Exit, Voice, and Loyalty.* Cambridge, Mass.: Harvard University Press.

Hobcraft, John. 1997. "The Consequences of Female Empowerment for Child Well-Being." Paper presented at IUSSP Conference, Lund, Sweden, April.

Kalleberg, Arne L. 1995. "Part-Time Work and Workers in the United States: Correlates and Policy Issues." *Washington and Lee Law Review* 52, no. 3: 771–798.

Kelly, Joan Berlin, 1986. "Divorce: The Adult Perspective." In Arlene S. Skolnik and Jerome H. Skolnik, eds., *Family in Transition,* 5th ed., pp. 304–337. Boston: Little, Brown.

Kitson, Gay. 1992. *Portrait of a Divorce.* New York: Guilford Press.

Martin, Teresa Castro, and Larry L. Bumpass. 1989. "Recent Trends in Marital Disruption." *Demography* 26, no. 1: 37–51.

McDonald, Gerald W. 1980. "Family Power: An Assessment of a Decade of Theory and Research, 1970–1979." *Journal of Marriage and the Family* 42, no. 2 (November): 841–851.

McLanahan, Sara S., and Kelly. 1999. "The Feminization of Poverty: Past and Future." In Janet Saltzman Chafetz, ed., *Handbook of the Sociology of Gender,* pp. 127–146. New York: Kluwer.

McLanahan, Sara S., Annemette Sorensen, and Dorothy Watson. 1989. "Sex Differences in Poverty, 1950–1980." *Signs* 15, no. 11: 102–112.

Michael, Robert T. 1988. "Why Did the U.S. Divorce Rate Double within a Decade?" *Research in Population Economics* 6: 367–399.

Moore, Kristin A. 1995. *Report to Congress on Out-of-Wedlock Childbearing.* Hyattsville, Md.: National Center for Health Statistics.

Oppenheimer, Valerie. 1997. "Comment on 'The Rise of Divorce and Separation in the United States, 1880–1990.'" *Demography* 34: 467–472.

Pearce, Diana, 1978. "The Feminization of Poverty: Women, Work, and Welfare." *Urban and Social Change Review* 11: 128–136.

Petersen, Trond, and Laurie A. Morgan. 1995. "Separate and Unequal: Occupation-Establishment Sex Segregation and the Gender Wage Gap." *American Journal of Sociology* 101, no. 2: 329–365.

Presser, Harriet B. 1994. "Employment Schedules, Gender, and Household Labor." *American Sociological Review* 59: 348–364.

Raley, R. Kelly. 1996. "Cohabitation, Marriageable Men, and Racial Differences in Marriage." *American Sociological Review* 61, no. 6: 973–983.

Rosenfeld, Rachel A., and Gunn Elisabeth Birkelund. 1995. "Women's Part-Time Work: A Cross-National Comparison." *European Sociological Review* 11: 111–134.

Ruggles, Steven B. 1997a. "Reply to Oppenheimer and Preston." *Demography* 34: 475–479.

———. 1997b. "The Rise of Divorce and Separation in the United States, 1880–1990." *Demography* 34: 455–466.

South, Scott, and Glenna Spitze. 1986. "Determinants of Divorce over the Marital Life Course." *American Sociological Review* 51, no. 4 (August): 583–590.

Spain, Daphne, and Suzanne M. Bianchi. 1996. *Balancing Act: Motherhood, Marriage, and Employment among American Women.* New York: Russell Sage Foundation.

Spanier, Graham, and Linda Thompson. 1984. *Parting: The Aftermath of Separation and Divorce.* Beverly Hills, Calif.: Sage.

Svedin, D. G. 1994. Mans och kvinnors syn pa skilsmassoorsaker och upplevda konsekvenser av skilsmassan: I Rapporten Hearing om Skilsm Ssor Och Famil-jesplittring. 1993. Dokument 1994: 1. Fran Kommitten for FN:S Familjear. Socialdepartementet.

Taeuber, Cynthia. 1991. *Statistical Handbook on Women in America.* Phoenix: Oryx Press.

Thomas, Duncan. 1990. "Intra-Household Resource Allocation." *Journal of Human Resources* 25, no. 4: 635–664.

Tzeng, Jessie M., and Robert D. Mare. 1995. "Labor Market and Socioeconomic Effects on Marital Stability." *Social Science Research* 24: 329–351.

Waldfogel, Jane. 1998. "Understanding the 'Family Gap' in Pay for Women with Children." *Journal of Economic Perspectives* 12: 137–156.

Wallerstein, Judith S., and Joan Berlin Kelly. 1980. *Surviving the Breakup: How Children and Parents Cope with Divorce.* London: Grant McIntyre.

Wellington, Allison J. 1993. "Changes in the Male/Female Wage Gap, 1976–1985." *Journal of Human Resources* 28: 383–411.

———. 1994. "The Male/Female Wage Gap among Whites: 1976 and 1985." *American Sociological Review* 59, no. 6: 839–848.

Maid in L. A.

PIERRETTE HONDAGNEU-SOTELO

LIVE-IN NANNY/HOUSEKEEPER JOBS

For Maribel Centeno, newly arrived from Guatemala City in 1989 at age twenty-two and without supportive family and friends with whom to stay, taking a live-in job made a lot of sense. She knew that she wouldn't have to spend money on room and board, and that she could soon begin saving to pay off her debts. Getting a live-in job through an agency was easy. The *señora,* in her rudimentary Spanish, only asked where she was from, and if she had a husband and children. Chuckling, Maribel recalled her initial misunderstanding when the *señora,* using her index finger, had drawn an imaginary "2" and "3" in the palm of her hand. "I thought to myself, well, she must have two or three bedrooms, so I said, fine. 'No,' she said. 'Really, really big.' She started counting, 'One, two, three, four . . . two-three rooms.' It was twenty-three rooms! I thought, *huy!* On a piece of paper, she wrote '$80 a week,' and she said, 'You, child, and entire house.' So I thought, well, I have to do what I have to do, and I happily said, 'Yes.'"

"I arrived on Monday at dawn," she recalled, "and I went to the job on Wednesday evening." When the *señora* and the child spoke to her, Maribel remembered "just laughing and feeling useless. I couldn't understand anything." On that first evening, the *señora* put on classical music, which Maribel quickly identified. "I said, 'Beethoven.' She said, 'Yeah,' and began asking me in English, 'You like it?' I said 'Yes,' or perhaps I said, '*Sí,*' and she began playing other cassettes, CDs. They had Richard Clayderman and I recognized it, and when I said that, she stopped in her tracks, her jaw fell open, and she just stared at me. She must have been thinking, 'No schooling, no preparation, no English, how does she know this music?'" But the *señora,* perhaps because of the language difficulty, or perhaps because she felt upstaged by her live-in's knowledge of classical music, never did ask. Maribel desperately wanted the *señora* to respect her, to recognize that she was smart, educated, and cultivated in the arts. In spite of her best status-signaling efforts, "They treated me," she said, "the same as any other girl from the countryside." She never got the verbal recognition that she desired from the *señora.*

Maribel summed up her experiences with her first live-in job this way: "The pay was bad. The treatment was, how shall I say? It was cordial, a little, uh, not racist, but with very little consideration, very little respect." She liked caring for the little seven-year-old boy, but keeping after the cleaning of the twenty-three-room house, filled with marble floors and glass tables, proved physically impossible. She eventually quit not because of the polishing and scrubbing, but because being ignored devastated her socially.

Compared to many other Latina immigrants' first live-in jobs, Maribel Centeno's was relatively

Source: Pierrette Hondagneu-Sotelo, "Maid in L.A." In *Domestica: Immigrant Workers Cleaning and Caring in the Shadows of Affluence,* Berkeley: University of California Press, 2001: 30–37. Used with permission of University of California Press.

good. She was not on call during all her waking hours and throughout the night, the parents were engaged with the child, and she was not required to sleep in a child's bedroom or on a cot tucked away in the laundry room. But having a private room filled with amenities did not mean she had privacy or the ability to do simple things one might take for granted. "I had my own room, with my own television, VCR, my private bath, and closet, and a kind of sitting room—but everything in miniature, Thumbelina style," she said. "I had privacy in that respect. But I couldn't do many things. If I wanted to walk around in a T-shirt, or just feel like I was home, I couldn't do that. If I was hungry in the evening, I wouldn't come out to grab a banana because I'd have to walk through the family room, and then everybody's watching and having to smell the banana. I could never feel at home, never. Never, never, never! There's always something invisible that tells you this is not your house, you just work here."

It is the rare California home that offers separate maid's quarters, but that doesn't stop families from hiring live-ins; nor does it stop newly arrived Latina migrant workers from taking jobs they urgently need. When live-ins cannot even retreat to their own rooms, work seeps into their sleep and their dreams. There is no time off from the job, and they say they feel confined, trapped, imprisoned.

"I lose a lot of sleep," said Margarita Gutiérrez, a twenty-four-year-old Mexicana who worked as a live-in nanny/housekeeper. At her job in a modest-sized condominium in Pasadena, she slept in a corner of a three-year-old child's bedroom. Consequently, she found herself on call day and night with the child, who sometimes went several days without seeing her mother because of the latter's schedule at an insurance company. Margarita was obliged to be on her job twenty-four hours a day; and like other live-in nanny/housekeepers I interviewed, she claimed that she could scarcely find time to shower or brush her teeth. "I go to bed fine," she reported, "and then I wake up at two or three in the morning with the girl asking for water, or food." After the child went back to sleep,

Margarita would lie awake, thinking about how to leave her job but finding it hard to even walk out into the kitchen. Live-in employees like Margarita literally have no space and no time they can claim as their own.

Working in a larger home or staying in plush, private quarters is no guarantee of privacy or refuge from the job. Forty-four-year-old Elvia Lucero worked as a live-in at a sprawling, canyon-side residence, where she was in charge of looking after twins, two five-year-old girls. On numerous occasions when I visited her there, I saw that she occupied her own bedroom, a beautifully decorated one outfitted with delicate antiques, plush white carpet, and a stenciled border of pink roses painstakingly painted on the wall by the employer. It looked serene and inviting, but it was only three steps away from the twins' room. Every night one of the twins crawled into bed with Elvia. Elvia disliked this, but said she couldn't break the girl of the habit. And the parents' room lay tucked away at the opposite end of the large (more than 3,000 square feet), L-shaped house.

Regardless of the size of the home and the splendor of the accommodations, the boundaries that we might normally take for granted disappear in live-in jobs. They have, as Evelyn Nakano Glenn has noted, "no clear line between work and non-work time," and the line between job space and private space is similarly blurred.[1] Live-in nanny/housekeepers are at once socially isolated and surrounded by other people's territory; during the hours they remain on the employers' premises, their space, like their time, belongs to another. The sensation of being among others while remaining invisible, unknown and apart, of never being able to leave the margins, makes many live-in employees sad, lonely, and depressed. Melancholy sets in and doesn't necessarily lift on the weekends.

Rules and regulations may extend around the clock. Some employers restrict the ability of their live-in employees to receive telephone calls,

---

[1] Evelyn Nakano Glenn, *Issci Nisei, Warbride,* Philadelphia, PA: Temple University Press, 1986: p. 141.

entertain friends, attend evening ESL classes, or see boyfriends during the workweek. Other employers do not impose these sorts of restrictions, but because their homes are located on remote hillsides, in suburban enclaves, or in gated communities, their live-in nanny/housekeepers are effectively kept away from anything resembling social life or public culture. A Spanish-language radio station, or maybe a *telenovela,* may serve as their only link to the outside world.

Food—the way some employers hoard it, waste it, deny it, or just simply do not even have any of it in their kitchens—is a frequent topic of discussion among Latina live-in nanny/housekeepers. These women are talking not about counting calories but about the social meaning of food on the job. Almost no one works with a written contract, but anyone taking a live-in job that includes "room and board" would assume that adequate meals will be included. But what constitutes an adequate meal? Everyone has a different idea, and using the subject like a secret handshake, Latina domestic workers often greet one another by talking about the problems of managing food and meals on the job. Inevitably, food enters their conversations.

No one feels the indignities of food more deeply than do live-in employees, who may not leave the job for up to six days at a time. For them, the workplace necessarily becomes the place of daily sustenance. In some of the homes where they work, the employers are out all day. When these adults return home, they may only snack, keeping on hand little besides hot dogs, packets of macaroni and cheese, cereal, and peanut butter for the children. Such foods are considered neither nutritious nor appetizing by Latina immigrants, many of whom are accustomed to sitting down to meals prepared with fresh vegetables, rice, beans, and meat. In some employers' homes, the cupboards are literally bare. Gladys Villedas recalled that at one of her live-in jobs, the *señora* had graciously said, "'Go ahead, help yourself to anything in the kitchen.' But at times," she recalled, "there was nothing, nothing in the refrigerator! There was nothing to eat!" Even in lavish

kitchens outfitted with Subzero refrigerators and imported cabinetry, food may be scarce. A celebrity photographer of luxury homes that appear in posh magazines described to a reporter what he sees when he opens the doors of some of Beverly Hills' refrigerators: "Rows of cans of Diet Coke, and maybe a few remains of pizza."[2]

Further down the class ladder, some employers go to great lengths to economize on food bills. Margarita Gutiérrez claimed that at her live-in job, the husband did the weekly grocery shopping, but he bought things in small quantities— say, two potatoes that would be served in half portions, or a quarter of a watermelon to last a household of five all week. He rationed out the bottled water and warned her that milk would make her fat. Lately, she said, he was taking both her and the children to an upscale grocery market where they gave free samples of gourmet cheeses, breads, and dips, urging them all to fill up on the freebies. "I never thought," exclaimed Margarita, formerly a secretary in Mexico City, "that I would come to this country to experience hunger!"

Many women who work as live-ins are keenly aware of how food and meals underline the boundaries between them and the families for whom they work. "I never ate with them," recalled Maribel Centeno of her first live-in job. "First of all, she never said, 'Come and join us,' and secondly, I just avoided being around when they were about to eat." Why did she avoid mealtime? "I didn't feel I was part of that family. I knew they liked me, but only because of the good work I did, and because of the affection I showered on the boy; but apart from that, I was just like the gardener, like the pool man, just one more of their staff." Sitting down to share a meal symbolizes membership in a family, and Latina employees, for the most part, know they are not just like one of the family.

Food scarcity is not endemic to all of the households where these women work. In some homes, ample quantities of fresh fruits, cheeses,

---

[2]Irene Lacher, "An Interior Mind," *Los Angeles Times,* March 16, 1997, E1.

and chicken stock the kitchens. Some employer families readily share all of their food, but in other households, certain higher-quality, expensive food items may remain off-limits to the live-in employees, who are instructed to eat hot dogs with the children. One Latina live-in nanny/housekeeper told me that in her employers' substantial pantry, little "DO NOT TOUCH" signs signaled which food items were not available to her; and another said that her employer was always defrosting freezer-burned leftovers for her to eat, some of it dating back nearly a decade.

Other women felt subtle pressure to remain unobtrusive, humble, and self-effacing, so they held back from eating even when they were hungry. They talked a lot about how these unspoken rules apply to fruit. "Look, if they [the employers] buy fruit, they buy three bananas, two apples, two pears. So if I eat one, who took it? It's me," one woman said, "they'll know it's me." Another nanny/housekeeper recalled: "They would bring home fruit, but without them having to say it, you just knew these were not intended for you. You understand this right away, you get it." Or as another put it, "*Las Americanas* have their apples counted out, one for each day of the week." Even fruits growing in the garden are sometimes contested. In Southern California's agriculture-friendly climate, many a residential home boasts fruit trees that hang heavy with oranges, plums, and peaches, and when the Latina women who work in these homes pick the fruit, they sometimes get in trouble. Eventually, many of the women solve the food problem by buying and bringing in their own food; early on Monday mornings, you see them walking with their plastic grocery bags, carting, say, a sack of apples, some chicken, and maybe some prepared food in plastic containers.

The issue of food captures the essence of how Latina live-in domestic workers feel about their jobs. It symbolizes the extent to which the families they work for draw the boundaries of exclusion or inclusion, and it marks the degree to which those families recognize the live-in nanny/housekeepers as human beings who have basic human needs.

When they first take their jobs, most live-in nanny/housekeepers do not anticipate spending any of their meager wages on food to eat while on the job, but in the end, most do—and sometimes the food they buy is eaten by members of the family for whom they work.

Although there is a wide range of pay, many Latina domestic workers in live-in jobs earn less than minimum wage for marathon hours: 93 percent of the live-in workers I surveyed in the mid-1990s were earning less than $5 an hour (79 percent of them below minimum wage, which was then $4.25), and they reported working an average of sixty-four hours a week. Some of the most astoundingly low rates were paid for live-in jobs in the households of other working-class Latino immigrants, which provide some women their first job when they arrive in Los Angeles. Carmen Vasquez, for example, had spent several years working as a live-in for two Mexican families, earning only $50 a week. By comparison, her current salary of $170 a week, which she was earning as a live-in nanny/housekeeper in the hillside home of an attorney and a teacher, seemed a princely sum.

Many people assume that the rich pay more than do families of modest means, but working as a live-in in an exclusive, wealthy neighborhood, or in a twenty-three-room house, provides no guarantee of a high salary. Early one Monday morning in the fall of 1995, I was standing with a group of live-in nanny/housekeepers on a corner across the street from the Beverly Hills Hotel. As they were waiting to be picked up by their employers, a large Mercedes sedan with two women (a daughter and mother or mother-in-law?) approached, rolled down the windows, and asked if anyone was interested in a $150-a-week live-in job. A few women jotted down the phone number, and no one was shocked by the offer. Gore Vidal once commented that no one is allowed to fail within a two-mile radius of the Beverly Hills Hotel, but it turns out that plenty of women in that vicinity are failing in the salary department. In some of the most affluent Westside areas of Los Angeles—in Malibu, Pacific Palisades, and Bel Air—there are live-in nanny/housekeepers earning $150 a week. And in 1999, the *Los Angeles Times* Sunday classified ads still listed live-in nanny/housekeeper jobs with pay as low as $100 and $125.[3] Salaries for live-in jobs, however, do go considerably higher. The best-paid live-in employee whom I interviewed was Patricia Paredes, a Mexicana who spoke impeccable English and who had legal status, substantial experience, and references. She told me that she currently earned $450 a week at her live-in job. She had been promised a raise to $550, after a room remodel was finished, when she would assume weekend housecleaning in that same home. With such a relatively high weekly salary she felt compelled to stay in a live-in job during the week, away from her husband and three young daughters who remained on the east side of Los Angeles. The salary level required that sacrifice.

But once they experience it, most women are repelled by live-in jobs. The lack of privacy, the mandated separation from family and friends, the round-the-clock hours, the food issues, the low pay, and especially the constant loneliness prompt most Latina immigrants to seek other job arrangements. Some young, single women who learn to speak English fluently try to move up the ranks into higher-paying live-in jobs. As soon as they can, however, the majority attempt to leave live-in work altogether. Most live-in nanny/housekeepers have

been in the United States for five years or less; among the live-in nanny/housekeepers I interviewed, only two (Carmen Vasquez and the relatively high-earning Patricia Paredes) had been in the United States for longer than that. Like African American women earlier in the century, who tired of what the historian Elizabeth Clark-Lewis has called "the soul-destroying hollowness of live-in domestic work,"[4] most Latina immigrants try to find other options.

Until the early 1900s, live-in jobs were the most common form of paid domestic work in the United States, but through the first half of the twentieth century they were gradually supplanted by domestic "day work." Live-in work never completely disappeared, however, and in the last decades of the twentieth century, it revived with vigor, given new life by the needs of American families with working parents and young children—and, as we have seen, by the needs of newly arrived Latina immigrants, many of them unmarried and unattached to families. When these women try to move up from live-in domestic work, they see few job alternatives. Often, the best they can do is switch to another form of paid domestic work, either as a live-out nanny/housekeeper or as a weekly housecleaner. When they do such day work, they are better able to circumscribe their work hours, and they earn more money in less time.

[3]Employment Classified Section 2, *Los Angeles Times,* June 6, 1999, 69.

[4]Clark-Lewis, Elizabeth. 1994. *Living In, Living Out: African American Domestics in Washington, D.C., 1910–1940.* Washington, D.C.: Smithsonian Institution Press. Pp. 123.

Selling in Minnesota

BARBARA EHRENREICH

For sheer grandeur, scale, and intimidation value, I doubt if any corporate orientation exceeds that of Wal-Mart. I have been told that the process will take eight hours, which will include two fifteen-minute breaks and one half-hour break for a meal, and will be paid for like a regular shift. When I arrive, dressed neatly in khakis and clean T-shirt, as befits a potential Wal-Mart "associate," I find there are ten new hires besides myself, mostly young and Caucasian, and a team of three, headed by Roberta, to do the "orientating." We sit around a long table in the same windowless room where I was interviewed, each with a thick folder of paperwork in front of us, and hear Roberta tell once again about raising six children, being a "people person," discovering that the three principles of Wal-Mart philosophy were the same as her own, and so on. We begin with a video, about fifteen minutes long, on the history and philosophy of Wal-Mart, or, as an anthropological observer might call it, the Cult of Sam. First young Sam Walton, in uniform, comes back from the war. He starts a store, a sort of five-and-dime; he marries and fathers four attractive children; he receives a Medal of Freedom from President Bush, after which he promptly dies, making way for the eulogies. But the company goes on, yes indeed. Here the arc of the story soars upward unstoppably, pausing only to mark some fresh

milestone of corporate expansion. 1992: Wal-Mart becomes the largest retailer in the world. 1997: Sales top $100 billion. 1998: The number of Wal-Mart associates hits 825,000, making Wal-Mart the largest private employer in the nation. Each landmark date is accompanied by a clip showing throngs of shoppers, swarms of associates, or scenes of handsome new stores and their adjoining parking lots. Over and over we hear in voiceover or see in graphic display the "three principles," which are maddeningly, even defiantly, nonparallel: "respect for the individual, exceeding customers' expectations, strive for excellence."

"Respect for the individual" is where we, the associates, come in, because vast as Wal-Mart is, and tiny as we may be as individuals, everything depends on us. Sam always said, and is shown saying, that "the best ideas come from the associates"—for example, the idea of having a "people greeter," an elderly employee (excuse me, associate) who welcomes each customer as he or she enters the store. Three times during the orientation, which began at three and stretches to nearly eleven, we are reminded that this brainstorm originated in a mere associate, and who knows what revolutions in retailing each one of us may propose? Because our ideas are welcome, more than welcome, and we are to think of our managers not as bosses but as "servant leaders," serving us as well as the customers. Of course, all is not total harmony, in every instance, between associates and their servant-leaders. A video on "associate honesty" shows a cashier being caught on videotape as he pockets

Source: Pages 143–169 from *Nickel and Dimed: On (Not) Getting By in America* by Barbara Ehrenreich. Copyright © 2001 by Barbara Ehrenreich. Reprinted by permission of Henry Holt and Company, LLC.

some bills from the cash register. Drums beat ominously as he is led away in handcuffs and sentenced to four years.

The theme of covert tensions, overcome by right thinking and positive attitude, continues in the twelve-minute video entitled *You've Picked a Great Place to Work.* Here various associates testify to the "essential feeling of family for which Wal-Mart is so well-known," leading up to the conclusion that we don't need a union. Once, long ago, unions had a place in American society, but they "no longer have much to offer workers," which is why people are leaving them "by the droves." Wal-Mart is booming; unions are declining: judge for yourself. But we are warned that "unions have been targeting Wal-Mart for years." Why? For the dues money of course. Think of what you would lose with a union: first, your dues money, which could be $20 a month "and sometimes much more." Second, you would lose "your voice" because the union would insist on doing your talking for you. Finally, you might lose even your wages and benefits because they would all be "at risk on the bargaining table." You have to wonder—and I imagine some of my teenage fellow orientees may be doing so—why such fiends as these union organizers, such outright extortionists, are allowed to roam free in the land.

There is more, much more than I could ever absorb, even if it were spread out over a semester-long course. On the reasonable assumption that none of us is planning to go home and curl up with the "Wal-Mart Associate Handbook," our trainers start reading it out loud to us, pausing every few paragraphs to ask, "Any questions?" There never are. Barry, the seventeen-year-old to my left, mutters that his "butt hurts." Sonya, the tiny African American woman across from me, seems frozen in terror. I have given up on looking perky and am fighting to keep my eyes open. No nose or other facial jewelry, we learn; earrings must be small and discreet, not dangling; no blue jeans except on Friday, and then you have to pay $1 for the privilege of wearing them. No "grazing," that is, eating from food packages that somehow become open;

no "time theft." This last sends me drifting off in a sci-fi direction: *And as the time thieves headed back to the year 3420, loaded with weekends and days off looted from the twenty-first century . . .* Finally, a question. The old guy who is being hired as a people greeter wants to know, "What is time theft?" Answer: Doing anything other than working during company time, anything at all. Theft of *our* time is not, however, an issue. There are stretches amounting to many minutes when all three of our trainers wander off, leaving us to sit there in silence or take the opportunity to squirm. Or our junior trainers go through a section of the handbook, and then Roberta, returning from some other business, goes over the same section again. My eyelids droop and I consider walking out. I have seen time move more swiftly during seven-hour airline delays. In fact, I am getting nostalgic about seven-hour airline delays. At least you can read a book or get up and walk around, take a leak.

On breaks, I drink coffee purchased at the Radio Grill, as the in-house fast-food place is called, the real stuff with caffeine, more because I'm concerned about being alert for the late-night drive home than out of any need to absorb all the Wal-Mart trivia coming my way. Now, here's a drug the drug warriors ought to take a little more interest in. Since I don't normally drink it at all—iced tea can usually be counted on for enough of a kick—the coffee has an effect like reagent-grade Dexedrine: my pulse races, my brain overheats, and the result in this instance is a kind of delirium. I find myself overly challenged by the little kindergarten-level tasks we are now given to do, such as affixing my personal bar code to my ID card, then sticking on the punch-out letters to spell my name. The letters keep curling up and sticking to my fingers, so I stop at "Barb," or more precisely, "B*A*R*B*," drifting off to think of all the people I know who have gentrified their names in recent years—Patsy to Patricia, Dick to Richard, and so forth—while I am going in the other direction. Now we start taking turns going to the computers to begin our CBL, or Computer-Based Learning, and I become transfixed by the HIV-inspired module entitled "Bloodborne Pathogens," on what to do in the event that pools of human blood should show up on the sales floor. All right, you put warning cones around the puddles, don protective gloves, etc., but I can't stop trying to envision the circumstances in which these pools might arise: an associate uprising? a guest riot? I have gone through six modules, three more than we are supposed to do tonight—the rest are to be done in our spare moments over the next few weeks—when one of the trainers gently pries me away from the computer. We are allowed now to leave.

There follows the worst of many sleepless nights to come. On the drive home along the interstate, a guy doing over eighty passes me on the right at a few angstroms' distance, making the point that any highway has far more exits than you can see, infinitely many—final exits, that is. At this hour, which is nearly midnight, it takes me fifteen minutes to find a parking place, and another five to walk to the apartment, where I find that Budgie, distraught by my long absence, has gone totally postal. Feathers litter the floor under his cage, and he refuses to return to it even after a generous forty-five minutes of head time. I want to be fresh for my first day in plumbing tomorrow—Menards is still my choice—but a lot of small things have been going wrong, and at this level of finances, nothing wrong is ever quite small enough. My watch battery ran out and I had to spend $11 to get it replaced. My khakis developed a prominent ink stain that took three wash cycles ($3.75) and a treatment with Shout Gel ($1.29) to remove. There was the $20 application fee at the Park Plaza, plus $20 for the belt I need for Menards, purchased only after comparison shopping at a consignment store. And why hadn't I asked what that knife and tape measure are going to cost? I discover that the phone is no longer taking incoming calls or recording voice mail, so who knows what housing opportunities I have missed. Around two in the morning, I pop a Unisom to counteract the still-raging caffeine, but at five Budgie takes his revenge, greeting the prospect of dawn, which is still comfortably remote, with a series of scandalized squawks.

I am due at Menards at noon. At this point, although I have not formally accepted either job, I realize I am officially employed at both places, Wal-Mart and Menards. Maybe I'll combine both jobs or just blow off Wal-Mart and go for the better money at Menards. But Wal-Mart, with its endless orientation, has, alas, already sunk its talons into me. People working more than one job—and in effect I would be doing that for a day by going from my three-to-eleven stint at Wal-Mart to a day at Menards—have to take sleep deprivation in stride. I do not. I am shaky, my brain fried like that egg in the Partnership for a Drug-Free America commercial. How am I going to master the science of plumbing products when I can barely summon the concentration required to assemble a breakfast of peanut butter and toast? The world is coming at me in high-contrast snapshots, deprived of narrative continuity. I call Menards and get Paul on the line to clear up what exactly my shift is supposed to be. Steve—or was it Walt?—said noon till eleven, but that would be eleven hours, right?

"Right," he says. "You want to be full-time, don't you?"

And you're going to pay me ten dollars an hour?

"Ten dollars?" Paul asks, "Who told you ten?" He'll have to check on that; it can't be right.

Now thoroughly unnerved, I tell him I'm not working an eleven-hour shift, not without time and a half after eight. I don't tell him about the generations of workers who fought and sometimes died for the ten-hour day and then the eight, although this is very much on my mind.[1] I just tell him I'm going to send my knife, my vest, and my tape measure back. In the days that follow I will try to rationalize this decision by telling myself that, given Wal-Mart's position as the nation's largest private employer, whatever I experience there will

---

[1] Under the Fair Labor Standards Act it is in fact illegal not to pay time and a half for hours worked above forty hours a week. Certain categories of workers—professionals, managers, and farmworkers—are not covered by the FLSA, but retail workers are not among them.

at least be of grand social significance. But this is just a way of prettifying yet another dumb mistake, the one involving all that coffee. The embarrassing truth is that I am just too exhausted to work, especially for eleven hours in a row.

Why hadn't I asked all these questions about wages and hours before? For that matter, why hadn't I bargained with Roberta when she called to tell me I'd passed the drug test—told her $7 an hour would be fine, as long as the benefits included a free lakeside condo with hot tub? At least part of the answer, which I only figured out weeks later, lies in the employers' deft handling of the hiring process. First you are an applicant, then suddenly you are an orientee. You're handed the application form and, a few days later, you're being handed the uniform and warned against nose rings and stealing. There's no intermediate point in the process in which you confront the potential employer as a free agent, entitled to cut her own deal. The intercalation of the drug test between application and hiring tilts the playing field even further, establishing that you, and not the employer, are the one who has something to prove. Even in the tightest labor market—and it doesn't get any tighter than Minneapolis, where I would probably have been welcome to apply at any commercial establishment I entered—the person who has precious labor to sell can be made to feel one down, way down, like a supplicant with her hand stretched out.

It's Saturday and the time has come to leave my free lodgings and neurotic avian roommate. A few hours before my hosts are scheduled to return, I pack up and head down to Twin Lakes, where—no big surprise—I find out that all the second-story rooms have been taken. The particular room I'd requested, which looks out on a backyard instead of a parking lot, is now occupied by a woman with a child, the owner tells me, and he is good enough to feel uncomfortable about asking them to move to a smaller one. So I decide that this is my out and call another weekly rental place on my list, the Clearview Inn (not its real name), which has two big advantages: it's about a twenty-minute drive

from my Wal-Mart, as opposed to at least forty-five in the case of Twin Lakes, and the weekly rate is $245, compared to $295. This is still scandalously high, higher in fact than my aftertax weekly pay will amount to. But in our latest conversation Hildy has promised me a room with kitchenette by the end of next week, and I am confident I can get a weekend job at the supermarket I applied to, in bakery if I am lucky.

To say that some place is the worst motel in the country is, of course, to set oneself up for considerable challenge.[2] I have encountered plenty of contenders in my own travels—the one in Cleveland that turned into a brothel at night, the one in Butte where the window looked out into another room. Still, the Clearview Inn leaves the competition in the dust. I slide $255 in cash (the extra $10 is for telephone service) under the glass window that separates me from the young East Indian owner—East Indians seem to have a lock on the midwestern motel business—and am taken by his wife to a room memorable only for its overwhelming stench of mold. I don't have enough Claritin-D for this situation, a point I have to make by holding my nose, since her English does not extend to the concept of allergy. Air freshener? she suggests when she catches my meaning. Incense? There is a better room, her husband says when we return to the office, but—and here he fixes me with a narrow-eyed stare—I'd better not "trash" it. I attempt a reassuring chuckle, but the warning rankles for days: have I been fooling myself all these years, thinking I look like a mature and sober person when in fact anyone can see I'm a vandal?

Room 133 contains a bed, a chair, a chest of drawers, and a TV fastened to the wall. I plead for and get a lamp to supplement the single overhead

---

[2]I may have to withdraw my claim. Until it was closed for fire code violations in 1997, the Parkway Motel in southern Maryland boasted exposed electrical wires, holes in room doors, and raw sewage on bathroom floors. But if price is entered into the competition, the Clearview Inn may still win, since the Parkway was charging only $20 a day at the time (Todd Shields, "Charles Cracks Down on Dilapidated Motels," *Washington Post,* April 20, 1997).

bulb. Instead of the mold smell, I now breathe a mixture of fresh paint and what I eventually identify as mouse droppings. But the real problems are all window- and door-related: the single small window has no screen, and the room has no AC or fan. The curtain is transparently thin; the door has no bolt. Without a screen, the window should be sensibly closed at night, meaning no air, unless I'm willing to take my chances with the bugs and the neighbors. Who are the neighbors? The motel forms a toilet-seat shape around the parking lot, and I can see an inexplicable collection. A woman with a baby in her arms leans in the doorway of one room. Two bunches of teenagers, one group black and the other white, seem to share adjoining rooms. There are several unencumbered men of various ages, including an older white man in work clothes whose bumper sticker says, "Don't steal, the government hates competition"—as if the income tax were the only thing keeping him from living at the Embassy Suites right now. When it gets dark I go outside and look through my curtain, and yes, you can see pretty much everything, at least in silhouette. I eat the deli food I've brought with me from a Minneapolis supermarket and go to bed with my clothes on, but not to sleep.

I am not a congenitally fearful person, for which you can blame or credit my mother, who never got around to alerting me to any special vulnerabilities that went with being a girl. Only when I got to college did I begin to grasp what rape involves and discover that my custom of exploring strange cities alone, on foot, day or night, looked more reckless to others than eccentric. I had no misgivings about the trailer park in Key West or the motel in Maine, but the trailer's door had a bolt, and both had effective shades and screens. Here, only the stuffiness of the air with the window shut reminds me that I'm really indoors; otherwise I'm pretty much open to anyone's view or to anything that might drift in from the highway, and I wouldn't want to depend on my hosts for help. I think of wearing earplugs to block out the TV sounds from the next room and my sleep mask to cut the light from the Dr Pepper sign on the pop machine in the parking lot. Then I

decide it's smarter to keep all senses on ready alert. I sleep and wake up, sleep and wake up again, listen to the cars coming and going, watch the silhouettes move past my window.

Sometime around four in the morning it dawns on me that it's not just that I'm a wimp. Poor women—perhaps especially single ones and even those who are just temporarily living among the poor for whatever reason—really do have more to fear than women who have houses with double locks and alarm systems and husbands or dogs. I must have known this theoretically or at least heard it stated, but now for the first time the lesson takes hold.

So this is the home from which I go forth on Monday to begin my life as a Wal-Martian. After the rigors of orientation, I am expecting a highly structured welcome, perhaps a ceremonial donning of my bright blue Wal-Mart vest and a forty-five minute training on the operation of the vending machines in the break room. But when I arrive in the morning for the ten-to-six shift, no one seems to be expecting me. I'm in "softlines," which has a wonderful, sinuous sound to it, but I have no idea what it means. Someone in personnel tells me I'm in ladies' wear (a division of softlines, I learn) and sends me to the counter next to the fitting rooms, where I am passed around from one person to the next—finally ending up with Ellie, whose lack of a vest signals that she is management. She sets me to work "zoning" the Bobbie Brooks knit summer dresses, a task that could serve as an IQ test for the severely cognitively challenged. First the dresses must be grouped by color—olive, peach, or lavender, in this case—then by decorative pattern—the leafy design on the bodice, the single flower, or the grouped flowers—and within each pattern by size. When I am finished, though hardly exhausted by the effort, I meet Melissa, who is, with only a couple of weeks on the job, pretty much my equivalent. She asks me to help her consolidate the Kathie Lee knit dresses so the Kathie Lee silky ones can take their place at the "image," the high-traffic corner area. I learn, in a couple of hours of scattered exchanges, that Melissa was a waitress before this job, that her husband works in construction and her children are grown. There have been some disorganized patches in her life—an out-of-wedlock child, a problem with alcohol and drugs—but that's all over now that she has given her life to Christ.

Our job, it emerges in fragments throughout the day, is to keep ladies' wear "shoppable." Sure, we help customers (who are increasingly called "guests" here as well), if they want any help. At first I go around practicing the "aggressive hospitality" demanded by our training videos: as soon as anyone comes within ten feet of a sales associate, that associate is supposed to smile warmly and offer assistance. But I never see a more experienced associate do this—first, because the customers are often annoyed to have their shopping dazes interrupted and, second, because we have far more pressing things to do. In ladies' wear, the big task, which has no real equivalent in, say, housewares or lawn and garden, is to put away the "returns"—clothes that have been tried on and rejected or, more rarely, purchased and then returned to the store. There are also the many items that have been scattered by customers, dropped on the floor, removed from their hangers and strewn over the racks, or secreted in locations far from their natural homes. Each of these items, too, must be returned to its precise place, matched by color, pattern, price, and size. Any leftover time is to be devoted to zoning. When I relate this to Caroline on the phone, she commiserates, "Ugh, a no-brainer."

But no job is as easy as it looks to the uninitiated. I have to put clothes away—the question is, Where? Much of my first few days is devoted to trying to memorize the layout of ladies' wear, one thousand (two thousand?) square feet of space bordered by men's wear, children's wear, greeting cards, and underwear. Standing at the fitting rooms and facing toward the main store entrance, we are looking directly at the tentlike, utilitarian plus sizes, also known as "woman" sizes. These are flanked on the left by our dressiest and costliest line (going up to $29 and change), the all-polyester Kathie Lee

collection, suitable for dates and subprofessional levels of office work. Moving clockwise, we encounter the determinedly sexless Russ and Bobbie Brooks lines, seemingly aimed at pudgy fourth-grade teachers with important barbecues to attend. Then, after the sturdy White Stag, come the breezy, revealing Faded Glory, No Boundaries, and Jordache collections, designed for the younger and thinner crowd. Tucked throughout are nests of the lesser brands, such as Athletic Works, Basic Equipment, and the whimsical Looney Tunes, Pooh, and Mickey lines, generally decorated with images of their eponymous characters. Within each brand-name area, there are of course dozens of items, even dozens of each *kind* of item. This summer, for example, pants may be capri, classic, carpenter, clam-digger, boot, or flood, depending on their length and cut, and I'm probably leaving a few categories out. So my characteristic stance is one of rotating slowly on one foot, eyes wide, garment in hand, asking myself, "Where have I seen the $9.96 Athletic Works knit overalls?" or similar query. Inevitably there are mystery items requiring extra time and inquiry: clothes that have wandered over from girls' or men's, clearanced items whose tags haven't been changed to reflect their new prices, the occasional one-of-a-kind.

Then, when I have the layout memorized, it suddenly changes. On my third morning I find, after a few futile searches, that the Russ shirt-and-short combinations have edged Kathie Lee out of her image. When I groaningly accuse Ellie of trying to trick me into thinking I'm getting Alzheimer's, she's genuinely apologetic, explaining that the average customer shops the store three times a week, so you need to have the element of surprise. Besides, the layout is about the only thing she *can* control, since the clothes and at least the starting prices are all determined by the home office in Arkansas. So as fast as I can memorize, she furiously rearranges.

My first response to the work is disappointment and a kind of sexist contempt. I could have been in plumbing, mastering the vocabulary of valves, dangling tools from my belt, joshing around with

Steve and Walt, and instead the mission of the moment is to return a pink bikini top to its place on the Bermuda swimwear rack. Nothing is heavy or, as far as I can see, very urgent. No one will go hungry or die or be hurt if I screw up; in fact, how would anyone ever know if I screwed up, given the customers' constant depredations? I feel oppressed, too, by the mandatory gentility of Wal-Mart culture. This is ladies' and we are all "ladies" here, forbidden, by storewide rule, to raise our voices or cuss. Give me a few weeks of this and I'll femme out entirely, my stride will be reduced to a mince, I'll start tucking my head down to one side.

My job is not, however, as genteel as it at first appears, thanks to the sheer volume of clothing in motion. At Wal-Mart, as opposed to say Lord & Taylor, customers shop with supermarket-style shopping carts, which they can fill to the brim before proceeding to the fitting room. There the rejected items, which are about 90 percent of try-ons, are folded and put on hangers by whoever is staffing the fitting room, then placed in fresh shopping carts for Melissa and me. So this is how we measure our workload—in carts. When I get in, Melissa, whose shift begins earlier than mine, will tell me how things have been going—"Can you believe, eight carts this morning!"—and how many carts are awaiting me. At first a cart takes me an average of forty-five minutes and there may still be three or four mystery items left at the bottom. I get this down to half an hour, and still the carts keep coming.

Most of the time, the work requires minimal human interaction, of either the collegial or the supervisory sort, largely because it's so self-defining. I arrive at the start of a shift or the end of a break, assess the damage wrought by the guests in my absence, count the full carts that await me, and plunge in. I could be a deaf-mute as far as most of this goes, and despite all the orientation directives to smile and exude personal warmth, autism might be a definite advantage. Sometimes, if things are slow, Melissa and I will invent a task we can do together—zoning swimsuits, for example, a nightmarish tangle of straps—and giggle, she in her

Christian way, me from a more feminist perspective, about the useless little see-through wraps meant to accompany the more revealing among them. Or sometimes Ellie will give me something special to do, like putting all the Basic Equipment T-shirts on hangers, because things on hangers sell faster, and then arranging them neatly on racks. I like Ellie. Gray-faced and fiftyish, she must be the apotheosis of "servant leadership" or, in more secular terms, the vaunted "feminine" style of management. She says "please" and "thank you"; she doesn't order, she asks. Not so, though, with young Howard—*assistant manager* Howard, as he is uniformly called—who rules over all of softlines, including infants', children's, men's, accessories, and underwear. On my first day, I am called off the floor to an associates' meeting, where he spends ten minutes taking attendance, fixing each of us with his unnerving Tom Cruise–style smile, in which the brows come together as the corners of the mouth turn up, then reveals (where have I heard this before?) his "pet peeve": associates standing around talking to one another, which is, of course, a prime example of time theft.

A few days into my career at Wal-Mart, I return home to the Clearview to find the door to my room open and the motel owner waiting outside. There's been a "problem"—the sewage has backed up and is all over the floor, though fortunately my suitcase is OK. I am to move into Room 127, which will be better because it has a screen. But the screen turns out to be in tatters, not even fastened at the bottom, just flapping uselessly in the breeze. I ask for a real screen, and he tells me he doesn't have any that fit. I ask for a fan and he doesn't have any that work. I ask why—I mean, this is supposedly a working motel—and he rolls his eyes, apparently indicating my fellow residents: "I could tell you stories . . ."

So I lug my possessions down to 127 and start trying to reconstruct my little domestic life. Since I don't have a kitchen, I have what I call my food bag, a supermarket bag containing my tea bags, a few pieces of fruit, various condiment packets salvaged from fast-food places, and a half dozen string cheeses, which their labels say are supposed to be refrigerated but I figure are safe in their plastic wraps. I have my laptop computer, the essential link to my normal profession, and it has become a matter of increasing concern. I figure it's probably the costliest portable item in the entire Clearview Inn, so I hesitate to leave it in my room for the nine or so hours while I'm away at work. During the first couple of days at Wal-Mart, the weather was cool and I kept it in the trunk of my car. But now, with the temperature rising to the nineties at midday, I worry that it'll cook in the trunk. More to the point at the moment is the state of my clothing, most of which is now residing in the other brown paper bag, the one that serves as a hamper. My khakis have a day or two left in them and two clean T-shirts remain until the next trip to a Laundromat, but a question has been raised about the T-shirts. That afternoon Alyssa, one of my co-orientees, now in sporting goods, had come by ladies' to inquire about a polo shirt that had been clearanced at $7. Was there any chance it might fall still further? Of course I had no idea—Ellie decides about clearancing—but why was Alyssa so fixated on this particular shirt? Because one of the rules is that our shirts have to have collars, so they have to be polos, not tees. Somehow I'd missed this during orientation, and now I'm wondering how long I have before my stark-naked neck catches Howard's attention. At $7 an hour, a $7 shirt is just not going to make it to my shopping list.

Now it's after seven and time to resume my daily routine at the evening food-gathering phase. The town of Clearview presents only two low-priced options (there are no high-priced options) to its kitchenless residents—a Chinese all-you-can-eat buffet or Kentucky Fried Chicken—each with its own entertainment possibilities. If I eat out at the buffet I can watch the large Mexican families or the even larger, in total body mass terms, families of Minnesota Anglos. If I eat KFC in my room, I can watch TV on one of the half dozen available channels. The latter option seems somehow less lonely, especially if I can find one

of my favorite programs—*Titus* or *Third Rock from the Sun*. Eating is tricky without a table. I put the food on the chest of drawers and place a plastic supermarket bag over my lap, since spills are hard to avoid when you eat on a slant and spills mean time and money at the Laundromat. Tonight I find the new sensation, *Survivor,* on CBS, where "real people" are struggling to light a fire on their desert island. Who are these nutcases who would volunteer for an artificially daunting situation in order to entertain millions of strangers with their half-assed efforts to survive? Then I remember where I am and why I am here.

Dinner over, I put the remains in the plastic bag that served as a tablecloth and tie it up tightly to discourage the flies that have free access to my essentially screenless abode. I do my evening things—writing in my journal and reading a novel—then turn out the lights and sit for a while by the open door for some air. The two African American men who live in the room next door have theirs open too, and since it's sometimes open in the daytime as well, I've noticed that their room, like mine, has only one bed. This is no gay tryst, though, because they seem to take turns in the bed, one sleeping in the room and the other one napping in their van outside. I shut the door, put the window down, and undress in the dark so I can't be seen through the window. I still haven't found out much about my fellow Clearview dwellers—it's bad enough being a woman alone, especially a woman rich enough to have a bed of her own, without being nosy on top of that. As far as I can tell, the place isn't a nest of drug dealers and prostitutes; these are just working people who don't have the capital to rent a normal apartment. Even the teenagers who worried me at first seem to have mother figures attached to them, probably single mothers I hadn't seen before because they were at work.

Finally I lie down and breathe against the weight of unmoving air on my chest. I wake up a few hours later to hear a sound not generated by anyone's TV: a woman's clear alto singing two lines of the world's saddest song, lyrics indecipherable, to the accompaniment of trucks on the highway.

Morning begins with a trip, by car, to the Holiday gas station's convenience store, where I buy a pop container full of ice and a packet of two hard-boiled eggs. The ice, a commodity unavailable at the motel, is for iced tea, which I brew by letting tea bags soak in a plastic cup of water overnight. After breakfast I tidy up my room, making the bed, wiping the sink with a wad of toilet paper, and taking the garbage out to the Dumpster. True, the owner's wife (or maybe she's the co-owner) goes around from room to room every morning with a cleaning cart, but her efforts show signs of deep depression or possibly attention deficit disorder. Usually she remembers to replace the thin little towels, which, even when clean, contain embedded hairs and smell like cooking grease, but there's nothing else, except maybe an abandoned rag or bottle of air freshener, to suggest that she's been through on her rounds. I picture an ad for a "traditional-minded, hardworking wife," a wedding in her natal village, then—plop—she's in Clearview, Minnesota, with an Indian American husband who may not even speak her language, thousands of miles from family, a temple, a sari shop.[3] So I clean up myself, then do my hair with enough bobby pins to last through the shift, and head off for work. The idea is to make myself look like someone who's spent the night in a regular home with kitchen and washer and dryer, not like someone who's borderline homeless.

The other point of my domestic rituals and arrangements is to get through the time when I can't be at work, when it would look weird to be hanging around in the Wal-Mart parking lot or break room. Because home life is more stressful than I have consciously acknowledged, and I would be dreading my upcoming day off if I weren't confident of spending it on the move to better

quarters at the Hopkins Park Plaza. Little nervous symptoms have arisen. Sometimes I get a tummy ache after breakfast, which makes lunch dicey, and there's no way to get through the shift without at least one major refueling. More disturbing is the new habit of plucking away at my shirt or my khakis with whichever hand can be freed up for the task. I have to stop this. My maternal grandmother, who still lives on, in a fashion, at the age of a hundred and one, was a perfect model of stoicism, but she used to pick at her face and her wrist, creating dark red circular sores, and claimed not to know she was doing it. Maybe it's an inheritable twitch and I will soon be moving on from fabric to flesh.

I arrive at work full of bounce, pausing at the fitting room to jolly up the lady on duty—usually the bossy, self-satisfied Rhoda—because the fitting room lady bears the same kind of relation to me as a cook to a server: she can screw me up if she wants, giving me carts contaminated with foreign, nonladies' items and items not properly folded or hangered. "Here I am," I announce grandiosely, spreading out my arms. "The day can begin!" For this I get a wrinkled nose from Rhoda and a one-sided grin from Lynne, the gaunt blonde who's working bras. I search out Ellie, whom I find shooting out new labels from the pricing gun, and ask if there's anything special I need to be doing. No, just whatever needs to be done. Next I find Melissa to get a report on the cartage so far. Today she seems embarrassed when she sees me: "I probably shouldn't have done this and you're going to think it's really silly . . ." but she's brought me a sandwich for lunch. This is because I'd told her I was living in a motel almost entirely on fast food, and she felt sorry for me. Now *I'm* embarrassed, and beyond that overwhelmed to discover a covert stream of generosity running counter to the dominant corporate miserliness. Melissa probably wouldn't think of herself as poor, but I know she calculates in very small units of currency, twice reminding me, for example, that you can get sixty-eight cents off the specials at the Radio Grill every Tuesday, so a sandwich is something to consider. I

---

[3] I thank Sona Pai, an Indian American graduate student in literary nonfiction at the University of Oregon, for giving me a glimpse into the Indian American motel-operating community and the lives of immigrant brides.

set off with my cart, muttering contentedly, "Bobbie Brooks turquoise elastic-waist shorts" and "Faded Glory V-neck red tank top."

Then, in my second week, two things change. My shift changes from 10:00–6:00 to 2:00–11:00, the so-called closing shift, although the store remains open 24/7. No one tells me this; I find it out by studying the schedules that are posted, under glass, on the wall outside the break room. Now I have nine hours instead of eight, and although one of them is an unpaid dinner hour, I have a net half an hour a day more on my feet. My two fifteen-minute breaks, which seemed almost superfluous on the 10:00–6:00 shift, now become a matter of urgent calculation. Do I take both before dinner, which is usually about 7:30, leaving an unbroken two-and-a-half-hour stretch when I'm weariest, between 8:30 and 11:00? Or do I try to go two and a half hours without a break in the afternoon, followed by a nearly three-hour marathon before I can get away for dinner? Then there's the question of how to make the best use of a fifteen-minute break when you have three or more urgent, simultaneous needs—to pee, to drink something, to get outside the neon and into the natural light, and most of all, to sit down. I save about a minute by engaging in a little time theft and stopping at the rest room before I punch out for the break (and, yes, we have to punch out even for breaks, so there's no padding them with a few stolen minutes). From the time clock it's a seventy-five-second walk to the store exit; if I stop at the Radio Grill, I could end up wasting a full four minutes waiting in line, not to mention the fifty-nine cents for a small-sized iced tea. So if I treat myself to an outing in the tiny fenced-off area beside the store, the only place where employees are allowed to smoke, I get about nine minutes off my feet.

The other thing that happens is that the post–Memorial Day weekend lull definitely comes to an end. Now there are always a dozen or more shoppers rooting around in ladies', reinforced in the evening by a wave of multigenerational gangs—Grandma, Mom, a baby in the shopping cart, and a gaggle of sullen children in tow. New tasks arise, such as bunching up the carts left behind by customers and steering them to their place in the front of the store every half hour or so. Now I am picking up not only dropped clothes but all the odd items customers carry off from foreign departments and decide to leave with us in ladies'—pillows, upholstery hooks, Pokémon cards, earrings, sunglasses, stuffed animals, even a package of cinnamon buns. And always there are the returns, augmented now by the huge volume of items that have been tossed on the floor or carried recklessly to inappropriate sites. Sometimes I am lucky to achieve a steady state between replacing the returns and picking up items strewn on the racks and the floor. If I pick up misplaced items as quickly as I replace the returns, my cart never empties and things back up dangerously at the fitting room, where Rhoda or her nighttime replacement is likely to hiss: "You've got three carts waiting, Barb. What's the *problem*?" Think Sisyphus here or the sorcerer's apprentice.

Still, for the first half of my shift, I am the very picture of good-natured helpfulness, fascinated by the multiethnic array of our shoppers—Middle Eastern, Asian, African American, Russian, former Yugoslavian, old-fashioned Minnesota white—and calmly accepting of the second law of thermodynamics, the one that says entropy always wins. Amazingly, I get praised by Isabelle, the thin little seventyish lady who seems to be Ellie's adjutant: I am doing "wonderfully," she tells me, and—even better—am "great to work with." I prance from rack to rack, I preen. But then, somewhere around 6:00 or 7:00, when the desire to sit down becomes a serious craving, a Dr. Jekyll/Mr. Hyde transformation sets in. I cannot ignore the fact that it's the customers' sloppiness and idle whims that make me bend and crouch and run. They are the shoppers, I am the antishopper, whose goal is to make it look as if they'd never been in the store. At this point, "aggressive hospitality" gives way to aggressive hostility. Their carts bang into mine, their children run amok. Once I stand and watch helplessly while some rug rat pulls everything he can reach off the racks, and the thought that abortion is wasted on the unborn must show on my face, because his mother finally tells him to stop.

I even start hating the customers for extraneous reasons, such as, in the case of the native Caucasians, their size. I don't mean just bellies and butts, but huge bulges in completely exotic locations, like the backs of the neck and the knees. This summer, Wendy's, where I often buy lunch, has introduced the verb *biggiesize,* as in "Would you like to biggiesize that combo?" meaning double the fries and pop, and something like biggiesizing seems to have happened to the female guest population. All right, everyone knows that midwesterners, and especially those in the lower middle class, are tragically burdened by the residues of decades of potato chips and French toast sticks, and I probably shouldn't even bring this up. In my early-shift, Dr. Jekyll form, I feel sorry for the obese, who must choose from among our hideous woman-size offerings, our drawstring shorts, and huge horizontally striped tees, which are obviously designed to mock them. But compassion fades as the shift wears on. Those of us who work in ladies' are for obvious reasons a pretty lean lot—probably, by Minnesota standards, candidates for emergency IV nutritional supplementation—and we live with the fear of being crushed by some wide-body as she hurtles through the narrow passage from Faded Glory to woman size, lost in fantasies involving svelte Kathie Lee sheaths.

It's the clothes I relate to, though, not the customers. And now a funny thing happens to me here on my new shift: I start thinking they're mine, not mine to take home and wear, because I have no such designs on them, just mine to organize and rule over. Same with ladies' wear as a whole. After 6:00, when Melissa and Ellie go home, and especially after 9:00, when Isabelle leaves, I start to *own* the place. Out of the way, Sam, this is Bar-Mart now. I patrol the perimeter with my cart, darting in to pick up misplaced and fallen items, making everything look spiffy from the outside. I don't fondle the clothes, the way customers do; I slap them into place, commanding them to hang straight, at attention, or lie subdued on the shelves

in perfect order. In this frame of mind, the last thing I want to see is a customer riffling around, disturbing the place. In fact, I hate the idea of things being sold—uprooted from their natural homes, whisked off to some closet that's in God-knows-what state of disorder. I want ladies' wear sealed off in a plastic bubble and trucked away to some place of safety, some museum of retail history.

One night I come back bone-tired from my last break and am distressed to find a new person, an Asian American or possibly Hispanic woman who can't be more than four and a half feet tall, folding T-shirts in the White Stag area, *my* White Stag area. It's already been a vexing evening. Earlier, when I'd returned from dinner, the evening fitting room lady upbraided me for being late—which I actually wasn't—and said that if Howard knew, he probably wouldn't yell at me this time because I'm still pretty new, but if it happened again . . . And I'd snapped back that I could care less if Howard yelled at me, which is a difficult sentiment to fully convey without access to the forbidden four-letter words. So I'm a little wary with this intruder in White Stag and, sure enough, after our minimal introductions, she turns on me.

"Did you put anything away here today?" she demands.

"Well, yes, sure." In fact I've put something away everywhere today, as I do on every other day.

"Because this is not in the right place. See the fabric—it's different," and she thrusts the errant item up toward my chest.

True, I can see that this olive-green shirt is slightly ribbed while the others are smooth. "You've *got* to put them in their right places," she continues. "Are you checking the UPC numbers?"

Of course I am not checking the ten or more digit UPC numbers, which lie just under the bar codes—nobody does. What does she think this is, the National Academy of Sciences? I'm not sure what kind of deference, if any, is due here: Is she my supervisor now? Or are we involved in some kind of test to see who will dominate the 9:00–11:00 time period? But I don't care, she's pissing me off, messing with my stuff. So I say, only without the numerals or the forbidden curse word, that (1) plenty of other people work here during the day, not to mention all the customers coming through, so why is she blaming me? (2) it's after 10:00 and I've got another cart full of returns to go, and wouldn't it make more sense if we both worked on the carts, instead of zoning the goddamn T-shirts?

To which she responds huffily, "I don't *do* returns. My job is to *fold*."

A few minutes later I see why she doesn't do returns—she can't reach the racks. In fact, she has to use a ladder even to get to the higher shelves. And you know what I feel when I see the poor little mite pushing that ladder around? A surge of evil mirth. I peer around from where I am working in Jordache, hoping to see her go splat.

I leave that night shaken by my response to the intruder. If she's a supervisor, I could be written up for what I said, but even worse is what I thought. Am I turning mean here, and is that a normal response to the end of a nine-hour shift? There was another outbreak of mental wickedness that night. I'd gone back to the counter by the fitting room to pick up the next cart full of returns and found the guy who answers the phone at the counter at night, a pensive young fellow in a wheelchair, staring into space, looking even sadder than usual. And my uncensored thought was, At least you get to sit down.

This is not me, at least not any version of me I'd like to spend much time with, just as my tiny coworker is probably not usually a bitch. She's someone who works all night and naps during the day when her baby does, I find out later, along with the information that she's not anyone's supervisor and is in fact subject to constant criticism by Isabelle when the two overlap. What I have to face is that "Barb," the name on my ID tag, is not exactly the same person as Barbara. "Barb" is what I was called as a child, and still am by my siblings, and I sense that at some level I'm regressing. Take away the career and the higher education, and maybe what you're left with is this original Barb, the one who might have ended up working at Wal-Mart for real if her father hadn't managed to climb out of the mines. So it's interesting, and more than a little disturbing, to see how Barb turned out—that she's meaner and slyer than I am, more cherishing of grudges, and not quite as smart as I'd hoped.

Members Only: Organizational Structure and Patterns of Exclusion

DIANA KENDALL

Historically, elite women's volunteer groups have been viewed as informal structures somewhat akin to a coffee klatch. For example, a number of years ago a male executive with the American Symphony Orchestra League said, "Give me six women, a tea pot and a handful of cookies—and I will give you a symphony orchestra."[1] Even though elite women volunteers in the past may have casually sat around a table, devising ways to raise money to support orchestras and other nonprofit causes, many contemporary women participate in volunteer organizations that are much more formally organized. The membership practices of these bureaucratically structured organizations are set forth in written bylaws that have been voted on and approved by the membership. As we will see, these bylaws can be used in a manner that excludes entire categories of other women—even on the basis of race or religion—although on their face, the provisions do not appear to have that purpose. However, spokespersons for organizations such as the Junior League and women's orchestra volunteer groups emphasize that their groups have been restructured in recent years to change their "elitist" public image. An example is this comment by a member of the New Orleans Junior League:

> [Our members] took off the white gloves and put on the work gloves. But people often have a warped view of

the Junior League. Many people think of the organization as exclusively for wealthy New Orleans women who sit around all day sipping tea in lush, perfectly manicured gardens. We're not just ladies who lunch. We have lawyers, doctors . . . women who are busy working during the day. [The Junior League] is run by women, and women do all the work.[2]

Another example is this statement by the president of the Junior League of Dallas:

> We have an open admission policy. Definitely not a little social club. [We] are dedicated [and] welcome anyone who is willing to work. To join, you have to have a sponsor. You can pick up a sponsor form at the Junior League office. You may not think you know someone to sponsor you, but you'll find there are Junior Leaguers in your church, your company, your PTA and many other organizations.[3]

Similarly, a recent publication by the American Symphony Orchestra League's Volunteer Council emphasized that orchestra volunteer groups are assessing the effectiveness of their organizations, structures, and image in regard to issues such as membership diversity. Do these statements reflect a new attitude and direction or do some organizations continue to do things the way they have "always been done"? My observations indicate that a little of both is true: Although some organizations I have analyzed are in the process of making major changes, this process is slow in some groups and virtually nonexistent in others.

To understand how elite women's organizations operate in the twenty-first century, it is necessary to examine the historical roots of such groups.

Source: Diana Kendall, "Members Only: Organizational Structure and Patterns of Exclusion," in *The Power of Good Deeds,* Rowman and Littlefield, 2002: 143–164. Used with permission of Rowman and Littlefield.

PAST PRACTICES WITH CURRENT RELEVANCE: THE HISTORY OF EXCLUSION IN ELITE WOMEN'S ORGANIZATIONS

Many of the earliest elite women's clubs in the United States were organized for purely social purposes, and the formal organizational structure blocked from membership all women but those who were in the inner social circle or who otherwise were acceptable to established members. For example, the Colony Club in New York City and similar clubs in Boston, Philadelphia, and San Francisco were founded by white socialites who required that any new member be from a family listed in the *Social Register.*[4] When the Junior League was founded in 1901, all of its members were debutantes or former debutantes. Criticized for their seemingly frivolous lives of partying and conspicuous consumption, the founders of the League decided to start an organization that would combine social activities with community service work so that the members could show that they were accepting their social obligation to the community. Consequently, the Junior League for the Promotion of the Settlement Movement—the organization's original name—started settlement houses to improve child health, nutrition, and literacy, particularly among recent immigrants. Racial-ethnic and class distinctions between the members of the League and the beneficiaries of their largesse were great: The recent immigrants frequently did not speak English, were poor, and lacked the social skills that League members prided themselves on possessing.

The founding of the Junior League and the subsequent changes in this organization show how white women of the upper classes have largely maintained the exclusivity of many of their organizations while, at the same time, doing good deeds that serve a diverse clientele that would not be invited to membership in the group itself. From its origins, the Junior League practiced exclusivity in its membership, a fact that contemporary organizational leaders have worked to diminish in significance. Some African American members of local branches of the League are aware that racial

discrimination historically was a fact in their organization. One African American woman who has served as a League president in a southern city referred to it as the League's "unwritten, cultural ban" against nonwhite members until the mid-1970s.[5] The organization today is quite different from its original debutante membership and it no longer has unwritten racial or religious bans, allowing more Jewish, African American, and Latina women to become members. Changes in racial and ethnic composition are most apparent in a few of the League's leadership positions, such as the presidency of the national organization, the Association of Junior Leagues International, where some recent presidents have been Cuban American or African American. Similarly, among the 285 Junior Leagues, an estimated two dozen African American, Latina, and Asian American women have served as president.[6] However, about 96 percent of all Junior League members are white Americans, and even the women of color who serve as officers of the international organization and of the local Leagues fit class-based criteria typical of its white (Anglo) officers, such as having a successful career or a prominent family.

The norm of exclusivity remains strongest in elite women's social/community service organizations where there are many members who fit the Old Money or Old Name family categories. Women whose families have resided in the same city for many years and whose relatives have been active in elite women's and men's organization often believe that membership in these prestigious organizations should continue to be restricted. Judith, a sustaining member of the Junior League in one city, expressed her concerns about changes in her local League:

> Now, don't get me wrong. I'm not a snob, and I don't think that the League should shut its doors on anyone. Discrimination is bad, and our community projects are planned to benefit people all over town. But, I will say that things have changed on the membership front over the past years. We have gone from having our "first Jewish member" to bringing in new members who are Hispanic or black. Several "old timers" were commenting the other day that we used to know everybody in the League

and now there are so many new faces that we don't recognize. I know that diversity is good, but I don't know that bringing more people [of diverse racial and ethnic groups] into the organization actually means that we talk to each other a whole lot more. At the earliest meetings black provisionals [women who are new members] mingle with everybody and don't all sit together. But as the year goes by, they start doing everything together like "peas in a pod." They sit together at meetings, work on the same projects, and generally "hang out" together. It seems that several of the black women were members of the same sorority, and apparently they enjoyed being together. But what's more important than all of this is that our organization is very successful and that we make a significant contribution to [city] each year through the groups we support, and that's what really counts, isn't it?

In some cases, when women believe that it has gotten to where "just anybody" can become a member of their formerly exclusive organization, the women either quit participating or form a new group where they believe they can exert more control over who becomes a member or an officer of the club. For example, some members of Junior Leagues stated that they believed that "political correctness has overtaken the League," giving other exclusive women's organizations a greater chance to recruit members who would like the prestige of being a member of a highly selective organization more akin to those elite men's clubs that have resolutely held onto the sanctity of "Members Only" and have protected their membership rosters from outsiders. However, other members believe that elite women's organizations such as the Junior League that have welcomed greater diversity in their membership and leadership ranks are "on the right path"— that "change was long overdue"—but that these groups still have far to go before they are actually seen as welcoming minority women into the organization.

Due to the existence of other, parallel organizations, being seen as "welcoming" minority group members into an organization does not necessarily mean that those individuals would want to join previously all-white groups, or conversely that whites (Anglos) would want to join a previously all-African American organization.

HOW RACIAL EXCLUSION LED TO PARALLEL ELITE WOMEN'S ORGANIZATIONS

A number of elite women's organizations, including the Junior League, were founded on patterns that denied membership to women—either intentionally or unintentionally—on the basis of race, ethnicity, religion, and/or class. Throughout the United States, women who were identified as white ethnics (such as Irish Americans and Italian Americans), members of religious minorities such as Jews or Catholics, and African Americans were categorically excluded from membership in elite white women's organizations. Even women from prominent families, such as Rose Kennedy (wife of Joseph Kennedy and mother of President John F. Kennedy), were refused membership in the Junior League for reasons such as being a Roman Catholic. Because of these patterns of overt discrimination, parallel women's organizations comprised of women from excluded racial, ethnic, and religious categories were founded in many cities. New Haven, Connecticut, for example, was home to seven different Leagues or their equivalent when August B. Hollingshead conducted a study there in the 1950s. According to Hollingshead's classification:

> The top ranking organization is the New Haven Junior League which draws its membership from "Old Yankee" Protestant families whose daughters have been educated in private schools. The Catholic Charity League is next in rank and age—its membership is drawn from Irish-American families. In addition to this organization there are Italian and Polish Junior Leagues within the Catholic division of the society. The Swedish and Danish Junior Leagues are for properly connected young women in these ethnic groups, but they are Protestant. Then too, the upper-class Jewish families have their Junior League. The principle of parallel structures for a given class level, by religion, ethnic, and racial groups, proliferates throughout the community.[7]

As Hollingshead's work shows, parallel structures of elite volunteer organizations were founded by women from somewhat similar class positions who did not have access to membership in the most prestigious women's organizations. One of the earliest parallel organizations founded by African American women was the National Association of Colored Women's Clubs (NACWC), which was created by an 1896 merger of the national Federation of Afro-American Women, the Women's Era Club of Boston, and the Colored Women's League of Washington, D.C. The NACWC had as its stated goals advancing the education of women and children, improving conditions for family living, and promoting understanding so that justice might prevail. The NACWC was similar to the Junior League in that it sought to unite women for service to the community; however, the NACWC has particularly emphasized the importance of improving the quality of life in the black community. Its motto is "Lifting as We Climb," and the group focuses on improving the condition of people of color who are the victims of race- and class-based oppression.[8]

Other elite African American women's organizations have structures and functions similar to those of the predominantly white Junior League. The Girl Friends, founded in New York in 1927, has about forty chapters that sponsor fundraising events such as debutante cotillions and provide many hours of community service.[9] Jack and Jill of America, a membership-by-invitation-only social group, was founded in 1938. Although it is the mothers who are invited to membership, this organization primarily benefits middle- and upper-class African American children. Today, the 220 chapters of Jack and Jill constitute a national network for African American children and their families, providing them with opportunities for social service, education, and other projects.[10] African American college students I have talked with about this organization fondly—or not so fondly—recall how much emphasis their parents placed on attending academic awards dinners and parties sponsored by Jack and Jill. As one young woman stated, "With my parents, it was be-there-or-else when it came to Jack and Jill."

The Links, Inc., another prestigious African American women's organization, has been described as "the black equivalent of the Junior League."[11] Founded in Philadelphia in 1946, The Links has a membership of over 10,000 women in 270 chapters located in 40 states and several other nations. The Links defines itself as "a group of friends committed to civic, educational, and cultural activities, with the singular purpose of serving community needs for the improvement of life and the pursuit of excellence."[12] Members estimate that, during the more than fifty years of this organization's existence, the group has donated more than $15 million to various charities and programs, and its members provide more than one million hours of volunteer service annually.

Membership in The Links is considered by many elite African Americans to be an exceptional honor. Briana, a professional African American woman in her late 30s, described it as follows:

> I'm proud to be a member. Links is well organized. We have elected officers at the national level, and they're excellent. One recent president was an attorney, and believe me, she's a dynamic public speaker. At the national level, the president and former presidents are top notch, and they keep the organization running smoothly, along with the members of the Executive Council. Because of the national organization we have shown our concern for people in African countries as well as the U.S. We've been at the cutting edge on programs to revitalize African American families and communities. We've also worked with education and programs promoting good health. I could go on and on . . . but I'd sum this up by saying that we've done as much as the Junior League, but we are not as well known because we don't get all the publicity they do.

Statements by women like Briana have been expressed by other members of the African American community such as author Lawrence Otis Graham, who provided the following account of how happy his family was when his mother was invited to join The Links:

> As my mother and every other woman in her crowd would have told you, getting accepted into the Links was a big deal, and it was not something you'd ever need to explain if you were in the company of the right kind of people. In this case, some would say the right kind of people didn't include whites or blue-collar blacks.[13]

According to Graham, membership in The Links is so valuable because:

> For fifty years, membership in the invitation-only national organization has meant that your social background, lifestyle, physical appearance, and family's academic and professional accomplishments passed muster with a fiercely competitive group of women who—while forming a rather cohesive sisterhood—were nonetheless constantly under each other's scrutiny. Each of the 267 local chapters brings together no more than fifty-five women, most of them either professional, socialites, volunteer fund-raisers, educators, or upper-class matrons, and is added to only when a current member dies or moves to another city.[14]

As Graham's statement suggests, one of the reasons membership in The Links (or other elite women's organizations) is so valuable is because of its scarcity—not everyone who wants to become a member will be invited to join. The history of The Links's intraracial practices of exclusivity—and sometimes exclusion—has been described by social historian Stephen Birmingham, who notes that even in the 1970s its membership was restricted by covert practices such as an emphasis on skin color: "Most Links are so fair-skinned that some blacks wonder why Links call themselves a black group at all."[15] Despite the many positive contributions The Links has made to improving the quality of life for the African American community and the society at large, organizational leaders have felt a need in recent years to try to shed the group's appearance of elitism, just as some predominantly white women's organizations have sought to do. Patricia Russell-McCloud, a recent national president of The Links, stated the problem as follows:

> I think that because membership in this organization is by invitation only, it creates an aura of mystique, and it lessens the knowledge and understanding of the mission. Therefore, the stereotypical portrayal that gets attached relates possibly, and unfairly, to an upper middle class that is insensitive to the greater needs in the community. But our record speaks for itself, and in the past and now our purpose has been demonstrated, our commitment firm.[16]

According to Russell-McCloud, Links members have been stereotyped as rich ladies who wear white gloves and sponsor teas and socials, whereas she views the organization as an activist group involved in many domestic and international projects.[17] The concerns that this former president expressed remain an issue with some members of The Links, as well as with women who were not invited to join the group. Cassandra, an African American college student, described her mother's frustration when she learned that her nomination for membership had been turned down:

> [A local chapter of Links] really hurt my mamma's feelings. So, I'm not going to have anything to do with them when I graduate even though my [sorority] background would probably make it easy for me to get in. My mamma does lots of good things in [city] and she is somebody you can always count on. But she isn't fancy. She doesn't wear those expensive designer clothes—even though she could afford them if she wanted to—and she wasn't in the "best" sorority, but they had no good reason to tell her sponsor "no."

Like other elite women's organizations, the membership practices of The Links may vary somewhat from city to city; however, the racial and ethnic composition of the group has remained largely unchanged, and parallel organizations of elite white and African American women volunteers remain in the cities in my study.

It has been more difficult to trace the development of parallel organizations of elite Latinas, perhaps because patterns of exclusion of Latinas have been somewhat different from those applied to African American women. In some cities, affluent Latinas have been welcomed into elite white women's social/community service organizations more readily than have African American women. In cities where there is a large population of Mexican Americans, Cuban Americans, or other groups that trace their origins to Latin America, many elite Latinas fully participate in previously all-white organizations such as the Junior League. In a few cases, affluent Latinas have succeeded white (Anglo) elite women as leaders of prestigious groups previously associated with Anglo elites. An example is the Society of Martha Washington in Laredo, Texas—which . . . holds a lavish annual debutante presentation. Originally, this prestigious group was composed primarily of affluent Anglo women; however, in a city that is currently about 95 percent Latino/a, the board of directors, many members of the group, and the "royalty" honored at the annual Martha Washington debutante ball are affluent Latinas or women who are married to Latinos. A recent president of the Society of Martha Washington, for instance, was Libby Casso, an Anglo who married her college sweetheart, Alfonso Casso, Jr., and who identifies her three children as being "Hispanic." At the annual ball, many of those chosen to be royalty, including those chosen to portray George and Martha Washington, are now Latinos and Latinas, whereas in the past this organization and its fundraising events were considered to be social events for rich Anglos.[18]

At the national level, Latina leaders of formerly all-white (Anglo) women's organizations such as the Junior League have also emerged in recent years. An example is Clotilde Dedecker, the Cuban American president of the Association of Junior Leagues International, who was the first Latina to hold that post. As president of the League, Dedecker described her organization as being so inclusive that it now advertises in newspapers and on billboards for new members;[19] however, others have disputed this claim because League chapters, like other elite women's organizations, have bylaws stating that new members must be proposed by several existing members of the organization. Women who might be interested in joining but do not know current members may be unlikely to pursue their interest and thus turn elsewhere for their volunteer work. But current members defend the membership policies that exist as a part of the organization's bureaucratic structure.

JOINING THE CLUB: BUREAUCRACY MAINTAINS BARRIERS

In the past, a symphony fundraising group may have been started by a group of women meeting over cookies and tea at someone's home, but this is no longer the way in which elite women's symphony leagues and other charitable groups are structured. At the local, state, and national levels, the organizational structure of women's community service and fundraising groups have all of the characteristics of other bureaucratic organizational structures. Sociologists have utilized Max Weber's ideal type construct of bureaucracy in research involving for-profit and governmental organizations. As the following discussion will show, this model can also be applied to nonprofit organizations, particularly those that have not only local chapters or affiliates but also regional and national associations.

To Weber, bureaucracies are the most rational and efficient means of attaining organizational goals, and certain ideal-type characteristics are found in bureaucratic organizations: (1) standardization through the application of specific rules and procedures; (2) a division of labor (specialization); (3) a hierarchy of authority (chain of command); (4) impartiality in personnel matters; and (5) employment based on technical qualifications, resulting in recruiting experts who have a career pattern.[20] The first three of these are most applicable to the structure of elite women's organizations because these characteristics help them to attain goals that would not be possible if the women acted individually or conducted the group's activities informally. The latter two characteristics are inapplicable to these groups themselves, although they are true of the paid staffs that support these organizations.

Evidence of the bureaucratic organizational structure in elite women's organizations can be found in the way in which the groups have formalized their relationships, not only with one another (within the umbrella of national and regional organizations) but also under the law. The women in these organizations have incorporated their groups and established a board of directors that is held responsible for the fiscal management and administrative operations of the organization. The women in volunteer organizations would agree with Weber's emphasis on the importance of efficiency in getting the job done and in achieving organizational goals in a timely manner, because most of the women are involved in a variety of competing activities that also vie for their time and attention. Although some elite women are "full-time moms," or are otherwise not employed outside their own household, a growing number of elite women volunteers are employed either full or part time and have young children living in their household. Consequently, across class lines, today's women volunteers want the time they donate to an organization to be well used, and, in some cases, they want the organization to log the number of hours they have worked, to show the significance of their nonpaid contributions to the charity or arts organization.

BYLAWS AS THE GROUND RULES FOR MEMBERSHIP

The seemingly neutral bylaws of some elite women's organizations establish the guidelines by which new members are selected. It is the manner in which existing members use those provisions, however, that determines how inclusive of outsiders the group actually is. Most elite women's organizations are corporations created under relevant state law, in this case, under the Texas Non-Profit Corporation Act. One major reason for being incorporated is to prevent any of the women from having personal liability for the actions or obligations of the organization itself. Thus, the corporation has liability for its debts, yet—as long as the women adhere to the requisite "corporate formalities" prescribed by state law—the members and officers will have no such liability. However, adhering to corporate formalities requires written articles of incorporation (a "charter") that are filed with the state government. It means having written bylaws, having a board of directors or trustees, and having elected officers. These written, formal documents become the basis for the rules and procedures of the organization itself.

The bylaws of the organization are, among other things, the ground rules for membership

categories, including the rights and responsibilities that go with each of the membership categories (such as who may be elected to an office and—if the group holds debutante presentations—which category or categories of members are eligible to have their children selected as "royalty"). According to Weber, rules are standardized and are provided to members in written format, so that clear-cut guidelines are established. For this reason, most elite women's organizations publish their bylaws in their annual yearbook and provide a copy to all members.

When a question arises, such as how to propose a person for membership, existing members are referred to the bylaws and are told to fill out the appropriate form. After completing the membership proposal form, the current member is responsible for getting the requisite number of signatures—sometimes as many as four—from other members in good standing who are willing to sponsor the candidate. The form must be submitted to the membership chair by a specified date in order for the candidate to be considered. The membership chair, who typically serves on the organization's board of directors, holds one of the many elected or appointed positions that are set forth in the bylaws. Although positions such as membership chair and provisional- or new-member chair have little meaning in the for-profit organizational environment, these are very influential positions and serve as a source of social power in many elite women's groups.

The bylaw provisions have an effect on the kinds of people who are invited to become new members. The "admission to membership" section of the bylaws of one organization sets forth, for example, the deadline by which membership applications must be submitted and who is eligible to sponsor a candidate for membership:

> An active member in good standing [who has completed the requirements for new members and fulfilled her annual membership obligations] may sign her name on four applications per year. Her name may appear only twice as the main proposer. Associate members [who have served eight years as active members in good standing and have requested a change to associate status] may second

two candidates. One of the sponsors of a candidate must attend the sponsor orientation meeting prior to the candidate being considered for admission by the committee. If the candidate is found to have the required qualifications, the Admissions Committee shall vote upon her eligibility for membership. Upon a favorable vote of at least four members of the Admissions Committee, such a candidate shall be issued an invitation to join the organization.

The nomination form for membership in this organization requires that proposed candidates have an interest in the organization, a commitment to volunteerism, and have demonstrated previous interest in the organization by donating time and money to its fundraising projects. However, other factors are also taken into consideration. The form asks the sponsoring member to indicate the following: "How long has this woman lived in the city?" and "Does she have a personal acquaintance with her sponsors?" New member proposal forms typically ask for information about the candidate's membership in other groups such as alumnae sorority organizations, other nonprofit boards, and evidence of "active" participation in school and church work. In all of the organizations I examined, the membership process included at least the following steps: (1) a membership proposal form must be completely filled out, (2) the candidate's sponsor (who is a member) must get from two to four signatures (depending on the organization) from other members in good standing, (3) the candidates for membership are discussed and voted on, sometimes one at a time, by a membership committee and, in some cases, by the full membership at one of its monthly meetings, (4) candidates who are approved by the membership committee must also be accepted by the organization's board of directors, (5) the candidate is notified that she will be "invited to membership" if she is willing to assume all the responsibilities and fulfill all the requirements for active membership in the organization as set forth in the bylaws and other rules, (6) the organization holds an announcement party or new members luncheon and prints biographies of the women in the organization's newsletter, and (7) new members

serve out a provisional year in which they are more closely scrutinized to see that they fulfill the obligations of their new status before officially becoming an "active" member of the organization.

Bylaws and informal group "understandings" pertaining to membership—regardless of their original intent—partly determine what type of women will be invited to become members of elite organizations. According to some women in these organizations, explicit membership rules have the following positive functions: they typically state the various categories of membership and what the expectations are of women in each of these categories; they state the number of women who can be in some categories (e.g., active members) at any one time, thus limiting membership to a workable size; and these membership caps give women the distinct impression that they are fortunate to be one of the "chosen" because membership in the organization is a finite resource not necessarily available to all who might desire to become members. This practice reinforces the referent power of the group because scarcity of membership positions enhances the group's social attractiveness to other women. However, most members would not justify the membership limits in those terms. Rather, they would agree that capping the membership at a specific number and not admitting new members beyond this point has the function of ensuring that the organization does not grow so large that it is "unwieldy," as one organization's president stated:

> Just because our membership is limited to [a given number], does not mean that we try to keep anybody out. It just means that we don't have houses large enough for monthly meetings with more women than that. I'm sure that somewhere in the past, our leaders decided on what they thought was a good number, and we've stuck with it because it works for us.

However, as another women implied, this membership cap can be used to exclude women deemed to be "unacceptable" candidates:

> I like it that our bylaws state a set number of members: If we have a candidate who is not accepted for membership, we can tell her sponsors that there were only a few "open slots" that year and that the competition was real stiff for those.

For some women, exclusivity is an important incentive for joining voluntary organizations. In her study of upper-class women's social clubs, Susan Ostrander found that exclusivity of association was particularly important to those women who wanted to associate only with those who have similar interests and values.[21] Today's members may be more subtle when they express the same concern, framing their preferences in terms of finding new members who are "congenial" and will "fit in with the rest of the group."

As noted above, there are potentially exclusionary effects of bylaws pertaining to membership because these rules set parameters regarding who may, or may not, become a member. Requirements that women be put up for membership by existing members limits the access of other women, particularly individuals from other racial, ethnic, or religious categories, from consideration for membership. Then, members can truthfully state, "Well, no African American women were nominated for membership this year, so we have no new black members."

Since the bylaws are the formal means by which women's organizations establish the number and composition of their membership, perhaps it is no surprise that "bylaw fights" such as the one described at the beginning of the chapter may take place in some organizations if individuals seek to modify existing rules and procedures. However, the bylaws of women's groups that operate under the "umbrella" of a larger (state, regional, national, or even international) organization may be encouraged to have a more "open door" admissions policy at the national level because gaining a wider diversity of members not only brings new people and ideas into the group but also sends a message that the organization is not racist or elitist.

DIVISION OF LABOR: WHO DECIDES WHO GETS TO JOIN

Like organizational rules and procedures, division of labor—another of Weber's ideal characteristics

of bureaucracy—plays a central part in membership policies and practices. Division of labor refers to the process of dividing up tasks so that they are performed by different people and thus are performed in the most optimal manner. Because elite women volunteers are not paid employees or career professionals in a for-profit work environment, a clear statement of the division of labor—what important tasks must be accomplished and who is responsible for doing them—is integral to the organization's success. As found in the organizational rules, the division of labor includes the titles of officers and the heads of standing committees and in what the specific duties of each shall be. By dividing the tasks into a variety of unpaid administrative duties—such as the treasurer and the newsletter chair—and into leadership positions relating to specific fundraising projects, the women can specialize in certain tasks within the organization. Chairing the membership committee is an example. Although many guidelines for membership are set forth in writing, other factors considered by the typical membership committee are more nebulous (such as how well a candidate is known by other women and how suitable she is for membership). Barbara, a white woman in her 50s, described her duties as chair of a membership committee:

> I am honored to chair this committee because when you get right down to it, the decisions we make are crucial to the lifeblood of the [organization]—we help the general membership select those women who are best suited to become "one of us." Because of the needs of our constituency and the time-consuming fundraising projects we have each year, we need to be able to count on dedicated volunteers who, if they say they'll be there, will indeed *be there with bells on,* ready to do their jobs with a smiley face. Compatibility with existing members is really important, too. You can let in one or two bad apples, and it really sours the feelings of other members, especially if the newcomer is a gossiper, griper, or doesn't have good manners. When you work in close proximity on important projects and events, going along to get along is essential.

In Barbara's organization, the membership committee can strike a candidate from the list of potential members who will later be voted on by the entire membership. In other organizations, the membership committee makes the final choices about new members and reports its decision to the larger constituency. Women selected to chair the membership committee are trusted, often long-term members. According to Hallie, the former president of one elite women's organization:

> If you ask me, heading up the membership committee is one of the most important tasks we ask members of our group to take on. The year I was president-elect, several members of the board told me to be really careful who I appointed to that position because she needed to be "balanced." I decided that they meant the membership chair had to balance the needs of the organization against the wishes of membership candidates and their sponsors.

As Hallie's statement indicates, elite women's organizations typically have individuals such as members of the board of directors or other long-term members who provide suggestions to incoming officers and, sometimes from behind the scenes, provide direction for people who take on leadership positions in the organization. In other words, as the division of labor becomes established in elite women's organizations, a core of women emerge who "run" the organization and have coercive power over others because they have the ability to "punish" them (at least in limited ways) if they do not fulfill the "core's" expectations as to how other members and potential members should behave. Organization leaders possess coercive power in that they can mete out negative sanctions, such as harsh criticism, rejection of a member's proposed new membership candidate, or refusal to vote for a member's daughter to be presented as a debutante. This "core" group of influential members is often described as "running the show" by some newer members and by longer-term members who consider themselves to be "outside the loop" when it comes to the decision-making process. Audrey, a relatively new member of a prestigious women's volunteer organization, referred to this phenomenon as the "outsider on the inside" feeling:

> My husband and I had moved to [city] about two years before I become a member. My mother had old friends here, and she asked them to put me up for membership.

> Apparently, there wasn't any problem because the next thing I knew I was being invited to join and come to a new member orientation. The women are very cordial, and I've attended a number of the meetings. However, one day I noticed that there were a lot of "insider" jokes among the women, and that these same women were the ones that everybody was always praising. If some major decision had to be made, they'd say, "We've got to ask so-and-so. She'll know what we should do." After I had been a member long enough to nominate a woman for membership, I asked questions about how to do this. When I asked how membership decisions were made, I was told: "It's like magic . . . it either happens or it doesn't happen. After the committee meets you will be told whether or not your candidate was accepted." When I asked if I could put in a good word for her in addition to the letter of recommendation I had written, I was told rather curtly that the organization worked best if members who weren't on the board just let other people do their jobs. My friend didn't get in that year, and I was told that there just weren't enough places for all of the outstanding candidates for that year.

As described by Audrey, the division of labor in some elite women's organizations is firmly established, serving as a source of power for the women in the "core" group, and challenges to their power are discouraged.

HIERARCHY OF AUTHORITY: PRESSURE FOR AND RESISTANCE TO CHANGE

Division of labor in elite women's organizations is intricately linked to the organization's hierarchical structure—Weber's ideal-type hierarchy of authority. By definition, hierarchy of authority means that each lower position in an organization is under the control and supervision of a higher one, with the further proviso that all of the persons in the chain of command need to recognize the necessity and legitimacy of the higher positions. In elite women's groups, committees responsible for fulfilling various organizational functions do not operate in isolation, with the chair and committee members making their own plans and establishing their own budget. For a lavish fundraising event such as a debutante ball, wine tasting dinner, designer showhouse, or "luxury" holiday bazaar, for example the chair is told how much of the organization's money she can spend on the project and, in some groups, it is understood that committee chairs and members who exceed the budget will be responsible for making up the difference out of their own pockets.

In addition to a hierarchy of authority at the local level, many elite women's organizations have state and/or national associations that are a part of the larger organizational bureaucracy. State and national associations of elite women's organizations have elected officers (who typically are unpaid volunteers), paid staff members, and numerous advisory boards and councils made up of delegates from local chapters or leagues. The Links, Inc., an elite African American women's organization, is an example. Established more than 50 years ago, The Links has more than 10,000 members in 270 chapters located in 40 states, Washington, D.C., the Bahamas, and Frankfurt, Germany. The local chapters are mainly supported by membership dues and fundraising activities that benefit scholarship programs and community service projects. In 1949, members of local Links chapters established a national organization that holds annual meetings, has elected officials, and oversees the National Foundation of The Links, Inc., the philanthropic arm of the organization.

Predominantly white elite women's organizations such as the Junior League and symphony orchestra leagues have state and national bureaucracies. Local Junior Leagues participate in the Association of Junior Leagues, Inc. (AJLI), the umbrella organizations for the 285 Junior League chapters located in four countries. According to a recent president of the AJLI, "Our Association is . . . about growing something: It is about growing our collective future. The Leagues add value to the communities; the Association exists to add value to the work of the Leagues."[22] Although state and national organizations of The Links, the Junior Leagues, and symphony orchestra leagues serve in an advisory capacity to the local organizations, this hierarchy influences how local chapters conduct their business. Generally, the national groups want to bring about at least the appearance of greater openness in membership; however, at the local level, some members are resistant to change,

especially if it means that they have less control over membership decisions that determine with whom they will associate.

How do women's volunteer associations reach out to a wider diversity of people and meet their fundraising goals while also providing elite women with a "comfort zone" in which they associate primarily with others like themselves? One answer has been the tiering of volunteer groups under larger umbrella organizations such as the American Symphony Orchestra League. The volunteer groups that are to be "less selective" and thus less exclusive often indicate their presence on Web sites where visitors can find information on "how to get involved" or "volunteer opportunities." Some have membership forms that can be filled out on the Web site, and people are invited to fill out a survey form indicating areas of interest in which they would like to help out. However, a visit to some Web sites reveals the tiers of membership and what demographics are included in each group. An example is the Dallas Symphony Orchestra League (DSOL) Web site, which states: "Membership is open to anyone interested in supporting the Symphony through special projects and committees." The Web site visitor learns that the demographics for this group are: "Women, generally over the age of 40. Open to anyone. Daytime meetings." The fundraising projects of the DSOL include a Neiman Marcus Fashion Show and Luncheon, a Presentation Ball, the Junior Symphony Ball, and the Dallas Symphony Derby. With daytime meetings and these fundraisers, this group largely appeals to older, nonemployed women. By contrast, the Junior Group of the DSOL has this requirement for membership: "Candidates are recommended for membership. Active membership must be proposed and is limited to 225 women under 45." The Junior Group requires that members purchase symphony tickets, attend three general meetings a year (which are held in the daytime), and participate in a variety of fundraising and service activities each year. While the DSOL and the Junior Group follow the more traditional model of elite women's organizations, two "professional" groups are open to business and professional men and women; one has luncheon meetings whereas the other has evening meetings.

The formal organizational structure of some elite volunteer organizations has been modified to bring in a greater diversity of people; however, other groups remain relatively resistant to change. It is in these organizations that we find vestiges of past exclusionary practices based on race, ethnicity, religion, or class that now are perpetuated in a different way. Informal networks within elite women's organizations are a primary way in which officers and others in the established "inner circle" are able to maintain social power. They gain control of the organization and restrict membership to those with whom they think they would be compatible. An example of how the informal network may control membership is Trudy, a white woman who was rejected by an elite white women's organization because it was believed that she "would not fit in." One member of the group described the situation as follows:

> I knew that [women's names] were putting [Trudy] up for membership, but when the new members were announced, she wasn't among them. I didn't think much about it until the same thing happened two years in a row. When I asked [other members] about it, one of them said that [the membership committee chair] had asked them not to propose [Trudy] again next year. [The chair] told them the general consensus of the membership committee was that Trudy "would not fit in," given that she was a known troublemaker in another organization. Apparently, she had started arguments and spread rumors, and wasn't a "team player." She was described as too loud . . . flamboyant . . . and that her hair style was "too much" for the organization. Personally, I think some members saw her as a "climber" even though she had been a hard worker for [another organization].

During several years of participant observation, I learned that Trudy was not invited to join several of the most prestigious women's volunteer organizations in her city. It was interesting to observe that she had a number of skills but that many of the "older guard" did not want to be associated with her on a more permanent basis as a member of their club. Trudy's case is not the exception; women in other organizations with "closed" memberships described similar situations but nearly

always emphasized that none of these had to do with race, ethnicity, religion, or how much money a particular woman has.

Most members are aware that their organizations have a statement such as this in their bylaws: "The Club shall not discriminate on the basis of race, color, religion, national origin, age, or disability in the admission of candidates to membership." However, requirements for sponsorship of new members and numerical restrictions to membership serve the latent purpose of limiting membership to "friends," "friends of friends," and others who are similarly situated in terms of class and race/ethnicity. For example, the phrase that follows immediately after the "nondiscrimination" clause in one organization's bylaws states, "Active membership shall be limited to 150." This membership limit serves as an official way to restrict the size of the organization and, in an unofficial way, to limit changes in the composition of its membership. A women who has been proposed for membership may not be invited to join because of any number of factors, but her sponsors may be told that there are simply no new member slots available this year or that those who are invited to become new members have been on a waiting list for several years.

The formal organizational structure of many elite women's groups is carefully guarded by those who have been members of the club for long periods of time and by newer members who believe that they benefit from the norm of exclusivity. Although some women attempt to maintain the status quo through existing bureaucratic channels, other women typically work through informal networks to maintain exclusivity and to gain social power. Informal networks serve as an integral part of elite women's organizations and have a significant influence in the "formal" decisions that are made by the group.

Like other sectors of the society, some elite women's organizations may decide that it is desirable to have racial and ethnic diversity in the membership. Based on the overall membership figures for elite, previously all-white women's organizations, however, it appears that women of color are very limited in their overall numbers in such groups. Likewise, white (Anglo) women typically are not members of traditionally black elite women's organizations. In elite white women's organizations, highlighting the few members who are from diverse racial, ethnic, or religious categories—particularly those who have risen to the top positions in the organization's hierarchy—makes it possible for the group to convey the appearance of diversity while maintaining the elitist, essentially all-white prestigious organization that controls privileged ties and rituals. Similarly, the most prestigious organizations for women of color may exclude women based on their family background, skin color, appearance, or other attributes that are not strictly within the scope of organizational bylaws and other policies.

CONCLUSION

For many women at the top economic tiers of society, being invited to join a prestigious women's philanthropic organization has a special meaning that might not be easily understood by nonelites. The women I interviewed and the observations that I recorded show a similar pattern: Many elite women gain social power and personal rewards through their membership in by-invitation-only women's groups and, for these women, those rewards equal—or exceed—the rewards they might receive in paid employment. Across racial and ethnic categories, these organizations are a source of empowerment for privileged women, and they provide a setting in which they can interact with like-minded women "who will understand who I am and why I want to participate in the betterment of my community," as one woman stated.

In both historically white and historically black organizations, certain commonalities are apparent. Primary among these is the bureaucratic structure that makes it possible for the women to accomplish major fundraising and community service projects. However, the same bureaucracy also provides the women with the means whereby they can

retain the exclusivity of the organization's membership and "hand-pick" new members. Rules and policies, the division of labor, and a hierarchy of authority may serve as a buffer against incursion by "outsiders." Requirements that new members be recommended by existing members may exclude some women who would desire to participate in the group's beneficial community service projects but fear rejection by the members if they seek to join.

Within elite organizations, change-oriented women quickly learn that organized resistance will be mounted against the changes that they propose. Those who resist changes in membership policies, for example, can use the existing bureaucratic structure to fight proposed changes. Women who resist change can also use their informal social networks to subvert change. Buffy, a member of several elite women's organizations, described how she had used existing rules to maintain the status quo in a group:

> Some women have no sense of tradition—they always want to throw out the baby with the bath water—"Let's change the bylaws!" is what they say when someone says "The bylaws won't let us do that." But instead, I say, "If it ain't broke, don't fix it." We need to have a really good reason to make a change, and frankly I've seen very few in my many years on boards.

Women such as Buffy resist change in the organizations where they consider themselves to be the "grande dames." Less-established members come to realize that they can suggest changes in the organization only at the risk of frustrating—and frequently angering—more long-term members who are deeply entrenched in the organization's leadership and advisory roles.

With resistance to change—and the fact that some women may believe that no change is necessary—it is not surprising that there are racially and ethnically separate elite women's organizations and that change, if at all, comes very slowly despite changes in the demographic composition of the population throughout the United States. Although opening up the membership of elite historically white women's organizations to greater diversity has been an issue among privileged white women, the women of color I interviewed or observed were less concerned about this topic with regard to historically black organizations. Those who were involved in The Links, The Girl Friends, or similar groups saw themselves as uniquely related to other women of color because of shared goals of racial uplift and a common "history of discrimination that is not easily understood by those who have not experienced it," as Viola stated.

Are separate, parallel organizations of elite white women volunteers and elite women of color problematic for individuals? Do these parallel structures offer equal social power for participants? Do parallel structures maintain and perpetuate racial and ethnic divisions within the next generation of social elites? . . .

NOTES

1. Winzenried, Rebecca. 2001. "Not Your Mother's Volunteer Group." *Symphony: The Magazine of the American Symphony Orchestra League* (July–August): Pp. 72.

2. Ermann, Natalie. 1997. "A League of Their Own: Two Women's Groups Celebrate Anniversaries." *New Orleans Magazine* (December): Pp. 37.

3. Schwartz, Marilyn. 2000. "Joke's On You: Junior League Has Grown Up." *Dallas Morning News* (NAT 11). Retrieved June 6, 2001, from *http://ajili.org/jokesonyou.html*.

4. Birmingham, Stephen. 1968. *The Right People*. New York: Little, Brown.

5. Yeomans, Jeannie. 2000. "Junior League Remakes Itself for the 21st Century." Retrieved June 6, 2001, from *http://ajili.org/remakes.html*.

6. Yeomans, Jeannie. 2000.

7. Hollingshead, August B. 1952. "Trends in Social Stratification: A Case Study." *American Sociological Review* 17, no. 6 (December): Pp. 685–686.

8. NACWC. 2000. "National Association of Colored Women's Clubs, Inc." A Legacy of Strength." Retrieved November 25, 2000 from *http://expert.cc.perdue.edu/~wov/NACWHistory.html*.

9. Birmingham, Stephen. 1977. *Certain People: America's Black Elite*. New York: Little, Brown; Graham, Lawrence Otis. 2000. *Out Kind of People: Inside America's Black Upper Class*. New York: HarperPerennial.

10. Graham, 2000.

11. Birmingham, 1977: Pp. 74.

12. Columbia Chapter of The Links, Inc. 2000. "Purpose and Projects." Retrieved November 30, 2000 from *http://www.midnet.sc.edu/links*.

13. Graham, 2000: Pp. 102.

14. Graham, 2000: Pp. 102.

15. Birmingham, 1977.

16. *Ebony*, 1996. "The Links: Women's Organization Celebrates 50th Anniversary." *Ebony* 51, No. 9: 108–112.

17. Graham, 2000.

18. Rodriguez, Gregory. 2000. "We're Patriotic Americans Because We're Mexicans." *Salon.com* (February 24). Retrieved November 9, 2000, from *http://www.salon.com/news/feature/2000/02/24/laredo*.

19. Bumiller, Elisabeth. 2000. "The Refugee from Cuba Who Grew Up to Head the Junior League." *New York Times* (August 24): A15.

20. Weber, Max. 1958. *From Max Weber: Essays in Sociology*. Translated and edited by Hans H. Gerth and C. Wright Mills. New York: Oxford University Press. Pp. 196–244.

21. Ostrander, Susan. 1984. *Women of the Upper Class*. Philadelphia: Temple University Press.

22. Dedecker, Clotilde. 1999. "President Dedecker's Annual Speech." Annual Conference 1999. Association of Junior Leagues International. Retrieved June 5, 2000, from *http://www.ajili.org/clotilespeech.html*.

Lesbian and Gay Occupational Strategies

M. V. LEE BADGETT AND MARY C. KING

This essay is an initial attempt to think about whether lesbians and gay men might tend to be in different occupations than straight people, and to consider how being in different occupations might affect lesbians' and gay men's earnings. Due to discrimination, socialization, and family responsibilities, both gender and ethnicity significantly influence occupational distributions—the proportions of different groups found in different occupations (Reskin 1994; King 1992). For similar reasons, we might expect sexual orientation to influence occupational distribution. Factors that specifically affect the occupational distribution of lesbians and gay men may be roughly divided into two categories: those relating to discrimination against lesbians and gay men, and those stemming from same-sex family structures.

The first section of the essay develops an analytical framework, based on economics, with which to think about the occupational strategies of lesbians and gay men—that is, the ways that being gay is likely to affect job and career decisions. The second section presents data on the occupational distributions of gay and straight people and on the degree of acceptance of homosexuality prevailing in different occupations. The statistics in the second section

are based on data from the General Social Survey (GSS), a nationally representative survey conducted by the National Opinion Research Center. Since 1989, the GSS has included several sets of questions allowing the identification of respondents' sexual orientations and attitudes toward homosexuality, along with their occupations, education, and other characteristics. The third section includes a discussion of the limitations of the work presented here and plans for further research.

ANALYTICAL FRAMEWORK

Economic analysis is often conducted in the language of unfettered personal choice, as if individuals are able to make completely free choices about those aspects of their lives examined by economists, subject to "constraints" generally having to do with financial means and, sometimes, discrimination. When examining the occupational distributions of two different groups, as we do here with gay and straight people, economists are not really investigating the entire process by which anyone comes to his or her occupation, a process that includes many factors such as an assessment of what's realistically available to people of different circumstances in different places at different times. Economists in the neoclassical paradigm, which we are using, are looking for differences at the margin. In other words, we are assuming that gay and straight people face similar labor markets with similar limitations due to their class, ethnicity, location, and gender, and we are looking for differences in occupations that stem solely from differences in sexual orientation.

Using this perspective, we may expect lesbians and gay men to enter different occupations than straight women and men for two reasons: (1) the potential for discrimination against lesbians and gay men may vary in different occupations, and (2) lesbians and gay men may have different expectations than straight women and men about the way in which their work life will mesh with their family life.

Discrimination Against Lesbians and Gay Men in Different Occupations

Beth Schneider (1986, 464) has called the need to "manage a disreputable sexual identity at the workplace" the most persistent problem lesbians and gay men face in their daily lives. The potential for discrimination against lesbians and gay men is evident from the public's ambivalent attitudes about homosexuality. A 1993 Gallup poll (Moore 1993) found that 80 percent of respondents believed that gay people should "have equal rights in terms of job opportunities," although only 46 percent favored specifically protecting gay people with civil-rights laws. In the same survey, however, 45 percent of men and 30 percent of women "prefer that homosexuals stay in the closet." Of the 818 adults surveyed in a national 1993 *Washington Post* poll (Warden 1993), 69 percent said that they "feel comfortable" working with a gay person, but 53 percent believe that "it is wrong for two consenting adults to have a homosexual relationship," a finding consistent with many previous polls (Herek 1991).

Lesbians and gay men have good reason to expect that they will be discriminated against at work if people know of their sexual orientation. A 1987–88 survey of 191 employers in Anchorage, Alaska revealed that 18 percent would fire, 27 percent would not hire, and 26 percent would not promote homosexuals (Brause 1989). A recent review of 21 surveys of lesbians and gay men found that between 16 and 46 percent of survey respondents reported having experienced some form of discrimination in employment—in hiring, promotion,

discharge, or harassment (Badgett, Donnelly and Kibbe 1992). Using GSS data, Badgett (1995) finds evidence that discrimination against gay men and lesbians lowers their earnings.

However, unlike discrimination based upon easily observable characteristics such as color or gender, discrimination against lesbians and gay men is analogous to that based on religion or national origin, which depends on the knowledge or suspicion that an employee has the stigmatized characteristic. Gay people who do not reveal their sexual orientation at work can be described as "passing—that is, providing a facade of heterosexuality" (Escoffier 1975). Passing entails the need to dissemble, to hide one's personal life, to avoid discussions of families and relationships, to come alone to work-related social events, and, often, to endure derogatory conversations about lesbians and gay men (Escoffier 1975; Herek 1991; Woods 1993). When career advancement depends in part on socializing, passing may carry economic as well as psychological costs (Escoffier 1975).

Gay employees may voluntarily disclose their sexual orientation or may be unable to hide it, given military discharge records, arrests and/or convictions, marital status, residential neighborhood, or silences in conversations and gossip. Lesbians and gay men who voluntarily reveal their sexual orientation to employers or coworkers for psychological or political reasons risk loss of income and diminished prospects for career advancement. However, disclosure provides psychological relief, as it ends the need for passing, allowing people to be themselves at work. And politically, disclosure has the potential to educate people or to promote greater understanding and acceptance of homosexuality.

It makes sense to assume that lesbians and gay men will attempt to minimize the impact of anti-gay discrimination on their work lives. Depending on their preference for being out at work, a gay worker will avoid occupations in which either:

1. it is relatively difficult to pass as heterosexual, *or*
2. the penalties for disclosure of a gay identity are relatively high because of institutional policies or coworker attitudes.

Occupations in which it would be most difficult to pass are those that involve high levels of social interaction, either on or off the job (Escoffier 1975); examples include sales and social services (Schneider 1986).

Occupations in which it may be easier to pass but in which the penalties for disclosure are relatively high are more diverse. These include occupations that:

- explicitly exclude people who are or are presumed to be lesbian or gay, such as military occupations and some jobs requiring security clearances
- exclude gay people in historical and current practice, such as elementary school teaching and law enforcement
- require work with children, a source of public contention and fear (Schneider 1986)
- require supervision of other employees, since authority is socially as well as officially conferred (Reskin and Padavic 1994)
- are traditionally imbued with a feminine or masculine identity, such as craft work (Baron 1991)
- are occupations dominated by men, who are reported to be more hostile than women to lesbians and particularly to gay men (Herek 1991)
- require more contact with the public.

In addition, we may expect to find lesbians and gay men concentrated in:

- the "gay ghetto" occupations, i.e., those publicly associated with gay men, such as positions in the arts, interior decorators, librarians, and waiters (Escoffier 1975)
- occupations found predominantly in large cities such as New York and San Francisco, where the best known gay communities exist.

It is difficult to determine whether discrimination against lesbians and gay men is likely to be greater in the private or the public sector. Civil-service hiring procedures appear to benefit women and ethnic minorities, and might afford some protection to lesbians and gay men. On the other hand, many workplaces that have been particularly hostile to gay people are found in the public sector, including elementary schools, police and fire departments, jails, intelligence agencies, and the military. Lesbians and gay men who have been politically motivated by the experience of prejudice, discrimination, and harassment may choose to work in nonprofit organizations dedicated to social change, where we also find women and ethnic minorities overrepresented, if not overly well-paid, relative to white men (Burbridge 1994; Kleiman 1994).

Finally, Beth Schneider (1986) has suggested that penalties for coming out are higher for jobs that pay more, since an employee with a high income has more to lose, and she has presented some evidence that people with high incomes are less willing to come out at work. Schneider mentions that this might be less true for lesbians than for gay men, since occupational segregation by gender limits women's employment options. It may also be true that the decision to remain closeted is different from the decision to avoid occupations with high penalties for disclosure. In other words, gay men and lesbians in highly paid positions might be especially careful to avoid disclosure of their homosexuality without steering away from such positions altogether. However, we believe that losing a relatively poorly paid position is in fact likely to exact a relatively greater cost than losing a well-paid job. People in well-paid jobs generally have more options when looking for work and may be expected to have more financial security to weather a period of unemployment and job search. A lawyer who is fired can work as a waitress, but a fired waitress cannot work as an attorney, and lawyers usually have more physical, social, and financial resources than waitresses.

Since the package of job characteristics includes income and status as well as institutional and personal attitudes toward gay people, a gay employee will make decisions based on the whole package. Because of the importance of the workplace environment, we expect that lesbians and gay men may enter less financially rewarding occupations than they would if they were straight, trading income and status for a job in which it is easier to pass or where the penalties for disclosure are relatively low, including jobs traditionally associated with lesbians and gay men or concentrated in areas with large gay communities.

Economists would describe these occupational strategies as pursuing a compensating differential, in other words, a tradeoff a worker faces between pay and work environment—between a job with lower pay and a more pleasant work environment and one with higher pay and less pleasant work conditions. The classic example of a compensating differential is the relatively high pay of garbage collectors. Although the concept of compensating differentials is well developed, many economists question the extent to which such differentials actually exist. It's certainly easier to think of examples of pleasant, high-status jobs that pay well and unpleasant, low-status jobs that pay poorly than the reverse.

However, we can imagine that a lesbian might choose a lower-paying occupation or a job in a tolerant environment over a better-paying one in a workplace hostile to disclosure of her sexual orientation. This kind of compensating differential operates for women who leave the trades, where they face greater levels of sexual harassment, for female-dominated occupations that are relatively poorly paid (Bergmann 1986; Martin 1988). Such a differential may be said to be operating for members of ethnic minorities who have been pushed by harassment and hostility out of particular jobs and entire occupations (Hill 1985).

Of course, the compensating differential is not an intrinsic characteristic of the job, but results from coworkers' attitudes and behavior. Harassment can be seen as a tactic to reserve particular jobs and workplaces for the incumbent social group. Fire departments have provided many examples in recent years of severe harassment of people of color and white women who have attempted to work in jobs previously held exclusively by white men. It may be difficult in practice for researchers working with quantitative data to distinguish employee harassment from hiring and promotion discrimination, since both operate to keep target populations out of good jobs. Certainly management bears the responsibility for both on the job.

Occupational Strategies Related to Family Structure

Lesbians' and gay men's expectations about their future family structures might lead them to choose different occupations from those entered by straight women and men. If it is true that gay relationships are less stable than those of straight couples (Blumstein and Schwartz 1983), then gay people need to plan for more independent and autonomous futures. And regardless of the relative stability of relationships, no legal protections exist for gay partners who forgo their own career advancement in the interest of their families. Certainly neither lesbians nor gay men can currently expect to receive health and other work-related benefits through a partner, as very few employers provide benefits to domestic partners. Consequently, both lesbians and gay men might foresee the need to support themselves through adulthood and into retirement, and the need to establish benefits under their own names. Likewise, gay people must establish credit on an individual basis.

While they share all of these considerations, lesbians and gay men are likely to have different expectations about family life and its impact on their career choices. Lesbians might anticipate that their partners are likely to earn significantly less than the (male) partners of straight women, regardless of class, ethnicity, or educational level, given the significant wage gap between men and women at all levels of education and in all occupations. They would thus expect to have to earn a higher individual income than straight women to achieve a particular standard of living. Moreover, if, on average, lesbians have fewer children than straight women, then lesbians would be less likely to voluntarily work part-time, combining childrearing and paid work, as more women than men currently do. Lesbians who do have children have more incentive to work full-time in order to obtain benefits than straight women, who may obtain benefits for themselves and their children through marriage.

Many economists believe that women tend to work in female-dominated occupations because these pay best over the long run to people who work intermittently, depending upon the needs of their families (Polachek 1981), but empirical research has discredited this line of reasoning (England 1982). However, if it does retain any power to explain occupational segregation by gender, we would expect that lesbians would be less likely to choose to work in typical "women's jobs" to the extent that they are less likely to raise children. Finally, straight women may work in low-paid female occupations to retain a badge of femininity as an asset in the marriage market (Bergmann 1986), an asset that lesbians may not value.

Gay men, on the other hand, can anticipate that their partners will have higher incomes and fewer children than the partners of straight men. Except for the necessity of securing their own benefits, gay men have fewer family-based incentives than straight men to pursue well-paid work, since they are less likely to be responsible for the support of children or a partner. However, having fewer children may also free both lesbians and gay men to devote more time and energy to education, training, and work, which should result in higher pay. Finally, it may be true that lesbians and gay men receive less support from their parents and other family members for schooling, down payments, starting a business, or emergencies; if this is so, they are likely to have less opportunity for advancement and thus need to work harder to ensure their own financial security.

In short, lesbians have greater family-based incentives than do straight women to aim for full-time, better-paid jobs with benefits, even if they violate some gender norms in the process. Thus, the influence of family considerations runs counter to the strategy most likely to help a lesbian avoid discrimination—one that gives up higher income and benefits in return for a gay-tolerant work environment.

Gay men may have less responsibility for family welfare. However, they do need to ensure their financial security independently, and they may receive less support from their families of origin. If gay men on average have less incentive than straight men to pursue highly paid work, this might be expected to amplify an occupational strategy that trades pay for lower levels of discrimination and harassment.

EMPIRICAL EVIDENCE

Description of the Data

Finding reliable random samples of the population with information on sexual orientation as well as economic and social characteristics is very difficult. Students of the gay community have been forced to rely on small, unrepresentative data sets generated either by marketing surveys of gay publications or by snowball sampling techniques, which involve researchers interviewing all of their own contacts, then all of the contacts of their contacts, and so on. Both kinds of samples appear to overrepresent gay people who are white, professional, relatively affluent, urban, middle aged, well-educated, politically oriented, and, of course, willing to identify themselves to surveyers as gay (Larson 1992; Gluckman and Reed 1993; Badgett 1995).

One underutilized but valuable survey, the General Social Survey (GSS) conducted by the National Opinion Research Center, has collected data on a variety of economic, demographic, and attitudinal characteristics, and in 1989 began asking respondents about their sexual behavior (Davis and Smith 1991). The GSS contains no specific variables on sexual orientation or identity, but it allows respondents who have had same-sex partners to be identified. Here, then, people who have had at least one same-sex sexual partner are behaviorally identified as lesbian, gay, or bisexual, behavioral identification being highly correlated with a self-identified gay or bisexual orientation (Lever, et al. 1992). People who have had a gay period in their lives but who currently behave and may identify as straight are also included in the "gay" category. The questions on sexual behavior were self-administered, accompanied by assurances of confidentiality.

Because of the design of the GSS, not all respondents were asked all questions in each survey. After eliminating those responses without information on sex partners, attitudes, or occupation, and a few with missing data on other variables, the sample pooled from the 4,426 respondents in the 1989–91 surveys contained 996 men and 1,156 women. Of this subsample, 3 percent of the women and 5 percent of the men reported having had at least one same-sex sexual partner since the age of eighteen (our definition of behaviorally lesbian, gay, or bisexual), a proportion that falls within the range determined in studies of sexual orientation (Gonsiorek and Weinrich 1991).

In addition to data on occupation, age, education, race, sex, and place of residence, the GSS asked about attitudes toward homosexuals in two ways. One series of three questions asked respondents whether an admitted male homosexual should be allowed to speak in the respondent's community, to teach in a college or university, or to have a book in the respondent's local public library. Those answering yes to these questions were coded as "gay-tolerant." A separate question asked if the respondent thought that sexual relations between two adults of the same sex were always wrong, almost always wrong, wrong only sometimes, or not wrong at all. For this question, one coding of gay-tolerant included just those answering "not wrong at all"; another specification also included those answering "wrong only sometimes."

Are the People in Some Occupations More Tolerant?

One measure of the potential magnitude of anti-gay discrimination in different occupations is to assess the attitudes of people working in those occupations. Table 1 shows this cross-tabulation for two of the tolerance questions, which were consistent in their ordering with the other questions. People in the professional and technical occupations hold more tolerant attitudes, regardless of the measure, and those in craft and operative occupations are the least tolerant. The tolerance rankings are the same for men and women, with one exception: men in clerical and sales positions are more tolerant of sex between two adults of the same sex than are men in managerial positions, while women in clerical/sales and managerial positions are roughly the same in terms of tolerance.

These patterns could simply reflect the unequal distribution of occupations across regions, urban and rural areas, educational levels and age groups, or could point to particular work cultures in the different occupations, all of which might be related to tolerance. If these other factors are the main influence on tolerance, then getting more education or moving might be more important strategies than occupational choice for lesbians and gay men seeking a tolerant workplace. To see if there is a relationship strictly between tolerance and occupation, we estimated what are called probit models for the

TABLE 1   Measures of Tolerance within Occupations

Occupation	Would Allow Homosexual College Teacher (%)		Believe that Sex Between Two Adults of Same Sex is not Wrong (%)	
	Women	Men	Women	Men
Professional/Technical	81.0	86.7	26.2	24.6
Managerial	67.8	73.3	16.1	15.8
Clerical/Sales	66.3	71.4	14.0	21.1
Service	63.7	63.5	12.2	14.1
Craft/Operative	54.6	54.2	9.8	5.4

Source: Authors' tabulations from General Social Survey 1989–91, in Davis and Smith 1991.

attitude measures, using race, age, education, marital status, region, urban residence, sexual orientation, and occupation as independent variables. The effect of this statistical procedure is to hold constant the effect of factors such as region and urban residence, so as to see what the separate effect of occupation is on the degree of acceptance people express toward homosexuality.

The results of the probit procedure were fairly consistent for men and women, regardless of the survey question asked. Using the effect of occupational category generated by the probit procedure, we found the ranking of occupations by the level of tolerance to be much the same as in Table 1. People in professional/technical and managerial occupations are always among the most tolerant in their answers to the first set of civil liberties questions, along with men in clerical/sales positions. People in craft and operative jobs again appear to be the least tolerant, though women in these positions are less inclined than men to feel that gay sexual behavior is wrong. These results may be due to greater numbers of men in clerical and sales positions and women in craft and operative positions who are either gay themselves or more likely to know someone who is gay, given the overrepresentation of lesbians in craft/operative work and of gay men in clerical/sales jobs (see next section) and the correlation between acquaintance with gay people and tolerance (Herek and Glunt 1993).

However, the occupational parameters are rarely statistically significant; in other words, the effects seen here could be the result of an unusual sample of people rather than some systematic effect of occupation on level of tolerance. This is evidence that the markedly different levels of tolerance evinced by people in different occupational groups summarized in Table 1 may be a smoke screen, obscuring the more important underlying relationships between tolerance and education, urban residence, and age, the three variables that appear to be the most significant for predicting tolerance. It may be, however, that a larger sample and a more detailed occupational breakdown would reveal a greater role for occupational differences as well.

Are Lesbians and Gay Men Found in Tolerant Occupations?

Lesbians and gay men do appear to be distributed differently among occupations compared to heterosexuals, even when occupations are very broadly defined, as shown in Table 2. Lesbians in this sample are significantly less likely to hold professional/technical or clerical/sales positions and more likely to be engaged in service of craft/operative jobs than heterosexual women. Gay men are overrepresented in professional/technical, clerical/sales, and service categories and underrepresented in managerial and craft/operative positions, relative to heterosexual men.

TABLE 2   Occupational Distribution by Sexual Orientation and Gender, 1989–91

	Women			*Men*		
Occupation	*Lesbian/Bi*	*Heterosexual*	*All*	*Gay/Bi*	*Heterosexual*	*All*
Prof/Technical	11.4	20.8	18.1	32.0	18.9	14.9
Managerial	11.4	10.2	11.1	12.0	16.8	13.9
Clerical/Sales	14.3	36.6	40.9	18.0	14.6	16.8
Service	34.3	17.8	17.7	12.0	8.4	9.6
Craft/Operative	28.6	14.6	12.2	26.0	41.3	44.7
N=	35	1,121		50	946	

Sources: Data by sexual orientation comes from the General Social Survey, 1989–91, Davis and Smith 1991; data for all men and women comes from *Employment and Earnings,* January 1990.

At first glance, the concentration of lesbians in craft/operative positions would seem to confirm the prediction that lesbians are likely to trade conformity to gender roles to obtain better-paid positions with benefits. However, earnings equations performed by Badgett (1995) on these same data indicate that lesbians earn no more, and perhaps less, than comparable heterosexual women, in part due to lesbians' occupational distribution. What is odd is that lesbians appear to be in different and somewhat less conventional occupations than straight women, but they are neither earning more nor are they clustered in the more tolerant occupations; indeed, lesbians are concentrated in the least tolerant occupations. The lesbians and straight women in this sample have equal levels of education, but the lesbians are on average younger and less likely to be white. It may be that the lesbians are in relatively lower-paying occupations because of discrimination, because they have not yet trained for or been promoted to better jobs, or in order to reduce their potential losses from disclosure or discrimination, as Beth Schneider argues. A larger sample is needed to perform the sophisticated statistical analysis which could determine the relative influence of age and ethnicity on lesbians' and gay men's occupations. A larger sample would also allow us to identify particular jobs that are attractive to or problematic for lesbians, due to levels of customer contact, team-work, or other issues. Identifying the specific jobs in which lesbians are concentrated may help us to understand why lesbians appear to be clustered in relatively poorly paying and intolerant occupations.

Gay men's occupational distribution may indicate that they are avoiding or are unable to enter craft and operative jobs, which stereotypically entail the greatest emphasis on masculinity as a prerequisite for the work (or perhaps for the work culture). Again, the gay and straight men in this sample have equal levels of education; indeed, all four groups average 13.6 years of education. Perhaps gay men with less education are concentrated in clerical, sales, and service occupations rather than craft and operative positions, because

these jobs are not only outside of the masculine preserve in the labor market but are also concentrated in urban areas—as are the gay men in this sample, 55 percent of whom live in large urban areas (SMSAs) in comparison to 46 percent of the straight men.

Further, gay men are underrepresented in management, where hiring and promotion depend on very subjective assessments of ability, allowing a wide latitude for excluding people. They are overrepresented in professional/technical positions, where access is more often mediated by credential. It may be that socially subordinate groups in general find the credentialing process easier to pursue than promotion; for instance, the ratio of white women and African Americans in management compared to those in the professions is much lower than for white men (King 1992). Gay men do seem to be concentrated in the more tolerant occupational groups.

However, this sample is quite small, including only thirty-five lesbian and bisexual women and fifty gay and bisexual men, and it cannot be relied on for more than the suggestion of large patterns. Further, the sample as a whole may be slightly skewed toward professional and managerial employees, especially for men, as is indicated by the data in the columns for all working women and men, taken from the larger 1990 *Employment and Earnings* sample.

DISCUSSION AND CONCLUSION

Several issues complicate straightforward predictions of occupational strategies based on sexual orientation. First is the timing of one's realization of one's own sexual orientation. If, as suggested by Escoffier (1975), many lesbians and gay men do not identify as gay until their early twenties, many will already be well into an occupation or on an occupational path that has been influenced by other factors such as gender, class, ethnicity, and personal aptitudes and tastes.

Second, gender, ethnicity, and class have been shown to be very influential in sorting people into occupations, and these factors may explain some of the puzzles raised in this paper. The lesbians in this sample are younger, more likely to be non-white, and more likely to live in the South than the straight women, while the gay men are slightly older and more likely to live in a large urban area than the straight men. For these reasons, the lesbians in our sample have been more restricted in the occupations they could enter than the gay men. This may explain why they appear to be concentrated in less well-paid and less tolerant occupations than straight women, but not to face sexual orientation-based pay discrimination in these occupations, while gay men appear to be overrepresented in well-paid and tolerant occupations but to face sexual orientation-based pay discrimination in those occupations (Badgett 1995; see also previous chapter, this volume).

Third, we have assumed that lesbians and gay men are identical to straight women and men in every way except their sexual orientation. We have also treated lesbians and gay men as if they were the same except for their likely partners. An approach which investigated the impact of the different cultures, networks, opportunities, and experiences that combine to shape occupational distributions might contribute significantly to our understanding of gay occupational distributions.

In short, a larger sample and perhaps a more qualitative approach—including interviewing—are needed to pursue the questions raised here. With a larger sample, we could (1) see how gay and straight people are distributed among occupations defined more specifically than we were able to here; (2) use more sophisticated statistical techniques to separate the influences of education, location, age, gender, and ethnicity from the effect of sexual orientation; and (3) test the validity of our results: that lesbians are concentrated in less well-paid and less tolerant occupations, and that gay men are clustered in better-paid, more tolerant occupations but earn less than comparably situated straight men. We hope that data from the 1990 U.S. Census, a huge, nationally representative sample and the first Census in which couples could identify themselves as gay, will allow us to explore these questions in far greater depth.

Finally, the development of the gay civil-rights movement over the last few decades suggests that the occupational options for gay people have changed and will continue to change. Several examples demonstrate the tremendous possibilities. First, many explicit barriers have fallen, with openly gay and lesbian people working in government jobs or as police officers or teachers, for instance. Second, the development of the gay-rights movement has involved taking control of important institutions serving the lesbian, gay, and bisexual communities, a trend intensified by the HIV epidemic and the subsequent formation of support institutions. These trends have led to new entrepreneurial opportunities and employment options in gay bars, bookstores, restaurants, newspapers, magazines, hotels, health services, and political organizations. And third, many of the barriers related to intolerant attitudes are apparently susceptible to change. Gay workers are organizing workplace groups to fight for equal employment opportunities and equal benefits (e.g., domestic partner benefits), and much effort has gone into increasing gay visibility and directly educating coworkers and supervisors on lesbian and gay issues. If the composition of these groups' leaders is any indication, however, most of these efforts are directed at the managerial and professional levels of coworkers, increasing the tolerance level—and the attractiveness to lesbian and gay workers—of those occupations that are already relatively tolerant.

ACKNOWLEDGMENTS

The authors would like to thank Johanna Brenner, Connie Ledbetter, Clifford Lehman, Vicky Lovell, Lisa Saunders, Harold Vatter, Bill Weber, Mary Young and our editors for their insightful comments.

REFERENCES

Badgett, M. V. Lee. "The Wage Effects of Sexual Orientation Discrimination." *Industrial and Labor Relations Review,* Vol. 48, No. 4 (July 1995): 726–739.

Badgett, M. V. Lee, Colleen Donnelly, and Jennifer Kibbe. "Pervasive Patterns of Discrimination Against Lesbians and Gay Men: Evidence from Surveys Across the United States." Washington, DC: National Gay and Lesbian Task Force Policy Institute, 1992.

Baron, Ava (ed.). *Work Engendered: Toward A New History of American Labor.* Ithaca, NY: Cornell University Press, 1991.

Bergmann, Barbara. *The Economic Emergence of Women.* New York: Basic Books, 1986.

Blumstein, Philip, and Pepper Schwartz. *American Couples: Money, Work, Sex.* New York: William Morrow & Company, 1983.

Brause, Jay. "Closed Doors: Sexual Orientation Bias in the Anchorage Housing and Employment Markets." *Identity Reports: Sexual Orientation Bias in Alaska.* Anchorage, AK: Indentity Incorporated, 1989.

Burbridge, Lynn. "The Reliance of African American Women on Government and Nonprofit Employment." Unpublished paper presented at the Allied Social Science Associations (ASSA) meetings in Boston, January 1994.

Davis, James Allan, and Tom W. Smith. General Social Surveys, 1972–1991 (machine-readable data file). Principal Investigator, James A. Davis; Director and Coprincipal Investigator, Tom W. Smith. NORC ed. Chicago: National Opinion Research Center, producer, 1991; Storrs, CT: The Roper Center for Public Opinion Research, University of Connecticut, distributor.

England, Paula. "The Failure of Human Capital Theory to Explain Occupational Sex Segregation." *Journal of Human Resources,* Vol. 17, No. 3 (Summer 1982).

Escoffier, Jeffrey. "Stigmas, Work Environment, and Economic Discrimination Against Homosexuals." *Homosexual Counseling Journal,* Vol. 2, No. 1 (January 1975): 8–17.

Gonsiorek, John C., and James D. Weinrich. "The Definition and Scope of Sexual Orientation," in John C. Gonsiorek and James D. Weinrich (eds.), *Homosexuality: Research Implications for Public Policy.* Newbury Park, CA: Sage Publications, 1991.

Herek, Gregory M. "Stigma, Prejudice and Violence Against Lesbians and Gay Men," in John C. Gonsiorek and James D. Weinrich (eds.), *Homosexuality: Research Implications for Public Policy.* Newbury Park, CA: Sage Publications, 1991.

Herek, Gregory M., and Eric K. Glunt. "Interpersonal Contact and Heterosexuals' Attitudes Toward Gay Men: Results from a National Survey." *The Journal of Sex Research,* Vol. 30, No. 3 (August 1, 1993).

Hill, Herbert. "Race and Ethnicity in Organized Labor: The Historical Sources of Resistance to Affirmative Action," in Winston Van Horne and Thomas Tonnesen (eds.), *Ethnicity and the Work Force.* Madison, WI: University of Wisconsin System, 1985.

King, Mary C. "Occupational Segregation by Race and Sex, 1940–1988." *Monthly Labor Review,* Vol. 115, No. 4 (April 1992): 30–37.

Kleiman, Carol. "At Non-Profit Agencies, Women Lag Men in Salary and Power." *San Diego Union Tribune,* Sept. 27, 1994, c-6.

Larson, Kathryn. "The Economic Status of Lesbians: The State of the Art." Unpublished paper presented at the ASSA meetings in New Orleans, January 1992.

Lever, Janet, David Kanouse, William H. Rogers, Sally Carson, and Rosanna Hertz. "Behavior Patterns and Sexual Identity of Bisexual Males." *The Journal of Sex Research,* Vol. 29 (1992): 141–67.

Martin, Molly (ed.). *Hard-hatted Women: Stories of Struggle and Success in the Trades.* Seattle: Seal Press, 1988.

Moore, David W. "Public Polarized on Gay Issue." *The Gallup Poll Monthly,* No. 331 (April 1993).

Polachek, Solomon. "Occupational Self-Selection: A Human Capital Approach to Sex Differences in Occupational Structure." *Review of Economics and Statistics,* Vol. 63, No. 1 (February 1981).

Reskin, Barbara. "Segregating Workers: Job Differences by Ethnicity, Race and Sex." Paper presented at the ASSA meetings in Boston, January 1994.

Reskin, Barbara, and Irene Padavic. *Women and Men at Work.* Thousand Oaks, CA: Pine Forge Press, 1994.

Schneider, Beth. "Coming Out at Work." *Work and Occupations,* Vol. 13, No. 4 (November 1986): 463–87.

U.S. Department of Labor, Bureau of Labor Statistics, *Employment and Earnings,* Vol. 37, No. 1 (January 1990).

Warden, Sharon. "Attitudes on Homosexuality." *Washington Post,* April 25, 1993, A18.

Woods, James D. *The Corporate Closet: The Professional Lives of Gay Men in America.* New York: Free Press, 1993.

The Sexual Division of Labor, Sexuality, and Lesbian/Gay Liberation
Toward a Marxist-Feminist Analysis of Sexuality in U.S. Capitalism

JULIE MATTHAEI

In this paper, I will try to draw out some of the ways in which the economic sphere—especially the division of labor between the sexes—has contributed to the construction of sexuality during the past century and a half in the United States. I will show how economic forces have helped create both heterosexual and homosexual relationships—with emphasis on the latter, which have received very little attention from economists. I will also argue that the late twentieth century emergence of a lesbian and gay political movement—and of a feminist movement in which lesbians have played key roles—constitutes a direct challenge to the sexual division of labor and gender. Since I cover a broad sweep of history, this analysis will be, of necessity, sketchy. In particular, I will not be able to address adequately the class and racial-ethnic variations in sexuality. Nor can I integrate the many noneconomic factors that have contributed to the changing construction of sexuality. However, I hope to be able to show that the economy has played an important part in shaping and transforming sexuality.[1]

This paper builds predominantly upon the work of historians of sexuality, and on basic feminist theory. There is little recent work on sexuality written from a Marxist or radical economics perspective.

Marxist economic theory essentially ignores the family and sexuality; when necessary, it assumes heterosexuality. Marxist-feminist theory has focused on the institution of heterosexuality as key to patriarchy; it has shown how the sexual division of labor, and in particular the exclusion of women from high-paying jobs, has forced women into unequal marriages with men, which include the provision of unpaid domestic labor to their husbands.[2] However, these analyses essentially equate sexuality with marriage, and usually ignore homosexuality.[3] Furthermore, as Ann Ferguson (1989, 1991) has pointed out, these analyses have utilized a "rational self-interested" view of the individual, which cannot comprehend either "unconscious libidinal motivations" or the motivations of individuals by "symbolic definitions of gender, racial, sexual and family identity," all of which are key to understanding gender and sexuality (Ferguson 1989: 32). Rhonda Gottlieb's path-breaking article, "The Political Economy of Sexuality" (1984), examined some of the basic aspects of sexuality in capitalism, including the male-centeredness of heterosexual sex, the grounding of heterosexuality and male-defined sexuality in the sex-typing of jobs, and the egalitarian aspects of many homosexual relationships. Unfortunately, there has been no response to it (not one citation in the *Social Science Citation Index!*). Here I will try to address the topic of economics and sexuality from a radical economics framework, as does Gottlieb, but with a more historical focus.

Source: "The Sexual Division of Labor, Sexuality, and Lesbian/Gay Liberation: Towards a Marxist Feminist Analysis of Sexuality in U.S. Capitalism." *Review of Radical Political Economics* 27:2 (June 1995).

I find this to be a difficult topic, and it is one in which I am by no means an expert. However, I think that it is important that economists, especially Marxist-feminists, along with feminist social scientists in general—all of whom have remained more or less silent on the subject—begin to include an analysis of sexuality in their work. In not accounting for sexuality, they relegate it to an extrasocial given. One result is that they end up assuming heterosexuality and erasing homosexuality. For example, Marxist-feminist and feminist analyses of the family, of housework, and of reproduction almost always assume a heterosexual family. In doing so, they erase gays and lesbians, thereby contributing to our oppression. It has been gay and lesbian studies, centered in history and the humanities, that has done the most both to recognize the existence of homosexuality and to analyze sexuality itself (including heterosexuality) as a social construct.

SEXUALITY AS SOCIALLY, AND ECONOMICALLY, CONSTRUCTED

One of the most valuable insights of Marxist economics is the recognition that individuals are constructed—i.e., produced and reproduced as social beings—by the relationships that they enter into with other members of their society. Economic relationships constitute a key part of this social production of the individual. Not only is a certain type of person constructed by a certain type of economy—for example, advanced capitalism constructs an individuated, consumption-oriented, self-seeking person—but also, economic relationships differentiate people, for example by class, race-ethnicity, and gender. This social constructionist view of the individual is the polar opposite of the prevailing neoclassical view, which starts with a predetermined individual whose preferences, along with those of other isolated individuals, determine the economy (for a neoclassical analysis of sexuality, see Posner 1992[4]).

The social constructionist view of sexuality or sexual preference, in turn, rejects biological explanations of sexual desire, behavior, and identity. Jeffrey Weeks, a historian of sexuality and a leader in the development of the social constructionist school, has written:

> We tend to see sexuality as a protean force, drawing on the resources of the body, providing the energy for myriad manifestations of desire, and having unique effects. But the more we explore this "special case" of sex, the more variegated, ambivalent and racked by contradiction it seems. There is, I would argue, no simple relationship between "sex" and "society" . . . no easy fit between biological attributes, unconscious fantasy and desire, and social appearance and identity. The mediating elements are words and attitudes, ideas and social relations. The erotic possibilities of the human animal, its generalized capacity for warmth, intimacy and pleasure, can never be expressed "spontaneously" without intricate transformation; they are organized through a dense web of beliefs, concepts and social activities in a complex and changing history. (Weeks 1985: 4)

A social constructionist view of sexuality views it as neither genetically/naturally determined nor as a purely self-conscious moral choice. Social institutions and practices not only direct and restrict one's sexual behavior, but also give this behavior its content and meaning. "Each society seems to have a limited range of potential storylines for its sexual scripts," as Stephen Epstein has noted (1987: 24).[5] Theorizing about sexuality involves studying the social construction of a constellation of possible sexual behaviors at a particular place and time. Thus, neither heterosexuality nor homosexuality is either "natural" or universal; both are socially produced. Even if biologists were able to identify a genetic marker that appeared to be correlated with homosexual behavior of some sort (which they have not), this marker could not in any way be understood to determine or create homosexuality as a culturally specific set of social concepts and practices.[6]

TIME AND PLACE MATTER: SEXUALITY AS HISTORICAL AND CULTURAL

The growth of the gay liberation and feminist movements in the 1970s engendered the development of the field of lesbian and gay history. The earliest studies were essentially searches for the lesbians and gay men of all times and places whose sexuality had been obscured by earlier historians. However, as the field developed breadth and sophistication, the rising social constructionist school criticized such studies as "essentialist" for incorrectly positing a cross-historical lesbian or gay identity. Indeed, historians of sexuality have criticized the very idea of "gay history," since the concepts that construct sexuality have varied so greatly across time.[7]

As far as I know, there are no universals about human sexuality that hold true for all time periods and societies. In the United States, sexual practices have changed very rapidly in the past 150 years, along with capitalist development; the very concepts of heterosexual and homosexual persons did not even arise until the early twentieth century, as we will discuss below. Neither is homophobia/heterosexism—prejudice against and fear of homosexuals/homosexual behavior—a universal given throughout human history. Consider, for example, the oft-admired Greeks, who viewed man-boy love (including sex) as one of the highest forms of love. Or certain Native American nations, including the Kaska and Navajo, in which lesbians were highly valued (Amott and Matthaei 1991: 37). Neither is there an unambiguous one-to-one correspondence between the economic system that characterizes a society and its sexual practices—compare the tolerance for homosexuality in the Netherlands with the repression presently practiced in Great Britain.

These historical and cross-cultural differences make difficult any historical study of sexuality (or indeed, of any social construct, be it the family, gender, or whatever). In this study, I try to stake out a conceptual middle ground between the extremes of total historical specificity (which precludes meaningful cross-historical comparison) and of universalization (which falsely projects the present social practices onto the past).

An additional problem one encounters when analyzing sexuality, even within a particular historical period, is the variation of sexuality across race-ethnicity, gender, and class. A person's sexuality is

not, in the metaphor of Elizabeth Spelman (1988), a discrete "pop-bead" on his or her necklace of identity that takes the same form regardless of the gender, class, or race-ethnicity it is combined with. We are all aware of the significant interconnections between sexuality and gender—indeed, few would presume to discuss sexuality without specifying the genders of the participants. However, race-ethnicity and class also differentiate sexuality in important ways. For example, in the nineteenth century, white middle- and upper-class women were constructed as relatively asexual, endangered by the lust of Black men (for which the latter were lynched), while free Black women, viewed by the dominant white society as oversexed and "loose," were not allowed to protest against their rape by white men (hooks 1981: ch. 2). Where I can, I will specify the class and racial-ethnic aspects of the sexualities studied; unfortunately, the available literature upon which I have based this paper usually slights or simply ignores the sexual practices of those who are poor or of color.

THE SEXUAL DIVISION OF LABOR, THE SOCIAL CONSTRUCTION OF GENDER, AND HOMOPHOBIA

Economic institutions, in particular the organization of work into men's and women's work, have played an important role in the social construction of family and sexuality. Until very recently, it was simply accepted that individuals could not and would not be permitted to perform the work of the "opposite sex." God-given, biological differences in abilities between the sexes, it was argued, made only males fit for men's work, and only females fit for women's. For example, only females/women were seen to possess the "maternal instincts" necessary for the raising of small children.

This sexual division of labor, present in all previously known societies, has assigned the biological sexes (males, females) to different and complementary work activities, men's work and women's work, respectively. In general, women's work has centered on caring for children within the family, while men's work has been focused outside of the family, involving interfamilial relationships, such as market-oriented production or political activity. When wage labor developed, jobs were typed either men's or women's work—if not in general, then at least within a particular region or workplace (Matthaei 1982: ch. 9). Among European Americans in the United States, the sexual division of labor has always involved the political and economic domination of women by men; among certain Indian nations, on the other hand, the gender differences it constructed did not involve the subordination of women to men (Amott and Matthaei 1991: ch. 3).

The sexual division of labor plays a key role in constructing gender identity—masculinity and femininity, or manhood and womanhood—because preparation for and involvement in different and complementary work activities makes the sexes into different and complementary genders, masculine men and feminine women. However, this division of labor is only one part of the social construction of gender, which begins much earlier. One's gender identity is assigned at birth, according to one's perceived biological sex, and is imprinted upon the infant and child's personality at every level, from clothing to recreation to vocabulary and way of speaking. Most people, then, by the time they are adults, accept their assigned gender identities as given and immutable parts of themselves—and actively attempt to prove and reprove them to others by doing things appropriate to their gender and by distancing themselves from behaviors attributed to the "opposite sex."[8]

While gender roles have been viewed, by society, as emerging naturally out of the biological differences between the sexes, they are in fact social constructs that are achieved only through a great deal of limiting and molding of a person's being (Hubbard, Henifin, and Fried 1982). This limiting and molding is not always successful. For example, females and males whose physiques and characters predispose them for the incorrect gender role (e.g., large, strong, and aggressive females, or small, slight, sensitive males) may find it difficult

to become women and men, respectively. They may even find themselves criticized and taunted by parents and schoolmates for their deviant-for-their-sex looks or behavior. While such social ostracism may work to pressure some people into heightened efforts to "fit in," it can also succeed in convincing others that their efforts to conform to their correct gender roles are doomed—that they are really "men in women's bodies" (or vice versa) or belong to some in-between gender.[9] Some individuals, especially females as we will see, consciously choose to reject their gender roles for those of the opposite sex. Those who cross gender lines in this way often take up the sexuality connected with their new gender roles, forming heterogenderal (cross-gender) but homosexual (same-sex) relationships: for example, a masculine female with a feminine female, or an effeminate male with a masculine male.

THE SEXUAL DIVISION OF LABOR, MARRIAGE, AND SEXUALITY IN THE NINETEENTH CENTURY

An essential part of gender identity has been the social requirement to marry and form a family with a member of the opposite sex and gender. Women marry only men, and men only women. The sexual division of labor has provided much of the incentive for marriage, as well as the glue keeping these marriages together, since it makes the genders economically and socially complementary and in need of one another. In this way, gender, and the sexual division of labor that accompanies it, can be seen as involving "compulsory heterosexuality," i.e., as forcing males and females to marry one another (Rich 1980).

As capitalism developed in the United States, the sexual division of labor concentrated income in the hands of men within each racial-ethnic group and class (with the exception of enslaved African Americans). Within each of these groups, men's jobs were much higher paying than women's, and the work of homemaking and child care was assigned to wives, daughters, and domestic servants (mostly female). Hence, most women needed fathers or husbands to provide them with sufficient income to survive and support their children, while most men needed wives to take care of their children and their homes.[10] Once women were married, their inability to survive financially without their husbands placed them in a subordinate position, forced to serve their husbands in whatever ways necessary to "keep them." In this sense, a husband became a woman's "meal ticket," and many women were constrained from leaving unhappy or even dangerous marriages by their financial dependence upon their husbands. So although chosen marriages based in love increasingly replaced marriages arranged by parents (Matthaei 1982: 116–118), women did have to consider a man's financial position before deciding whether to accept a marriage proposal.

If economic forces pressured adults to marry the opposite sex, organized religion both propounded the necessity of marriage and attempted to restrict sexuality to it. Nineteenth-century Protestantism defined "good sex" as being only procreative sex within marriage. All other kinds of sexuality—from fornication (sexual intercourse between unmarried members of the opposite sex) to sodomy (any erotic physical relations that could not result in pregnancy, including anal sex between same- or opposite-sex partners, masturbation, and oral sex)—were assumed to be sins that tempted individuals, especially men, but that should be resisted (D'Emilio 1983: 104; Katz 1983: 140–5; Weeks 1977: 4, 12). Birth control and abortion were illegal. Further, love was not linked with sexual passion; indeed, the white middle- and upper-class idea of "true love" at this time involved nothing erotic—it was an "affinity between two disembodied souls," which could be of the same or opposite sexes (Snitow, Stansell, and Thompson 1983: 14).

However, other factors reduced the incidence of marriage and the confinement of sexual acts to marriage. First, a variety of economic and social forces made it difficult for many to marry. The social practice of marrying within one's class and race (laws against "miscegenation" were on the books in many states until the 1950s!), combined with regional imbalances in the numbers of men and women, limited the availability of potential partners. The migration to the West Coast, among both whites and Asians, was disproportionately male, restricting opportunities for marriage; in California in 1850, there were twelve men for every woman, and the imbalance was much greater among Asians (Amott and Matthaei 1991: 201). Among African Americans, the problem was not the sex ratio but their status as property; marriages of enslaved African Americans had no legal recognition, and were often broken up by profit-seeking owners. For American Indians, this period was one of displacement and genocide, clearly disruptive of marriage relationships (Amott and Matthaei 1991: 16–7). In 1890, 16 percent of women and 28 percent of men between the ages of 25 and 44 were reported to be single and never married; almost 22 percent of women and 30 percent of men were reported to be single, widowed, or divorced (U.S. Department of Commerce 1976: 21); substantial numbers were also married, but separated.

Second, the sexual division of labor provided less financial incentive for men to marry than it did for women. Given their access to higher wage jobs, most men were able to live independently off of their earnings, purchasing in the market most of the services which a wife provided, from meals to laundry to sex and companionship.[11] Indeed, some men chose never to marry, a choice they could make much more easily than could women, who often remained single for lack of a marriage proposal.

Third, sexuality within marriage was restricted, at least among the most-studied white middle and upper classes. Much has been made of the Victorian view of white women's sexuality—i.e., their lack of sexual feelings—and certainly this view was present, if not omnipresent. Historians have also pointed out the objective reasons that married women had for trying to limit their sexual relations with their husbands, factors that may have contributed to the ideology of woman's sexlessness. For one thing, birth control was illegal and difficult to obtain, and many women feared the dangers of miscarriage and pregnancy as well as the extra work of each additional child. In addition, the construction of marital sexuality, within the patriarchal power relations of marriage, was around the husband's sexual gratification (Gottlieb 1984: 144–50); women often found it brutish, even violent, and far from sexually arousing—an unpleasant duty to be performed. Furthermore, since men commonly exposed themselves to venereal diseases through their relations with prostitutes, wives often feared contracting these dreaded illnesses from sexual intercourse with their husbands. Indeed, nineteenth-century feminists formed a "Voluntary Motherhood" movement, centered on the assertion of every woman's right to say no to sex with her husband (and hence to the possibility of pregnancy and motherhood) (Degler 1980: ch. II; Gordon 1976: ch. 5). The lesser interest of women in sexuality—plus the concentration of income in men's hands—helped fuel men's pursuit of sex outside marriage from prostitutes.

THE SEXUAL DIVISION OF LABOR AND FEMALE AND MALE PROSTITUTION

The nineteenth-century view of sexuality as either procreation or sin, however, was not successful in restricting it to marriage. As we have seen above, many people were not married. And while unmarried women were expected to remain "chaste" or risk losing their marriageability and being saddled with "illegitimate" children, unmarried men were expected to need and seek out sexual outlets—to "sow their wild oats"—even if this was viewed as sinful. Even though married women were expected to be sexual only with their husbands, married men were actively encouraged, if backhandedly, toward sexual relations outside marriage. The social construction of masculinity as driven by sexual desires, or lust, for sexual objects; the practice of men paying for their fiancees' and wives'

expenses, i.e., purchasing women's sexual services; the restriction of sex within many marriages; and the gender and class differences that distributed money unevenly—all of these factors contributed to the establishment of sexuality as an industry, i.e., prostitution, that catered to men and employed a class of women who became unmarriageable (Gilfoyle 1992).

The existence of women prostitutes who serviced men of all classes is well documented. If sex within marriage was to be passionless, rare, and aimed at procreation, then men could appease their sexual desires outside of marriage with "bad" girls. And for working-class girls and women who lacked good marriage prospects or simply chose not to marry, prostitution offered much higher pay than the pittance they could earn at the other jobs that were open to them. Many working-class girls became professional prostitutes, especially within the cities; others, called "charity girls" in the nineteenth century, provided sexual favors to men in exchange for gifts, meals, and entertainment that were otherwise out of their financial reach (Peiss 1983). Among whites, prostitution was very common in the cities, as well as in all parts of the woman-scarce West. Free Black women, whose job opportunities were especially restricted, often turned to prostitution in southern cities, where they served both Black and white clientele (Amott and Matthaei 1991: 150). The sex imbalance in Chinese and Japanese immigration (25 men to 1 woman among Japanese immigrants, for example, in 1900) made for a very profitable prostitution business: women were sold or kidnapped in their home countries, sent to the United States, and kept as slaves/prostitutes (Amott and Matthaei 1991: 201, 219).

What is perhaps less well known is that male prostitution was also very common (indeed, the word "gay" in the nineteenth century referred to a prostitute [Weeks 1977: 42]). Weeks estimates that about half of the prostitutes in Europe in the late nineteenth-century cities were young men; I have not found comparable data for the United States, but male prostitution appears to have been common, especially in large cities. Weeks points out the continuity between male heterosexual and homosexual sex/prostitution: the interest was in sex; encounters were usually casual, not long term; the prostitute was a sex object, performing sexual services in exchange for money or gifts; the client was a man with money to spend.

Male prostitutes were very similar to female ones: young; working class; interested in pay that was many times what they could earn at their jobs; servicing their clients' sexual needs, usually by bringing them to orgasm. Some were full-time "professionals," who worked out of brothels or "boy-houses"; they often dressed like women. Detective Gardener describes a New York brothel in 1892: "In each room sat a (male) youth, whose face was painted, eye-brows blackened, and whose airs were those of a young girl. Each person talked in a high falsetto voice, and called the others by women's names." German sexologist Magnus Hirschfeld wrote of meeting, in Chicago, "a Negro girl on Clark Street who turned out to be a male prostitute" (Karz 1976: 63, 77).

There were also many part-time male prostitutes, who were working-class youth employed in low-wage jobs: sailors, soldiers, laborers, newspaper boys, messenger boys, and the like (Weeks 1989: 207; Katz 1976: 64, 78). For this group, prostitution was a way to supplement very low-wages or, like the charity girls, to give them access to "the better life." A gay academic wrote Hirschfeld a long letter describing the homosexual life, including this description of part-time male prostitutes:

> In the vicinity of Denver there is a military fort with a force of a few hundred men. Last summer a soldier from there propositioned me on the street in Denver. I've heard that this happens quite frequently in San Francisco and Chicago. I recall meeting a soldier who was a prostitute long ago in San Antonio, Texas, and last summer I met a young sailor from Massachusetts. The latter was on leave and looking for homosexual intercourse out on the street late at night. In all of these cases it was difficult to tell whether the soldiers were really homosexual or just prostitutes, or whether they

> went with men for lack of anything better. It's never easy to draw the line, and things are so expensive nowadays that someone could easily be moved to earn a little pocket money in one way or the other. (Katz 1976: 78)

Some men may have become male prostitutes because it gave them a way to live out aspects of the feminine gender role to which they were attracted—feminine dress, a desire to be a passive sexual partner, erotic attraction to a man. In a sense, they wanted to be women, and were doing "women's work" of prostitution. In some cases, such effeminate males actually "treated" their sexual partners: one study of Newport, Rhode Island, sailors in 1919 found that a gang of effeminate sailors would "take a sailor to a show or to dinner, offer him small gifts, or provide him with a place to stay when he was on overnight leave; in exchange, the sailor allowed his host to have sex with him that night, within whatever limits the sailor cared to set." Some of these gay sailors provided sexual services to civilian men in exchange for money, while others had steady relationships with masculine men they referred to as their "husbands" (Chauncey 1990: 299, 303).

While most sexuality in nineteenth-century capitalism involved the cash nexus, either overtly in prostitution, or covertly in marriage, casual male homosexual relations also could take the form of a sexual encounter in which both partners satisfied sexual needs and no exchange of money or gifts was necessary. After all, men were constructed as lustful beings, who desired sex for its own sake. Plus, there was no problem of unwanted pregnancy as in heterosexual sex. The male homosexual subculture that emerged in this period involved "cruising places" where men could meet—certain streets, beaches, woods, bars, or bath houses—to engage in mutually satisfying casual sex. Often, relationships crossed class lines. Gender roles were often involved, including "balls" where males dressed as women. Sometimes race differences were played on: one sexologist discovered, in St. Louis, a group of Black male butlers, cooks, and chauffeurs, who dressed as women for their encounters with white, masculine males (Katz 1976: 66–67, 75–76).

FEMALES WHO LIVED AS MEN: LESBIANISM AS A RESPONSE TO GENDER INEQUALITY AND OPPRESSION

While the sexual division of labor helped pressure women into heterosexual marriage, its rigid confines also led some females to reject womanhood and heterosexuality.[12] Some of these rebels worked as feminists to challenge gender roles in society at large. Others rebelled privately by becoming men: they dressed as men, did men's work, and married women. Many "passed" so effectively that they were not found out until their deaths, at which time their femaleness was cause for great surprise and, often, media attention. Murray Hall became a well-known New York City politician; his death, and femaleness, were covered in the *New York Times* and the New York *Daily Tribune*. One of Hall's acquaintances was quoted as saying: "While he was somewhat effeminate in appearance and talked in a falsetto voice, still his conduct and actions were distinctively masculine. This revelation [of Hall's femaleness] is a stunner to me and, I guess, to everybody else who knew him" (Katz 1976: 356).

Accounts of the lives of passing women indicate that many if not most of them were driven into passing by the inequality and oppression involved in the sexual division of labor—in particular, by the gender-typing of jobs and the restriction of females/women to low-paid jobs. Many passing women directly referred to their inability to survive on women's wages in explaining their decisions to take up the masculine gender. A female who called herself Charles Warner wrote in the 1860s:

> When I was about 20 I decided that I was almost at the end of my rope. I had no money and a woman's wages were not enough to keep me alive. I looked around and saw men getting more money and more work, and more money for the same kind of work. I decided to become a man. It was simple, I just put on men's clothing and applied for a man's job. I got it and got good money for those times, so I stuck to it (Berube 1979:1).

According to the *Day Book* tabloid newspaper of Chicago, Cora Anderson, an American Indian, studied nursing with Marie White, who was white, at the Provident Hospital in Chicago. The two formed a relationship but found it difficult to survive on nurses' wages—and Cora was unwilling to accede to sexual harassment: "Two-thirds of the physicians I met made a nurse's virtue the price of their influence in getting her steady work. Is it any wonder that I determined to become a member of this privileged sex, if possible?" The two moved to Cleveland as the Kerwinnieos, with Cora becoming the husband, Ralph. "This disguise also helped me to protect my chum as well as myself. She could stay in the home, and believe me, as long as society, with its double code and double standards of morals, is as it is now, the only place for a woman is in the home." Ralph worked as a bellboy and later for a manufacturer. Later, Ralph left Marie to marry another woman. Marie responded by exposing Ralph as a passing woman, and Cora/Ralph was charged with "disorderly conduct" (Katz 1976: 385–90).

Another passing woman, Caroline Hall, decided to live as "Mr. Hall," according to a *New York Times* story in 1901, because of her "belief that women were not afforded as many opportunities in the world as men." She was an artist who was "an excellent rifle shot," and, as a man, traveled in Italy as a painter, entering and winning several rifle contests. She/he met and became domestic partners with Giuseppina Boriani (Katz 1976: 365–68).

It appears that passing women were from all classes and races. Edward Stevenson wrote of a group of about ten women, most likely African American, who passed as men to work as porters, train agents, switchmen, and cooks for the New York Central Railway in 1903 (Katz 1976: 378–79). Mary Fields, an ex-slave, passed and found employment as a stagecoach driver (Faderman 1991: 44). It was also common for women who wished to fight in wars to pass as men; many were found out when they were wounded in battle. One Civil War expert estimated that 400 females fought as men in that war; one such female, accepted as a man, was a spy who "posed" as a woman! (Katz 1976: 323, 345–46, 363, 909–910). I have found references to females passing as men to practice medicine in the early 1800s (U.S. Dept. of Labor 1974: 21–23) and in the early 1900s (Faderman 1991: 317), and to female (passing as men) sailors (Katz 1976: 905–914).

Sometimes daughters started the process of gender switching at the behest of their parents. For example, Lucy Ann Lobdell, the only child of a farm couple, took on men's work to help her parents, both of whom were disabled by illness. When she reached adulthood, she decided to actually take up life as a man. As she explained:

> First, my father was lame, and in consequence, I had worked in-doors and out [on the farm, and hunting]; and as hard times were crowding upon us, I made up my mind to dress in men's attire to seek labor, as I was used to men's work. And as I might work harder at house-work, and get only a dollar per week, and I was capable of doing men's work, and getting men's wages, I resolved to try . . . to get work away among strangers. (Katz 1976: 333)

During her life as a man, Lucy (who took the name of Joseph) supported herself as a hunter and trapper, and married a woman who had been abandoned by her husband and was living on charity. Lucy/Joseph had to work to hide her femaleness. While changing one's gender wasn't acceptable in her society, in contrast, among the Canadian Kaska nation, it was common and accepted for families lacking sons to urge one of their daughters to become a man (Amott and Matthaei 1991: 37).

While anecdotal evidence points to many passing women who formed long-term relationships with other women, the evidence leaves many questions unanswered. For example, we cannot determine whether it was the economic disadvantage of being a woman or the potential for partnering with another woman that was more likely to be the primary impetus for a woman to pass. And what of the female/women partners of passing women? Some, it appears, were not aware that their husbands were female.[13] Others married "men" they knew to be females, because of love or perhaps because of bad experiences they had with male

men.[14] Males passing as women seem to have been much less common, probably because of the clear loss in economic power and social status that this involved.

SIMILARS ATTRACT: THE GENDER DIVIDE, ROMANTIC FRIENDSHIPS, AND "GAY" JOBS

Even for those who did not reject their assigned gender role, the rigid sexual division of labor of the nineteenth century tended to spawn intimate homosocial (and perhaps homosexual) relationships, especially between women, because of the vast social chasm it opened up between the sexes. Men's and women's work and social lives were so disparate, their interests and sensibilities so opposed, that real intimacy between them was difficult to achieve, and usually not expected. As Carroll Smith-Rosenberg writes:

> If men and women grew up as they did in relatively homogeneous and segregated sexual groups, then marriage represented a major problem in adjustment. From this perspective we could interpret much of the emotional stiffness and distance that we associate with Victorian marriage as a structural consequence of contemporary sex-role differentiation and gender-role socialization. With marriage, both women and men had to adjust to life with a person who was, in essence, a member of an alien group. (Smith-Rosenberg 1979: 331)

In contrast, members of the same gender had a good deal in common; they could understand one another's feelings, thoughts, and experiences, and hence achieve emotional and intellectual intimacy.

Not only did the rigid sexual division of labor make the genders so different as to seem alien to one another, but also the nineteenth-century idea of love, as a nonsexual meeting of souls, was easily applied to same-sex relationships. What historians have called "romantic friendships" were common between middle- and upper-class women in the late nineteenth and early twentieth centuries; all of the documented examples I have seen appear to have been among white women, but it is probable that they also occurred among other racial-ethnic groups. Unlike the relationships between a passing woman and another woman, these relationships were homogenderal: that is, these (female) women were attracted to a person of their same, feminine, gender. These women had intense, emotionally and physically intimate love relationships with other women before and during their marriages with men (Smith-Rosenberg 1979; Faderman 1981). For most of these women, their "romantic friendships" were more passionate and intimate than their marriages; for example, "rural women developed a pattern of . . . extended visits that lasted weeks and sometimes months, at times even dislodging husbands from their beds and bedrooms so that dear friends might spend every hour of every day together" (Smith-Rosenberg 1979: 319).

Close friendships among men—also viewed as love relationships—were also common, given the gulf between the genders. While there has been less attention paid to these relationships, they were probably widespread. Discussions of love between men were common in mid-nineteenth-century popular novels, letters, and diaries, in which "American men loved each other, sought verbal and physical forms for the expression of that love, located it in a tradition, and worried about its place in a social order" (Martin 1990: 170). The celebrated poet Walt Whitman spoke of "adhesiveness," love between men, as coexisting with "amativeness" between the sexes, but finessed the question of sexuality (Weeks 1977: 34, 52–53); the German sexologist Hirschfeld wrote in 1914, "Strongly sublimated homosexuality is also common in America; a good example is provided by the poet of comradely love, Walt Whitman" (Katz 1976: 77). Not pressured by financial need into marriage, men could remain bachelors or maintain their friendships after marriage.

The rigid sexual division of labor also created homosexuality in another way: jobs that isolated the employee with his/her coworkers tended to spawn homosocial and homosexual relationships, as did the sex segregation of other social institutions. Military and maritime employment, cattle

herding (cowboys), and other men's employments in the woman-scarce West encouraged close relationships and sexuality among men. Prostitution, which marginalized and isolated women from the mainstream and from marriage, as well as exercised their sexuality, generated loving relationships that were often sexual among women: "They spent all their free time together, traveled together, protected each other, loved each other" (Faderman 1991: 37; see also Nestle 1987: 157–77). The sex-segregated schools that were viewed as preparation for segregated gender roles also, because of their homosocial environment, encouraged homosexual relationships, as did the sex-segregated prison system (Faderman 1991: 19–20, 36–37). Interestingly, women in reform schools formed same-sex relationships across racial (Black-white) lines in which "the difference in color . . . [took] the place of difference in sex," with Black women taking the masculine role (Otis, quoted in Faderman 1991: 38).[15]

LESBIAN CAREER WOMEN AND BOSTON MARRIAGES: A VARIATION ON THE ROMANTIC FRIENDSHIP THEME

In the nineteenth and early twentieth centuries, women whom historians have called "social homemakers" worked to expand woman's traditional work of homemaking and, indeed, the boundaries of womanhood; some of these social homemakers were explicitly feminist. While few directly attacked the sexual division of labor, these activists did argue for (middle class) women's right to a college education (to prepare themselves better for motherhood), and for women's claims on emerging professions that they viewed as naturally feminine—teaching, social work, librarianship, and nursing, as well as social activism/social homemaking itself. Black as well as white women participated in this movement and in the emerging women's professions, although Black women encountered virulent discrimination in both (Matthaei 1982: 173–86; Amott and Matthaei

1991: 152–54). As Lillian Faderman has pointed out (1991: ch. 1), access to such jobs gave educated, middle-class females the economic wherewithal to live with other females as life partners, without one member of the couple having to pass as a man (an opportunity working class-women did not have). Indeed, "Many of the leaders of this [social homemaking] movement, including Jane Addams, Vida Scudder, and Frances Willard, not only rejected marriage, but lived with women in intense emotional (and probably sexual) love relationships" (Amott and Matthaei 1991: 125). One suspects that their rejection of heterosexual marriage in favor of relationships with women was a factor underlying their commitment to expanding women's professional options.

Not only did education and career open up women's possibility of nonmarriage, but they also restricted a woman's marriage options: in white middle-class society, paid careers were seen to be incompatible with the full-time dedication to homemaking and mothering expected of wives. (Indeed, marriage bars—employer policies to fire female employees upon marriage and/or refuse to hire married women—were common, especially in teaching and clerical work, through the 1940s [Goldin 1990: 160–71]). Thus, the movement for women's college education, and the participation in feminine careers it encouraged and made possible, discouraged those women from heterosexual marriage (Matthaei 1982: ch. 11). Because a college education prepared women for labor force careers, rates of nonmarriage were much higher among college graduates than among nongraduates; one study found that 35 percent of women college graduates born before 1897 had not married by the age of 50, compared to 8 percent of nongraduates (Matthaei 1982: 259).

Thus, the development of women's education and careers both reduced women's opportunities for marriage and increased their ability to form live-in relationships with one another. Women who had formed close emotional (and maybe sexual) relationships in college no longer had to subordinate

these "romantic friendships" to marriage, as in previous times, but could set up households together (Faderman 1991: ch. 1; Matthaei 1982: ch. 11). As Jessie Taft, a sociologist, wrote in 1916:

> Everywhere we find the unmarried woman turning to other women, building up with them a real home, finding in them the sympathy and understanding, the bond of similar standards and values as well as the same aesthetic and intellectual interests, that are often difficult of realization in a husband. . . . One has only to know professional women to realize how common and how satisfactory is this substitute for marriage. (Quoted in Matthaei 1982: 260)

Such arrangements were so common in the East that they were called "Boston marriages."

It is interesting to note that these relationships, like the romantic friendships that preceded them, were homogenderal and were usually with members of the same class and race. Sometimes, both women were professionally employed. For example, Katharine Coman (professor of economics) and Katharine Lee Bates (professor of English, and writer of the words to "America the Beautiful"), lived and worked together at Wellesley College (my employer); Katharine Lee Bates wrote a book of poetry to Katharine Coman, entitled *Yellow Clover* (1922), whose dedication reads, in Latin, "How can it be wrong to love one so dear?" (Schwartz 1979). However, it appears that it was more common for one woman to take on the role of primary provider, and for the other to take on a wifely/motherly role (Vicinus 1992: 482–83; Faderman 1981: ch. 5). The same-class, same-race quality of these relationships contrasts with the prevalence of cross-class and cross-race sexual liaisons among male homosexuals.

THE TWENTIETH CENTURY: THE EMERGENCE OF HETEROSEXUALS AND HOMOSEXUALS

Two important and related changes in the social conceptualization of sexuality occurred as the nineteenth century gave way to the twentieth: the growing connection of sexuality to pleasure and love, and the emergence of "homosexuals" and "heterosexuals." These changes can be connected, at least indirectly, to the process of capitalist development: in particular, as we will see, to the rise of consumerism and to the emergence of a secular and scientific view of the world. Figure 1 lists some of the key aspects of this new view of sexuality, and contrasts it with the nineteenth-century view.

Historian Jonathan Katz (1983) notes that the view of sex as a pleasurable activity for both sexes accompanied the rise of consumerism and the decline of the work ethic that characterized advanced capitalism in the early-twentieth-century United States. Pleasure was to be sought after, through sexuality as well as consumption. The growing acceptance of birth control signified the acceptance of sexual intercourse for its own sake, not for procreation. While all sexual behavior was not seen as involving love, true love now was thought to properly include both sexual passion and the friendship/companionship of the earlier era.

One would think that this revolutionary shift would have eased if not eliminated the stigmatization of homosexual sexual relations—which are intrinsically nonprocreative, and hence clearly centered on pleasure and love. But this was not the case. Instead, the seeking of pleasure through homosexual sexual relations was in the process of being pathologized by "sexologists" in the medical profession, who attempted to analyze such relations scientifically.

In the late nineteenth century, the expanding medical profession began to develop the concept of "inversion" to describe individuals who took on the gender role of the opposite sex, and engaged in heterogenderal, homosexual sexual relations. Among males, the "invert" was the one who acted or dressed in feminine ways, including those who took the "feminine" role in homosexual sexual encounters—i.e., men who were "cocksuckers" or who liked to be anally penetrated. (Men who looked and acted masculine, and who played the "masculine" role in sex with men were not similarly labeled and pathologized.) Similarly, the female invert was the passing woman, the female who dressed like a man and took on the masculine gender role, including an active role in sexuality—and not her partner, if the latter took a feminine role (Chauncey 1989).

	19th Century	Early 20th Century	Late 20th Century
System of Conceptualization	Religious	Medical	Lesbian/Gay Liberationist
"Good" Sex	Procreative	Heterosexual	Safe, informed, consensual
"Bad" Sex	Nonprocreative	Homosexual	Unsafe, nonconsensual, uninformed
View of Homosexual Desire	Felt by all, but not to be acted upon because evil	Only felt by minority of "homosexuals," as result of illness or congenital defect	Can coexist with heterosexual desire; differing views of origins (biological vs. socialization vs. choice)
Problem with Homosexual Sex	Nonprocreative, hence sinful	An illness, requiring treatment by medical profession	Not a problem

FIGURE 1   Contrasting Views of Sexuality.

By the early twentieth century, medicine's focus began to shift from gender role transgression in general to sexual object choice: "homosexuality" was the illness from which *all* engaged in same-sex sexual relations were thought to suffer, regardless of the gender role they took in those relations or in life in general (Chauncey 1989). Thus, sex-object choice became a key aspect of an individual's identity. One was either heterosexual and normal, or homosexual and abnormal. The latter identity was seen as the result of illness or congenital flaws, and required treatment by the medical profession, especially by its emerging field of psychiatry. In this way, love and/or sexual relationships with members of one's own sex were increasingly viewed as the behavior of a minority of physically "deviant" homosexuals, anathemas to the vast majority of "normal" heterosexuals (Katz 1983: 142–55). Increasingly, then, individuals who felt emotionally close or who were sexually attracted to members of their own sex—and/or were emotionally or sexually indifferent to or alienated from members of the opposite sex—would begin to accept this new view, define themselves as homosexual, and look for support in the growing homosexual subculture.

The new view of sexuality was tightly tied into gender roles, the sexual division of labor, and heterosexual marriage. Sexually healthy individuals were thought to feel sexual passion for members of the opposite sex, passion that they eventually consummated in love-based heterosexual marriage (although nonprocreative heterosexual sex outside of marriage was increasingly accepted) (Katz 1983: 147–50). Conversely, those who engaged in homosexual sex were not viewed as real women or men, no matter how tightly they conformed to other aspects of their gender roles; they became a sort of "third sex," a new kind of person. This tight connection between sexuality and gender increased pressures on all individuals to conform to other, nonsexual aspects of their gender roles, for fear of being stigmatized as lesbian or gay (Goodman et al. 1983: 36).

While the sexual division of labor remained a cornerstone of heterosexuality during this period,

it still contained contradictions that ended up encouraging homosexual behavior. The genders continued to be constructed as "opposite," so that emotional intimacy and mutually satisfying sexuality were difficult to achieve between the genders; at the same time, common experiences and world views—and, for women, common oppression by men—continued to draw together members of the same gender. Many females were unwilling to swallow women's roles "whole hog," given the financial insecurities, subordinate position, and risk of harassment and spousal abuse that were involved. Many males, in turn, found the responsibility of supporting a wife and children overwhelming and unappealing. Others probably simply did not "feel" masculine or feminine enough to consider themselves "normal heterosexuals," especially when another category, homosexual, was defined and connected in the public mind to deviance from assigned gender roles. Indeed, homosexuality, now seen as an identity and way of life (even if a stigmatized one), provided a way to escape restrictive gender roles, as did growing subcultures which supported and validated these choices (Weeks 1991: 69–75). A massive rural-to-urban migration supported these emerging communities by bringing gays together and providing them with relative anonymity.

To establish sexual relationships with members of the same sex, gender roles had to be subverted, amended, played with, or simply rejected. Some females continued to pass as men. Jazz musician Billy Tipton started passing in the 1930s in order to play with the all-male swing bands of that era, and was not "found out" until her death in 1989 (Faderman 1991: 317). Ester left her husband and grown sons in Puerto Rico and moved to New York City, where she took up life as a man taxi-cab driver and lived with her female lover, a prostitute, during the 1950s (Nestle 1987: 40–41).

However, increasing numbers of females who rebelled against womanhood, especially those from the working class, identified themselves not as men but as gay women who were "butch"; modified versions of "passing women," they tried to find jobs where they could dress in pants (such as truck or cab driver, or factory worker), and formed relationships with "fems" who dressed like women. In the working-class lesbian subculture's version of heterogenderality, both women were usually employed, but other aspects of masculine/feminine difference were taken on (Faderman 1991: ch. 7; Kennedy and Davis 1993: 64–65).

Among middle- and upper-class women, romantic friendships and Boston marriages continued. However, the passionate love involved in such same-sex relationships became increasingly suspect and viewed not as a complement to heterosexual marriage but rather as an unacceptable "homosexual" substitute. "Throughout most of the twentieth century . . . the enriching romantic friendship that was common in earlier eras is thought to be impossible, since love necessarily means sex and sex between women means lesbian and lesbian means sick" (Faderman 1981: 311).[16] In contrast to working-class lesbian culture, most lesbian career women seemed to prefer androgynous roles and homogenderal relationships (Faderman 1991: 178–87).

Male homosexuality appears to have been more prevalent than lesbianism: Kinsey found in 1948 that over one-third of his sample of men had had sex to orgasm with a man after adolescence (D'Emilio and Freedman 1988: 291) D'Emilio suggests that the greater prevalence of homosexuality among men was due to their greater economic independence and; hence, their greater ability to live outside of marriage (1983: 106). While long-term, monogamous relationships have become increasingly common (especially after the onset of the AIDS epidemic), a large part of gay male life has revolved around casual sex, available at cruising spots, bars, and baths to both married and single men. As Richard Mohr points out, "[male] homosexual relations cut across all social classifications but gender," creating an equalizing or democratizing tendency in the subculture they create (1992: 198)[17] And men's demand for homosexual sex has continued to provide employment for some young gay males; for example, a recent *Boston Globe*

article described the division of turf into the "boys' block" (male prostitutes), the "girls' block" (male transvestites and transsexuals), and the "real girls" area (female prostitutes) (Jacobs 1992: 20).

LABOR DEMAND AND SEXUALITY DURING THE DEPRESSION AND WORLD WAR II

I have argued that the restriction of women to lower-paid jobs has provided a major economic motive for heterosexuality among women. Lillian Faderman provides an interesting, economically based analysis of the restriction of lesbianism and encouragement of heterosexual marriage in the 1930s. During this decade, high male unemployment generated a groundswell of anger against employed women—particularly against career women of women living independently of men—generating discrimination against women in jobs that could be filled by men "who had families to support." Even the dean of one women's college (Barnard) actively discouraged graduates from paid employment, claiming that this sacrifice would provide a service to their community. Professional women were increasingly portrayed as unwomanly, and their numbers dropped by over 50,000 between 1930 and 1940, even though the female labor force grew by over 500,000 during that period (U.S. Census 1930: 279; U.S. Census 1940: 75). In sum, during the depression years, both economic and social pressures toward heterosexual marriage were strengthened for middle-class young women.

At the same time, Faderman found that some middle- and upper-class married women, both Black and white, maintained lesbian relationships, one of the most famous being Eleanor Roosevelt.[18] And lesbianism was not uncommon among the substantial numbers of working-class women who dropped through the economic cracks into poverty and homelessness; living the life of hobos, they wore pants, joined with other women for protection, and formed intimate relationships that were sometimes self-consciously lesbian (Faderman 1991: 94–99).

The war economy during World War II shifted the balance between homosexuality and heterosexuality. In dire need of soldiers, the military established a secret policy of toleration of homosexuality in its ranks, as long as it was private and not disruptive. Young men were drafted in large numbers; most gay men appear to have been able to slip through the crude examination that was supposed to screen out homosexuals. Many more "came out" in homosexual relationships within the intimate, high-pressure atmosphere of the barracks (Berube 1990; D'Emilio 1992: 65–66).

In stark contrast to the 1930s, employers now actively recruited women into high-paid war-industry jobs in the cities. This facilitated the development of lesbian relationships: "As wage earners working in well-paying defense jobs, wearing men's clothes to do 'men's work,' and living, working, and relaxing with each other, many women for the first time fell in love with other women, socialized with lesbians, and explored the gay nightlife that flourished in the crowded cities" (Berube 1990: 384–85). Women wearing pants to war-industry jobs began to legitimize that practice among women, making it easier for masculine lesbians to "pass" as heterosexual (Faderman 1991: 125–26), while the absence of men from city streets made it safe for women to be out together without male escorts (Kennedy 1994). Some women enlisted in the Women's Army Corps, which both attracted women-loving women and put women in intimate contact with one another. A WAC lecture to officer candidates explained that, in this work situation, it was natural for women to have relationships "that can become an intimacy that may eventually take some form of sexual expression. It may appear that, almost spontaneously, such a relationship has sprung up between two women, neither of whom is a confirmed active homosexual" (Berube 1990: 385–86).

THE 1950S: GOVERNMENT-SPONSORED ANTIGAY DISCRIMINATION

If World War II exerted major pressures against the traditional sexual division of labor and toward

women's paid employment, lesbianism, and male homosexuality, the immediate postwar period brought a major backlash consciously aimed at reversing all of these trends. As historian Allan Berube describes:

> Churches, the media, schools, and government agencies conducted a heavy-handed campaign to reconstruct the nuclear family, to force women back into their traditional roles, and to promote a conservative sexual morality. A tactic of this campaign was to isolate homosexual men and women and identify them, like Communists, as dangerous and invisible enemies (Berube 1990: 391).

The military conducted antigay witch hunts, purging thousands of lesbians and gay men from its ranks. Antigay hearings were held in the U.S. Senate, in which it was argued that homosexuals were unfit to be federal employees because they were "generally unsuitable" (due to being abnormal and lacking in emotional stability and moral fiber) as well as because they were "security risks" in certain positions (because they could be blackmailed on the basis of their homosexuality, due to the federal policy of firing them!). President Eisenhower signed an Executive Order barring homosexuals from federal jobs; firing was allowed on the basis of anonymous, unsubstantiated accusations; no appeal was allowed beyond the employee's department. Many state governments followed suit, as did private employers and colleges and universities. Gay and lesbian bars were not a refuge: police raided them and released the names of those arrested to the newspapers, which commonly published them (D'Emilio and Freedman 1988: 292–95; Faderman 1991: ch. 6; Berube 1990: 391–93).

Many lesbians and gay men lost their jobs and careers; those who did not struggled to hide their gayness "in the closet" and lived in perpetual fear of being discovered; many probably chose to give up their gay lifestyles, and many others were deterred from even considering homosexuality. Whether gay or heterosexual, women workers lost their jobs to returning GIs. The pressure on both sexes to "be straight" was strong. Women married and sought happiness in caring for husbands and children; men married and shouldered the provider role, anxious to show they were not among the 50 percent of men who Kinsey had found were attracted to their own sex. But a small and brave group of men and women insisted on living gay lives, mostly in cities, and even founded groups that constituted the beginning of the lesbian and gay movement (D'Emilio 1992: 78–79; Kennedy and Davis 1993).

THE DECLINE OF THE SEXUAL DIVISION OF LABOR AND THE ATTENUATION OF THE ECONOMIC BASIS OF HETEROSEXUALITY

Cyclical and war-related ups and downs in women's labor-force participation in the '30s, '40s and '50s did not prevent an overall, secular increase in the entrance of women into the paid labor force full- or part-time—from less than 20 percent of all women in 1900 to 69 percent in 1991 (Matthaei 1982: 142; U.S. Census Bureau 1993: 394). This change was the result of a variety of factors. The growth of needs and consumerism from the 1920's on drew homemakers into the labor force as part of their job of filling family needs. Middle-class women entered higher education as training for homemaking, but this education inadvertently prepared them for paid careers and spawned the career woman. The rapid growth of jobs that had been typed feminine, especially clerical jobs, also helped draw women into the labor force (Matthaei 1982: Part 3). After 1970, the movement of women into the labor force gained further momentum as men's average real wages began a long-term decline. As a result, a major part of the sexual division of labor in marriage—the assignment of wage-earning to the husband and only the husband—began to break down to the point that by 1993, 59 percent of married women held paid jobs (U.S. Census Bureau 1993: 399).

The movement of married women into the paid labor force has been accompanied by a second major change in the sexual division of labor. As women began to spend more years of their lives in the paid labor force, and hence to view their jobs

not as temporary stints before marriage but as lifelong careers, they began to challenge women's exclusion from the higher paid and higher status "men's jobs" more vigorously. The demand for access to these jobs—i.e., for an end to gender discrimination in employment—became a key demand of the feminist movement, as did a demand for men to share in women's traditional work of homemaking and childrearing (Matthaei 1982: Part 3).

As an increasing share of women are employed, and more of these are in better paid jobs, more and more women have become able to support themselves, and even their children, independently of husbands or fathers. For example, in 1992, 11 million women—almost one third of the women who were employed full-time—held managerial or professional jobs; their median earnings of $562/week exceeded the overall median earnings for full-time employed men, which were $505/week (U.S. Census Bureau 1993: 426). Two million of the women who headed families with children but without husbands—one-quarter of the total—lived on annual family incomes of above $25,000 (U.S. Census Bureau 1993: 464).

The increase in the numbers of women who are economically independent of men has had an important effect on sexuality. The economic pressure toward heterosexual marriage has decreased for growing numbers of women, as has the pressure to remain in unhappy marriages. Concurrently, men's overall sense of economic responsibility for women in marriage has declined (Ehrenreich 1983), further fueling women's increasing participation in and commitment to the labor force. The divorce rate has sky-rocketed; the share of women who were married dropped from 71 percent in 1970 to 60 percent in 1992, and the share of those who were either divorced or never married rose from 16 percent to 30 percent (U.S. Census 1993: 53).[19]

At the same time, economic independence from men made it economically feasible for some women to structure their lives around lesbian relationships. A 1989 random phone survey, for example, found the median income for full-time full-year workers was $19,643 among all employed women, but $26,331 among employed lesbians (Badgett 1993: 19).[20] This could be both because higher incomes allow women to live without men, and because women who are lesbians expect to have to support themselves and/or their lovers, and hence invest in more training and stay on the job longer than comparable heterosexual women.

FEMINISM, LESBIAN/GAY LIBERATION, THE ATTACK ON THE SEXUAL DIVISION OF LABOR AND GENDER, AND THE CONSERVATIVE RESPONSE

There have been many noneconomic factors contributing to the rise of the feminist and lesbian/gay liberation movements, including the continued persecution of gays and lesbians, the legacy of the civil-rights movement, and the growing secularization of U.S. society. Here I want to focus on the relationship between these movements and the sexual division of labor.

The feminist movement of the 1970s and 1980s was closely linked to lesbianism. On the one hand, lesbians had a higher stake than heterosexual married women in accessing well-paid jobs, since lesbians did not have access to "family wages" through husbands. Furthermore, lesbians had already crossed gender lines in other ways—dress, choice of sexual partner—and were less fearful of losing their "womanhood" and attractiveness to men if they took on "men's jobs" than were heterosexual women. Thus lesbians made up a disproportionate part of the ranks of feminists among all class and racial-ethnic groups. Indeed, French feminist Monique Wittig has argued that feminism has provided lesbian activists with a closeted way of pushing their agenda of dismantling the sexual division of labor and gender roles.[21]

Furthermore, feminist analysis and the movement—especially its radical feminist, socialist feminist, and lesbian feminist components (e.g., Koedt, Levine, and Rapone 1973; Sargent 1981; and Johnston 1973, respectively)—have resulted in the "coming out" of many involved. First, feminists

developed a critique of the sexual division of labor and of gender roles as being both restrictive to all and oppressive to women. Second, they directly criticized heterosexual marriage because of its subordination of women to men as unpaid servants and sexual objects. Third, many feminists put forth lesbianism as a viable alternative—even, some argued, *the* appropriate feminist choice, a form of resistance to patriarchy that is more symmetrical and egalitarian than heterosexuality (e.g., Johnston 1973; Radicalesbians 1973; Rich 1980). Many of the leading early feminist theorists—such as Adrienne Rich, Andrea Dworkin, Gayle Rubin, Charlotte Bunch, Mary Daly, Audre Lorde, Barbara Smith, Cherrie Moraga, and Susan Griffin—were "out" lesbians. Fourth, feminism has brought like-minded women together as coparticipants in support and action groups, providing them with potential sexual/love partners.

In other words, feminist movement[22] has encouraged women to challenge and even deviate from traditional gender roles; it has highlighted the oppressiveness of traditional heterosexuality; it has supported and even advocated lesbianism as an option for women; it has encouraged women to pursue "men's" jobs (and fought to open these higher-paying jobs to women), jobs that allow them to survive economically without men; and it has brought women in close and cooperative contact with other like-minded women. When criticized as being lesbian or prolesbian, some feminist groups (such as the early NOW) tried to distance feminism from lesbianism. However, most feminist groups have instead responded by openly supporting their lesbian members and by adding the demand for lesbian and gay civil rights to their platforms.

Meanwhile, the 1969 Stonewall rebellion against a police raid of a gay bar began a growing, out-of-the-closet movement of gay men and lesbians that has asserted our rights to live and love. While the early movement was tied into radical feminism and to the Left, it has become increasingly centered on a liberal agenda of gaining rights and protection from discrimination for lesbians and gays (Seidman 1993). By the early nineties, the movement had succeeded in making antigay discrimination illegal in a number of states. Gay and lesbian couples are demanding and beginning to win recognition as families, with access to spousal benefits and the right to parent. This extension of rights and legal protections to lesbians and gays is gaining increasing public acceptance as a logical extension of civil rights and antidiscrimination principles central to the U.S. ethical/legal system.[23]

Indeed, during his 1992 presidential campaign, Clinton courted the lesbian/gay vote by promising to end discrimination in the military. He reneged on this promise once in office, in the face of vociferous opposition from the military and Congress, and instead compromised with a modest reform: under the new "don't ask, don't tell" policy, the military agreed not to investigate a service member's sexuality, but service members are prohibited from being "out" on their jobs. The terms of the debate on the issue also represented a minor step forward in public discourse. Those who argued against the proposed changes did not use either the religious argument (gays are immoral) or the medical one (gays are mentally or physically compromised). Rather, they argued that the presence of "out" gays in the military would "threaten unit cohesion," an argument centered on the inefficiencies caused by homophobia rather than by homosexuals themselves.

A new, "social" view of sexuality is being put forward by lesbian/gay and feminist movements, in which "bad" sex is sex that creates unwanted children, sex that exposes the participants to disease (especially AIDS), or sex into which either participant has been forced against his/her will (see Figure 1). Our society, it is argued, has the responsibility to support "good" sex by educating us all about sexuality, including reproduction, birth control options, and safe sex; by exposing, condemning, and punishing rape and child sexual abuse; and by supporting an individual's right to engage in homosexual (as well as heterosexual) sex if she/he so chooses, through education, antidiscrimination, and other measures.

In these ways, then, feminism and the lesbian and gay movements, encouraged by and combined with economic developments, have attacked the core of the sexual division of labor—the assignment of individuals to men's or women's work, on the basis of their sex—as well its main corollaries—gender identity as given by sex, and marriage as the union of different and complementary genders. Gender differences are themselves being eroded, as each gender's work and sexual options are expanded, so that gender now has less and less consistent meaning beyond biological sex. If a female/woman can do anything that a male/man can do and still be a woman (and vice versa), then woman is not any different from man, other than biologically.

New principles are arising. The right to choose from among all jobs for which one is qualified, regardless of one's gender. The notion that full individuality (for both males and females) involves participation in family, economy, and polity. The conception of marriage as a union of socially similar beings, be they of the same or opposite sexes (Matthaei 1982: ch. 13, Conclusion; Matthaei 1988). The new concept of "sexual preference," which suggests that sexual orientation is not inborn but rather a choice between two desirable options, a choice that *all* individuals make. The category of bisexual: individuals who refuse to acknowledge an exclusive sexual preference. If gender further fades into sex, we can expect an entirely new set of sexual categories, perhaps not even called "sexual," to emerge (see Figure 1).

The radical nature of these changes, both won and proposed, has called forth a strong conservative reaction, a reaction that has coalesced in the religious and "pro-family" arms of the "New Right." Their goal is to roll back the gains of the feminist and gay movements and to reestablish the "traditional family": a heterosexual married couple with children, in which the husband/breadwinner commands and the wife/full-time homemaker submits. As they see it, "the homosexual movement is nothing less than an attack on our traditional, pro-family values" (Schwartz and Rueda 1987: 8). Key to their ideology is a religious view of sexuality that virtually replicates the nineteenth-century view we have discussed above: homosexual acts, as well as birth control and sex outside of marriage, are seen as sinful because they prevent or cannot lead to the birth of legitimate children; abortion is viewed as murder, pure and simple.[24] In the fall of 1992, the religious right won passage in Colorado of an amendment that prevented state agencies from protecting lesbians and gay men from discrimination; the amendment was later overturned by the courts. A similar but stronger measure was put forward in Oregon that, besides banning nondiscrimination policies, also required government-funded organizations to represent homosexuality as "abnormal, wrong, unnatural, and perverse"; the measure was narrowly defeated. For the 1994 elections, the religious right backed antigay initiatives in ten states; however, only two made it onto ballots (Idaho and Oregon), and both were defeated by voters. However, the Republican take-over of the House and Senate has brought a heightened threat of federal antigay legislation. Meanwhile, the religious right has also been active in local school board elections, their goal being to block or roll back progressive curricular reform, such as the inclusion of gay and lesbian families in New York City's "rainbow curriculum." With the backing of a number of semi-independent, well-financed organizations that have trained thousands of committed activists, and with powerful allies in the now-dominant Republican Party, the New Right poses a real threat to the realization of the goals, both liberal and radical, of the feminist and gay rights movements (Cagan 1993; *Gay Community News* 1994: 5–6; Hardisty 1993; *Momentum* 1994: 1).

ACKNOWLEDGMENTS

I would like to thank Sumangala Kailasapathy for research assistance. An earlier draft of this paper was presented at "The Economics of Sexual Orientation: Theory, Evidence, and Policy" panel, sponsored by the Union for Radical Political Economics (URPE) at the annual Allied Social Science Associations (ASSA) meetings in Anaheim, California in January 1993. I have benefited from comments made at that session, and at presentations of the paper at the Washington, DC, Economic History Seminar and at the Homo-Economics Conference in the spring of 1994. I would also like to thank the members of the Wellesley Faculty Seminar on Lesbian and Gay Studies, and Laurie Nisonoff, Jayati Lal, and Ann Davis—the reviewers at *The Review of Radical Political Economics*—for their comments and help.

NOTES

Reprinted with permission, with minor changes, from *The Review of Radical Political Economics,* June 1995.

1. A short note regarding my methodology is in order here. My method of argument is an historical and dialectical one, and may discomfort those who think in linear terms, as it did one reviewer. For example, I argue simultaneously that the sexual division of labor is a main force in cementing heterosexual marriage, and that it contains contradictions that help construct homosexual relationships. I do not believe that historical processes can be adequately analyzed through an econometric logic according to which each "independent variable" is thought to have a consistent effect.

2. See, for example, Hartmann (1979), Folbre (1982), and Delphy (1984).

3. Walby (1990) is an exception, as is Ehrlich (1981); neither was trained as an economist. Ferguson (1989), whom I discuss next, is a philosopher.

4. Building on Becker, Posner (1992) argues that an individual's sexual behavior is determined by a combination of genetic predisposition (along Kinsey's range from purely homosexual to purely heterosexual) and rational choice. The latter is then influenced by a number of factors, from sex ratios in the population to urbanization to social policy.

5. As also quoted in Vicinus (1992: 469).

6. See LeVay and Hamer (1994) and Byne (1994) for a recent rehashing of the "gay gene" debate.

7. For more on the constructionist-essentialist debate, see Stein (1990) (especially the essay by Boswell), Vance (1991), and Escoffier (1992).

8. The concept of gender identity, including the difference between sex and gender, is key to women's studies; see, for example, Oakley (1972). The sexual division of labor is a central concept in the work of Marxist-feminist economists and feminist anthropologists; see, for example, Hartmann (1979), Rosaldo and Lamphere (1974), and Amott and Matthaei (1991: ch. 2). More recently, queer theorist Judith Butler has analyzed gender as "an identity tenuously constituted in time, instituted in an exterior space through a

stylized repetition of acts" (1990: 140). These "acts and gestures, articulated and enacted desires create the illusion of an interior and organizing gender core" (136).

9. See, for example, Morris (1975), the eloquent autobiography of a male who underwent a sex change operation to realize his feminine identity; and Feinberg (1993), in which the main character is taunted and ostracized for not being feminine enough, eventually finds an identity as a butch lesbian, and thinks of herself as a "he-she." Kennedy and Davis (1993) report that "butch identity was based in various combinations of masculine inclination and sexual interest in women" (327).

10. This differs from the neoclassical analysis of the sexual division of labor in marriage. The latter argues that utility-maximizing individuals freely choose marriage and specialization because it increases their total utility. Specialization results either from different innate preferences, from different relative abilities to do home and market work, and/or from sex discrimination (women receiving less return than men to their human capital investments).

11. Indeed, historian John D'Emilio (1983) argues that the development of capitalism and wage labor enabled homosexuality, especially male homosexuality, by enabling individuals to provide for their needs outside of a traditional family context. In my opinion, this argument is much stronger for men than it is for women.

12. For a discussion of the historical antecedents of the passing woman, see Vicinus (1992).

13. For example, Dr. Eugene de Savitsch wrote in 1958 of the case of Nicholas de Raylan, a female who passed as a man, in the early 1900s. His/her second wife wept at his death, "declaring that talk of his being a woman was nonsense." The postmortem showed him to be female. "An imitation penis and testicles made of chamois skin and stuffed with down were suspended in the right place by means of a band around the waist" (Katz 1976: 380).

14. For example, the July 25, 1863, *Fitcher's Trades' Review* had a story on a "Curious Married Couple."

> In 1731, a girl named Mary East was engaged to be married to a young man for whom she entertained the strongest affection; but upon his taking to evil courses, or, to tell the whole truth, being hanged for highway robbery, she determined to run no risk of any such disappointment from the opposite sex in future. A female friend of hers having suffered in some similar manner, and being of the like mind with herself, they agreed to pass for the rest of their days as man and wife. . . . The question of which should be the husband was decided by lot in favor of Mary East. (Katz 1978: 343–44).

15. The women were physically segregated by race to some degree within the reform schools.

16. Recent analysts note that even in the mid- and late-nineteenth century, romantic friendships, while acceptable, were viewed as involving potential threats to traditional marriage (Martin 1990; Vicinus 1992).

17. Mohr (1992) quotes Paul Goodman as writing, "Its [queer life's] promiscuity can be a beautiful thing. . . . I have cruised rich, poor, middle class, and petit bourgeois; black, white, yellow and brown; scholars, jocks, Gentlemanly C's, and dropouts; farmers, seamen, railroad men, heavy industry, light manufacturing, communications, business, and finance; civilian, soldiers and sailors, and once or twice cops (1977: 219–21)."

18. Faderman's and others' claims that Eleanor had a homosexual relationship with Lorena Hickock have been hotly disputed or, more commonly, simply ignored by many mainstream biographers.

19. These data were standardized by age. This is not to say that all women have become economically independent. For a substantial share of women, the choice to stay single or to divorce is still a choice to live in poverty; indeed, over one third of all women heading households without husbands present lived in poverty in 1991 (U.S. Census 1993: 471). Many of these women were divorced or abandoned by their husbands. Thus, while a larger share of women is economically independent from men, overall, women's per capita access to resources has declined (Albelda 1988).

20. In this volume, Badgett reports a later research finding showing no significant difference between the average incomes of straight women and lesbians. She also discusses the limitations of all research to date on lesbian and gay incomes, given the paucity of data.

21. Talk by Wittig at Wellesley College in the mid-1980s. Clearly it is impossible to accurately ascertain the numbers of lesbians in different parts of the feminist movement, due to so many of them being in the closet; however, my personal experiences in many parts of the feminist movement over the past fifteen years, as well as my reading on the subject, lead me to this conclusion.

22. I use the term "feminist movement" instead of "the feminist movement" to emphasize the many different forms feminist organizing has taken, as suggested by bell hooks in her *Feminist Theory: From Margin to Center* (1984).

23. A Gallup poll of Americans reported in *Newsweek* on September 14, 1992, p. 37, found that 67 percent approved of health insurance for gay spouses, 70 percent approved of inheritance rights for gay spouses, and 58 percent approved of Social Security for gay spouses. Significant minorities approved of legally sanctioned gay marriages and adoption rights for gays (35 percent and 32 percent, respectively).

24. One difference, however, is that they do not seem to assume that all feel attractions to members of their own sex. For example, Schwartz and Rueda (1987: 8) write of homosexuality as a "disordered sexual condition" that leads to evil acts in *Gays, AIDS and You* (quoted in Hardisty 1993: 3).

REFERENCES

Albelda, Randy, et al. 1988. *Mink Coats Don't Trickle Down: The Economic Attack on Women and People of Color.* Boston: South End Press.

Amott, Teresa, and Julie Matthaei. 1991. *Race, Gender and Work: A Multicultural Economic History of Women in the United States.* Boston: South End Press.

Badgett, M. V. Lee. 1993. The Economic Well-Being of Lesbians and Gay Men: Pride and Prejudice. Paper Presented at a Union of Radical Political Economics-sponsored Session of the 1993 Allied Social Science Associations Meetings. Anaheim, CA.

Bates, Katharine Lee. 1922. *Yellow Clover: A Book of Remembrance.* New York: E. P. Dutton.

Berube, Alan. 1979. Lesbian Masquerade. *Gay Community News.* November 17, 1979.

———. 1990. Marching to a Different Drummer: Lesbian and Gay GIs in World War II. In *Hidden from History: Reclaiming the Gay and Lesbian Past,* edited by Duberman, Vicinus, and Chauncey, pp. 383–94. New York: Penguin.

Butler, Judith. 1990. *Gender Trouble: Feminism and the Subversion of Identity.* New York: Routledge.

Byne, William. 1994. The Biological Evidence Challenged. *Scientific American* 270(5): 50–55.

Cagan, Leslie. 1993. Community Organizing and the Religious Right: Lessons From Oregon's Measure Nine Campaign. An Interview with Suzanne Pharr. *Radical America* 24(4): 67–75.

Chauncey, George. 1989. From Sexual Inversion to Homosexual: The Changing Medical Concept of Female "Deviance." In *Passion and Power: Sexuality in History,* edited by K. Peiss, et al., pp. 87–119. Philadelphia: Temple University Press.

———. 1990. Christian Brotherhood or Sexual Perversion? Homosexual Identities and the Construction of Sexual Boundaries in the World War I Era. In *Hidden from History: Reclaiming the Gay and Lesbian Past,* edited by Duberman, Vicinus, and Chauncey, pp. 294–317. New York: Penguin.

Degler, Carl N. 1980. *At Odds: Women and the Family in America from the Revolution to the Present.* New York: Oxford University Press.

Delphy, Christine. 1984. *Close to Home: A Materialist Analysis of Women's Oppression.* Amherst: University of Massachusetts Press.

D'Emilio, John. 1983. Capitalism and Gay Identity. In *Powers of Desire: The Politics of Sexuality,* edited by Snitow, Stansell, and Thompson. New York: Monthly Review Press.

———. 1992. *Making Trouble: Essays on History, Politics and the University.* New York: Routledge.

D'Emilio, John, and Estelle Freedman. 1988. *Intimate Matters: A History of Sexuality in America.* New York: Harper & Row.

Duberman, Martin, Martha Vicinus, and George Chauncey, Jr. (eds.). 1990. *Hidden from History: Reclaiming the Gay & Lesbian Past.* New York: Penguin.

Ehrenreich, Barbara. 1983. *The Hearts of Men: American Dreams and the Flight from Commitment.* Garden City, NY: Anchor Press/Doubleday.

Ehrlich, Carol. 1981. The Unhappy Marriage of Marxism and Feminism: Can It Be Saved? In *Women and Revolution,* edited by Lydia Sargent. Boston: South End Press.

Escoffier, Jeffrey. 1992. Generations and Paradigms: Mainstreams in Lesbian and Gay Studies. In *Gay and Lesbian Studies,* edited by Minton, pp. 7–88. New York: Haworth Press.

Epstein, Stephen. 1987. Gay Politics, Ethnic Identity: The Limits of Social Constructionism. *Socialist Review* 17(3&4): 9–54.

Faderman, Lillian. 1981. *Surpassing the Love of Men: Romantic Friendship and Love between Women from the Renaissance to the Present.* New York: William Morrow.

———. 1991. *Odd Girls and Twilight Lovers: A History of Lesbian Life in Twentieth-Century America.* New York: Penguin.

Feinberg, Leslie. 1993. *Stone Butch Blues.* Ithaca, NY: Firebrand Books.

Ferguson, Ann. 1989. *Blood at the Root: Motherhood, Sexuality, and Male Dominance.* London: Pandora.

———. 1991. *Sexual Democracy: Women, Oppression, and Revolution.* San Francisco: Westview Press.

Folbre, Nancy. 1982. Exploitation Comes Home: A Critique of the Marxian Theory of Family Labour. *Cambridge Journal of Economics* 6(4) : 317–29.

Gay Community News. October. 1994. "Bigot Busters v. Religious Right: Bigot Busters Win" 20(3) : 5–6.

Gilfoyle, Timothy. 1992. *City of Eros: New York City, Prostitution, and the Commercialization of Sex, 1720–1920.* New York: W. W. Norton.

Goldin, Claudia. 1990. *Understanding the Gender Gap: An Economic History of American Women.* New York: Oxford University Press.

Goodman, Gerre, et al. 1983. *No Turning Back: Lesbian and Gay Liberation for the '80s.* Philadelphia: New Society Publishers.

Goodman, Paul. 1977. The Politics of Being Queer. *Nature Heals: The Psychological Essays of Paul Goodman.* Edited by Taylor Stoehr, pp. 216–25. New York: Free Life Editions.

Gordon, Linda. 1976. *Woman's Body, Woman's Right.* New York: Grossman Publishers.

Gottlieb, Rhonda. 1984. The Political Economy of Sexuality. *Review of Radical Political Economics* 16: 143–66.

Hardisty, Jean. 1993. Constructing Homophobia: Colorado's Right-Wing Attack on Homosexuals. *The Public Eye: A Publication of Political Research Associates* (March): 1–10.

Hartmann, Heidi. 1979. Capitalism, Patriarchy, and Job Segregation by Sex. In *Capitalist Patriarchy and the Case for Socialist Feminism,* edited by Z. Eisenstein, pp. 206–247. New York: Monthly Review Press.

hooks, bell. 1981. *Ain't I A Woman: Black Women and Feminism.* Boston: South End Press.

Hubbard, Ruth, Mary Sue Henefin, and Barbara Fried (eds.). 1982. *Biological Woman—The Convenient Myth: A Collection of Feminist Essays and a Comprehensive Bibliography.* Cambridge, MA: Schenkman.

Jacobs, Sally. 1992. Cruising and Losing: Young Men Barter Flesh, Dismal Future. *Boston Sunday Globe,* December 20, pp. 1, 20.

Johnston, Jill. 1973. *Lesbian Nation: The Feminist Solution.* New York: Simon and Schuster.

Katz, Jonathan. 1976. *Gay American History: Lesbians and Gay Men in the U.S.A.* New York: Discus/Avon Books.

———. 1983. *Gay/Lesbian Almanac.* New York: Harper & Row.

Kennedy, Elizabeth. 1994. Codes of Resistance in the Buffalo Lesbian Community of the 1950s: Class, Race and the Development of Lesbian Identity. Talk Given at Wellesley College, February 22.

Kennedy, Elizabeth, and Madeline Davis. 1993. *Boots of Leather, Slippers of Gold: The History of a Lesbian Community.* New York: Routledge.

Koedt, A., A. Levine, and A. Rapone (eds.). 1973. *Radical Feminism.* New York: Quadrangle/The New York Times.

LeVay, Simon, and Dean Hamer. 1994. Evidence for a Biological Influence in Male Homosexuality. *Scientific American* 270(5): 44–49.

Martin, Robert K. 1990. Knights-Errant and Gothic Seducers: The Representation of Male Friendship in Mid-Nineteenth-Century America. In *Hidden from History: Reclaiming the Gay and Lesbian Past,* edited by Duberman, Vicinus, and Chauncey, pp. 169–82. New York: Penguin.

Matthaei, Julie. 1982. *An Economic History of Women in America: Women's Work, the Sexual Division of Labor, and the Development of Capitalism.* New York: Schocken Books.

———. 1988. Political Economy and Family Policy. In *The Imperiled Economy, Book 2,* edited by Robert Cherry, et al. New York: Union for Radical Political Economics and Monthly Review Press.

Momentum: The Newsletter for Members of the Human Rights Campaign Fund. " '94 Voters Reject Anti-Gay Discrimination" (Winter 1994): 1.

Mohr, Richard. 1992. *Gay Ideas: Outing and Other Controversies.* Boston: Beacon Press.

Morris, Jan. 1975. *Conundrum.* New York: New American Library.

Nestle, Joan. 1987. *A Restricted Country.* Ithaca, NY: Firebrand Books.

Oakley, Ann. 1972. *Sex, Gender, and Society.* San Francisco: Harper & Row.

Peiss, Kathy. 1983. "Charity Girls" and City Pleasures: Historical Notes on Working-Class Sexuality, 1880–1920. In *Powers of Desire,* edited by Snitow, Stansell, and Thompson. New York: Monthly Review Press.

Posner, Richard A. 1992. *Sex and Reason.* Cambridge: Harvard University Press.

Radicalesbians. 1973. The Woman-Identified Woman. In *Radical Feminism,* edited by Koedt, Levine and Rapone. New York: Quadrangle/The New York Times.

Rich, Adrienne. 1980. Compulsory Heterosexuality and Lesbian Existence. *Signs: Journal of Women in Culture and Society* 5(4): 631–60.

Rosaldo, Michelle, and Louise Lamphere (eds.). 1974. *Woman, Culture, and Society.* Stanford, CA: Stanford University Press.

San Francisco Lesbian and Gay History Project. 1990. "She Even Chewed Tobacco"; A Pictorial Narrative of Passing Women in America. In *Hidden from History: Reclaiming the Gay and Lesbian Past,* edited by Duberman, Vicinus, and Chauncey, pp. 183–94. New York: Penguin.

Sargent, Lydia (ed.). 1981. *Women and Revolution: A Discussion of the Unhappy Marriage of Marxism and Feminism.* Boston: South End Press.

Schwartz, Judith. 1979. Yellow Clover: Katharine Lee Bates and Katherine Coman. *Frontiers* 4(1): 59–67.

Schwartz, Michael, and Enrique Rueda. 1987. *Gays, AIDS and You.* Old Greenwich, CT: Devin Adair Company.

Seidman, Stephen. 1993. Identity and Politics in a "Postmodern" Gay Culture: Some Historical and Conceptual Notes. In *Fear of a Queer Planet,* edited by Michael Warner, pp. 105–42. Minneapolis: University of Minnesota Press.

Smith-Rosenberg, Carroll. 1979. The Female World of Love and Ritual. In *A Heritage of Her Own: Toward a New Social History of American Women,* edited by Nancy F. Cott and Elizabeth H. Pleck, pp. 311–342. New York: Simon and Schuster.

Snitow, Ann, Christine Stansell, and Sharon Thompson (eds.). 1983. *Powers of Desire: The Politics of Sexuality.* New York: Monthly Review Press.

Spelman, Elizabeth. 1988. *Inessential Woman: Problems of Exclusion in Feminist Thought.* Boston: Beacon Press.

Stein, Edward (ed.). 1990. *Forms of Desire: Sexual Orientation and the Social Constructionist Controversy.* New York: Garland Publishing.

U.S. Department of Commerce. Bureau of the Census. 1930. *Census of Occupations. Occupations: General Report.* Washington, D.C.: GPO.

———. 1940. *Census of the U.S. Population: Vol. III: The Labor Force. Part I: U.S. Summary.* Washington, DC: GPO.

———. 1975. *Historical Statistics of the U.S.: Colonial Times to 1970.* Washington, DC: GPO.

———. 1993. *Statistical Abstract of the United States.* Washington, DC: GPO.

U.S. Department of Labor. 1974. *Nontraditional Occupations Women of the Hemisphere—The U.S. Experience.* Washington, DC: GOP.

Vance, Carol. 1991. Anthropology Rediscovers Sexuality: A Theoretical Comment. *Social Science Medicine* 33(8): 876–84.

Vicinus, Martha. 1992. "They Wonder to Which Sex I Belong": The Historical Roots of the Modern Lesbian Identity. *Feminist Studies* 18(3): 467–98.

Walby, Sylvia. 1990. *Theorizing Patriarchy.* London: Basil Blackwell.

Weeks, Jeffrey. 1977. *Coming Out: Homosexual Politics in Britain, from the Nineteenth Century to the Present.* New York: Quartet Books.

———. 1985. *Sexuality and its Discontents: Meanings, Myths, and Modern Sexualities.* London: Routledge and Kegan Paul.

———. 1989. Inverts, Perverts, and Mary-Annes. In *Hidden from History: Reclaiming the Gay and Lesbian Past,* edited by Duberman, Vicinus, and Chauncey, pp. 195–211. New York: Penguin.

———. 1991. *Against Nature: Essays on History, Sexuality and Identity.* London: Rivers Oram Press.

CHAPTER
5

Citizenship, Capitalism, Globalization, and Class

We have thus far looked at neighborhood and work as they are influenced by the key identities of race, ethnicity, nationality, sex, and sexual preference. Our focus now broadens to consider these issues on a global level: What does global inequality mean for those of us living in the United States? What kinds of disparities do different populations face in the world based on race, ethnicity, and sex? How can we make sense of inequality from the vantage point of neighborhood and community (the local and particular) while trying to understand national and international issues? Are issues that are enormously complex reduced to the check-out stand: Do we or do we not enjoy the low prices of clothing produced in sweat shops; of soccer balls stitched by children; of technology assembled by young women who earn a pittance even by local standards? Now more than ever, consumption becomes an act of conscience, and as the social scientists and commentators in chapter 5 show, so much more than that.

All of these authors, in different ways, address themselves to the meaning and the conundrum of globalization. Bear in mind that globalization, like social class, is not new. Marx and Engels make reference to the global marketplace in their manifesto; colonialism (whether Spanish, Dutch, British, or French) was based on the exploitation of labor and land and the creation of subjugated peoples. In this context, it may seem absurd to ask the question: Is globalization something that creates greater inequality, making of the many a great global proletariat while simultaneously creating a much smaller first world transnational bourgeoisie? Could inequality be fueled by other forces? While these authors don't agree on the answer to this question, they do document how important it is to understand the intersection once again of race and sex, free and unfree labor, in a stratified global economy.

For Howard Winant, in a selection from *The World Is a Ghetto* (2001), the crucial variable in understanding global inequity is race. Despite the abolition of colonial rule in the postwar period and the end of explicit policies based on presumed racial superiority and inferiority, white entitlement is still seen in the disparities of quality of life indicators worldwide: life expectancy, quality of education, and literacy itself have much to do with skin color and citizenship. Winant describes the contour of the problem as a north–south "planetary correlation of darkness and poverty." He outlines a new world racial system more pernicious than the old because it presents itself as colorblind and egalitarian. In the wealthier, northern nations, Winant argues, the key issues for most working people are the effects of deindustrialization and massive reductions in the welfare state; in poorer, southern nations, where cheaper labor lives, industries operate at low cost. Thus, globalization isn't colorblind; it is based on the continuation of white hegemony.

Glenn Firebaugh's piece challenges the emerging conventional wisdom that globalization has increased inequality, what he calls the Trade Protest Model. He poses an alternative hypothesis: that the changing shape of global inequality has shifted from across-nation to within-nation inequality. Firebaugh argues that across-nation inequality has decreased due to the change in economies from agriculturally based to industrial ones. His analysis is supported by Ralf Dahrendorf's (1959) look at the degree of inequality under feudalism: that for all the excesses and ills of the industrial age, industrialization provides a higher standard of living than does subsistence farming. However, within national boundaries, the initial "price" of industrialization will be a jump in income inequality.

Historian David Landes in the excerpt included here presents us with a series of lessons learned from the "losers" in the global marketplace. His *The Wealth and Poverty of Nations* (1998) attempts to answer the question that forms the subtitle of the book: Why some are so rich and some so poor. Landes surveys those nations that fell behind in the boom of the 1990s, analyzing Latin America, the formerly Communist countries of Eastern Europe, postcolonial Africa and the Middle East.

The rest of these selections look at specific aspects of globalization that other authors in our collection have looked at domestically. For example, Loïc Wacquant's idea of "advanced marginality" in urban ghettos around the world connects to earlier pieces on residential segregation; Leslie Sklair's intriguing extension of William Domhoff's "ruling class" thesis to an argument for the existence of a (self-conscious) transnational capitalist class ties back to our first chapter on social class. Issues seen domestically, these authors make clear, are not isolated but must be considered from a global perspective.

Wacquant takes on the issue of the transformation of urban poverty in Western capitalist societies. Although called by different names (e.g., "the underclass" and "the new poverty"), advanced marginality results in violent inner cities that authorities across different nation-states need to contain. Wacquant presents four "logics" that explain the contours of urban poverty; among them, the paradox of poverty in the midst of plenty and the deteriorating social contract provided by the welfare state. Is Europe becoming "Americanized" with new racial and religious ghettos in its major cities?

Sklair revisits present-day use and abuse of immigrant labor internationally. Sklair (2001) contends that what keeps such a system in place is the "transnational capitalist class." That is, capitalism and its keepers no longer belong to any one nation-state, but rather the capitalist class transcends national boundaries. The notion of a global capitalist class can be empirically tested through networks of membership in elite organizations, corporate boards, and policy-planning specialists. Furthermore, argues Sklair, a transnational dominant class need not work in any (or every) specific country.

Another measure of inequality and power is access to technology, specifically, Internet technology. Pippa Norris, in *Digital Divide* (2001), provides data on who uses the Internet in the European Union. Access to the Internet can be a proxy measure of the kind of work one does (and thus the kind of earnings potential one has), and more directly, to household income, since dial-up modem technology and phone time is very expensive in Europe. The digital divide thus becomes another parameter of stratification, one of "information poverty," as Norris puts it. Of course, there are some important differences: age, more than income, influences the likelihood of being connected. Older people are less likely to adopt new technologies, and so it has always been.

Source: Ralf Dahrendorf. 1959. *Class and Class Conflict in Industrial Society.* Stanford, CA: Stanford University Press.

We end this chapter on global forces with a disturbing look at "disposable people," Bales's (1999) term for the enslavement of workers in the global economy. The old slavery system, represented in the Americas by the enslavement of Africans, was one in which the slave represented a substantial investment; therefore, it behooved the owner to keep the slave alive. Bales suggests that the new slavery is fueled by the growth in global population, especially in countries with large numbers of children and convulsed by massive social and economic changes. The new slavery, unlike the old, makes no claim to permanent servitude, but short-term ownership of other human beings is perhaps more brutal because disposable people can be used up. Examples of this new kind of servitude include debt bondage, where a person sells himself or herself or is sold to pay off a debt, called "contract" slavery. Contract slavery is most common in the world of sex work; a girl expects one kind of work and finds herself imprisoned in a brothel, working off her purchase price. So, if chattel slavery has virtually disappeared as too costly, debt bondage and contract slavery have taken its place.

Racism: From Domination to Hegemony

HOWARD WINANT

RACISM: FROM DOMINATION TO HEGEMONY

At the turn of the twenty-first century the world has largely dispensed with the overt racial hierarchies that existed before the post–World War II racial break: colonialism, racially demarcated labor reserves, explicit policies of segregation and apartheid, and candid avowals of racial superiority and inferiority all appear today as hopeless atavisms, relics of a benighted past. International organizations like the UN have for decades made opposition to racism a central priority. And the globalized "culture industry"—from Hollywood to Bollywood, from Disney to Globo to Benneton—has produced a continuing stream of anti-racist messages: legitimating interracial romance and friendship, stigmatizing prejudice and discrimination, and fostering the hybridization of cultures and styles.

Yet as all this anti-racist policy-making, multiculturalism, and hybridization proceeds, the vast gaps between North and South, haves and have-nots, whites and "others," also persist. Pick any relevant sociological indicator—life expectancy, infant mortality, literacy, access to health care, income level—and apply it in virtually any setting, global, regional, or local, and the results will be the same: the worldwide correlation of wealth

and well-being with white skin and European descent, and of poverty and immiseration with dark skin and "otherness." Sure, there are exceptions: there are plenty of exploited white workers, plenty of white welfare mothers both urban and rural, plenty of poor whites throughout the world's North; and there are a smattering of wealth-holders "of color" around the world too. But these are outliers in the planetary correlation of darkness and poverty.

In analyzing patterns of inequality, of stratification, it is impossible fully to distinguish the effects of race and class. These factors interact both locally and globally; they have shaped each other over historical time and continue to do so in the present. For instance, is the black worker at General Motors' plant in Ohio, or at Volkswagen's plant in the ABC region of São Paulo for that matter, so much worse off than the white worker beside him (or her) on the assembly line? Not so much. The real local discrepancies are between those who have fairly reliable, even unionized jobs, and those relegated to poverty and the informal economy. And then there are the global discrepancies: auto workers' wages in the ABC, heartland of the highly developed Brazilian manufacturing economy, home base of the *Confederação Unificado dos Trabalhadores* (CUT—the militant Brazilian trade union confederation), and site of some of the most desirable jobs in the national economy, average about 10 percent of U.S. wages for the same work.

Nor do we have to look at stratification to recognize the continuing significance of race. When we turn to the world political system, to the social structure of domination and subjugation, to the allocation of voice and voicelessness, the point is confirmed again. A worldwide political class exercises power from corporate boardrooms and government ministries alike: how multiracial, how committed to racial equality, is this select group? Of course at the commencement of the twenty-first century, after the end of colonialism and the conclusion of the Gold War, political rule can claim to be democratic almost everywhere. But democracy now means little more than that the citizenry "periodically enjoys the right to withold their acclaim," as Jürgen Habermas remarked (Habermas 1997; see also Habermas 1996).

In such a system the racial gradations of power and powerlessness can sometimes be confusing, but long-standing patterns of racial hierarchy still hold. Do citizens of the core nations of the metropolitan North, do the whites of the world, exercise much political power? No, they do not. How much "freedom" (in the sense of the relative absence of coercion, the availability of personal autonomy) do they possess relative to the racialized "others" both in the northern metropoles and "down home" in the world's South? There are two answers. First, in a given local/national setting—in Los Angeles or Frankfurt, Fortaleza or Durban—whites experience a sense of belonging, a sense of entitlement, that blacks, immigrants, racialized "others," rarely if ever enjoy. Second, on a global level, however disfranchised, however yoked to a low-skilled and inadequately paid job, however resentful of those in command, however manipulable by racists both "old" and "new," the ordinary *schmo* in the world's North—in the still largely white bastions of Europe and North America and ("honorary white") Japan—disposes of a greater basket of life chances, greater freedom, than most of his or her southern brothers and sisters could even imagine.

Culturally too the old system rules. Whence cometh the ideals, the near universal representations, the recognizable icons and idols: where do Michael Jordan and Michael Jackson and Michael Mouse live? In Hollywood, of course (or perhaps in Orlando)! Whose names adorn the canonical bookshelves, whose artworks hang in the museums, whose films does the world stand in line to see? Yes, here again there are exceptions: there is the vast treasurehouse of black music that rules the audio world from Bensonhurst to Bahia, even if it is harnessed to the profit-making imperatives of global media conglomerates; there is not only Hollywood but also Bollywood; there is Chris Ofili, who scandalized New York Mayor Giuliani with his painting *Black Madonna.* But "McWorld" (Barber 1995) is still a largely northern place.

To make sense of these developments and dilemmas, we must rethink the concept of racism. Just as the meaning of race has proved to be malleable and fungible, changing dramatically in the years since World War II, for example, so too the meaning of *racism* has changed over time. The attitudes, practices, and institutions of the epochs of colonialism, segregation, or apartheid may not have been entirely eliminated, but neither do they operate today in the same ways as they did half a century ago. Employing a similar logic, it is reasonable to question whether concepts of racism that were developed in the early postwar period, when the limitations of both nationalist revolution and moderate programs of reform had not yet been encountered, could possibly remain adequate to explain racial dynamics and conflicts in the twenty-first century.

Today racism operates in societies and institutions that explicitly condemn prejudice and discrimination. In the era that succeeded the post–World War II racial break, the conflicts between anti-racist movements and reform-oriented regimes resulted in a new pattern of racial rule, one that makes concessions without surrendering fundamental power. Put somewhat differently: after half a millennium in which global power and capitalist development had been based on racial domination, opposition to the coercive rule required by this old world racial system simply became too strong. Faced with increasingly assertive demands for democracy and national liberation—demands that sometimes reached revolutionary levels of mobilization and involved prolonged armed conflict—the world racial system underwent a transition *from domination to hegemony.* Segregation and colonialism—at least in their explicit, state-enforced forms—were abandoned as the principal instrumentalities of racial rule.

But having conceded this much, northern rule, metropolitan rule, capitalist rule, found its stability largely restored. The new world racial system could maintain much of the stratification and inequality, much of the differential access to political power and voice, much of the preexisting cultural logic of collective representation and racial hierarchy, without recourse to comprehensive coercion or racial dictatorship. Since the political energy and support available to its movement adversaries was limited, a new era of world racial equilibrium could be proclaimed. Opposition was now effectively reduced: since the moderates had been effectively satisfied by reforms, only radical groups remained restive; they could be contained by a combination of marginalization and repression.

In the age of racial hegemony, then, what forms does racism take? To the extent that the transition from domination to hegemony has been accomplished, it is racism's reinforced structural role, its "cleaned-up," "streamlined," and "mainstream" manifestations, that allow it to survive and indeed go largely politically unchallenged at the dawn of the twenty-first century.

Today racism must be identified by its consequences. Racism has been largely—although not entirely, to be sure—detached from its perpetrators. In its most advanced forms, indeed, it has no perpetrators; it is a nearly invisible, taken-for-granted, commonsense (Gramsci) feature of everyday life and global social structure.

Under these conditions—racial hegemony—racism may be defined as *the routinized outcome of practices that create or reproduce hierarchical social structures based on essentialized racial categories.* This definition seeks a comprehensiveness that may not be fully attainable. It leaves enough room to contain the old, instrumental, forms of racism—such as prejudice and discrimination, racial code words, and the like—but focuses attention on new, structural forms that

can operate more or less automatically. It incorporates the analyses that critiqued the European new racism (Barker 1981; Taguieff 2001 [1988]; Miles 1993; Wieviorka 1995; Ansell 1997; Gilroy 1999), but seeks to place that important work in a global framework.

There can be no timeless and absolute standard for what constitutes racism, because social structures undergo reform (and reaction) and discourses are always subject to rearticulation. The concept of racism should not be invested with any permanent content. Instead racism should be seen as a property of certain—but by no means all—political projects that link the *representation* and *organization* of race, that engage in the "work" of racial formation. Such an approach focuses on the "work" essentialism does for domination, and the "need" domination displays to essentialize the subordinated. It allows comparison of different national/regional cases of racial formation, such as those I have presented here. All these countries/regions are in transition from racial domination to racial hegemony. The case study settings both overlap and diverge: each has a unique location and genealogy, yet all partake in the world racial system; all were reshaped during the post–World War II racial break.

OF OUR POLITICAL STRIVINGS

The tremendous accomplishments of the anti-racist and anti-colonial movements that succeeded World War II have now been incorporated. In the decades after the war it seemed at times that these movements might not only found independent postcolonial states, but that they might reorganize global society, even demolish capitalism. At the start of the twenty-first century, however, the outlook is far less promising. At the local/national level many formerly powerful anti-racist movements have lost their adherents and some their political moorings. Some are reduced to defending the limited racial reforms won in earlier moments, for example, affirmative action policies, against the specious claims of public institutions that they are now color-blind, meritocratic, post-racial. Other movements and activists put their energies into multicultural projects, which (again defensively) advocate pluralism and tend to reduce racism to a strictly cultural phenomenon. At the global level the still-impoverished nations of the former Third World, even the formerly revolutionary and still officially communist ones, seek direct private investment and curry favors from the gnomes of London, Zurich, and the IMF.

In earlier times and places—say, during the later 1960s in the United States—it seemed that the "Third World within" might finally achieve the power and claim the wealth so long denied it: redistribution of resources, community control, massive rebuilding of the inner cities, black power (and red power, brown power, yellow power) would accomplish in a "second reconstruction" what had been denied and betrayed one hundred years earlier. But today, at the turn of the twenty-first century, the ghettos, barrios, and reservations are still neglected, still occupied by trigger-happy police, still immiserated; and no serious political movement is in sight.

The vast social movements that democratized the old world racial system, that did away with official policies of racial exclusion, disfranchisement, segregation, and degradation, have now lost a great deal of their support. Formerly they could lead whole peoples in the direction of emancipation; now they struggle to define their purpose. The disruption of the old world racial system during and after the post–World War II racial break has given rise to a "new world racial system" characterized not by racial domination, but instead by racial hegemony. This new system can maintain white supremacy better than the old one could. This system of racial hegemony can present itself as color-blind and multicultural, not to mention meritocratic, egalitarian, and differentialist, all the while restricting immigration, exporting industry (and pollution) to the low-waged South, and doing away with the welfare state in the North.

So while some racial mobility has been achieved, fierce racial inequalities persist: globally they mirror the North-South patterns that colonial rule developed and the *Pax Americana* has continued. In local settings, racial inequalities also continue

to operate: by and large the descendants of slaves, indigenous and occupied peoples, refugees, and migrants continue to be subjugated to the descendants of landholders and slavemasters, occupiers and European settlers.

While some political power has passed from colonialists' and segregationists' hands into darker hands, both the global political system and its local variants have survived and prospered in the transition to a new world racial system. Contemporary political systems of rule—both global and local—descend rather directly from the old world racial system. How independent are the rulers of southern nation-states, even relatively developed ones like South Africa and Brazil, from the discipline of world financial markets and institutions like the IMF? How effective is political representation—black, immigrant, indigenous—even in settings where those formerly excluded on racial grounds can now vote?

Culturally too the transition to hegemony has been contradictory. Well before the post–World War II break the world's "others" were crucial sources of signification: artistic, musical, philosophical, religious, and scholarly insights and techniques were deeply rooted outside the West, even though the "big heads" of Europe laid claim to sole possession of advanced knowledge in all these areas. Already adept at reworking these cultural riches, in the period after the break the metropolitan "culture industries" moved to take possession them, to commodify and purvey them on a global scale. But although ready, willing, and able to market reggae, soka, or samba, say, anywhere in the world, the metropolitan powers still claimed to possess the superior cultures, to live in the home of reason and the center-stage of history (Sen 2000; Davidson 1992). They still required the *difference* of the world's "others," whose cultures they purported now to value far more than in the past, in order to define their own identities.

So what's left after all this conflict and accommodation? Is the picture so bleak that the legacy of half a millennium of resistance to racial rule must now be abandoned? After the tremendous upsurge of the break, after the partial but real triumphs of recent decades, has the worldwide movement for racial equality and justice, for emancipation and self-determination, finally been defeated, not by force and repression, but by co-optation and incorporation? How should racial hegemony be confronted politically, or even politically understood?

The definitive answer to this question cannot be given on paper. Only in political action, in organization and mobilization, will present-day racial dilemmas and contradictions be resolved. Researchers and writers, even those who identify with movements for social justice, are ultimately led by those movements. They cannot, and I cannot, presume to offer political prescriptions.

Yet it is clear that despite recent setbacks, fertile ground remains for new anti-racist initiatives. However successfully the new world racial order was able to incorporate the anti-racist and anti-colonial demands asserted during the break, it was not able fully to transform the inequalities and injustices that generated those demands. It could defuse and blunt the basis of racial opposition, but it could hardly eliminate it. Under no circumstances could the system move "beyond race," despite its claims to post-raciality, color-blindness, multiculturalism, and so on.

So what's left? The fundamental elements of resistance to racial injustice and inequality that remain intact, that have been largely untouched by the incorporative initiatives of the new world racial system, may form building-blocks for the new anti-racist movements. Both in the case study countries/regions and more generally, counter-hegemonic movements may emerge as significant challenges to the world racial system.

There are three fundamental reasons, three incluctable social facts, that suggest that the struggle against white supremacy will continue around the world: first, *global racial inequality and injustice remain;* second, *race-consciousness endures;* and third, *racial politics is pervasive.* In what follows I present the arguments for these three claims, necessarily in a brief and schematic

way. I then conclude with some notes on the Duboisian legacy.

Global Racial Inequality and Injustice Remain

Indeed, they are more visible now, in the age of the Internet and globalized media, than ever before. Where there is injustice and oppression, there is resistance. A powerful argument can be made that opposition to injustice is the main form that political opposition takes in the modern world (Moore 1978).

In all the national/regional case studies examined here, racial stratification remains a significant issue: that unemployment levels are higher and income levels lower for those with dark faces across the world is hardly news. The complex phenomenon known as globalization is itself a major mechanism of resource redistribution—but mainly in a regressive direction.

In the world's North globalization tends toward deindustrialization. The work that can be exported consists of the less skilled factory jobs that are held by immigrants and the working poor—who are disproportionately people "of color." Much of the low-waged work that remains in the metropolitan countries is located in sweatshops, in agriculture, in the service sector, and in the informal economy. Assaults on the welfare state—both on the spending and revenue side—also have regressively redistributive consequences. Many of these developments—competition for jobs, association of immigrants and non-whites with crime, objections to the welfare state and calls for tax reduction—are framed racially.

In the world's South globalization takes the form of neo-liberal economic discipline. The ability to extract primary resources at low cost, unburdened by government regulation, labor organization, or environmental restrictions, is the primary force driving globalization here. Often the importation of factory work doesn't mean serious industrial development or foreign direct investment: more likely it involves an ongoing search for easy acquisition of resources and for cheap and submissive labor. Such policies combine with the austerity and compulsory debt-service enforced upon the South by the International Monetary Fund to maintain much of the population of the South—not only those in countries decolonized only after World War II but even the great majority in an industrially developed country like Brazil—in a state of impoverishment (Greider 1997).

This is an outline—very schematically summarized here—of current world patterns of economic inequality and injustice. Although often seen in terms of global *social* stratification, in terms of environmental destruction, and in terms of gender inequalities (sweatshops and *maquilas,* for example, tend to exploit women at high levels), these injustices are rarely characterized as *racial.* Yet is it not clear that they flow fairly continuously from patterns established in the now-departed colonial epoch?

A movement against the depredations of globalization has begun to appear, drawing on a range of supporters: chiefly environmentalists, trade unions, and religious groups (as well as assorted radical groups committed to direct action). In demonstrations against the World Trade Organization (WTO) in Seattle in 1999, and against the IMF and World Bank in Washington, DC in 2000, this coalition first attracted major attention. Protests in Geneva, Paris, Bangkok, and Prague have also taken place. Real questions have been raised as to how much support the anti-WTO (or anti-globalization) movement can count on from the world's South, where impoverishment is severe enough to make even employment in a sweatshop or *maquila* seem desirable, and where even relatively progressive governments sympathetic to trade unionism—such as the ANC government in South Africa—are subject to immense pressure from the world's financial power-centers. As of yet this movement has exhibited relatively little racial awareness. It remains to be seen if this initiative will acquire the depth and organizational strength needed to operate on a global scale, but it is already achieving limited results

(somewhere between substantive and symbolic) in respect to its demands for debt relief.

Race-Consciousness Endures

One of the most important accomplishments of the worldwide racial mobilizations that confronted colonialism and white supremacy during and after World War II was their reinterpretation (or if one prefers this term, their rearticulation) of the meaning of race and the significance of racial identity. Building upon the immense labors of their ancestors and predecessors, these movements systematically fostered awareness and pride among the world's subjugated and subaltern peoples. To be sure, the creation and nurturing of race-consciousness is a highly uneven and contradictory process. It combines potentially emancipatory elements, such as rejection of stereotypes and "internalized racism," with potentially chauvinistic and even fascist ones (Gilroy 1996). Although in many cases it was the work of revolutionary nationalism to awaken and enunciate concepts of pride, solidarity, and cultural awareness among the racially subordinated, these projects were themselves undertaken by insurgent elites, as we have learned from subalternity theory. . . . They did not preclude, and in some cases actively fostered, new forms of subordination and voicelessness among black, native, or colonized peoples. They could not avoid, and in some cases actively participated in, the degradation of race-consciousness into a commodified and depoliticized form (dashikis, kente cloth, blaxploitation films, etc.).

Yet with all these limitations there has been an indisputably enormous increase in racial awareness throughout the world as a consequence of the upheavals of the break and its aftermath. This awareness is open to further articulation, and by no means inherently emancipatory. There can be no permanent formulas here. Yet the vastly augmented presence of race-consciousness in the world, although contradictory and flexible, still works as a sort of transnational inoculation against post-racialism in all its forms: notably the color-blind viewpoint in the United States and the racial differentialism evident in Europe.

This expanded awareness also acts as a reminder to those on the left who have remained committed to an outmoded notion of anti-racism as integration pure and simple—for example, some in the South African ANC who remain die-hard adherents to the vision of non-racialism articulated in the 1955 Freedom Charter—that the old world racial system is definitively dead, and that a new vision of racial justice and equality must be developed. The fact that race-consciousness has expanded so much in the aftermath of the break also has consequences in Brazil, where it works to erode the tenacious ideology of racial democracy. The old charge that to criticize or even to acknowledge the presence of racism was *ipso facto* to perpetuate it, is less tenable today, due to the growing debates and discussions about race in the political sphere, in popular media, in religious venues, and in everyday life.

Racial Politics Is Pervasive

Despite the decline of anti-racist movements in the new world racial order, a significant legacy of the break and its aftermath remains relatively intact. It is the pervasiveness of racial politics, the recognition that racial hierarchies and systems of signification permeate social institutions from the most comprehensive and global to the most small-scale and experiential. A notable and intriguing feature of race is its ubiquity, its presence in both the "smallest" and the "largest" features of social relationships, institutions, and identities. Much of the impetus behind the "politicization of the social," the reconceptualization of politics that has occurred in recent decades, was derived from anti-racist social movements. The democratizing challenge posed after World War II to "normal" systems of domination and power, "accepted" divisions of labor, and "rational-legal" means of legitimation, all had inescapable racial dimensions. Racially based movements, then (and the "second wave" feminism that followed and was inspired by them), problematized the public-private distinction

basic to preexisting political cultures. After World War II, the range of political issues that existed, and the number and sorts of political actors afforded any voice, was greatly expanded beyond the political norms of the years before the break.

These transformations were also reflected in political theory and political sociology, where older approaches to democratic theory, social movements, and the state were challenged, for example, by "political process" models (McAdam 1982; Morris and Mueller 1992). Recognition of the pervasiveness of politics also appears in the revival of interest in pragmatist sociology, in symbolic interactionism, in "constitution" theories of society (Joas 1996; Giddens 1984), and in the belated revival of interest in the work of W. E. B. Du Bois (West 1989; Lewis 1993, Winant 1997).

Mention of Du Bois brings me to the final points I want to make. Du Bois's astonishing career stretched from the eventide of the U.S. Civil War to the aftermath of the postwar racial break. He lived to see the sun set on the great colonial empires whose ravages he had opposed for seventy years, and to greet the dawn of the modern civil rights movement in the United States, for which he had laid so much groundwork. In a less well-known speech, given at a conference in 1960, Du Bois (then 92 years of age) contemplated the consequences of these victories, and of the new political situation that black people would find themselves in their aftermath:

> [W]hat we must now ask ourselves is when we become equal American citizens what will be our aims and ideals and what we will have to do with selecting these aims and ideals. Are we to assume that we will simply adopt the ideals of Americans and become what they are or want to be and that we will have in this process no ideals of our own?
>
> That would mean that we would cease to be Negroes as such and become white in action if not completely in color. We would take on the culture of white Americans doing as they do and thinking as they think.
>
> Manifestly this would not be satisfactory. Physically it would mean that we would be integrated with Americans losing first of all, the physical evidence of color and hair and racial type. We would lose our memory of Negro history

and of those racial peculiarities which have long been associated with the Negro. We would cease to acknowledge any greater tie with Africa than with England or Germany. We would not try to develop Negro music and Art and Literature as distinctive and different, but allow them to be further degraded as is the case now. We would always, if possible, marry lighterhued people so as to have children who are not identified with the Negro race, and thus solve our racial problem in America by committing race suicide. (Du Bois 1973 [1960], 149–150)

Du Bois confronted this tendency, not very different from the color-blind position of the present day, with the same radical democratic alternative he had been proposing over the course of the entire century. He recognized at its dawning the outlines of the new world racial system that would not be fully realized for many decades. He identified very early the limits of the moderate civil rights vision: the United States could not undo its deep commitment to white supremacy, at least not without a fundamental social upheaval. Blacks would be asked to absorb the costs of their inclusion, not whites. The price black people would be asked to pay in return for full inclusion was self-negation: the repudiation of their particularity and the unlearning of their history. Determined to maintain both the demand for full equality and the integrity of black identity, Du Bois *refused to choose* between the two terms of "American" and "Negro."

Du Bois ends his talk with a series of revolutionary commitments: the world, he says, is "going socialist." Black people should support a socialist transition in the United States as the only route to full equality; they should also dedicate their resources to self-determination and autonomous development for their own community. Du Bois also reiterates his long-standing commitments to pan-Africanism and the well-being (again, within the socialist framework), of the formerly colonized peoples of the South.

What can we take from this talk today? As I have noted, the injunction against race "suicide" remains convincing. The socialist alternative that Du Bois embraced (and about which he was perhaps willfully naive) is dead: the Stalinist and Maoist systems were certainly no democratic alternative for blacks in the United States or the "wretched of the earth" in general. Without repudiating the ideals of socialism—of cooperation, egalitarianism, and democratic self-rule—we probably have to reject Du Bois' complacency about the "actually existing forms" that socialism took at this time.

Yet at the same time the contours of the Duboisian political formula of racial dualism—what he calls "the possibility of black folk and their cultural patterns existing in America without discrimination and on terms of equality" (150)—seems, if extrapolated to a global level, a good starting-point for revisioning a political program for the next century or so. This vision remains strong. It continues as a radical pole of attraction. It is a "North Star" that shines yet.

To return to the Duboisian dictum with which I began this [essay]: at the start of the twenty-first century the world as a whole, and various national societies as well, are far from overcoming the tenacious legacies of colonial rule, apartheid, and segregation. All still experience continuing confusion, anxiety, and contention about race. Yet the legacies of epochal struggles for freedom, democracy, and human rights persist as well.

Despite the enormous vicissitudes that demarcate and distinguish national conditions, historical developments, roles in the international market, political tendencies, and cultural norms, racial differences still operate as they did in centuries past: as a way of restricting the political influence, not just of racially subordinated groups, but of all those at the bottom end of the system of social stratification. In the contemporary era, racial beliefs and practices have become far more contradictory and complex. The old world racial order has not disappeared, but it has been seriously disrupted and changed. The legacy of democratic, racially oriented movements, and anti-colonialist initiatives throughout the world's South, remains a force to be reckoned with. But the incorporative (or if one prefers this term, hegemonic) effects of decades of reform-oriented state racial policies have had a profound result as well: they have removed much of the motivation for sustained, anti-racist mobilization.

In this unresolved situation, it is unlikely that attempts to address worldwide dilemmas of race and racism by ignoring or transcending these themes, for example, by adopting so-called color-blind or differentialist policies, will have much effect. In the past the centrality of race deeply determined the economic, political, and cultural configuration of the modern world. Although recent decades have seen an efflorescence of movements for racial equality and justice, the legacies of centuries of racial oppression have not been overcome. Nor is a vision of racial justice fully worked out. Certainly the idea that such justice has already been largely achieved—as seen in the color-blind paradigm in the United States, the non-racialist rhetoric of the South African Freedom Charter, the Brazilian rhetoric of racial democracy, or the emerging racial differentialism of the European Union—remains problematic.

Will race ever be transcended? Will the world ever "get beyond" race? Probably not. But the entire planet still has a chance of overcoming the stratification, the hierarchy, the taken-for-granted injustice and inhumanity that so often accompanies the race-concept. Like religion or language, race can be accepted as part of the spectrum of the human condition, while it is simultaneously and categorically resisted as a means of stratifying national or global societies. Nothing is more essential in the effort to strengthen our commitments to democracy and social justice, and indeed to global survival and prosperity, as we enter a new millennium.

REFERENCES

Ansell, Amy Elizabeth. *New Right, New Racism: Race and Reaction in the United States and Britain.* New York: New York University Press, 1997.

Barber, Benjamin R. *Jihad vs. McWorld,* New York: Times, 1995.

Barker, Martin. *The New Racism: Conservatives and the Ideology of the Tribe.* London: Junction, Racism 1981. *Radical America* 5, no. 2 (1971).

Davidson, Basil. *The Black Man's Burden: Africa and the Curse of the Nation-State.* New York: Random House, 1992.

Du Bois, W. E. B. "Whither Now and Why" [1960]. In idem. *The Education of Black People: Ten Critiques 1906–1960.* Edited by Herbert Aptheker. Amherst: University of Massachusetts Press, 1973.

Giddens, Anthony. *The Constitution of Society: Outline of the Theory of Structuration.* Berkeley: University of California Press, 1984.

Gilroy, Paul. "Revolutionary Conservatism and the Tyrannies of Unanimism." *New Formations* 28 (Spring 1996).

Gilroy, Paul. "The End of Anti-Racism." In Martin Bulmer, and John Solomos, eds. *Racism* New York: Oxford University Press, 1999.

Greider, William. *One World, Ready or Not: The Manic Logic of Global Capitalism.* New York: Touchstone, 1997.

Habermas, Jürgen. *Between Facts and Norms: Contributions to a Discourse Theory of Law and Democracy.* Translated by William Rehg. Cambridge, MA: MIT Press, 1996.

Habermas, Jürgen. *A Berlin Republic: Writings on Germany.* Translated by Steven Rendall. Lincoln: University of Nebraska Press, 1997.

Joas, Hans. *The Creativity of Action.* Translated by Jeremy Gaines and Paul Keast. Chicago: University of Chicago Press, 1996.

Lewis, David Levering. *W. E. B. Du Bois: Biography of a Race, 1868–1919.* New York: Henry Holt, 1993.

McAdam, Doug. *Political Process and the Development of Black Insurgency, 1930–1970.* Chicago: University of Chicago Press, 1982.

Miles, Robert. *Racism after "Race Relations."* London: Routledge, 1993.

Moore, Barrington, Jr. *Injustice: The Social Bases of Obedience and Revolt.* White Plains: M. E. Sharpe, 1978.

Morris, Aldon, and Carol McClurg Mueller, eds. *Frontiers in Social Movement Theory.* New Haven: Yale University Press, 1992.

Sen, Amartya. "East and West: The Reach of Reason." *The New York Review of Books,* July 20, 2000.

Taguieff, Pierre-André. *Les Fins de l'Anti-racisme: Essai.* Paris: Editions Michalon, 1995.

West, Cornel. *The American Evasion of Philosophy: A Genealogy of Pragmatism.* Madison: University of Wisconsin Press, 1989.

Wieviorka, Michel. *The Arena of Racism.* Translated by Chris Turner. Thousand Oaks, CA: Sage, 1995.

Winant, Howard. "Racial Dualism at Century's End." In Wahneema Lubiano, ed. *The House That Race Built: Black Americans, US Terrain.* New York: Pantheon, 1997.

The Reversal of Historical Inequality Trends

GLENN FIREBAUGH

[The hypothesis presented in this essay] posits a new geography of global income inequality. The new geography of inequality—not to be confused with the "new economic geography" that arose in economics in the 1990s (Fujita, Krugman, and Venables 1999)—refers to the new pattern of global income inequality caused by the recent phenomenon of declining inequality across nations accompanied by (in many places) rising inequality within nations. This phenomenon, which began in the last third of the twentieth century and continues today, results in a "new geography" because it represents the reversal of trends that trace back to the early stages of Western industrialization. Put in the perspective of an individual, the new geography of global income inequality means that national location—while still paramount— is declining in significance in the determination of one's income.

Despite a recent surge of interest in global inequality, researchers have largely overlooked its changing contour. Studies of global income inequality over the last decades of the twentieth century have been preoccupied with the problem of global divergence, that is, the presumed problem of worsening income inequality for the world as a whole (for example, Wade 2001; Milanovic 2002). This preoccupation with global divergence is misguided, first, because global income inequality almost certainly declined over this period and, second, because the focus on the level of global income inequality has diverted attention from the changing nature of global income inequality in recent decades. Global income inequality is no worse today than it was in the 1960s and 1970s, but global income inequality is nevertheless changing— it is gradually shifting from inequality across nations to inequality within nations. The rising importance of within-nation inequality and declining importance of between-nation inequality represents a historic change, since it involves the reversal of a trend that began with the uneven industrialization of the world that started more than two centuries ago.

This chapter contrasts the New Geography Hypothesis with the popular view that globalization—by which I mean the increased interconnectedness of localities, particularly the deepening of economic links between countries—has led to growing global income inequality:

Globalization → global inequality.

For short, I call this popular view the Trade Protest Model, because the protests against the World Trade Organization in Seattle and elsewhere were driven at least in part by the assumption that global trade is exacerbating global inequality. To place the New Geography Hypothesis in context, it is useful first to examine five myths that underlie the globalization → global inequality model.

MYTHS OF THE TRADE PROTEST MODEL

Under the heading "Siege in Seattle," the December 13, 1999, issue of the U.S. magazine *Newsweek* gave this account of the protests surrounding the meeting of the World Trade Organization in Seattle, Washington:

> Until last week, not so many Americans had even heard of the WTO. Fewer still could have identified it as the small, Geneva-based bureaucracy that the United States and 134 other nations set up five years ago to referee global commerce. To Bill Clinton, it is a mechanism that can allow America to do well and good at the same time. But to many of the 40,000 activists and union members who streamed into Seattle—a clean, scenic city that has grown rich on foreign trade—the WTO is something else again: a secretive tool of ruthless multinational corporations. They charge it with helping sneaker companies to exploit Asian workers, timber companies to clear-cut rain forests, shrimpers to kill sea turtles and a world of other offenses.

Media accounts grappled with the sheer diversity of the protesters, from leaders of U.S. labor to members of environmental groups to a leading Chinese dissident.[1] The common thread seemed to be, as the *New York Times* (1999) put it, the view that the WTO is a "handmaiden of corporate interests whose rulings undermine health, labor and environmental protections around the world." According to *The Economist* (1999), "The WTO has become a magnet for resistance to globalisation by both old-fashioned protectionists and newer critics of free trade."

Some of the protest groups emphasized rising inequality as among the most noxious consequences of increasing trade globalization. For example, Ralph Nader's Public Citizen group portrays the WTO as a tool of big business "which is harming the environment and increasing inequality" (*The Economist* 1999), and representatives of 1,448 nongovernmental organizations protesting

the WTO signed a statement claiming that "globalisation has three serious consequences: the concentration of wealth in the hands of the multinationals and the rich; poverty for the majority of the world's population; and unsustainable patterns of production and consumption that destroy the environment" (*New Scientist* 1999). Note that two of the three consequences—concentration of wealth and impoverishment of the majority—tie globalization directly to growth in inequality.

Global income inequality is the result of the interplay of multiple causes, of course, so serious analyses are unlikely to give an unqualified endorsement to the notion that globalization has automatically resulted in an explosion in global income inequality. Global inequality existed before the recent growth in world trade, and it would persist if nations suddenly stopped trading. Nonetheless, popular literature on globalization has tended to fuel the belief in a globalization-led explosion in global income inequality by making claims that purport to be grounded in the findings of serious scholarly analyses. Upon closer inspection, however, many of the claims fly in the face of available empirical evidence. This section examines the key myths that underlie the globalization → global inequality model.

Myth 1. The Myth of Exploding Global Income Inequality. A steady drumbeat of reports and articles claims that the world's income is becoming more and more unequally distributed. Here is a sample:

- "Globalization has dramatically increased inequality between and within nations" (Jay Mazur, 2000, in *Foreign Affairs*).
- "The very nature of globalization has an inherent bias toward inequality. . . . One would have to be blind not to see that globalization also exacerbates the disparity between a small class of winners and the rest of us" (Paul Martin, Canada's prime minister, June 1998, quoted in Eggertson 1998).
- "Along with ecological risk, to which it is related, expanding inequality is the most serious problem facing world society" (Anthony Giddens, 1999).
- "Thus, overall, the ascent of informational, global capitalism is indeed characterized by simultaneous

---

[1] The business editor of the *Evening Standard* (December 1, 1999) described the demonstrators "in their Nike trainers, excitedly loading their Fuji film to take pictures with their Canons, chatting on their Nokia mobiles and dancing at the intersections to music from their Sonys" as "walking advertisements for the global economy."

economic development and underdevelopment, social inclusion and social exclusion. . . . There is polarization in the distribution of wealth at the global level, differential evolution of intra-country income inequality, and substantial growth of poverty and misery in the world at large" (Manuel Castells, 1998, p. 82, emphasis omitted).

What we will find subsequently is that global income inequality has not exploded but in fact leveled off and then declined in the last part of the twentieth century. Although income inequality rose somewhat in the average nation, income inequality declined across nations. Since between-nation inequality is the larger component of global income inequality, the decline in between-nation income inequality more than offset the rise in within-nation income inequality. As a result, global income inequality declined in the last years of the twentieth century. Sherlock Holmes was right: it *is* a capital mistake to theorize in advance of the facts (Doyle 1955, p. 507). With respect to global income inequality, much mischief has been done by theorizing about global income inequality on the basis of the views expressed above. Theorizing based on the widespread view of exploding global income inequality is theorizing based on facts that aren't.

Myth 2. The Myth of Growing Income Inequality Across Nations, as Rich Nations Surge Ahead and Poor Nations Fall Further Behind.

The first myth—exploding global inequality—is based on a second myth, the myth that inequality is growing across nations. The second myth is as widespread as the first, and it has been fueled by widely circulated reports of international agencies:

- "Figures indicate that income inequality between countries has increased sharply over the past 40 years" (World Bank 2000b, *World Development Report 2000/2001*, p. 51).
- "The average income in the richest 20 countries is 37 times the average in the poorest 20—a gap that has doubled in the past 40 years" (International Monetary Fund 2000, p. 50).
- "Gaps in income between the poorest and richest people and countries have continued to widen. In 1960 the 20% of the world's people in the richest countries had 30 times the income of the poorest

20%—in 1997, 74 times as much . . . Gaps are widening both between and within countries" (United Nations Development Program 1999, *Human Development Report 1999*, p. 36).
- "It is an empirical fact that the income gap between poor and rich countries has increased in recent decades" (Ben-David, Nordström, and Winters 1999, World Trade Organization special study, p. 3).
- "In 1960, the Northern countries were 20 times richer than the Southern, in 1980 46 times. . . . [I]n this kind of race, the rich countries will always move faster than the rest" (Sachs 1992, *The Development Dictionary*, p. 3).

The myth of growing income inequality across nations is based in large part on a misinterpretation of the widely cited finding (for example, World Bank 2000b, p. 50) that income growth has tended to be slower in poor nations than in rich nations. As we shall see, this positive cross-country association between income level and income growth rate conceals the critical fact that the poor nations that are falling badly behind contain no more than 10 percent of the world's population, whereas the poor nations that are catching up (largely in Asia) contain over 40 percent of the world's population. When nations are weighted by population size—as they must be if we want to use between-nation inequality to draw conclusions about global income inequality—we find that income inequality across nations peaked sometime around 1970 and has been declining since. This peaking of between-nation income inequality circa 1970 is particularly interesting in light of Manuel Castells's (1998, p. 336) well-known claim that a "new world" originated in the late 1960s to mid-1970s. Ironically, though, Castells characterizes the world born in this period as a world of sharply increasing global inequality, and many other globalization writers make the same error. . . .

This book will debunk myth number 2 first by replicating the United Nations/World Bank results and then by demonstrating how they have been misinterpreted. In addition to the weighting problem just mentioned, the claims of growing inequality often ignore nations in the middle of the income distribution, focusing instead on selected nations at the tails. When the entire income distribution is used, and when individuals are given equal weight, we find that—far from growing—income inequality across nations declined in the late twentieth century.

Myth 3. The Myth That Globalization Historically Has Caused Rising Inequality Across Nations.
Contrary to this myth, the trend in between-nation inequality historically has not followed changes in the trend in world economic integration. First, although it is true that between-nation income inequality increased dramatically over the nineteenth and early twentieth centuries, Peter Lindert and Jeffrey Williamson (2000) argue that the period of rising inequality across nations began *before* the period of true globalization started, so globalization apparently did not cause the upturn. Second, the sharp decline in globalization between World War I and World War II did not result in declining inequality across nations (to the contrary, between-nation income inequality shot up rapidly over the period). Finally, as this book emphasizes, income inequality across nations has declined in recent decades, during a period when globalization has presumably reached new heights. (I say "presumably" because globalization is itself a contentious issue: see Guillén 2001. Nonetheless virtually all agree that the world has become more economically integrated over recent decades, even if the degree of globalization is often overstated, as Chase-Dunn, Kawano, and Brewer 2000, among others, have noted.) In short, the rise in global inequality predates the rise in globalization, global inequality has risen while globalization was declining, and currently global inequality is declining while globalization is rising. It is hard then to make the case historically that globalization is the cause of rising income inequality across nations (O'Rourke 2001).

Myth 4. The Myth of a Postindustrial World Economy.
In reading the globalization literature it is easy to lose sight of the fact that, until recently, most of the world's people were engaged in agriculture. So the world's workforce is barely postagricultural, much less postindustrial. This

book makes the point that the primary engine still driving the growth in world production is more manufacturing. A new information age might be on the way, but it is not here yet—at least it is not here for most of the world's people. It is important to look ahead, of course, and it is hard to argue against the view that the world will eventually be postindustrial. The death of industrialization is nonetheless much exaggerated, as is the view that we are rapidly approaching an information-based global economy (Quah 1997). Estimates of the composition of global output, albeit rough approximations, rule out the claims of some globalization writers that we live in a new economic era quite unlike the era of the last generation. Industrialization was important in the nineteenth century, it was important in the twentieth century, and it remains important in most regions of the world in the twenty-first century. A preoccupation with postindustrialization in the face of the continuing diffusion of industrialization results in an incomplete and distorted story of global income inequality that deemphasizes the critical role of the continuing spread of industrialization to all regions of the world. Computers are important, but they are not all-important. In accounting for recent trends in global income inequality, this book argues that the bigger story is industrial growth in Asia, not technological growth in the West.

Myth 5. The Myth of International Exchange as Inherently Exploitative.
Globalization involves increased exchange over national boundaries. One might posit that increased exchange worsens global inequality under some historical conditions and reduces it under other conditions. Until those historical conditions are identified and understood, the effect of globalization on global income inequality at any point in time is an open question to be settled empirically.

But if international exchange is inherently exploitative, as some theories of world stratification insist, then rising exchange implies rising exploitation, and the Trade Protest Model is true virtually by definition. The Trade Protest Model then becomes:

Globalization → more exploitation of poor nations by rich nations → greater global inequality

Note that this elaboration of the Trade Protest Model reveals how high the theoretical stakes are with regard to empirical tests of the globalization → global income inequality model, since the failure of globalization to lead to rising global income inequality would undermine exploitation theories (for example, dependency theories) as well as undermining the Trade Protest Model.

[E]vidence [exists] that increasing international exchange over recent decades has been accompanied by declining—not rising—income inequality across nations. Other studies also document declining between-nation income inequality over recent decades, as we shall see. The decline in between-nation inequality has significant theoretical implications. The assumption of inherent exploitation favoring rich nations in international exchange is the linchpin of some theoretical schools. But if international exchange were inherently exploitative, we would not expect to observe declining inequality across nations during a period of rising international trade. Yet the assumption persists, suggesting that in some theories the notion of inherent exploitation is so essential that it enjoys creedal status as a doctrine to be believed rather than as a hypothesis to be tested.

CAUSES OF THE REVERSAL: AN OVERVIEW

I argue that the world's spreading industrialization and growing economic integration in the late twentieth century and the early twenty-first have reversed the historical pattern of uneven economic growth favoring richer nations. The conventional view, just elaborated, is that globalization has exacerbated global income inequality. The evidence presented here challenges that view. In reality globalization has offsetting effects—by spurring industrialization in poor nations, globalization raises inequality within many nations and compresses inequality across nations. The net effect has been a reduction in global income inequality in recent decades, since the reduction in between-nation income inequality has more than offset the growth in within-nation income inequality.

The new pattern of rising within-nation and falling between-nation income inequality has multiple causes. The most important cause is spreading industrialization—the diffusion of industrialization to the world's large poor nations. The diffusion of industrialization to poor regions compresses inequality across nations and boosts inequality within them. The effect of spreading industrialization on between-nation inequality is reinforced by the effect of the growing integration of national economies. Growing economic integration tends to dissolve institutional differences between nations. The convergence of institutional economic goals and policies compresses inequality across nations by (in some instances at least) removing impediments to growth in poor nations.

There are at least four other significant causes of the new geography of global inequality. The first is technological change that reduces the tyranny of space in general and more particularly reduces the effect of labor immobility across national boundaries. This technological change works to reduce inequality across nations. The second is a demographic windfall that has benefited some poor Asian nations in recent decades and promises to benefit other poor nations in the near future. This effect also operates to compress global income inequality, by reducing between-nation inequality. The third is the rise of the service sector, especially in richer nations. Growth in this sector has boosted income inequality within nations, and it is likely to do so in the future as well. The fourth is the collapse of communism, which also boosted within-nation inequality. This is a nonrecurring event, however, so its effect on within-nation inequality is limited to a specific point in history, the 1990s.

In short, the decline in between-nation income inequality that began in the late twentieth century was caused by deepening industrialization of poor nations, by growing economic integration that dissolves institutional differences between nations, by technological change that reduces the effects of labor immobility across national boundaries, and by a demographic windfall that has benefited some poor nations and promises to benefit others in the future. The growth in within-nation income inequality was caused by the deepening industrialization of poor nations, by the growth of the service sector, and by the collapse of communism. Each of these causes will be elaborated and argued in the last two chapters of the book. To set the context for that discussion—as well as to anticipate the empirical findings that constitute the bulk of the book—it is useful to summarize evidence indicating that we are in fact in the midst of an inequality transition.

THE INEQUALITY TRANSITION

The industrialization of richer nations in the nineteenth century and first half of the twentieth caused income inequality across nations to explode. As a result, global income inequality shifted from inequality within nations to inequality across nations. Now, however, poorer nations are industrializing faster than richer ones are, and between-nation inequality is declining while within-nation inequality appears to be rising. If this turnaround continues, future historians will refer to an inequality transition that accompanied world industrialization. That transition is from within-nation inequality to between-nation inequality back to within-nation inequality, with the late twentieth century as the period when the shift back to within-nation income inequality began.

Phase 1 of the Transition: from Within- to Between-Nation Inequality

Phase 1 of the inequality transition coincides with the period of Western industrialization that began in the late eighteenth century and ended in the second half of the twentieth century. The first phase

of the inequality transition was characterized by unprecedented growth in income inequality across nations. As Lant Pritchett (1996, p. 40) puts it, "the overwhelming feature of modern economic history is a massive divergence in per capita incomes between rich and poor countries." The evidence is incontrovertible. First, it is clear that current levels of between-nation income inequality would not have been possible earlier in human history. Again quoting Pritchett (1997, pp. 9–10): "If there had been no divergence, then we could extrapolate backward from present income of the poorer countries to past income assuming they grew at least as fast as the United States. However, this would imply that many poor countries must have had incomes below $100 in 1870 [in 1985 U.S. dollars]. Since this cannot be true, there must have been divergence."

Second, Pritchett's conclusion that "there must have been divergence" is supported by estimates of between-nation income inequality in the nineteenth century. Consider the recent estimates of Bourguignon and Morrisson (1999). Bourguignon and Morrisson use the Maddison (1995) data to estimate changes in the level of between-nation income inequality from 1820 to 1992. Because their objective is to estimate total world income inequality—not just between-nation income inequality—Bourguignon and Morrisson begin by disaggregating national income data into vintiles (5 percent groups, that is, twenty income groups per nation). National boundaries have changed over the past two centuries, of course, and nations have come and gone over the past two centuries. Even in nations where boundaries remained constant, we do not always have income data for the entire period. To overcome these problems, Bourguignon and Morrisson grouped the 199 nations with income data in 1992 into 33 homogeneous groups, each of which represented at least 1 percent of the world population or world GDP in 1950. The 33 groups include single nations (such as China and the United States) as well as large groups of small nations and small groups of medium-sized nations. From these 660 data points (33 nation groups × 20) it is a straightforward matter to apply the population-weighted

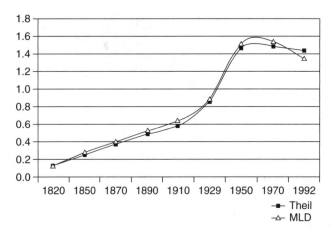

FIGURE 1   Ratio of Between-Nation to Within-Nation Income Inequality for 33 Nation Groups, 1820–1992. Based on Table 2.1. Theil and MLD are Measures of Inequality.

formulas for the Theil index and the mean logarithmic deviation (MLD)—two measures of inequality—to calculate summary measures of the world's total inequality for different years. By collapsing the 199 nations into 33 groups, Bourguignon and Morrisson are able to extend their inequality series back to 1820. Note that, to the extent that their grouping strategy introduces bias, the bias is in the direction of underestimating between-nation inequality and inflating within-nation inequality, since some of the inequality within the nation groups is actually between-nation inequality. But that bias should not affect our basic conclusions about the relative growth in between-nation and within-nation income inequality over the past two centuries.[2]

The results are striking (Figure 1). Two facts stand out. First, the *B/W* ratio—the ratio of between-nation to within-nation income inequality—is much higher now than it was in the early stages of Western industrialization. The increase in the *B/W* ratio

reflects both a rise in between-nation income inequality and a decline in within-nation income inequality since 1820 (Table 1). By far the greater change is in between-nation income inequality, however. The Theil index for between-nation income inequality (actually, inequality between nation *groups*) shot up from 0.061 in 1820 to 0.513 in 1992, and the MLD shot up from 0.053 in 1820 to 0.495 in 1992. As anticipated, then, the Industrial Revolution of the past two centuries has increased income inequality across nations, but the magnitude of the increase is stunning. There has been a metamorphosis from a world where poverty was the norm in all nations to a richer world with much lower poverty rates (Bourguignon and Morrisson 1999, table 1) but also with much greater income inequality across nations. Because the steep rise in between-nation income inequality was not accompanied by an increase in inequality within nations, where you live—your nation—is much more important in determining your income in today's world than it was in the preindustrial world.

The second fact that stands out is that the growth in the *B/W* ratio stalled in the second half of the

---

[2] In estimating global inequality, the key is the reliability of the data for larger nations, since global income inequality is driven largely by patterns in those nations.

TABLE 1 Trends in Income Inequality Between and
Within 33 Homogeneous Nation Groups,
1820–1992

	Between Nation Groups		*Within Nation Groups*	
Year	*Theil*	*MLD*	*Theil*	*MLD*
1820	.061	.053	.472	.388
1850	.128	.111	.477	.393
1870	.188	.162	.485	.399
1890	.251	.217	.498	.408
1910	.299	.269	.500	.413
1929	.365	.335	.413	.372
1950	.482	.472	.323	.309
1970	.490	.515	.324	.330
1992	.513	.495	.351	.362

Estimates: Between nation groups: From Bourguignon and Morrisson (1999),
based on Maddison (1995) data set. *Within nation groups:* From Bourguignon
and Morrisson (1999), based on updating of Berry, Bourguignon, and Morrisson (1983a,b) for the post–World War II period and on various sources (for
example, Lindert 1999; Morrisson 1999) for the pre–World War II period. As
this book was going to press, Bourguignon and Morrisson (2002) published
modestly revised estimates for inequality. By collapsing vintiles to deciles,
they report slightly lower estimates of inequality within the nation groups, but
the fundamental conclusions are the same.

Note: Income measures are adjusted for purchasing power parity, and
inequality measures are based on income vintiles (see Bourguignon and
Morrisson 1999 for elaboration).

Source: Bourguignon and Morrisson (1999), table 3.

twentieth century. The *B/W* ratio stopped growing
in the second half of the twentieth century because
growth in inequality across the nation groups has
slowed dramatically since 1950. In the four decades
after 1950, income inequality across the nation
groups increased by 6 percent using the Theil index
and by 5 percent using the MLD. Over the four
decades prior to 1950, the Theil had grown about
60 percent and the MLD had grown about 75 percent. Apparently the most dramatic effects of Western industrialization on between-nation inequality
are over. After more than a century of sharp divergence in national incomes, the trend has been much
more stable in recent years. This finding is in line
with the findings of others (for example, Schultz
1998; Firebaugh 1999; Melchior, Telle, and Wiig
2000; Goesling 2001) who, drawing on data for
individual nations instead of nation groups, find
that between-nation income inequality is no longer
rising. As we shall see later, between-nation income

inequality declined in the late twentieth century
when income data for the 1990s are added to data
for the 1970s and 1980s.

Finally, it should be emphasized that the results
here are so strong that the historical story they tell
of increasing inequality across nations and of a rising *B/W* ratio cannot be dismissed as due to error in
the data. To be sure, income estimates for the nineteenth century are gross approximations for many
nations. But even if we make the extreme assumption that incomes are so drastically overstated for
poorer nations in 1820 (or so drastically understated
for richer nations in 1820) that the Theil and the
MLD estimates understate between-nation income
inequality in 1820 by a factor of three, that would
still mean that between-nation income inequality
tripled from 1820 to 1992 (from 0.18 to 0.51 based
on the Theil index and from 0.16 to 0.50 for the
MLD), and the *B/W* ratio still would have more than
tripled for both inequality measures.

Phase 2 of the Transition: from Between-Nation Back to Within-Nation Inequality

The second phase of the inequality transition began in the second half of the twentieth century, with the stabilization of between-nation income inequality in the 1960–1990 period and the decline in between-nation inequality beginning in earnest in the 1990s. Social scientists hardly have a stellar track record for predictions, especially with regard to sweeping predictions such as the one made here. Nonetheless there is sufficient theory and evidence that we can plausibly forecast that the *B/W* ratio will continue to decline in the twenty-first century.

The prediction of a declining *B/W* ratio is based on two separate conjectures. The first conjecture is that between-nation income inequality will decline, and the second conjecture is that within-nation income inequality will rise, or at least will not decline. These conjectures are based on the causes of the current trends, which I expect to continue and in some cases to intensify. (I am assuming that there will be no cataclysmic upheaval in the twenty-first century, such as a global war or a worldwide plague.) Recall the causes listed earlier for the inequality turnaround in the late twentieth century. I expect the major causes to continue, so between-nation income inequality will decline because of the continued industrialization of poor nations, because of the continued convergence of national economic policies and institutions arising from growing economic integration of national economies, because of the declining significance of labor immobility across national borders, and because of a demographic windfall for many poor nations. Within-nation income inequality will rise—or at least not decline—because of the continued industrialization of poor nations and because of continued growth in the service sector. Because between-nation inequality is the larger component, global income inequality will decline. . . .

The conjecture of declining global income inequality is out of step with much of the globalization literature. A recurring theme in that literature is

that we have entered a new information-based economic era where productive activity is becoming less dependent on physical space, as a rising share of the world's economic output is produced in electronic space that knows no national borders (Sassen 2000). This phenomenon is possible because of the emergence of a global economy where income—and hence income inequality—is becoming increasingly rooted in knowledge rather than in capital goods (Reich 1991). What do these developments imply for global income inequality? For many globalization writers, the answer is clear: global inequality is bound to worsen because of the growing "global digital divide" that enlarges the gap between the "haves" and the "have-nots" (Campbell 2001; Ishaq 2001; Norris 2001).

Empirical evidence presented subsequently suggests otherwise, however, and the theoretical argument that a shift to a knowledge-based global economy would worsen global income inequality is shaky as well. It is not hard to think of reasons why the shift from an industrial-based to a knowledge-based global economy would reduce, not increase, inequality across nations. Knowledge is mobile, especially with today's telecommunication technologies that permit virtually instant worldwide codification and distribution of knowledge. In addition, because knowledge can be given away without being lost, the notion of property rights is more problematic in the case of knowledge, so it is harder to concentrate and monopolize knowledge across nations than it is to concentrate and monopolize capital goods across nations. Hence the switch to a knowledge-based global economy should mean that one's income is increasingly determined by how much knowledge one obtains and uses as opposed to where one lives. The tighter link between knowledge and income in turn implies declining income inequality across nations and rising inequality within nations since—absent institutional barriers . . .—the variance in individuals' ability to obtain and benefit from knowledge is greater within nations than between them.

. . . [T]he issue of how the new information age will affect global inequality in the near term

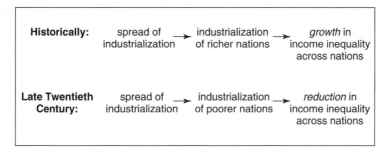

FIGURE 2   Industrialization and Between-Nation Income Inequality: Historically and in the Late Twentieth Century.

is not as decisive as often imagined, since as already noted, the coming of the information age is often much exaggerated. What is still most important in today's world is industrialization for the many, not digitization for the few. Historically the spread of industrialization has been the primary force driving the growth in between-nation income inequality. The initially richer nations of the West were the first to industrialize, and the poorer nations of Asia and Africa lagged behind. The new geography of inequality is also driven by the spread of industrialization, but the effects are different today: now the spread of industrialization means the diffusion of manufacturing technology to the world's largest poor regions. In recent decades inequality has declined across nations as industrialization has been an engine of growth in the most populous poor regions of the world, especially East Asia. That growth has worked both to compress inequality across nations (Figure 2) and to boost inequality within the industrializing nations.

The significance of this continuation of world industrialization has been lost in much of the literature on globalization, because of preoccupation with the idea that we are witnessing the emergence of a new knowledge-based technology regime. To be sure, in the categories used to classify world production, the output of the so-called service sector is estimated to exceed the output of the industrial sector for the world as a whole (World Bank 1997,

table 12). Yet much of the service sector—an amorphous sector that includes wholesale and retail trade, the banking industry, government, the transportation industry, the commercial real estate industry, and personal services (including health care and education)—has arisen to grease the wheels of industry. Aside from the growth in personal services and government, much of the growth in the service sector has been for services for producers, not consumers—for example, the rise of an engineering industry to design better machines, and the growth of a banking industry and a commercial real estate industry for commercial transactions. In addition, many of the other so-called service industries—the transportation industry that distributes manufactured goods, for example, and the specialized retailing industry that sells the goods—benefit producers as well as consumers. In short, a significant portion of the growth in service industries over the past century can be seen as ancillary to the industrialization process.

REFERENCES

Ben-David, Dan, Håkan Nordström, and L. Alan Winters. 1999. *Trade, Income Inequality, and Poverty.* WTO Special Study no. 5. Geneva: World Trade Organization.

Bourguignon, François, and Christian Morrisson. 1998. "Inequality and development: The role of dualism." *Journal of Development Economics* 57:233–257.

Bourguignon, François, and Christian Morrisson. 1999. "The size distribution of income among world citizens: 1820–1990." Draft. June.

Campbell, Duncan. 2001. "Can the digital divide be contained?" *International Labour Review* 140:119–141.

Castells, Manuel. 1993. "The informational economy and the new international division of labor." Chapter 2 in *The New Global Economy in the Information Age*, ed. Martin Carnoy, Manuel Castells, Stephen S. Cohen, and Fernando Henrique Cardoso. University Park: Pennsylvania State University Press.

Castells, Manuel. 1998. *End of Millennium*. Malden, Mass.: Blackwell.

Chase-Dunn, Christopher. 1975. "The effects of international economic dependence on development and inequality: A cross-national study." *American Sociological Review* 40: 720–738.

Chase-Dunn, Christopher, Yukio Kawano, and Benjamin D. Brewer. 2000. "Trade globalization since 1795: Waves of integration in the world-system." Special millennium issue, edited by Glenn Firebaugh, of the *American Sociological Review* 65:77–95.

Doyle, Arthur Conan. 1955. *A Treasury of Sherlock Holmes*. Selected and with an introduction by Adrian Conan Doyle. Garden City, N.Y.: Hanover House.

The Economist. 1996. "Economic growth: The poor and the rich." Pp. 23–25. May 25.

The Economist. 1999. "The battle in Seattle." U.S. edition. November 27.

Eggertson, Laura. 1998. "Rich-poor gap next issue for Martin." *Toronto Star.* June 3, p. A6.

Firebaugh, Glenn. 1999. "Empirics of world income inequality." *American Journal of Sociology* 104:1597–1630.

Fujita, Masahisa, Paul Krugman, and Anthony J. Venables. 1999. *The Spatial Economy: Cities, Regions, and International Trade*. Cambridge: MIT Press.

Giddens, Anthony. 1999. "Globalization: An irresistible force." *The Daily Yomiuri,* June 7, p. 8.

Goesling, Brian. 2000. "World income inequality: How much is between nations and how much is within?" M.A. thesis. Department of Sociology, Pennsylvania State University.

Goesling, Brian. 2001. "Changing income inequalities within and between nations: New evidence." *American Sociological Review* 66:745–761.

Guillén, Mauro F. 2001. "Is globalization civilizing, destructive, or feeble? A critique of five key debates in the social science literature." *Annual Review of Sociology* 27:235–260.

International Monetary Fund (IMF). 2000. "How we can help the poor." *Finance and Development* (December). (*http://www.imf.org/external/pubs.*)

Ishaq, Ashfaq. 2001. "On the global digital divide." *Finance and Development* 38:44–47.

Lindert, Peter. 1999. "Three centuries of inequality in Britain and America." In *Handbook of Income Distribution*, ed. A. B. Atkinson and F. Bourguignon. Amsterdam: Elsevier.

Lindert, Peter, and Jeffrey G. Williamson. 2000. "Does globalization make the world more unequal?" Paper presented at the "Globalization in Historical Perspective" preconference,

National Bureau of Economic Research, Cambridge, Mass. November.

Maddison, Angus. 1995. *Monitoring the World Economy, 1820–1992*. Paris: OECD.

Mazur, Jay. 2000. "Labor's new internationalism." *Foreign Affairs* 79:79–93.

Melchior, Arne, Kjetil Telle, and Henrik Wiig. 2000. *Globalization and Inequality: World Income Distribution and Living Standards, 1960–1998*. Studies on Foreign Policy Issues. Oslo: Royal Norwegian Ministry of Foreign Affairs.

Milanovic, Branko. 2002. "True world income distribution, 1988 and 1993: First calculation based on household surveys alone." *Economic Journal* 112:51–92.

Morrisson, Christian, 1999. "Historical perspectives on income distribution: The case of Europe." In *Handbook of Income Distribution*, ed. A. B. Atkinson and F. Bourguignon. Amsterdam: Elsevier.

New Scientist. 1999. Editorial. December 4.

New York Times. 1999. "National guard is called to quell trade talk protests." December 1.

Norris, Pippa. 2001. *Digital Divide: Civic Engagement, Information Poverty, and the Internet Worldwide*. Cambridge and New York: Cambridge University Press.

O'Rourke, Kevin H. 2001. "Globalization and inequality: Historical trends." National Bureau of Economic Research. Draft. April.

Pritchett, Lant. 1996. "Forget convergence: Divergence past, present, and future." *Finance and Development* (June):40–43.

——1997. "Divergence, big time." *Journal of Economic Perspectives* 11:3–17.

Quah, Danny T. 1996. "Convergence empirics across economies with (some) capital mobility." *Journal of Economic Growth* 1:95–124.

Quah, Danny T. 1997. "Increasingly weightless economies." *Bank of England Quarterly Bulletin* (February):49–55.

Reich, Robert B. 1991. *The Work of Nations: Preparing Ourselves for Twenty-first-Century Capitalism*. New York: Knopf.

Sassen, Saskia. 2000. "Territory and territoriality in the global economy." *International Sociology* 15:372–393.

Schultz, T. Paul. 1998. "Inequality in the distribution of personal income in the world: How it is changing and why." *Journal of Population Economics* 11:307–344.

United Nations Development Program. 1999. *Human Development Report 1999*. New York: Oxford University Press.

Wade, Robert. 2001. "Global inequality: Winners and losers." *The Economist*. April 28.

World Bank. 1990. *World Development Report 1990*. Oxford: Oxford University Press.

World Bank. 1997. *World Development Report 1997: The State in a Changing World*. Oxford: Oxford University Press.

World Bank. 2000b. *World Development Report 2000/2001: Attacking Poverty*. New York: Oxford University Press.

Losers

DAVID S. LANDES

Strung out behind the leaders and followers—in the sense of those who are keeping pace or catching up—are most of the world's peoples.

By comparison with East Asia, the rest of the world looks like a study in slow motion, or even one step forward, two steps back. The Middle East has much going for it, in particular, huge oil revenues (some $2 trillion [$10^{12}$] in the twenty years after 1973), but its political, social, and cultural institutions do not ensure security of enterprise or promote autonomous technological development. Also, cultural attitudes, and above all, gender biases, inhibit industrial undertakings. One result is high rates of unemployment and underemployment, made worse and angrier by education: people who have been to school expect more.[1]

To be sure, well-meaning governments in the region have tried to substitute for private initiative. Thus Egypt, recalling the industrial projects of Muhammad Ali one hundred years earlier, decided after World War II to invest in cotton-spinning mills. The idea seemed fool-proof. Egypt grew the finest long-fiber cotton in the world; why not work it up and gain the value added? The trouble was, the yarn turned out by these callow mills was not of international quality, while foreign growers sought to upgrade their raw cotton and weavers looked for ways to make high-quality cloth with poorer varieties. Never underestimate the ingenuity of good technicians: before the Egyptians could turn around, they were stuck with poor cloth for the home market and had lost part of their export market for raw cotton. Egypt, unfortunately, was not the only example of industry aborted. The African continent abounds in projects and disappointments.

Failure hardens the heart and dims the eye. Up to now, Middle Eastern losers have sought compensation in religious fundamentalism and military aggression. On the popular level, prayer and faith console the impotent and promise retribution. Hence the apocalyptic tone of much Muslim preaching and discourse: the End will bring redress. Meanwhile, the strong resort to force. They find it easier to seize and screw than to make and do. So for Iraq, which thought to get rich quicker by grabbing oil and looting houses in Kuwait than by manufacturing salable commodities. Why buy arms if not to use them?

Will these counterproductive tendencies pass? Impossible to say. They are not accidental but visceral. The international experts keep their chin up (that's what they're paid for) and offer modest recipes for improvement. Thus the World Bank, with its talk of "adjustment," reminds us that good policies pay. What are good policies? Realistic, competitive exchange rates, low or no budget deficits, low or no barriers to trade, markets, markets, markets.

Such "improvements in the macroeconomic framework" do help. They clear major distortions and obstacles. But they do not come easy. How does one eliminate budget deficits when half the workforce is employed by the state unproductively and political stability is tied to inefficiency? (This kind of problem afflicts even rich nations. Look at Europe and the Maastricht criteria for the euro currency.)

And that's only the beginning. The real work of building structures and institutions remains. Besides, what happens when the oil is gone?*

Latin America has had almost two hundred years of political independence to graduate to economic independence. It remains, however, a mixed area, wanting in local initiatives, technologically patchy, entrepreneurially needy. This pattern of arrested development reflects the tenacious resistance of old ways and vested interests. In particular, the apparently rational focus on land and pastoralism (long live comparative advantage!), reinforced by social and political privilege, bred powerful, reactionary elites ill-suited and hostile to an industrial world. This disjuncture, when combined with social discontents—so many poor—invited antidemocratic, though populist, solutions *(caudillismo),* terrible when durable, destructive when fragile.

So industry came late. This need not be a handicap; lateness has its advantages. But everything depends on the quality of enterprise and the technological capability of the society. In most of Latin America, industry came in under the shelter of import substitution: high tariffs, discriminatory legislation and regulations, nontariff barriers to imports. As we know from American experience in the nineteenth century and Japanese in the twentieth, such measures may work in a context of energetic emulation, of exigent, world-level (export-capable) standards, of domestic competition.

In Latin America, this impulse was largely wanting. Not everywhere. Some industry is on the cutting edge. But most is well behind the frontier, panting behind protective walls.

This protection has been justified by national interest or by anticolonialist ideologies that, if pushed to their logical conclusion, would suggest an end to all exchange with the more advanced industrial nations abroad. (Latin America has been a field of dichotomous perspective: center vs. periphery, neocolonialists vs. victims, bad guys against good.) Fortunately, that has not happened. Such exercises in pure reason (or unreason) are more suited to scholars' studies than to the halls of government, as President Cardoso of Brazil, once a flag-bearer of the dependency school, has now discovered.

We should not underestimate the importance of that discovery: just because something is obvious does not mean that people will see it, or that they will sacrifice belief to reality. In the effort to have things both ways, or every way, to appease old interests, to encourage new, to keep the foreigner away while bringing him in, most Latin nations have resorted to the manipulation of trade and money: import barriers and quotas, differential rates of exchange, a carapace of restrictions that some have called the "inward-looking model"—and, of course, to borrowing.[2]

Such measures can provide temporary relief, but at a heavy price: constant adjustments, currency black markets, runaway inflations, high transaction costs, a chilling of foreign investment. Even so, some Latin American countries were able to borrow ridiculously large sums from official international lenders (World Bank, IMF) and from private commercial banks, acting with the encouragement of their governments and, no doubt, tacit assurances of a rescue safety net. Much of this money found its way back to secret private accounts in the United States, Switzerland, and other cozy shelters.

The combination of mismanagement, profligacy, corruption, and open-ended borrowing—development without efficiency constraints—cannot long endure. Such structures are intrinsically brittle,

---

* Field, *Inside the Arab World,* p. 21, points out that at rates of extraction in the early 1990s, oil in the Gulf has 130 years to go. (The assumption, of course, is that we know what's there. People are still looking.) But that's the Gulf; for other oil producers in the Middle East and North Africa, the end is nearer. Meanwhile progressive exhaustion is an incentive to a search for new energy technologies. In the end, for oil as now for coal, a fair amount may be left in the ground.

because everyone is straining to the limit and everything is interconnected. Sooner or later, someone gets worried; the balance sheets do not balance; the lenders get cold feet; it becomes impossible to pay old debts with new. Panic!

This happened in the Mexican peso crisis of 1994–95. It couldn't have come at a worse (some would say, a better) time, just after the American administration managed to squeeze through the North American Free Trade Agreement (NAFTA) by calling in every political chip and committing to a mountain of anti-economic favors. Now it had to find tens of billions to reassure the market and give investors and monetary allies the time to pull their chestnuts out. But this time it could not get fast action from a recalcitrant, narrow-minded Congress. Not to worry: the technicians, led by economist Lawrence Summers, found some $20 billion lying quietly in an account established over half a century earlier with the profits realized in the 1930s by repudiating obligations in gold. These ill-gotten gains had been set aside at the time to protect the American dollar . . . Well, one could say that a collapse of the peso and the liquidation of American holdings in Mexico would have done terrible damage to NAFTA and the American dollar . . . Those $20 billion plus another $30 billion cobbled together from international lending organizations saved the day. The American government subsequently made much of quick repayment by Mexico, and the press played down, or never noticed, the fact that the Mexicans had to borrow the money. New debt for old.

The heart of the matter is Latin America's need to go on borrowing, if only to pay interest on older loans. A research student from Latin America once complained to me about this burden of old debt and the vexatious, small-minded foreign insistence on repayment. "You don't have to repay," I pointed out; "a sovereign nation can always repudiate." "Yes," he replied, "but then where shall we go to borrow more?" Exactly. Now, however, the banks are wary, and international lending organizations are tying their support to fiscal and trade reform in the direction of openness. The code word is "adjustment"—surely a good thing. A more open market is a force for rationality and efficiency, a reordering of economic activity in the direction of comparative advantage, a constraint on corruption and favoritism. And the prospect of aid may be an incentive to cooperation in the struggle against the drug trade—an industry whose growth can only be guessed at.[3] No guarantees. But better a push in the right direction than a return to the *status quo ante.*

Among the heaviest losers in this period of record-breaking economic growth and technological advance were the countries of the Communist-Socialist bloc: the Soviet Union at the bottom of the barrel, Romania and North Korea almost as bad, and a range of satellite victims and emulators struggling to rise above the mess. Best off were probably Czechoslovakia and Hungary, with East Germany (the DDR) and Poland trailing behind. The striking feature of these command economies was the contradiction between system and pretensions on the one hand, performance on the other. The logic was impeccable: experts would plan, zealots would compete in zeal, technology would tame nature, labor would make free, the benefits would accrue to all. From each according to his ability; to each according to his deserts; and eventually, to each according to his needs.[*]

The dream appealed to the critics and victims of capitalism, admittedly a most imperfect system— but as it turned out, far better than the alternatives. Hence the Marxist economies long enjoyed a willfully credulous favor among radicals, liberals, and progressives in the advanced industrial nations;

---

[*] The Soviets anticipated and perhaps taught the Germans. The "tens of thousands" of slave labor deaths incurred building the White Sea–Baltic canal (early 1930s)—picks, shovels, and wheelbarrows against snow, ice, and hunger—were justified by the allegedly redemptive character of the work, which would turn enemies of the people into good socialists. The slogan: "We will instruct nature and we will receive freedom." Compare the motto at the entrance to the Nazi death camps: *Arbeit macht frei*—Work makes free. On the Soviet dream (nightmare) of ruthless gigantism (gods do not weep), see Josephson, " 'Projects of the Century.' "

and a passionate, almost religious endorsement by the militant "anti-imperialist" leaders of the world's poor countries. Many colonies, now independent, turned to the socialist paradigm with a hunger and passion that defied reality.[4]

These favorable predilections long concealed the weaknesses of such command economies. In fact, although the Russian state was capable of mobilizing resources for specific projects, technique was generally backward and overall performance shoddy. The impressive production data were intrinsically and deliberately exaggerated. They should have been heavily discounted for propaganda; also for deterioration and unsold (unsalable) commodities. (Except for caviar, vodka, and folkloric mementoes, nothing Russia made could compete on the world market.) Apartment buildings hung nets around the perimeter to protect pedestrians from falling tiles or stones. Thrifty consumers paid a small fortune for tiny, primitive motor vehicles and then waited years for delivery. Even after they got a car, they found replacement parts unobtainable, and motorists routinely took their windshield wipers with them when they parked their automobiles. Electrical appliances were at the mercy of fluctuating house current. National income data excluded services, for reasons of economic doctrine—only real product counted. But in fact, the less said about services the better: inconveniences balanced advantages. No friend like a good plumber. Or someone in the *nomenklatura,* the privileged elite, with their special stores and clubs, their access to foreign imports, their quasi-exemption from dregs and dross.

Some see this endemic mess as a dirty secret of the system: rulers nourished privation by way of rewarding favorites, building desire in the ambitious, and dulling the rest in the tedium of endless queues. The capitalist economies stimulated labor by the prospect of reward: "ya pays yer money an ya takes yer choice." Communism offered "singing tomorrows." But waiting had to be paid for, and tomorrow never came. When did the people in the queues work? The joke had it, they made believe they worked, and the state made believe it paid them.

The worst aspect of the system, however, was its indifference to, nay, its contempt for, good housekeeping and human decency. Prosperity forgone was bad enough. In a world that had once created and still preserved some beautiful things, the new system mass-produced ugliness: buildings and windows out of true; stained and pocked exteriors, raw cement block; equipment out of order, rusting machinery, abandoned metal corpses—in short, raging squalor.

Necessarily, what the system did to things, it did to people. How to survive in a wasteland dotted with junkheaps? In a world of systematic contempt for humanity? "White coal," they called the people shipped in jammed, fetid freight cars to useless labor and oblivion in frigid wastes. (The USSR anticipated here the death trains and marches of Nazi Germany.) Some, spared or overlooked, heroically maintained oases of warmth and culture in tiny flats and rooms. Many more drowned disappointment and despair in vodka.

Still, nature's gifts remained. The greatest asset of the revolutionary regime was the unspoiled natural treasures it inherited from a late-developing economy. It ran these down with the recklessness that comes with self-proclaimed virtue.

One *place* and one *event* stand for the whole. The place is the Aral Sea, once the fourth largest body of fresh water on the face of the earth, today a dying hole—half the original surface, a third of its volume, reeking with chemicals, fish gone, air hot and poisoned. Children in the region die young, one in ten in the first year. Decades of insolent plans, haste and waste, tons of pesticide, herbicide, and fertilizer, false economies such as unlined irrigation trenches enabled the Soviet Union to grow lots of cotton ("white gold"), while reversing gains in life expectancy and leading the way backward.[5]

Aral, moreover, was not unique, though it was a worst case. In general, Soviet projects for diversion and reversal of water and for construction of industrial plants in previously clean settings took no account of environment. Priority went to virtual jobs and economic growth, and the bigger and more costly the task, the more ennobling. Siberia especially was seen as a *tabula rasa,* empty tundra, space and more space, to do with as one pleased: rivers to be turned backwards, the snows of the north to water the deserts of the south. Creation corrected: communism saw itself as antireligious and scientific, but it aimed at making gods of men. The biggest of these megalomaniacal schemes, which would have altered global climate, had to be abandoned. Prometheus fortunately re-bound.

Aral was the *place.* The *event* was the meltdown of the atomic power reactors at Chernobyl in the Ukraine in 1986. The fire burned out of control for five days and spread more than 50 tons of radioactive poison across White Russia (Belarus), the Baltic states, and parts of Scandinavia—far more than the bombs at Hiroshima and Nagasaki combined. The prevailing winds blew north-northwestward, but no one will convince those Turks who later came down with blood diseases or the thousands of pregnant women from Finland to the Adriatic who had precautionary abortions that they were not victims too. Among the unquestioned casualties were the brave men sent in to fight the fire and clean up afterwards. They were promised special compensation and did not always get it. Relief funds disappeared down the local party maw. The workers' exposure was systematically understated, so that they did their job at the price of a lingering death. (Could they have said no?) Withal, the task was apparently botched: the core was not completely smothered; "the situation" not stabilized.[*]

The area around the plant has become a place of fear. Is the fear justified? The definitive answer may not come for decades: low levels of radiation work slowly. Some scientists speak of fifty years. By then all the victims will be dead. The residents of the area have chosen caution and terror. Most have left and not returned; but some never left and some have come back to take advantage of empty land. One such diehard, a woman of sixty-five, reassures herself that she is still feeling fine. She has rules of thumb: plant apple seeds deep in the ground; eat no more than ten kilos of mushrooms; "if you feel too much radiation, you have to drink some vodka." Her neighbor believes what she sees: "Look at this place. Where do you see any radiation? If anything, this place is better now that there are less people." And some try to laugh about their plight. They tell the joke about the farmer who is selling apples under a big sign, APPLES FROM CHERNOBYL. "You must be mad," says a passerby. "No one wants to buy apples from Chernobyl." "Sure they do," says the vendor. "Some people buy them for their mother-in-law, others for their wife."[6] (And maybe others for their husband.)

As a result, although other accidents and natural catastrophes may have cost more lives—the chemical leak at Bhopal, India, in 1984, perhaps—none has been more damaging to reputation and prestige.[†] Repugnance and repudiation were in direct proportion to the technological arrogance and gigantism that inspired and sanctified Soviet programs and projects.[7] The socialist command economy was tarred with incompetence, credulity, stupidity, and indifference to the public weal—among other sins—the more so because of clumsy attempts at concealment and mitigation. "It is now clear that the political repercussions from Chornobyl accelerated the collapse of the Soviet empire."[8]

A dozen nuclear plants on the Chernobyl model are still in operation.

Pretense and promises are vulnerable to truth and experience. When the dream vanished, when

---

[*] This was not what the Soviet authorities told the public; or, for that matter, what the International Atomic Energy Agency was ready to admit. Cf. Alexander R. Rich, "10 Years Later, Chernobyl's True Story Is Hard to Nail Down," *Boston Globe,* 26 April 1996, p. 21.

[†] The human cost of Chernobyl may never be known. Officials, including medical personnel, were under great pressure to minimize casualties. (Contrast Bhopal, where the injured had a financial incentive to make claims.) Feshback and Friendly, *Ecocide in the USSR,* p. 152, think doctors cleared out because they feared public anger. They may have feared radiation more.

people came to know the difference between the systems, communism lost its legitimacy. The walls came down and the Soviet Union collapsed, not by revolution, but of abandonment.

> . . . the ecological inheritance [of Africa] could never have been less than difficult. Africa was "tamed" by its historical peoples, over many centuries, against great handicaps not generally present in other continents, whether in terms of thin soils, difficult rainfall incidence, a multitude of pests and fevers, and much else that made survival difficult.[9]

All the ills that have hurt Latin America and the Middle East are exponentially compounded in sub-Saharan Africa: bad government, unexpected sovereignty, backward technology, inadequate education, bad climate, incompetent if not dishonest advice, poverty, hunger, disease, overpopulation—a plague of plagues. Of all the so-called developing regions, Africa has done worst: gross domestic product per head increasing, maybe, by less that 1 percent a year; statistical tables sprinkled with minus signs; many countries with lower income today than before independence. The failure is the more poignant when one makes the comparison with other parts: in 1965, Nigeria (oil exporter) had higher GDP per capita than Indonesia (another oil exporter); twenty-five years later, Indonesia had three times the Nigerian level.[10]

The pain of reality hurts more for the initial exhilaration. With independence, the burden of exploitation would be lifted. Time now for rewards. Some early growth figures seemed to confirm this: "Some areas—like the Rhodesias, the Belgian Congo, Morocco, Gabon, Kenya—were given as growing at 6 to 11 per cent per year, rates among the highest in the world."[11] Few people deflated these estimates to take account of upward bias in countries moving toward urbanization and a growing share of monetized, hence countable, transactions. And no one paused to ask why the colonial powers were so quick to leave. People wanted Africa to do well. Here is a Western observer, writing in 1962:

> Africans in general are the most present-minded people on earth. . . . Without significant exception, all African leaders

> . . . share the passionate desire to acquire all the good things which western civilization has produced in the two millennia of its history. They want especially to get the technological blessings of American civilization, and to do so as quickly as possible. The lack of historical consciousness of their people gives the African leaders a great advantage in moving rapidly toward this goal of modernization.[12]

And yet . . . Basil Davidson, Africanist of unquestioned sympathy and bona fides, writes sadly of the moment of disillusion—that point when the Africans of one or another place realized that freedom was not an automatic gateway to happiness and prosperity.[13]

Specialists in these matters distinguish between food security and food self-sufficiency; Africa is wanting on both scores. A large and increasing number of people—and that means women and children especially—are hungry and malnourished, whether for want of purchasing power or for bad distribution. Recalling the anarchy of the late Roman empire, city and country are at war with each other. The new bureaucrats try to squeeze the land and pay less than market value. The farmers hold back or give up. The rootless urbanites have learned tastes that cannot be satisfied locally. So, even in the best of circumstances, the land produces too little food or the wrong kind of food, and must bring it in from outside, at a growing cost to earnings and balance of payments. No other part of the globe is so much prisoner to survival.[14]

Unlike other poor regions, moreover, Africa's shortfalls in food supply afflict, not the food buyers in the cities, but the small farmers who scratch the soil and raise the livestock.* Here nature—material impediments and climatic variations—plays a

---

* Typically the farmers will get enough to eat (will feed themselves first) if the government does not expropriate food supplies for distribution in cities or for sale abroad. So in Europe during World War II. But in the Soviet Union, seizure of farm crops in the 1930s in the Ukraine led to a ghastly famine that killed millions. But then, this was the intent. These were nationalists and kulaks, marked as enemies of the Revolution. For a brief, vivid description of this atrocious crime, see Moynahan, *The Russian Century,* pp. 114–22. To know this is to understand the eventual collapse of a rotten regime.

nasty role, not only swinging widely from fat years to lean, but cumulating trends over longer periods. In the quarter century from 1960 to 1984, food output did not keep up with population, and only a rapid increase in imports kept nourishment up to inadequate (as against catastrophic) levels. Market forces encouraged the trend: food grains from the United States, for example, could be had in Lagos in 1983 at a quarter of the locally grown price.[15] Import dependency (6 percent of caloric intake in 1969–71, 13 percent in 1979–81) switched tastes from old, boring staples to new cereals, while new urban eating habits led to an increased demand for meat by those who could not afford it. In this way, more and more of Africa's food crops went to animal feed. All along, the highest natural rates of population growth in the world (3+ percent per year) were pushing farmers on to marginal soils that quickly wore out. Or driving them from country to slums in the city.[16] In countries where political agencies are fragile and ineffective, the scars of mismanagement do not easily heal, and the good and bad do not balance.

One should not blame these outcomes on smallholder ignorance or incapacity, for in Africa, as much as anywhere, farming methods and reproductive behavior mix old values and rituals with a rational response to material circumstances. African farmers are not fools, and children start paying their way early in a land where firewood and water are scarce and much time is spent foraging and carrying. The result is a reasonable preference for large families. Large families are also proof of virility and a source of pride.[17] In general, the women do as they are told, especially in those cultures where polygamy prevails; and when the men come home, for they often work far off, they have their way, often at great risk to health. AIDS? Forget condoms; the men don't like them. And the women? "They have so many other problems to think of, why should they think about something that kills you in 10 years?"[18]

In the latter days of empire, some governments and foreign advisers tried to remedy these ills, although their calculations were often distorted by extraneous motives and personal interest. Take agriculture. Even before independence, some colonial rulers tried to correct for past mistakes and indifference and to introduce "modern" methods.

The "mother" of all such projects was the British groundnut (in American English, peanut) scheme, launched and sunk in Tanganyika over the period 1946–54 and "intended to demonstrate what the state was capable of . . . when it harnessed modern Western technology and expertise."[19] The idea came originally from the managing director of the United Africa Company, a subsidiary of Unilever, a company reputed to know its oil. The plan was vetted and approved at British cabinet level. The immediate objective: to alleviate British postwar oil and fat shortages without spending dollars (buy colonial). In the words of Food Minister John Strachey, "On your success depends, more than on any other single factor, whether the harassed housewives of Britain get more margarine, cooking fat and soap, in the reasonably near future."[20]

The ultimate aim was to "raise the standard of living of the African peasant" by demonstrating the possibilities of modern technology. To be sure, these peanuts were not destined for consumption by Africans, hungry as they might be; but the peasants would see (would be given an "ocular demonstration," in bureaucratese) and copy the superiority of large-scale, mechanized agriculture. No hands; everything would be done by machine: bulldozers, tractors, rooters, sowers, combines.

At the same time, as though to prove the virtues of British-style socialism (the project was intended, among other things, to demonstrate a superior alternative to Soviet ideology), the British Labour government sent officials to teach the African employees how to strike for higher pay. This altruism succeeded beyond expectations. The natives took up spears, idled the tractors, blocked the roads, stopped the railway. Police had to be brought in; the union leaders, put in prison. The strike failed, but the natives had learned a thing or two.[21]

The planners went in without a plan. They chose a central site because it was empty. It was empty because it had no water. Members of the mission acknowledged "a total lack of any experience of mechanised agriculture." No one had ever tried this kind of thing. Information on rainfall patterns and their effect on yields was wanting; ditto regarding the soil; and estimates on cost of clearing bush drew on experience with airstrips during the war. Supplies took the form of leftover army stores from the Philippines, some useful, some worthless, all the worse for neglect. The mission had no engineering expert. As one member, an accountant, put it: "It was all guesswork, and our guess was as good as anybody else's."

Both British housewives and African peasants had a long wait in prospect. African farmers raised peanuts in some areas, but they (usually the women) did so at enormous pain and effort, scratching and clawing every step of the way. Even so, they did better than these machines, which for all their steel, rubber, and internal combustion engines, sickened in the African climate. Breakdowns were common, repair shops lacking, and what would they have done anyway without replacement parts? Clearance of the gnarled brush and roots was a nightmare. It cost ten times original estimates, and the ground, once cleared, dried to brick hardness. Very soon the projectors had to scale back expectations and substitute sunflowers for some of the peanut bushes. The changes did not help. Nature refused to cooperate, and yields were far below expectations.

The effects on the local economy and society were deplorable. The British employees had enough money to buy the natives out of food, and the natives in turn got jobs with the project and gave up traditional cultivation. So food production went down and large amounts had to be imported to feed those who were supposed to be producing a surplus for export. Liquor came in too; and prostitutes, charging "stupendous fees of five shillings and more";[22] and thieves—all the afflictions and corruptions of unexpected wealth. Meanwhile the British tried to teach the natives the virtues of working-class solidarity and equality. The natives saw this as a subversion of order and morality.

By 1950, failure was inescapable; time now for remorse and liquidation. The groundnut does not lend itself to mass cultivation. Economic yields require intensive farming. The plan to grow in huge 30,000 acre units proved utterly impractical. It took four years to dispose of the equipment and installations. The British turned as much as possible over to the government of newly independent Tanganyika, which saw these ill-favored leftovers as nuisance more than assets. It wasn't hard for observers to note that the money could have been put to better use.

Needless to say, the fiasco hurt British prestige and discouraged other "imaginative schemes of economic development." Would these have done better? The record is not encouraging, except to ever renewable planners and technicians, who seem to use these projects as children might a dollhouse, and who learn with every failure. I would not depreciate the motives and deeds of these experts. They remain our hope for large-scale, long-range amelioration. Yet nothing is more inebriating and seductive than making a world and feeling virtuous for it. In the end, the British shrugged the failure off. The nation was tired and had better things to worry about than peanuts in Africa.

The British groundnut scheme was not the exception. Colonial governments were liable to these temptations, which held out the irresistible promise of doing well while doing good. The French tried for cotton on the Niger River, upstream from Timbuktu (today Mali), from the 1910s to the 1940s. Again Africa was to supply European needs—this time the potential demand by French spinners, pressed to find precious dollars for American cotton. The colonial administrators involved were concerned to protect their African constituents, even against themselves, while ensuring a supply of raw cotton that could compete on the world market. The French also wanted to preserve freedom of enterprise where possible. So, with consummate Gallic logic, they came up with a compromise formula: the peasants had a "strict obligation" to grow cotton from dawn to dusk, but complete freedom to sell it.[23] Then the French uprooted and replanted peasants and made them plant cotton bushes, and if the peasants made trouble or brought in unsatisfactory cotton, they were marched off to jail. It was, some like to think, a loose, easygoing jail—enough though to make the point.

One would like to think that liberation changed all that, but in fact the new governments had their own schemes of economic development and social engineering, inspired by a new world of peripatetically eager experts and technicians—eager to spend money, to do good, to wield power. These doers, be it said, had no trouble imagining schemes, the bigger the better. And when the schemes failed?

> That is the fault of the West. The West told us to build power stations, bridges, factories, steel mills, phosphate mines. We built them because you said so, and the way you told us. But now they don't work, you tell us we must pay for them with our money. That is not fair. You told us to build them, you should pay for them. We didn't want them.[24]

Much of the gap between expectation and realization came from un-preparedness. The postcolonial Africans had no experience of self-government, and their rulers enjoyed a legitimacy bounded by kinship networks and clientelist loyalties. Abruptly, these new nations were pressed into the corset of representative government, a form alien to their own traditions and unprepared by colonial paternalism. In some instances, this transition had been preceded by a war of liberation, which mobilized passion and identity. But the legacy was rule by a strongman, autocratic embodiment of the popular will, hence slayer of democracy. Stability depended on one man's vigor, and when he weakened or died (or was helped to die), the anarchy of the short-lived military coup followed.

The governments produced by this strong-man rule have proved uniformly inept, with a partial exception for pillage. In Africa, the richest people are heads of state and their ministers.[25] Bureaucracy has been inflated to provide jobs for henchmen; the economy, squeezed for its surplus. Much (most?) foreign aid ends in numbered accounts abroad.[26] These kleptocrats have much to gain by living in Switzerland, near their banks. But maybe money alone is not enough.

Basil Davidson gives us two case studies in incoherence. The first, Zaire (ex-Belgian Congo), was a skeleton of a state. The tyrant Mobutu Sese Seko ruled in the capital Kinshasa and a few other cities, and in those localities where foreign companies were extracting mineral wealth. All of these paid him tribute, and his accounts in Switzerland were said to total billions of dollars. Between these few points of effective control, the only transport was by air, for the roads below are neither passable nor safe. Under Belgian rule in 1960, the Congo had 88,000 miles of usable road; by 1985 this was down to 12,000 miles, only 1,400 of them paved. But then dirt roads are better than holed and cracked hard surfaces. Paving is only as good as its maintenance.

Almost the whole of the country and the society was in but not of the pseudo-nation. In the east, foreign invaders were driving foreign refugees to their death while supporting rebellion against Kinshasa. In the capital, the parliamentary opposition denounced rebel plans and warned against a new despotism: "We are not getting rid of one strongman to replace him with another." The rebel reply: "If the opposition leader "wants to pilot a ship that is going down," he'd better learn to swim.[27] Meanwhile Western agents worked to persuade Mobutu into retirement (or keep him in office) while jockeying for influence with what might follow. The primary Western concern was to keep getting those minerals out. The French also wanted to keep Zaire in the francophone orbit, as though the dignity of France depended on it. (The Belgians had thrown up their hands long ago.) The Americans . . . well, it wasn't clear what might be the American interest, except maybe to "stick it" to the French.

In the midst of this anarchy, international relief agencies tried to keep refugees alive but had to break off every time marauders drew near. Some emergency supplies got in, but for whom? Some mineral resources were still getting out, but for whom? The capture by rebels in April 1997 of the country's diamond capital portended a change in regime. Without revenues, Mobutu could not pay his troops, now given to pillage (a soldier's got to live); nor could he hold the hearts of the great powers, even if he spoke French. Footnote: Zaire had vanished by then from the tables of the World Bank. This was prescient: the victorious rebels, after forcing Mobutu out in June, changed the name of the country back to (the Republic of) Congo.

The second case is Benin, formerly Dahomey. This country's biggest products from 1960 to 1989 were Marxist-Leninist propaganda and political coups. The official statistics showed product and trade as almost nonexistent. Yet Benin was planting and harvesting palm oil and peanuts. It simply did not yield up its product to the authorities or to official markets. Just about everything moved in parallel channels. These yielded the farmer more than he would ever get from an official marketing board, and the farmer bought off the swollen bureaucracy. On the record, then, Benin is an empty husk with big negative trade balance and negative growth; but it's really a smuggling machine.

The lesson one draws from these and similar instances is that Africa is not so badly off as it appears, just worse. Look at a photo or TV screen, at these prostrate fly-specked children, all bones, saggy skin, bulging eyes and belly, and you are overwhelmed by the misery. You *know* that the children you are looking at are dead by the time you see them. Look at another scene, especially in the picturesque pages of the *National Geographic,* and you marvel at the smiles and vigor of the dancers or traders in an exotic landscape. The continent bears witness to hope and hopelessness, courage and despair. Circumstances are appalling, but somehow people find ways to cope, survive, die, yet multiply.

Meanwhile the international placemen and experts sing their little songs of innocence and inexperience. "Adjustment" is the current refrain: a touch of freedom here, of market and exchange rate realism there, and things will be better, may even get well. One of the games economists play may be called "statistical misinference." Compare more or less comparable numbers from different countries and draw conclusions, past and future. So with Africa: as we saw earlier, comparing Nigeria

and Indonesia, Africa has done less well than East Asian countries that started at a lower level. (One can make a similar invidious comparison between Turkey and South Korea.) But why not turn that around? If Indonesia could do so well, why not Nigeria? The same World Bank report that deplores African performance in 1965–90 cites Asian figures for 1965 ("conditions similar to those in Africa in 1990") to envisage African growth over the next quarter century. Equal levels at different times constitute for these experts similar conditions. Oh yes, the proportion of children in school was higher in Asia, but that is easily remedied. Otherwise, no problem. Of cultural and institutional differences, nothing.

News item: The United Nations, in collaboration with the World Bank and the International Monetary Fund, has announced a plan to raise $25 billion over the next decade, over and beyond what these international agencies can find (much to come from private sources), and invest it in African improvement.[28] At present twenty-two of the twenty-five poorest countries in the world are in Africa, and 54 percent of Africans live below the UN poverty line; what's more, Africa is the only region where poverty is expected to increase over the next ten years. How much can $25 billion do? Well, as of 1994, the debts of African nations totaled $313 billion (almost 2.5 times total export income), so the $25 billion could pay the interest for one year. In the meantime, of $231 billion in direct foreign investment in the Third World in 1995, some $2 billion, less than 1 percent, went to Africa. Businessmen know to go elsewhere.

No matter: accentuate the positive. The worse the situation, the greater the potential for improvement. Better policies (structural adjustment) can/will put Africa back on the growth track. But there would still be lots to do. The continent's problems go much deeper than bad policies, and bad policies are not an accident. Good government is not to be had for the asking. It took Europe centuries to get it, so why should Africa do so in mere decades, especially after the distortions of colonialism? And how about no government? At the moment, for example, Somalia is a political vacuum: even if one wants to send help, what address to send it to? "We don't even know how to send them a message."[29]

In a fragile world, good policies are hostages to fortune. In Africa, as in much of the world only more so, the clocks go backward as well as forward.

NOTES

1. Cf. Ishac Diwan, "Hard Time for More Labor Economics," *Forum* (Newsletter of the Economic Research Forum for the Arab Countries, Iran & Turkey), 2, 2 (July–August 1995), 1–3; and N. Fergany, "Unemployment in Arab Countries: The Menace Swept Under the Rug," *ibid.,* pp. 4–5.

2. Bulmer-Thomas, *Economic History of Latin America,* p. 278.

3. The U.N. International Drug Control Programme, in its first World Drug Report, estimates the trade in illicit drugs at $400 billion—about 8 percent of total world trade. Between 28 and 53 percent of Bolivia's export revenues are estimated to come from narcotics; some 6 percent of Colombia's GDP—*Financial Times,* 26 June 1997, p. 4. Guesses all.

4. For a fascinating insight into the fairy-tale economics of the Socialist countries, in this case, the German Democratic Republic, see Merkel and Mühlberg, eds., *Wunderwirtschaft.*

5. Feshbach and Friendly, *Ecocide in the USSR,* ch. 4; Kaplan, *Ends of the Earth,* p. 277; David Filipov, "A Sea Dies, Mile by Mile," *Boston Globe,* 23 March 1997, p. A-1.

6. Filipov, "In Chernobyl Soil, Fatalism Thrives," *Boston Globe,* 21 April 1996, p. 17.

7. Cf. Josephson, " 'Projects of the Century' " p. 546 and *passim.*

8. Shcherbak, "Ten Years of the Chornobyl Era," p. 44. See also Marples, *Social Impact;* Medvedev, *Truth About Chernobyl;* Michael Specter, "10 Years Later, Through Fear, Chernobyl Still Kills in Belarus," *N.Y. Times,* 31 March 1996, p. A-1.

9. Davidson, *Black Man's Burden,* p. 216.

10. World Bank, *Adjustment in Africa,* p. 17. See also the Bank's *World Development Report 1997: The State in a Changing World.* One difficulty with these numbers is that the margin of error is huge. On the one hand, African authorities make up figures as needed. On the other, all manner of parallel economic activities escape measurement. Do these biases even out?

11. Kamarck, *Economics of African Development,* p. 17.

12. H. J. Spiro, *Politics in Africa,* cited in Kamarck, *Economics,* p. 48.

13. Davidson, *The Black Man's Burden,* p. 197.

14. On all this, see Platteau, "Food Crisis in Africa."

15. *Ibid.,* p. 451.

16. Some welcome this premature urbanization as the seedbed of modernity, democracy, and business enterprise. Cf. A. Frachon, "L'Afrique n'est plus rurale," *Le monde,* 10–11 November 1996.

17. Cf. Dasgupta, "Population, Poverty, and the Local Environment."

18. J. C. McKinley, Jr., "Anguish of Rwanda Echoed in a Baby's Cry," *N.Y. Times,* 21 February 1996, p. A-8. See also Howard W. French, "Migrant Workers Take AIDS Risk Home to Niger," *N.Y. Times,* 8 February 1996, p. A-3.

19. Havinden and Meredith, eds., *Colonialism and Development,* p. 276.

20. *Ibid.,* p. 278.

21. I take this from Evelyn Waugh's account, *Tourist in Africa,* p. 98.

22. *Ibid.,* p. 99.

23. Roberts, "The Coercion of Free Markets," p. 224; also Davidson, *Black Man's Burden,* p. 217.

24. An educated and traveled police captain in Mali, quoted in Biddlecombe, *French Lessons,* p. 247.

25. George B. N. Ayittey, "The U.N.'s Shameful Record in Africa," *Wall St. J.,* 26 July 1996, p. A-12.

26. According to Ayittey, the United Nations estimated that some $200 billion was shipped from Africa to foreign banks in 1991 alone—equal to 90 percent of sub-Saharan Africa's GDP. *Ibid.*

27. H. W. French, "Personal Rivals Fight to Finish in War in Zaire," *N.Y. Times,* 6 April 1997.

28. Barbara Crossette, "U.N., World Bank and IMF Join $25 Billion Drive for Africa," *N.Y. Times,* 17 March 1996, p. A-6. The New York–based *African Observer* denounced the scheme as a charade, cooked up by Boutros Boutros-Ghali by way of promoting his campaign for renewal as secretary-general of the UN (if so, it didn't help)—Ayittey, "U.N.'s Shameful Record."

29. *N.Y. Times,* 17 March 1996, p. A-6.

Urban Marginality in the Coming Millennium

LOÏC WACQUANT

INTRODUCTION

All social phenomena are, to some degree, the work of collective will, and collective will implies choice between different possible options. . . . The realm of the social is the realm of modality (Mauss, 1929, p. 470).

This paper analyses the modalities whereby new forms of urban inequality and marginality have arisen and are spreading throughout the advanced societies of the capitalist West. The argument unfolds in two steps.

First, I sketch a compact characterisation of what I take to be a new regime of urban marginality. This regime has been ascendant for the past three decades or so, since the close of the Fordist era defined by standardised industrial production, mass consumption and a Keynesian social contract binding them together under the tutelage of the social welfare state. Yet its full impact lies ahead of us because its advent is tied to the most advanced sectors of our economies—this is why I refer to it here as 'advanced marginality'. Identifying the distinctive properties of this consolidating regime of urban marginality helps us to pinpoint what exactly is new about the 'new poverty' of which the city is the site and fount.

Secondly, I turn to the question that implicitly informs or explicitly guides European debates on the resurgence of destitution, division and tension in the metropolis: namely, are we witnessing an epochal convergence of urban poverty regimes across the Atlantic? It is argued that we are not: urban relegation follows different social and spatial dynamics on the two continents. Yet European societies must beware of pursuing public policies that isolate distinct urban zones and populations, thereby encouraging them to pursue divergent and even oppositional life strategies that can set off self-reinforcing cycles of social involution not unlike those that underlie ghettoisation in the US.

Despite its title, then, this paper is not a contribution to the fadish celebration of '2000'. Rather, it is an attempt to diagnose the social forces and forms with which our current urban predicament is pregnant and that promise to shape the metropolis of tomorrow—unless we exercise our 'collective will' and act to check mechanisms and steer trends in a different direction.

SYMPTOMS OF ADVANCED MARGINALITY

The close of the 20th century is witnessing a momentous transformation of the roots, make-up and consequences of urban poverty in Western society. Along with the accelerating economic modernisation caused by the global restructuring of capitalism, the crystallisation of a new international division of labour (fostered by the frantic velocity of financial flows and workers across porous national boundaries) and the growth of novel knowledge-intensive industries based on

Source: Loïc Wacquant, "Urban Marginality in the Coming Millennium," *Urban Studies,* Vol. 36, No. 10, 1999: 1639–1647. Used with permission of Loic Wacquant.

revolutionary information technologies and spawning a dual occupational structure, has come the modernisation of misery—the rise of a new regime of urban inequality and marginality. (For a fuller argument, see Wacquant, 1996a.)

Where poverty in the Western metropolis used to be largely residual or cyclical, embedded in working-class communities, geographically diffuse and considered remediable by means of further market expansion, it now appears to be increasingly long-term if not permanent, disconnected from macroeconomic trends and fixated upon disreputable neighbourhoods of relegation in which social isolation and alienation feed upon each other as the chasm between those consigned there and the rest of society deepens.

The consolidation of this new regime of urban marginality is treading diverse routes and taking different forms in the various countries of the First World. In the US and in the UK, it has been greatly facilitated by the policy of wholesale state retrenchment pursued by conservative and liberal parties alike over the past two decades and by the rigid or rising spatial and social separation of white and coloured in the major urban centres. In other nations with strong corporatist or social-democratic welfare states and less segregated cities, such as the countries of northern Europe and Scandinavia, it has been partly attenuated but not wholly deflected. And it has become embroiled with the vexed question of the integration of Third World migrants and refugees, as expressed in the anguish over the crystallisation of immigrant 'ghettos' gripping the continent from Marseille to München and Brussels to Brindisi (see, for example, Hadjimichalis and Sadler, 1995; Mingione, 1996).

Whatever the label used to designate it—'underclass' in the US and in the UK; 'new poverty' in the Netherlands Germany and Northern Italy; 'exclusion' in France, Belgium and Nordic countries—the telltale signs of the new marginality are immediately familiar to even the casual observer of the Western metropolis: homeless men and families vainly scrambling about for shelter, beggars on public transport spinning heart-rending tales of

personal disaster and dereliction, soup kitchens teeming with not only drifters but also the unemployed and the underemployed; the surge in predatory crime and the booming of informal (and more often than not illegal) street economies spearheaded by the trade in drugs; the despondency and rage of youths shut out from gainful employment and the bitterness of older workers made obsolete by deindustrialisation and technological upgrading; the sense of retrogression, despair and insecurity that pervades poor neighbourhoods locked into a seemingly unstoppable downward spiral of deterioration; and mounting racial violence, xenophobia and hostility towards and amongst the poor. Everywhere, state élites and public policy experts have become acutely concerned with preventing or containing the 'disorders' brewing within and around expanding enclaves of urban decline and abandonment. Hence the sprouting of research on urban decline and destitution supported by various national and transnational bodies, including the European Commission (with its Targeted Socio-economic Programme on exclusion and integration), the OECD, and even NATO on the European side, and major philanthropic foundations in the US.

FOUR STRUCTURAL LOGICS FUEL THE NEW MARGINALITY

But the distinctive structural properties of 'modernised misery' are much less evident than its concrete manifestations. Schematically, the emerging regime of marginality may be characterised as the product of four logics that jointly reshape the features of urban poverty in rich societies. These features stand in stark contrast with the commanding traits of poverty in the era of Fordist expansion from the close of World War II to the mid-1970s.

THE MACROSOCIAL DYNAMIC: THE RESURGENCE OF SOCIAL INEQUALITY

The new urban marginality results not from economic backwardness, sluggishness or decline, but from rising inequality in the context of overall economic advancement and prosperity. Arguably the most puzzling attribute of the new marginality is that it is spreading in an era of capricious but sturdy growth that has brought about spectacular material betterment for the more privileged members of First World societies. Notwithstanding ritual talk of 'crisis' among politicians, all leading capitalist countries have seen their GNP expand and collective wealth increase rapidly over the past three decades. Opulence and indigence, luxury and penury, copiousness and deprivation have flourished right alongside each other. Thus the city of Hamburg, by some measurements the richest city in Europe, sports both the highest proportion of millionnaires and the highest incidence of public assistance receipt in Germany, while New York City is home to the largest upper class on the planet but also to the single greatest army of the homeless and destitute in the Western hemisphere (Mollenkopf and Castells, 1991).

The two phenomena, though apparently contradictory, are in point of fact linked. For the novel forms of productivity and profit-seeking in the 'high-tech', degraded manufacturing and business and financial service sectors that drive *fin-de-siècle* capitalism are splitting the workforce and polarising access to, and rewards from, durable employment. Post-industrial modernisation translates, on the one hand, into the multiplication of highly skilled positions for university-trained professional and technical staff and, on the other, into the deskilling and outright elimination of millions of jobs for uneducated workers (Sassen, 1991; Carnoy *et al.*, 1993). What is more, today, jobless production and growth in many economic sectors are not a utopian possibility but a bittersweet reality. Witness the virtual emptying of the harbour of Rotterdam, perhaps the most modern in the world and a major contributor to the rise of unemployment in this Dutch city to above the 20 per cent mark.

The more the revamped capitalist economy advances, the wider and deeper the reach of the new marginality, and the more plentiful the ranks of those thrown into the throes of misery with neither respite nor recourse, even as official unemployment drops and income rises in the country. In September 1994, the US Bureau of the Census reported that the US poverty rate had risen to a 10-year high of 15.1 per cent (for a staggering total of 40 million poor persons) despite 2 years of robust economic expansion. Meanwhile, the European Union officially tallies a record 52 million poor, 17 million unemployed and 3 million homeless—and counting—in the face of renewed economic growth and improved global competitiveness.

Put differently, advanced marginality appears to have been 'decoupled' from cyclical fluctuations in the national economy. The consequence is that upswings in aggregate income and employment have little beneficial effect upon life-chances in the neighbourhoods of relegation in Europe and the US, while downswings cause further deterioration and distress within them. Unless this disconnection is somehow remedied, further economic growth promises to produce more urban dislocation and depression among those thrust and trapped at the bottom of the emerging urban order.

The Economic Dynamic: The Mutation of Wage Labour

The new urban marginality is the by-product of a double transformation of the sphere of work. The one is quantitative and entails the elimination of millions of low-skilled jobs under the combined press of automation and foreign labour competition and dispersion of basic conditions of employment, remuneration and social insurance for virtually all but the most protected workers.

From the time when Friedrich Engels wrote his classic exposé on the condition of the working class in Manchester's factories to the crisis of the great industrial heartlands of Euro-American capitalism a century and a half later, it was rightly assumed that expanding wage labour supplied a viable and efficacious solution to the problem of urban poverty. Under the new economic regime, that assumption is at best dubious and at worst plain wrong.

First, a significant fraction of the working class has been rendered redundant and composes an 'absolute surplus population' that will probably never find regular work again. At any rate, given the loosening of the functional linkage between macroeconomic activity and social conditions in the poor enclaves of the First World metropolis, and considering the productivity increases permitted by automation and computerisation, even miraculous rates of growth could not absorb back into the workforce those who have been deproletarianised—that is, durably and forcibly expelled from the wage labour market to be replaced by a combination of machines, cheap immigrant labour and foreign workers (Rifkin, 1995).

Secondly, and more importantly, the character of the wage–labour relation itself has changed over the past two decades in a manner such that it no longer grants fool-proof protection against the menace of poverty even to those who enter it. With the expansion of part-time, 'flextime' and temporary jobs that carry fewer benefits, the erosion of union protection, the diffusion of two-tier pay scales, the resurgence of sweat-shops, piece rates and famine wages, and the growing privatisation of social goods such as health coverage, the wage labour contract has become a source of fragmentation and precariousness rather than of social homogeneity and security for those consigned to the peripheral segments of the employment sphere (see, for example, European Economic Community, 1989; Mabit, 1995; MacDonald and Sirianni, 1996). In short, where economic growth and the correlative expansion of the wage sector used to provide the universal cure against poverty, today they are part of the malady.

The Political Dynamic: The Reconstruction of Welfare States

The fragmentation and desocialisation of labour are not the only factors fuelling the rise of the new urban poverty. For, alongside market forces, welfare states are major producers and shapers of urban inequality and marginality. States not only deploy programmes and policies designed to 'mop up' the most glaring consequences of poverty and to cushion (or not) its social and spatial impact. They also help to determine who gets relegated, how, where and for how long.

States are major engines of stratification in their own right and nowhere more so than at the bottom of the socio-spatial order (Esping-Andersen, 1993): they provide or preclude access to adequate schooling and job training; they set conditions for labour market entry and exit via administrative rules for hiring, firing and retirement; they distribute (or fail to distribute) basic subsistence goods, such as housing and supplementary income; they actively support or hinder certain family and household arrangements; and they co-determine both the material intensity and the geographical exclusivity and density of misery through a welter of administrative and fiscal schemes.

The retrenchment and disarticulation of the welfare state are two major causes of the social deterioration and destitution visible in the metropolis of advanced societies. This is particularly obvious in the US, where the population covered by social insurance schemes has shrunk for two decades while programmes targeted to the poor were cut and increasingly turned into instruments of surveillance and control. The recent 'welfare reform' concocted by the Republican congress and signed into law by President Clinton in the summer of 1996 is emblematic of this logic (Wacquant, 1997a). It replaces the right to public aid with the obligation to work, if necessary at insecure jobs and for sub-standard wages, for all able-bodied persons, including young mothers with dependent children. It drastically diminishes funding for assistance and creates a life-time cap on welfare support. Lastly, it transfers administrative responsibility from the federal government to the 50 states and their counties, thus aggravating already existing inequalities in access to welfare and accelerating the incipient privatisation of social policy.

A similar logic of curtailment and devolution has presided over wholesale or piece-meal modifications of social transfer systems in the UK, Germany, Italy and France. Even the Netherlands and Scandinavian countries have implemented measures designed to reduce access to public support and to stem the growth of social budgets. Everywhere the mantra of 'globalisation' and the fiscal strictures imposed by the Maastricht Treaty have served to justify these measures and to excuse social disinvestment in formerly working-class areas highly dependent on state provision of public goods. The growing shortcomings of national welfare schemes have led regional and local authorities to institute their own stop-gap support programmes (especially in response to homelessness and long-term unemployment).

The irrelevance of the 'national state' has become a commonplace of intellectual conversation the world over. It is fashionable nowadays to bemoan the incapacity of central political institutions to check the mounting social dislocations consequent upon global capitalist restructuring. But large and persistent discrepancies in the incidence and persistence of poverty, as well as in the living standards, (im)mobility and spatial distinctiveness of the urban poor in different countries suggest that news of the passing of the national welfare state has been greatly exaggerated. As of the late 1980s, tax and transfer programmes lifted most poor households near the median national income level in the Netherlands (62 per cent) and France (52 per cent); in West Germany only a third of poor families escaped poverty thanks to government support and in the US virtually none. Extreme destitution has been eliminated among children in Scandinavian countries, while it plagues one child in six (and every other black child) in the US (these data are drawn from McFate *et al.,* 1995; a more analytical overview can be found in Kangas, 1991). States do make a difference—that is, when they care to. Therefore, it is imperative to bring them back to the epicentre of the comparative sociology of urban marginality as *generative* as well as *remedial* institutions.

The Spatial Dynamic: Concentration and Stigmatisation

In the post-war decades of industrial expansion, poverty in the metropolis was broadly distributed throughout working-class districts and tended to affect a cross-section of manual and unskilled labourers. By contrast, the new marginality displays a distinct tendency to conglomerate in and coalesce around 'hard core', 'no-go' areas that are clearly identified—by their own residents, no less than by outsiders—as urban hellholes rife with deprivation, immorality and violence where only the outcasts of society would consider living.

Nantua in Philadelphia, Moss Side in Manchester, Gutleutviertel in Hamburg, Brixton in London, Niewe Westen in Rotterdam, Les Minguettes in Lyon's suburbs and Bobigny in the Parisian periphery: these entrenched quarters of misery have 'made a name' for themselves as repositories for all the urban ills of the age, places to be shunned, feared and deprecated. It matters little that the discourses of demonisation that have mushroomed about them often have only tenuous connections to the reality of everyday life in them. A pervading territorial stigma is firmly affixed upon the residents of such neighbourhoods of socioeconomic exile that adds its burden to the disrepute of poverty and the resurging prejudice against ethnic minorities and immigrants (an excellent analysis of this process of public stigmatisation is offered by Damer, 1989, in the case of Glasgow).

Along with territorial stigmatisation comes a sharp diminution of the sense of communality that used to characterise older working-class locales. Now the neighbourhood no longer offers a shield against the insecurities and pressures of the outside world; it is no longer a familiar and reaffirming landscape suffused with collective meanings and forms of mutuality. It turns into an empty space of competition and conflict, a danger-filled battleground for the daily contest of survival and escape. This weakening of territorially based communal bonds, in turn, fuels a retreat into the sphere of privatised consumption and strategies of distancing

('I am not one of them') that further undermine local solidarities and confirm deprecatory perceptions of the neighbourhood.

We must remain alert to the possibility that this may be a transitional (or cyclical) phenomenon eventually leading to the spatial deconcentration or diffusion of urban marginality. But for those presently consigned at the bottom of the hierarchical system of places that compose the new spatial order of the city, the future is now. Relatedly, it must be stressed that such neighbourhoods of relegation are creatures of state policies in matters of housing, urban and regional planning. Fundamentally, then, their emergence, consolidation and eventual dispersion are essentially political issues.

The Spectre of Transatlantic Convergence

One question is at the back of everyone's mind when it comes to the deterioration of social conditions and life-chances in Old World metropolis: does the rise of this new marginality signal a structural *rapprochement* between Europe and the US on the model of the latter (see, for instance, Cross, 1992; Musterd, 1994; van Kempen and Marcuse, 1999; Haüßerman *et al.,* in press). Framed in such simplistic, either/or, terms, the question hardly admits of an analytically rigorous answer. For regimes of urban marginality are complex and capricious beasts; they are composed of imperfectly articulated ensembles of institutional mechanisms tying together economy, state, place and society that do not evolve in unison and, moreover, differ significantly from country to country with national conceptions and institutions of citizenship. It is therefore necessary first to rephrase this query.

If by convergence, one means the wholesale 'Americanisation' of urban patterns of exclusion in the European city leading down the path of *ghettoisation* of the kind imposed upon Afro-Americans since they urbanised at the beginning of this century (i.e. the formation of a segmented, parallel, socio-spatial reality serving the dual purpose of

exploitation and ostracisation of a bounded ethno-racial category), then the answer is clearly negative (Wacquant, 1996b). Contrary to first impressions and superficial, media-driven accounts, the changeover of the continental metropolis has not triggered a process of ghettoisation: it is not spawning culturally uniform socio-spatial ensembles based on the forcible relegation of stigmatised populations to enclaves where these populations evolve group- and place-specific organisations that substitute for and duplicate the institutional framework of the broader society, if at an inferior and incomplete level.

There is no Turkish ghetto in Berlin, no Arab ghetto in Marseilles, no Surinamese ghetto in Rotterdam and no Caribbean ghetto in Liverpool. Residential or commercial clusters fuelled by ethnic affinity do exist in all these cities. Discrimination and violence against immigrants (or putative immigrants) are also brutal facts of life in all major urban centres of Europe (Wrench and Solomos, 1993; Björgo and White, 1993). Combined with their typically lower-class distribution and higher rates of joblessness, this explains the disproportionate representation of foreign-origin populations in urban territories of exile. But discrimination and even segregation are not ghettoisation. Such immigrant concentrations as exist are not the product of the institutional encasement of the group premised on rigid spatial confinement— as evidenced by rising rates of intermarriage and spatial diffusion when education and class position improve (Tribalat, 1995). Indeed, if anything characterises the neighbourhoods of relegation that have sprouted across the continent as mechanisms of working-class reproduction have floundered, it is their extreme ethnic heterogeneity as well as their incapacity to supply the basic needs and encompass the daily round of their inhabitants—two properties that make them *anti-ghettos.*

If convergence implies that self-reinforcing cycles of ecological disrepair, social deprivation and violence, resulting in spatial emptying and institutional abandonment, are now operative on the continent, then again the answer is negative because European areas of urban exile remain, with few exceptions (such as southern Italian cities), deeply penetrated by the state. The kind of 'triage' and purposive desertion of urban areas to 'economise' on public services that has befallen the American metropolis is unimaginable in the European political context with its fine-grained bureaucratic monitoring of the national territory. At the same time, there can be no question that the capacity of European states to govern territories of relegation is being severely tested and may prove unequal to the task if recent trends toward the spatial concentration of persistent joblessness continue unabated (Engbersen, 1997).

Finally, if convergence is intended, more modestly, to spotlight the growing salience of ethnoracial divisions and tensions in the European metropolis, then the answer is a qualified and provisional yes, albeit with the following strong provisos. First, this does not necessarily imply that a process of 'racialisation' of space is underway and that the societies of the Old World are witnessing the formation of 'minorities' in the sense of ethnic communities mobilised and recognised as such in the public sphere. Secondly, ethnoracial conflict is not a novel phenomenon in the European city: it has surged forth repeatedly in the past century during periods of rapid social and economic restructuring—which means also that there is little that is distinctively 'American' about it (Moore, 1989).

Finally, and contrary to the American pattern, putatively racial strife in the cities of the Old World is fuelled not by the growing gap between immigrants and natives but by their greater propinquity in social and physical space. Ethnonational exclusivism is a nativist reaction to abrupt downward mobility by the autochthonous working class before it expresses a profound ideological switch to a racist (or, rather, racialist) register. Notwithstanding fadish blanket pronouncements about the 'globalisation of race,' the increased salience of ethnicity in European public discourse and everyday life pertains as much to a politics of class as to a politics of identity.

Coda: Coping with Advanced Marginality

In their effort to respond to emergent forms of urban relegation, nation-states face a three-pronged alternative. The first, middle-ground, option consists of patching up the existing programmes of the welfare state. Clearly, this is not doing the job, or the problems posed by advanced marginality would not be so pressing today. The second, regressive and repressive, solution is to criminalise poverty via the punitive containment of the poor in increasingly isolated and stigmatised neighbourhoods, on the one hand, and in jails and prisons, on the other. This is the route taken by the US following the ghetto riots of the sixties (Wacquant, 1997b; Rothman, 1995). One cannot dismiss its appeal among segments of the European ruling class, even in the face of the colossal social and fiscal costs entailed in the mass confinement of poor and disruptive populations. Incarceration rates have risen through much of the continent over the past two decades and imprisonment is a seductive stop-gap solution to mounting urban dislocations even in the most liberal societies (Christie, 1997). But, aside from the powerful political and cultural obstacles to the wholesale confinement of misery inherent in the make-up of social-democratic states in Europe, punitive confinement leaves untouched the root causes of the new poverty.

The third, progressive, pathway points to a fundamental reconstruction of the welfare state that would put its structure and policies in accord with emerging economic and social conditions. Radical innovations, such as the institution of a universal citizen's wage (or basic income grant) that would sever subsistence from work, are needed to expand social rights and check the deleterious effects of the mutation of wage labour (van Parijs, 1996). In the end, this third option is the only viable response to the challenge that advanced marginality poses to democratic societies as they prepare to cross the threshold of the new millennium.

REFERENCES

Björgo, T. and White, R. (Eds) (1993) *Racist Violence in Europe.* New York: St Martin's.

Carnoy, M., Castells, M., Cohen, S. S. and Cardoso, F. H. (1993) *The New Global Economy in the Information Age: Reflections on Our Changing World.* University Park, PA: Pennsylvania State University Press.

Christie, N. (1997) *An essay in penal geography.* Unpublished manuscript, Department of Criminology, Universitet Oslo.

Cross, M. (Ed.) (1992) *Ethnic Minorities and Industrial Change in Europe and North America.* Cambridge: Cambridge University Press.

Damer, S. (1989) *From Moorepark to 'Wine Alley': The Rise and Fall of a Glasgow Housing Scheme.* Edinburgh: Edinburgh University Press.

Engbersen, G. (1997) *In de schaduw van morgen: Stedelijke marginaliteit in Nederland.* Amsterdam: Boom.

Esping-Andersen, G. (Ed.) (1993) *Changing Classes: Stratification and Mobility in Post-industrial Societies.* Newbury Park, CA: Sage.

European Economic Community (1989) *Underground economy and irregular forms of employment: synthesis report and country monographs.* Brussels. (mimeograph).

Hadjimichalis, C. and Sadler, D. (Eds) (1995) *Europe at the Margins: New Mosaics of Inequality.* New York: Wiley and Sons.

Haüberman, H., Kronauer, M. and Siebel, W. (Eds) (in press) *Die Neue Armut und Exklusion in der Stadt.* Frankfurt: Suhrkamp.

Kangas, O. (1991) *The Politics of Social Rights.* Stockholm: Institute for Social Research.

Kempen, R. van and Marcuse, P. (Eds) (1999) *The New Spatial Order of Cities.* Cambridge: Blackwell.

Mabit, R. (Ed.) (1995) *Le travail dans vingt ans: Rapport de la Commission présidée par Jean Boissonnat.* Paris, Odile Jacob.

MacDonald, C. L. and Sirianni, C. (Eds) (1996) *Working in the Service Economy.* Philadelphia: Temple University Press.

Mauss, M. (1929) Les civilisations: éléments et formes, in: *Oeuvres, vol. 2: Représentations collectives et diversité des civilisations* (1968). Paris: Editions de Minuit.

McFate, K., Lawson, R. and Wilson, W. J. (Eds) (1995) *Poverty, Inequality, and Future of Social Policy.* New York: Russell Sage Foundation.

Mingione, E. (Ed.) (1996) *Urban Poverty and the Underclass.* Oxford: Basil Blackwell.

Mollenkopf, J. H. and Castells, M. (Eds) (1991) *Dual City: Restructuring New York.* New York: Russell Sage Foundation.

Moore, R. (1989) Ethnic division and class in western Europe, in: R. Scase (Ed.) *Industrial Societies: Crisis and Division in Western Capitalism and State Socialism,* pp. 115–143. London: Allen and Unwin.

Musterd, S. (Ed.) (1994) Special issue on 'A Rising European Underclass?', *Built Environment,* 20(3).

Parus, P. van (1996) *Refonder la solidarité.* Paris: Editions du Cerf.

Rifkin, J. (1995) *The End of Work: The Decline of the Global Work Force and the Dawn of the Post-market Era.* New York: G.P. Putnam's Sons.

Rothman, D. (1995) American criminal justice policies in the 1990s, in: T. G. Blomberg and S. Cohen (Eds) *Punishment and Social Control,* pp. 29–44. New York: Aldine de Gruyter.

Sassen, S. (1991) *The Global City: New York, London, Tokyo.* Princeton, NJ: Princeton University Press.

Tribalat, N. (1995) *Faire France: Une enquête sur les immigrés et leurs enfants.* Paris: La découverte.

Wacquant, L. (1996a) The rise of advanced marginality: notes on its nature and implications, *Acta Sociologica,* 39, pp. 121–139.

Wacquant, L. (1996b) Red belt, black belt: racial division, class inequality and the state in the french urban periphery and the American ghetto, in: E. Mingione (Ed.) *Urban Poverty and the Underclass,* pp. 234–274. Oxford: Basil Blackwell.

Wacquant, L. (1997a) Les pauvres en pâture: la nouvelle politique de la misère en Amérique, *Hérodote,* 85, Spring, pp. 21–33.

Wacquant, L. (1997b) Vom wohltätigen Staat zum strafenden Staat: Über den politischen Umgang mit dem Elend in Amerika, *Leviathan: Zeitschrift für Social- und Politikwissenschaft,* 25, pp. 50–66.

Wrench, J. and Solomos, J. (Eds) (1993) *Racism and Migration in Western Europe.* New York: Berg.

Globalizing Class Theory

LESLIE SKLAIR

Classes, however defined, are generally thought of as operating within the sphere of the nation-state. The consensus in sociology and related disciplines is that countries have classes and although the activities of some classes might spill over into other, particularly geographically or culturally contiguous countries, classes are rarely conceived outside the nation-state, a problematic but common synonym for countries and societies (Mann 1997). The main purpose of this article is to argue that a transnational capitalist class is in the making. It is domiciled in and identified with no particular country but, on the contrary, is identified with the global capitalist system.

THEORIZING THE DOMINANT CLASS

How do we go about rethinking the concept of class and class structure in transnational terms? The theories of national capitalist classes of Connell (1977), Useem (1984), Scott (1997), and Domhoff (1996) provide good starting places. Connell's work on class in Australia is notable for a bold if inconclusive attempt to connect the idea of a ruling class with the idea of a ruling culture, the problem of hegemony, at the conscious and unconscious levels. This is dangerous territory but it suggests how the culture-ideology of consumerism works. Global capitalism survives and capitalists prosper because

people are persuaded to consume beyond their basic needs (though these needs may change and expand over time). Patterns of consumption have to be sustained that will more or less keep the mines, fields, factories, and offices of the global economy in work. As these become ever more productive due to improvements in technology and industrial organization, even more consumption is required to keep the system going. Slump and depression are not malfunctions of the economy so much as malfunctions of the social organization of consumption: to borrow and adapt a slogan from the British Conservative Party, the culture-ideology of consumerism isn't working! Therefore, the prime culture-ideology task of global capitalism is to ensure that as many people as possible consume as much as possible, by inculcating beliefs about the intrinsic value of consumption as a "good thing" and the key component of the "good life." Thus, as Ewen (1976) argued so eloquently, the captains of industry have to be reinforced by the captains of consciousness. After persuading people that the meaning of life is in their possessions, global capitalism has to prioritize the importance of constantly changing and upgrading these possessions, thus the realms of fashion, style, novelty, difference.

The system is integrated through the "inner circle," the group within the capitalist class that organizes big business and promotes its interests in all spheres (Useem 1984). This idea provides two direct inputs for global system theory. First, Useem's use of network analysis is one useful technique for measuring how far, if at all,

Source: Leslie Sklair, "Globalizing Class Theory," in *The Transnational Capitalist Class,* Malden, MA: Blackwell Publishers, 2001: Used with permission of Blackwell Publishers.

the denationalization and globalization of the transnational capitalist class has gone. Second, Useem's study itself is a comparison of two cases, the USA and Britain, with obvious implications for widening the comparison, for example across industrial sectors as well as between other countries.

Scott is one of the few class theorists who, albeit briefly, even considers the possibility that the capitalist class could cross borders. He argues that until the demographic relations of national capitalist classes change so that social relations between members in different nation-states are as important as social relations between members in the same nation-state, then a transnational capitalist class cannot be said to exist (Scott 1997: 312). But this is to define class membership in terms of who marries whom, who consorts with whom, rather than in terms of ownership and control of the means of production and economic interests. Naturally, people who live in the same place, speak the same language, enjoy the same food and leisure pursuits, will tend to interact and intermarry more than people who live far apart, speak different languages, and enjoy themselves in different ways. But these differences need not be consequences of "national" characteristics. Indeed, the facts of a globalizing world are that more people are more mobile than ever before, use of a few common "global" languages (notably English) is greater than ever before, and "global tastes" in food, clothing, cultural pursuits of various types, sport, etc. are more widespread than ever before. Therefore, that members of a transnational capitalist class and their offspring who live for the most part in one country tend to marry partners and interact mostly with those who live in the same country seems less important than the fact that they also partake differentially in recognizable global patterns of capital accumulation, consuming, and thinking.

Insofar as globalization is changing the structure and dynamics of the capitalist class, it is necessary to start to explore in addition to capitalist classes in separate countries, the possibility of the emergence of a transnational capitalist class. The members of a TCC will have specific relations with national actors, agencies, and institutions in separate countries as well as actors, agencies, and institutions that cannot sensibly be described as "national." Those who own and control the means of production, distribution, exchange, and consumption have always been central to the conception of class. In the global context, the transnational capitalist class plays the central role in the struggle to commodify everything, the goal of the culture-ideology of consumerism. That some of these capitalists and their allies can find themselves, from time to time, in different and competitive class situations is a second-order problem, though it can be of decisive importance for the historical development of industries, class relations, and political systems in particular places, for example, within cities or countries or even continents. Nevertheless, for the global capitalist system as a whole, these intra-class struggles are less important than what binds the members of the class together globally, namely their common interest in the protection of private property and the rights of private individuals to accumulate it with as little interference as possible. Consequently, capitalists in the USA or Japan or Brazil or Germany or India may have more interests in common with each other than they have with their noncapitalist fellow citizens.

Domhoff's class dominance theory, a critical dialogue with the power elite thesis of Mills (1956), is the most challenging sociological account of the dominant class, and though he restricts it to the USA it provides a sound basis on which to globalize class theory. State autonomy theorists claim that the state has "interests and goals of its own, carried out by elected and appointed officials" (Domhoff 1996: 1). To this, Domhoff counters: "The idea of the American state having any significant degree of autonomy from the owners and managers of banks, corporations, and agribusinesses is a theoretical mistake based in empirical inaccuracies" (ibid., p. 3). The main empirical errors are the claims that the federal government has great independence from classes and interest groups; that independent experts are important;

and that competition between parties leads them to be responsive to voters. The class dominance perspective is based on three methods of research: analysis of membership networks (the institutional connections between people and between organizations), money flows (between people and institutions), and outputs of networks (which involves content analysis of texts). Domhoff accepts Dahl's three tests for the existence of a ruling elite. Is it a well-defined group? Is there a fair sample of cases where elite preferences run counter to the preference of others? Do the preferences of the elite prevail? Class dominance theory sets out to prove that "there is (1) a small social upper class (2) rooted in the ownership and control of a corporate community that (3) is integrated with a policy-planning network and (4) has great political power in both political parties and dominates the federal government in Washington" (ibid., p. 18). The method involves a synthesis of research focused on class and research focused on organization, connected through the structured agency of boards of directors of major corporations and other central organizations.

This straightforward methodology, common in much theoretically-informed empirical social science, incorporates both agency and structure, in this case investigating individuals who are powerful by virtue of their institutional positions and the institutions from which they derive their power. Taking this into the global arena, research on the transnational capitalist class is at the same time research on corporations. The three interlocking networks of elite rule in the USA, the most thoroughly researched case, are increasingly those of the TCC globally: networks of members of the upper class, the corporate community, and the policy-planning specialists. Evidence amassed by Domhoff and others over decades (see Scott, ed., 1990), demonstrates that an upper class does exist in the USA (and elsewhere) whose members are identified through an institutional network of schools, clubs, resorts, and intermarriage, and that it is a wealth-holding class. Domhoff argues that these people bring a class perspective to the executives they meet

on corporate boards, while executives bring an organization perspective to the upper class through their stewardship of the corporations. Successful corporate executives, notably those recruited onto the boards of banks and major TNCs, are not usually upper class in origins, but are incorporated to inculcate values of profit-seeking, corporate expansion and the practice of good public relations. Policy-planning networks of corporate experts, charitable foundations, and think-tanks complete the interlocking and solidarity of the elite.

Class dominance theory is highly controversial. Most sociology and politics textbooks conclude that while there might be something in elite or dominant class theory, versions of pluralist polyarchy (competing elite-like groups vying for power in a more or less open fashion) are more likely explanations of who gets what, when, and how. The differences between class dominance theory and pluralist polyarchy are small but fundamental. Both are antagonistic to the liberal democratic theory that most of the major decisions are made by politicians who simply respond to the will of the majority as expressed through democratic processes. Whereas pluralist polyarchy explains the origins and wielding of power in a nondeterminate fashion (power originates from different sources and no one source ever has a monopoly), class dominance theory argues that decisive long-term power flows from control of economic resources, more accurately from the ownership and control of the means of production. So, while military, religious, ethnic, aristocratic, political, or any other elites can and do wield power, unless they also own and control the major means of production or enjoy the support of those who do, they will be unable to hold onto their power. Their power will always be fatally vulnerable to seizure by those who do own and control the means of production, if and when they decide that their vital interests are threatened. And so, more often than not, it has proved throughout history. The capitalist class does not need to rule directly in the sense that a government or dictatorship rules, but no government or dictatorship that works actively against the interests of those who own and control the means of production can survive for long. Many governments and dictatorships have avoided this dilemma by themselves seizing ownership and control over the means of production and many more in the contemporary world thrive on turning politics into a form of business. As Robinson argues: "Promoting polyarchy and promoting neo-liberal restructuring has become a singular process in US foreign policy" (1996: 55). While radical and requiring a flexible definition of "neo-liberal restructuring," this thesis is less easy to deny now than it would have been at any time in the past for most governments.

This raises the perennial issue of the relationship between the state in capitalist society and the capitalist class. It is interesting to reflect that the Marxist thesis that the state acts like the executive committee of the bourgeoisie is actually a possible empirical consequence of pluralist polyarchy research. Some propose a stronger version of the thesis, arguing that the state is nothing but the executive committee of the bourgeoisie. In practice, the difference between these positions is not always of great importance, particularly for those who suffer when state agencies violently suppress the rights of workers and citizens as well as when they do so by nonviolent administrative means. If governments legislate in the interests of the capitalist class then it makes little difference whether they do this as if they were acting in these interests directly or not. The truly fundamental change that capitalist globalization has introduced into the state–class argument is that, for the first time in human history, there is indeed a material and ideological shift towards selling business as such as the only real business of the planet and its inhabitants. So, in the global capitalist system, agents and agencies of the state (among other institutions) fulfill the role of facilitators of the global capitalist project. James O'Connor summarizes very well a first approximation of the role of the state in capitalist society:

the conditions of production are not produced in accordance with the laws of the market. . . . There must be some agency, therefore, whose task it is either to produce the conditions of

production or to regulate capital's access to them. In capitalist societies, this agency is the state. Every state activity, including every state agency and budgetary item, is concerned with providing capital with access to labor power, nature, or urban space and infrastructure. (O'Connor 1994: 166)

Global system theory would revise this powerful statement to reflect the evidence that states are no longer monolithic bodies (even if they once were) and that the forces of globalization have pitted groups of globalizing bureaucrats and politicians and the agencies and institutions they control, against localizing bureaucrats and politicians and their bases of power and influence. While there are virtually no actively anticapitalist states left, within most states and transnationally there are continuing struggles for and against capitalist globalization. These struggles take place within state and nonstate agencies, parliaments, and social movements of many types. O'Connor's thesis, therefore, needs to be expanded to acknowledge these struggles.

Does class dominance theory work outside as well as inside the nation-state? For class dominance theory to be correct transnationally there is no necessity for it to be correct for any particular country. It is possible that a transnational capitalist class dominates globally while particular countries are dominated by other groups, for example elites or status groups made up of those who control the state apparatus or military or ideological or religious organizations and symbols. This may be the case in some countries with feeble capitalist classes. Further, the local capitalist class may not dominate in given parts of a country or throughout a country, but nevertheless the transnational capitalist class may dominate in strategic localities (like cities or communities with valuable natural resources). Where it sees its vital interests at stake, the transnational capitalist class can take control and exert its power even where there is no local dominating capitalist class. In such cases it often acts through alliances between local rulers and those who own and control the major corporations. An authority on the mining industry expresses this idea clearly: "The history of RTZ is thus the history of a worldwide political infrastructure consisting of alliances between RTZ and its potential competitors; between the company and national governments; and between the company and power brokers within the local communities where it operates" (Moody 1996: 47).

Extractive industries illustrate the point that whereas in the past much of the globe was of little interest to capitalists, for contemporary capitalism almost the whole world is of potential commercial interest, because of intense pressure that has built up within corporations to find new natural and labor resources and to exploit new markets. This is a direct consequence of two world-historical forces: first, the unprecedented productive capacities of global capitalism and, second, the hegemony of the culture-ideology of consumerism that has been constructed to solve the problem of the underconsumption of the fruits of this production.

The capitalist system, however, is not the only global system or, more accurately, it is not the only social system that has global aspirations. It competes for global hegemony with the international system of states, with global systems of religions, the global environmentalist system, and perhaps others. Nevertheless, it is the dominant global system precisely because the TCC owns and controls of most of the planet's means of production.

There have been several attempts to theorize such a transnational dominant class, and all have found a place for the transnational corporations. Concepts of the international bourgeoisie, more or less a staple of dependency theorists (see Frank 1972), the corporate international wing of the managerial bourgeoisie (Sklar 1987), and the international corporate elite (Fennema 1982) have been proposed. The Gramscian turn in International Relations has provided another source of insight. Cox (1987: 271) writes of "an emerging global class structure" and Gill (1990: 94ff) identifies a "developing transnational capitalist class fraction." All of these contributions are, at best, ambivalent about state-centrism. In order to move

forward, I believe, it is necessary to make a decisive break with state-centrism and this involves a critical deconstruction of the ideas of "national interest" and "national economy." If it is to mean anything more than internationalization, globalization must at least mean that capitalists (or any other globalizing forces) seek to transcend the national in search of the global. As an attempt to build on this rich literature, the concept of transnational practices and its political form, the TCC, is a step towards consolidating the theoretical link between globalization and the dominant class.

STRUCTURE AND DYNAMICS OF THE TRANSNATIONAL CAPITALIST CLASS

The transnational capitalist class can be analytically divided into four main fractions:

1. TNC executives and their local affiliates (the corporate fraction);
2. globalizing bureaucrats and politicians (the state fraction);
3. globalizing professionals (the technical fraction);
4. merchants and media (the consumerist fraction).

The first and dominant group is composed of those who own and control the major corporations, subsumed under the generic label of TNC executives. This includes both those who are leading salaried employees of the corporations (the conventional use of corporate executives) and those who have executive power to make and influence key decisions, notably the so-called non-executive directors and other major owners and their representatives. The other three groups—globalizing bureaucrats and politicians, globalizing professionals, and consumerist elites—are supporting members of the TCC. Some Marxist scholars may object that only those who actually own the means of production can properly be called capitalists and be members of the capitalist class, local or transnational. However, the globalization of capitalism can only be adequately understood when ownership and control of money capital is augmented with ownership and control of other types of capital, notably political, organizational, cultural, and knowledge capital (Bourdieu 1996, Scott, ed., 1990).

The composition of the transnational capitalist class, therefore, reflects the different types of capital that must be mobilized to further the direct interests of the global capitalist system. While the four groups are analytically distinct in that they serve different though complementary functions for global capital in the abstract, concretely the individuals in them overlap to a considerable degree. Some TNC executives, for example, spend time as state bureaucrats (globalizing and localizing); and bureaucrats and politicians, professionals, and especially members of consumerist elites work directly for corporations. The capitalist class is defined here as those who own and control the major means of production, distribution, and exchange through their ownership and control of money and other forms of capital. In a theme that will be argued in detail in subsequent chapters, class hegemony does not simply happen as if by magic. The capitalist class expends much time, energy, and resources to make it happen and to ensure that it keeps on happening.

Together, the leading representatives of these fractions constitute a transnational dominant class in some respects. The transnational capitalist class opposes and is opposed not only by those who reject capitalism as a way of life and/or an economic system but also by those capitalists who reject globalization. Some localized, domestically oriented businesses can share the interests of globalizing corporations and prosper, but many cannot and fail to enrich their owners. Influential business strategists and management theorists commonly argue that to survive, local business must globalize (for example, Kanter 1996). Inward-oriented government bureaucrats, politicians, and professionals who reject globalization and espouse extreme nationalist ideologies are comparatively rare, despite the recent rash of civil wars in economically marginal parts of the world. While there are anticonsumerist elements in most societies, there are few cases of a serious anticonsumerist party winning political power anywhere in the world.

The transnational capitalist class is transnational (and globalizing) in several respects.

a. The economic interests of its members are increasingly globally linked rather than exclusively local and national in origin. The property and shares of those who own and control the major corporations are becoming more globalized as are their corporations. The intellectual products of members of the TCC increasingly serve the interests of globalizing rather than localizing capital. These outcomes follow directly from the shareholder-driven growth imperative that lies behind the globalizing of the world economy and the increasing difficulty of enhancing shareholder value in purely domestic firms. The richest and most powerful corporations in the world and those who own and control them, with few exceptions, tend to be globalizing in terms of foreign economic activities, aspirations to world-class operations, the rhetoric and practices of global corporate citizenship, and global visions. While for many practical purposes the world is still organized in terms of discrete national economies, the TCC increasingly conceptualizes its interests in terms of markets, which may or may not coincide with a specific nation-state, and the global market, which clearly does not.

Purely "domestic firms" may be defined as those serving the market of one sovereign state, employing only co-nationals, whose products consist entirely of domestic services, components, and materials. That this appears to be a ridiculously narrow definition for the realities of contemporary economies suggests that the concept of economic globalization has some plausibility. Apart from small localized firms, the exceptions are mainly state-owned enterprises (SOEs) and quasi-monopolistic utility and services corporations. The facts that SOEs are being run more like TNCs and/or are being privatized and frequently sold to TNCs, and that quasi-monopolies are being rapidly deregulated, enhance rather than detract from this argument. Van der Pijl (1993: 30) traces the point when the "national identity" of the corporations "had to be abandoned" to the 1970s. While few would go this far, there is sufficient evidence to show that globalizing corporations today are not the same as the corporations of the past. There are countless explanations from economists, and from management, international business, and organization theorists (exhaustively surveyed in Dunning, 1992–4), of how and why the TNCs, under a variety of labels, differ from firms in the past. My interest here is in how the TNCs relate to the global capitalist system, which includes changing business sectors, regulatory frameworks, political regimes, and climates of opinion on social and environmental questions.

In the early 1970s, the Conference Board, a business think-tank based in New York, commissioned research on this topic. One respondent in the study stated that: "Multinational corporations are not really multinational. They are national companies with units abroad" (quoted in LaPalombara and Blank 1976: 111). In the course of my own interviews in the *Fortune* Global 500, this quotation was read out and comments invited. In the majority of cases the respondents commented, some quite forthrightly, that this was an old-fashioned and specifically American idea of how corporations operate and that no corporation aspiring to global competitiveness could afford to think in these terms any more. . . . Whether all those who own and control major corporations, or the corporations as they present themselves to the public, actually transcend national stereotypes is, of course, another matter.

b. The TCC seeks to exert economic control in the workplace, political control in domestic and international politics, and culture-ideology control in everyday life through specific forms of global competitive and consumerist rhetoric and practice. The focus of workplace control is the threat that jobs will be lost and, in the extreme, the economy will collapse unless workers are prepared to work longer hours and for less pay in order to meet foreign competition. This has been called "the race to the bottom" by radical critics (see Brecher and Costello 1994; Ranney 1994). While this is not new—capitalists have always fought against reductions in the length of the working day and increases in wages—its global scope is unprecedented.

This race to the bottom is reflected in local electoral politics all over the world, in rich and poor countries alike, where the major parties have few substantial strategic (even if many tactical) differences, and in the sphere of culture-ideology, where consumerism is rarely challenged. Paradoxically, the rhetoric and ideology of global capitalism has become inextricably bound up with the demand for ever-rising standards of living, which makes the debate around renewable resources and irreversible environmental damage more and more difficult to engage in seriously. The central question that the issue of capitalist class control raises is: how does the TCC exert its control successfully in the interests of the global capitalist project? The answer that global system theory provides is in terms of the grip that the TNC-generated culture-ideology of consumerism has on the mass of the world's population.

c. Members of the TCC have outward-oriented global rather than inward-oriented local perspectives on most economic, political, and culture-ideology issues. The growing TNC and international institutional emphasis on free trade and the shift from import substitution to export promotion strategies in most developing countries since the 1980s have been driven by members of the TCC working through government agencies, business professionals, elite opinion organizations, and the media. Some of the credit for this apparent transformation in the way in which big business works around the world is attached to the tremendous growth in business education since the 1960s, particularly in the US and Europe, but increasingly all over the world. By 1990 there were around 200 business schools in the USA offering graduate degrees in international business. A spokesman for one of the most prestigious, the Wharton School, commented: "We wanted to be a school of management of the world that just happens to be headquartered in Philadelphia" (Carey 1990: 36). Between 26 and 40 percent of all Wharton students on graduate business programs were then from outside the USA. Research on INSEAD in Paris suggests that transnational business schools were beginning to have a significant impact on the behavior and ideology of European executives as well (Marceau 1989). There is now a huge literature in the popular and academic business press on the making of the global executive and the globalization of business and management (see Warner 1997, *passim*) that confirms that this is a real phenomenon and not simply the creation of a few "globaloney" myth-makers.

d. Members of the TCC tend to share similar lifestyles, particularly patterns of higher education (increasingly in business schools) and consumption of luxury goods and services. Integral to this process are exclusive clubs and restaurants, ultra-expensive resorts in all continents, private as opposed to mass forms of travel and entertainment and, ominously, increasing residential segregation of the very rich secured by armed guards and electronic surveillance. These gated communities are being studied all over the world, in Istanbul (Bartu 1999), Bangalore (King 1999), Los Angeles (Davis 1999), and other world cities.

e. Finally, members of the TCC seek to project images of themselves as citizens of the world as well as of their places of birth. Leading exemplars of this phenomenon include Jacques Maisonrouge, who in the 1960s became the chief executive of IBM World Trade (Maisonrouge 1988); Percy Barnevik, credited with the creation of ABB and often portrayed as spending most of his life in his corporate jet (Taylor 1991); Helmut Maucher, former CEO of Nestlé's far-flung global empire (Maucher 1994); David Rockefeller, the key figure in the Trilateral Commission (Gill 1990); Akio Morita, founder of Sony (Morita and Reingold 1987); and Australian-born Rupert Murdoch, who actually changed his nationality to pursue his global media interests (Shawcross 1992).

The concept of the transnational capitalist class implies that there is one central inner circle that makes system-wide decisions, and that it connects in a variety of ways with subsidiary members in communities, cities, countries, and supranational regions. Despite real geographical and sectoral conflicts, the whole of the transnational capitalist class shares a fundamental interest in the continued accumulation of private profit. What the inner circle of the TCC does is to give a unity to the diverse economic interests, political organizations, and cultural and ideological formations of those who make up the class as a whole. As in any social institution, fundamental long-term unity of interests and purpose does not preclude shorter-term and local conflicts of interests and purpose, both within each of the four fractions of the TCC and between them. The culture-ideology of consumerism is the fundamental value system that keeps the system intact, but it permits a relatively wide variety of choices, notably "emergent global nationalisms" as a way of satisfying the needs of the different actors and their constituencies within the global system. The four fractions of the TCC in any geographical and social area, whether analyzed in terms of bloc, region, country, city, society, or community, perform complementary functions to integrate the whole. The achievement of these goals is facilitated by the activities of agents and organizations that are connected in a complex network of local and global interlocks.

A crucial component of the integration of the TCC is that most of the senior members of its inner circle will occupy a variety of interlocking positions. The core of the system is the interlocking corporate directorates that have been the subject of detailed studies for some time in many countries (Mizruchi and Schwartz 1987; Scott, ed., 1990, vol. III; Stokman et al. 1985). Those in the core frequently have extensive connections outside the direct ambit of the corporate sector, the civil society as it were servicing the state-like structures of the corporations. Leading capitalists and corporate executives serve on the boards of think-tanks, charities, scientific, sports, arts, and culture bodies, universities, medical foundations, and similar institutions, just as leaders of these institutions often occupy places on corporate boards (see Scott, ed., 1990, vol. I, parts II and III; Useem 1984). While there is little evidence of widespread direct transnational (nonstate) or international (state-based) interlocking, there are indications of changes. Major corporations are beginning to see the advantages of bringing more nationalities on to main and subsidiary boards, and the idea that those who control companies headquartered in one country have to be nationals of that country is slowly eroding. With the dramatic increase of cross-border strategic alliances—what Dunning (1997) calls globalizing alliance capitalism—the penetration of all social institutions by the corporations is likely to increase. It is in this sense that the claims "the business of society is business" and "the business of our society is global business" become legitimated in the global capitalist system. Business, particularly the TNC sector, then begins to monopolize symbols of modernity and postmodernity like free enterprise, international competitiveness, and the good life, and to transform most, if not all, social spheres in its own image. Table 1 summarizes the structure of the transnational capitalist class.

The particular places where the TCC operates in the unfolding era of globalization, while broadly similar in fundamentals insofar as they are parts of the global capitalist system, all have their peculiarities. So the homogenizing effects of capitalist globalization, one defining characteristic of the phenomenon, and the peculiarities and uniqueness of history and culture, are always in tension. This tension creates a globalizing dialectic. The thesis is the historical local of communities, real and imagined of all types, the relatively recent

TABLE 1   Structure of the Transnational Capitalist Class

	Economic Base	*Political Organization*	*Culture-Ideology*
TNC executives (corporate fraction)	corporate salaries, shares	peak business organizations	cohesive culture-ideology of consumerism
Globalizing bureaucrats and politicians (state fraction)	state salaries, perks	state and interstate agencies, corporatist organizations	emergent global nationalism and economic neoliberalism
Globalizing professionals (technical fraction)	salaries and fees, perks	professional and corporatist organizations, think-tanks	economic neoliberalism
Globalizing merchants and media (consumerist fraction)	corporate salaries, perks, shares	peak business organizations, mass media, selling spaces	cohesive culture-ideology of consumerism

invention of the nation-state being the most prominent in the modern era. The antithesis is the emerging global, of which the global capitalist system driven by the transnational capitalist class is the dominant, though not the only, force. The synthesis is as yet unformulated. "Going global" is the tendency of contemporary capitalism, but it is neither inevitable nor irreversible.

REFERENCES

Bartu, A. 1999. "Redefining the Public Sphere through Fortified Enclaves: A View from Istanbul." *WALD International Conference,* Istanbul.

Bourdieu, P. 1996. *The State Nobility: Elite Schools in the Field of Power.* Cambridge: Polity Press.

Brecher, J. and T. Costello. 1994. *Global Village or Global Pillage: Economic Reconstruction from the Bottom Up.* Boston: South End Press.

Carey, P. 1990. "The Making of a Global Manager." *North American International Business* June: 36–41.

Connell, R. W. 1977. *Ruling Class, Ruling Culture.* Cambridge: Cambridge University Press.

Cox, R. W. 1987. *Production, Power, and World Order: Social Forces in the Making of History.* New York: Columbia University Press.

Davis, M. 1999. *Ecology of Fear: Los Angeles and the Imagination of Disaster.* New York: Metropolitan Books.

Domhoff, W. G. 1996. *State Autonomy or Class Dominance? : Case Studies on Policy Making in America.* Hawthorne, NY: Aldine de Gruyter.

Dunning, J. 1997. *Alliance Capitalism and Global Business.* London and New York: Routledge.

Ewen, S. 1976. *Captains of Consciousness.* New York: McGraw-Hill.

Fennema, M. 1982. *International Networks of Banks and Industry.* The Hague: Martinus Nijhoff.

Frank, A. G. 1972. *Lumpenbourgeisie: Lumpendevelopment.* New York: Monthly Review Press.

Gill, S. 1990. *American Hegemony and the Trilateral Commission.* Cambridge: Cambridge University Press.

Kanter, R. M. 1996. *World Class: Thriving Locally in the Global Economy.* New York: Simon and Schuster.

King, A. 1999. "Suburb/Ethnoburb/Globurb: Framing Transnational Urban Space in Asia." *WALD International Conference,* Istanbul.

LaPalombara, J. and S. Blank. 1976. *Multinational Corporations and National Elites: A Study in Tensions.* New York: The Conference Board.

Maisonrouge, J. 1988. *Inside IBM: A European's Story.* London: Collins.

Mann, M. 1997. "Has Globalization Ended the Rise and Rise of the Nation-state?" *Review of International Political Economy* 4: 472–96.

Marceau, J. 1989. *A Family Business? The Making of an International Business Elite.* Cambridge: Cambridge University Press.

Maucher, H. 1994. *Leadership in Action: Tough-minded Strategies from the Global Giant.* New York: McGraw-Hill.

Mills, C. W. 1956. *The Power Elite.* New York: Oxford University Press.

Mizruchi, M. and M. Schwartz (eds.) 1987. *Intercorporate Relations: The Structural Analysis of Business.* Cambridge: Cambridge University Press.

Moody, R. 1996. "Mining the World, the Global Reach of Rio Tinto Zinc." *The Ecologist,* March/April: 46–52.

Morita, A. and E. Reingold. 1987. *Made in Japan: Akio Morita and Sony.* London: Collins.

O'Connor, J. "Is Sustainable Capitalism Possible?" In M. O'Connor, ed., op. cit.

O'Connor, M (ed.) 1994. *Is Capitalism Sustainable?* New York: Guildford Press.

Overbeek, H. (ed.) 1993. *Restructuring Hegemony in the Global Political Economy: The Rise of Transnational Neoliberalism in the 1980s.* London: Routledge.

Ranney, D. 1994. "Labor and an Emerging Supranational Corporate Agenda." *Economic Development Quarterly* 8: 83–91.

Scott, A. 1990. *Ideology and the New Social Movements.* London: Unwin Hyman.

Scott, J. 1997. *Corporate Business and Capitalist Classes.* Oxford: Oxford University Press.

Scott, J. (ed.) 1990. *The Sociology of Elites.* Aldershot: Edward Elgar, 3 vols.

Shawcross, W. 1992. *Murdoch.* Sydney: Random House.

Sklar, R. 1987. "Postimperialism: A Class Analysis of Multinational Corporate Expansion." In *Postimperialism,* eds. D. Becker, J, Frieden, S, Schatz, and R, Sklar. Boulder, Colo.: Lynne Rienner.

Stokman, F. N., R. Ziegler, and J. Scott (eds.) 1985. *Networks of Corporate Power: A Comparative Analysis of Ten Countries.* Cambridge: Polity Press.

Taylor, W. 1991. "The Logic of Global Business: An Interview with ABB's Percy Barnevik." *Harvard Business Review* 69: 90–105.

Useem, M. 1984. *The Inner Circle.* New York: Oxford University Press.

van der Pijl, K. 1993. "The Sovereignty of Capital Impaired: Social Forces and Codes of Conduct for Multinational Corporations." In H. Overbeek, ed., op. cit.

Warner, M. (ed.) 1997. *Concise Encyclopedia of Business & Management.* London and New York: Thompson Business Press.

Digital Divide

PIPPA NORRIS

WHO IS ONLINE?

Income

The digital divide is a multidimensional phenomenon tapping many social cleavages but differences of resources are commonly assumed to be among the most important, meaning the capacities based primarily on the income, occupation, and education that people bring to using new forms of info-tech. *Falling through the Net* emphasized that household income was one of the strongest predictors of Internet access in America. U.S. Census data show that home ownership of PCs quadrupled from 1984 to 1997, but this period saw growing disparities in ownership among social strata based on household income, race, and education. An OECD study, drawing on data from France, Japan, and the United States, confirmed the substantial disparity in the availability of personal computers in the home for different levels of household income, with the size of the gap between the lowest and highest income groups widening from 1995 to 1998. Economic resources, including personal or household income, influence the ability to afford home computers and modems, related software, and the monthly ISP and telephone or broadband cable connection charges. Telephone costs can be substantial in Europe, especially where charges for local calls are metered by

Source: Pippa Norris, "Digital Divide," in *Digital Divide: Civic Engagement, Information Poverty, and the Internet Worldwide,* Cambridge University Press, 2001: 77–92. Reprinted with the permission of Cambridge University Press.

the minute, with these bills outweighing the initial investment in computer hardware within a few years. The OECD's *Information Technology Outlook 2000* study found that the growth in Internet demand has been driven by a combination of faster connection speeds, improved reliability and service, easier technical use, and declining access costs. Dial-up telephone modems currently remain the most popular mode of household access, used in two-thirds of all homes in OECD member states, although more advanced forms of delivery are gradually becoming more available, including cable, DSL, ISDN, and wireless.

How far does household income determine Internet access? Table 1 summarizes trends in the social profile of Internet users within Europe from 1996 to 1999, for comparison across all major social cleavages. Figure 1 illustrates the size of the gap in Internet access between the most and least affluent quartile household incomes, with the nations ranked across the chart by their overall level of Internet penetration. Three major findings stand out. First, as expected, the income gap in Internet users across the whole of Europe proved substantial; on average the wealthiest European households were almost three times more likely to be online than the poorest ones. Overall 37 percent, of those living in the most affluent households were online, compared with only 14 percent, of those in the poorest homes. There was a consistent and significant association between household income and levels of Internet access across all EU countries, with the single exception of Greece.

TABLE 1   Trends in the Social Profile of Internet Users in Europe, 1996–99

	Percent Online Spring 1996	*Percent Online Spring 1999*	*Change*
All EU-15	5	20	+15
Age			
15–25	9	32	+23
26–44	7	24	+17
45–64	5	16	+11
65+	1	3	+2
HH income category			
−	4	14	+10
−	3	14	+11
+	5	22	+17
++	10	37	+27
Age finished education			
Up to 15	1	5	+4
16–19 years	4	15	+11
20+	9	33	+24
Gender			
Men	6	22	+16
Women	4	17	+13
Occupational status			
Managers	14	44	+30
Other white collar	8	29	+21
Manual worker	3	15	+12
Home worker	2	8	+6
Unemployed	3	10	+7
Student	13	44	+31

Sources: Eurobarometer 44.2, spring 1996; 47.0, spring 1997; 50.1, fall 1998; and 51.0, spring 1999.

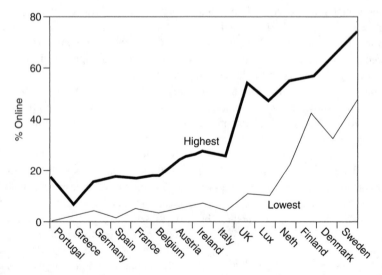

FIGURE 1   Percent Online by Household Income, EU-15, 1999.

Source: Eurobarometer 51.0, spring 1999.

Moreover, across Europe the relative size of the gap between rich and poor stayed roughly constant from spring 1996 to spring 1999, rather than increasing or diminishing. During these years the EU Internet population grew at a rate of roughly 10 percent per annum but this did not lead to any closure of the digital divide by income. Finally, the comparison of societies that are leaders and laggards in the Information Age gives no support to the normalization thesis claim that income differentials necessarily diminish as Internet use widens throughout the population; if anything the reverse. Despite relatively widespread use of the Internet in Britain, for example, the most affluent households were five times more likely to be online than the poorest. The variations among European countries suggest that many factors within each nation may influence the income gap in Internet access, such as state initiatives to make wired computers widely available through community centers, unemployment offices, and schools, as well as levels of market competition driving down the financial costs of hardware, software, and access charges. But the differential between rich and poor families evident in such countries as Britain, Luxembourg, and Denmark mean that, at least during the emerging years, we would not expect the income gap to close automatically as the Internet diffuses more widely throughout society.

Occupation

Related patterns in the workforce can also be expected to be important for many reasons. Professional and managerial jobs in the service sector facilitate 24/7 Internet connections at the office, often through high-speed LAN networks, as well as providing training assistance and technical support. Companies also commonly provide managers and executives with mobile equipment such as laptops, digital personal assistants, and cell phones, as well as subsidizing home access charges, to facilitate connectivity with the office. Professional, managerial, and executive salaries provide the resources to afford consumer durables like computers and high-speed cable connections for the home and family,

and multiple-connection household intranets. In contrast, manual workers, although using computers as part of the industrial manufacturing process, are less likely to experience Internet access at work or to acquire the skills and experience in the workplace that breed comfort and familiarity with the Web at home. Governments in Britain, Germany, and Sweden have emphasized the need to bring the unemployed into the knowledge economy, through the provision of networked computers and training in job centers and unemployment offices. Nevertheless, even with these initiatives, those seeking work are likely to be among the most marginalized and poorest members of society. There are reasons to believe that occupational status may prove less important for Internet access as use diffuses more widely; during the last five years home access has doubled in America, with remarkably little increase in the proportion using the Internet from work.

Figure 2 shows the distribution of Internet access by the respondent's occupation in the workforce in the fifteen member states of the EU. The pattern confirms that managers and professionals are almost twice as likely to use the Internet as those in other white-collar jobs including clerical assistants and service sector employees, and managers are almost three times as likely to use the Internet as manual workers. Access for the unemployed fell just below the level of manual workers. Again, the gap between the info-rich and poor varied across nations but it proved largest among certain leader societies including the United Kingdom, Finland, and Denmark, and slightly more marked than the disparities already observed by household income.

Education

The related divide in Internet use by educational attainment is well established in many American studies, where college graduates are among those most familiar with the Internet. Wilhelm, for example, concluded that education was a stronger determinant of connectivity in America than any other demographic or social variable. Many reasons can be given for this pattern. Schools and colleges

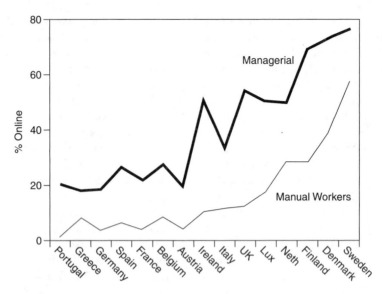

FIGURE 2   Percent Online by Occupation, EU-15 1999.

Source: Eurobarometer 51.0, spring 1999.

provide an environment that is exceptionally rich in all forms of info-tech and indeed these have usually been among the first institutions wired to the Net in most countries. Education can be expected to improve the general capacity for analytical reasoning and information filtering, which helps cope with the flow of information available online, as well as strengthening numeracy, literacy, English-language, and keyboard skills. Schools and colleges commonly provide students with free email and Web hosting facilities, computer labs, as well as direct hands-on experience of surfing the Internet for research, and training support or technical backup for using common software packages. College education is also closely related to subsequent occupational status and income, which we have already observed are important, as well as being linked to generational patterns of diffusion, illustrated by the popularity of programs for music sharing such as Napster on college campuses. Figure 3 illustrates the relationship between the age of finishing education and use of the Internet in European member states. The results confirm the expected disparities by education, showing similar

results to the inequalities evident in the workforce. In Europe, those with a college education are seven times more likely to be online than those who left school at 15. Indeed education proved one of the strongest predictors of connectivity: more than 40 percent of college students in Europe are online, a figure ranging up to 80 percent of all students in Sweden and Finland.

Gender

The gender gap within the online community has been the subject of widespread study. Some surveys have reported that this difference has closed recently in America; for example the Pew Internet and American Life tracking survey suggested that by spring 2000 the surge in the number of women online had produced gender parity, although women and men continued to differ in their attitudes toward new technology and in their behavior online. Nevertheless the evidence about the gender gap remains inconclusive; for example, AC Nielsen's *Net Watch* surveyed thirteen nations in North America, Europe, and Asia in spring 2000,

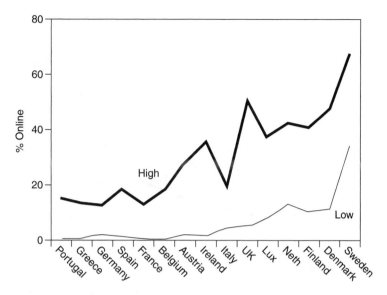

FIGURE 3   Percent Online by Education, EU-15 1999.
Source: Eurobarometer 51, spring 1999.

and reported that women were less likely to be online in every country, including the United States, with almost twice as many male to female Internet users in Germany, Hong Kong, and Taiwan. Many plausible reasons may account for any gender differences in use of computer technology and within the online community. Bolt and Crawford reviewed a wide range of evidence suggesting that girls and women are less likely to use computers because of their early experiences within school class-rooms, reflecting long-standing gender differences in attitudes toward science and technology, as well as the typical contents of computer games and websites available for children. The position of women as primary caregivers in the home and family may also play a role, since we have already observed the importance of work environments for Internet access. In Europe, the evidence on male and females within the online community in Figure 4 shows that the gender gap proves the weakest predictor of Internet use among all the factors we have considered so far, with the difference between women and men becoming statistically insignificant in Belgium,

Denmark, France, Portugal, the United Kingdom, and Finland. Nevertheless a significant online gender gap was evident elsewhere, especially in the Netherlands, Sweden, and Italy.

Generation

The generational difference in adaptation to new technologies is perhaps the most significant for the future diffusion of the Internet, and yet the most taken for granted in policy circles. The pattern in Figure 5 shows that early adopters in Europe were concentrated among the youngest age groups, with minimal use in most of Europe among senior citizens—this despite the fact that the Internet seems well suited to the needs of the elderly, as a fairly sedentary population with considerable leisure time, especially for social networking, hobbies, and services such as the home delivery of groceries. The typical age profile may flatten in the future because there is a large potential market among the elderly if access to the Internet becomes more commonly delivered through dedicated plug-and-play email units, and services like Web-TV, rather than

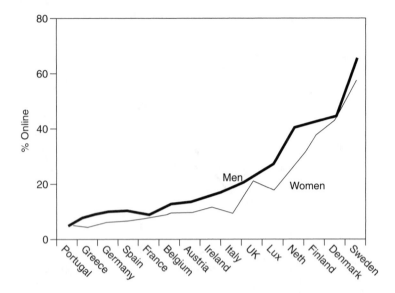

FIGURE 4   Percent Online by Gender, EU-15, 1999.
Source: Eurobarometer 51.0, spring 1999.

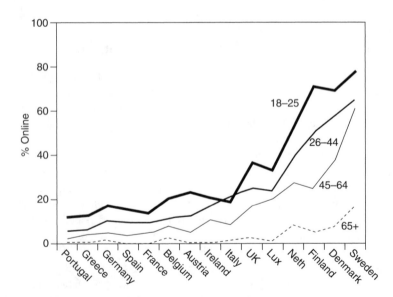

FIGURE 5   Percent Online by Age Group, EU-15, 1999.
Source: Eurobarometer 50.1.

via more technically demanding computers. At present, the online community in Europe largely excludes the retired population. The generation gap within the Nordic region, where the Internet has penetrated most widely, proves the largest of any social cleavage observed so far. The youngest group is ten times as likely to be online than the oldest group; overall almost a one-third of all Europeans under 25 are online, compared with only 3 percent of the over-65 year-olds. The Napster generation is already experiencing a virtual world as they develop that is different from formative lives of their parents and grandparents.

The evidence so far suggests that the familiar social profile of online users in the United States is also evident throughout Western Europe. Trends in these societies since the mid-1990s confirm that, contrary to the "normalization" thesis, the resource-based inequalities that we have already observed grew in significance as Internet use gradually diffused more widely (Figure 6). Multivariate analysis predicting use of the Internet in spring 1996 and 1999 helps to distinguish the relative weight of the factors discussed so far and confirms the significance of these patterns. The order of the variables in the OLS regression models followed the standard logic of the classic "funnel of causality". The demographic variables of age and gender were entered first, followed by the resource variables of household income, education, and the respondent's occupation, the latter coded as manual or nonmanual. The country variables were then entered as dummy variables (0/1) to determine if the national differences in Internet use remain significant even after controlling for social background.

The results of the models confirm that all the demographic factors discussed [here] were significantly associated with Internet use in Europe (see Table 1). In particular, the gender and age differences remained significant predictors of Internet use even after controlling for income, education, and occupation, suggesting that resources are only one part of the explanation here. Moreover the national-level country variables usually continued to be significant, even after controlling for social background. This indicates that the structure of opportunities within each nation . . . influences Internet use even after controlling for individual-level differences in occupation and income. For example, a well-paid college-educated company manager living in Stockholm or Copenhagen would still be more likely to surf the Web or use email than an equivalent colleague working in Madrid or Athens. The macrolevel context is important, including such factors as state initiatives to widen access through education and training, and market competition in the pricing of computer hardware and ISP connectivity.

Turning to the analysis of changes over time, the comparison of the same models run in 1996 and 1999 demonstrate that, far from equalizing, the digital divide in Europe expanded during these years; the inequalities of access by income, education, occupational status, and age become stronger and only the gender gap weakened over time. It is likely that the social profile of users may possibly flatten further within the next decade, if Internet access spreads even more widely to become ubiquitous in almost all European households, as commonplace as a VCR or refrigerator. Nothing that we have said disproves the claims that the "normalization" thesis could still be true in the longer-term. But the European evidence indicates a growing digital divide between the information-rich and poor during the emergent Internet era, in addition to the widening North–South global disparities documented in the previous chapter, with no evidence to date that these gaps are starting to close or normalize in leading societies where use of the Internet has become most pervasive.

RELATIVE INEQUALITIES IN THE INFORMATION SOCIETY

The fact that there are absolute differences in access to the Internet is hardly surprising. However, the question remains whether the *relative* disparities in access to the Internet are substantially different or similar to the distribution of other common forms of information and communication technology,

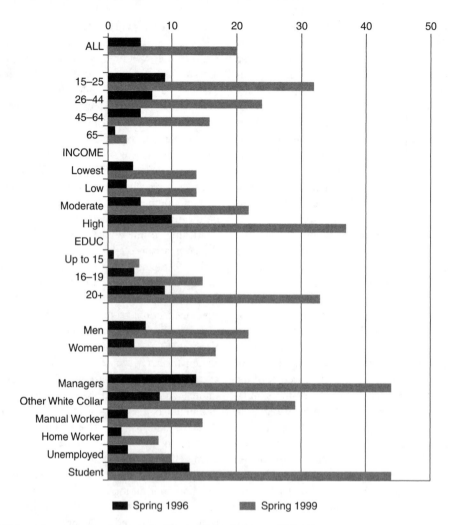

FIGURE 6   Change in the Percent Online by Social Group, EU-15.
Source: Eurobarometers 1996 and 1999.

such as VCRs and cable TV. Like gambling at Rick's bar, some popular accounts are shocked— *shocked*—to discover social inequalities on the Internet. We should not be. As in the previous chapter, the more realistic approach compares relative inequalities in computers access and Internet use with disparities in the distribution of other common forms of information technologies. The spring 1999 Eurobarometer survey monitored whether people had access to or used ten different types of information technology, including the Internet, as well as VCRs, facsimile machines, and personal computers. If we establish that patterns of income, educational, or occupational inequalities are similar across all types of communication and information technologies, then this suggests broad explanations of this phenomenon relating to deep-rooted patterns of social stratification endemic in modern societies. Households with Internet access can be expected to possess multiple consumer durables for entertainment and communications, such as satellite or cable TVs, pagers and fax machines, home entertainment centers, and mobile phones. Conversely, if the distribution of Internet access differs from use of other types of info-tech, then we should search for explanations based on the distinctive characteristics of the Internet per se, such as the financial costs of gaining online access, the cognitive skills and computing experience required for surfing, language barriers to use of the Web in non–English-speaking countries, and the way people respond to the type of materials and services available online (e.g., music, entertainment, and shopping). Both relative and absolute inequalities can be regarded as equally important, but the

analysis of the former provides deeper insights into the causes of this phenomenon and therefore also its potential solution.

The correlations shown in Table 2 indicate that Internet use is significantly associated with access to all forms of communication technologies, including noncomputer related machines such as VCRs and cable TV. Reflecting parallel patterns at national level documented in the previous chapter, this suggests that individuals living in affluent households with many different forms of consumer durables designed for traditional forms of home entertainment and communication are also most likely to access networked computers. Ownership of personal computers is related to all sorts of other common

TABLE 2   Explaining Internet Use in Europe, 1996 and 1999

	1996			1999		
	R	*Sig.*	*B*	*R*	*Sig.*	*B*
Demographics						
Age	−.085	.000	−.035	−.168	.000	−.642
Gender	.058	.000	.588	.052	.000	.327
Resources						
Education	.095	.000	.303	.153	.000	.609
Income	.055	.000	.783	.141	.000	.439
Class	.056	.000	.827	.077	.000	.574
Nation						
Greece	−.035	.000	−1.43	−.073	.000	−1.72
Germany	−.006	.849	−.035	−.067	.000	−1.30
France	−.037	.000	−.774	−.057	.000	−1.24
Spain	−.027	.000	−1.03	−.055	.000	−1.36
Portugal	−.007	.012	−.563	−.054	.000	−1.44
Belgium	−.015	.000	−.628	−.052	.000	−1.20
Austria	−.001	.923	.020	−.041	.000	−.93
Italy	−.018	.000	−.507	−.036	.000	−.91
Ireland	.010	.104	.359	−.029	.000	−.73
United Kingdom	.069	.000	.966	.000	.432	.23
Netherlands	.035	.000	.578	.021	.000	.45
Finland	.055	.000	.784	.035	.000	.65
Denmark	.038	.000	.573	.049	.000	.89
Sweden	.068	.000		.099	.000	1.77
Cox-Snell R2	.073			.278		
Nagelkerke R2	.209			.431		
Percent correct	94.5			83.8		

Notes: The table reports the coefficients predicting the use of the Internet based on binary logistic regression models. Use of the Internet is measured as a dichotomy where 1 = yes and 0 = no. Luxembourg, which is close to the Europe mean, is excluded from the standardized household income scale. Age in measured in years. Education is measured as years finished full-time education. Income is measured from the standardized household income scale. Class is based on the manual/nonmanual occupation for the head of household. Gender is 1 = male and 0 = female.

Source: Eurobarometer 47, spring 1996 (No. 65178) and spring 1999.

TABLE 3   Use of New and Old Media in Europe, 1999

	Internet	*Computer*	*CD ROM*	*Modem*	*VCR*	*Fax*	*Sat. TV*	*Cable TV*	*Video-text*
Computer	0.61								
CD-ROM	0.59	0.70							
Modem	0.91	0.67	0.65						
VCR	0.19	0.31	0.26	0.21					
Fax	0.44	0.45	0.43	0.47	0.22				
Satellite TV	0.12	0.14	0.13	0.12	0.12	0.13			
Cable TV	0.14	0.16	0.16	0.15	0.15	0.14	0.24		
Teletext TV	0.19	0.25	0.22	0.21	0.32	0.18	0.16	0.10	
Videotext	0.09	0.12	0.11	0.11	0.07	0.14	0.06	0.13	−0.02

Note: Q: "*Do you use, or do you have access to . . .*" The figures represent individual-level simple correlations (R) without any controls.

Source: Eurobarometer 51.0, spring 1999 EU-15.

household gadgets from deep-fat fryers to video cameras and clock radios. There can obviously be many exceptions; for example, less affluent students, low-paid service professionals, and office clerical workers are commonly in work environments where the Internet is easily available even if they lack home access. Nevertheless, the association between use of computer and other types of household consumer durables implies that broad and deep-rooted patterns of social stratification are the major explanation for patterns of Internet diffusion.

To test this further, multivariate models were run as before with three dependent variables, the percentage of the population using the Internet (% Online), a broader New Media index summarizing access to a computer, CD-ROM, and modem, as well as the Internet, and an Old Media index including access to traditional technologies, including a VCR, fax, satellite TV, cable TV, teletext TV, and videotext. Most strikingly, comparison of the results across all three models shows that similar social and demographic factors explaining online participation also help predict access to new *and* old media technologies (see Table 4). The digital divide is striking but far from new. The relative strength of the coefficients varied slightly across models; for example, education and occupation were slightly more strongly associated with the new than old media. Nevertheless the headline finding concerns the striking similarities across models. This pattern

confirms that important social inequalities exist in the virtual world. Since the mid-1990s, the global divide between leader and laggard nations, and the social divide among subpopulations even within leader nations, have expanded substantially. In Europe, as in the United States, the sweeping tide of the Internet has left behind many poorer households, manual workers, the less educated, the elderly, and women. Yet, there is nothing distinctive about these social and regional inequalities in the virtual world, which also characterize access to the Information Society delivered via older media technologies such as cable or satellite TV, VCRs, and fax machines. We may be less concerned about the implications of lack of access to cable TV or VCRs than lack of access to the Internet, but this insight has important implications for policy initiatives designed to overcome the social barriers to digital access. The results suggest that such programs as training in keyboard skills or wiring schools may help to overcome the digital divide but they are likely to have limited effect given the deep-rooted socioeconomic barriers to access.

At the same time it is true that in the emerging knowledge economy the evidence of trends in Internet use remains limited, and we remain at the bottom of the diffusion curve. The situation could change in the near future and the social profile of the online community could be transformed if costs fall dramatically, driven by the proliferation of subscription-free and unmetered access services,

TABLE 4   Explaining Use of New and Old Media in Europe, 1999

	Percent Online		New Media		Old Media	
	Beta	*Sig.*	*Beta*	*Sig.*	*Beta*	*Sig.*
Demographic						
Age (years)	−0.12**		−0.16**		−0.18**	
Gender (male)	0.06**		0.05**		0.07**	
Resources						
HH income	0.16**		0.21**		0.25**	
Education	0.12**		0.15**		0.06**	
Manual occupation	0.09**		0.12**		0.06**	
Region						
North (1) South (0)	0.23**		0.21**		0.25**	
Constant	0.21		0.81		2.19	
Adjusted R²	0.19		0.26		0.24	

** Sig. > p. = .01

Notes: The figures represent standardized beta coefficients using OLS regression models. **Percent Online:** Have access to or use the Internet or World Wide Web (0 = no/1 = yes). **New Media Index:** four-point scale measuring use or access to computer plus CD-ROM plus modem plus Internet. **Old Media Index:** six-point scale measuring use or access to VCR plus Fax plus Satellite TV plus Cable TV plus Teletext plus Videotext.

Source: Eurobarometer 51.0, spring 1999.

greater competition, and the increasing availability of broadband services, as many predict. Companies also forecast a proliferation of Web appliances delivering a cut-down version of the Internet outside the box. Although there are reasons to be skeptic about industry hype, eTForecast estimate that there are currently 21.5 million Web-enabled appliances in use globally, such as cell phones and personal assistants. The projected figures for 2005 are 596 million globally: 115.4 million for the United States and 126.4 million for Western Europe. Web delivery via mobile phones has proved particularly popular in Japan where home PCs are not common. The popular distribution of powerful but relatively inexpensive units such as Play Station II also facilitates new ways of accessing the Internet. The consequences of these developments for the digital divide remain to be determined but their lower costs could help close the divide.

CONCLUSIONS: SOCIAL STRATIFICATION AND INTERNET ACCESS

The explanation for the digital divide is often assumed to lie in certain characteristics of this technology, such as the need for computing skills

and affordable online connections. The policy solutions designed to ameliorate the digital divide commonly focus on just these sorts of fixes, such as wiring schools and classrooms, training teachers, and providing community access in poorer neighborhoods. Certainly this can do no harm. But will these initiatives work in terms of diversifying the online population? The results of this analysis suggest that, unfortunately, it seems unlikely. The policy fixes are too specific, the problem of social inequalities too endemic.

[This] analysis . . . demonstrates that the heart of the problem lies in broader patterns of social stratification that shape not just access to the virtual world, but also full participation in other common forms of information and communication technologies. The results suggest that there is no need to try to explain the online gender gap, for example, by theories specific to this type of technology, such as women's supposed "computer phobia," attitudes toward computers in the classroom, or the lack of nonaggressive computer games and websites suitable for young girls. All this may, or may not, be true. But it turns out that these are flimsy general explanations for why fewer women than men are online, because women are also less likely than men to have access to technologies delivering mass entertainment such as cable TV and VCRs. Even in affluent societies, poorer families lacking such common consumer durables as cable TV, VCRs, and automobiles are likely to lack Internet access as well.

In the longer run, technological and economic developments may well alter the market for Internet access, reducing costs, simplifying technical skills, and thereby widening usage. Generational trends are likely to be particularly important in terms of the long-term patterns of use, as younger groups eventually replace the older population. Public policy initiatives such as wiring all schools are likely to contribute to ameliorating some of the major disparities in computing skills and knowledge. Nevertheless none of these developments is likely to alter long-established patterns of social stratification in the short term. Moreover, even if the Internet eventually reaches 85 to 95 percent of the population, there are still multiple layers of access and use. TV sets essentially come in only a couple of flavors. The box can be bigger or smaller, analog or digital, single speaker or home theater, cheaper or more expensive, and so on, but basically a TV is a TV is a TV, making no demands beyond how to switch the power button, with perhaps 100+ channels but still nothing to watch. In contrast, levels of Internet access can vary substantially. Today people living in poorer neighborhoods may be able to surf the Web from public libraries, schools, and community centers, or even cyber cafés, but this is not the same as having automatic access via high-speed connections at home and the office. Nor is it the same as having all Internet, all the time, downloadable via personal appliances, digital assistants, and cellular phones for today's wired road warriors in planes, ships, and trains. Internet technology is not going to stand still as long as the market continues to demand ever smaller, faster, and improved forms of delivery. . . .

NOTES

1. NTIA. 1999. *Falling through the Net.* Washington, DC: U.S. Department of Commerce. www.ntia.doc.gov. ntiahome/fttn99

2. Fosbert Kominski and Eric Newburger. 1999. "Access Denied: Changes in Computer Ownership and Use 1984–1997." Paper presented at the annual meeting of the American Sociological Association, Chicago.

3. OECD. 2000. *Information Technology Outlook,* Paris: OECD. Figure 7. P. 86.

4. OECD. 2000. *Information Technology Outlook,* Paris: OECD. P. 82.

5. The statistical difference between groups was measured by ANOVA. In Greece, the difference by income group proved statistically insignificant, in large part because so few Greeks from any social sector were online.

6. The June 1995 Pew survey reported that the U.S. online population split almost evenly between those gaining access from home (9 percent) or work (15 percent). In contrast, the September 1999 Pew survey found that there was a greater edge for home access (37 percent) over work access (21 percent). See Pew Research Center for the People and the Press June 2000. "Internet Sapping Broadcast News Audience." www.people-press.org/media00rpt.htm Similar trends toward home access have been found elsewhere, see OECD. 2000. *Information Technology Outlook:* Paris: OECD.

7. Anthony G. Wilheim, 2000. *Democracy in the Digita. Age: Challenges to Political Life in Cyberspace.* New York: Routledge. P. 56.

8. The Pew Internet Project Report, 10 May 2000. "Tracking Online Life. How Women Use the Internet to Cultivate Family and Friends." www.pewinternet.org/reports

9. AC, Nielsen. October 25, 1999. *Net Watch.* www. acuiglsen.com/products/reports/net-watch

10. David Bolt and Ray Crawford, 2000. *Digital Divide: Computers and Our Children's Future.* New York: TV Books. Chapter 3.

11. It should be noted that OLS results are presented here and the analysis was confirmed by logistic regression analysis in Table 4.4, producing identical results.

12. IDC. June 8, 2000. "Western European Internet Access Industry Continues to Reinvent itself." www.idc.com/emea/ press/PR/ECM060800PR.sim

13. eTForecast. June 12 2000. "By 2005 33% of U.S. Internet Users Will Use Web Appliances." www.etforecasts.com/ pr/pr600.htm

14. For example, dedicated email units currently cost at about $100 in the United States, compared with $500 or more for an inexpensive basic PC.

New Slavery in the Global Economy

KEVIN BALES

THE RISE OF THE NEW SLAVERY

For thousands of years people have been enslaved. Slavery echoes through the great epics of the distant past. Ancient Egypt, ancient Greece, and the Roman Empire all made slavery integral to their social systems. Right through the American and Brazilian slave economies of the last century, legal, old-style slavery persisted in what is now called the developed world. But slavery never disappeared; instead, it took a different form. The basic fact of one person totally controlling another remains the same, but slavery has changed in some crucial ways.

Two factors are critical in the shift from the old slavery to the explosive spread of the new. The first is the dramatic increase in world population following World War II. Since 1945 the world population has almost tripled, increasing from about 2 billion people to more than 5.7 billion. The greatest growth has been in those countries where slavery is most prevalent today. Across Southeast Asia, the Indian subcontinent, Africa, and the Arab countries, populations have more than tripled and countries are flooded with children. Over half the population in some of these countries is under the age of fifteen. In countries that were already poor, the sheer weight of numbers overwhelms the resources at

hand. Without work and with increasing fear as resources diminish, people become desperate and life becomes cheap. Especially in those areas where slavery had persisted or was part of the historical culture, the population explosion radically increased the supply of potential slaves and drove down their price.

The second crucial factor is that at the same time that the population was exploding, these countries were undergoing rapid social and economic change. In many developing countries modernization brought immense wealth to the elite and continued or increased the impoverishment of the poor majority. Throughout Africa and Asia the last fifty years have been scarred by civil war and the wholesale looting of resources by home-grown dictators, often supported by one of the superpowers. To hold on to power, the ruling kleptocrats have paid enormous sums for weaponry, money raised by mortaging their countries. Meanwhile traditional ways of life and subsistence have been sacrificed to the cash crop and quick profit. Poor families have lost their old ways of meeting a crisis. Traditional societies, while sometimes oppressive, generally relied on ties of responsibility and kinship that could usually carry people through a crisis such as the death of the breadwinner, serious illness, or a bad harvest. Modernization and the globalization of the world economy have shattered these traditional families and the small-scale subsistence farming that supported them. The forced shift from subsistence to cash-crop agriculture, the loss of common land,

Source: Kevin Bales, "New Slavery in the Global Economy," in *Disposable People: New Slavery in the Global Economy,* Berkeley, University of California Press, 1999: 12-22. Used with permission of University of California Press.

and government policies that suppress farm income in favor of cheap food for the cities have all helped bankrupt millions of peasants and drive them from their land—sometimes into slavery.

Although modernization has had good effects, bringing improvements in health care and education, the concentration of land in the hands of an elite and its use of land to produce cash crops for export have made the poor more vulnerable. Because the political elites in the developing world focus on economic growth, which is not just in their collective self-interest but required by global financial institutions, little attention is paid to sustainable livelihoods for the majority. So while the rich of the developing world have grown richer, the poor have fewer and fewer options. Amid the disruption of rapid social change, one of those options is slavery.

The end of the cold war only made matters worse. William Greider explains it well:

> One of the striking qualities of the post–Cold War globalization is how easily business and government in the capitalist democracies have abandoned the values they putatively espoused for forty years during the struggle against communism—individual liberties and political legitimacy based on free elections. Concern for human rights, including freedom of assembly for workers wishing to speak for themselves, has been pushed aside by commercial opportunity. Multinationals plunge confidently into new markets, from Vietnam to China, where governments routinely control and abuse their own citizens.

In fact, some of these countries *enslave* their own citizens, and others turn a blind eye to the slavery that generates such enormous profits.

The Old Slavery Versus the New Slavery

Government corruption, plus the vast increase in the number of people and their ongoing impoverishment, has led to the new slavery. For the first time in human history there is an absolute glut of potential slaves. It is a dramatic illustration of the laws of supply and demand: with so many possible slaves, their value has plummeted. Slaves are now so cheap that they have become cost-effective in many new kinds of work, completely changing how

they are seen and used. Think about computers. Forty years ago there were only a handful of computers, and they cost hundreds of thousands of dollars; only big companies and the government could afford them. Today there are millions of personal computers. Anyone can buy a used, but quite serviceable, model for $100. Use that $100 computer for a year or two, and when it breaks down, don't bother to fix it—just throw it away.

The same thing happens in the new slavery. Buying a slave is no longer a major investment, like buying a car or a house (as it was in the old slavery); it is more like buying an inexpensive bicycle or a cheap computer. Slaveholders get all the work they can out of their slaves, and then throw them away. The nature of the relationship between slaves and slaveholders has fundamentally altered. The new disposability has dramatically increased the amount of profit to be made from a slave, decreased the length of time a person would normally be enslaved, and made the question of legal ownership less important. When slaves cost a great deal of money, that investment had to be safeguarded through clear and legally documented ownership. Slaves of the past were worth stealing and worth chasing down if they escaped. Today slaves cost so little that it is not worth the hassle of securing permanent, "legal" ownership. Slaves are disposable.

Around the world today the length of time a slave spends in bondage varies enormously. Where old-style slavery is still practiced, bondage lasts forever. A Mauritanian woman born into slavery has a good chance of remaining so for the rest of her life. Her children, if she has any, will also be slaves, and so on down the generations. But today most slaves are temporary; some are enslaved for only a few months. It is simply not profitable to keep them when they are not immediately useful. Under these circumstances, there is no reason to invest heavily in their upkeep and indeed little reason to ensure that they survive their enslavement. While slaves in the American South were often horribly treated, there was nevertheless a strong incentive to keep them alive for many years. Slaves were like valuable livestock: the plantation owner needed to make back his investment. There was also pressure to breed them and produce more slaves, since it was usually cheaper to raise new slaves oneself than to buy adults. Today no slaveholder wants to spend money supporting useless infants, so female slaves, especially those forced into prostitution, are prevented from conceiving. And there is no reason to protect slaves from disease or injury—medicine costs money, and it's cheaper to let them die.

The key differences between the old and new slavery break down like this:

OLD SLAVERY	NEW SLAVERY
Legal ownership asserted	Legal ownership avoided
High purchase cost	Very low purchase cost
Low profits	Very high profits
Shortage of potential slaves	Surplus of potential slaves
Long-term relationship	Short-term relationship
Slaves maintained	Slaves disposable
Ethnic differences important	Ethnic differences not important

Looking at a specific example will clarify these differences. Perhaps the best studied and best understood form of old slavery was the system in the American South before 1860. Slaves were at a premium, and the demand for them was high because European immigrants were able to find other work or even start their own farms in the ever-expanding West. This demand for slaves was reflected in their price. By 1850 an average field laborer sold for $1,000 to $1,800. This was three to six times the average yearly wage of an American worker at the time, perhaps equivalent to around $50,000 to $100,000 today. Despite their high cost, slaves generated, on average, profits of only about 5 percent each year. If the cotton market went up, a plantation owner might make a very good return on his slaves, but if the price of cotton fell, he might be forced to sell slaves to stay in business. Ownership was clearly demonstrated by bills of sale and titles of ownership, and

slaves could be used as collateral for loans or used to pay off debts. Slaves were often brutalized to keep them under control, but they were also recognized and treated as sizable investments. A final distinctive element was the extreme racial differentiation between slaveholder and slave, so strong that a very small genetic difference—normally set at being only one-eighth black—still meant lifelong enslavement.

In comparison, consider the agricultural slave in debt bondage in India now. There land rather than labor is at a premium today. India's population has boomed, currently totaling three times that of the United States in a country with one-third the space. The glut of potential workers means that free labor must regularly compete with slave, and the resulting pressure on agricultural wages pushes free laborers toward bondage. When free farmers run out of money, when a crop fails or a member of the family becomes ill and needs medicine, they have few choices. Faced with a crisis, they borrow enough money from a local landowner to meet the crisis, but having no other possessions, they must use their own lives as collateral. The debt against which a person is bonded—that is, the price of a laborer—might be 500 to 1,000 rupees (about $12 to $23). The bond is completely open-ended; the slave must work for the slaveholder until the slaveholder decides the debt is repaid. It may carry over into a second and third generation, growing under fraudulent accounting by the slaveholder, who may also seize and sell the children of the bonded laborer against the debt. The functional reality is one of slavery, but its differences from the old slavery reflect five of the seven points listed above.

First, no one tries to assert legal ownership of the bonded laborer. The slave is held under threat of violence, and often physically locked up, but no one asserts that he or she is in fact "property." Second, the bonded laborer is made responsible for his or her own upkeep, thus lowering the slaveholder's costs. The slaves may scrape together their subsistence in a number of ways: eking it out from the foodstuffs produced for the slaveholder, using their "spare time" to do whatever is necessary to bring in food, or receiving some foodstuffs or money from the slaveholder. The slaveholders save by providing no regular maintenance, and they can cut off food and all support when the bonded laborer is unable to work or is no longer needed.

Third, if a bonded laborer is not able to work, perhaps because of illness or injury, or is not needed for work, he or she can be abandoned or disposed of by the slaveholder, who bears no responsibility for the slave's upkeep. Often the slaveholder keeps an entirely fraudulent legal document, which the bonded laborer has "signed" under duress. This document violates several current Indian laws and relies on others that either never existed or have not existed for decades, yet it is normally used to justify holding the bonded laborer. It also excuses the abandonment of ill or injured slaves, for it specifies responsibilities only on the part of the bonded laborer; there are none on the part of the slaveholder. Fourth, the ethnic differentiation is not nearly so rigid as that of the old slavery. As already noted, bonded laborers may well belong to a lower caste than the slaveholder—but this is not always the case. The key distinction lies in wealth and power, not caste.

Finally, a major difference between the old and new slavery is in the profits produced by an enslaved laborer. Agricultural bonded laborers in India generate not 5 percent, as did slaves in the American South, but over 50 percent profit per year for the slaveholder. This high profit is due, in part, to the low cost of the slave (i.e., the small loan advanced), but even so it reflects the low returns on old-fashioned smallscale agriculture: indeed, almost all other forms of modern slavery are much more profitable.

Agricultural debt bondage in India still has some characteristics of the old slavery, such as the holding of slaves for long periods. A better example of the new slavery is provided by the young women lured into "contract" slavery and put to work in prostitution in Thailand. A population explosion in Thailand has ensured a surplus of potential slaves, while rapid economic change has led to new poverty and desperation. The girls are often initially drawn from rural areas with the promise of work in restaurants or factories. There is no ethnic difference—these are Thai girls enslaved by Thai brothel owners; the distinction between them, if any, is that the former are rural and the latter urban. The girls might be sold by their parents to a broker, or tricked by an agent; once away from their homes they are brutalized and enslaved, then sold to a brothel owner. The brothel owners place the girls in debt bondage and tell them they must pay back their purchase price, plus interest, through prostitution. They might use the legal ruse of a contract—which often specifies some completely unrelated job, such as factory work—but that isn't usually necessary. The calculation of the debt and the interest is, of course, completely in the hands of the brothel owners and so is manipulated to show whatever they like. Using that trick, they can keep a girl as long as they want, and they don't need to demonstrate any legal ownership. The brothel does have to feed the girl and keep her presentable, but if she becomes ill or injured or too old, she is disposed of. In Thailand today, the girl is often discarded when she tests positive for HIV.

This form of contract debt bondage is extremely profitable. A girl between twelve and fifteen years old can be purchased for $800 to $2,000, and the costs of running a brothel and feeding the girls are relatively low. The profit is often as high as 800 percent a year. This kind of return can be made on a girl for five to ten years. After that, especially if she becomes ill or HIV-positive, the girl is dumped.

The Forms of the New Slavery

Charted on paper in neat categories, the new slavery seems to be very clear and distinct. In fact, it is as inconveniently sloppy, dynamic, changeable, and confusing as any other kind of relation between humans. We can no more expect there to be one kind of slavery than we can expect there to be one kind of marriage. People are inventive and flexible, and the permutations of human violence and exploitation are infinite. The best we can do with slavery is to set down its dimensions and then test any particular example against them.

One critical dimension is violence—all types of slavery depend on violence, which holds the slave in place. Yet, for one slave, there may be only the threat of violence while, with another, threats may escalate into terrible abuse. Another dimension is the length of enslavement. Short-term enslavement is typical of the new slavery, but "short" may mean ten weeks or ten years. Still another aspect is the slave's loss of control over his or her life and ongoing "obligation" to the slaveholder. The actual way in which this obligation is enforced varies a great deal, yet it is possible to use this dimension to outline three basic forms of slavery:

1. *Chattel slavery* is the form closest to the old slavery. A person is captured, born, or sold into permanent servitude, and ownership is often asserted. The slave's children are normally treated as property as well and can be sold by the slaveholder. Occasionally, these slaves are kept as items of conspicuous consumption. This form is most often found in northern and western Africa and some Arab countries, but it represents a very small proportion of slaves in the modern world. . . .

2. *Debt bondage* is the most common form of slavery in the world. A person pledges him- or herself against a loan of money, but the length and nature of the service are not defined and the labor does not reduce the original debt. The debt can be passed down to subsequent generations, thus enslaving offspring; moreover, "defaulting" can be punished by seizing or selling children into further debt bonds. Ownership is not normally asserted, but there is complete physical control of the bonded laborer. Debt bondage is most common on the Indian subcontinent. . . .

3. *Contract slavery* shows how modern labor relations are used to hide the new slavery. Contracts are offered that guarantee employment, perhaps in a workshop or factory, but when the workers are taken to their place of work they find themselves enslaved. The contract is used as an enticement to trick an individual into slavery, as well as a way of making the slavery look legitimate. If legal questions are raised, the contract can be produced, but the reality is that the "contract worker" is a slave, threatened by violence, lacking any freedom of movement, and paid nothing. The most rapidly growing form of slavery, this is the second-largest form today. Contract slavery is most often found in Southeast Asia, Brazil, some Arab states, and some parts of the Indian subcontinent. . . .

These types are not mutually exclusive. Contracts may be issued to chattel slaves in order to conceal their enslavement. Girls trapped into prostitution by debt bondage will sometimes have contracts that specify their obligations. The important thing to remember is that *people are enslaved by violence and held against their wills for purposes of exploitation.* The categories just outlined are simply a way to help us track the patterns of enslavement, to clarify how slavery might be attacked.

A small percentage of slaves fall into a number of other readily identifiable kinds of slavery. These tend to be specific to particular geographical regions or political situations. A good example of slavery linked to politics is what is often called *war slavery;* this includes government-sponsored slavery. In Burma today, there is widespread capture and enslavement of civilians by the government and the army. Tens of thousands of men, women, and children are used as laborers or bearers in military campaigns against indigenous peoples or on government construction projects. The Burmese military dictatorship doesn't suggest that it owns the people it has enslaved—in fact, it denies enslaving anyone—but the U.S. State Department and human rights organizations confirm that violence is used to hold a large number of people in bondage. Once again, the motive is economic gain: not to generate profits but to save transportation or production costs in the war effort, or labor costs in construction projects. One major project is the natural gas pipeline that Burma is building in partnership with the U.S. oil company Unocal, the French oil company Total, and the Thai company PTT Exploration and Production. These three companies are often featured in international and global mutual investment funds. The Thai company, which is owned in part by the Thai government, is recommended by one mutual fund as a "family" investment. In the pipeline project thousands of enslaved workers, including old men, pregnant women, and children, are forced at gunpoint to clear land and build a railway next to the pipeline. War slavery is unique: this is slavery committed *by* the government, whereas most slavery happens in spite of the government.

In some parts of the Caribbean and in western Africa, children are given or sold into domestic service. They are sometimes called "restavecs." Ownership is not asserted, but strict control, enforced by violence, is maintained over the child. The domestic services performed by the enslaved child provide a sizable return on the investment in "upkeep." It is a culturally approved way of dealing with "extra" children; some are treated well, but for most it is a kind of slavery that lasts until adulthood.

Slavery can also be linked to religion, as with the Indian *devadasi* women . . . or the children who are ritual slaves in Ghana. Several thousand girls and young women are given by their families as slaves to local fetish priests in southeastern Ghana, Togo, Benin, and southwestern Nigeria. In a custom very alien to Western sensibilities the girls are enslaved in order to atone for sins committed by members of their families, often rape. The girls may, in fact, be the products of rape, and their slavery is seen as a way of appeasing the gods for that or other crimes committed by their

male relatives. A girl, who *must* be a virgin, is given to the local priest as a slave when she is about ten years old. The girl then stays with the priest—cooking, cleaning, farming, and serving him sexually—until he frees her, usually after she has borne several children. At that point the slave's family must provide another young girl to replace her. Ghana's constitution forbids slavery, but the practice is justified on religious grounds by villagers and priests.

As can be seen from these cases, slavery comes in many forms. Moreover, slavery can be found in virtually every country. A recent investigation in Great Britain found young girls held in slavery and forced to be prostitutes in Birmingham and Manchester. Enslaved domestic workers have been found and freed in London and Paris. In the United States farmworkers have been found locked inside barracks and working under armed guards as field slaves. Enslaved Thai and Philippine women have been freed from brothels in New York, Seattle, and Los Angeles. This list could go on and on. Almost all of the countries where slavery "cannot" exist have slaves inside their borders—but, it must be said, in very small numbers compared to the Indian subcontinent and the Far East. The important point is that slaves constitute a vast workforce supporting the global economy we all depend upon.

What Is to Be Done?

This text of selected readings outlines the parameters of the essential debates in social stratification, the competing theories concerning the dividing line of social class, and demonstrates that no reading of social class is complete without careful attention to race, ethnicity, nationality, sex, sexual preference, and country of residence. Now it is time to return to some of the questions posed at the beginning of our text. Three stand out. First, is inequality inevitable? Second, is it enough to study differences? Third, should the social sciences be more proscriptive?

Howard Winant suggests that others must come forward to chart the direction of any social movement. There is an uncomfortably close relationship, after all, between social analysis and social engineering (if social scientists had that kind of power). However, having looked at various and insightful analyses of the problem of inequality, we would be remiss to stop short of considering what might be done to counter it. Thus, we turn to four commentators, two of whom are gray eminences who point to different ways in which we can challenge inequality: through policy promoting more public spending and social welfare, through a vigorous defense of democracy, through working with egalitarian social movements, and through envisioning if not *the* good society, at least a pretty good one.

Jeff Faux looks at the importance of public investment in a deteriorating infrastructure. The infrastructure of a nation-state is crucial to the health of the populace. Thus, he argues for investing in goods from which we all benefit: good roads, safe bridges, clean and modern schools, and so forth. Faux challenges the standard political wisdom of public debt by looking at public entitlement—and provides a possible blueprint by suggesting means by which we could pay for the services so desperately needed.

Amartya Sen, a Nobel Prize winner in economics, writes about the virtues of democracy as a universal value in a piece originally published in the *Journal of Democracy*. Sen makes a compelling and moving argument for democracy, employing references to historical and contemporary comparative examples. For example, famine is a depressingly regular occurrence in the world, but Sen can find no instance of famine in countries that have a free press and a democratic system of governance. Democracy is characterized not by majority rule but by the political freedom that invites participation, by the importance of expressing claims, and by the opportunity to learn from others in the community. Above all else, we shouldn't reduce democracy to a franchise owned by one group of people or one party.

Philip Green looks further at collaborative political activity in addressing the question of social solidarity. He writes that "the goal of egalitarians is to forge a union out of many solidarities." This is much easier said than done because solidarities that are not common can compete against one another as readily as they can work together, but Green's larger question is an important one. What are our obligations to—our solidarity with—other people in the world? Where, and with whom, does egalitarianism begin? Does egalitarianism mean going against our own interests as workers? As citizens?

Immanuel Wallerstein's extensive body of work on the capitalist world system has put the lie to the idea that any one power is indefatigable. U.S. hegemony in business, in military might, in food production, began to be eclipsed some thirty years ago. Wallerstein believes that we are in the midst of a transition to another world system and that now is the time to ask questions about building a better society. Do we want to continue on the same path? Will we be able to? The presumed virtues of the current world system—that is, material abundance, liberal political structures, and a longer life span in which to enjoy it all—draws critics who in various ways challenge this portrait. So, what is the choice with which we are faced? We can choose to continue on the course of inequality, where some have much more than everybody else, or we can choose democracy and equality.

The title of Wallerstein's book, *Utopistics,* brings us full circle to the beginnings of the social sciences: in a time of crisis and change, how do we build a better society? What do you envision? What will be your place in the new world system and the place of your children? Most importantly, what is to be done?

In this collection we've tried to present for your perusal some of the best minds at work in the social sciences and related fields today. Because this is an edited collection, some of the work presented may be best read in its larger context. However, we hope that this collection convinces you to keep reading and thinking about these issues and about the tangled difficulties posed by inequality. Inequality as a concept, as a thing, *is* inevitable. However, the extent of economic inequality that leads to terrible human suffering and exploitation is not. The final selection is an original essay written for this book that documents the breadth and depth of today's inequalities and something of the human toll they take.

Public Investment
for a Twenty-first Century Economy

JEFF FAUX

Investment is the act of shaping the future. Public investment in infrastructure is a major way democratic people shape their collective future and is an essential complement to private investment. Government spending on schools, roads, bridges, and basic research and development is a foundation upon which the private sector builds profit-making enterprises.

Public investment is also a generator of specific private investment opportunities. America's history is studded with grand economic sectors opened up by government and profited on by business. Early in our republic's life, we built canals and highways and provided land for towns and schools in the territories. Government financed the first assembly lines, subsidized the railroads to settle the West, and developed long-range radio technologies. It created the suburbs after World War II and explored space. Government leadership developed the jet engine, the computer, and the Internet. Each of these programs generated jobs and businesses. Just as important, they spun off technological advances that became what Robert Heilbroner calls economic "klondikes"—massive veins of investment opportunities that have been the building blocks of American prosperity.

Finally, public infrastructure is a major way a democratic society balances the tendency of the market to concentrate wealth and economic opportunity. By providing commonly owned spheres of "enabling" activity accessible to all—schools to all students, roads to all truckers, telecommunications to all businesses—public infrastructure extends the web of upward mobility to a widening circle of the population. And by providing the public sector with leverage over resources, infrastructure spending allows government to redirect resources to citizens and regions that the market leaves behind in its pursuit of narrower, shorter-term goals.

Not all basic infrastructure is financed by direct government expenditures. Railroads were subsidized with undeveloped land; airlines with rights to airspace and a flight control system; and radio and television by privileged access to the public's airwaves. In these and other cases, public and private funds and interests were and are co-mingled.

Because of the alarming deterioration of public support for traditional infrastructure—education and training, public works, and civilian research and development—the bulk of this brief essay is addressed to those sectors. But the reader should also be aware that the deregulation of telecommunications, transportation, electric utilities, and even finance also has the potential for eroding the opportunity-widening functions of public infrastructure.

Source: From *Back to Shared Prosperity: The Growing Inequality of Income in America.* ed. Ray Marshall (Armonk, NY: M.E. Sharpe, 2000): 211–218. Copyright © 2000 by M.E. Sharpe, Inc. Reprinted with permission. All rights reserved. Not for Reproduction.

THE IMPORTANCE
OF PUBLIC INFRASTRUCTURE

Until very recently, standard statistical descriptions of the economy (e.g., the basic national income accounts) treated all government spending as consumption and thereby ignored the contribution that public investment makes to productivity and overall economic growth. Economists who have studied the issue in depth have found that public investment produces substantial gains in productivity, private investment, and overall economic growth. Studies of physical infrastructure spending by David Aschauer, Alicia Munnell, and Sharon Erenburg found that every dollar of public investment raises private investment another forty-five to fifty cents. Indeed, Aschauer, Munnell, Douglas Holtz-Ekins, and Amy Schwartz concluded that, because of years of neglect, investment in public infrastructure now produces a higher return (measured by increases in productivity) than investment in the private sector. Although government reports now make some attempt to separate capital from operating expenditures, the way in which macroeconomic data are collected, analyzed, and discussed still systematically undervalues public investment.

Economists may quarrel over its exact contribution, but there is little doubt among serious observers that public investment plays a major role. In 1995, over 400 prominent economists wrote an open letter to the president and the Congress warning of the dangers of neglecting public investment. "Just as business must continually reinvest in order to prosper," they wrote, "so must a nation. Higher productivity—the key to higher living standards—is a function of public as well as private investment." They concluded that "compared with what we need in order to compete and to make all segments of our society productive, we are still not investing enough."

In this new global economy, public investment is even more important than it used to be. Where private investment has become foot-loose—forcing American workers to compete with workers from countries where wage growth is deliberately kept below productivity growth by public policy—public investment, in both human and physical capital, is by its very nature targeted at improving the competitiveness of those who produce in America. Indeed, those who urge us to "embrace" the global marketplace have a special obligation to assure that we raise the level of public investment.

Today, by any measure, public investment in the United States is falling further behind that necessary to maintain a productive and stable society. A decreasing share of gross domestic product is devoted to federal non-defense spending (including transfers to state and local governments) for physical infrastructure, education and training, and research and development. In 1996, it was some 40 percent less than it was twenty years earlier. The sharp downward shift in the share of GDP going to public investment occurred in 1981, after which the federal government invested considerably less in real terms than in the previous fifteen years.

Nor has the slack been made up by state and local governments. As a share of GDP, state and local government spending on capital projects and for education has fallen since the early 1970s.

Internationally, the United States now invests relatively less in its basic infrastructure than other major industrial nations. For more than two decades, it has ranked lowest in public works spending among the G-7 nations.

For the past decade, the existence of a large federal fiscal deficit has been the excuse for squeezing public sector investment. When President Clinton early in his term decided to make balancing the budget his economic priority, the concerns of supporters of public investment were assuaged by the promise that once balance was achieved, the government could return to neglected public investments.

The budget could have been balanced in a number of ways, including tax increases. But the process was concentrated on cutting discretionary spending—the source of public investment funds. Moreover, it was accompanied by rhetoric, for example, "The era of big government is over," that tended to deny the importance of public spending to the country's economic health. Not surprisingly, the political constituency for public investment became intimidated and discouraged. As a result, after the budget was balanced in 1998, the debate over how to use the surplus centered around Republican demands for tax cuts and a defensive Democratic strategy that purported to save the surplus for Social Security. Public investment needs were largely forgotten.

In his budget for the fiscal year 2000, the president proposed a small spate of programs—some of which did reflect new investments in education. But overall, the downward trend in domestic spending was continued. The president's plan called for a further reduction of domestic spending's share of GDP by fiscal year 2004, from 3.5 to 3.2 percent.

In addition, the devolution of highly visible and politically sensitive social-service programs to the states will put increasing pressure on their budgets. As Timothy Bartik has suggested, there is already a systematic bias against state and local government spending on infrastructure because local taxpayers must pay all the costs while the benefits often spill over to others.

Two decades of neglect have already taken a huge toll on our public capital. A comprehensive survey of public- and private-sector expert estimates of physical, human, and technological capital needs in 1991 concluded that, in order to keep from widening the gap between needs and actual investment, the federal government should have been spending a minimum of $60 billion and possibly as much as $125 billion. The estimates were based on a modest definition of investment; it did not include spending on health, housing, environmental cleanup, public safety, and other purposes that also add to our nation's economic strength. The 1991 investment gap was as follows:

HUMAN RESOURCES (BILLIONS OF DOLLARS)

Education and Training	$23.3–45.0
Children	6.1–12.5
Physical Capital	22.7–54.8
Research and Development	10.8–13.5
Total Investment	$62.9–125.8

Since then, new studies have shown even wider gaps. For example, in 1996, the General Accounting Office reported that the nation's schools needed another $100 billion just to fix up public school buildings—repair the roofs, get the rats out of the basements, and wire the school rooms for computers. The Republican congressional leadership was completely unresponsive. The president suggested spending $5 billion over three years.

The human side of the ongoing public investment crisis was reflected in a recent interview with the retired chief engineer of New York City. Speaking of the deterioration of the city's crucial web of bridges, he noted that a bridge is in fact a series of interlocking flexible parts that, if not lubricated, will crack. In 1900, the city had 200 people painting and lubricating the Williamsburg Bridge. Now there are three. "You can take your hand and go right through the concrete—the bridge has moved so much because they didn't lubricate the bearing plates."

THE PUBLIC BALANCE SHEET

Despite the growing gap, public investment has virtually disappeared in the national discussion over economic policy. It is now completely overwhelmed by the obsession with cutting back government spending. The problem is symbolized by "national debt clocks"—clicking away with so many dollars a second. The device is used as a prop by politicians (and often affixed to billboards) to frighten the populace with the nightmare of government spending out of control.

The debt clock is a half-truth, which is often worse than a lie. It reflects an absurd accounting notion that is concerned exclusively with the liability side of the ledger, ignoring the assets. Also missing is another dial—the value of what we are getting for government borrowing.

This is not just a problem of public accounting; it points to the misguided moral motivation behind many people's concerns with the public debt (i.e., the concern with the kind of economic future we are leaving our children and grandchildren). It is frequently claimed that "every new American baby is presented with an $18,000 debt"— representing its per capita share of the federal government's outstanding liabilities. Indeed, if that were the complete story, we would be guilty of burdening our children's future. But in fact, the newborn baby is also entitled to a share of the federal government's assets that, as indicated below, are just a shade lower than its per capita liabilities. Moreover, the child is also entitled to its share of assets financed by that public debt and now owned by state and local governments—schools, highways, water systems, and so on. Beyond that, the child is eligible to share in the nation's productive private assets, many of which would not exist if they had not been stimulated by public investment.

Part of the problem is, of course, politics. The national debt clock is sponsored by people interested in discrediting government. And part of the problem lies in bad economics.

But part of the problem is also with the way that we keep the federal books. First, all expenditures, whether for operations or capital investment, are lumped together in one year. Thus, both a one-year subsidy to a farmer and an investment in a bridge that takes three years to build and will bring the farmer's goods to market more rapidly over the next fifty years are lumped together in the federal budget. No sensible business or householder manages its own finances this way. A business or household knows that its financial health depends not on just how much cash it takes in and spends each year, but also on the condition of its "balance sheet," a comparison of assets and liabilities. When a family borrows money to buy a house, it does not normally consider itself to be worse off because in that one year it ran a deficit (i.e., the cost of the house is more than its annual income). On the contrary, it considers itself to be better off because it has bought an asset that can rise in value. The same is true for a business buying a new plant or a piece of machinery that will last more than a year. As with households and business, the question is not the size of the government's debt, but on what one has used the proceeds. If a family borrows to buy a

house, it may improve its financial condition because it now has an asset. If it borrows to take a vacation, it probably will not.

From 1980 to 1993, the federal government's debt rose more than 400 percent. During that time per capita liabilities rose from $12,130 to $18,110. Per capita federally owned and financed assets actually dropped, from $17,670 to $17,109. In 1980, the balance sheet of the U.S. government showed that assets exceeded liabilities by 27 percent. By 1993, liabilities were some 4 percent greater than assets. Had we maintained our national assets at the same level that they were in 1980—that is, had we used the increase in the national debt for investment—the federal balance sheet would still be in the black.

A balance sheet approach is not by any means a definitive measure of the government's health or, more importantly, the effect of government investment on the economy. It does not, for example, adequately capture the effects of education, health care, and similar investments that, in the new global economy, are arguably more important than traditional public works. But it serves as a proxy for the shift away from investment—and to remind us that the composition of spending is as important as its totals.

It is often argued that the problem of government investment is not that we are not spending enough, but that the government is not spending it wisely enough. There is always need for more improvement in the efficiency of the public sector. But there is no serious evidence that the public sector is less efficient than it was in the past, when the valuable investments we are currently living on were made. Indeed, a good case can be made that the public sector as a whole is more efficient than it used to be. Moreover, many of the measures used to denounce the public sector—like the calculation of liabilities without assets—are misleading. Thus, for example, it is commonly charged that funding of the public schools has doubled with no commensurate rise in SAT scores. But the great bulk of the increase in school funding has been for special education—largely to extend school services to the physically and mentally handicapped. One can argue the merits of such policy, but spending on such disadvantaged groups cannot be expected to affect the performance on SATs. Moreover, SAT scores, after declining between 1965 and 1975, have held steady since, which is a remarkable performance considering that one-third more students (primarily those who rank lower in school achievement) take the SATs than in the 1970s. Finally, as a very labor-intensive service, education costs should be expected to rise somewhat faster than the costs of other goods and services. Adjusted for inflation, education spending has risen a modest 1 percent per year. More money is not the sole answer to the problem of education in America, but in a market economy, little improvement can be expected without it. If money were not important, we would not see the huge disparity in funding between schools in upper- and lower-income neighborhoods.

WHERE WILL THE MONEY COME FROM?

Despite the growing investment gap in each of the three major public investment categories—education and training, infrastructure, and research and development—the problem of funding remains.

Capital Budgeting

The first step toward solving the money problem is to keep in mind that there is nothing wrong with borrowing if the proceeds are dedicated to investment that generates a return greater than the cost of borrowing. And in any sensible accounting system, investments would be separated from operating expenditures and amortized over time. The revenue stream can come from the tax proceeds of a more efficient economy and, where appropriate, fees or tolls from specific projects. The treatment of less-tangible investments such as education and training is more complex than, say, the investment in fixed assets such as bridges or schools. But the U.S. government already has developed statistical

techniques for doing so. In any event, it is hard to argue that in an information age, the improvement of skills for the working population is not an investment in the future. Thus, if it makes sense for an individual to borrow for his or her education, it surely makes sense for the U.S. government to borrow to educate its people.

Beyond education and training there are other human investments that one can argue are equally important—spending on children's nutrition, public health, and public safety. Indeed, many argue that the reason not to have a capital budget is that there are so many government activities that might arguably be considered as investments that a capital budget would rationalize borrowing for any purpose. This is an exaggeration, but in any event, it would be healthy to have a public debate over defining public investment. Certainly, there is little reason to hide these problems from the public.

Capital budgeting is not compatible with the demand to put the budget, as we now calculate it, into permanent balance. But it is compatible with federal fiscal responsibility. For example, the current Republican-led Congressional Budget Office has pointed out that it is not necessary to achieve balance in order to assure a sustainable budget as far into the future as we can see. A budgetary strategy aimed at stabilizing the ratio of national debt to GDP would permit us to run permanent deficits on the order to 1.5–2 percent of GDP. Without going to a full-fledged capital budget, we could raise the level of public investment by this amount (representing over $130–175 billion in 1999) and remain within the bounds of sensible fiscal discipline.

Infrastructure Bank

Even within the balanced-budget framework, there remains a number of strategies to raise public infrastructure investments. For example, as suggested by financier Felix Rohatyn and former New York City budget director Carol O'Cleireacain, the federal government could create an off-budget infrastructure fund with a fixed long-term revenue stream—say a gasoline or energy tax. The fund would permit a much-needed investment catch-up within the confines of fiscal austerity. A $10 billion revenue stream could generate $25 billion in federal investment over the first ten years, much of which would be concentrated in the nation's cities, not only to repair and replace much-neglected transportation and water systems and other capital stock, but also to provide jobs and opportunities. These investments become the backbone of a twenty-first-century program of urban revitalization, and the jobs created would not simply be pick-and-shovel jobs. Today's public work construction requires computer skills and technical knowledge that would represent career opportunities for thousands of young people in the inner city.

Human Capital

Money for more investment in education and training could come from a small dedicated tax on financial securities. Such a tax would have the added benefit of helping to discourage financial market speculation and reduce market volatility. It would also be highly and appropriately progressive, shifting resources from often empty and speculative "investment" in stocks and bonds to real productive investment in people.

A 0.25 percent tax on all stock transactions, for example, with an appropriately weighted tax applied to bonds, options, futures, currency swaps, and other financial instruments would raise over $30 billion per year with little impact on the normal functioning of financial markets. The costs of transactions on the major stock exchanges have fallen rapidly over the last twenty years. So even if the full cost of the tax is passed on to the buyers of financial instruments, average transaction costs would be raised only to their 1982 levels.

Finding the Peace Dividend

We now plan to spend as many real dollars on defense in the year 2000 as we did in 1975—in the midst of the cold war, when the Soviet Union, armed to the teeth, was threatening to bury us.

The rationale is that we must be prepared to fight two simultaneous wars with "rogue states"—North Korea, Cuba, Libya, Syria, Iraq, or Iran. The *combined* military budgets of these nations in 1995 was at most $15 billion, as opposed to a $265 billion U.S. military budget. We are spending roughly $80 billion for the defense of Western Europe alone at a time when the Soviet Union has disappeared and the former communist nations of Eastern Europe are clamoring to join the Western alliance. We spend at least $35 billion to maintain a bloated and unaccountable Central Intelligence Agency at cold war levels.

Defense experts such as William Kaufmann and Lawrence Korb estimate that we could easily cut another $40 billion a year from the Clinton military budget, and more from the even greater military spending advocated by the Republican leadership. Such a cut would still leave the United States with by far the single most powerful military force in the world.

The prize here is not just the saving of money. It is the opportunity to find civilian uses for the technical resources that the nation has bought and paid for in the decades of high defense spending. Successful conversion can happen only if it is linked to a public investment strategy, because there is almost no private market for the technology we built to fight the cold war. Either we continue to waste it by producing and exporting weapons that neither we nor the rest of the world needs, dismantle it and lose our investment, or apply it to the great internal development project of rebuilding America.

Other Potential Sources of Dedicated Taxes

The United States is the least-taxed economy in the advanced world. One reason is that our tax system remains riddled with preferences and unequal treatment. The politics of tax policy make it extremely difficult to eliminate many of these tax loopholes because the benefits are general (deficit reduction) and the costs are specific to industries, individuals, and firms. But if the benefits were dedicated to specific public investments, whose case has been effectively argued, the potential for raising revenues could be enhanced.

Many billions of dollars for investment might be shifted from tax expenditures that do neither the economy nor the society any good. Examples include loopholes through which foreign corporations avoid paying U.S. taxes, interest subsidies to state and local bonds used for private purposes, and specific tax preferences for the insurance, thrift, mining, pharmaceutical, and timber industries. Other possibilities include the taxation of air and water pollution, which in effect would represent a collection of rent for the use of the public's domain.

Public Leadership

Implicit in the call for expanded infrastructure investment is an assumption of a civilian public sector capable of allocating resources and understanding the long-term needs of the economy. After at least two decades of systematic ideological attack, this assumption is problematic. The reason for some of the opposition to more public investment is the widespread conviction that the government is, by its very nature, incompetent. In fact, the decline in public confidence in government over the last twenty years has mirrored the decline in public investment. Yet the bulk of the American people remain convinced that the government should be responsible for providing opportunities for work, training, social services, and the regulation of the marketplace. A 1995 Harris poll for *Business Week* showed 70 percent or more of the electorate thought the federal government had a responsibility for providing a job for those willing to work, providing continued access to job training, providing a minimum level of health care, and making sure that business sells safe products.

One clue on how to solve this puzzle is a comparison of the civilian government's leadership role in America's past economic development. Unlike many other nations, where civilian government *per se* is accepted as important, government in America has by and large been successful when it has been "mission" oriented, when its energy has been applied to specific national goals—creating a barge canal network, a transcontinental rail-road track, a space program, or a more productive agriculture. For most of the past half-century, the overriding public investment task has been prevailing in the cold war. In fact, the two major civilian infrastructure efforts of the post–World War II period— education and highways—were promoted as part of national defense. With the end of the cold war, it may well be that in order to obtain the political support for investing in a twenty-first-century infrastructure, we need to define a new national task for the twenty-first century—the domestic redevelopment of the United States, its cities, its transportation systems, its telecommunications networks, and, most of all, its people.

Democracy as a Universal Value

AMARTYA SEN

In the summer of 1997, I was asked by a leading Japanese newspaper what I thought was the most important thing that had happened in the twentieth century. I found this to be an unusually thought-provoking question, since so many things of gravity have happened over the last hundred years. The European empires, especially the British and French ones that had so dominated the nineteenth century, came to an end. We witnessed two world wars. We saw the rise and fall of fascism and Nazism. The century witnessed the rise of communism, and its fall (as in the former Soviet bloc) or radical transformation (as in China). We also saw a shift from the economic dominance of the West to a new economic balance much more dominated by Japan and East and Southeast Asia. Even though that region is going through some financial and economic problems right now, this is not going to nullify the shift in the balance of the world economy that has occurred over many decades (in the case of Japan, through nearly the entire century). The past hundred years are not lacking in important events.

Nevertheless, among the great variety of developments that have occurred in the twentieth century, I did not, ultimately, have any difficulty in choosing one as the preeminent development of the period: the rise of democracy. This is not to deny that other

occurrences have also been important, but I would argue that in the distant future, when people look back at what happened in this century, they will find it difficult not to accord primacy to the emergence of democracy as the preeminently acceptable form of governance.

The idea of democracy originated, of course, in ancient Greece, more than two millennia ago. Piecemeal efforts at democratization were attempted elsewhere as well, including in India.[1] But it is really in ancient Greece that the idea of democracy took shape and was seriously put into practice (albeit on a limited scale), before it collapsed and was replaced by more authoritarian and asymmetric forms of government. There were no other kinds anywhere else.

Thereafter, democracy as we know it took a long time to emerge. Its gradual—and ultimately triumphant—emergence as a working system of governance was bolstered by many developments, from the signing of the Magna Carta in 1215, to the French and the American Revolutions in the eighteenth century, to the widening of the franchise in Europe and North America in the nineteenth century. It was in the twentieth century, however, that the idea of democracy became established as the "normal" form of government to which any nation is entitled—whether in Europe, America, Asia, or Africa.

The idea of democracy as a universal commitment is quite new, and it is quintessentially a product of the twentieth century. The rebels who forced restraint on the king of England through

Source: Amartya Sen. "Democracy as a Universal Value." *Journal of Democracy* 10:3 (1999), 3–17. © National Endowment for Democracy and The Johns Hopkins University Press. Reprinted with permission of The Johns Hopkins University Press.

the Magna Carta saw the need as an entirely local one. In contrast, the American fighters for independence and the revolutionaries in France contributed greatly to an understanding of the need for democracy as a general system. Yet the focus of their practical demands remained quite local—confined, in effect, to the two sides of the North Atlantic, and founded on the special economic, social, and political history of the region.

Throughout the nineteenth century, theorists of democracy found it quite natural to discuss whether one country or another was "fit for democracy." This thinking changed only in the twentieth century, with the recognition that the question itself was wrong: A country does not have to be deemed fit *for* democracy; rather, it has to become fit *through* democracy. This is indeed a momentous change, extending the potential reach of democracy to cover billions of people, with their varying histories and cultures and disparate levels of affluence.

It was also in this century that people finally accepted that "franchise for all adults" must mean *all*—not just men but also women. When in January of this year I had the opportunity to meet Ruth Dreyfuss, the president of Switzerland and a woman of remarkable distinction, it gave me occasion to recollect that only a quarter century ago Swiss women could not even vote. We have at last reached the point of recognizing that the coverage of universality, like the quality of mercy, is not strained.

I do not deny that there are challenges to democracy's claim to universality. These challenges come in many shapes and forms—and from different directions. Indeed, that is part of the subject of this essay. I have to examine the claim of democracy as a universal value and the disputes that surround that claim. Before I begin that exercise, however, it is necessary to grasp clearly the sense in which democracy has become a dominant belief in the contemporary world.

In any age and social climate, there are some sweeping beliefs that seem to command respect as a kind of general rule—like a "default" setting in a computer program; they are considered right

unless their claim is somehow precisely negated. While democracy is not yet universally practiced, nor indeed uniformly accepted, in the general climate of world opinion, democratic governance has now achieved the status of being taken to be generally right. The ball is very much in the court of those who want to rubbish democracy to provide justification for that rejection.

This is a historic change from not very long ago, when the advocates of democracy for Asia or Africa had to argue for democracy with their backs to the wall. While we still have reason enough to dispute those who, implicitly or explicitly, reject the need for democracy, we must also note clearly how the general climate of opinion has shifted from what it was in previous centuries. We do not have to establish afresh, each time, whether such and such a country (South Africa, or Cambodia, or Chile) is "fit for democracy" (a question that was prominent in the discourse of the nineteenth century); we now take that for granted. This recognition of democracy as a universally relevant system, which moves in the direction of its acceptance as a universal value, is a major revolution in thinking, and one of the main contributions of the twentieth century. It is in this context that we have to examine the question of democracy as a universal value.

THE INDIAN EXPERIENCE

How well has democracy worked? While no one really questions the role of democracy in, say, the United States or Britain or France, it is still a matter of dispute for many of the poorer countries in the world. This is not the occasion for a detailed examination of the historical record, but I would argue that democracy has worked well enough.

India, of course, was one of the major battlegrounds of this debate. In denying Indians independence, the British expressed anxiety over the Indians' ability to govern themselves. India was indeed in some disarray in 1947, the year it became independent. It had an untried government, an undigested partition, and unclear political alignments, combined with widespread communal violence and social disorder. It was hard to have faith in the future of a united and democratic India. And yet, half a century later, we find a democracy that has, taking the rough with the smooth, worked remarkably well. Political differences have been largely tackled within the constitutional guidelines, and governments have risen and fallen according to electoral and parliamentary rules. An ungainly, unlikely, inelegant combination of differences, India nonetheless survives and functions remarkably well as a political unit with a democratic system. Indeed, it is held together by its working democracy.

India has also survived the tremendous challenge of dealing with a variety of major languages and a spectrum of religions. Religious and communal differences are, of course, vulnerable to exploitation by sectarian politicians, and have indeed been so used on several occasions (including in recent months), causing massive consternation in the country. Yet the fact that consternation greets sectarian violence and that condemnation of such violence comes from all sections of the country ultimately provides the main democratic guarantee against the narrowly factional exploitation of sectarianism. This is, of course, essential for the survival and prosperity of a country as remarkably varied as India, which is home not only to a Hindu majority, but to the world's third largest Muslim population, to millions of Christians and Buddhists, and to most of the world's Sikhs, Parsees, and Jains.

DEMOCRACY AND ECONOMIC DEVELOPMENT

It is often claimed that nondemocratic systems are better at bringing about economic development. This belief sometimes goes by the name of "the Lee hypothesis," due to its advocacy by Lee Kuan Yew, the leader and former president of Singapore. He is certainly right that some disciplinarian states (such as South Korea, his own Singapore, and postreform China) have had faster rates of economic growth than many less authoritarian ones (including India, Jamaica, and Costa Rica). The "Lee hypothesis," however, is based on

sporadic empiricism, drawing on very selective and limited information, rather than on any general statistical testing over the wide-ranging data that are available. A general relation of this kind cannot be established on the basis of very selective evidence. For example, we cannot really take the high economic growth of Singapore or China as "definitive proof" that authoritarianism does better in promoting economic growth, any more than we can draw the opposite conclusion from the fact that Botswana, the country with the best record of economic growth in Africa, indeed with one of the finest records of economic growth in the whole world, has been an oasis of democracy on that continent over the decades. We need more systematic empirical studies to sort out the claims and counterclaims.

There is, in fact, no convincing general evidence that authoritarian governance and the suppression of political and civil rights are really beneficial to economic development. Indeed, the general statistical picture does not permit any such induction. Systematic empirical studies (for example, by Robert Barro or by Adam Przeworski) give no real support to the claim that there is a general conflict between political rights and economic performance.[2] The directional linkage seems to depend on many other circumstances, and while some statistical investigations note a weakly negative relation, others find a strongly positive one. If all the comparative studies are viewed together, the hypothesis that there is no clear relation between economic growth and democracy in *either* direction remains extremely plausible. Since democracy and political liberty have importance in themselves, the case for them therefore remains untarnished.[3]

The question also involves a fundamental issue of methods of economic research. We must not only look at statistical connections, but also examine and scrutinize the *causal* processes that are involved in economic growth and development. The economic policies and circumstances that led to the economic success of countries in East Asia are by now reasonably well understood. While different empirical studies have varied in emphasis, there is by now broad consensus on a list of "helpful policies" that includes openness to competition, the use of international markets, public provision of incentives for investment and export, a high level of literacy and schooling, successful land reforms, and other social opportunities that widen participation in the process of economic expansion. There is no reason at all to assume that any of these policies is inconsistent with greater democracy and had to be forcibly sustained by the elements of authoritarianism that happened to be present in South Korea or Singapore or China. Indeed, there is overwhelming evidence to show that what is needed for generating faster economic growth is a friendlier economic climate rather than a harsher political system.

To complete this examination, we must go beyond the narrow confines of economic growth and scrutinize the broader demands of economic development, including the need for economic and social security. In that context, we have to look at the connection between political and civil rights, on the one hand, and the prevention of major economic disasters, on the other. Political and civil rights give people the opportunity to draw attention forcefully to general needs and to demand appropriate public action. The response of a government to the acute suffering of its people often depends on the pressure that is put on it. The exercise of political rights (such as voting, criticizing, protesting, and the like) can make a real difference to the political incentives that operate on a government.

I have discussed elsewhere the remarkable fact that, in the terrible history of famines in the world, no substantial famine has ever occurred in any independent and democratic country with a relatively free press.[4] We cannot find exceptions to this rule, no matter where we look: the recent famines of Ethiopia, Somalia, or other dictatorial regimes; famines in the Soviet Union in the 1930s; China's 1958–61 famine with the failure of the Great Leap Forward; or earlier still, the famines in Ireland or India under alien rule. China, although it was in many ways doing much better economically than India, still managed (unlike India) to have a famine, indeed the largest recorded famine in world

history: Nearly 30 million people died in the famine of 1958–61, while faulty governmental policies remained uncorrected for three full years. The policies went uncriticized because there were no opposition parties in parliament, no free press, and no multiparty elections. Indeed, it is precisely this lack of challenge that allowed the deeply defective policies to continue even though they were killing millions each year. The same can be said about the world's two contemporary famines, occurring right now in North Korea and Sudan.

Famines are often associated with what look like natural disasters, and commentators often settle for the simplicity of explaining famines by pointing to these events: the floods in China during the failed Great Leap Forward, the droughts in Ethiopia, or crop failures in North Korea. Nevertheless, many countries with similar natural problems, or even worse ones, manage perfectly well, because a responsive government intervenes to help alleviate hunger. Since the primary victims of a famine are the indigent, deaths can be prevented by recreating incomes (for example, through employment programs), which makes food accessible to potential famine victims. Even the poorest democratic countries that have faced terrible droughts or floods or other natural disasters (such as India in 1973, or Zimbabwe and Botswana in the early 1980s) have been able to feed their people without experiencing a famine.

Famines are easy to prevent if there is a serious effort to do so, and a democratic government, facing elections and criticisms from opposition parties and independent newspapers, cannot help but make such an effort. Not surprisingly, while India continued to have famines under British rule right up to independence (the last famine, which I witnessed as a child, was in 1943, four years before independence), they disappeared suddenly with the establishment of a multiparty democracy and a free press.

I have discussed these issues elsewhere, particularly in my joint work with Jean Dr'eze, so I will not dwell further on them here.[5] Indeed, the issue of famine is only one example of the reach of democracy, though it is, in many ways, the easiest case to analyze. The positive role of political and civil rights applies to the prevention of economic and social disasters in general. When things go fine and everything is routinely good, this instrumental role of democracy may not be particularly missed. It is when things get fouled up, for one reason or another, that the political incentives provided by democratic governance acquire great practical value.

There is, I believe, an important lesson here. Many economic technocrats recommend the use of economic incentives (which the market system provides) while ignoring political incentives (which democratic systems could guarantee). This is to opt for a deeply unbalanced set of ground rules. The protective power of democracy may not be missed much when a country is lucky enough to be facing no serious calamity, when everything is going quite smoothly. Yet the danger of insecurity, arising from changed economic or other circumstances, or from uncorrected mistakes of policy, can lurk behind what looks like a healthy state.

The recent problems of East and Southeast Asia bring out, among other things, the penalties of undemocratic governance. This is so in two striking respects. First, the development of the financial crisis in some of these economies (including South Korea, Thailand, Indonesia) has been closely linked to the lack of transparency in business, in particular the lack of public participation in reviewing financial arrangements. The absence of an effective democratic forum has been central to this failing. Second, once the financial crisis led to a general economic recession, the protective power of democracy—not unlike that which prevents famines in democratic countries—was badly missed in a country like Indonesia. The newly dispossessed did not have the hearing they needed.

A fall in total gross national product of, say, 10 percent may not look like much if it follows in the wake of a growth rate of 5 or 10 percent every year over the past few decades, and yet that decline can decimate lives and create misery for millions if the burden of contraction is not widely shared but allowed to be heaped on those—the unemployed or the economically redundant—who can least bear it. The vulnerable in Indonesia may not have missed democracy when things went up and up, but that lacuna kept their voice low and muffled as the unequally shared crisis developed. The protective role of democracy is strongly missed when it is most needed.

THE FUNCTIONS OF DEMOCRACY

I have so far allowed the agenda of this essay to be determined by the critics of democracy, especially the economic critics. I shall return to criticisms again, taking up the arguments of the cultural critics in particular, but the time has come for me to pursue further the positive analysis of what democracy does and what may lie at the base of its claim to be a universal value.

What exactly is democracy? We must not identify democracy with majority rule. Democracy has complex demands, which certainly include voting and respect for election results, but it also requires the protection of liberties and freedoms, respect for legal entitlements, and the guaranteeing of free discussion and uncensored distribution of news and fair comment. Even elections can be deeply defective if they occur without the different sides getting an adequate opportunity to present their respective cases, or without the electorate enjoying the freedom to obtain news and to consider the views of the competing protagonists. Democracy is a demanding system, and not just a mechanical condition (like majority rule) taken in isolation.

Viewed in this light, the merits of democracy and its claim as a universal value can be related to certain distinct virtues that go with its unfettered practice. Indeed, we can distinguish three different ways in which democracy enriches the lives of the citizens. First, political freedom is a part of human freedom in general, and exercising civil and political rights is a crucial part of good lives of individuals as social beings. Political and social participation has *intrinsic value* for human life and well-being. To be prevented from participation in the political life of the community is a major deprivation.

Second, as I have just discussed (in disputing the claim that democracy is in tension with economic development), democracy has an important *instrumental value* in enhancing the hearing that people get in expressing and supporting their claims to political attention (including claims of economic needs). Third—and this is a point to be explored further—the practice of democracy gives citizens an opportunity to learn from one another, and helps society to form its values and priorities. Even the idea of "needs," including the understanding of "economic needs," requires public discussion and exchange of information, views, and analyses. In this sense, democracy has *constructive* importance, in addition to its intrinsic value for the lives of the citizens and its instrumental importance in political decisions. The claims of democracy as a universal value have to take note of this diversity of considerations.

The conceptualization—even comprehension—of what are to count as "needs," including "economic needs," may itself require the exercise of political and civil rights. A proper understanding of what economic needs are—their content and their force—may require discussion and exchange. Political and civil rights, especially those related to the guaranteeing of open discussion, debate, criticism, and dissent, are central to the process of generating informed and considered choices. These processes are crucial to the formation of values and priorities, and we cannot, in general, take preferences as given independently of public discussion, that is, irrespective of whether open interchange and debate are permitted or not.

In fact, the reach and effectiveness of open dialogue are often underestimated in assessing social and political problems. For example, public discussion has an important role to play in reducing the high rates of fertility that characterize many developing countries. There is substantial evidence that the sharp decline in fertility rates in India's more literate states has been much influenced by public discussion of the bad effects of high fertility rates on the community at large, and especially on the lives of young women. If the view has emerged in, say, the Indian state of Kerala or of Tamil Nadu that a happy family in the modern age is a small family, much discussion and debate have gone into the formation of these perspectives. Kerala now has a fertility rate of 1.7 (similar to that of Britain and France, and well below China's 1.9), and this has been achieved with no coercion, but mainly through the emergence of new values—a process in which political and social dialogue has played a major part. Kerala's high literacy rate (it ranks higher in literacy than any province in China), especially among women, has greatly contributed to making such social and political dialogue possible.

Miseries and deprivations can be of various kinds, some more amenable to social remedies than others. The totality of the human predicament would be a gross basis for identifying our "needs." For example, there are many things that we might have good reason to value and thus could be taken as "needs" if they were feasible. We could even want immortality, as Maitreyee, that remarkable inquiring mind in the *Upanishads,* famously did in her 3000-year-old conversation with Yajnvalkya. But we do not see immortality as a "need" because it is clearly unfeasible. Our conception of needs relates to our ideas of the preventable nature of some deprivations and to our understanding of what can be done about them. In the formation of understandings and beliefs about feasibility (particularly, *social* feasibility), public discussions play a crucial role. Political rights, including freedom of expression and discussion, are not only pivotal in inducing social responses to economic needs, they are also central to the conceptualization of economic needs themselves.

UNIVERSALITY OF VALUES

If the above analysis is correct, then democracy's claim to be valuable does not rest on just one particular merit. There is a plurality of virtues here, including, first, the *intrinsic* importance of political participation and freedom in human life; second, the *instrumental* importance of political incentives in keeping governments responsible and accountable; and third, the *constructive* role of democracy in the formation of values and in the understanding of needs, rights, and duties. In the light of this diagnosis, we may now address the motivating question of this essay, namely the case for seeing democracy as a universal value.

In disputing this claim, it is sometimes argued that not everyone agrees on the decisive importance of democracy, particularly when it competes with other desirable things for our attention and loyalty. This is indeed so, and there is no unanimity here. This lack of unanimity is seen by some as sufficient evidence that democracy is not a universal value.

Clearly, we must begin by dealing with a methodological question: What is a universal value? For a value to be considered universal, must it have the consent of everyone? If that were indeed necessary, then the category of universal values might well be empty. I know of no value—not even motherhood (I think of *Mommie Dearest*)—to which no one has ever objected. I would argue that universal consent is not required for something to be a universal value. Rather, the claim of a universal value is that people anywhere may have reason to see it as valuable.

When Mahatma Gandhi argued for the universal value of non-violence, he was not arguing that people everywhere already acted according to this value, but rather that they had good reason to see it as valuable. Similarly, when Rabindranath Tagore argued for "the freedom of the mind" as a universal value, he was not saying that this claim is accepted by all, but that all do have reason enough to accept it—a reason that he did much to explore, present, and propagate.[6] Understood in this way, any claim that something is a universal value involves some counterfactual analysis—in particular, whether people might see some value in a claim that they have not yet considered adequately. All claims to universal value—not just that of democracy—have this implicit presumption.

I would argue that it is with regard to this often *implicit* presumption that the biggest attitudinal shift toward democracy has occurred in the twentieth century. In considering democracy for a country that does not have it and where many people may not yet have had the opportunity to consider it for actual practice, it is now presumed that the people involved would approve of it once it becomes a reality in their lives. In the nineteenth century this assumption typically would have not been made, but the presumption that is taken to be natural (what I earlier called the "default" position) has changed radically during the twentieth century.

It must also be noted that this change is, to a great extent, based on observing the history of the twentieth century. As democracy has spread, its adherents have grown, not shrunk. Starting off from Europe and America, democracy as a system has reached very many distant shores, where it has been met with willing participation and acceptance. Moreover, when an existing democracy has been overthrown, there have been widespread protests, even though these protests have often been brutally suppressed. Many people have been willing to risk their lives in the fight to bring back democracy.

Some who dispute the status of democracy as a universal value base their argument not on the absence of unanimity, but on the presence of regional contrasts. These alleged contrasts are sometimes related to the poverty of some nations. According to this argument, poor people are interested, and have reason to be interested, in bread, not in democracy. This oft-repeated argument is fallacious at two different levels.

First, as discussed above, the protective role of democracy may be particularly important for the poor. This obviously applies to potential famine victims who face starvation. It also applies to the destitute thrown off the economic ladder in a financial crisis. People in economic need also need a political voice. Democracy is not a luxury that can await the arrival of general prosperity.

Second, there is very little evidence that poor people, given the choice, prefer to reject democracy.

It is thus of some interest to note that when an erstwhile Indian government in the mid-1970s tried out a similar argument to justify the alleged "emergency" (and the suppression of various political and civil rights) that it had declared, an election was called that divided the voters precisely on this issue. In that fateful election, fought largely on this one overriding theme, the suppression of basic political and civil rights was firmly rejected, and the Indian electorate—one of the poorest in the world—showed itself to be no less keen on protesting against the denial of basic liberties and rights than on complaining about economic deprivation.

To the extent that there has been any testing of the proposition that the poor do not care about civil and political rights, the evidence is entirely against that claim. Similar points can be made by observing the struggle for democratic freedoms in South Korea, Thailand, Bangladesh, Pakistan, Burma, Indonesia, and elsewhere in Asia. Similarly, while political freedom is widely denied in Africa, there have been movements and protests against such repression whenever circumstances have permitted them.

THE ARGUMENT FROM CULTURAL DIFFERENCES

There is also another argument in defense of an allegedly fundamental regional contrast, one related not to economic circumstances but to cultural differences. Perhaps the most famous of these claims relates to what have been called "Asian values." It has been claimed that Asians traditionally value discipline, not political freedom and thus the attitude to democracy must inevitably be much more skeptical in these countries. I have discussed this thesis in some detail in my Morganthau Memorial Lecture at the Carnegie Council on Ethics and International Affairs.[7]

It is very hard to find any real basis for this intellectual claim in the history of Asian cultures, especially if we look at the classical traditions of India, the Middle East, Iran, and other parts of Asia.

For example, one of the earliest and most emphatic statements advocating the tolerance of pluralism and the duty of the state to protect minorities can be found in the inscriptions of the Indian emperor Ashoka in the third century B.C.

Asia is, of course, a very large area, containing 60 percent of the world's population, and generalizations about such a vast set of peoples is not easy. Sometimes the advocates of "Asian values" have tended to look primarily at East Asia as the region of particular applicability. The general thesis of a contrast between the West and Asia often concentrates on the lands to the east of Thailand, even though there is also a more ambitious claim that the rest of Asia is rather "similar." Lee Kuan Yew, to whom we must be grateful for being such a clear expositor (and for articulating fully what is often stated vaguely in this tangled literature), outlines "the fundamental difference between Western concepts of society and government and East Asian concepts" by explaining, "when I say East Asians, I mean Korea, Japan, China, Vietnam, as distinct from Southeast Asia, which is a mix between the Sinic and the Indian, though Indian culture itself emphasizes similar values."[8]

Even East Asia itself, however, is remarkably diverse, with many variations to be found not only among Japan, China, Korea, and other countries of the region, but also *within* each country. Confucius is the standard author quoted in interpreting Asian values, but he is not the only intellectual influence in these countries (in Japan, China, and Korea for example, there are very old and very widespread Buddhist traditions, powerful for over a millennium and a half, and there are also other influences, including a considerable Christian presence). There is no homogeneous worship of order over freedom in any of these cultures.

Furthermore, Confucius himself did not recommend blind allegiance to the state. When Zilu asks him "how to serve a prince," Confucius replies (in a statement that the censors of authoritarian regimes may want to ponder), "Tell him the truth even if it offends him."[9] Confucius is not averse to practical caution and tact, but does not forgo the recommendation to oppose a bad government (tactfully, if necessary): "When the [good] way prevails in the state, speak boldly and act boldly. When the state has lost the way, act boldly and speak softly."[10]

Indeed, Confucius provides a clear pointer to the fact that the two pillars of the imagined edifice of Asian values, loyalty to family and obedience to the state, can be in severe conflict with each other. Many advocates of the power of "Asian values" see the role of the state as an extension of the role of the family, but as Confucius noted, there can be tension between the two. The Governor of She told Confucius, "Among my people, there is a man of unbending integrity: when his father stole a sheep, he denounced him." To this Confucius replied, "Among my people, men of integrity do things differently: a father covers up for his son, a son covers up for his father—and there is integrity in what they do."[11]

The monolithic interpretation of Asian values as hostile to democracy and political rights does not bear critical scrutiny. I should not, I suppose, be too critical of the lack of scholarship supporting these beliefs, since those who have made these claims are not scholars but political leaders, often official or unofficial spokesmen for authoritarian governments. It is, however, interesting to see that while we academics can be impractical about practical politics, practical politicians can, in turn, be rather impractical about scholarship.

It is not hard, of course, to find authoritarian writings within the Asian traditions. But neither is it hard to find them in Western classics: One has only to reflect on the writings of Plato or Aquinas to see that devotion to discipline is not a special Asian taste. To dismiss the plausibility of democracy as a universal value because of the presence of some Asian writings on discipline and order would be similar to rejecting the plausibility of democracy as a natural form of government in Europe or America today on the basis of the writings of Plato or Aquinas (not to mention the substantial medieval literature in support of the Inquisitions).

Due to the experience of contemporary political battles, especially in the Middle East, Islam is often portrayed as fundamentally intolerant of and hostile to individual freedom. But the presence of diversity and variety *within* a tradition applies very much to Islam as well. In India, Akbar and most of the other Moghul emperors (with the notable exception of Aurangzeb) provide good examples of both the theory and practice of political and religious tolerance. The Turkish emperors were often more tolerant than their European contemporaries. Abundant examples can also be found among rulers in Cairo and Baghdad. Indeed, in the twelfth century, the great Jewish scholar Maimonides had to run away from an intolerant Europe (where he was born), and from its persecution of Jews, to the security of a tolerant and urbane Cairo and the patronage of Sultan Saladin.

Diversity is a feature of most cultures in the world. Western civilization is no exception. The practice of democracy that has won out in the *modern* West is largely a result of a consensus that has emerged since the Enlightenment and the Industrial Revolution, and particularly in the last century or so. To read in this a historical commitment of the West—over the millennia—to democracy, and then to contrast it with non-Western traditions (treating each as monolithic) would be a great mistake. This tendency toward oversimplification can be seen not only in the writings of some governmental spokesmen in Asia, but also in the theories of some of the finest Western scholars themselves.

As an example from the writings of a major scholar whose works, in many other ways, have been totally impressive, let me cite Samuel Huntington's thesis on the clash of civilizations, where the heterogeneities *within* each culture get quite inadequate recognition. His study comes to the clear conclusion that "a sense of individualism and a tradition of rights and liberties" can be found in the West that are "unique among civilized societies."[12] Huntington also argues that "the central characteristics of the West, those which distinguish it from other civilizations, antedate the modernization of the West." In his view, "The West was West long before it was modern."[13] It is this thesis that—I have argued—does not survive historical scrutiny.

For every attempt by an Asian government spokesman to contrast alleged "Asian values" with alleged Western ones, there is, it seems, an attempt by a Western intellectual to make a similar contrast from the other side. But even though every Asian pull may be matched by a Western push, the two together do not really manage to dent democracy's claim to be a universal value.

WHERE THE DEBATE BELONGS

I have tried to cover a number of issues related to the claim that democracy is a universal value. The value of democracy includes its *intrinsic importance* in human life, its *instrumental role* in generating political incentives, and its *constructive function* in the formation of values (and in understanding the force and feasibility of claims of needs, rights, and duties). These merits are not regional in character. Nor is the advocacy of discipline or order. Heterogeneity of values seems to characterize most, perhaps all, major cultures. The cultural argument does not foreclose, nor indeed deeply constrain, the choices we can make today.

Those choices have to be made here and now, taking note of the functional roles of democracy, on which the case for democracy in the contemporary world depends. I have argued that this case is indeed strong and not regionally contingent. The force of the claim that democracy is a universal value lies, ultimately, in that strength. That is where the debate belongs. It cannot be disposed of by imagined cultural taboos or assumed civilizational predispositions imposed by our various pasts.

NOTES

1. In Aldous Huxley's novel *Point Counter Point,* this was enough to give an adequate excuse to a cheating husband, who tells his wife that he must go to London to study democracy in ancient India in the library of the British Museum, while in reality he goes to see his mistress.

2. Adam Przeworski et al., *Sustainable Democracy* (Cambridge: Cambridge University Press, 1995); Robert J. Barro, *Getting It Right: Markets and Choices in a Free Society* (Cambridge, Mass.: MIT Press, 1996).

3. I have examined the empirical evidence and causal connections in some detail in my book *Development as Freedom,* forthcoming from Knopf in 1999.

4. See my "Development: Which Way Now?" *Economic Journal* 93 (December 1983); *Resources, Values, and Development* (Cambridge, Mass.: Harvard University Press, 1984); and my "Rationality and Social Choice," presidential address to the American Economic Association, published in *American Economic Review* in March 1995. See also Jean Dr'eze and Amartya Sen, *Hunger and Public Action* (Oxford: Clarendon Press, 1987); Frances D'Souza, ed., *Starving in Silence: A Report on Famine and Censorship* (London: Article 19 International Centre on Censorship, 1990); Human Rights Watch, *Indivisible Human Rights: The Relationship between Political and Civil Rights to Survival, Subsistence and Poverty* (New York: Human Rights Watch, 1992); and International Federation of Red Cross and Red Crescent Societies, *World Disaster Report 1994* (Geneva: Red Cross, 1994).

5. Dr'eze and Sen, *Hunger and Public Action.*

6. See my "Tagore and His India," *New York Review of Books,* 26 June 1997.

7. Amartya Sen, "Human Rights and Asian Values," Morgenthau Memorial Lecture (New York: Carnegie Council on Ethics and International Affairs, 1997), published in a shortened form in *The New Republic,* 14–21 July 1997.

8. Fareed Zakaria, "Culture is Destiny: A Conversation with Lee Kuan Yew," *Foreign Affairs* 73 (March–April 1994): 113.

9. *The Analects of Confucius,* Simon Leys, trans. (New York: Norton, 1997), 14.22, 70.

10. *The Analects of Confucius,* 14.3, 66.

11. *The Analects of Confucius,* 13.18, 63.

12. Samuel P. Huntington, *The Clash of Civilizations and the Remaking of World Order* (New York: Simon and Schuster, 1996), 71.

13. Huntington, *The Clash of Civilizations,* 69.

Equality and Democracy

PHILIP GREEN

COMPETING SOLIDARITIES

An egalitarian society . . . cannot be founded on merely materialistic premises. It can only be founded in deeply held feelings of social solidarity—social solidarity of the particular kind that results in collaborative political activity. What is this solidarity?

It begins in recognition that the so-called atomized individual of classical liberal ideology is a myth. That myth has been treated as a reality, of course, by the free market ideologues who find it useful in furthering their own economic interests. But it has also been ascribed an undeserved status of reality by its opponents. Whether they be traditional Marxists wanting to criticize capitalism or latter-day communitarians wanting to criticize liberal pluralism, these opponents have found it useful to ascribe to their enemy (capitalism, liberalism) something that is manifestly not true: that it *creates* "atomized individuals." On the contrary: capitalism (for the Marxist critics of capitalism are much more correct than the communitarian critics of liberalism) *pulverizes* both communities and thus individuals. It never, however, succeeds in eliminating their fundamental connection; which is not local and parochial, as the communitarians have it, but human.

There is indeed solidarity; there is indeed a General Will. It would be a strange individual who has

Source: Philip Green, "Equality and Democracy," In *Equality and Democracy,* New York: The New Press, 1998: 171–184.

never had the experience of voluntarily submitting his or her own desires to those of a more general sociality. More precisely, however, there are competing solidarities—of nation, community, religion, ethnicity, gender, sexuality, class—and many general wills, not just one. Rather than surrendering themselves to some preestablished unity, the goal of egalitarians is to forge a unity out of many solidarities.

To suggest that this might be easy would be the thinnest pretense. We have already seen how historically burdened perceptions of racial difference can divide an entire polity and how class distance can fracture a mass political movement. The example of two other, equally burdensome types of divisive solidarity makes this point even more clear, for many of us accept them without even the faintest intellectual unease.

The first of these has to do with the geographical boundaries of equality among peoples. I do not mean by this the familiar and conventional question of what *nations,* or the peoples who compose them, owe each other; that is just a matter of *realpolitik,* once the assumption of multiple and competing nationhood has been accepted without reservation. I mean to ask instead the quite different question: what do *individuals* who live in separate national jurisdictions owe each other?[1] If a majority of the U.S. Congress, genuinely representing a majority of the American people, had voted to declare war on North Vietnam, would that have made it "right"? Who should have participated in that vote? As Robert Nozick has remarked, there's no intellectually principled reason for stopping majority rule at the water's edge. Again, I know that the shirt I buy labeled Made in Indonesia is made by viciously oppressed, mostly female labor, but do I have any obligations of solidarity with those women, such as I felt with "American" farm laborers during the various produce boycotts called by Cesar Chavez's farm workers union?

Clearly, any consideration of such questions by me or any other inhabitant of the world's most technologically advanced and powerful capitalist society can only be partial and painfully tentative. It can only take off from, and build on, the work of those spokespersons who can genuinely try to speak for what Fanon called "les damnees de la terre," because they have inhabited the same life-world as, or at the very least lived side by side with, those people whose material needs are so often markedly different from, and vastly greater than, the expressed needs of the Western working class.[2]

From this very limited "First World" standpoint, the beginning of any answer to the questions I've asked above is obviously that, the artificiality of national boundaries aside, my most immediate obligations are to those persons who have an historical reason to expect them from me, and who might be expected to feel similar obligations to me in return. But that's only the beginning of an answer. The boundaries are still artificial, historical tradition or not, compared to the unavoidable universality of any ethical principle, such as the principle of equality. It's no use saying, as Michael Walzer and other communitarians say, that principles of justice must be based on "shared understandings" and that therefore justice is primarily local; or that, as various post-modernists assert, ideals such as "justice" and "equality" are nothing but socially variable linguistic constructions.[3] Stated so baldly, neither of these positions is tenable.

Quite to the contrary, I would suggest that there's not an iota of misunderstanding, linguistic or historical, between Indonesian workers who think that they are oppressed by domestic tyranny and exploited by Western imperialism and American economists and industrialists who preach the rationality of market choice and "comparative advantage." If representatives of each group were to read Marx (as some of them probably have), whether in a common language or in separate translations, they would all understand him perfectly well. They would have intellectual disagreements (is the labor theory of value defensible, and can a notion of fair exchange be founded on it?), and practical disagreements based on considerations of self-interest and power. But neither group would have the faintest doubt that they were arguing about the nature of economic justice, and neither would be influenced in any great degree by purely local traditions or by varying semiotic codes.

You own it, I don't own it, and you say that therefore you can do anything you want with it, even if I am badly injured by your actions. This language is a universal language par excellence, and it's understood and resisted as such in every corner of the globe. Summing up examples of resistance and revolutionary practice (on a small scale) from all over the globe, two critics of "globalization" conclude:

> If capitalist globalization is an infection, it can be said to coexist with many other types of infection. Were we not bedazzled by images of the superior morphology of global capitalism, it might be possible to theorize the global integration of noncapitalist economic relations and noneconomic relations to see capitalist globalization as coexisting with, and even facilitating, the renewed viability of noncapitalist globalization.[4]

The exact nature of the resistance will certainly be based on particularistic traditions—Walzer's "shared understandings." The communal decentralism of the Indian village, for example, produces a different idea of what ought to be done than do the Jacobinism and Bonapartism of France; but this is a difference about how, not whether, to pursue a commonly understood goal.[5]

In the same way, many Afghani or Irani women reading Mary Wollstonecraft's *Vindication of the Rights of Women* or Mill's *The Subjection of Women* for the first time might well reject their argument. But many others would accept it (and have accepted it); and in any case every female reader would know exactly what Mill, for instance, meant when he wrote, "I consider it presumption in any one to pretend to decide what women are or are not, can or cannot be, by natural constitution. They have always been hitherto kept, as far as regards spontaneous development, in so unnatural a state, that their nature cannot but have been greatly distorted and disguised . . ."[6] The principles of ideologically inspired dismissal on the one hand, and of logical reasoning on the other, are again universally visible; and the notion of equality that they reject or to which they appeal varies only in the details of its implementation, never in its core meaning.

To put these two examples as one, the Indonesian or Philipine women who are conscripted as women (by husbands, by fathers, and often by armed force) into literal wage slavery, brutalized by local tyrants, exploited by overseas corporations, and ignored by happy American consumers are being subjected to a much harsher version of the same regimen, based on the same sexual division of labor, as are American women conscripted into "paid work" by "welfare reform." If notions of equality are thought by American social critics to demand that those Americans who benefit from the exploitation of female labor abolish the conditions in which it is exploited, how can that demand not weigh even more heavily on those of us who benefit (as we all in fact do) from its much more horrific version? And if, more generally, we seek to limit the power of American-based corporations to close factories or to poison workers in Ohio or Illinois or North Carolina, then how can we not seek the same control over what those corporations do in Indonesia or the Philipines or Brazil?

Of course we, whoever we are, can't fix the whole world and ought not even to try. In the post-Reagan era, after all, most Americans have yet to put up any significant resistance to the despoiling of lives, neighborhoods, and the natural environment by corporations operating right in front of our eyes. Here Walzer is certainly correct: wherever the search for justice may lead us ultimately it does begin, like charity, at home. The notion that "we" should investigate working conditions in Indonesia and then shouldn't buy shirts made there but that it's all right to buy chickens raised and killed by exploited workers in North Carolina or Maine without paying any great attention to what goes on in their employment is incoherent. And few people will be impressed by it.

I do not intend these remarks as an argument about what policies the United States should adopt; overseas workers probably look to the American Congress with about the same degree of hope that sheep would feel in the presence of a convocation of wolves. The argument, rather, is about what principles egalitarians have to advocate and stand by. For there is a coherent principle at stake here: the case against the exploitation of one is ineluctably a case against the exploitation of all. Obversely, the case for more equality is a case for the greater equality of all, not just of a favored few. Whatever legislative or cultural changes egalitarians in the rich nations of the globe advocate, therefore, at a minimum have to advance the interests of the most exploited and the least advantaged *wherever* they might be found.

There is certainly a limitation on what might be intended by that last assertion. Whatever those "alien" interests are, we must understand them at first in an abstract and institutional form. Most of us who aren't saints can't live our lives in single-minded dedication to the world's poorest people, nor can or should any American policy-makers, even if some day they might truly be egalitarians themselves, try to fine-tune either legislation or trade policies so as to serve the interests of oppressed workers in Jakarta. Instead, the universality of the principle of equality has two implications at a minimum.

First, neither the well-off nor even the poor deserve support if they try to better their material condition at the expense of those who are worse off than they are. Second, those who struggle (or say they struggle) to create, maintain, or improve institutions of democratic equality in their own polity ought to show their solidarity with those who struggle for those goals anywhere else; or else we are visibly confusing a class interest with a general one. More concretely, this means that American (or German or Swedish) egalitarians considering the condition of the working classes in Indonesia or the Philipines or Brazil and their obligations to those classes would have to remind themselves of the following realities when rendering any analysis of American (or German etc.) political economy.

Workers in the United States and other Western capitalist societies possess the basic civil liberty of the right to vote and in some more limited degree the rights to organize unions and to bargain collectively; as well as (in the United States) various compensatory protections such as those created by the National Labor Relations Act of 1936, the Fair Labor Standards Act of 1940, the Occupational Safety and Health Act, the Civil Rights Act of 1964, and so on. All of these rights and protections (except the vote) have been under severe threat in the United States since their inception, and most have been seriously curtailed. They still exist in principle, however, and organized labor struggles to defend and extend them. The obligation of American labor (or any organized Western European labor) and its supporters is therefore to encourage and (if called upon to do so) aid, all struggles of overseas labor for those same institutions.

By the same token, most women in the West effectively have the right not to be sold into wage slavery, not to be conscripted into prostitution, and not to be excluded from legal protections available to male workers. Again, for many women these rights are under threat, or at least lack effective enforcement; but their condition is the exception rather than the rule. In contrast, working-class or rural women in many poor countries (where, as Cynthia Enloe has remarked, "cheap labor" is really a euphemism for subjugated female labor), are subject to all those oppressions, without any recourse to the law.[7] American and other Western egalitarians, and certainly those who work for sexual equality, are consequently obliged to support the struggles of women in poorer countries to achieve simple, formal, legal equality.

There is a serious problem here, however, in all the Western capitalist societies but especially in the United States. Although the American state is complicit with capital against the interests of American workers, it does function to protect those workers whenever their economic interests are coterminous with those of capital. In fact, despite the passage of NAFTA the American state is still one of the most protectionist states in the world, and organized American workers on the whole fight for more rather than less protection against overseas or multinational capital. This can be seen not only in requests for tariff protection generally, but in, for example, the effort to require Mexico to incorporate labor legislation as part of NAFTA.

One would think that the American labor movement ought to consider itself duty bound, therefore, to support rather than to oppose the protectionism of labor movements in poorer countries with poorer working classes: sauce for the gander. But this is not as simple a demand as it sounds. American economic nationalists (not all but some of whom will be found in the labor movement) often formulate the problem of poor economies in the concept of competition from "cheap labor," an evidently racist and sexist formulation that has the rhetorical effect of blaming the exploited rather than those who exploit them. Genuine solidarity with those who supply "cheap labor" is unthinkable; it would be like solidarity with scabs. Conversely, from the standpoint of exploited labor and peasant agriculture in the non-Western world, the chief exploiter, hiding behind the veil of the "multinational corporation," is American capital itself, which still dominates world financial and consumer markets and with which American labor has reached at least a partial accommodation.

In the poorer countries of the world, the "success" of global capitalism is for local elites and a minority of workers only. To most others the global market brings devastation and dislocation in its wake, and in the absence of a nationalist revolution governments can usually be counted on to be nothing more than a brutal occupying army for overseas capital. Though there may be a commonality of interest between American workers who don't want their jobs exported overseas and overseas workers and villagers who don't want to be raped by the penetrations of American capital, the latter are often in the position of resisting and attacking precisely that which is "American." Their consequent interpretation of the global capitalist world as an evil American empire is as alien and unacceptable to most American ears as it is accurate.

From an egalitarian standpoint, however, "anti-Americanism" (and sometimes, though not as often, anti-Westernism in general) is the very essence of the overseas working-class and peasant struggle against domination by capital. The struggle for more equality, therefore, requires an understanding of the world's super-exploited masses, including also the often nonwhite and bitterly resented reserve army of labor in the United States, not as "cheap labor" but as "oppressed labor." More, it requires the spirit of solidarity with those oppressed in their struggles rather than of resentment against them as labor market competitors, even if that is to an extent what they inevitably must be.

Undoubtedly, for specific people this may not always be possible. There is a serious issue, for example, posed by the problem of immigration. When well-off Californians support legislation depriving "illegal aliens" of their ordinary human rights ("illegal" according to whose laws and according to what concept of national boundaries?), thereby securing for themselves a labor pool of defenseless, indentured domestic servants, their position is so transparently hypocritical as to be morally indefensible. But African American workers (or would-be workers) in Southern California who support the same legislation are genuinely trying to protect themselves against a competition that on the whole they cannot withstand.

Still, it's essential for all of us, including even those who seem to be bearing the major costs of immigration, to be aware that among the reasons Mexican (and other Central American and Caribbean) workers come to the United States in such large numbers are that in their national homelands they lack certain basic legal protections and economic rights taken for granted even in the capitalist United

States, and that the industrial, agricultural, and natural resource sectors that super-exploit their labor do so under the protective umbrella of an American economic policy and imperial politics that has always subjected Central America to a subordinate status. And it's also crucial for all of us to be aware that it's the historical racism of the American polity, economy, and labor movement that has forced many African Americans into the position of hapless competitor for the lowest rung on the economic ladder; not the nasty competitive nature of Latin Americans with whom they must ultimately be allies.

The never-ending, unstoppable flow of Mexican citizens (and of course U.S. citizens too, although for different reasons) across what is in reality a purely notional, totally porous border, suggests an underlying unity of persons and lives beneath apparent fragmentation. Since, as I've noted, both African American citizens of the United States and Latin American citizens of its neighbors to the south have experienced the historical disaster of being relegated to the margins by uneven economic and political development, they have both suffered the same frustration and deprivation—that is, the denial of fundamental human needs.[8]

To ignore this underlying equivalence is again to try to gain equality on the cheap, rather than confront its real history, its real enemies, and its real costs. To substitute a politics based on group envy for a politics based on recognizable human need is to ensure failure. Turned against each other, the oppressed become blackmailers of each other on behalf of those who benefit from their joint enmity. Contrarily, the principle of solidarity based on recognition of human need knows no boundaries.

Solidarity, I have insisted, is the fundamental ethos of equality. Surely, though (Marx to the contrary), we cannot expect an international solidarity of workers of the same intensity as those local solidarities entrenched by centuries of national development. That is true. But if the spirit of egalitarian solidarity is not extended, at least in principle, to those who are exploited by institutions that most of us in the affluent world, even wage workers, think of as "our own," the movement for more equality will self-destruct. It cannot survive in the face of mortal competition among those who seek it.

The second example of partial solidarities is sexual solidarity, seemingly less global in its scope and effects than the division of nations, but in fact also a crucial obstacle to the pursuit of equality. Again, it often goes unrecognized that sexual solidarity is a two-way affair. It becomes noticed when women oppose their mistreatment by men (e.g., "feminism") or the gender hierarchy of state and society. But as Shannon Faulkner could testify, an exclusive and often oppressive kind of masculine solidarity stands behind that mistreatment.

Male solidarity comes in many guises. Most familiarly, a certain kind of sexual solidarity exists among men in occupations based mostly on physical strength or at least physical performance. Among these men this sexual solidarity often passes for class solidarity, but the truth about this solidarity is revealed by its targets of choice. Assertive women, gays, and "pansy intellectuals" are as much as or more its enemy than capitalists, since the behavior of the former has more resonance in those aspects of life within the average man's immediate control. Who will do the dishes, what makes a good movie, what's worth doing on a Friday night, and above all what makes a man a "real man"—these issues, the immediately observable material of daily life, can easily define one's entire world. Even among men in the learned professions . . . , legitimate authority is more often than not associated with the ability to demonstrate (or intimate) physical force, and masculinity with the power not to have one's decisions be subjected to a woman's judgment. In every social class, of course, these temptations of manhood have diminished in the wake of the feminist revolution; but they remain as bastions of privilege and major obstacles to a wider solidarity.

Women's sexual solidarity is not as focused as men's, since women's labor is rarely as collectivized. It tends to be strongest in the nonwage realms of life, and is on the whole a defensive reflex rather than an aggressive opposition. But most of all, female sexual solidarity, unlike its male counterpart, does prefigure a more encompassing, and more egalitarian, solidarity. The solidarity of those who demand the end of privilege, unlike the solidarity of those who struggle to maintain it, can (and sometimes does) lead beyond itself. On some occasions at least feminist solidarity has consisted of the effort to forge a common bond out of competing solidarities among women. Just so, egalitarian politics consists of the effort, as manifested both . . . in policies . . . and in interventions aimed at counter-ideological persuasion, to forge a common bond out of these competing, more parochial, solidarities.

How this is to be done in practice, however, is obviously the concern of activists more than theorists. To become more than simply an abstract theory, the theory of equality awaits a mass movement founded on the politics of equality (that is, democratic participation) to demand it; and leaders committed to democratic participation, to help that mass movement define itself. We can only guess what will be the issues that unite various peoples who are now united in that movement. They will almost certainly be issues around which people in different nations and from widely differing backgrounds will be able to congregate, having to do with the penetration of daily life, space, and culture by the aggressive, impersonal, and unforgiving institutions of global capital.

NOTES

1. Rawls, for example, discusses only what in the European tradition is rather optimistically called "the law of nations." (op. cit., pp. 378–79). Michael Walzer, who differs from Rawls on many other points, also adopts the integrity of the nation-state as a principle in his *Just and Unjust Wars* (New York: Basic Books, 1977). He discusses whether "we" should have intervened in South Africa, e.g., but not whether "I" should or should not have helped run guns to the A.N.C. The only major contemporary exception is Amartya K. Sen, who, not surprisingly, writes from the standpoint of an Indian rather than European or North American economic theorist.

2. Most notable, perhaps, is Eqbal Ahmad, "The Neo-Fascist State: Notes on the Pathology of Power in the Third World," *Arab Studies Quarterly* vol. 3 no. 2 (spring 1981), 170–80. See also Vandana Shiva, *The Violence of the Green Revolution: Third World Agriculture, Ecology, and Politics* (London: Zed Books, 1991) and M. R. Bhagavan, "A Critique of

India's Economic Policies and Strategies," *Monthly Review* vol. 39 no. 3 (July–August 1987), pp. 56–79; Carlos Maria Vilas, *Between Earthquakes and Volcanoes: Market, State, and the Revolutions in Central America* (New York: Monthly Review Press, 1995), or the extensive Spanish-language bibliography in Joseph Collins and John Lear, *Chile's Free-Market Miracle: A Second Look* (Oakland, Calif.: The Institute for Food and Development Policy, 1995); Larbi Sadiki, "Al-La Nidam—an Arab View of the New World (Dis)Order," *Arab Studies Quarterly* vol. 17 no. 3 (summer 1995), pp. 1–22; and Samir Amin, *Capitalism in the Age of Globalization: The Management of Contemporary Society* (London: Zed Books, 1997).

3. See, for example, Walzer's *Spheres of Justice*, pp. 28–30 (although it's doubtful if the liberal social democrat Walzer is himself a "communitarian" in the contemporary sense of that epithet); for a representative instance of postmodernist discourse, the essays (especially Butler's) in Seyla Benhabib, Judith Butler, Drucilla Cornell, and Nancy Fraser, *Feminist Contentions: A Philosophical Exchange* (New York: Routledge, 1995).

4. See J. K. Gibson-Graham, "Querying Globalization," in *Rethinking Marxism* vol. 9 no. 1, 1996–97, 1–27; 21. ("J.K. Gibson-Graham" is the pen name of Julie Graham and Katherine Gibson.) Writing from a much different perspective Ben Barber, in his *Jihad vs. McWorld* (New York: Times Books, 1995), in effect explains the resurgence of Islamic fundamentalism as a result of uneven development; and he predicts that in the end it will be defeated by the culture of "McWorld." The missing term here, as he notes himself, is democracy; and we could say alternatively that what is missing (perhaps temporarily) from this polarity, and what his analysis neglects to consider, is any effective democratic opposition to capitalism on a global rather than merely local scale.

5. This argument does not necessarily vitiate Walzer's notion of "shared understandings," since he might agree (my reading of *Spheres of Justice* is that he does agree) that in this particular case *every* cultural tradition holds certain kinds of economic domination or monopoly to be wrong.

6. John Stuart Mill, *The Subjection of Women* (Arlington Heights, Ill.: Harlan Davidson, 1980), p. 56. Although we owe this perfected logical point to Mill, he is otherwise in fact less free of traditional attitudes about women than Wollstonecraft.

7. On the role of gender in the globalized political economy see Enloe's "The Globetrotting Sneaker," *Ms.,* vol. 5 no. 5 (March/April 1995), pp. 10–15.

8. See Manning Marable, *How Capitalism Underdeveloped Black America: Problems in Race, Political Economy, and Society* (Boston: South End Press, 1983).

A Substantially Rational World, or Can Paradise Be Regained?

IMMANUEL WALLERSTEIN

If, indeed, as I have been contending, we are in a long and difficult transition from our existing world-system to another one or ones, and if the outcome is uncertain, there are two large questions before us: what kind of world do we in fact want; and by what means, or paths, are we most likely to get there? These are long-standing questions that many have posed for a long time, certainly over the past two centuries. But the first question has usually been asked in terms of utopias, and I wish to address it in terms of utopistics, that is, the serious assessment of historical alternatives, the exercise of our judgment regarding the substantive rationality of possible alternative historical systems. And the second question has been asked in terms of the inevitability of progress, and I wish to present it in terms of the end of certainty, the possibility but the non-inevitability of progress.

We are all familiar with the principal claims about our existing historical system. Those who argue that it represents the best of all possible worlds tend to emphasize three asserted virtues: material abundance and convenience; the existence of liberal political structures; the lengthening of the average life span. Each of these is argued by comparison with all known previous historical systems. On the other hand, the case *against* the merits of our existing historical system argues virtually the opposite of this same

list of three. Where the advocates see material abundance and convenience, the critics see acute inequality and polarization, arguing that material abundance and convenience exist only for the few. Where the advocates see liberal political structures, the critics see the absence of significant popular participation in decision making. Where the advocates see longer life spans, the critics stress the seriously degraded quality of life.

These are indeed hoary debates, but it might be useful to review the criticisms in the light of the positive assessments, in order to see what conclusions we might draw about what needs to be satisfied in any alternative system we might want to construct, now that the issue will be before us. It should be evident from what I have already said, that I fall on the side of the critics and do not consider the present world-system the best of all possible worlds. I am not even sure it is the best of all worlds we have already known. Still, I do not want to reargue this case here.[1] It is in some ways irrelevant to demonstrate what I consider to be the limitations of our existing world-system. I have been arguing that enough people consider it to have limitations such that it is not going to survive. The real question before us is what we want to replace it.

Before I can address that question, however, I must lay one ghost to rest. It is the misdeeds of

Source: Immanuel Wallerstein, "A Substantially Rational World, or Can Paradise be Regained?" in *Utopistics,* New York: The New Press, 1998: 65–90.

[1] I have already done so in the Wei Lun Lectures at the Chinese University of Hong Kong in 1992, entitled "Capitalist Civilization," which have been reprinted as the second part of *Historical Capitalism, with Capitalist Civilization* (London: Verso, 1995).

what some have taken to calling, in recent years, "historical socialism," referring primarily to the set of Marxist-Leninist states that were once called the "socialist bloc." But by analogy and extension, the term is often used to cover many of the national liberation movements and even the Social Democratic parties in the pan-European world. Let us review this story briefly because it has been used to suggest that no alternative to our existing system is realistic or even remotely desirable. The three main charges against historical socialism are (1) the arbitrary use of state (and party) authority; at its worst, state-directed terror; (2) the extension of privileges to a Nomenklatura; and (3) extensive economic inefficiency deriving from state involvement in the economy and resulting in holding back rather than promoting the increase of social value.

Let me start by admitting that these charges are largely true, certainly the first two charges, as a historical assessment of the state regimes that existed under the aegis of these parties. What one can immediately say, however, is that it has been equally true that a lot of regimes not under the aegis of these parties could also be said to have made arbitrary use of state authority and even state-directed terror, to have given extensive and excessive privilege to groups linked to or preferred by the state authorities, and to have been incredibly inefficient, thereby no doubt holding back the increase of social value. It does not excuse the authorities of any so-called socialist state to note that these characteristics have been standard fare of most state regimes throughout the historical trajectory of the modern world-system. Indeed, these practices are so widespread that one might wonder why their vices are not laid at the feet of the system itself, rather than at institutions (regimes) within the system. May it not be that it was the system as a whole that bred such regimes and that needed this kind of regime for its smooth functioning?

To be sure, some will reply, not all state regimes have been like this. But even the best of regimes, at their best moments, were scarcely innocent in terms of these various vices. More important, to the extent

that some regimes were (or looked) better, they were those of the so-called liberal states. And all these liberal states were to be found in a very narrow corner of the world-system, located in the wealthy areas, and known only in recent times. It is not difficult to explain the reasons. They are those that are usually offered: the very large middle stratum resident within the boundaries of these countries; the relative satisfaction of this group with their share of the global pie; the consequent institutionalization of the "rule of law," which protected this middle stratum, although it also served to protect others somewhat. But, all these features were dependent on the reality of the polarization of the existing world-system. To assert that the roots of the liberal regimes were internal and "cultural" is to misread history and to ignore the relative strength of various contributing factors to the global results. In any case, as we have often seen, the liberalism of liberal states was always more precarious than we are wont to admit.

Whatever the explanation for the limitations of so-called socialist states, it should be remembered that they were never autonomous entities and always operated within the framework of the capitalist world-economy, constrained by the operations of the interstate system, and did not—could not—represent the workings of an alternative historical system. That is not to say, however, that we cannot learn from this experience in pursuing our exercise in utopistics. We have gotten useful lessons about the consequences of particular mechanisms, which are at the very least food for thought.

If we are making a fundamental historical choice in the next fifty years, what is it between? Clearly, our choice is between a system (analogous to the present one in some fundamentals) in which some have significantly greater privileges than others, and one that is relatively democratic and egalitarian. All known historical systems have in fact been of the former kind up to now, although some have been worse in this regard than others. Indeed, I would argue that our existing system has been quite possibly the worst, in that it has shown the greatest polarization precisely because of its presumed virtue, the incredible expansion of the production of value. With much, much more value produced, the difference between the top stratum and the rest could be and has been far greater than in the other historical systems, even if it is true that the top stratum of the present system has included a larger percentage of the system's overall population than that of preceding historical systems.

Still, the mere fact that all prior historical systems have been unequal, undemocratic systems is no argument that one could not envisage one that was relatively democratic and egalitarian. After all, we have been talking about this possibility for a long time now, and it is clearly attractive to a lot of people. In our present system, what guarantees the inequalities and therefore necessarily the absence of real democratic participation in collective decision making is the primacy of the endless accumulation of capital. What people fear is that if one eliminates this primacy, one would have to sacrifice either relative productive efficiency or a free and open society. Let us investigate if either of these consequences is a necessary correlate of eliminating the primacy of the endless accumulation of capital. Could one devise a structure that would give primacy to maximizing the quality of life to everyone (presumably the original Benthamite liberal ideal) while at the same time limiting and controlling the means of collective violence so that everyone felt relatively and equally secure in their person and enjoyed the widest possible range of individual options without threatening the survival or equal rights of others (presumably the original John Stuart Mill ideal)? This might be called realizing liberal ideals worldwide in the context of an egalitarian system, or democracy as it is theorized, as opposed to the modified and hidden autocracies we have deceptively labeled democratic regimes.

This would not by itself fulfill the objective of a democratic, egalitarian system. It would have to be the case that everyone would be able to work at a satisfying job or jobs, and that, in case of special as well as unexpected need, assistance would be socially available. And finally, we would need to know that the resources of the biosphere were being

adequately preserved, so that there would be no intergenerational losses and therefore no intergenerational exploitation.

What might accomplish this? Let us start with the issue of remuneration. Generally, it is argued that monetary reward is an incentive for quality work. And I suppose generally this is sometimes true. But it is one thing to reward an artisan for quality artisanship and another thing to reward an executive for obtaining extraordinary profits for a corporation. They are different in two ways. It is clear that good artisanship is quality work. But the obtaining of extraordinary profits is only quality work if one accepts the priority of the endless accumulation of capital. It is hard to justify it on any other grounds. The second difference is the size of the reward. Increasing an artisan's income by 10 or even 25 percent for quality work is quite different from increasing an executive's income by 100 or even 1000 percent.

Is it really true that an industrial manager will only work well if he receives the kind of bonuses he can obtain in the present system? I believe it is absurd to think so. We have the clear example of many kinds of professionals (such as university professors) who are stimulated to work well not primarily by the relatively small increases in material rewards but rather by a combination of honors and increased control over their own work time. People do not usually win Nobel Prizes because they are spurred on by the endless accumulation of capital. And there are a remarkably large number of persons in our present system whose incentives are not primarily monetary. Indeed, if honor and increased control of one's own work time were more generally available as rewards, would not many more people find them inherently satisfying?

If we then added to this somewhat changed set of social priorities a much improved system of career selection, such that more people were able to do the kind of work they found, for whatever reasons, more satisfying, perhaps anomie would be greatly reduced. And if we allowed, encouraged, and organized multiple career roles, within each year and/or successively over time, who knows with what arrangements we might increase general satisfaction? This would, in addition, make much more possible the equalization of family responsibilities, about which we have been talking so much in recent years—and doing so relatively little, I should add.

Greed is a very corrosive emotion, and our present system encourages it, virtually lauds it, because it rewards it. Are we really arguing that no society can be free if greed is morally leashed in some way, and in which countervalues are incorporated into our superegos? Some say charity can balance greed. But charity does not demonstrate the absence or even the diminution of greed. It can well be merely the guilt offering of the greedy. Charitable contributions only represent true charity—that is, dearness, affection, high regard, as its etymology tells us—when it is performed as a duty derived from the claims of justice, not when it is a peace offering to the gods.

Efficiency is a desirable phenomenon, but it is a means to some end. What is the end to which we have been putting it? Can we put it to other ends? For example, if we increase the production of steel or computers or grain—that is, if we demonstrate that they can be produced at the same level of quality for lower cost of real inputs—why are we doing this? If there were no rewards for increasing capital accumulation but there were rewards for meeting real needs or for extending distribution, is it truly inconceivable that those who ran the operation would not work efficiently? Surely that can't be so, or we could not justify the entire range of activities we call professional activity. Is it really clear that, on average, today's big businessmen are more efficient than small-town architects or garage mechanics? I have never seen evidence to this effect, and it contradicts my initial observations of the social scene. If efficiency at capital accumulation were the only consideration, are not the drug lords of the world magnificent tributes to the capacity of greed to stimulate productivity?

Are large organizations more efficient than small ones? Once again, it depends on the criteria. Surely size affects cost, but not always in a strictly linear direction. In any case, in our present system,

the size of productive operations has to do with a lot more than productive efficiency. It has to do with optimizing the evasion of taxes and regulations, or the benefits of relative monopoly versus the benefits of reducing coordination costs, or of shifting risk burdens in times of world economic expansion versus times of world economic contraction. These are all considerations that disappear once you eliminate the priority of the endless accumulation of capital. Left to itself, considerations of efficiency would probably lead to a great variety in terms of sizes of economic activity. There would be fewer giant structures, no doubt, and a greater number of medium-size ones, instead of the relentless juggernaut of increase of size—the world concentration of capital and therefore of ownership and organized structures—that exists in the present system.

Suppose all economic structures were defined as nonprofit structures, but non-state control were an open, even a very widely used, option. We have known this system for centuries now in the so-called nonprofit hospitals. Are they notoriously less efficient, and less medically competent, than private or state hospitals? Not at all, to my knowledge. Indeed, probably the opposite. Why must this be restricted to hospitals? Could one not have a nonprofit electricity company on the model of the nonprofit hospital? Of course, one might argue that the trend today, even in hospitals, is to move toward the model of private-for-profit structures. No doubt, but this is precisely the result of the commodification of everything, which is at the base of our present system. Is it improving efficiency? Is it improving health care? The main argument its proponents use is that it will keep down health costs. Personally, I doubt that it will do this. What it will more likely do is reallocate money that has heretofore been expended on health care to the accumulation of capital. Is that really desirable? Who desires it?

So the first structural element I offer as a possible base of an alternative system is the erection of nonprofit decentralized units as the underlying mode of producing within the system. It could offer the same incentives for efficiency—probably greater ones—than our present system. And it would avoid the fear that centralization, especially through state mechanisms, makes experimentation and diversity unlikely and leads, over time, both to authoritarian decision making and to bureaucratic sloth. But this still leaves questions of how these units might relate to one another, and on what basis. It also does not address the issue of the internal organization of these production units, what we might call workplace democracy.

How would multiple nonprofit productive enterprises fit together? Perhaps precisely in the way the theoretical model of laissez-faire tells us: through the market, the real market and not the monopolistically controlled world market we have in the present system. Would we need some kind of regulation? Some, no doubt, akin perhaps to traffic lights on a busy road. It need not involve agencies engaging in planning the production. The regulation might be limited to counteracting fraud, improving information flows, and sending up warning signals about over- and underproduction.

Nor is it necessary that these nonprofit production units be internally autocratic. The interests of workers might still differ from those of managers. Some mode of negotiation would continue to be essential, with unions or some such institution representing collective worker interests. And some form of worker participation in decision making at the top would still need to be implemented. A mode of worker freedom to move between employing organizations, without losing lifetime benefits, would need to be established. (That is to say, the lifetime benefits would have to be vested in some structure outside the production organization itself.) Also, a method for adjusting the size of the workforce to the needs of production would need to be developed, along with some kind of mechanism to ensure that workers could find alternative, satisfying employment. Finally, a system of penalizing true sloth and incompetence would have to be constructed. We could long debate the details of how to meet each of these needs. And even once decided, they would be constantly under renewed discussion. The

point is that none of them presents an inherently insuperable obstacle that people of good will could not resolve, more or less, within the framework of a world-system not driven by the endless accumulation of capital.

What, then, about the issues we have been discussing so much and so vigorously in recent years: the inequalities of race, of gender, and of nation. Any world-system that does not do a whole lot better than our present one in this regard is not worth struggling to achieve. I will not say that eliminating the priority given to the endless accumulation of capital will automatically ensure equality of race, gender, and nation. What I will say is that it would eliminate one of the most potent reasons for the inequalities. After that, the real work begins, unencumbered by this heavy constraint. Perhaps with the elimination—or at least reduction—of economic fears, at the very least the murderous element may disappear.

One of the central issues that has been under discussion has been the outcomes within the present system in terms of distribution of positions and rewards. The reality of the existing system is that the outcomes of job allocation and actual quality of life are deeply tilted in terms of race, gender, and nation. The defenders of the existing system argue that this is simply the result of using meritocracy as the criterion, and that this criterion represents a morally virtuous mode of distribution. The critics say that meritocracy hides institutionalized biases in distribution, which affect the ability to compete on adult age "tests" long before the candidates come to the starting line.

In fact, both are right. Meritocracy does represent a democratizing pressure, but it is also true that in our present system, the decks are stacked. Let us analyze what meritocracy really involves, however. Suppose we give a test, any test, to a group of one hundred people and get quantified results. Is it the case that person 38 in the ranking is truly and significantly more qualified than person 39? The very idea is absurd. What we could probably say, if this is a test of competence, is that the top ten are quite good and the bottom ten quite poor, and that the eighty that are in-between are just that, in-between. Suppose, then, we were asked to allocate fifty positions as the result of such a test. Should we give them to the top fifty? Another possibility would be to award ten places to the top ten, eliminate the bottom ten from consideration, and draw lots among the in-between eighty for the forty positions. Of course, I am inventing the exact percentages, but testing of any kind is a limited mechanism of discerning capacity and certainly cannot rank people plausibly throughout the continuum. Yet it is true that there is always a minority that is exceptionally qualified and another minority that is exceptionally unqualified. As long as we take account of this but remember that these two categories are relatively small, we can move toward a random distribution of positions among the rest. Just doing that would drastically reduce institutionalized racism-sexism.

Remember, I am not proposing utopia. I am proposing routes to greater substantive rationality. The serious reduction of these inequalities will take much collective work. Still, it should be intrinsically possible to envisage a social world in which the discriminations had become at most minor, instead of continuing to be fundamental to the operation of the historical system as they currently are. Today, they poison all of social life, everywhere. They dominate our mentalities. They wreak untold havoc, physical and psychological, not only on those who belong to the oppressed groups but on those who belong to the dominant groups. The evil results are not getting better; they're getting worse. These inequalities are morally unacceptable and unresolvable within the framework of our existing world-system. Fortunately, this system is on its way out. The question is, what is on its way in?

Would we then have a classless society? This too I doubt, in the sense that ending polarization does not mean ending variation, including variation in class position. But as with race, gender, and nation, it means transforming the distinction from one that is deep-rooted and corrosive into one that could be relatively minor and limited in its impact. There is no fundamental reason we could not overcome the three greatest consequences of class differences: unequal access to education, to health services, and to a guaranteed decent income throughout life. It should not be difficult to place all three of these needs outside commodification, to be provided by nonprofit institutions and paid for collectively. We do this now for such things as water supply and, in many countries, libraries. Some say that the worldwide costs would then get out of hand. They might, but there are many solutions to the question of collective cost allocations other than commodification. It is a social decision we cannot avoid and should not want to avoid.

Could we prevent the creation of Nomenklaturas? Since public office would no longer be the only rapid guarantee of better access to education, health, and lifetime minimal income (because these would be universal), and because there would be no outlets for profit-making economic structures, what would be the point of a Nomenklatura? We might actually attain, for the first time, the Weberian ideal, a disinterested civil service, in which all members entered it because it offered them job satisfaction, and not for all the other reasons they enter it today. Of course, an essential element in avoiding a Nomenklatura would be a truly democratic set of political institutions. And here the idea of limited terms of office, so dear to conservative forces at the present time, might be quite useful. But nothing will work unless the majority of the population feel that they really have a considerable impact on political decision making, an impact that has to go far beyond the simple veto power of being able once every few years to vote against the "ins."

Here we run into the question of how one gets widespread participation, and sense of participation, in ways that cannot be channeled, and thereby distorted, by the massive investment of money in media campaigns. Once again, a knotty question, but scarcely an insurmountable one. For one thing, where will the huge sums come from if there is not the endless accumulation of capital? And, given the technological advances these days in information flows, could not matters be organized in such a way that there were not financial imbalances between competing points of view? Once again, not at all technically impossible. This might not be enough to guarantee a sense of real democracy, but it would be a beginning. Here, too, the real work would only begin, not end, with the establishment of this kind of historical system.

As to the preservation of the biosphere, there is one simple, viable, and necessary element in its achievement. We must require all production organizations to internalize all costs, including all costs necessary to ensure that their productive activity neither pollutes nor uses up the resources of the biosphere. That is, immediate restoration and/or cleanup costs would become integral to the production process and therefore to production costs. This, of course, would not be enough by itself, but it would, at the minimum, ensure that waste would never be casual. There would still be differences of views about the consequences of particular productive activity to the biosphere. There are no scientifically definitive answers. Ultimately, these questions come down to political choices. Is x really more important than y? It is often a choice between present and future consumption, between generations living and yet to be born, between risks calculated in one realm of the universe against risks calculated in another. These are social judgments and should be made democratically, involving all who are affected by the decisions.

The underlying issue is the measured evaluation of social costs, and the problem is how to make such evaluation truly collective. It is not a question restricted to ecological issues. When we consider health costs, should we spend more on the children or more on the aged? Should the real income of the healthier, mid-lifetime working population be reduced, and by how much, to cover the more marginal of these health expenditures for the young, the old, and those needing special care? In our present system, these are choices made on the basis of individual egotisms, tempered perhaps by some limited collective interference. As the costs go up, and as the social demand for democracy and equality goes up, the results of our present system seem

more and more absurd and unreasonable. But how do we collectively evaluate this? What is substantively rational in terms of the allocation of our less-than-unlimited resources? Surely, we cannot know without open, wide-ranging discussion involving as many people as possible. But how can we best institutionalize this, and on a world level, without removing the arena of decision from the inputs and control of ordinary people?

In this search for substantive rationality, for the good society (or at least the better society), one thing we have on our side is human creativity. Here, there is no limit to the potential. What we know about complex systems is that they are self-organizing and that they repeatedly invent new formulas, new solutions for existing problems. I do not, however, wish to sneak in here a concept of inevitable progress, because creativity is not necessarily or always positive. What works is not necessarily what is morally good. And the morally good is not achieved simply by preaching it. As almost all the religions of the world tell us, God gave us free will, and therefore the intrinsic possibility of both good and evil. Hence, we come to the political question, how do we get there, or what can we do in the next twenty-five to fifty years that will move us to a more substantively rational historical social system?

This brings us back to the period of transition, to the period of hell on earth. We shall not witness a simple, laid-back political debate, a friendly discussion among choir boys. It will be a struggle, conducted on a life-and-death level. For we are talking about laying the bases for the historical system of the next five hundred years. And we are debating whether we want to have simply one more kind of historical system in which privilege prevails and democracy and equality are minimized, or whether we want to move in the opposite direction, for the first time in the known history of humanity.

The first thing to look at is how those who currently have privilege will react, are indeed reacting. One cannot expect that any significant segment of those who have privilege will relinquish it without struggle, simply on the ground of some appeal to their ethical responsibilities or even to their historical vision. One must assume that they will seek to preserve privilege. Any other presumption is implausible and unrealistic. Even so, we do not know what their strategy will be.

The optimal strategy by which to defend privilege—the one most likely to be efficacious—has long been a matter of debate among those who hold privilege, and it is not a question upon which social science has offered us any definitive evidence up to now. To start with the simple, there is the division of views between those who believe that repression (at least judicious repression) is the key, and those who believe that concessions that give away a small portion of the pie in order to save the rest are the secret. One can try a mix of both formulas, of course, but then the question remains, in what proportion and in what sequence?

The fact that historically both methods have been used is not in itself evidence that both methods work equally well, or that the one or ones that worked well in the past will work well in the present, or that the one that worked well during the ongoing normal trajectory of our present historical system would work well in the period of bifurcation and transition. What we can say is that the accumulated knowledge of world history and the vastly improved means of world communication ensure that there will be more intelligent reflection, more conscious decision making on the part of the privileged during this historical transition than during any previous one. The privileged are inevitably better informed and thereby socially smarter than they have been. They are also far wealthier, and they have far stronger and more effective means of destruction and repression than they ever did before.

One would think they would be able to do very well. Of course, they will have the standard problem. They are not an organized, disciplined sectarian group. They are an amorphous, quite varied group of beneficiaries of the existing state of things. Some are more powerful and wealthy than others, and by far. Some are more intelligent and sophisticated than others. Some are indeed organized into smallish groups, others quite adrift. And of course, they are in competition with each other just as much as they have a collective, class interest in certain outcomes.

Still, they find themselves collectively in structural difficulties, as I have been arguing. This means that they have to do something. The question, however, is not only what but when. Shall they simply pursue short-run advantage now until the system more visibly cracks? Or shall they take their losses immediately, on the presumption that a stitch in time will save nine? This question is all the more difficult depending on whether we are talking of the superpowerful or merely the ordinarily privileged. The former may find it easier to take short-term losses than the latter, in order to safeguard their long-term privilege.

The biggest problem for those with privilege comes with the awareness of systemic crisis, if and when they finally attain it and fully integrate this expectation into their operational procedures. At that point, it is quite probable that they would seek to implement the di Lampedusa principle—to change everything (or seem to do so) in order that nothing change (although it seems to do so). This is extremely tricky. The first problem is to invent the change (less easy and less obvious than one might think). The second is to delude a large part of one's own camp. The third is to delude the opponents.

What kind of alternative can they invent? I am not at all sure. Could anyone have predicted in fifteenth-century Europe what kind of alternative a disintegrating feudal stratum would invent to save itself? And if one had predicted, how likely is it that one would have foreseen our present capitalist world-economy, which has had precisely the di Lampedusa result: a capitalist system that is different in most ways from the feudal system except in the crucial outcome of ensuring inegalitarian results, and in many cases to the very same strata, at least for the first several centuries. I am certainly not going to try to do the invention for them. I would guess, however, that the method most likely to succeed would be one that incorporated a lot of the terminology of the discontented.

Twenty years ago I would have said that the program would come in the guise of Marxism, but for many reasons this seems far less likely now. It may well come under the pretext of ecology, or of multiculturalism, or of women's rights. I am not suggesting anything suspect about the current proponents of these various causes, all three of which seem to me to be indispensable forms of rebellion against the abuses of our current world-system. But rhetoric is co-optable, even when movements resist co-option. And movements, as we have seen, find it very difficult over time not to bend in the wind, especially if they can obtain some portion of their immediate objectives thereby.

The privileged need more than merely adopt a radically different rhetoric, however. They have to use the rhetoric to establish a radically different set of institutions. And here they have two more problems. One lies in their own camp, and in two forms. The first is that what may be good for a group as a worldwide whole may not at all be good for subgroups among the privileged. The losing subgroups will, of course, be unwilling to go along, and that can disrupt the political viability of the operation. It is impossible even to attempt to predict the details.

But the second form of difficulty within the camp of the privileged presents even greater dilemmas. Suppose that some clever group works out an effective di Lampedusa strategy. Many of their camp may not understand what is going on, and so may not be willing to support it politically (or indeed financially). What can be done then? The proponents could, of course, spell it out in black and white, but that defeats the whole purpose of a di Lampedusa strategy. So they will have to argue for it discreetly and indirectly, which may or may not rally the troops.

And this leads directly to the third form of difficulty: how to persuade the vast majority that the non-change is really change, that transformation is indeed in the direction of a more substantively rational world, rather than merely changing the form of substantive irrationality. The key element of a di Lampedusa strategy is never to proclaim the real

strategy too openly, but to insist on the surface strategy. An Ayn Rand approach, the glorification of the right of strong individuals to reap their unequal returns, has never really worked, to my knowledge. It is even less likely to work now, although the momentary attraction of neoliberal theorizing may seem to be counterevidence. I would contend that the public reaction is already there and quite visible, and that we shall hear distinctly less of neoliberal arguments as we move into the twenty-first century. Still, the camp of the privileged must tread a difficult tightrope: explaining enough to their side to rally the troops, but not so much that it will afford the other side evidence and motives for fierce opposition. It will not be easy, and it is another element absolutely impossible to foresee in detail.

As for those who are the oppressed in our existing system, how will they act? They have at least as many problems as do the privileged. If the latter are a heterogeneous, amorphous group, the oppressed are even more so. If the camp of the privileged contains a wide range of immediate and even long-term interests within their camp, so does the camp of their opponents. And of course, compared to the privileged, the oppressed have less current power, less current organization, less current wealth at their disposal to pursue any global political battle. Especially, one should add, a battle that will take place in such multiform ways—open violence, quasi-polite electoral and legislative battles, theoretical debates within the structures of knowledge, and public appeals to strange and often muted rhetoric.

I cannot really say more about this, except that the concept of a rainbow coalition is probably the only viable one, but one tremendously difficult to implement. And the tactic of demanding that the privileged live up to their liberal rhetoric would no doubt wreak havoc, but is again very difficult to implement. What should be clear is that I have not proposed a program but merely some elements that should enter into the discussion of a program— of how one could institutionalize a more substantively rational historical system, and of how one might traverse the period of transition in order to end up there. These proposals need to be debated, supplemented, or replaced by better ones. And the debate must be worldwide.

We must now return to the original assertions about the structure of systems. Remember the pattern. They are born; they live long lives according to some rules; and at some point they come into crisis, bifurcate, and transform themselves into something else. The last period, the transition period, is particularly unpredictable, but also particularly subject to individual and group input, what I have called the increase in the free will factor. If we wish to seize our opportunity, which seems to me a moral and political obligation, we must first recognize the opportunity for what it is, and of what it consists. This requires reconstructing the framework of knowledge so that we can understand the nature of our structural crisis, and therefore our historical choices for the twenty-first century. Once we understand the choices, we must be ready to engage in the struggle without any guarantee that we shall win it. This is crucial, since illusions only breed disillusions and are therewith depoliticizing. Finally, our tactical action—our intellectual, moral, and political judgments—must be at one and the same time straightforward and clear, but nonetheless subtle and medium-run. We are called upon to be wary of a deceitful opponent and trusting in the fundamental good faith of allies who do not share all our backgrounds or needs or predispositions, or indeed interests. This may seem like a formula for superpersons. I believe it is rather a formula for those who hope to achieve a more substantively rational, better world than the one in which we live.

There is one final question I must address. Will people in power just yield their privilege? Of course not; they never do. Sometimes they concede parts of it, but only as a tactic to retain most of it. People in power have never been as powerful or as wealthy as they are in the contemporary world. And people out of power (or at least many of them) have never been as badly off, certainly relatively, and to a considerable extent, absolutely. So the polarization is the greatest it has ever been, which means that noble renunciation of privilege is the least likely outcome.

That being said, it is irrelevant to my thesis. I have argued that there exist structural limitations to the process of endless accumulation of capital that governs our existing world, and that these limitations are coming to the fore currently as a brake on the functioning of the system. I have argued that these structural limitations—what I have called the asymptotes of the operative mechanisms—are creating a structurally chaotic situation that will be both unpleasant to live through and thoroughly unpredictable in its trajectory. Finally, I have argued that a new order will emerge out of this chaos over a period of fifty years, and that this new order will be shaped as a function of what everyone does in the interval—those with power in the present system, and those without it. This analysis is neither optimistic nor pessimistic, in the sense that I do not and cannot predict whether the outcome will be better or worse. It is, however, realistic in trying to stimulate discussion about the kinds of structure that might actually serve us all better and the kinds of strategies that might move us in those directions. So, as they say in East Africa, *harambee!*

Confronting Intersecting Inequalities

SONIA HANSON, PETER KIVISTO, AND ELIZABETH HARTUNG

The traditional political fault line that divides the left from the right speaks to widely divergent views about whether building an egalitarian society is desirable. The left, whether its expression is communist, social democratic, or liberal, has argued that equality must be a goal in the effort to create a society that does not exploit or oppress some in order to enhance the situation of others. From this side of the political divide, a truly just society must be an egalitarian one. In contrast, the right contends that inequality is not only natural and therefore inevitable but also often proves to be beneficial. If, in the past, inequality was justified in religious terms, appealing to the idea of God's hierarchal order in which each person had his or her appropriate place, today the right is more likely to appeal to the idea of meritocracy. Sometimes this takes on a biological essentialism, as with Social Darwinians a century ago or the authors of *The Bell Curve* (1994) more recently. In other instances, there is a distinctly psychological cast to the account. Thus, conservatives justify the inequality of privilege on the basis of certain individuals' presumed value to society and on such personal attributes as diligence, a strong work ethic, intelligence, competitiveness, and so forth. From this ideological perspective, the poor are poor because of their own personal character failings. Inequality can actually serve them well insofar as it serves to goad them to change their errant ways.

In the current epoch of global capitalism, defined by neoliberal economic policies that have been promoted aggressively by the right-of-center administrations in the most powerful nations of the world, the pursuit of equality does not appear to be on their agenda. Instead, policies have been promoted that allow markets to operate increasingly free from the intervention of the state. Markets are seen as generators of wealth, and any intrusion into the "natural" functioning of markets is criticized for stifling economic growth. Thus, the welfare state is seen as an impediment to growth, and for this reason, efforts to reduce it have been pursued vigorously. The logic of this economic strategy is based on the assumption that when those at the top are permitted to increase their wealth, the impact of their increased wealth benefits not only them but the rest of society as well, as added wealth trickles down throughout the class structure. In such a scenario, levels of inequality may increase, but everybody is better off for it. Therefore, according to exponents of neoliberalism, any attempt to implement redistributive policies that are designed to reduce existing levels of inequality ought to be rejected.

The problem with this position is that it is based on ideology rather than empirical evidence or a clearly articulated moral vision about what a just and fair society would look like. It fails to adequately account for the wide range of negative impacts of inequality on individuals and on communities. It also fails to account for the fact that once in place, inequality perpetuates itself—becoming what

Charles Tilly (1998) refers to as "durable inequality." As he points out, such inequality speaks less to ideas such as meritocracy or the functionally beneficial character of inequality, and more to the capacity of those with power, wealth, and privilege to effect strategies of closure that prevent those who are lower on the social ladder from climbing up the rungs.

Before neoliberalism and the collapse of the Soviet Union, there were three major egalitarian positions from the left. The product of revolutionary upheaval, communism was the experiment that began in the Soviet Union and then, after World War II, spread to China and a number of other Third World nations. It called for the replacement of market economies by state-run, or command, economies. The result was a rigid bureaucratic system that proved to be highly ineffective and inhumane. Since communist states did not permit the emergence of pluralist democratic systems, the result was a repressive and authoritarian society. The police apparatus succeeded in stifling dissent for many decades, but by the 1980s, the failures of the system to deliver a decent standard of living for a majority of the population was evident. Ultimately—with perhaps the collapse of the Berlin Wall symbolically signaling the end—Soviet-style communism was abandoned.

The two other egalitarian models were found not in the developing world but in the most advanced industrial nations: social democracy (sometimes called democratic socialism) and liberalism. Both the former, seen clearly in the Scandinavian nations, and the latter, seen most clearly in the United States, preserved a capitalist market economy while creating a welfare state designed to address the negative consequences of a capitalist economy. Capitalism creates goods and services that benefit society as well as simultaneously generates extremes in inequality. In the case of the United States, the welfare state largely came into being during the Depression, the product of Franklin Roosevelt's New Deal policies, which, for example, created the Social Security system, unemployment insurance, and a host of other "safety net"

measures. The welfare state expanded during Lyndon Johnson's Great Society initiatives, which included the creation of the Medicare and Medicaid programs.

At some level, the difference between liberalism and democratic socialism are matters of degree. During the period from the end of World War II to the 1980s, both liberal and social democratic states succeeded in reducing the levels of inequality, the latter to a greater extent than the former. Social democracy is more likely to promote a mixed economy wherein some sectors of the economy are state-owned or run, whereas in liberalism such ownership is very limited (e.g., municipally owned water systems). In addition, social democracies have far more comprehensive welfare states, delivering what are sometimes called cradle-to-grave benefits. Thus, social democratic nations provide universal health insurance to their citizens; liberalism in practice does not. This means that while all Scandinavian citizens receive health insurance, at present nearly 20 percent of Americans do not have such coverage. Social democracies, in part because of their tax systems and in part because of the high level of provision of public goods (e.g., comprehensive public transportation systems, universal access to higher education) are much more egalitarian than their liberal counterparts. Thus, the gap between the wealthiest and the poorest is far more pronounced in the United States than in Scandinavia. Likewise, the level of poverty is higher in the former than in the latter.

Both systems confronted serious challenges to their capacity to manage inequality by the 1970s, leading to a frontal assault on the welfare state by advocates of neoliberalism. The 1970s set the stage, as a number of challenges presented themselves. Edward Broadbent (2001: 7) summarized the situation as follows: "Lower growth rates, higher oil prices, an aging population, and the transformation of industry from large, unionized blue-collar enterprises into smaller, unorganized manufacturing and service employment produced unanticipated problems for the welfare state." In short, the advent of what became known as postindustrial economies, with the attendant process of deindustrialization and the expansion of a global economy, meant that the welfare state was vulnerable. The election of Ronald Reagan in the United States and Margaret Thatcher in Britain signaled the political triumph of business forces intent on rolling back as far as possible the welfare state. Similar campaigns occurred in all of the advanced industrial nations. They proved to be most successful in introducing the neoliberal alternative to the welfare state in liberal rather than social democratic nations, chiefly perhaps because in the latter the link between equality and a sense of a community of shared fate was more deeply embedded in their respective national cultures. Whatever the differences, Broadbent (2001: 8) is correct when he writes, "In many democracies, the march to equality has not only stopped, it has been reversed."

In the next section, we turn to the case of the United States to assess the current level of inequality, with a focus on its class-based, racial, and gendered character.

INEQUALITY IN THE UNITED STATES IN THE EARLY TWENTY-FIRST CENTURY

That the United States is the advanced industrial nation with the highest level of inequality in the world is virtually undisputed by scholars today. There are a variety of ways that social scientists attempt to understand the extent and the scope of inequality. One of the most commonly used measuring sticks is income distribution. Employing this measure, we find a highly skewed distribution pattern. In 2003, the bottom fifth of all households with the lowest incomes received only 3.4 percent of the total income earned that year, while the second quintile earned 8.7 percent, the middle quintile 14.8 percent, the next to the top quintile 23.4 percent, and the top quintile earned 49.8 percent. In other words, the top 20 percent of the population possessed nearly half of all earned income (DeNavas-Walt, Proctor, and Mills 2004: 8). These distribution figures are the most recent in a significant trend that began in the 1970s. During the past thirty years, beginning

in 1974, the percentages earned by the lowest quintile fell 2.1 percent, the second quintile lost 3.3 percent, and the third quintile lost 2.7 percent. The fourth quintile has shown small up and down fluctuations, currently down 0.6 percent, and the percent of total income of the top quintile has increased 8.8 percent (Danziger and Gottschalk 1995: 42, Jones and Weinberg 2000: 4).

A similar trend is demonstrated by evaluating income inequality over time. During the 1980s, the entire income structure expanded dramatically, with the top stretching upward away from the center and the center moving up away from the bottom. In the 1990s, the gap between the 90th and 50th percentile continued to grow, increasing inequality between the top tenth and the rest of the population, while at the same time the difference between the 50th and 10th percentiles shrank. Since 1999, however, it appears that the decreasing inequality in the bottom half of the income structure has stopped and has shown signs of increasing while the widening disparity between the top and the middle persists (Mishel, Bernstein, and Boushey 2003: 152). In fact, the highest incomes have continuously increased at rather rapid rates. In 1979, about 13,500 U.S. taxpayers claimed incomes equivalent to $1 million or more. By 1994, the number earning this much had exceeded 68,000 (Kingston 2000: 159–160). The disparities between the salaries of executives and their employees have widened considerably as CEO and other executive-level salaries have soared, particularly since the 1990s. The use of stock options as a key component of many executive pay packages has led to much higher levels of income inequality (Frydman and Saks 2004).

Frank and Cook (1995) have explored the runaway incomes at the top of the distribution, which are fed by "winner-take-all" markets. The most popular musicians, athletes, actors, artists, authors, car manufacturers, and even producers of food and ordinary household items increasingly tend to receive a disproportionate amount of the monetary benefits in their respective markets, pushing those of only slightly lesser quality (and sometimes of equal quality) far down the income scale if not out of the market entirely. Indeed, the mean income of the top 5 percent of earners in the United States nearly doubled in a decade, from $138,000 in 1991 to $260,000 in 2001, while earners further down the distribution ladder made comparatively meager gains (U.S. Census 2003).

However, while the income and wage distributions do provide a glimpse of the extent of inequality in the United States, a factor that even more profoundly gets at the heart of inequality is wealth. Wealth, determined by a household's assets minus debts, is distributed even more unevenly than income. Wealth is an especially important consideration shaping economic security in changing times. The wealthiest people in the society have in their wealth a buffer from downward economic trends and family and other crises that is not always available to the middle class, and when it is, it is far more limited—and is largely absent from the working class and the poor. If a household experiences financial hardship—the loss of a job, illness, and so forth—wealth is the cushion that breaks a fall. Given this reality, a significant portion of the U.S. population live in very vulnerable circumstances. Only one third of households has any (or has negative) financial assets, and the average family in 1988 held $3,700 in net financial assets, enough to sustain them at the poverty line for a mere three months (Oliver and Shapiro 1997: 69). The economic precariousness of the entire bottom half of the population is in stark contrast to their more affluent counterparts. In 1992, the wealthiest quintile possessed a whopping 84 percent of the wealth in the United States (Mishel, Bernstein, and Boushey 2003: 281) and was the beneficiary of 99 percent of the wealth gain between 1983 and 1989. The bottom 80 percent of households received a mere 1 percent of the increase (Marshall 2000: 5).

Much of this social class inequality tracks along lines defined by race and gender. First considering race, in 2003 the median income was about $55,000 for Asian households; $48,000 for non-Hispanic white households; $33,000 for Hispanic, American Indian, and Alaska Native households;

and $30,000 for African American households (DeNavas-Walt, Proctor, and Mills 2004: 4–10). Likewise, whereas only 8.2 percent of non-Hispanic whites were living at or below the poverty line in 2003, 11.8 percent of Asians, 22.5 percent of Hispanics, 23.9 percent of American Indians and Alaska Natives (2002–2003 average), and 24.3 percent of blacks lived in poverty. Even when they are found in the same occupations and work full-time and year-round, Asian men earn 94 percent of the income of white men, Hispanic men only 86 percent, and black men only 84 percent (Xu and Leffler 1996: 119).

Wealth is similarly divided along racial lines. While a quarter of white households possess no wealth or negative wealth, 61 percent of black and 54 percent of Hispanic households fit into this category. While 38 percent of white households lack the financial assets to survive for three months at the poverty line, as many as 73 percent of Hispanic households and 80 percent of black households live in this precarious financial position (Oliver and Shapiro 1997: 86–87). Viewed another way, the median white household possesses $7,000 in net financial assets in contrast to the zero assets held by the median black household. The median white household has over eight times the net worth of the median black household (Mishel, Bernstein, and Boushey 2003: 284).

Even considering only middle-class households, whether defined by income ($25,000 to $50,000, calculated with 1988 dollars), college education, or white-collar occupation, black households possess only 35 percent of the net worth of white households by the first definition, 23 percent by the second, and 15 percent by the third. In terms of financial assets—that which can help prevent financial disaster in extenuating circumstances—black households have 1 to 4 percent that of whites, with white-collar black households having no net financial assets whatsoever, a figure that excludes equity in a home or vehicle (Oliver and Shapiro 1997: 94). This means that the average black middle-class family has to rely almost entirely on income alone for its middle-class standard of living and cannot withstand a single financial obstacle without it becoming a potential financial catastrophe.

The disparity in earnings by gender has significantly decreased in recent decades; however, the gap between women and men remains, and it is not an insignificant gap. In 1984, full-time, year-round working women of privileged racial groups—white and Asian—made 68 to 77 percent that of white men *in the same occupations;* men of the least privileged racial groups—Hispanic and black—earned 84 to 86 percent that of white men (Xu and Leffler 1996: 119). However, since 1984, women of all races combined (irrespective of occupation) have jumped from an average $0.64 per men's dollar to $0.76 per men's dollar. Whereas men's incomes have made little progress since 1973 (then $27,802, and $29,101 in 2001), women's incomes have increased 72 percent—up from $9,649 in 1973 to $16,614 in 2001 (U.S. Census 2001).

This can be construed as welcome change in the right direction. However, substantial inequalities still exist for women. While the median earnings gap between women and men may be decreasing, this does not reveal the fact that most of women's pay increase is occurring in the lower and middle rungs of the income distribution and to a far lesser degree at the top (Blau and Kahn 1997); this is particularly the case for black women (Bernhardt, Morris, and Handcock 1995). Since 1983, the greatest income distribution change for men occurred in the category of those earning $75,000 and above—an increase of 5.7 percentage points. For women, the most progress was made in the lowest income group—those with negative earnings to making $2,499, a drop of 7.3 points (U.S. Census 2001). The phrase "glass ceiling" used in reference to women's low rates of advancement in upper-level income brackets is affirmed by these figures.

Motherhood is one major factor that stunts financial compensation for women, especially if they are unmarried. Budig and England (2001) found that women pay a "wage penalty" of about 7 percent per child, only a third of which is explained by differences in work experience or interrupted employment. Three fifths of the impoverished population in the United States is composed of women (Rank 2004: 32). The "feminization of poverty" is especially evident among unmarried mothers (including divorcees, widows, and the never married) and their children. For the 10.5 percent of people living in female-headed households in 2002, 35.2 percent were at or below the poverty line, nearly three times the rate for all people, 12.1 percent (Rank 2004: 31). McLanahan and Booth (1989) contend that most single mothers become poor as a result of divorce. Post-divorce women earn a mere 67 percent of the prior family income, while their ex-husbands garner about 90 percent of what they had brought in before the marital breakup. Making matters worse, although most women have custody of their children, 60 percent receive no child support at all (Furstenberg, Morgan, and Allison 1987), and the payments are meager for many of those who do.

THE CONSEQUENCES OF INEQUALITY: CONSTRAINTS ON EQUAL OPPORTUNITY

What are the implications of these existing levels of inequality on life chances? This is the topic we turn to in the following section. While a vast majority of Americans claim to embrace the idea of equal opportunity (but not equality of outcomes), the issue becomes one of sorting out the various ways that existing levels of inequality impede the realization of creating an equal opportunity society. In this section, we explore the following issues: (1) quality of life issues associated with physical and mental health; (2) food and nutrition; (3) housing and neighborhood quality; (4) crime; (5) environmental risk; (6) schooling and the development of human capital; and (7) social capital.

It should be stressed at the outset that this is only a snapshot of aspects of the consequences of inequality. What is clear is that inequality is a complex and multidimensional phenomenon. What follows is by no means intended to be comprehensive. Rather, its purpose is to illustrate some of the key multifaceted elements involved in determining the varied impacts of inequality on different sectors of the disadvantaged population.

Physical and Mental Health

Inequality in the United States is in no way limited simply to economics. The "losers" in this unequal society endure a number of consequences deriving from their lower socioeconomic status (SES), consequences that pervade virtually all aspects of life. One of these is a generic term called "quality of life." While this term can be used to account for a number of factors, we concentrate here on only two: mental and physical health.

Numerous studies have demonstrated that low SES is correlated with a wide range of psychological disorders (Merva and Fowles 2000). Although the direction of causality is still debated, Marva and Fowles's study of the mental health of laid-off workers suggests that financial privation, at least in some cases, precedes psychiatric distress. Furthermore, it appears that not only is *absolute* economic deprivation strongly associated with mental health but so too is *relative* deprivation. Increasing inequality causes those in the lower rungs of the wage scale to feel alienated from the rest of society and to increasingly view themselves as inadequate.

Mental health problems frequently result from the negative impacts of poverty and inequality, and once individuals are suffering from a mental illness, they become less likely to find or keep gainful employment. Add to this that the mentally ill are often left untreated, particularly if they do not have insurance to pay for counseling or medication. More of the poor with treatable mental illnesses go untreated than is the case with the general population.

Pressure to "keep up with the Joneses" is strong throughout the society, but for those at the bottom it is especially stressful because success seems to be out of reach. Indeed, the lower class is no less influenced than the middle class by the values of a consumer culture, despite that there are so many goods and services that they cannot possibly afford to purchase (Caplovitz 1967: 12). If all members of a consumption-oriented society confront the problem of seeing their desires always unmet because there is always something more that one might possess, the frustrations are more intense for those who have access to so much less than others. The result is stress. These stressors often result in not only mental health problems but also violence; indeed, wage inequality is positively associated with accident mortality, homicide, and aggravated assault. Single, low-income mothers are among the most likely to develop stress-related disorders (Merva and Fowles 2000). Hughes and Thomas (1998) demonstrate that African Americans experience a lower quality of life (measurements include life satisfaction, marital happiness, degree of trust, happiness, anomie, and health) than whites, even when classified as middle or upper class. The authors suggest that this is because of a "racial tax"—the harmful psychological effects of a long historical legacy of racism.

The physical health consequences of inequality are no less serious. Regardless of the exact measurement used, low-income level and poor health are strongly linked. For example, impoverished African Americans have disproportionately high incidences of high blood pressure, heart problems, diabetes and its complications, and sudden infant death syndrome (Mullahy and Wolfe 2001: 284). Cancer (among males), sickle-cell anemia, tuberculosis, hypertension, arteriosclerosis, and AIDS also affect significantly higher percentages of blacks than whites (Pearson 1994). Because of the high concentration of blacks among the poor, it is likely that these are related to poverty and not only to racism. Life expectancy is another factor that varies considerably by race, gender, SES, and also location. Geronimus and her colleagues (2001) found that the life expectancy at age 16 of a black man living in urban poverty is 42 years. Likewise, black women have shorter life expectancies, and spend more time disabled by poor health, than white women.

This difference may be because those in poverty tend to exhibit more unhealthy behaviors than the rest of the population (Mullahy and Wolfe 2001: 285). Smoking, in particular, appears to be concentrated among those of low SES and among racial minorities (Williams and Collins 1995). The disparity in health is also in large part due to an underuse of health care. One third of the African American deaths above the white death rate are the result of treatable conditions (Williams and Collins 1995). Much of this is certainly because access to health care is severely limited for low SES Americans, and the number of people without health insurance has recently increased. In 2003, 15.6 percent of the population was without coverage, amounting to 45 million people, 1.4 million more than in 2002 (DeNavas-Walt, Proctor, and Mills 2004: 14). Employer-provided health insurance is decreasing as health care costs increase, and those who still have insurance via an employer are expected to pay larger portions of the premiums even as quality of care is decreasing because of the increasing adoption of managed care plans (Davis 2000). These recent trends most sharply affect the lower classes—as income level decreases, so does access to quality health insurance—and racial minorities, particularly Hispanics, of whom nearly a third have no health coverage (DeNavas-Walt, Proctor, and Mills 2004: 15).

Living in hazardous neighborhoods and being exposed to injurious work conditions further endangers the physical health of the disadvantaged. Individuals at the bottom of the social structure are more likely to hold jobs that involve heavy lifting; awkward body postures; exposure to toxic substances, dust, fumes, explosives, acids, and other harmful substances; as well as long hours of mechanical, routinized actions (William and Collins 1995). These hazards are also correlated with race. For example, steelworkers occupying the most dangerous positions in the production process are three times more likely to be black than white (Evans and Kantrowitz 2002). All of these take a toll on the bodies and on the life expectancies of the most disadvantaged sectors of the society.

Food and Nutrition

Hunger is another problem that disproportionately affects racial minorities, low-income households, and female-headed households. Alaimo, Briefel, Frongillo, Jr., and Olson (1998) estimate

that 4.1 percent of the overall U.S. population—between 9 and 12 million people—does not have enough food to eat either occasionally or frequently. However, in their study of Minneapolis–St. Paul, 15.2 percent of Mexican Americans fell into this category; even when controlling for other economic and demographic factors, twice as many Mexican Americans as whites claimed to experience food deficiency. Nearly 8 percent of African Americans reported food deficiency compared to 2.5 percent of non-Hispanic whites, which at least in part is attributable to disparities in SES. Obviously, SES plays an enormous role in food sufficiency; 14 percent of the low-income population[1] does not have enough food at times. Other studies report even higher percentages of hunger levels. Forty-five percent of children living under the poverty line in 2002 suffered food insecurity. America's Second Harvest, the nation's largest food relief distributor, came to the assistance of 23.3 million people in 2001; the median income for those helped was well below the poverty line (Rank 2004: 38). Getting enough food to eat can be especially problematic for the poor during the winter months. Bhattacharya, Deleire, Haider, and Currie (2002) found that while both the rich and poor increase heating expenditures in very cold times, the poor compensate for this increase by reducing their food expenditures by about the same cost. While the rich tend to increase their food intake, the poor eat about 200 fewer calories per day than in warmer months. This "heat or eat" dilemma significantly impacts the nutrition and the health of the poor.

Making matters worse, Chung and Myers (1999) demonstrate that food actually costs more for the urban poor. They found a $16.62 difference in market-basket prices, or the cost for a week's worth of food that meets minimum nutritional requirements, between chain and non-chain grocery stores. Because many chain stores are not located in or near

---

[1]Low income is defined in this study as households having a "poverty index ratio (PIR; ratio of family income to the federal poverty line times 100) less than or equal to 130 percent of the poverty line" (422).

urban poor neighborhoods, and many poor people do not have cars or adequate public transportation, residents have little choice but to shop at closer but more expensive non-chain stores. Furthermore, these non-chain stores carry a far smaller selection of certain types of foods, particularly fresh produce, meat, and dairy products, (Barnes, 2005: 67–93).

But food insufficiency also affects households in the lower-middle income range,[2] particularly those with children headed by employed females; when other factors are controlled, these households are 5.5 times more likely to suffer food deficiency than other households. In part, this deficiency appears to be the result of difficulties associated with affording childcare during work hours while not being eligible for federal assistance, such as food stamps. This situation is particularly acute for female-headed households. The adverse effects of hunger are obvious: malnutrition not only affects an individual's health in various ways but also impedes children's physical and cognitive development (Alaimo, Briefel, Frongillo, Jr., and Olson, 1998).

Inequality does not only impact food in terms of insufficiency and hunger. Many people conceive of eating disorders as being primarily white, middle- to upper-class female phenomena, resulting from social pressures to conform to our culture's thin ideal of beauty. However, Thompson (1992) asserts that these disorders have class, race, and sexual orientation dimensions as well. She claims that some women develop bulimia, anorexia, unhealthy dieting, and binging as a means of coping with such "traumas" as discrimination and high levels of stress based on the factors just mentioned. For example, many women living in poverty respond to the stress of their lives by using food as a drug. Excessive eating can produce effects similar to alcohol consumption, is far cheaper, and does not result in hangovers that would hinder productivity. This phenomenon can explain one of the paradoxes of contemporary poverty. While there is hunger, it is also true that poor people are more likely to be overweight than the general population. Obesity and its related problems, such as hypertension and diabetes, result not only from overeating but from eating cheaper but unhealthy foods, particularly those high in saturated fat.

Housing and Neighborhood Quality

Inequality also profoundly affects housing and neighborhood quality. Housing discrimination based primarily on race remains an endemic problem in the United States, which, combined with a shortage of decent affordable housing, is responsible for the concentration of poverty in select geographic areas (Massey, Gross, and Shibuya 1994). While some of the most overt forms of housing discrimination are far less obvious since the civil rights era, new and more subtle modes of discrimination persist, many of them difficult to detect. For example, Yinger (1986) has demonstrated that housing agents show blacks 36 percent fewer apartments than they show whites; more to the point, they purposefully do not introduce them to apartments located in predominantly white neighborhoods. To make matters worse, even when SES is controlled, blacks looking to procure housing in black neighborhoods are significantly less likely to be approved for a loan than are their white counterparts (Massey and Fong 1990). This anomaly is caused in part by redlining practices and in part by discriminatory lending policies. And when blacks do move into predominantly white areas, they often must endure the antagonisms directed at them by white residents. Whites searching for new homes tend to avoid these neighborhoods, and as a result, minority households will eventually dominate them. The above is true for Hispanics as well, though to a lesser extent.

What is the result of this geographic segregation? Massey and Fong (1990) show that while highly educated black communities can truly uphold a "separate but equal" status with socioeconomically similar white communities, poorer and less-educated blacks experience neighborhood conditions

---

[2]Low middle income includes "PIR 131% to 185% of the poverty line" (422).

inferior to other impoverished populations because of their relative concentration in urban inner city settings. These are neighborhoods characterized by what Massey and Denton (1993) call "hypersegregation." Police protection, firefighting, sanitation services, and similar municipal services tend to be of poorer quality in low SES areas, and children have fewer places to play and an even smaller numbers of *safe* recreation areas (Evans and Kantrowitz 2002). More youth in these neighborhoods drop out of high school, have decreased childhood IQ, and become pregnant as teenagers (Brooks-Gunn, Duncan, Klebanov, and Sealand, 1993; Crane 1991). Those who live in impoverished and racially segregated (especially African American, but to a lesser degree Mexican American) neighborhoods suffer significantly higher mortality rates, even when variance in individual characteristics is controlled (LeClere, Rogers, and Peters 1997). Wilson (2000) is particularly concerned about "jobless ghettoes" that continue to grow in inner cities, which are plagued with crime, prostitution, drug trafficking, and gang activity. Often, potential employers do not welcome individuals raised in these locales, in part because of discrimination but also because of the underdevelopment of skills in these communities; unfortunately, this inability to find work only reinforces and thus perpetuates disadvantage.

Crime and Punishment

Socioeconomic and racial inequality also negatively affect crime and violence. In terms of racial inequality, in 2002, 49 percent of all murder victims were black and 49 percent were white, while only 13 percent of Americans are black and 80 percent are white (Bureau of Justice 2002, Rasmussen 2003). Blacks are seven times more likely than whites to commit murder and six times more likely to be murdered (Bureau of Justice 2002). Turning to another type of crime, households earning less than $7,500 were victims of burglary and assault at significantly higher rates than higher earning households (Bureau of Justice 2003). Why blacks and those of low SES are so much

more likely to be exposed to crime is the object of much speculation. Of interest to this discussion, Harer and Steffensmeier (1992) have shown that for whites, low SES is strongly correlated with violent crime. For blacks, on the other hand, this is not the case.

A possible explanation is put forward by Alba, Logan, and Bellair (1994). In their study, which focused on suburbs, they also found that black SES, and additionally family structure and other personal traits, do not explain the race's disproportionately large exposure to crime. Rather than these factors, they suggest that the culprit is the residential segregation process that locates blacks—even if affluent—in crime-prone areas. Sampson, Raudenbush, and Earls (1997) show that neighborhoods characterized by a high percentage of disadvantaged households (including high levels of lower class families, minority households, and female-headed households), immigrants, and residential instability are less likely to have strong ties to one another and to uphold informal social control, such as watching over neighbors' property, keeping track of neighbors' kids, and so forth. Thus, they experience much higher rates of crime and violence because they lack the control necessary to prevent these things from happening.

In general, insofar as high levels of inequality are associated with high crime levels, and socioeconomic inequality and racial inequality are intertwined, it is not surprising that disadvantaged racial minorities are involved in crime at a greater rate than the general population, both as offenders and victims. Evidence suggests that this is particularly the case in instances of violent crime (Blau and Blau 1982).

The significance of class location and racial identity is reflected in the state's punishment practices for criminal violations. The United States imprisons far more of its citizens per capita than any other advanced industrial nation. It incarcerates approximately 600 individuals per 100,000. The average for other advanced industrial nations ranges from around 55 to 120 per 100,000. The rate in Scandinavian countries, for example, is one tenth the U.S. rate (Currie 1998). Moreover, the United States sends people to prison for much longer periods of time than is the case in other economically comparable nations. The typical prisoner in both state and federal prisons is relatively young and relatively poor. It is also the case that blacks disproportionately constitute the largest plurality of the current prison population. At the beginning at this century the United States imprisoned almost 1.5 million individuals, 44 percent of whom were black, compared to 35 percent white, 19 percent Latino, and 2 percent other (Human Rights Watch 2002).

A similar scenario can be seen in the use of the death penalty—a practice that has been abolished in virtually all other advanced industrial nations. Costanzo (1997: 84) summarizes the nature of the racial disparities in capital punishment cases in the following way:

> Those who are accused of murdering a white victim are more likely to be charged with a capital crime; those convicted of killing a white victim are more likely to receive a death sentence; black defendants who are convicted of killing a white person are the group most likely to receive the death penalty; [and] white defendants who murder black victims are the group least likely to receive a death sentence.

While 58 percent of the defendants executed between 1976 and 2004 were white, at 34 percent, blacks are overrepresented. Moreover, as of 2004, blacks and whites had nearly reached parity in terms of their respective percentages of the death row population, with blacks registering at 42 percent and whites at 46 percent (NAACP Legal Defense Fund 2004).

The capacity of the state to punish its citizenry is a reflection of its monopoly on the power to do so. The need to punish large numbers of citizens is related to levels of inequality. It is not fortuitous that the United States has the highest level of inequality among the advanced industrial nations and it also has, by far, the highest level of incarceration and is the only one routinely using the death penalty. Social control, in short, is more problematic and difficult to achieve in highly unequal societies.

Environmental Risk

Those at the bottom of the social class system and the racial hierarchy are endangered not only by greater violence and crime but also by environmental hazards. Because minimizing pollution and toxic wastes is costly, plants that produce these by-products tend to carefully locate themselves in areas where land is less expensive, where residents are not likely to protest their presence, and where challenges to their mishandling of wastes is least likely. These locations are found in low-SES and minority communities (Krieg 1998). In the Southeast, 26 percent to 42 percent of households proximal to (within the same census tract as) a hazardous waste landfill live in poverty. Other sources of environmental dangers plague the disadvantaged as well. As many as 68 percent of urban African American children living in households earning less than $6,000 yearly suffer dangerous levels of lead in their blood. On the other hand, white children in families above $15,000 experience unsafe lead levels at a rate of only 12 percent. Likewise, impoverished children are nearly 40 percent more likely to be exposed to cigarette smoke in the home than are those above the poverty line. Air pollution (CO and NO_2) from stoves and heating systems is also far more prevalent in low-income homes. Water pollution affects primarily rural, low-SES populations, including poor Mexican Americans residing near the nation's southern border. As noted earlier, a variety of environmental risks are associated with various low-income occupations (Evans and Kantrowitz 2002).

While these and related environmental risks have profound effects on their victims' health, often due to daily exposure year after year, other less apparent environmental factors also deeply influence the lives of the urban poor. First, exposure to high levels of noise pollution is also linked with low SES. Not only does constant clamor often result in hearing damage but also it has been shown to elevate stress, to impede the execution of complex tasks, to hinder children's mastery of reading, and to undermine the development of certain crucial "interpersonal processes" related to the emergence of altruism and the control of aggression. Furthermore, it may also spur feelings of helplessness and inhibit motivation—apparently from the individual's inability to control the noise.

Overcrowding (less than one room per resident) is yet another environmental risk factor associated with SES. Living in crowded conditions has virtually the same result as noise exposure and also contributes to the spread of infectious diseases. Overcrowding is not limited to the home. This also translates to outdoor space, both in the yard as well as in park areas: children in low-income New York City neighborhoods average about 17 square yards of park space per child, whereas the rest of the city's children each have 40 square yards (Evans and Kantrowitz 2002).

While many environmental risks, such as air pollution, are shared by all sectors of the population, it is clearly the case that environmental risks in general disproportionately impact lower income people and disadvantaged racial minorities.

Schooling and the Development of Human Capital

Race and social class inequality, more than gender inequality, result in vast educational disadvantages for lower class and minority children. These inequities appear to be rooted in three main factors: unequal funding for schools, family structure and parental involvement in their child's education, and discrimination. First, school funding is based largely on local property taxes. This means that schools located in areas populated primarily with lower class households are going to have significantly smaller budgets than schools in wealthier middle- to upper-class districts. However, this inequality is exacerbated in the inner cities, where lower class youth and racial minorities are likely to be concentrated. Operating inner-city schools tends to be more expensive than running suburban schools. The school properties themselves tend to cost more, and the upkeep and insurance of the buildings, which are often old and subject

to frequent vandalism, demands a larger portion of the educational budget than elsewhere. Furthermore, other needs of inner cities, such as large police forces and fire departments, compete with the neighborhood schools for limited local tax revenues (Spratlen 1973).

Despite *Brown v. Board of Education of Topeka,* the 1954 landmark Supreme Court decision that found that segregated schools led to racially unequal educational opportunities, a half century after the decision, American schools are undergoing a process of resegregation. In a recent study conducted by Harvard's Civil Rights Project, the researchers determined that the gains made in the 1960s and 1970s have eroded and, particularly in the 1990s, the rate of resegregation has increased dramatically. At present, 70 percent of black students attend schools that contain predominantly minority student populations, while Latinos have also witnessed increasing levels of educational segregation (Orfield 2004). Thus, minority students, particularly poorer ones, increasingly attend public schools that are inferior to those of their white counterparts.

In general, less money is spent per capita on the education of low-SES and minority youth than on higher social class whites. Somewhat more debated is the effect of this inequity on disadvantaged students. The frequently cited Coleman Report, which appeared in 1966, convinced many that school characteristics, most of which can be linked directly to the school's economic resources, have very little bearing on student achievement. The report argued that the single most important factor was the role played by parents. However, more recent research has contradicted this finding. School resources and class size both appear to affect students' test scores, and going to underprivileged schools has been demonstrated to be as strong a predictor as intelligence of low future SES (Walters 2001; Pong 1998). It is not surprising that youth who attend schools that use dated textbooks, that have inadequate or no science labs, inadequate library materials, underpaid teachers, and large classrooms; and that lack access to computer technologies are at a significant disadvantage compared to youth who attend schools with well-paid instructors, who are provided individualized attention, and who have access to up-to-date educational materials.

Coleman was not entirely wrong: family characteristics and parental involvement do affect education by race and SES as well. Roscigno and Ainsworth-Darnell (1999) have shown that high-SES parents tend to provide their children with more household educational resources (periodicals, reference materials, computers, books, calculators); enroll their children in more nonschool classes involving art, music, or dance; and take their children on more cultural trips to museums, historical sites, concerts, and so forth. Interestingly, while white students who receive these household benefits appear to benefit from them (as measured by higher grades and test scores), black students do not receive the same educational return.

Parental interaction with their children also facilitates educational success. Hence, children in single-parent households tend to operate at an educational disadvantage; single parents supervise their children's homework less often and generally have less contact with their children. Pong (1998) provides evidence that a high level of parental involvement in a school boosts student achievement. However, since single working parents generally have little time available to attend PTA meetings and other such activities, their students do not receive this benefit to their education to the same extent as more privileged students in two-parent households. Finally, female-headed households are disproportionately characteristic of minority families and lower class families, reflecting the interactive impact of race, class, and gender.

Finally, simple discrimination appears to explain much of the leftover disparity in educational achievement between blacks and whites. The racial difference in academic success is profound. African Americans on average are as many as four years behind white students in reading, math, science, and writing. They are more likely to be held back a grade. They are less likely to attend and complete college. They are vastly underrepresented at the top of national test distributions. Although black students at higher SES schools score higher on the SAT than do those at lower SES schools, they do not perform as well as their white classmates (Hallinan 2001). While many of these differences can be explained by the aforementioned economic and family factors, these do not fully account for the differences. Although discrimination is far less easy to operationalize, it seems highly likely that racial discrimination also plays a part in educational inequality (Hedges and Nowell 1999).

Although women do not experience significant educational differences from men before graduating from high school, there are gender disparities in higher education. In many ways, of the many inequalities discussed in this essay, education may be the arena in which women and men are nearly equal, with women sometimes even surpassing men. A slightly higher percentage of women (among whites and in virtually all minority groups; see Hoffman, Llagas, and Snyder 2003: 95) enroll in college and graduate with two-year, bachelors, master's, and professional degrees compared to men. However, only 37.3 percent of PhD degrees were earned by women in 1992, and they remain a minority among college and university faculty. Additionally, women tend to be disproportionately enrolled in less selective schools; men still enroll in and receive degrees from choice institutions at higher rates than women (Jacobs 1996).

Many of these factors related to higher education provide evidence for the perpetuation of racial disparities. A smaller percentage of African Americans and Hispanics enroll in colleges and universities than do whites; in 2000, 39 percent of 18- to 24-year-old whites were enrolled, 31 percent of blacks, and 22 percent of Hispanics (Hoffman, Llagas, and Snyder 2003: 93). Additionally, the percentage of degrees earned by blacks decreases as the level of the degree increases, earning 11 percent of associate's degrees, 9 percent of bachelor's, 8 percent of master's, 7 percent of professional, and 5 percent of doctorate degrees. For Hispanics, the respective percentages are 9 percent, 6 percent, 4 percent, 5 percent, and 3 percent (Hoffman, Llagas, and Snyder 2003: 96–97).

Education has a direct effect on the development of human capital, or one's skill, education, and experience that can be used to secure a quality position or to advance in the job market. As mentioned earlier, lower class students and racial minorities do not receive educations equivalent to their more advantaged counterparts and therefore are often at a human capital disadvantage that starts early in childhood. Insofar as the school system in the nation fails to provide genuinely equal educational opportunities, it serves to reinforce existing inequalities rather than contribute to overcoming them.

Women's human capital has made great gains in recent decades; women are completing undergraduate and some graduate degrees at higher rates than men. However, these high levels of education often do not translate into financial benefits comparable with men's. Partly as a function of earning degrees in female-dominated fields, women earn less money than men (Jacobs 1996: 169). Additionally, while not lacking in educational achievement, women may on average lag somewhat behind men in experience. Since the responsibilities of childrearing fall primarily upon women, many married women put their careers on hold or work part time, both of which decrease experience and depress earning potential (Budig and England 2001). These effects of household labor persist across class lines, although nonworking-class women experience a more significant drop in wages (Coverman 1983). However, this does *not* fully account for the difference between women's and men's earnings. Discrimination continues to play a role in persisting gender-based earnings differentials.

Social Capital

Inequality not only leads to vast discrepancies in social capital but also perpetuates it by deterring upward mobility for those at the bottom of the social structure and by facilitating it for those already near the top. Lin (2000: 786) describes social capital as "the quantity and/or quality of resources that an actor (be it an individual or group or community) can access or use through its location in a social network." Access to these resources, then, enables people to attain higher paying and more prestigious jobs as well as other quality of life benefits.

While social capital is important to the attainment of SES, its benefits are distributed highly inequitably by initial SES location, gender, and race. Since individuals tend to maintain social networks with others of similar characteristics, the networks of members of the lower class tend to consist primarily of other low-SES contacts. These connections tend to be lacking not only in the number of beneficial resources for socioeconomic advancement but also in the diversity of resources that are available to those of higher SES (Lin 2000). In his review of the literature, Portes (1998) explains that all too frequently for inner-city residents, social networks do not reach outside of the inner city, and their knowledge of and ability to obtain good jobs is therefore severely limited. Furthermore, since inner-city communities tend to be more transitory, even the social ties within these poor locales are likely to be less extensive and more tenuous as a result.

Clearly, these factors have implications for race as well. African Americans have less extensive networks than Hispanics and whites, with whites having the largest networks. Since blacks are often segregated in certain neighborhoods, their social networks consist largely of other African Americans, which is not advantageous in an economy more or less dominated by whites. Even in the middle and upper classes, blacks often have relatively few weak ties to white networks, instead forming strong social ties among themselves (Lin 2000). These differences play out in explicit ways, for example, when a person seeking a job begins to turn to people he or she knows who might be of assistance. Blacks tend not to have the social capital that will work to their advantage. But social capital also works in more implicit ways, as well. The example of IQ scores, which are the product of the social forces that shape one's background, is revealing. Black children adopted by white families tend to demonstrate higher IQ scores than those adopted by black families, but black children adopted by black families that have ties to racially diverse networks or predominantly white networks have higher IQs than those in black families that do not have these social network characteristics (Moore 1987). It appears that disparities in social capital between blacks and whites contribute to the lower socioeconomic attainment of blacks.

Social capital also varies greatly by gender. McPherson and Smith-Lovin (1982) have shown that although women and men on average have the same number of memberships in organizations, women are members of much smaller organizations than are men. Thus, men have more social contacts (men average 600 contacts via these groups, women 185). Furthermore, the type of organization differs between men and women. Women predominantly take part in organizations concerned with domestic matters, whereas men are far more involved in work-related organizations.

This disparity is exaggerated during childrearing years. Munch, McPherson, and Smith-Lovin (1997) suggest that especially when children are around 3 years old, childcare responsibilities tend to restrict mothers' social contacts significantly in terms of both network size and contact frequency. They further suggest that these social ties, while lessening somewhat as children grow older, may never reach their pre-parenting extent, strength, and richness. Men, on the other hand, do not experience any of these significant, lasting effects on social networks as a result of having young children. In sum, women's social capital provides fewer socioeconomic benefits than that of men, because women's smaller networks provide them primarily domestic information, and their focus on childrearing severely limits beneficial social contacts for a number of years.

Durable Inequalities

Although this survey of the extent of inequality in the contemporary United States and its implications in such varied areas of social life as physical and mental health, food and nutrition, housing and neighborhood quality, crime and punishment, environmental risk, schooling and human capital development, and social capital only manages to skim the surface, it does reveal the depth of the levels of inequality and the deleterious consequences they have on the life chances of the more disadvantaged sectors of the population. It also indicates the complexity of inequality, a complexity that contributes to its durability (McCall 2001; Tilly, 1998).

GLOBAL INEQUALITY

Complicating the situation considerably is that we live in an increasingly global and therefore interdependent world. Inequality in the United States occurs in a context of a country that is by global standards one of the world's wealthy nations. To put its patterns of inequality into relief, we briefly turn to a global frame of analysis. Specifically, we provide summary evidence regarding (1) the levels of inequality among rich nations; (2) a comparison of rich and poor nations; and (3) levels of inequality within poor nations.

Rich Nations

Although, as previously mentioned, the United States is one of the most unequal Western nations, many other wealthy nations have high levels of inequality as well. George and Wilding (2002: 49–51) describe some of the ways in which globalization and other trends promote the interests of wealthy businesses, often at the expense of the lower social classes within those nations. Perhaps most importantly, labor's "bargaining power" has diminished significantly in recent decades. Since corporations have become increasingly mobile, able to relocate themselves in countries where labor is cheap, workers in advanced industrial countries (AICs) have had to settle for less in order to retain their jobs. Just as in the United States, income distributions in the United Kingdom and Italy, among others, have demonstrated rising levels of inequality in the last quarter century. Likewise, work conditions are deteriorating. "More use of temporary, short-term contracts, more use of part-time and shift work, [and] the proliferation of low-paid jobs" are some of the circumstances workers increasingly find themselves facing (George and Wilding 2002: 50).

Unemployment is a mounting problem in AICs as their factory jobs decrease in number, a problem which disproportionately affects those at the bottom of the social class system. In the face of all of this, social welfare benefits in many AICs are in a period of constriction, so fewer needy individuals are eligible, or those who are eligible receive less. In many (but not all) rich countries, social security pensions have been or are being reduced, the age at which one can begin to receive these pensions is being pushed higher (e.g., Sweden and Germany), more years of paying into the pension system are being required, and means testing is increasingly being employed to reduce old age benefits (including in Australia, Canada, Denmark, Finland, the Netherlands, New Zealand, and Norway). Unemployment compensation benefits have been similarly reduced (George and Wilding 2002: 71–72).

In all, inequality for the world's wealthiest nations is substantial, but not to the extent that one finds in the United States. De Nardi, Ren, and Wei (2000) evaluate the income inequality within five of these countries: Canada, Finland, Germany, Sweden, and the United States. Whereas the ratio of the average disposable income[3] of the top 20 percent to the bottom 20 percent is 9:1 in the United States, it is only 6:1 in Canada, 5:1 in Germany, 5:1 in Finland, and 4:1 in Sweden.

Rich Versus Poor Nations

While the inequality within the United States and other rich countries appears vast, in terms of income, only 25 to 33 percent of world inequality is comprised of inequality *within* nations. On the contrary, approximately 70 percent of individual income disparities are directly linked to one's nation of residence. In an even broader perspective, Firebaugh (2003: 10–11) breaks down income

inequality by larger world regions. In 1990, per capita income in the high-income regions of Western Europe and Western offshoots (Australia, Canada, New Zealand, and the United States) was approximately $17,000 and $21,000, respectively. In Southern and Eastern Europe and Latin America, the middle-income regions per capita income was between $4,700 and $8,000. Finally, in China, India, and Africa, average income was between $1,300 and $2,700, with the remaining parts of Asia earning $4,700 annually per capita; these are classified as low-income areas. To put world economic inequality in stark terms, the three wealthiest people in the world possess more than the gross domestic products of the 48 poorest nations together. The incomes of the poorest 2.5 billion people in the world—47 percent of the world's population—is equal to the worth of the richest 225 people (Yates 2003: 57).

This extensive spread, from a little above $1,000 to $21,000, has not always been so vast. In 1820, the top region of the world, Western Europe, earned per capita just under three times that of the world's lowest average income locale, Africa ($1,300 and $450, respectively, 1990 dollars). Clearly, similar to the trend within the United States and other Western nations, the world income distribution demonstrates increasingly vast inequalities. However, there are important differences. The income gap between advanced industrial countries and industrially developing countries (IDCs) has remained static for over two decades, with the AICs earning twenty-one times more than the IDCs. While all levels of the U.S. distribution have seen absolute positive change over time, average incomes in the poorest 48 IDCs have actually dropped over these two decades while those of other IDCs and AICs were rising (George and Wilding 2002: 88–89). Viewed through a long-term lens, although Firebaugh (2003) points out that in general people in the later twentieth and twenty-first centuries have better living standards than their early nineteenth-century forebears, those in the bottom income nations have experienced significantly less economic growth. Whereas the high-income United States has multiplied its 1820 per

---

[3]Includes all forms of income after taxes; figures only include individuals age 25 to 60.

capita income by a factor of nearly 18, Africa, at the bottom of the income heap, only tripled its 1820 average income.

While living on the bottom in the United States is wrought with difficulty, even those with median incomes in poor nations often live in absolute penury. Eighty-five percent of the population of Uganda lives on less than one dollar per day, as does 72 percent of Mali, 64 percent of Zambia, 61 percent of Madagascar, 45 percent of Ghana, 42 percent of Malawi, 36 percent of Bangladesh, and 35 percent of India. The fact that these countries are all located in Africa and South Asia is no coincidence; the populations living at this level of poverty in sub-Saharan African and South Asian nations average 46 percent and 40 percent respectively, while numerous countries in other regions of the world have percentages at or near zero, including Chile, the Czech Republic, Jordan, Thailand, Turkey, and certainly wealthy Western nations (UN Statistics 2004a; George and Wilding 2002).

Clearly, this extreme poverty has numerous negative consequences for individuals' lives. One of these consequences is undernutrition. Perhaps contrary to what one would think, some of the most impoverished nations are not the *most* hungry; indeed, many of those subsisting on less than $1 daily work in agriculture and hence do not rely solely upon their meager incomes for food. In 2000, 70 to 75 percent of the populations of Afghanistan, Burundi, the Democratic Republic of the Congo, Somalia, and Tajikistan were undernourished, and around half those of Angola, Haiti, Mozambique, Sierra Leone, and Zambia suffered the same plight. A large percentage of children under five years of age are "moderately or severely underweight" in the poorest regions of the world; 48 percent in Bangladesh and Nepal, 47 percent in India and Ethiopia, 45 percent in Burundi and Cambodia, and 40 percent in Eritrea and Niger. This figure is a mere 1.4 percent in the United States, and zero percent of Hungary is hungry (UN Statistics 2004a).

Poor nutrition is only one of several contributors to the poor health of the world's poorest individuals. Many do not have access to clean water.

While virtually 100 percent of the people of Western nations have improved drinking water sources, 80 to 100 percent in Latin America, 70 to 90 percent in most of Southern Asia, and 70 to 100 percent in some sub-Saharan African countries—many of the least developed nations—have very limited access to clean water. Only 13 percent of Afghanistan, 22 percent of Ethiopia, 29 percent of Somalia, and 34 percent of Chad and Cambodia have improved water sources. As for access to improved sanitation, most of sub-Saharan Africa does not possess this benefit; less than 10 percent of the populations of some of these countries receive any sanitation services. Less than half of many South and West Asian populations have access to improved sanitation (UN Statistics 2004a). Typhoid, cholera, and diarrhea are just some of the maladies that result from a lack of clean water and sanitation, and some of these diseases are fatal, especially to children. Urban areas in IDCs tend to be the most unsanitary in the world (George and Wilding 2002: 100–107).

Although perhaps the poorest nations have the most need for curative medicine, they in fact have very limited access to drugs. About half of sub-Saharan African countries have populations of which at least half do not have any access to drugs; 50 percent to 80 percent of the populations of the other half have access to needed medicine. Most of Southern Asia and Latin America have between 50 and 80 percent access, and over 80 percent of Western nations' populations have access to drugs, with the wealthiest individuals having over 95 percent access (UN Statistics 2004a).

These factors all contribute to wide variance in life expectancy. While Americans are expected to live to 74 (men) and 80 (women), and Japanese to 78 and 85 (in fact, women are expected to live into their eighties in many Western nations), in Zambia, the average male has a life expectancy of only 33 and women, 32. Sierra Leone, Malawi, Lesotho, Afghanistan, Angola, Botswana, Burundi, Central African Republic, Congo, Democratic Republic of the Congo, Ivory Coast, Kenya, Niger, Somalia, and Zimbabwe also have life expectancies only in the thirties and forties, which no doubt is due in part to the AIDS epidemic plaguing Africa (UN Statistics 2004b).

Inadequate housing is also a significant concern in poor countries. As it is for the poor in the United States, overcrowding is a major problem in numerous countries of the world. Pakistan is among the most crowded, with a national average of three people per room (more than one person per room is considered overcrowded). Syria, Nicaragua, Sri Lanka, Peru, Lesotho, India, Honduras, and Azerbaijan all average between two and three people per room, and numerous others fall between one and two per room, primarily from Asia, Southeastern Europe, and the Middle East, with a few from Latin America and Africa. Conversely, in the United States and the United Kingdom, there are only .5 people per room (UN Statistics 2004b).

In addition to health and housing, education is another factor that is often tied to the wealth of nations. Whereas 92.7 percent of American primary-school-age children are enrolled in school, only 8.2 percent of such Somalian children were enrolled in 1990. Burkina Faso, Djibouti, Niger, and the Democratic Republic of the Congo have enrollment rates of about 35 percent, and Burundi, Comoros, Chad, Eritrea, Ethiopia, Guinea-Bissau, Mali, Mozambique, Nigeria, Senegal, Sierra Leone, Sudan, Tanzania, and Uganda all have between 35 and 60 percent enrollment. These are among the lowest in the world. The low education rates of these African countries are matched only by Bhutan (14 percent), Haiti (22 percent), Afghanistan (27 percent), Saudi Arabia (59 percent), and Pakistan (59 percent) (UN Statistics 2004a). Not surprisingly, three of these countries are located in Southern Asia, one (Saudi Arabia) is very proximal to African countries with low enrollment rates, and Haiti is the poorest country in the Western hemisphere (World Factbook 2004). These low enrollment rates are accompanied by short educational life expectancies as well. Whereas an average American student attends school for 15 years, those native to the aforementioned nations generally stay in school only 2 to 5 years (UN Statistics 2004b). The inadequacy conveyed by these figures is often

exacerbated by poor education conditions. Underfed, tired children who must walk miles to school every morning and are taught by poorly educated teachers in a cramped, hot schoolroom are not going to get as much out of a year of education as the average student in a wealthy nation (George and Wilding 2002: 104).

Literacy rates are quite varied among these poor countries. While some, such as Burkina Faso, have rates as low as 19 percent (includes only persons age 15 to 24), 90 percent of Saudi Arabians in this age range are able to read and write. Most of the poorest countries have literacy rates between 45 percent and 75 percent. Most other countries of the world have literacy rates in the 80 to 100 percent range, and of these, the majority rank in the high 90s (UN Millennium 2004).

In most of the poor countries of the world, governments do not have the capacity to remedy endemic poverty. Although Westerners may lament social welfare benefit cuts in their own nations, in comparative perspective, they do quite well. Residents of Africa, Latin America, and Asia only receive 1.4 percent, 2.1 percent, and 3 percent of each region's GDP in social security pensions. Europeans, on the other hand, receive 12.1 percent of a much larger GDP in such pensions. George and Wilding (2002: 97) contend that the gap in other social welfare benefits between these regions is even broader. What this means for most developing countries is that as many as 80 percent of the population does not receive any social security; the figure is as high as 90 percent in sub-Saharan Africa. In the most poverty-stricken areas of the world, there are virtually no safety nets to ensure that individuals can access survival necessities.

Inequality Within Poor Nations

Even within poor countries, inequality is prevalent. In terms of income inequality, some are highly unequal, such as Zimbabwe and South Africa; although not poor, Brazil, Chile, and Paraguay also are IDCs with considerable income inequality. Indeed, when evaluated using the Theil index,

Africa was second only to Latin America in income inequality in 1995 (Firebaugh 2003: 161). Some nonwealthy nations are more equal in this respect, including Bangladesh, India, Pakistan, and Sri Lanka (George and Wilding 2002: 90). By the same measure, India had the second-lowest degree of inequality, topped only by Western Europe, and Asia as a whole ranked in the middle but demonstrated more equality than Western offshoots, including the United States (Firebaugh 2003: 161).

However, these same four nations just noted for greater levels of income equality, as well as others, have high levels of gender inequality. In some regions of the world, women are confined largely to home life; only 11 percent of women in the Middle East are earning independent incomes. Although elsewhere increasing numbers of women are entering the workplace, as many as one third to half of women laborers residing in these countries are expected to hand over all money earned to their husbands or other household heads (George and Wilding 2002: 114–115). Additionally, the quality of women's jobs is significantly lower than men's. They tend to get jobs with poorer working conditions, less security, lower wages, and fewer benefits. Like in the United States, the disparity between women's and men's pay is decreasing in many countries, but large gaps still persist. Women are more likely than men to be destitute, and they are more often undernourished. As more and more people all over the world are exposed to Western attitudes, divorce rates tend to rise, leaving female-headed households susceptible to increased poverty, hunger, and disease without the support of government welfare (George and Wilding 2002: 127).

Gender inequality permeates the educational systems of many poor countries as well. Two thirds of those who cannot read or write in the world are women, and there is little indication that this will change in the near future (United Nations 2000). Whereas in rich countries, women and men have very similar school enrollment rates, in poor nations, women tend to be highly underrepresented in school. In Yemen, 2.5 times as many men as women

are enrolled; in Afghanistan, over twice as many men are in school; and numerous other countries—primarily African—demonstrate slightly lesser yet still prevalent disparities (Yates 2003: 41).

Violence against women is also pervasive in poorer countries (although it is problematic everywhere in the world). In South Africa, Pakistan, India, and elsewhere, women live in fear of rape and domestic abuse, and perpetrators nearly always go unpunished. In Jamaica, wife-beating is regarded as a daily event. Men of Bangladesh generally consider the ability to hit one's wife to be a right; here and elsewhere, wife-beating not uncommonly turns into wife-murdering (Narayan 2000: 197). In some regions of the world where male children are strongly preferred over female children, such as in China, female infanticide and selective abortion practices kill girls. Particularly in parts of Africa where female virginity is carefully protected, female genital mutilation is regularly performed on young, often prepubescent girls.

Women are not the only ones who suffer from the inequality within IDCs. Slavery is one modern problem that disproportionately affects poor residents of poor countries. Although it is commonly believed that slavery is a phenomenon of the past—indeed, it is not legal anywhere in the world—leading slavery expert Kevin Bales (1999: 9) estimates that there are currently 27 million people in the world forcefully laboring without compensation; in fact, "there are more slaves alive today than all the people stolen from Africa in the time of the transatlantic slave trade." He reports that 15 to 20 million of these are bonded laborers in Bangladesh, India, Nepal, and Pakistan, or individuals who become slaves in order to repay a debt. Often, the owed amount is under $25, but there is no contracted amount of time after which the debt is considered repaid; sometimes generation after generation labors to work off such a debt. One example of bonded labor is prostitution prevalent in Thailand and India. Girls' parents are often tricked into selling their children to agents who in turn sell them to brothels, which can make nearly 800 percent profit off of the girl prostitutes (Bales 1999: 16–18). The remaining 7 to 12 million slaves are located primarily in Southeast Asia, North and West Africa, and some areas in South America. Perhaps shockingly, nearly every country in the world has some slaves; child slaves toil in such Western cities as London, Los Angeles, New York, and Zurich (Bales 1999: 3).

Modern slavery is different from old slavery. Unlike old slavery, today race and ethnicity may factor into who becomes a slave, but slave and slaveholder are often of the same ethnic background. They are generally not imported from a distant land, although they sometimes are taken from a neighboring country, but can frequently be snatched from a nearby town. Slaveholders prey on vulnerable populations, which are often women, almost always those who are poor, and sometimes members of a marginalized ethnic group or religion. With populations quickly growing in many already impoverished nations, labor becomes extremely cheap and the potential slave population flourishes (Bales 1999: 11–12). With such a glut of cheap slaves at their command, slaveholders can force them to labor under the most inhumane, abusive circumstances, even keeping them permanently chained to their workstations; then, when their bodies are too broken down to work, they can be simply thrown away and replaced with new slave labor. Using the aforementioned example, girl prostitutes are generally thrown into the streets once they grow too old or ill, or become HIV-positive. It is cheaper for holders to let slaves die than to care for their survival needs. While some slaves work for only a few months before being disposed of, others are enslaved for a lifetime (Bales 1999: 9–19).

NEOLIBERALISM AND ITS DISCONTENTS: THINKING ABOUT AN ALTERNATIVE FUTURE

Is it possible to create a just social order at either the national or global level if high levels of inequality exist? The evidence provided in this chapter combined with the empirical accounts and theoretical arguments advanced in the chapters of this book lead to the conclusion that the answer is a resounding no. Should market forces alone determine inequality levels, as neoliberals contend? Again, we conclude that the answer is no if we are seriously intent on promoting social justice.

This book is an exercise in sociological analysis. We have sought to explore the nature, the scope, the complexity, the durability, and the historically and socially conditioned character of inequality in its many guises. This distinguishes it from both an effort to articulate a philosophical defense of egalitarianism and an analysis of social policies, existing and potential, aimed or promoting more equality (for philosophic and policy discussions, see Gutmann, 1980; Walzer 1983; Baker 1987; Roemer 1994; Green 1998). This being said, we conclude with a brief summary of our sense of where we are today and how we might begin to pursue an alternative future that holds out the promise of a fairer, more humane, and just world.

As we read the current social landscape, we see two main justifications for inequality. One is based on a defense of tradition. This position can be seen in particular in fundamentalist religious circles— and all the major religions have fundamentalist elements—and has its most potent impact on gender inequality and inequality based on sexual orientation across the board and racial inequality in many instances. Fundamentalism often offers a religious gloss on inequality and a justification for the continued subservience and exclusion of historically disenfranchised groups.

The other justification derives from neoliberal ideology, which is underpinned by a brand of conservative philosophy that valorizes the individual, freedom, and the market above all else. Neoliberalism, contrary to fundamentalism, exhibits no allegiance to tradition. It does not place a premium on community and is disinterested in promoting equality. Indeed, neoliberalism arose as a significant political and economic platform by directly challenging the idea that inequality needed to be combated.

An alternative future would necessarily begin with a critique of both of these positions. Mounting such a critique ought to be three-pronged. First, it ought to make use of the abundant sociological literature on inequality to indicate that rather than being a naturally occurring condition, inequality is historically constructed and preserved on the basis of unequal access to political and economic power. Thus, contrary to fundamentalists, it need not be seen as either inevitable or necessary. Rather, the argument must be made that it can be changed: just as it was constructed, it can be deconstructed. Second, that same body of work can provide powerful testimony to the claim that inequality takes a profound toll on the most disadvantaged. Moreover, it also reveals that once in place, inequality tends to perpetuate itself as those at the top seek to protect their privileges, while those at the bottom are denied genuinely equal opportunities. Related to this, it can indicate the falsity of the neoliberal belief that trickle-down economic policies can compensate for rising levels of inequality. Or in other words, sociological inquiry can be used to make the case that contrary to the neoliberal assertion that a rising tide lifts all boats, neoliberalism actually appears to create a world that looks increasingly like a zero-sum game.

We believe that the collection of essays in this volume provides some of the tools necessary for mounting such a critique. But the rejection of defenses of inequality is only a precondition for thinking about what an egalitarian society might look like and exploring the realistic possibilities of reducing existing levels of inequality within the numerous economic, political, and cultural constraints imposed on such a project. A useful starting place, in our opinion, can be found in the suggestion of Philip Green (1998: 69) that we identify evidence of what he calls "surplus inequality," by which he means "inequality above and beyond the necessary inequalities of a complex division of labor, existing primarily to enhance the power and well-being of some people at the expense of others." Second, the relationship between equality and democracy needs to be articulated. Equality cannot occur without democracy, and the problem today is that there is not enough democracy. Not only are many nations non-democratic, but even those that are formal representative democracies are not sufficiently

democratic. Democracy needs to be expanded and deepened (Barber 1984, Young 2000) if anything resembling a just and egalitarian society—either at the national or global level—is to be possible. This is because such a society cannot emerge without political struggle, and ordinary people cannot possibly win that struggle without the democratic tools to do so.

REFERENCES

Alaimo, Katherine, Ronnette R. Briefel, Edward A. Frongillo, Jr., and Christine M. Olson. (1998). Food insufficiency exists in the United States: Results from the third National Health and Nutrition Examination Survey (NHANES III). *American Journal of Public Health, 88,* 419–426.

Alba, Richard D., John R. Logan, and Paul E. Bellair. (1994). Living with crime: The implications of racial/ethnic differences in suburban location. *Social Forces, 73,* 395–434.

Baker, John. (1987). *Arguing for equality.* London: Verso.

Bales, Kevin. (1999). *Disposable people: New slavery in the global economy.* Berkeley: University of California Press.

Barber, Benjamin. (1984). *Strong democracy: Participatory politics for a new age.* Berkeley: University of California Press.

Barnes, Sandra. 2005. *The cost of being poor: A comparative study of life in poor urban neighborhoods in Gary, Indiana.* Albany: SUNY Press.

Bernhardt, Annette, Martina Morris, and Mark S. Handcock. (1995). Women's gains or men's losses? A closer look at the shrinking gender gap in earnings. *The American Journal of Sociology, 101,* 302–328.

Bhattacharya, Jayanta, Thomas Deleire, Steven Haider, and Janet Currie. (2002). Heat or eat? Cold weather shocks and nutrition in poor American families. NBER Working Paper No. W9004.

Blau, Francine D., and Lawrence M. Kahn. (1997). Swimming upstream: Trends in the gender wage differential in the 1980s. *Journal of Labor Economics, 15,* 1–42.

Blau, Judith R., and Peter M. Blau. (1982). The cost of inequality: Metropolitan structure and violent crime. *American Sociological Review, 47,* 114–129.

Broadbent, Edward (Ed.). (2001). *Democratic equality: What went wrong?* Toronto: University of Toronto Press.

Brooks-Gunn, Jeanne, Greg J. Duncan, Pamela Kato Klebanov, and Naomi Sealand. (1993). Do neighborhoods influence child and adolescent development? *The American Journal of Sociology, 99,* 353–395.

Browne, Irene. (1999). Latinas and African American women in the U.S. labor market. In I. Browne (Ed.), *Latinas and African American women at work: Race, gender, and economic inequality* (pp. 1–31). New York: Russell Sage Foundation.

Budig, Michelle J., and Paula England (2001). The wage penalty for motherhood. *American Sociological Review, 66,* 204–225.

Bureau of Justice Statistics. (2002). Homicide trends in the U.S.: Trends by race. Online: *http://www.ojp.usdoj.gov/ bjs/homicide/race.htm.*

Bureau of Justice Statistics. (2003). Victim characteristics: Annual household income. Online: *http://www.ojp.usdoj. gov/bjs/cvict_v.htm.*

Caplovitz, David. (1967). *The poor pay more: Consumer practices of low-income families.* New York: The Free Press.

Chung, Chanjin, and Samuel L. Myers, Jr. (1999). Do the poor pay more for food? An analysis of grocery store availability and food price disparities. *The Journal of Consumer Affairs, 33,* 276–296.

Coleman, James S., Ernest Q. Campbell, Carol F. Hobson, James M. McPartland, Alexander M. Mood, Frederic D. Weinfeld, and Robert L. York. (1996). *Equality of educational opportunity.* Washington, D.C.: U.S. Government Printing Office.

Costanzo, Mark. (1997). *Just revenge: Costs and consequences of the death penalty.* New York: St. Martin's Press.

Cotter, David A., Joan M. Hermsen, and Reeve Vanneman. (1999). Systems of gender, race, and class inequality: Multilevel analyses. *Social Forces, 78,* 433–460.

Coverman, Shelley. (1983). Gender, domestic labor time, and wage inequality. *American Sociological Review, 48,* 623–637.

Crane, Jonathan. (1991). The epidemic theory of ghettos and neighborhood effects on dropping out and teenage childbearing. *The American Journal of Sociology, 96,* 1226–1259.

Currie, Elliott. (1998). *Crime and punishment in America.* New York: Metropolitan Books.

Danziger, Sheldon, and Peter Gottschalk. (1995). *America unequal.* New York: Russell Sage Foundation.

Davis, Karen. (2000). Health care for low-income people. In Marshal, R. (Ed.), *Back to shared prosperity: The growing inequality of wealth and income in America* (pp. 311–320). Armonk, NY: M. E. Sharpe.

De Nardi, Mariacristina, Liqian Ren, and Chao Wei. (2000). Income inequality and redistribution in five countries. Federal Reserve Bank of Chicago. *Economic Perspectives, 24,* 2–20.

DeNavas-Walt, Carmen, Bernadette D. Proctor, and Robert J. Mills. (2004). Income, poverty, and health insurance coverage in the United States: 2003. U.S. Census Bureau, Current Population Reports, P60-226. Washington D.C.: U.S. Government Printing Office.

Evans, Gary W., and Elyse Kantrowitz. (2002). Socioeconomic status and health: The potential role of environmental risk exposure. *Annual Review of Public Health, 23,* 303–331.

Firebaugh, Glenn. (2003). *The new geography of global income inequality.* Cambridge: Harvard University Press.

Frank, Robert H., and Philip J. Cook. (1995). *The winner-take-all society.* New York: The Free Press.

Frydman, Carola, and Raven E. Saks. (2004). "Historic Trends in Executive Compensation, 1936–2002." Harvard University, unpublished paper.

Furstenberg, Jr., Frank F., S. Philip Morgan, and Paul D. Allison. (1987). Paternal participation and children's well-being after marital dissolution. *American Sociological Review, 52,* 695–701.

George, Vic, and Paul Wilding. (2002). *Globalization and human welfare.* Houndmills, Basingstoke, Hampshire: Palgrave.

Geronimus, Arline T., John Bound, Timothy A. Waidmann, Cynthia G. Colen, and Dianne Steffick. (2001). Inequality in life expectancy, functional status, and active life expectancy across selected black and white populations in the United States. *Demography, 38,* 227–251.

Green, Philip. 1998. *Equality and democracy.* New York: The New Press.

Gutmann, Amy. (1980). *Liberal equality.* Cambridge: Cambridge University Press.

Hallinan, Maureen T. (2001). Sociological perspectives on black–white inequalities in American schooling. *Sociology of Education, 74,* 50–70.

Harer, Miles D., and Darrell Steffensmeier. (1992). The differing effects of economic inequality on black and white rates of violence. *Social Forces, 70,* 1035–1054.

Hedges, Larry V., and Amy Nowell. (1999). Changes in the black–white gap in achievement test scores. *Sociology of Education, 72,* 111–135.

Herrnstein, Richard J., and Charles Murray. (1994). *The bell curve: Intelligence and class structure in American life.* New York: The Free Press.

Hoffman, Kathryn, Charmaine Llagas, and Thomas D. Snyder. (2003). *Status and trends in the education of blacks.* (Report No. NCES-2003-034). Washington, D.C.: National Center for Education Statistics. (ERIC Document Reproduction Service No. ED481811)

Hughes, Michael, and Melvin E. Thomas. (1998). The continuing significance of race revisited: A study of race, class, and quality of life in America, 1972–1996. *American Sociological Review, 63,* 785–795.

Human Rights Watch. (2002). *Race and incarceration in the United States.* Human Rights Watch Backgrounder, February 27.

Jacobs, Jerry A. (1996). Gender inequality and higher education. *Annual Review of Sociology, 22,* 153–185.

Jones, Arthur F., and Daniel H. Weinberg. (2000). The changing shape of the nation's income distribution. U.S. Census Bureau, Current Population Reports, P60-204. Washington D.C.: U.S. Government Printing Office.

Kingston, Paul W. (2000). *The classless society.* Stanford, CA: Stanford University Press.

Krieg, Eric J. (1998). The two faces of toxic waste: Trends in the spread of environmental hazards. *Sociological Forum, 13,* 3–20.

LeClere, Felicia B., Richard G. Rogers, and Kimberley D. Peters. (1997). Ethnicity and mortality in the United States:

Individual and community correlates. *Social Forces, 76,* 169–198.

Lichter, Daniel T., and David J. Eggebeen. (1993). Rich kids, poor kids: Changing income inequality among American children. *Social Forces, 71,* 761–780.

Lin, Nan. (2000). Inequality in social capital. *Contemporary Sociology, 29,* 785–795.

Marshall, Ray. (2000). *Back to shared prosperity: The growing inequality of wealth and income in America.* Armonk, NY: M. E. Sharpe.

Massey, Douglas S., and Eric Fong. (1990). Segregation and neighborhood quality: Blacks, Hispanics, and Asians in San Francisco metropolitan area. *Social Forces, 69,* 15–32.

Massey, Douglas S., and Nancy A. Denton. 1993. *American apartheid: Segregation and the making of the underclass.* Cambridge, MA: Harvard University Press.

Massey, Douglas S., Andrew B. Gross, and Kumiko Shibuya. (1994). Migration, segregation, and the geographic concentration of poverty. *American Sociological Review, 59,* 425–445.

McCall, Leslie. (2001). *Complex inequality: Gender, class, and race in the new economy.* New York: Routledge.

McLanahan, Sara, and Karen Booth. (1989). Mother-only families: Problems, prospects, and politics. *Journal of Marriage and the Family, 51,* 557–580.

McPherson, J. Miller, and Lynn Smith-Lovin. (1982). Women and weak ties: Differences by sex in the size of voluntary organizations. *The American Journal of Sociology, 87,* 883–904.

Merva, Mary, and Richard Fowles. (2000). Economic outcomes and mental health. In R. Marshal (Ed.), *Back to shared prosperity: The growing inequality of wealth and income in America* (pp. 69–75). Armonk, NY: M. E. Sharpe.

Mishel, Lawrence, Jared Bernstein, and Heather Boushey. (2003). *The state of working America 2002/2003.* Ithaca, NY: Cornell University.

Moore, Elsie G. J. (1987). Ethnic social milieu and black children's intelligence test achievement. *The Journal of Negro Education, 56,* 44–52.

Mullahy, John, and Barbara L. Wolfe. (2001). Health policies for the non-elderly poor. In S. H. Danziger and R. H. Haveman (Eds.), *Understanding poverty* (pp. 278–313). New York: Russell Sage Foundation.

Munch, Allison, J. Miller McPherson, and Lynn Smith-Lovin. (1997). Gender, children, and social contact: The effects of childrearing for men and women. *American Sociological Review, 62,* 509–520.

NAACP Legal Defense Fund. (2004). *Racial statistics of executions and death row in the United States.* Online: http://www.naacpldf.org/deathpenaltyinfo.

Narayan, Deepa (with Raj Patel, Kai Schafft, Anne Rademacher, and Sarah Koch-Schulte). (2000). *Voices of the poor: Can anyone hear us?* New York: Oxford University Press.

Oliver, Melvin L., and Thomas M. Shapiro. (1997). *Black wealth/white wealth: A new perspective on racial equality.* New York: Routledge.

Pearson, Dale F. (1994). The black man: Health issues and implications for clinical practice. *Journal of Black Studies, 25,* 81–98.

Pong, Suet-ling. (1998). The school compositional effect of single parenthood on 10th-grade achievement. *Sociology of Education, 71,* 23–42.

Portes, Alejandro. (1998). Social capital: Its origins and applications in modern sociology. *Annual Review of Sociology, 24,* 1–24.

Rank, Mark Robert. (2004). *One nation, underprivileged: Why American poverty affects us all.* New York: Oxford University Press.

Rasmussen, David (2003). Annual estimates of the population by sex, race, and Hispanic or Latino origin for the United States: April 1, 2000 to July 1, 2003. University of Arkansas at Little Rock, Institute for Economic Advancement. Online: http://www.aiea.ualr.edu/research/demographic/population/NC-EST2003-03.pdf.

Roemer, John E. (1994). *Egalitarian perspectives: Essays in philosophical economics.* Cambridge: Cambridge University Press.

Roscigno, Vincent J., and James W. Ainsworth-Darnell (1999). Race, cultural capital and educational resources: Persistent inequalities and achievement returns. *Sociology of Education, 72,* 158–178.

Sampson, Robert J., Steven W. Raudenbush, and Felton Earls. (1997). Neighborhoods and violent crime: A multilevel study of collective efficacy. *Science, 277,* 918–924.

Spratlen, Thaddeus H. (1973). Financing inner city schools: Policy aspects of economics, political and racial disparity. *The Journal of Negro Education, 42,* 283–307.

Thompson, Becky Wangsgaard. (1992). "A way outa no way": Eating problems among African-American, Latina, and white women. *Gender and Society, 6,* 546–561.

Tilly, Charles. (1998). *Durable inequality.* Berkeley: University of California Press.

United Nations Statistics Division. (2000). Statistics and indicators on women and men: The world's women 2000. Online: http://unstats.un.org/unsd/demographic/products/indwm/edu2000.htm.

United Nations Statistics Division. (2004a). Millennium indicators database. Online: http://unstats.un.org/unsd/mi/mi_series_list.asp.

United Nations Statistics Division. (2004b). Demographic and social statistics: Social indicators. Online: http://unstats.un.org/unsd/demographic/products/socind/socind2.htm#edu.

U.S. Census Bureau. (2001). Historical income tables—people. Tables P-2, P-40, and P-54. Online: http://www.census.gov/hhes/income/histinc/incperdet.html.

U.S. Census Bureau. (2003). Historical income tables—households. Table H-3. Online: http://www.census.gov/hhes/income/histinc/h03.html.

Walters, Pamela Barnhouse. (2001). Educational access and the state: Historical continuities and discontinuities in racial inequality in American education. *Sociology of Education, 74,* 35–49.

Walzer, Michael. (1983). *Spheres of justice: A defense of pluralism and equality.* New York: Basic Books.

Williams, David R., and Chiquita Collins. (1995). US socioeconomic and racial differences in health: Patterns and explanations. *Annual Review of Sociology, 21,* 349–386.

Wilson, William J. (2000). Jobless ghettos: The social implications of the disappearance of work in segregated neighborhoods. In R. Marshal (Ed.), *Back to shared prosperity: The growing inequality of wealth and income in America* (pp. 85–94). Armonk, NY: M. E. Sharpe.

The World Factbook. (2004). Central Intelligence Agency. Online: *http://www.cia.gov/cia/publications/factbook/index. html.*

Xu, Wu, and Ann Leffler. (1996). Gender and race effects on occupational prestige, segregation, and earnings. In E. Ngan-Ling Chow, D. Wilkinson, and M. B. Zinn (Eds.), *Race, class, and gender: Common bonds, different voices* (pp. 107–124). Thousand Oaks, CA: Sage Publications.

Yates, Michael D. (2003). *Naming the system: Inequality and work in the global economy.* New York: Monthly Review Press.

Yinger, John. (1986). Measuring racial discrimination with fair housing audits: Caught in the act. *The American Economic Review, 76,* 881–893.

Young, Iris Marion. (2000). *Inclusion and democracy.* New York: Oxford University Press.